Praise for In Their Own Words

"Contemporary concerns in the study of history have made primary-source material from eyewitnesses increasingly interesting to a vast audience. . . . What makes Stiles's work so important is the quality of his editing." —*Library Journal*

Robber Barons and Radicals

"Powerful. . . . The genius of Stiles's approach is his panoramic view of post–Civil War America fighting for identity on many fronts. . . . A book of surprising passion." —*Library Journal*

"Interweaving revealing and often moving excerpts from contemporary documents with his own lucid narrative, T. J. Stiles has fashioned a compelling account of the Reconstruction era that followed the Civil War." —Eric Foner, DeWitt Clinton Professor of History, Columbia University

"T. J. Stiles has once again made history come alive. . . . The combination of rich, firsthand accounts with crisp connecting narrative allows us entry into the conflicts and promises of the last decades of the nineteenth century." —Louis P. Masur, author of *"The Real War Will Never Get in the Books": Selections from Writers During the Civil War*

Warriors and Pioneers

"Unique. . . . A thorough and accurate history of the westward expansion that began en masse in 1843. . . . Stiles presents history as a living thing, infused with life. Even if you have read a great deal about the conquest of the West, *In Their Own Words* might make that turbulent half century, for the first time, real." —*Statesman Journal* (Salem, OR)

"The next best thing to oral histories are contemporary writings. . . . T. J. Stiles includes white and Indian accounts for most of the major conflicts in the settlement of the West, including the gold rush, the war for the Black Hills, and the major campaigns to conquer the Indians." —*The Denver Post*

"An informative, entertaining primer. . . . Footnotes, maps, Stiles's narratives, and an introduction by historian Richard Maxwell Brown weave together these stories of conflict and conquest, putting them in a broader context of turbulent social, economic, and political forces that absorbed the Old West into mainstream America."

"Here is the West in the words of the array of diverse players on the vast and varied stage of the American past, words faithful to their time and place. . . . Stiles's informed commentary sets context and significance. Together, these voices of then and now form an illuminating and engaging volume."   —Robert M. Utley,
                                        author of *The Lance and the Shield: The Life and Times of Sitting Bull*

Civil War Commanders

"This skillful compilation of firsthand accounts by participants of the Civil War's most important battles offers readers rewarding fare. . . . *Civil War Commanders* is a valuable addition to the literature of the American *Iliad*."
        —James M. McPherson,
                author of *Battle Cry of Freedom: The Civil War Era*

"A chronological history of decisive events in a critical chapter in American history. Highly recommended."   —*Booklist*

"Treats the reader to a detailed perspective that is often lost. . . . This makes for interesting reading. . . . Overall, this is a well-organized and concise overview of the Civil War that is allowed to unfold through the words and actions of the participants."   —*Library Journal*

"This book moves the Civil War from the often unimaginative pages of a textbook into an exciting, first-person account of some of the war's major battles. . . . An interesting addition to any library."   —*KLIATT*

About the Author:

T. J. Stiles is the author of *Warriors and Pioneers; Civil War Commanders; Robber Barons and Radicals; The Citizen's Handbook: Essential Documents and Speeches from American History;* and *Jesse James.* His work has appeared in such publications as the *Los Angeles Times, The Denver Post, New York Daily News,* and *The People's Almanac Presents the Twentieth Century.* A native of Benton County, Minnesota, he studied history at Carleton College and Columbia University, and now lives in Brooklyn.

About the Introducer:

Daniel B. Botkin is president of the Center for the Study of the Environment in Santa Barbara, California, and director of the Program for Global Change at George Mason University in Fairfax, Virginia. He is the author of more than one hundred books and articles.

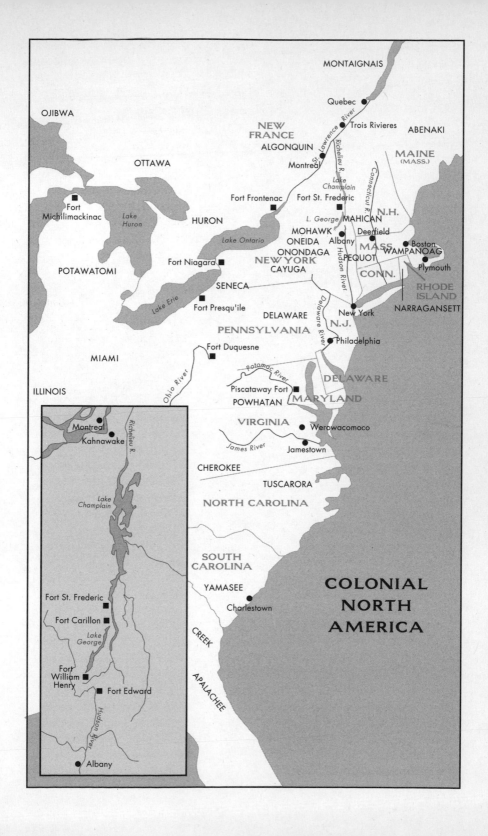

MONTAIGNAIS

OJIBWA

Quebec

NEW
FRANCE
ALGONQUIN

Trois Rivieres

ABENAKI

MAINE
(MASS.)

OTTAWA

Montreal

St. Lawrence River

Richelieu R.

Connecticut R.

Fort
Michilimackinac

Lake
Huron

Fort Frontenac

Fort St. Frederic

Lake
Champlain

N.H.

HURON

Lake Ontario

L. George

MAHICAN

MOHAWK

Deerfield

Boston

Fort Niagara

NEW YORK

ONEIDA

ONONDAGA

Albany

MASS

WAMPANOAG

CAYUGA

PEQUOT

Plymouth

POTAWATOMI

Lake Erie

SENECA

CONN.

RHODE
ISLAND

Fort Presqu'ile

Hudson River

Delaware River

NARRAGANSETT

DELAWARE

New York

MIAMI

PENNSYLVANIA

N.J.

Ohio River

Fort Duquesne

Philadelphia

ILLINOIS

Potomac River

DELAWARE

Piscataway Fort

MARYLAND

POWHATAN

VIRGINIA

Werowacomoco

James River

Jamestown

CHEROKEE

TUSCARORA

NORTH CAROLINA

SOUTH
CAROLINA

COLONIAL
NORTH
AMERICA

YAMASEE

Charlestown

CREEK

APALACHEE

Montreal

Kahnawake

Richelieu R.

Lake
Champlain

Fort St. Frederic

Fort Carillon

Lake
George

Fort
William
Henry

Fort Edward

Hudson River

Albany

IN THEIR OWN WORDS

THE COLONIZERS

Collected and Edited by

T. J. Stiles

With an Introduction by Daniel B. Botkin

A PERIGEE BOOK

A Perigee Book
Published by The Berkley Publishing Group
A member of Penguin Putnam Inc.
200 Madison Avenue
New York, NY 10016

First edition: April 1998

Published simultaneously in Canada.

The Penguin Putnam Inc. World Wide Web site address is
http://www.penguinputnam.com

Library of Congress Cataloging-in-Publication Data

In their own words / collected and edited by T. J. Stiles : with an
    introduction by Daniel B. Botkin.
        p.   cm. — (In their own words)
    "A Perigee book."
    Includes bibliographical references (p. xvii).
    ISBN 0-399-52390-1
    1. United States—History—Colonial period, ca. 1600–1775—
Sources. 2. United States—History—Colonial period, ca.
1600–1775—Biography. I. Stiles, T. J. II. Series: In their own
words (Berkley Publishing Group)
E162.I5   1998
973.2—dc21   97-41889
                                                              CIP

Printed in the United States of America

10   9   8   7   6   5   4   3   2   1

CONTENTS

V. Expansion
FROM OUTPOSTS TO EMPIRES

VI. By the Rivers of Babylon
AMERICAN CAPTIVITIES

VII. Conquest

PREFACE

Five years and four books ago, I began the *In Their Own Words* series with a simple idea: to trace history through the words of the participants. It's not exactly an original concept, of course: scholars have long produced collections of letters, diaries, and other primary sources, and many bookstores now offer reprints of the memoirs of historic figures. But such books demand a fair amount of previous knowledge, if they are to be enjoyed and appreciated; and most collections of sources simply don't read well. My purpose in this series was to bridge the gap between primary-source immediacy and narrative cohesion—to transform volumes of first-person accounts into chronological histories.

When my publisher bought the idea and I set to work, I faced two tasks: first, to find selections that combine readability with historical insight and information; and second, to weave those excerpts together with my own narrative—to turn otherwise unrelated fragments into a cohesive book.

After three books (this makes four), I think I'm getting the knack. In the first three volumes, I created something of a set within the series, by exploring the pivotal conflicts of the nineteenth century. The first, *Civil War Commanders,* provided a straightforward military history, largely through the memoirs of commanders from both sides. In the second, *Warriors and Pioneers,* I took on a more ambitious task: the fifty-year conquest of the Western frontier, in terms of the struggles between cultures and communities that so often led to violence. In the third book, *Robber Barons and Radicals,* I tackled a shorter but even more complex epoch: the twelve years of Reconstruction. With accounts from politicians, industrialists, and a pair of remarkable spokesmen for racial equality, I tried to portray a revolutionary moment in American history.

Taken together, I believe these three volumes offer insight into both the gritty reality and the larger meaning of the events that created our nation as we now know it. And I found each book to be a better realization of the concept of the series. Although these volumes will never get on the bestseller lists, they offer something unusual—and unusually rewarding, I hope—for the reader who happens across them.

With *The Colonizers,* the series makes a dramatic departure from the nineteenth-century focus of the first three volumes. I am literally going back to the beginning: the first 150 years of European settlement in North America. Given this dramatic shift in coverage, perhaps a few words about the selections and the approach are in order.

In any offering of primary sources, the knowledgeable reader will bemoan the absence of some accounts. Alas, there is not enough room to fit in everything worth reading—especially in a single volume that covers a century and a half. Furthermore, the number of issues to be addressed is vast: in recent decades, historians have stressed one after another, as they have plumbed the complexity and richness of life in North America during this period.

My first and simplest guideline is geographical: this book is about North America east of the Mississippi and north of Florida (that is, including French but excluding Spanish settlements). Second, it takes the European colonizers (as the title suggests) as the protagonists in this history. I should be clear: I treat the Native American peoples as equal contenders in the struggle for this continent, but the story told here begins with, and is driven by, the European invasion.

My third criterion is to provide a broad sense of movement and change—to show how the political, cultural, and demographic situation evolved over this 150 years. This leads to an emphasis on conflict (often armed), which distorts somewhat our understanding of daily life. The average person did not spend as much time in mortal peril as you might think from reading this book—but violent change played an enormous role in colonial history, and it cannot be avoided. I devote quite a bit of space to political and military issues; a rather traditional approach, perhaps, but essential to my desire to maintain a sense of movement through time.

In choosing precisely which conflicts to feature in the book, I have concentrated on pivotal clashes that resulted in lasting change. For the intercolonial rivalries, I focus heavily on the struggle between New France and the English colonies of New England and New York; this collision of armed Europeans had a wide impact on diplomacy, settlement, culture, and politics. For the struggles with Indians, I pay attention to those battles that similarly redefined patterns of settlement, power, and trade. On the other hand, I also delve into the alliances made between colonists and Native American nations. These links were decisive in the survival of many of the colonies, and led to a fascinating mingling of cultures.

Making these choices was not easy—and it became even harder when I considered the conflicts within the colonies. From the nineteenth century to the present day, scholars have churned out study after fascinating study of factional and religious disputes, as well as ethnic, social, and economic tensions. It seems that with each passing year, we discover that colonial America was a more complex place than we had thought. With my limited space, I am afraid that I have had to stick with many well-known stories, such as those of Captain John Smith and his rivals, Anne Hutchinson's Antinomians, Bacon's Rebellion, the Salem witch trials, and the introduction of slavery. Then again, the conflicts I have included became well known because they are both gripping and important.

But to return to my larger aims: my fourth goal is to evoke, in the midst of all this conflict and change, the diversity of colonial America—its ethnic, cultural, religious, and social richness. Here we glimpse what historian Edward Countryman calls the "collision of histories" that shaped the continent. This book takes the reader into Huron villages, onto Virginia plantations, into the German settlements of Pennsylvania, as well as into the patroonships of Dutch New Netherlands, the meeting houses of Massachusetts, the workshops of Philadelphia, the streets of Montreal, and the distant villages of Africa where unwilling immigrants began their American diaspora. As I depict the clashes of cultures and migrants and armed men, I wish to reveal the textures of life on these disputed shores. Critics of multiculturalism may rest assured: I do not propose that all these influences had an equal impact. Yet they all had *some* impact, and all are fascinating.

Most important of all, I wish to keep the reader's interest. This, too, may distort the impression this book gives of life in colonial North America; but a truly accurate book—one, say, that was largely devoted to accounts of planting, harvesting, mending clothes, and going to church—would be unreadable. I am unapologetically giving you the good parts. Here are many accounts of (and by) individuals who had adventures, faced dangers, dealt with terrible challenges, and somehow lived to tell about it. Many of these writers are famous, though many are not; in every case, I selected them because I find their accounts to be compelling, with a great deal to tell us about both the details of their daily lives and the great changes that overtook them.

I do *not* depict a steady march toward an inevitable United States, as the colonies were described in schoolbooks of old. Nor do I paint North America as a ripe fruit, destined to fall into the lap of the British Empire, as in traditional English textbooks. In these pages, the eastern seaboard writhes like a snakepit of military and political calculation, as Native Americans skillfully pitted the Europeans against traditional Indian foes, and as colonists looked to sachems, sagamores, and werowances for aid in their own rivalries. Here we see the tangle of influences that shaped daily life in North America, as words, customs, technology, and techniques from many cultures mingled along this extended frontier.

And hidden in these pages, there to be found by the attentive reader, is the epic invasion of pigs and pathogens—the environmental assault that undid the world the Indians had made. Native Americans did not live in a pristine state of nature before the Europeans arrived; they themselves had reshaped North American ecology more than once since their arrival from Asia tens of thousands of years before. But they were utterly unprepared for the onslaught of new animals (such as swine, sheep, and cattle) that invaded their cornfields and hunting grounds. They were especially unready for the invasion of viruses and bacteria—notably the dreaded smallpox, responsible for the deaths of hundreds of thousands. Yet some tribes forged successful strategies to meet the invisible assault—particularly the famed Five Nations of the Iroquois.

The most attention-getting import from Europe, of course, was the firearm—the most dramatic of the metallurgical products introduced into North America. After some initial shock (see Chapter 3 to witness the impact of gunpowder on unprepared Indian warriors), Native Americans took to muskets (along with such metalware as kettles, knives, and hatchets) with a vengeance. Indeed, Indians on the eastern half of the continent became utterly dependent on these imports; a century after the first European settlers arrived, a major theme in many native cultures would be traditional revivalism—the call to return to nearly forgotten ways, such as the use of the bow. And yet, dependent as they became, these innovations improved their lives and their military power, allowing them to defeat colonial forces on numerous occasions. Increasingly, the various cultures developed an interconnectedness that could not be easily severed.

What we are left with is a changing, constantly emerging world that was startlingly different from our own. The modern New Englander will be stunned by the brutal actions and intolerant decrees of her Puritan predecessors. The reader whose idea of Native Americans stems from the late-nineteenth-century Plains Indians will be taken aback by the shrewd political infighting of Powhatan, and staggered by the cruelty in a Huron village. The citizen who imagines a steady march to democracy will be appalled by Bacon's bloody rebellion and its even bloodier suppression. And a sad surprise awaits those who harbor illusions that any people in colonial North America—native or European—were virtuous in the modern sense; the accounts here reveal alien moral codes that we can scarcely decipher, let alone accept.

This is the world we came from, or the world we came to. It emerged out of the friction of peoples, a babble of tongues, a collision of histories. It would change many times before it would become our own—yet this world would always be a part of our own (as David Hackett Fischer so persuasively argued in *Albion's Seed: Four British Folkways in America*).

Mention of Fischer's book calls my attention to some other items I should discuss: sources and editing. The literature on the colonial period, of course, is vast; as this is not a scholarly monograph, I have refrained from much footnoting, nor do I offer an extensive listing of my sources. I should say, however, that I was particularly influenced by three books (preeminent among many, many others): first, the above-mentioned *Albion's Seed*. This provocative, staggeringly detailed study of the four main British culture groups that immigrated to the English colonies is truly a seminal work, and a source of many of my specific numbers and names. Second, Ian K. Steele's comprehensive *Warpaths: Invasions of North America* offers a well-balanced, thoroughly researched narrative of the entire span of relations between the colonies and Native Americans. It, too, proved a valuable source of data and interpretation. And the third book that influenced my own writing: *A New World: An Epic of Colonial America from the Founding of Jamestown to the Fall of Quebec* by the late Arthur Quinn. Professor Quinn's account is rhetorical hell on wheels: it roars through a century and a half, throwing dust in the face of the history's dry, scholarly monographs.

In editing the sources gathered here, I decided immediately to modernize spellings and intervene heavily with footnotes and bracketed comments where archaic usage pops up. I invite those who pine for original spellings to go to the many volumes of primary sources available in bookstores and libraries.

A few acknowledgments are in order. I've never much liked acknowledgments; I've always thought it would be more interesting to use the same space to get even with enemies and rivals. Sadly, I am not important enough to have enemies or rivals, so I am left with the thankless task of thanking.

First on my list is Daniel B. Botkin, who wrote a splendid introduction to this volume. My research was aided by Mr. Bertrand Tzeng, then of Columbia University. His interest in the project was piqued by the fact that he attended Jean de Brébeuf High School in Indianapolis. Poor Brébeuf: see chapters 7 and 10 to learn how he came to have Catholic high schools named after himself. Not a recommended path to fame. Martyrdom may be a better fate, however, than the one Mr. Tzeng has selected: he has since become a lawyer.

When it comes to my writing, I generally think that I know best. My editor, Mr. John Schline, usually agrees with me on that point, which accounts for our excellent working relationship. My wife, Ms. Nadine T. Spence, is another critic whose judgment I deeply respect; it is one reason why we are (happily) married. I am grateful to her for reviewing this manuscript with her sharp eye. In addition, the manuscript was reviewed by Mr. Dana Lowell and Mr. Peter Miller. Mr. Miller has provided a tremendous amount of help for this and the preceding volumes in the series.

Those who find acknowledgments to be insufferable will be happy to note that I have only one more person to thank. I must offer my appreciation and gratitude to Mr. Bill Harris, the managing editor for all of the *In Their Own Words* books. Mr. Harris works tremendously hard at his job, applying skill and dedication in equal amounts. He deserves a great deal of credit for the handsome look and fine editing of these volumes. Mr. Harris and I meet every week for a thirty-minute chess game over lunch; I cherish the hope that I may break even with him one day soon.

—T. J. Stiles

SOURCES

Andrews, Charles M., ed., *Narratives of the Insurrections: 1675–1690* (New York: Charles Scribner's Sons, 1915)

Bougainville, Louis Antoine de (translated and edited by Edward P. Hamilton), *Adventure in the Wilderness: The American Journals of Louis Antoine de Bougainville* (Norman: University of Oklahoma Press, 1964)

Bradford, William (edited by W. T. Davis), *Bradford's History of Plymouth Plantation* (New York: Charles Scribner's Sons, 1904)

Burr, George L., ed., *Narratives of the Witchcraft Cases: 1648–1706* (New York: Charles Scribner's Sons, 1914)

Champlain, Samuel de (ed. W. L. Grant), *Voyages of Samuel de Champlain, 1604–1618* (New York: Charles Scribner's Sons, 1907)

Church, Benjamin (edited by Thomas Church), *Entertaining Passages Relating to Philip's War Which Began in the Year, 1675* (Boston: B. Green, 1716)

Equiano, Olaudah, *The Interesting Narrative of the Life of Olaudah Equiano, or Gustavus Vassa, the African* (New York: W. Durell, 1791)

Franklin, Benjamin, *The Autobiography of Benjamin Franklin* (Boston: Houghton, Mifflin, and Company, 1906)

Kellogg, Louise Phelps, ed., *Early Narratives of the Northwest: 1634–1699* (New York: Charles Scribner's Sons, 1917)

Lincoln, Charles H., ed., *Narratives of the Indian Wars: 1675–1699* (New York: Charles Scribner's Sons, 1913)

Myers, Albert Cook, ed., *Narratives of Early Pennsylvania, West New Jersey, and Delaware: 1630–1707* (New York: Charles Scribner's Sons, 1913)

Rogers, Robert, *Reminiscences of the French War* (Concord: Luther Roby, 1831)

Salley, Alexander S., Jr., ed., *Narratives of Early Carolina: 1650–1708* (New York: Charles Scribner's Sons, 1911)

Thwaites, Reuben Gold, ed., *The Jesuit Relations and Allied Documents: Travels and Explorations of the Jesuit Missionaries in New France, 1610–1791* (Cleveland: Burrows Brothers, 1897); vols. V, VI, XXIV, LXXI

Tyler, Lynn, ed., *Narratives of Early Virginia* (New York: Charles Scribner's Sons, 1907)

Williams, John, *The Redeemed Captive Returning to Zion, or A Faithful History of the Remarkable Occurences in the Captivity and Deliverance of Mr. John Williams* (Northampton: Hopkins, Bridgman, and Co., 1853)

Winthrop, John (edited by E. James Kendall Hosmer), *Winthrop's Journal, "History of New England"* (New York: Charles Scribner's Sons, 1908)

INTRODUCTION

From the accounts of the settlers and explorers presented in *The Colonizers* we learn much about what it was like to participate in the European settlement of eastern North America. This is what is fascinating about T. J. Stiles's work. Their words tell us that they often viewed their experiences in terms of political and social events, including political and religious reasons that they made the dangerous crossing of the Atlantic Ocean, and the political and military exchanges between themselves and Native Americans. But because the colonization took place within an environmental context and a human cultural framework that greatly influenced events, it is important that we understand this context so that we can better understand both daily life and the larger developments that were taking place.

The European colonization of eastern North America was played out within an environmental theater that greatly affected the events and the experiences of the players. About this environment, we can make five generalizations. First, the colonization took place during a period of harsh climate; therefore it was a tough time to try to settle a continent. Second, contrary to our myth about the pristine character of American wilderness, the colonizers arrived at a landscape heavily modified by the Native Americans. Third, the settlement in turn brought new knowledge of the ecological conditions of a strange continent, which, along with later discoveries in Central and South America, in the world's tropics, and in Australia and New Zealand, led to irrevocable changes in the way we view nature. Fourth, the colonization was part of a broader unsettling of European ideas about the character of nature and the place of human beings in it. It took place at the beginnings of the scientific revolution, and much that we take for granted about natural resources, climate and weather, soils, rocks, and minerals, was not known. As a result, reactions of the colonizers to their new environment were different from how a time traveler from today would react to the same events. Fifth, the colonization was an ecological event of vast proportions. It had immense effects on the North American environment.

Our historical myth is that the colonizers discovered a wilderness sparsely populated by human societies that had little if any effect on nature. But recent environmental and anthropological research shows that this was not the case. Native Americans had greatly altered the landscapes of eastern

North America, and as a result the environment was much different than the colonizers would have experienced if there were no prior inhabitants.

Our myths about nature also mislead us into believing that the wilderness of North America was nature in a perfect balance, a set of ecosystems that were at their best and most glorious state—old-growth forests of huge, beautiful trees never disturbed, streams that flowed without changes in enduring channels. Moreover, we are led to believe that today we can recover exactly this mythological original state if we merely leave the environment alone. Then we would find ourselves surrounded by the same wilderness the colonizers experienced. But this isn't true. Modern environmental sciences tell us that natural ecosystems—the forests, lakes, rivers, coastal dunes, and wetlands of eastern North America—are always undergoing change. Thus the environment through which the colonizers trod was different from what we experience today, even when we visit our natural parks and wilderness areas and even when we attempt to restore former conditions.

This task of putting ourselves in the situation of the colonizers is all the harder for us because today, as a heavily technological society, we tend to look at major changes like that colonization through the periscope of technology—for many of us, colonization is the story of a civilization with more advanced technologies using its tools to overwhelm and destroy indigenous cultures. From this perspective, the material products of a culture drive history and were behind the colonization of eastern North America between 1600 and 1750. But much more was going on.

As I have discussed elsewhere, one of the profound discoveries of late-twentieth-century environmental sciences is that the environment is always changing.[1] In the seventeenth and eighteenth centuries, the predominant belief was in a permanent God-created balance of nature, with a place for every creature and every creature in its place, performing the work that God had meant for it. This belief persists into our own time, expressed in modified form. Most of the colonization of eastern North America took place during the Little Ice Age, the period between 1550 and 1700, one of the coldest times since the melting of the great continental ice sheets about 10,000 years ago. In northern Europe, summers as well as winters were colder; summers were wetter. Snow cover persisted longer. With longer snow cover and later springs, grain yields were low and people had to slaughter dairy cattle when their hay ran out.[2] Other crops failed. Wine harvests were poor and vineyard cultivation shifted southward. People starved. In Norway

[1] Botkin, Daniel B., *Discordant Harmonies: A New Ecology for the 21st Century* (New York: Oxford University Press, 1990) and *Our Natural History: The Lessons of Lewis and Clark* (New York: Grosset/Putnam, 1995).

[2] Lamb, H. H., "An approach to the study of the development of climate and its impact in human affairs," pp. 291–310 in T. M. L. Wigley, M. J. Ingram and G. Farmer (eds.), *Climate and History: Studies in Past Climates and Their Impact on Man* (New York: Cambridge University Press, 1981). This material appears on p. 303.

and in the Alps, mountain glaciers fingered their way downslope, riding over villages, blocking rivers, covering farms. Towns were abandoned in England and Scandinavia.[3] The 1690s were among the worst years. The year 1690 had a wet summer and a severe winter, which ruined harvests and caused widespread famine in Europe.

The cold climate was widespread beyond Europe. In the Kiangsi province of China, the centuries-old cultivation of oranges was abandoned in the late 1600s as a result of a number of years of frequent frost.[4] In Ethiopia, Portuguese travelers saw the snow line on the mountains coming down lower than they had before. In east Africa, mountain glaciers on Mt. Kenya and Kilimanjaro advanced downslope.

Indirect evidence suggests that the same bad weather occurred in eastern North America.[5] So when you try to put yourself in the place of the colonizers, you have to imagine their experiences as harsher in terms of weather than those of our century. Winters had longer periods of harsh weather; frosts tended to occur later in the spring and earlier in the fall than is the average of the twentieth century, so that growing seasons were shorter. It was a hard time to become a successful farmer in a new land with new crops, harder than if we tried to do the same today with our generally milder climate.

The experiences of Rev. John Williams of Deerfield, Massachusetts, recounted in this book, illustrate the tough weather. Captured by Indians in early 1704, he was forced to travel on foot through thick snow and to cross Lake Champlain when it was covered with ice in March.

Samuel de Champlain's experiences also reveal the harshness of the climate. In 1604, he explored the coast of New England, and then returned to the Island of St. Croix above modern-day Maine in early September. There, he wrote, "the snows began on the 6th of October." By December, he wrote that "the cold was sharp, more severe than in France, and of much longer duration," while the snow in the nearby mountains "was from three to four feet deep up to the end of the month of April."[6]

If the colonization had taken place a few centuries earlier—before the fourteenth century—the climate would have been much milder and therefore settlement in some ways easier. The period between the ninth and eleventh centuries was especially mild, and it was during this time that Greenland was settled and flourished, only to die off after the eleventh century.

[3] Le Roy Ladurie, E., *Times of Feast, Times of Famine: A History of Climate Since the Year 1000* (Garden City: Doubleday & Co., 1971), p. 426.

[4] Lamb, p. 304.

[5] Florn, H., and R. Fantechi, *The Climate of Europe: Past, Present and Future* (Boston: D. Reidel Pub. Co., 1984).

[6] Champlain, Samuel de, *Voyages of Samuel de Champlain, 1604–1618* (ed. W. L. Grant) (New York: Charles Scribner's Sons, 1907).

After this mild period, especially after 1300, there was an increase in storminess in the North Sea, with some evidence suggesting a similar increase in the Atlantic, so that the trip to the New World would have been smoother before the fourteenth century than it was at the time of the Pilgrims and the first settlement of Virginia.[7]

The arriving Europeans found a new environment with unfamiliar trees and animals, with rich unplowed soils, with new food crops, with a wealth of living and mineral resources. This aspect of pre-European settlement of eastern North America is of course familiar, but historic accounts by explorers and settlers about the degree of abundance of wild living resources continue to surprise us. Champlain, for example, found on the Island of St. Croix that, "in May and June, so great a number of herring and bass are caught there that vessels could be loaded with them." And nearby on the mainland, men of his party built houses near the coast and found that "around our habitation there is, at low tide, a large number of shellfish, such as clams, mussels, sea-urchins, and sea-snails, which were very acceptable to all."[8]

Peter Kalm, a Swedish botanist sent to the new world by Linnaeus to collect plants, arrived in Philadelphia in 1748, at the end of the period covered in *The Colonizers*. He traveled from there to Montreal. When he stopped in New York City, he observed that Manhattan Island was known to be a healthy place, which it would have been at the time, a magnificent bedrock island with woods and streams and cleansing sea breezes. There, shellfish were so plentiful, Kalm wrote, that the poor lived on "oysters and a little bread" while on nearby Long Island, one could fill a cart with oysters simply from what was washed in by the tide, without having to dig or wade in the water.

In 1612, explorer Samuel Argoll sailed on the Chesapeake Bay, and saw "a great store of cattle" which were "heavy, slow, and not so wild as other beasts in the wilderness."[9] He had seen buffalo—animals which our modern image of presettlement America place only in the plains of the West, the land of cowboys and Indians. Buffalo were observed widely in eastern North America but were rapidly driven out. In 1701 there was an attempt to domesticate buffalo in a new settlement on the James River in Virginia. One herd was reported in southwestern Georgia in 1686.[10] But buffalo were killed off in Georgia by 1780 and were last reported in South Carolina around 1775. Near Roanoke, Virginia, buffalo were common at a salt lick until the mid-eighteenth century.[11] But by the time of the Louisiana Purchase in 1803 (the year of the Lewis and Clark expedition, when buffalo were so abundant west of the Mississippi that they

---

[7] Lamb, p. 301.
[8] Champlain, cited previously.
[9] Haines, p. 73.
[10] Haines, p. 32.
[11] Haines, p. 74.

provided much of the expedition's diet), these animals were no longer found in eastern North America.

Some evidence suggests that before the arrival of Europeans, buffalo may have occupied one-third of North America, reaching their northern limit in the boreal forests of Canada, their southwestern limits in the chaparral of southwestern Texas. Interestingly, consistent with our new understanding that nature is dynamic and full of changes, there is some evidence that the buffalo had been pushing their way east and only reached the Atlantic during or just before the time of the colonizers.

Thus the wildlife that the colonizers saw and harvested were different in many ways from what you would see now in an area set aside as a nature preserve and left to return to what is believed to be a natural state. A Williamsburg, Virginia-like reconstruction of colonial life that included the environment of that time would have to add not only colder weather but vast quantities of shellfish and fin fish in the rivers and along the shore, and woodland buffalo on the landscape.

In some ways, the reactions of the colonizers to these abundant natural resources may surprise a modern reader. As you can read in *The Colonizers,* Thomas Mathew of the Virginia colony described the migration of passenger pigeons as "in breadth nigh a quarter of the mid-hemisphere, and of their length was no visible end; whose weights brake down the limbs of large trees whereon these rested at nights." Today, hearing of such an event, we might grab our binoculars and travel a long distance to see this remarkable sight and add the observation to our life list of birds seen. In the nineteenth century, people traveled by train to shoot the birds. But to the settlers in the Virginia colony, this strange event was taken as "ominous presages," Mathew wrote. "This sight put the old planters under the more portentous apprehensions, because the like was seen (as they said) in 1640, when the Indians committed the last massacre, but not after."

Many of the colonizers came to eastern North America for religious reasons and brought with them a set of beliefs about nature that included the ideas that human beings had dominion over nature, and we were above and separate from nature. These ideas were eloquently expressed in the eighteenth century by Georges Leclerc, Count de Buffon, a famous French naturalist, in his book *Histoire Naturelle, Générale et Particulière.* He wrote that although nature is the "external throne of the divine magnificence," people "among living beings" establish "order, subordination, and harmony." Human beings are granted by God "dominion over every creature," and it is our role to add "embellishment, cultivation, extension, and polish." It is man who "cuts down the thistle and the bramble, and he multiplies the vine and the rose." [12]

Among the Native Americans were a variety of related beliefs, but there

[12] Leclerc, G. L., *Natural History, General and Particular,* vol. 3, trans. W. Smellie (London: C. Wood, 1812), pp. 455–57.

was more of the sense that human beings are within and part of nature, neither above nor below it, neither owning nor ruling it. The colonization was thus an anthropological event—a confrontation among peoples with differing ideas about the character of nature and the relationship between human beings and nature.[13] Indeed, an argument can be made that these different approaches to nature, including whether one could have a sense of ownership of the landscape, and whether wildlife and forests were there to be exploited at will by those with dominion and dominance or to be sustained by those who were part of the system, were at the roots of conflicts that appear on the surface to be political and military conflicts.

It was a time when animals of the new world were perceived solely as commodities. William Penn, for example, wrote that there were animals "of diverse sorts, some for food and profit, and some for profit only," which is to say that the animals only had value if they were of direct economic use to people. Protection of endangered species and the conservation of nature were ideas of the future. Only a rare few of the colonists and explorers were concerned with what we call today natural history, biological conservation, or environment. In Peter Kalm's remarkable journey of his travels in 1748 and 1749, he wrote about the European colonists that "people are here (and in many other places) in regard to wood, bent only upon their own present advantage, utterly regardless of posterity. . . . [They take] little account of Natural History, that science being here (as in other parts of the world) looked upon as a mere trifle, and the pastime of fools."[14]

It was an attitude prevalent at that time, and not entirely lacking from our own. Here Kalm is complaining not only about the attitude toward nature that was prevalent, but also the lack of understanding of the need for scientific study and measurement—surveys, monitoring, data. In the twentieth century, managers of wild living resources understand the value of such studies for the conservation of these resources. While our general societal attitude has shifted to an appreciation of these resources, we are still only at the beginning stage in an appreciation of the value of scientific observation as a tool in conservation and management.

This is not to say that the Native Americans did not alter their environment. There is a tendency today to romanticize the relationship between Native Americans and nature to the point that we tend to believe that they made no changes except to gather a few foodstuffs. On the contrary, the Indians of eastern North America appear to be the cause of frequent forest fires. Many of the early explorers such as Henry Hudson mention that they saw many fires onshore, which they say were lit by the Indians. The explor-

[13] Glacken, Clarence J., *Traces on the Rhodian Shore: Nature and Culture in Western Thought from Ancient Times to the End of the Eighteenth Century* (Berkeley: University of California Press, 1967), p. 763.

[14] Kalm, P., *Travels in America: The America of 1750,* ed. A. B. Benson, English Version 1770 (New York: Dover, 1966), pp. 300 and 309.

ers gave various reasons for these fires: to clear the underbrush to make it easier to find wild game, to make travel easier, to drive the game away from the fire so that the animals could be caught more easily (a technique observed in this book by none other than Captain John Smith), and to clear the land for crops. Whatever the reasons, fire was more common than could be expected simply from lightning. These fires altered the appearance of the forests and the composition of species. Peter Kalm traveled through what is now New Brunswick, New Jersey, and wrote that the forests were primarily made up of large, old trees, clear of underbrush and young saplings in between. The trees were so widely spaced and the ground so clear among the trees that, Kalm related, one could easily drive a horse and carriage through the woods.

In contrast, a modern nature preserve has quite a different aspect. Hutcheson Memorial Forest near New Brunswick, New Jersey, is such a preserve. It was settled in 1701 by a Dutch family, the Mettlers, who maintained part of their holdings as a woodlot which they never harvested. The woodlot was purchased by Rutgers University in the 1950s to protect the last remaining uncut old-growth forest on the New Jersey piedmont. But by the second half of the twentieth century this forest had become a stand of many small trees with some scattered but aging old trees among them. The smaller trees formed such a dense stand that it was difficult to walk through the woods, let alone drive a horse and carriage. Peter Kalm had passed through a forest of oaks, hickories, and chestnut. The chestnut was gone by the 1950s from the blight introduced in the first decades of the twentieth century. But more curious, the oaks and hickories were not regenerating, but were being replaced by sugar maple, a species whose range was supposed to be to the north. The structure and species of the forest were changing in a preserve that was meant to protect these characteristics.

Modern ecological research has shown that fires occurred on average every ten years prior to 1701, when this location was first settled by Europeans, and that no fire had occurred since, as a result of fire suppression policies. The frequent Indian-lit fires cleared the underbrush, kept the fuel load down and thereby prevented destructively intense wildfires. The fires created the beautiful forest of large, old trees that people still believe were the true natural state of the landscape, in the sense that they developed without human influence. The fires favored oaks and hickories, which are better able to recover from burning than maples.

What we imagine to be the pristine state of nature, a nature essentially unaffected by human beings, but beautiful with abundant trees and wildlife, was in part the direct product of Native American activities. Fires, the growing of crops, and the hunting of wild game were several of the ways that the Indians altered the environment. These resulted in large landscape changes which have become our myth of the natural state of eastern North America.

The discoveries of strange creatures in North America, along with those elsewhere previously unknown to Europeans, forced a reexamination of ancient, great questions about the character of nature, the effects of nature on human beings, of human beings on nature, and on the relationship between the two. It provoked attempts by theologians to reconcile the discovery of new animals with the Bible.

The colonization took place during a major transition in European ideas about the character of nature everywhere, from the cosmos to the microbes. In the century when the Massachusetts Bay colonists built their homes and La Salle explored the Mississippi and Arkansas rivers, Galileo used the newly invented telescope to discover moons of Jupiter, spots on the sun, and the phases of Venus. Kepler demonstrated that the orbits of the planets were not circles but ellipses, a finding that at the time seemed contrary to the perfection of the universe created by a perfect God. And Antonie van Leeuwenhoek discovered "animalcules," tiny creatures visible only with the newly invented microscope.

The study of the anatomy of humans and other vertebrates was just beginning, and the parallels between our species and others were starting to yield new insights. One of the major medical discoveries of the seventeenth century was Harvey's understanding of the circulation of blood. Today we may have difficulty conceiving of a time when people did not understand that blood, which flowed so freely when an artery was cut, was circulating within the human body. Harvey's work is generally said to represent the beginnings of experimental physiology. Thus knowledge of the human body that we take for granted today was as little understood at the time of the colonizers as were natural ecosystems. From our modern biological perspective, the colonizers knew as little about themselves as they did of their surroundings. How different their perception, then, of nature and their role in it must have been.

The colonization was itself an ecological event whose ramifications are still being expressed. We know today that the introduction of new populations often has ecologically major effects, frequently disastrous to indigenous populations. This is indicated by the reports of the settlers at Plymouth about Indian villages abandoned because of an epidemic, probably smallpox brought by earlier European visitors. The colonization was the first stage in a post-colonization environmental history of North America, a time of discovery and initial exploitation of the continent's resources. This was followed by a period of intense exploitation which lasted until the beginning of the twentieth century, then a period of resource management for economic production and an initial approach to conservation, followed by modern environmentalism, beginning in the second half of the twentieth century.[15]

As you read the personal accounts of colonizers, remember that it was

[15] See Botkin, *Our Natural History: The Lessons of Lewis and Clark,* cited earlier.

a time of harsh weather, a time when science had yet had little impact on people's understanding of the natural world into which they were thrust, and that therefore their interpretations could differ considerably from ours. With this background, reading the accounts of the colonizers tells us not only about them, but about ourselves—about the myths and approaches to nature and natural resources that Europeans brought to this continent and still influence us. It helps us not only relive the colonization, but to rediscover ourselves.

—Daniel B. Botkin

A NOTE TO THE READER

In addition to providing introductions to the first-person accounts in this book, the editor has included original narrative to connect the selections and offer critical commentary. A heavy line appears at the beginning and end of these sections, marking off the editor's words from those of the historical writers. Within the first-person accounts, of course, the editor's insertions appear in brackets.

I

A VERY OLD WORLD

THE EUROPEANS ARRIVE

1
A SOLDIER OF FRANCE

We begin with a soldier of medieval France. A strange start, perhaps, for the story of what will become, at the end of this book, British North America. In 1604, however, nothing was foreordained to this particular soldier of France. He stood on the edge of a rare moment, when mere handfuls of men would direct the migrations of future millions, influence the survival or destruction of entire cultures, and shape the clash of empires. He and his peers would decide such things by a chance turn down this river or that, by a quirk of success in lobbying some royal court, or by simply surviving a killing winter in a primitive hut half a world from home. And the decisions, fortunes, and will of this particular individual, Samuel de Champlain, did more to shift the course of a continent than any other.

So we begin with a Frenchman, in a France we may certainly call medieval. Historically speaking, the year 1604 has been designated part of the Early Modern period: the Middle Ages had officially ended, even by the reckoning of his contemporaries, and the Renaissance was in full bloom. As Champlain prepared for his history-changing voyages, Galileo, Kepler, and Shakespeare were alive and well, working at the peak of their careers. Champlain belonged to a remarkable generation, and it is small wonder that we attach his age to ours with the phrase *Early* Modern.

But Champlain's world was far closer to the Dark Ages than to our own. It had virtually no sanitation, no medicine, no plumbing, no industry (as we could identify): the vast majority of human beings spent most of their waking moments producing, distributing, preparing, or worrying about food. The market economy we take for granted today existed only in strands and spots: there were thousands, perhaps millions, who went year in and year out without handling a penny in actual money. Famine—desperate, killing starvation that left villages strewn with families of the dead—swept the countryside regularly; smallpox and the plague, that most medieval of ailments, burned back and forth across the continent, carried by the vermin that crawled everywhere. It would be another sixty years yet before the last Great Plague hit London, along with the Great Fire, another common urban death machine. Dirt streets and the few miserable roads stretched along, clogged with manure, often human—running past wells in towns that would not

3

have proper drainage for centuries more. And the church still burned heretics.

France itself, as in the Kingdom of France, led Europe in the great activity of the Early Modern age: the erection of the nation-state. Historians have identified signs that the feudal, haphazard, ragged rule of medieval government was passing away in favor of rational, professional administration. Of course, this information would have startled, perhaps insulted a decent Frenchman of the day. He and his fellows still thought of society in terms of the classic three estates of medieval theory: those who fight (the nobility), those who pray (priests and monastic orders), and those who work (peasants and the small class of merchants). Birth, breeding, and fealty to one's hereditary master mattered more than merit in the pecking order of 1604. Champlain, for example, rose to prominence like a knight of old, by faithfully serving his liege lord—Henry, king of the mini-realm of Navarre and heir to the throne of France. And Henry needed all the faithful service he could get.

All through the late 1500s, a succession of savage wars had consumed the French countryside, as the wily Henry and his forces fought against the reigning house of Valois. A bitter religious dispute, a product of the Reformation, marked the conflict: traditional Catholics (gathered in the aptly named Catholic League, organized by the powerful Duke de Guise) rallied to oppose Henry of Navarre, and the Protestant Huguenots supported him. Indeed, we call this long series of sieges, battles, truces, and then more sieges and battles, the Wars of Religion. But it remained a dynastic struggle, in many ways as premodern as they come.[1]

Champlain (along with all the Frenchmen who first settled in North America) came of age in this time of startling ruthlessness and savagery. After the death of the Valois king Henry II and the rise of his vacillating brother Henry III, the two Catholic houses of Valois and Guise intrigued against each other. The Duke Henry de Guise launched a slaughter of all the Protestants in Paris, an event known as the Bartholomew's Day Massacre; Henry of Navarre, in town to marry the king's sister, survived by temporarily converting to Catholicism. Later, in what was called the War of the Three Henrys, Duke Henry de Guise forced King Henry III to flee Paris; the king joined forces with the now deconverted Henry of Navarre, and then had the duke assassinated. In return he was himself stabbed to death while besieging Paris. Henry of Navarre, as legitimate heir, claimed the throne; but Spanish troops poured into France to aid the Guise family and the Catholic League. Disease, looting, rape, and simple murder marked the path of the various armies as they wandered the land. And one of those wanderers was Samuel de Champlain.

Henry of Navarre won. He defeated the Spanish, routed the Catholic

---

[1] As if to highlight the medieval flavor of the times, in 1559 King Henry II died while jousting—as predicted, some said, by his court astrologer Nostradamus.

League armies, conquered the entire country except for the final prize: Paris. Finally, to seal his victory, he rediscovered his earlier, utilitarian love for Rome and reconverted to Catholicism. The Catholic League relented, and Henry of Navarre, head of the house of Bourbon and now King Henry IV of France, marched through the streets of the great city at the head of his troops. In a moment of remarkable candor, he explained his pendulum faith with the famous line, "Paris is well worth a mass."

Both the war and the subsequent reign of Henry IV, it should be said, offered hints that the medieval world was indeed passing away. Champlain and his comrades, for example, still carried age-old weapons for stabbing and cutting—heavy swords, long iron-pointed pikes, and axe-headed halberds favored by the Swiss mercenaries—but they now relied mainly on a matchlock musket known as the harquebus. This was a true innovation, one destined to separate Champlain from the peoples he would meet across the Atlantic. For the first time in human history, foot soldiers applied something other than muscle power in battle; now they used chemical power, the energy released when gunpowder is ignited.

But Champlain was a sailor first and a soldier second. As such, he was intimately acquainted with another great innovation—the oceangoing ship. During the last two centuries, shipwrights along the Atlantic coast had been perfecting hulls, sails, and rigging suited to the open sea. Champlain had also learned the relatively recent art of using an astrolabe, a device for navigating by the stars. Such techniques and technologies had released the great explosion of explorers over 100 years before, most famously in Columbus's voyage to the New World in 1492.

Columbus's journeys, however, had been financed by Spain. The Spanish could afford to simultaneously meddle in France's internal affairs and explore distant continents: They possessed the great empire of the age, encompassing southern Italy, the Netherlands, and other bits and pieces of Europe. Like France, it was a nation still shrouded in the Middle Ages: an awkwardly assembled collection of kingdoms and principalities, united only in the fact that one king held the throne of each. Even so, Spain was rich, powerful, and armed to the teeth. As the French spent their days calculating how to kill more of themselves, the Spanish had burned across Central and South America like an Early Modern blitzkrieg. By the time Henry of Navarre entered Paris as King Henry IV in 1594, Spain had already established an overseas empire teeming with subjects, cities, and silver mines.

Both the new king and his loyal servant Champlain were acutely aware of Spain's head start in the quest for an Atlantic empire. Henry had to spend a few more years, however, ejecting the last Spanish troops from French territory, a process completed in 1598. He longed to be a foreign-policy monarch, but domestic affairs called. For most of his reign, he labored to rebuild his shattered kingdom, reorganize its finances, institute a semblance of a bureaucracy, encourage economic development, and provide rights to the

Protestants—all with the aid of the able Duke de Sully. The entire time, however, Henry had his eyes on archrival Spain.

So did Champlain, but without such belligerence. The Spanish empire tugged at his yearning to explore. After the peace, he pulled strings with an uncle who had defected to the Spanish side and won a place on a voyage to New Spain. He marveled at what he saw, and when he came home he wrote an account of his travels (the start of a lifelong habit). The trip was a turning point in his life. His two great drives—a lust for adventure and a sense of duty—now had a specific focus: the New World. He had the knowledge (as a sailor) to go there, and the skills (as a soldier) to survive its perils. Most important, he had the will to go, and to keep going until he had stamped that world with his own mark.

As for Henry IV, he wanted to establish France across the Atlantic before it was too late. But the demands of strained finances required that he conduct his colony-making on the cheap. He floated deals with various parties, until he finally struck an agreement with the Company of New France. Private investors—rich nobles and merchants—would finance an expedition to North America to acquire the furs that were much in demand for fashionable hats. The king would get 10 percent of the profits and a foothold in the New World; the investors would keep 90 percent and gain a legal monopoly on the French fur trade. This sort of contract was a common expedient in cash-strapped France; most taxes, for example, were collected by tax farmers—private individuals who kept a part of the take. Yet the deal also set a long-term pattern of close royal involvement in colonial affairs.

Given Champlain's experience, knowledge, and skills, he made a natural officer of the Company, and he took part in the first voyage in 1603: a reconnaissance up the St. Lawrence River, first discovered by the French explorer Jacques Cartier seventy years earlier. He returned convinced that he had come close to finding the Northwest Passage, the legendary shortcut to the Pacific.

By now, Champlain's mission burned in his mind. This faithful soldier could serve his king by planting a colony of Frenchmen in the upper reaches of North America. He could serve his company by settling the fur trade on firm foundations. He could serve his countrymen by finding a route to the rich Asian trade in silk and spices. And he could serve his Church by winning the souls of those who lived across the Atlantic. Unlike his king, Champlain possessed a very real faith in the Catholic Church. In a cynical nation, in a self-serving age, Champlain cherished a rare virtue: sincerity.

In 1604, the executive director of the Company of New France, Pierre de Monts, appointed Champlain as one of his lieutenants for another voyage to New France. This time, they were to establish a lasting French colony in North America. Rather than try the St. Lawrence again, however, Monts decided to sail up the Bay of Fundy, above what is now the coast of Maine. That voyage was the start of the first serious, sustained effort to colonize

North America above Spanish Florida. Fortunately, Champlain himself wrote a detailed account of the journey after he returned to France—another volume in his ongoing travelogue. The New World, he discovered, was a very old world indeed. It was old to the Europeans, who had been traveling to the Newfoundland shores for a century or more, fishing and trading for furs. And it was unspeakably old to the native peoples, whose cultures and qualities he would later learn to admire as he risked his life to fight beside them.

In the passage below, Champlain begins by placing this effort in a grand historical perspective, evoking his own powerful sense of mission. That first attempt at a settlement has been excerpted from this selection—suffice it to say it was a brutal experience, as he and a handful of men suffered from scurvy, traded (and skirmished) with Native Americans, and explored the rocky coasts of what we now call New England. Eventually the Company lost its monopoly on the fur trade, and the settlers were ordered home after three years across the ocean.

Those three years were difficult for Champlain: he surely must have wondered how long he could keep beating the odds as men died all around him. Yet he also watched, wrote, and learned. The location of the first colony (on an island) had been a mistake, he noted; proper housing and food storage were essential; and the "savage" Indians were men he could deal with, at least as well as he had dealt with savages who plundered France for a generation in the name of religion.

Such was the knowledge and experience he carried into his next expedition—the decisive one, the voyage that firmly established France on North American soil. The dangers he would face, however, were even greater than those he had endured before, including hostile traders, starvation, scurvy—and treason.

Pestilence, Starvation, and Treason
by Samuel de Champlain

The inclinations of men differ according to their varied dispositions; and each one in his calling has his particular end in view. Some aim to gain, some at glory, some at the public weal. The greater number are engaged in trade, and especially that which is transacted on the sea. Hence arises the principal support of the people, the opulence and honor of states. That is what raised ancient Rome to the sovereignty and mastery over the entire world, and the Venetians to a grandeur equal to that of powerful kings. It has in all times caused maritime towns to abound in riches, among which Alexandria and Tyre are distinguished, and numerous others which fill up the regions of the interior with the objects of beauty and rarity obtained from foreign nations.

For this reason, many princes have striven to find a northerly route to China, in order to facilitate commerce with the Orientals, in the belief that this route would be shorter and less dangerous.

In the year 1496, the king of England commissioned John Cabot and his son Sebastian to engage in this search. . . . In the years 1534 and 1535, Jacques Cartier received a like commission from King Francis I [of France], but was arrested in his course. Six years after, Sieur de Roberval, having renewed it, sent Jean Alfonse of Saintonge farther northward along the coast of Labrador; but he returned as wise as the others. In the years 1576, 1577, and 1578, Sir Martin Frobisher, an Englishman, made three voyages along the northern coasts. . . .

So many voyages and discoveries without result, and attended with so much hardship and expense, have caused us French in late years to attempt a permanent settlement in those lands which we call New France, in the hope of thus realizing more easily this object; since the voyage in search of the desired passage commences on the other side of the ocean, and is made along the coast of this region. These considerations had induced Marquis de la Roche, in 1598, to take a commission from the king for the making of a settlement in the above region. . . . A year after, Captain Chauvin accepted another commission to transport settlers to the same region; but, as this was shortly after revoked, he prosecuted the matter no farther.

After the above, notwithstanding all these accidents and disappointments, Sieur de Monts [director of the Company of New France] desired to attempt what had been given up in despair, and requested a commission for this purpose of his Majesty, being satisfied that the previous enterprises had failed because the undertakers of them had not succeeded, in one nor even two years' time, in making the acquaintance of the regions and the people there, nor in finding harbors adapted for a settlement. He proposed to his Majesty a means for covering these expenses, without drawing anything from the royal revenues; viz. by granting him the monopoly of the fur-trade in this land. This having been granted to him, he made great and excessive outlays, and carried out with him a large number of men of various vocations. . . .

Sieur de Monts, by virtue of his commission, had published in all the ports and harbors of this kingdom the prohibition against the violation of the monopoly of the fur-trade accorded him by his Majesty, and gathered together 120 artisans, whom he embarked in two vessels; one of 120 tons, commanded by Sieur de Pont Gravé; another, of 150 tons, in which he embarked himself, together with several noblemen.

We set out from Havre de Grâce April 7, 1604. . . . [Champlain helped establish a fur-trading settlement in what is now Maine, and remained for three years. The Company's monopoly on France's fur imports expired, and the little colony was ordered home.]

Having returned to France after a stay of three years in New France, I proceeded to Sieur de Monts, and related to him the principal events of which I had been a witness since his departure, and gave him the map and plan of the most remarkable coasts and harbors there.

Some time afterward, Sieur de Monts determined to continue his undertaking, and complete the exploration of the interior along the great river St. Lawrence, where I had been by order of the late King Henry the Great[2] in the year 1603, for a distance of some hundred and eighty leagues. . . .

Now after Sieur de Monts had conferred with me several times in regard to his purposes concerning the exploration, he resolved to continue so noble and meritorious an undertaking, notwithstanding the hardships and labors of the past. He honored me with his lieutenancy for the voyage; and, in order to carry out his purpose, he had two vessels equipped, one commanded by Pont Gravé, who was commissioned to trade with the savages of the country and bring back the vessels, while I was to winter in the country.

Sieur de Monts, for the purpose of defraying the expenses of the expedition, obtained letters from his Majesty [the still-living Henry IV] for one year, by which all persons were forbidden to traffic in peltry [furs] with the savages. . . . I proceeded to Honfleur for embarkation, where I found the vessel of Pont Gravé in readiness. He left port on the 5th of April [1608]. I did so on the 13th, arriving at the Grand Bank on the 15th of May. . . .

On the 3rd of June, we arrived before Tadoussac,[3] distant from Gaspé from eighty to ninety leagues, which latter [Tadoussac] is a kind of cove at the mouth of the river Saguenay, where the tide is very remarkable on account of its rapidity. . . . I at once had the boat lowered, in order to go to the port and ascertain whether Pont Gravé had arrived.

While on the way, I met a shallop[4] with the pilot of Pont Gravé and a Basque, who came to inform me of what had happened to them because they attempted to hinder the Basque vessels from trading, according to the commission obtained by Sieur de Monts from his Majesty, that no vessels should trade without permission of Sieur de Monts, as was expressed in it; and that, notwithstanding the notifications which Pont Gravé made in behalf of his Majesty, they did not desist from forcibly carrying on their trade; and that they had used their arms and maintained themselves so well in their vessel that, discharging all their cannon upon that of Pont Gravé, and letting off many musket-shots, he was severely wounded, together with three of his men, one of whom died. Pont Gravé meanwhile made no resistance; for at the first shower of musketry he was struck down. The Basques came on

[2] Henry IV died on May 14, 1610, well after the events related here. He had finally put his domestic house in order and was preparing to go to war at last with Spain and Austria, when an assassin stabbed him to death.

[3] Tadoussac (still on today's maps) was the main meeting place for Indians and the French for fur trading. The trade was, technically, illegal for French subjects, but Basque merchants and fishermen hardly cared. The league mentioned here equaled roughly 2.8 miles.

[4] A shallop is a large open boat that can be fitted with a sail.

board of the vessel and took away all the cannon and arms, declaring that they would trade, notwithstanding the prohibition of the king, and that when they were ready to set out for France they would restore to him his cannon and ammunition, and that they were keeping them in order to be in a state of security. Upon hearing all these particulars, I was greatly annoyed at such a beginning, which might have easily been avoided.

Now, after hearing from the pilot all these things I asked him why the Basque had come on board our vessel. He told me that he came on behalf of their master, named Darache, and his companions, to obtain assurance from me that I would do them no harm when our vessel entered the harbor.

I replied that I could not give any until I had seen Pont Gravé. The Basque said that if I had need of anything in their power, they would assist me accordingly. What led them to use this language was simply their recognition of having done wrong, as they confessed, and the fear that they would not be permitted to engage in the whale-fishery. After talking at length, I went ashore to see Pont Gravé, in order to deliberate as to what was to be done. I found him very ill. He related to me in detail all that had happened. We concluded that we could only enter the harbor by force, and that the settlement must not be given up for this year, so that we considered it best, in order not to make a bad cause out of a just one and thus work our ruin, to give them assurances on my part so long as I should remain there, that Pont Gravé should undertake nothing against them, but that justice should be done in France, and their differences should be settled there.

Darache, master of the vessel, begged me to go on board, where he gave me a cordial reception. After a long conference, I secured an agreement between Pont Gravé and him, and required him to promise that he would undertake nothing against Pont Gravé, or what would be prejudicial to the King and Sieur de Monts; that, if he did the contrary, I should regard my promise as null and void. This was agreed to, and signed by each.

In this place were a number of savages who had come for trade in furs, several of whom came to our vessel with their canoes, which are from eight to nine paces long, and about a pace and a half broad in the middle, growing narrower toward the two ends. They are very apt to turn over, in case one does not understand managing them, and are made of birch bark, strengthened on the inside by little ribs of white cedar, very neatly arranged; they are so light that a man can easily carry one. Each can carry a weight equal to that of a pipe.[5] When they want to go overland to a river where they have business, they carry them with them. . . .

I set out from Tadoussac the last day of the month to go to Quebec. . . .

---

[5] A liquid measure, containing from 400 to 700 quarts.

ARRIVAL AT QUEBEC

I arrived there on the 3rd of July, when I searched for a place suitable for our settlement, but I could find none more convenient or better situated than the point of Quebec, so called by the savages, which was covered with nut-trees. I at once employed a portion of our workmen in cutting them down, so that we might construct our habitation there: one I set to sawing boards, another to making a cellar and digging ditches, another I sent to Tadoussac with the bark[6] for supplies. The first thing we made was the storehouse for keeping under cover our supplies, which was promptly accomplished through the zeal of all, and my attention to the work.

Some days after my arrival at Quebec, a locksmith conspired against the service of the king. His plan was to put me to death, and, getting possession of our fort, to put it into the hands of the Basques or the Spaniards, then at Tadoussac. . . . In order to execute his wretched plan, by which he hoped to make his fortune, he suborned four of the worst characters, as he supposed, telling them a thousand falsehoods, and presenting to them prospects of acquiring riches.

These four men, having been won over, all promised to act in such a manner as to gain the rest over to their side; so that, for the time being, I had no one with me in whom I could put confidence, which gave them still more hope of making their plan succeed: for four or five of my companions, in whom they knew that I put confidence, were on board of the barks, for the purposes of protecting the provisions and supplies necessary for our settlement. In a word, they were so skillful in carrying out their intrigues with those who remained, that they were on the point of gaining all over to their cause, even my servant, promising them many things which they could not have fulfilled.

Being now all agreed, they made daily different plans as to how they should put me to death, so as not to be accused of it, which they found to be a difficult thing. But the devil blindfolding them all and taking away their reason and every possible difficulty, they determined to take me while unarmed and strangle me; or to give a false alarm at night, and shoot me as I went out, in which manner they judged that they would accomplish their work sooner than otherwise. They made a mutual promise not to betray each other, on penalty that the first one who opened his mouth should be poniarded [stabbed with a dagger]. They were to execute their plan in four days, before the arrival of our barks, otherwise they would have been unable to carry out their scheme.

On this very day, one of our barks arrived with our pilot, Captain Testu, a very discreet man. After the bark was unloaded and ready to return to Ta-

---

[6] A bark is a ship with three to five masts, all square-rigged but the aftmost. Champlain probably used the term for a much smaller sailing vessel, however.

doussac, there came to him a locksmith named Natel, an associate of Jean du Val, the head of the conspiracy, who told him that he had promised the rest to do just as they did; but that he did not in fact desire the execution of the plot, yet did not dare to make a disclosure of it, from fear of being poniarded. Antoine Natel made the pilot promise that he would make no disclosure in regard to what he should say, since, if his companions should discover it, they would put him to death.

The pilot gave him his assurance in all particulars, and asked him to state the character of the plot which they wished to carry out. This Natel did at length, when the pilot said to him: "My friend, you have done well to disclose such a malicious design, and you show that you are an upright man, and under the guidance of the Holy Spirit. But these things cannot be passed by without bringing them to the knowledge of Sieur de Champlain, that he may make provision against them; and I promise you that I will prevail upon him to pardon you and the rest. And I will at once," said the pilot, "go to him without exciting any suspicion; and do you go about your business, listening to all they may say, and not troubling yourself about the rest."

The pilot came at once to me, in a garden which I was having prepared, and said that he wished to speak to me in a private place, where we could be alone. I readily assented, and we went into the wood, where he related to me the whole affair. I asked who had told it to him. He begged me to pardon him who made the disclosure, which I consented to do, although he ought to have addressed himself to me. He was afraid, he replied, that you would become angry, and harm him. I told him that I was able to govern myself better than that, in such a matter; and desired him to have the man come to me, that I might hear his statement. He went, and brought him all trembling with fear lest I should do him some harm. I reassured him, telling him not to be afraid; that he was in a place of safety, and that I should pardon him for all that he had done, together with the others provided he would tell me in full the truth in regard to the whole matter, and the motive which had impelled them to it.

"Nothing," he said, "had impelled them, except that they had imagined that, by giving up the place into the hands of the Basques or Spaniards, they might all become rich, and that they did not want to go back to France." He also related to me the remaining particulars in regard to their conspiracy.

After having heard and questioned him, I directed him to go about his work. Meanwhile, I ordered the pilot to bring up his shallop, which he did. Then I gave two bottles of wine to a young man, directing him to say to these four worthies, the leaders of the conspiracy, that it was a present of wine, which his friends at Tadoussac had given him, and that he wished to share it with them. This they did not decline, and at evening were on board the bark where he was to give them the entertainment. I lost no time in going there shortly after; and caused them to be seized, and held until the next day.

Then were my worthies astonished indeed. I at once had all get up, for it was about ten o'clock in the evening, and pardoned them all, on condition that they would disclose to me the truth in regard to all that had occurred; which they did, when I had them retire.

The next day I took the depositions of all, one after the other, in the presence of the pilot and sailors of the vessel, which I had put down in writing; and they were well pleased, as they said, since they had lived only in fear of each other, especially of the four knaves who had ensnared them. But now they lived in peace, satisfied, as they declared, with the treatment which they had received. The same day I had six pairs of handcuffs made for the authors of the conspiracy: one for our surgeon, named Bonerme, one for another, named La Taille, whom the four conspirators had accused, which, however, proved false, and consequently they were given their liberty.

This being done, I took my worthies to Tadoussac, begging Pont Gravé to do me the favor of guarding them, since I had as yet no secure place for keeping them, and as we were occupied in constructing our places of abode. Another object was to consult with him, and others on the ship, as to what should be done in the premises. He suggested that, after he had finished his work at Tadoussac, he should come to Quebec with the prisoners, where we should have them confronted with their witnesses, and, after giving them a hearing, order justice to be done according to the offense which they had committed.

I went back the next day to Quebec to hasten the completion of our storehouse, so as to secure our provisions, which had been misused by all of those scoundrels, who spared nothing, without reflecting how they could find more when these failed; for I could not obviate the difficulty until the storehouse should be completed and shut up.

Pont Gravé arrived some time after me, with the prisoners, which caused uneasiness to the workmen who remained, since they feared that I should pardon them, and that they would avenge themselves upon them for revealing their wicked design. We had them brought face to face, and they affirmed before them all that which they had stated in their depositions, the prisoners not denying it, but admitting that they had acted in a wicked manner, and should be punished, unless mercy might be exercised towards them; accusing, above all, Jean du Val, who had been trying to lead them into such a conspiracy from the time of their departure from France. Du Val knew not what to say, except that he deserved death, that all stated in the depositions was true, and that he begged for mercy upon himself and the others, who had given in their adherence to his pernicious purposes.

After Pont Gravé and I, the captain of the vessel, surgeon, mate, second mate, and other sailors had heard their depositions and face-to-face statements, we adjudged that it would be enough to put to death Du Val, as the instigator of the conspiracy; and that he might serve as an example to those who remained, leading them to deport themselves correctly in future, in the discharge of their duty; and that the Spaniards and Basques, of whom there were large numbers in the country, might not glory in the event. We adjudged that the three others might be condemned to be hung, but that they should be taken to France and put into the hands of Sieur de Monts, that such ample justice might be done them as he should recommend; that they should be sent with all the evidence and their sentence, as well as that of Jean du Val, who was strangled and hung at Quebec, and his head was put on the end of a pike, to be set up in the most conspicuous place on our fort.

DESCRIPTION OF OUR QUARTERS

After all these occurrences, Pont Gravé set out from Quebec on the 18th of September to return to France with the three prisoners. After he had gone, all who remained conducted themselves correctly in the discharge of their duty.

I had the work on our quarters continued, which was composed of three buildings of two stories. Each one was three fathoms long, and two and a half wide. The storehouse was six fathoms long and three wide, with a fine cellar six feet deep. I had a gallery [firing platform] made all around our buildings, on the outside, at the second story, which proved very convenient. There were also ditches, fifteen feet wide and six deep. On the outer side of the ditches, I constructed several spurs, which enclosed a part of the dwelling, at the points where we placed our cannon.

Before the habitation there is a place four fathoms wide and six or seven long, looking upon the riverbank. Surrounding the habitation are very good gardens, and a place on the north side some hundred or hundred and twenty paces long and fifty or sixty wide. Moreover, near Quebec there is a little river coming from a lake in the interior, distant six or seven leagues from our settlement. I am of the opinion that this river, which is north a quarter north-west from our settlement, is the place where Jacques Cartier wintered, since there are still, a league up the river, remains of what seems to have been a chimney, the foundation of which has been found, and indications of there having been ditches surrounding their dwelling, which was small. We found, also, large pieces of hewn, worm-eaten timber, and some three or four cannon-balls. . . .

While the carpenters, sawers of boards, and other workmen were employed on our quarters, I set all the others to work clearing up around our place of abode, in preparation for gardens in which to plant grain and seeds, that we might see how they would flourish, as the soil seemed to be very good.

Meanwhile, a large number of savages were encamped in cabins near us, engaged in fishing for eels, which begin to come about the 15th of September and go away on the 15th of October. During this time, all the savages subsist on this food, and dry enough of it for the winter to last until the month of February, when there are about two and a half, or at most three, feet of snow; and, when their eels and other things which they dry have been prepared, they go to hunt the beaver until the beginning of January. At their departure for this purpose, they intrusted to us all their eels and other things, until their return, which was on the 15th of December. But they did not have great success in the beaver-hunt, as the amount of water was too great, the rivers having overrun their banks, as they told us. I returned to them all their supplies, which lasted them only until the 20th of January. When their supply of eels gave out, they hunted the elk and such other wild beasts as they could find until spring, when I was able to supply them with various things. I paid special attention to their customs.

These people suffer so much from lack of food that they are sometimes obliged to live on certain shell-fish, and eat their dogs and the skins with which they clothe themselves against the cold. I am of the opinion that, if one were to show them how to live, and teach them the cultivation of the soil and other things, they would learn very aptly, for many of them possess good sense, and answer properly questions put to them. They have a bad habit of taking vengeance, and are great liars, and you must not put much reliance on them, except judiciously, and with force at hand. They make promises readily, but keep their word poorly.

The most of them observe no law at all, so far as I have been able to see, and are, besides, full of superstitions. I asked them with what ceremonies they were accustomed to pray to their God, when they replied that they had none, but that each prayed to him in his own heart, as he wished. . . . So, also, they believe that all their dreams are true; and, in fact, there are many who say that they have had visions and dreams about matters which actually come to pass or will do so. But, to tell the truth, these are diabolical visions, through which they are deceived and misled. This is all I have been able to learn about their brutish faith. All these people are well proportioned in body, without deformity, and are agile. . . .

All the time they were with us, which was the most secure place for them, they did not cease to fear their enemies to such an extent that they often at night became alarmed while dreaming, and sent their wives and children to our fort, the gates of which I had opened to them, allowing the men to remain about the fort, but not permitting them to enter, for their persons were thus as much in security as if they had been inside. I also had five or six men go out to reassure them, and to go and ascertain whether they could see anything in the woods, in order to quiet them. . . .

COMMENCEMENT OF THE WINTER AND ICE

On the 1st of October, I had some wheat sown, and on the 15th some rye. On the 3rd, there was a white frost in some places, and the leaves of the trees began to fall on the 15th. . . . On the 18th of November, there was a great fall of snow, which remained only two days on the ground, during which time there was a violent gale of wind. There died during this month a sailor and our locksmith of dysentery, so also many Indians from eating eels badly cooked, as I think.

On the 5th of February, it snowed violently, and the wind was high for two days. On the 20th, some Indians appeared on the far side of the river, calling to us to go to their assistance, which was beyond our power, on account of the large amount of ice drifting in the river. Hunger pressed upon these poor wretches so severely that, not knowing what to do, they resolved, men, women, and children, to cross the river or die, hoping that I should assist them in their extreme want. Having accordingly made this resolve, the men and women took the children and embarked in their canoes, thinking that they could reach our shore by an opening in the ice made by the wind; but they were scarcely in the middle of the stream when their canoes were caught by the ice and broken into a thousand pieces.

But they were skillful enough to throw themselves with the children, which the women carried on their backs, on a large piece of ice. As they were on it, we heard them crying out so that it excited intense pity, as before them there seemed nothing but death. But fortune was so favorable to these poor wretches that a large piece of ice struck against the side of that on which they were, so violently as to drive them ashore. On seeing this favorable turn, they reached the shore with as much delight as they ever experienced, notwithstanding the great hunger from which they were suffering. They proceeded to our abode, so thin and haggard that they seemed like mere skeletons, most of them not being able to hold themselves up. I was astonished to see them, and observe the manner in which they had crossed, in view of their being so weak and feeble. I ordered some bread and beans to be given them. So great was their impatience to eat them, that they could not wait to have them cooked. I lent them also some bark, which other savages had given me, to cover their cabins.

As they were making their cabin, they discovered a piece of carrion, which I had thrown out nearly two months before to attract the foxes, of which we caught black and red ones, like those in France, but with heavier fur. This carrion consisted of a sow and a dog, which had sustained all the rigors of weather, hot and cold. When the weather was mild, it stank so badly that one could not go near it. Yet they seized it and carried it off to their cabin, where they forthwith devoured it half cooked. . . .

This is the kind of enjoyment they experience for the most part of winter; for in summer they are able to support themselves, and to obtain provisions so as not to be assailed by such extreme hunger, in rivers abounding in fish, while birds and wild animals fill the country about. The soil is very good and well adapted for tillage, if they would but take pains to plant Indian corn, as all their neighbors do, the Algonquins, Ochasteguins [Hurons], and

Iroquois, who are not attacked by such extremes of hunger, which they provide against by their carefulness and foresight, so that they live happily in comparison with the Montagnais, Canadians, and Souriquois [Micmac] along the seacoast.

THE SCURVY AT QUEBEC

The scurvy began very late; namely, in February, and continued until the middle of April. Eighteen were attacked, and ten died; five others dying of dysentery. I had some opened, to see whether they were tainted, like those I had seen in our other settlements. They were found the same. Some time after, our surgeon died. All this troubled us very much, on account of the difficulty we had in attending to the sick. . . .

It is my opinion that this disease proceeds only from eating excessively of salt food and vegetables, which heat the blood and corrupt the internal parts. The winter is also, in part, its cause; since it checks the natural warmth, causing still greater corruption of the blood. There rise also from the earth, when first cleared up, certain vapors which infect the air: this has been observed in the case of those who have lived at other settlements. . . . From the month of April to the 15th of December, the air is so pure and healthy that one does not experience the slightest indisposition. But January, February, and March are dangerous, on account of the sicknesses prevailing at this time, rather than in summer. . . . As far as I have been able to see, the sickness attacks one who is delicate in his living and takes particular care of himself as readily as one whose condition is as wretched as possible. We supposed at first that the workmen only would be attacked with this disease; but this we found was not the case. . . . Yet I am confident that, with some good bread and fresh meat, a person would not be liable to it.

On the 8th of April, the snow had all melted; and yet the air was still very cold until May, when the trees begin to leaf out. Some of those sick with the scurvy were cured when spring came, which is the season for recovery. . . . On the 5th of June, a shallop arrived at our settlement with Sieur des Marais, a son-in-law of Pont Gravé, bringing us the tidings that his father-in-law had arrived at Tadoussac on the 28th of May. This intelligence gave me much satisfaction, as we entertained hopes of assistance from him. Only eight out of the twenty-eight at first forming our company were remaining, and half of these were ailing.

ONLY EIGHT SURVIVED. A more grim beginning could scarcely be imagined—it was hardly the triumphant arrival of a mighty European empire. Even before the killing winter began, Champlain only narrowly triumphed over desperate odds: first the Basque sailors, then the conspiracy against his life. His supposed followers truly showed themselves to be children of France's civil wars, quick to turn on a leader if there seemed to be penny's profit in it. But here, too, Champlain displayed his trademark discretion in both capturing and punishing the plotters, limiting blood vengeance to the ringleader alone. He had lived through the wars as well, but he had another experience the men lacked—three brutal winters in New France—and he knew he would need every man. As it turned out, if he had hung two, three, or four, the survivors might have numbered seven, six, or merely five.

And yet, the pious, destined Champlain did not despair. He apparently never asked why he had been one of the few to live while so many died. Rather, he directed his pity to the Indians who gathered nearby, desperate and starving—a wandering tribe overshadowed by the power and wealth of nearby nations, the corn-growing Algonquins, Hurons, and Iroquois. Their plight dismayed and astonished him; yet he never stopped to think what the natives might have seen in his band of twenty-eight dying Frenchmen, huddled half a world away from home. In his own earnest mind, he had a mission to fulfill: unlike Moses, God would not simply *show* him the promised land, He would offer him a dwelling place within it.

When Champlain called the natives "savages," he was speaking of their more primitive technology, of their lack of Christian faith, and, perhaps with a little disgust, of their strange habits. He did not underestimate them, or assume they were lesser beings. He had seen the darkest things that men could do, that *Frenchmen* could do, and he knew that true barbarism was always a prayer and a breastplate away. As the snows melted off, as the eight ragged survivors waited for the supply ship, Champlain was already seeing his "savage" neighbors as the key to the future—and his weather-beaten hut as the capitol of an empire.

2

A SOLDIER OF FORTUNE

In 1603, a few years after Henry of Navarre entered Paris in triumph, King James VI of Scotland journeyed to London to accept the English throne. The contrasts between the two new sovereigns could hardly be greater. Henry gained his crown by virtue of his generalship, his cunning, his sheer ruthlessness; James (now King James I of England) triumphed peacefully, through lack of a better candidate. Henry put an end to an era of weak government and began what would long be considered a golden age in France; James inaugurated a stumbling, exasperating reign, one overshadowed by his predecessor, Queen Elizabeth I.

Few dead monarchs have been so encrusted with myth as Elizabeth. But England's sense of loss upon her death rested on solid fact: she had enjoyed a long and, well, *glorious* reign. Blessed with rich political skills and extremely able advisers, she lived long enough to leave a lasting mark. She had inherited a weak, divided kingdom on the margins of Europe; when she died, she left behind a refurbished realm—not a great power, but certainly a pivotal one in European affairs.

When Elizabeth received the crown in 1558, England was still reeling from the reign of her sister Mary, a devout Catholic who tried to roll back the Protestant revolution launched by their father, Henry VIII. Henry had broken with Rome for dynastic reasons, but Protestant faith took on a life of its own, sweeping the population. Henry's son and short-lived successor Edward VI had encouraged the new popular devotion; but Edward's eldest sister (and his own successor) Mary despised it. She married Philip II, ruler of the Early Modern superpower of Spain. She restored Catholicism, and very publicly persecuted prominent Protestants. She didn't kill *that* many, but the executions had quite an effect on the popular imagination. When Protestant Elizabeth took the throne after Mary's brief reign, the English felt as if the millennium had arrived.

During the next fifty years, the queen seemed to produce one miracle after another. She had a gift for political theater and an appetite for administrative detail. In a church divided between two camps of Protestants—conservative, near-Catholic high churchmen and passionate, radical Calvinists—she let both sides believe she backed them. In a government divided between powerful aristocrats, each the patron of an army of office-seekers, she carefully balanced the various factions. In a realm where Parliament controlled taxation, she cultivated the leaders of the House of Commons to secure the revenues she desperately needed; yet she also applied fierce realism to her expenditures, slashing them to the roots. And the whole time, she badgered and battered Philip II, sending her buccaneers to plunder his colonies, bolstering the Dutch as they fought for independence from Spain, and routing the famed Armada invasion force.

But as the bells tolled in 1603 to mourn Elizabeth and welcome James, England faced serious corrosion long concealed by the shine of the Queen's golden age. For all her skillful politics, she had only balanced, not eradicated, bitter factionalism. The powerful Earl of Essex, for example, launched a rebellion in 1601; he was supported by men who felt slighted by Elizabeth's stinginess about offices and honors. The earl was executed, but he had set a bad example nonetheless.

In the countryside, the fires of militant Puritanism had been fed, ironically, by Elizabeth's conservative government. Her councilors had mobilized the nation to fight against a covert reconversion campaign by the Jesuits—priests of the Catholic Church's Society of Jesus, shock troops of the Counter-Reformation. Every county maintained parties of searchers that scoured the land for hidden priests. Neighbor turned against neighbor to turn in recusants—those who refused to partake in communion in the Church of England. The forces of Spain and the Papacy were not remote enemies to the English—they were, to borrow a phrase, under every bed.

Even Elizabeth's vaunted foreign policy suffered a serious blow in Ireland, where the Earl of Tyrone led a remarkably successful revolt against English rule. After years of brutal fighting, an uneasy peace settled in the year of her death. Her soldiers suffered a chronic lack of money in an age when war was very, very expensive; her notoriously penny-pinching ways prevented England from becoming a great military power. Time and time again, she forced warriors such as the buccaneering Sir Francis Drake to find their own funding.[7]

And so, in 1603, James trotted merrily down the length of England to his new capital, little suspecting the political quagmire that awaited him. On one hand, he faced the pressures and problems that had built up during his predecessor's long reign; on the other, he was virtually certain to seem a far lesser monarch, a pale shadow of the great queen. The situation demanded supreme tact, including the cultivation of powerful interests, the consultation of influential men, and a wariness of polarizing, absolutist statements.

But the newly crowned king did all he could to start out wrong. As ruler

---

[7] The expense of war burdened even the richest kingdoms. Spain's Philip II repeatedly declared bankruptcy, despite the influx of New World silver and gold. Drake's naval raids on New Spain were paid for by merchant investors.

of Scotland, he had crushed opposition among the nobility and in the church. He assumed he could do the same in the larger and more complex nation of England. At the Hampton Conference in 1604, he dismissed the pleas of the Puritans, alienating a growing number of his subjects. But that did not concern him; as Head of the Church, he made the rules of worship, and expected obedience.

And James never really understood the idea behind Parliament, particularly the House of Commons. Members of the Commons were hardly democratic representatives in the modern sense, yet they certainly reflected the opinions of the land-owning gentry who effectively ran the country. James had little regular income as king; each year, he had to ask the Commons for a "subsidy" (essentially a tax the gentry voted upon themselves). Elizabeth mastered this difficult relationship and used it well; James thought it a gross indignity, an assault upon the divine right of kings. The divine right of kings, in fact, was his favorite subject—he had written a book on it. It was also the least favorite subject in Parliament.

In this turbulent, pessimistic atmosphere, a group of aristocrats and merchants pooled their funds to form an organization known as the London Company. The joint stock company was a new type of institution in England, used primarily to facilitate foreign trade. The first had been created in 1572 for trade with Muscovy; more recently, in 1600, the East India Company had established itself to secure commerce with the Far East. But the London Company set its eyes on a different part of the world: the little-known shores of Virginia.

During Elizabeth's reign, the English had excelled in looting the New World, not in ruling it. The hated Spanish had built a mighty empire there, and the French (the Company men knew) had begun to found colonies of their own. Previously, Sir Walter Raleigh had made an attempt at Roanoke Island, but his colonists had mysteriously disappeared. However, Raleigh's failure did not put them off; the riches that Spain gathered seemed to await anyone with the determination to find them in parts still unexplored. Certainly things looked better overseas than at home.

In 1606, King James gave a charter to the Company, granting them a vaguely defined tract of land 100 miles by 100 miles, between the latitudes 34 degrees and 41 degrees north. They called this land "Virginia" (the London Company itself is better known as the Company of Virginia). It was an apt designation: to the English, it was virgin country; more to the point, it called forth the memory of the much-missed and never-married Queen Elizabeth. She had been called the Virgin Queen, perhaps less for her marital status than to make her a secular replacement for the Virgin Mary, whose Catholic cult had been eradicated in England. The Company might well have looked to North American shores as a place where they could rebuild the glory they knew under the lost monarch—a place where they could cel ebrate the old virtues of hating the Spanish, hating the Pope, and making a lot of money.

As the Company assembled its first expedition in 1606, its directors gathered three ships and 144 men, and prepared instructions for how they should evade detection by the Spanish. They told the voyagers to sail far up a river, away from the coast; they were to take matchlock muskets and cannons, as well as swords and breastplates. But the colonizers were mainly artisans and merchants—few were soldiers. They planned on making a profit not Sir Francis Drake's way, by stealing it, but the Spanish way: enslave the locals, plunder the natural resources (hopefully gold), etc. So as they set sail from that sceptered isle for unknown shores, they looked askance at one warrior among them, who talked loudly—and unbelievably—about his fantastic experiences as a soldier of fortune. The name of this blowhard was Captain John Smith.

Smith didn't quite fit in with Elizabethan (now Jacobean) England. It was true that he had fought against the despised Irish;[8] but years before he had departed at the age of sixteen or so to see the world and kill foreigners. He was not like the great heroes Drake and Raleigh; instead of going off to slaughter Catholics, as any self-respecting English soldier would, he fought *for* them, battling the Turks in distant Hungary.

Smith fought superbly well on his exotic adventures, and he learned skills that would prove invaluable on the American shores. But he had two terrible flaws. First, he had fought with the forces of darkness—that is, Catholicism—which could only have made him suspect in English eyes; and second, he had the temerity to brag about it, at length and with impossible-to-believe details. He didn't seem *reliable;* and as the small fleet made its way across the Atlantic, he began to seem positively dangerous.

What Smith's fellow future colonists failed to reckon on, however, was something he himself felt perfectly prepared for: the natives. Most members of the expedition expected the inhabitants of Virginia to fall before them as the Aztecs and Incas had collapsed before the Spanish. They were primitives, after all, savage and heathen. Perhaps only Smith knew that heathens could be as intelligent, devious, brave, and dangerous as any Christian. And little did any of them suspect that a true adversary awaited them—not a vaguely defined tribe or a poorly organized village, but a powerful ruler and a master of diplomacy.

Not many years after that first landing in Virginia, Captain John Smith published a set of accounts of the settlement—*A True Relation,* composed by Smith himself in 1608, and *The Proceedings of the English Colonies in Virginia,* stitched together from his friends' stories (and very likely edited and

---

[8] Historian Nicholas P. Canny has made the argument that the Elizabethan efforts to colonize nearby Ireland provided a model as the English invaded North America.

enhanced by Smith) and published in 1612. The picture that emerges is highly partisan; were we to believe it completely, there would be no doubt that there has never been a wiser, braver, or more dashing man than Captain John Smith. On the other hand, these tales give us a very early look at the very early days of Virginia, and they offer insight into the bitter factional disputes that divided the colonists.

Captain John Smith—savior or villain? Contemporary Native Americans would have little doubt; but all Europeans would be villains to them, with good reason. The colonists themselves could hardly decide, as they alternated between imprisoning Smith and asking him to rescue them. Either way, one thing is clear: in a nation of the pious, he was a man who worshiped survival.

Voyage to Virginia
by Thomas Studley and Anas Todkill

It might well be thought, a country so fair (as Virginia is) and a people so tractable, would long ere this have been quietly possessed, to the satisfaction of the adventurers [investors], and the eternizing of the memory of those that affected it. But because all the world do see a defailment, this following treatise shall give satisfaction to all indifferent readers, how the business has been carried, where no doubt they will easily understand and answer to their question, how it came to pass there was no better speed and success in those proceedings.

Captain Bartholomew Gosnoll, the first mover of this plantation, having many years solicited many of his friends, but found small assistance; at last prevailed with some gentlemen, as Edward Maria Wingfield, Captain John Smith, and diverse others, who depended a year upon his projects, but nothing could be effected, till by their great charge and industry it came to be apprehended by certain of the nobility, gentry, and merchants, so that his Majesty by his letters patent gave commission for establishing councils, to direct here and to govern and execute there. To effect this was spent another year, and by that time, three ships were provided, one of 100 tons, another of 40, and a pinnace[9] of 20. The transportation of the company was committed to Captain Christopher Newport, a mariner well practiced for the western parts of America. But their orders for government were put in a box, not to be opened, nor the governors known, until they arrived in Virginia.

On the 19th of December, 1606, we set sail, but by unprosperous winds were kept six weeks in the sight of England. . . . We watered at the Ca-

---

[9] A pinnace was a very small oceangoing ship, as suggested by the tounage.

naries, we traded with the savages at Dominica; three weeks we spent in refreshing ourselves amongst those West India isles. . . .

Gone from thence in search of Virginia . . . the first land they made, they called Cape Henry; where anchoring, Mr. Wingfield, Gosnoll, and Newport, with 30 others, recreating themselves on shore, were assaulted by five savages, who hurt two of the English very dangerously. That night [April 26, 1607] was the box opened and the orders read, in which Bartholomew Gosnoll, Edward Wingfield, Christopher Newport, John Smith, John Ratcliffe, John Martin, and George Kendall were named to be the council, and [ordered] to choose a president amongst them for a year, who with the council should govern. Matters of moment were to be examined by a jury, but determined by the major part of the council, in which the president had two voices [votes]. Until the 13th of May, they sought a place to plant in, then the council was sworn, Mr. Wingfield was chosen president, and an oration made, while Captain Smith was not admitted of [to] the council as the rest.

Now fell every man to work, the council [to] contrive the fort, the rest [to] cut down trees to make a place to pitch their tents; some provide[d] clapboard to reload the ships, some made gardens, some nets, etc. The savages often visited us kindly. The president's overweening jealousy would admit no exercise of arms, or fortification but the boughs of trees cast together in the form of a half moon by the extraordinary pains and diligence of Captain Kendall.

Newport, with Smith and 20 others, were sent to discover the head of the river: by diverse small habitations they passed, [and] in six days they arrived at a town called Powhatan, consisting of some 12 houses pleasantly seated on a hill; before it, three fertile isles; about it, many cornfields. The place is very pleasant, and strong by nature. Of this place the prince is called Powhatan, and his people Powhatans. To this place, the river is navigable, but higher within a mile, by reason of the rocks and isles, there is not passage for a small boat: this they call the Falls. The people in all parts kindly entreated them, till being returned within 20 miles of Jamestown, they gave just cause of jealousy.

But had God not blessed the discoverers otherwise than those at the fort, there had been an end to the plantation. For at the fort, where they arrived the next day, they found 17 men hurt, and a boy slain by the savages. And had it not chanced a crossbar shot from the ships struck down a bough from a tree amongst them, that caused them to retire, [then] our men had all been slain, being securely all at work and their arms in dry vats.

Hereupon the president was contented [that] the fort should be pallisaded, the ordnance [cannon] mounted, his men armed and exercised, for many were the assaults and ambuscades of the savages, and our men by their disorderly straggling were often hurt, when the savages by their nimbleness of their heels well escaped. What toil we had, with so small a power, to guard our workmen, watch all night, resist our enemies, and effect our business, to reload the ships, cut down trees, and prepare the ground to plant our corn, etc., I refer to the reader's consideration.

Six weeks being spent in this manner, Captain Newport (who was hired only for our transportation) was to return with the ships. Now Captain Smith, who all this time from their departure from the Canaries was restrained as a prisoner, upon the scandalous suggestions of some of the chief (envying his repute), who fained he intended to usurp the government, murder the council, and make himself king, that his confedcrates were dispersed in all the three ships, and that diverse of his confederates revealed it, would affirm it: for this he was committed [arrested].

Thirteen weeks he remained thus suspected, and by that time the ships should return, they pretended out of their commiserations to refer him to the council in England to receive a check, . . . make him so odious to the world as to touch his life, or utterly overthrow his reputation. But he much scorned their charity, and publicly defied the uttermost of their cruelty. He wisely prevented their policies, though he could not suppress their envies; yet so well he demeaned himself in this business, as all the company did see his innocence and his adversaries' malice, and those suborned to accuse him accused his accusers of subornation. Many untruths were alleged against him, but being so apparently disproved begat a general hatred in the hearts of the company against such unjust commanders. Many were the mischiefs that daily sprang from their ignorant (yet ambitious) spirits; but the good doctrine and exhortation of our preacher Mr. Hunt reconciled them, and caused Captain Smith to be admitted of [to] the council. The next day all received the communion: the day following the savages voluntarily desired peace, and Captain Newport returned for England with news, leaving in Virginia 100 [as of] the 15th of June, 1607. . . .[10]

WHAT HAPPENED TILL THE FIRST SUPPLY

Being thus left to our fortunes, it fortuned that, within ten days, scarce ten amongst us could either go or well stand, such extreme weakness and sickness oppressed us.[11] And thereat none need marvel, if they consider the cause and reason, which was this: while the ships stayed, our allowance was somewhat bettered by a daily proportion of bisket [an alcoholic beverage] which the sailors would pilfer to sell, give, or exchange with us, for money, sassafras, furs, or love. But when they departed, there remained neither tavern, beer-house, nor place of relief but the common kettle.

[10] Newport actually left Virginia on June 22, 1607.
[11] The colonists carried certain diseases with them, which soon spread; in addition, historians suspect they suffered salt poisoning from drinking water drawn from contaminated wells along the swampy tidewater shore.

Had we been as free from all sins as gluttony and drunkenness, we might have been canonized for saints. But our president would never have been admitted, for engrossing to his private [use] oatmeal, sack, oil, acquavitae, beef, eggs, or whatnot; but the kettle, that indeed he allowed equally to be distributed, and that [allowance] was half a pint of wheat, [and] as much barley, boiled with water, for a man a day, and this having fried some 26 weeks in the ship's hold contained as many worms as grains, so that we might truly call it rather so much bran as than corn.

Our drink was water; our lodgings, castles in the air. With this lodging and diet, our extreme toil in bearing and planting palisades so strained and bruised us, and our continual labor in the extremity of the heat had so weakened us, as were cause sufficient to have made us miserable in our native country, or any other place in the world. From May to September, those that escaped lived upon sturgeon and sea crabs. Fifty in this time we buried. The rest seeing the president's project to escape these miseries in our pinnace by flight (who all this time, had neither felt want nor sickness), so moved our dead spirits, as we deposed him [on September 10, 1607]; and established Ratcliffe in his place: Gosnoll being dead, Kendall deposed, Smith newly recovered; Martin and Ratcliffe were, by his care, preserved and relieved. But now was all our provision spent, the sturgeon gone, all helps abandoned, each hour expecting the fury of the savages; when God, the patron of all good endeavors, in that desperate extremity so changed the hearts of the savages that they brought such plenty of their fruits and provisions, as no man wanted. . . .

The new president and Martin, being little beloved, of weak judgment in dangers and less industry in peace, committed the managing of all things abroad to Captain Smith; who, by his own example, good words, and fair promises, set some to mow, others to bind thatch, some to build houses, others to thatch them, himself always bearing the greatest task for his own share, so that, in short time, he provided most of them lodgings, neglectful [of] any for himself.

This done, seeing the savages' superfluity [friendliness] beginning to decrease, [he] (with some of his workmen) shipped himself in the shallop to search the country for trade. The want [lack] of the language, knowledge to manage his boat without sailors, the want of a sufficient power (knowing the multitude of the savages), apparel for his men, and other necessities, were infinite impediments, yet no discouragement. Being but six or seven in company, he went down the river to Kecoughtan [an Indian village], where at first they scorned him as a starving man, yet he so dealt with them that the next day they loaded his boat with corn. And in his return, he discovered and kindly traded with the Werascoyacks. . . .

Smith perceiving (notwithstanding their late misery) not any regarded but from hand to mouth, the company being well recovered, caused the pinnace to be provided with things fitting to get provision for the year following. But in the interim, he made three or four journeys, and discovered the people of

Chickahominy. Yet what he carefully provided, the rest carelessly spent. Wingfield and Kendall, living in disgrace (seeing all things at random in the absence of Smith, the company's dislike of their president's weakness, and their small love to Martin's never-mending sickness) strengthened themselves with the sailors and other confederates, to regain their former credit and authority, or at least such means aboard the pinnace (being fitted to sail as Smith had appointed for trade), to alter her course, and to go for England.

Smith unexpectedly returning [in November 1607] had the plot discovered to him. Much trouble he had to prevent it, till with store of falcon [small cannon] and musket shot, he forced them stay or sink in the river, which action cost the life of Captain Kendall.[12] These brawls are so disgustful, as some will say they were better forgotten, yet all men of good judgment will conclude, it were better their baseness should be manifest to the world, than the business bear the scorn and shame of their excused disorders. The president and Captain Archer not long after intended also to have abandoned the country, which project also was curbed and suppressed by Smith.

The Spaniard never more greedily desired gold than he [Smith] victuals, which he found so plentiful in the river of Chickahominy, where hundreds of savages, in diverse places, stood with baskets expecting his coming. And now the winter approaching, the rivers became so covered with swans, geese, ducks, and cranes, that we daily feasted with good bread, Virginia peas, pumpkins, and putchamins, fish, fowl, and diverse sorts of wild beasts as fat as we could eat them: so that none of our tuftaffaty [silk-dressed] humorists desired to go for England.

But our comedies never endured long without a tragedy. Some idle exceptions being muttered against Captain Smith, for not discovering the head of Chickahominy river, and taxed by the council, to be too slow in so worthy an attempt: the next voyage, he proceeded so far that with much labor, by cutting . . . trees in sunder, he made his passage. But when his barge could pass no farther, he left her in a broad bay, out of danger of shot, commanding none should go ashore till his return; himself, with two English and two savages, went up higher in a canoe. But he was not long absent, when his men went ashore, whose want of government [discipline] gave both occasion and opportunity to the savages to surprise one George Casson, and much failed to have cut off the boat and all the rest.

Smith, little dreaming of that accident [and] being got to the marshes at the river's head, 20 miles in the desert [wilderness], had his two men slain (as is supposed) sleeping in the canoe, while himself by fowling [hunting birds] sought them victuals. . . . He was beset by 200 savages, 2 of them he slew, still defending himself with the aid of a savage, his guide, whom he

---

[12] Kendall was shot to death approximately December 1, 1607. Interestingly, archeologists recently uncovered the original Jamestown fort, along with the body of a colonist who had been shot.

bound to his arm and used as a buckler [shield], till at last, slipping into a
bog mire, they took him prisoner.

Powhatan's Prisoner
by Captain John Smith

Having two Indians for my guide and two of our own company, I set forward,
leaving seven in the barge. Having discovered 20 miles further in this desert, the
river still kept his depth and breadth, but much more combed with trees. Here
we went ashore (being some 12 miles higher than the barge had been) to refresh ourselves, during the boiling of our victuals. One of the Indians I took
with me to see the nature of the soil, and to cross the boughts [windings] of
the river; the other Indian I left with Master Robbinson and Thomas Emry,
with their matches lit,[13] and [an] order to discharge a piece [as a signal] for my
retreat, at the first sign of any Indian. But within a quarter of an hour I heard
a loud cry, and a hallowing of Indians, but no warning piece.

Supposing them surprised, and that the Indians had betrayed us,
presently I seized him [the guide] and bound his arm fast to my hand in a
garter, with my pistol ready bent to be revenged on him. He advised me to
fly, and seemed ignorant of what was done. But as we went discoursing, I
was struck with an arrow on the right thigh, but without harm; upon this occasion I spied two Indians drawing their bows, which I prevented in discharging a French pistol. By that [time] I had charged [reloaded] again,
three or four more did the like [shot their arrows]: for the first fell down and
fled; at my discharge, they did the like. My hinde [Indian prisoner] I made
my barricade. . . . Twenty or thirty arrows were shot at me but [fell] short.

Three or four times I had discharged my pistol ere the king of Pamunck,
called Opechancanough,[14] with 200 men, environed [surrounded] me, each
drawing their bow; which done they laid them upon the ground, yet without shot. My hinde treated [negotiated] betwixt them and me of conditions
of peace; he discovered [revealed] me to be the captain. My request was to
retire to the boat; they demanded my arms; the rest they said were slain; only
me would they preserve. The Indian importuned me not to shoot. In retiring, being in the midst of a low quagmire and minding them more than my
steps, I stepped fast into the quagmire. . . .

Thus surprised, I resolved to try their mercies. My arms I cast from me,

---

[13] Their muskets were matchlocks, which used a slowly burning cord, or match,
to ignite the gunpowder.

[14] Opechancanough was the brother and heir of Powhatan, the Indian chief
mentioned earlier. Powhatan's power will soon become apparent; Opechancanough
was his main lieutenant, and served as chief of the Pamunkey (a people who owed
allegiance to Powhatan).

till which none durst approach me. Being seized on me, they drew me out and led me to the king. I presented him with a compass dial, describing by my best means the use thereof; whereat he so amazedly admired, as he suffered me to proceed in a discourse of the roundness of the earth, the course of the sun, moon, stars, and planets. With kind speeches and bread he requited me, conducting me where the canoe lay and John Robbinson [was] slain, with 20 or 30 arrows in him. Emry I saw not.

I perceived by the abundance of fires all over the woods [that they had been hunting deer]. . . .[15] At each place I expected when they would execute me, yet they used me with what kindness they could. Approaching their town [Rasawrack], which was within six miles [of] where I was taken, . . . all the women and children, being advertised of this accident, came forth to meet them, the king well guarded with 20 bowmen, five flank and rear, and each flank before him a sword and a piece,[16] and after him the like, then a bowman, then I on each hand a bowman, the rest in file in the rear . . . , each his bow and a handful of arrows, a quiver at his back grimly painted; on each flank a sergeant, the one running always toward the front, the other toward the rear, each a true pace and in exceeding good order.

This being a good time continued, they cast themselves in a ring with a dance, and so each man departed to his lodging. The captain conducting me to this lodging, a quarter of venison and some ten pound of bread I had for supper; what I left was reserved for me, and sent with me to my lodging. Each morning three women presented me three great platters of fine bread; more venison than ten men could devour I had; my bown, points [lacings], and garters, my compass, and my tablet they gave me again. Though eight ordinarily guarded me, I wanted not what they could devise to content me; and still our longer acquaintance increased our better affection.

Much they threatened to assault our fort, as they were solicited by the king of Paspahegh [the Indian village nearest Jamestown]. . . . The king [Opechancanough] took great delight in understanding the manner of our ships and sailing the seas, the earth and skies, and of our God. What he knew of the dominions he spared not to acquaint me with, as of certain men . . . at a place called Ocanahonan, clothed like me; the course of our river, and that within four or five days journey of the Falls, was a great turning of salt water.

I desired he would send a messenger to [Jamestown], with a letter I would write, by which they should understand how kindly they used me, and that I was well, lest they should revenge my death. This he granted and sent three men, in such weather as in reason were impossible by any naked to be

[15] Smith had observed that the Indians would often hunt deer in large parties, setting fires to drive the animals toward parties of archers.

[16] The swords he refers to were clubs, often studded or tipped with sharp rocks or bits of copper. The "piece" is hard to explain, since this meant a musket, which the Indians did not possess. Perhaps he means a bow. The formation, however, indicates the unusually high degree of authority exerted by Opechancanough.

endured. Their cruel minds toward the fort I had diverted, in describing the ordnance and the mines in the fields, as also the revenge Captain Newport would take of them at his return. . . .

The next day after my letter, came a savage to my lodging with his sword, to have slain me; but being by my guard intercepted, with a bow and arrow he offered to have effected his purpose. The cause I knew not, till the king understanding thereof came and told me of a man a'dying, wounded with my pistol; he told me also of another I had slain, yet the most concealed they had any hurt. This was the father of him I had slain, whose fury to prevent the king presently conducted me to another kingdom, upon the top of the next northerly river. . . .

[After several days of travel among various villages,] I lodged at a hunting town of Powhatan's, and the next day arrived at Werowacomoco[17] upon the river of Pamunkey, where the great king is resident. . . . Arriving at Werowacomoco, their emperor proudly lying upon a bedstead a foot high, upon ten or twelve mats, richly hung with many chains of great pearls about his neck, and covered with a great covering of raccoons.[18] At [his] head sat a woman, at his feet another; on each side sitting upon a mat upon the ground were ranged his chief men on each side of the fire, ten in a rank, and behind them as many young women, each [with] a great chain of white beads over their shoulders, their heads painted in red; and with such a grave and majestical countenance as drove me into admiration to see such a state in a naked savage.

He kindly welcomed me with good words, and great platters of sundry victuals, assuring me his friendship, and my liberty within four days. He much delighted in Opechancanough's relation of what I had described to him, and oft examined me upon the same. He asked me the cause of our coming. I told him [of] being in [a] fight with the Spaniards our enemy, being overpowered, near put to retreat, and by extreme weather put to this shore; where landing at Chesapeake the people shot at us; but at Kequoughtan they kindly used us. We by signs demanded fresh water, [to which] they described [to] us [that] up the river was all fresh water. At Paspahegh also they kindly used us; our pinnace being leaky, we were forced to stay to mend her, till Captain Newport my father came to conduct us away.[19]

He demanded why we went further with our boat. I told him, in that I would have occasion to talk of the back sea [the Pacific], that on the other

[17] The name means "house of the werowance," or chief. This town was also known as Powhatan, after the powerful leader of this large Indian confederacy, and was located up the York River, on the northern bank.

[18] In the original, Smith spelled the name "rahaughcums."

[19] As the reader should realize, Smith lied as hard as he could to Powhatan. He had no trust in the Indian leader, who clearly overshadowed the tiny, disease-wracked, dissension-ridden colony. He craftily painted the sea captain Newport as a great war leader, soon to return. Powhatan, a wily statesman and empire builder, soon proved that he could lie as calmly and elaborately as Smith.

side of the main, where [there] was salt water. My father [Newport] had a child slain, which we supposed Monacan his enemy [had done], whose death we intended to revenge.[20]

After good deliberation, he began to describe me the countries beyond the Falls, with many of the rest; confirming what not only Opechancanough and an Indian which had been prisoner to Powhatan had before told me. . . . Many kingdoms he described me, to the head of the Bay, which seemed to be a mighty river [the Delaware] issuing from mighty mountains betwixt the two seas. . . .

I requited his discourse (seeing what pride he had in his great and spacious dominions, seeing that all he knew were under his territories) in describing to him the territories of Europe, which were subject to our great King whose subject I was, the innumerable multitude of his ships. I gave him to understand the noise of trumpets, and terrible manner of fighting . . . under Captain Newport, my father, whom I entitled the Meworames, which they call the king of all the waters.

At his [Newport's] greatness, he admired, and not a little feared. He desired me to forsake Paspahegh [Jamestown], and to live with him upon his river, a country called Capa Howasicke. He promised me to give me corn, venison, or what I wanted to feed us. Hatchets and copper we should make him, and none should disturb us. This request I promised to perform; and thus, having with all the kindness he could devise, sought to content me, [and] he sent me home with four men: one that usually carried my gown and knapsack after me, two other loaded with bread, and one to accompany me.

Smith's Return
by Thomas Studley and Anas Todkill

A month those barbarians kept him prisoner. Many strange triumphs and conjurations they made of him; yet he so demeaned himself amongst them, as he not only diverted them from surprising the fort, but procured his own liberty, and got himself and his company such estimation amongst them, that those savages admired him as a demigod. So returning safe to the fort [on January 2, 1608], once more he stayed the pinnace [in] her flight for England, which, till his return, could not set sail, so extreme was the weather, and so great the frost.

His relation of the plenty he had seen, especially at Werowacomoco, where inhabited Powhatan (that till that time was unknown) so revived again

---

[20] This particular lie seems to be a play on sympathies that Smith had already detected among Powhatan's people. As seen in the story of the father who came seeking revenge, the Powhatans had a healthy attachment to their children.

their dead spirits as all men's fear was abandoned. Powhatan having sent with this captain diverse of his men loaded with provisions, [but] he had conditioned, and so appointed his trusty messengers, to bring [back] but two or three of our great ordnances [cannons]. But the messengers being satisfied with the sight of one of them discharged, ran away amazed with fear, till means was used with gifts to assure them our loves. Thus you may see what difficulties still crossed any good endeavor, and the good success of the business, and being thus oft brought to the very period of destruction, yet you see by what strange means God hath still delivered it.

SICK, STARVING, QUARRELLING: The Jamestown colonists nearly wiped themselves out, without any help from the Indians. Their first target, even before they reached American shores, had been the loudmouth Smith. Upon their arrival, they quickly discovered that he could back up his insufferable talk with effective action. So they turned to him for guidance—some with reluctance, some with relief.

The internal divisions at Jamestown seem to echo those of Quebec—but with a crucial difference. Champlain's dissidents had been cutthroat plotters, hardened men who made a simple, ruthless calculation of the profit to be had. Jamestown's factions resemble nothing so much as petty parish politics, absurdly transplanted to a settlement on the edge of complete annihilation. Smith helped clarify matters—and gave himself a political leg up—by meeting Powhatan. No longer did the natives seem to be an ill-defined mass of hostile barbarians. Now the Indian enemy had a single face—an obviously powerful and calculating leader.

Even as Champlain contemplated alliances with his native neighbors, the English trembled before theirs. The French had the good fortune to plant themselves in a no-man's-land, in an area denuded of Indian settlements; Jamestown, on the other hand, sat in the middle of one of the most powerful and cohesive confederations in eastern North America.

It is difficult to know the actual political structure of Powhatan's realm; the early colonists used familiar words, such as "kingdom" and "empire," that can easily mislead. Hereditary kingship, sharply defined boundaries, and strong central rule were unknown to virtually all Native Americans. Yet perhaps the terms "king" and "emperor" are not so misleading after all, if we consider the history of such positions in Europe. Few monarchs had absolute power. The English king, for example, was hemmed in by Parliament and needed the support of influential aristocrats and merchants. The Holy Roman Empire covered all of central Europe—yet the emperor was elected by leading princes, and exerted little power outside the lands he had personally inherited. So when Captain John Smith described Powhatan as an emperor and his brother Opechancanough as king, he may not have been using the terms as James I and Henry IV wished them to be, but as they actually were—indicative of rank and leadership, not dictatorial power.

And leadership was one thing Powhatan could indeed boast of. For the last few decades, he had asserted himself over half a dozen or more tribes and communities: Rappahannock, Pamunkey, Chickahominy, Paspahegh (nearest to Jamestown), Appomattox, and Nansemond. He exerted a rare degree of authority for a Native American leader—a tribute to political gifts that rivaled those of the Virgin Queen herself. His wiles are apparent even through Smith's limited grasp of the local language: he would protect the English, he declared, but they, of course, would make him such implements as he required. They would be the newest members of his confederacy. And no more exploring, he added.

It is doubtful, however, that either Smith or Powhatan had much faith in the other at that first meeting. They eyed each other with intense calculation, weighing the benefits of alliance against the potential threat. Smith quickly grasped the ominous power of this formidable Native American leader—but he and his fellow colonists lacked the strength to attack him, even if they had so desired. In any event, they desperately needed the corn and game that only the Indians could provide. Powhatan, for his part, knew something of the Europeans; perhaps he had met some himself during his long and active life. He knew they made remarkably useful metal tools and other goods, and could serve as valuable new allies in his quarrels with neighboring tribes. On the other hand, he, too, sensed danger.

As the months dragged by, Powhatan turned to a subtle game of friendly overtures and military raids, to simultaneously control the English settlement and test its strength. He offered gifts of food even as he urged his vassals, the Paspahegh, to probe Jamestown's defenses. It was a rare reversal of the standard European experience in North America—for here the Indians were united behind a strong leader, and it was the colonists who were preoccupied and divided.

Corn, Fire, and Gold
by Walter Russell and Anas Todkill

All this time, our cares were not so much [as] to abandon the country, but the treasurer and council in England were . . . diligent and careful to supply us. Two tall ships they sent us, with near 100 men, well furnished with all things [that] could be imagined necessary, both for them and us. The one commanded by Captain Newport; the other, by Captain Nelson, an honest man and an expert mariner. But such was the leewardness of his ship, that (although he was within sight of Cape Henry), by stormy contrary winds, was forced so far to sea as the

West Indies was the next land [he reached], for the repair of his masts and relief of wood and water. But Captain Newport got in, and arrived at Jamestown
not long after the redemption of Captain Smith, to whom the savages, every
other day, brought such plenty of bread, fish, turkeys, squirrels, deer, and other
wild beasts; part they gave him as presents from the king, the rest, he as their
market clerk set the price how they should sell.

He had so enchanted those poor souls (being their prisoner) in demon-
strating unto them the roundness of the world, the course of the moon and
the stars, the cause of the day and night, the largeness of the seas, the qualities of our ships' shot and powder, the division of the world, with the diversity of the people, their complexions, customs, and conditions. All which
he fained [pretended] to be under the command of Captain Newport,
whom he termed to them his father; of whose arrival it chanced he so directly prophesied as they esteemed him an oracle. By these fictions he not
only saved his own life, and obtained his liberty, but he had them at that
command [that] he might command them what he listed. . . .

The president and the council so much envied his estimation amongst
the savages (though we all in general equally participated with him of the
good thereof) that they wrought it into their understandings, by their great
bounty in giving four times more for their [the Indians'] commodities than
he appointed, that their greatness and authority as much exceeded his, as
their bounty and liberality.

Now the arrival of this first supply so overjoyed us, that we could not
devise too much to please the mariners. We gave them liberty to truck or
trade at their pleasure. But in a short time, it followed that [something]
could not be had for a pound of copper, which before was sold for an ounce.
Thus ambition and sufference cut the throat of our trade, but confirmed
their opinion of Newport's greatness, wherewith Smith had possessed
Powhatan: especially by the great presents Newport often sent him, before
he could prepare the pinnace to go and visit him.

So [it was] that this savage also desired to see him. . . . When he went,
he was accompanied by Captain Smith and Mr. Scrivener (a very wise understanding gentleman newly arrived, and admitted of the council), and 30
or 40 chosen men for that guard. Arriving at Werowacomoco, Newport's
concept of this great savage bred many doubts and suspicions of treacheries,
which Smith, to make appear . . . needless, with twenty men well appointed
undertook to encounter (with that number) the worst that could happen. . . . These being kindly received ashore, with 200 or 300 savages were
conducted to their town.

Powhatan strained himself to the uttermost of his greatness to entertain
us, with great shouts of joy, orations of protestations, and the most plenty of
victuals he could provide to feast us. Sitting upon his bed of mats, his pillow of
leather embroidered (after their rude manner) with pearl and white beads, his
attire of a fair robe of skins as large as an Irish mantle; at his head and feet a

handsome young woman. On each side [of] his house sat 20 of his concubines, their heads and shoulders painted red, with a great chain of white beads about their necks; before those sat his chiefest men, in like order, in his arbor-like house. With many pretty discourses to renew their old acquaintance, the great king and our captain spent their time till the ebb left our barge aground; then renewing their feasts and mirth, we quartered that night with Powhatan.

The next day Newport came ashore, and received as much content as those people could give him. A boy named Thomas Savage was then given unto Powhatan, who Newport called his son, for whom Powhatan gave him Namontack his trusty servant, and one of a shrewd, subtle capacity. Three or four days were spent in feasting, dancing, and trading, wherein Powhatan carried himself so proudly, yet discreetly (in his savage manner), as made us all admire his natural gifts, considering his education.

As scorning to trade as his subjects did, he bespoke Newport in this manner: "Captain Newport, it is not agreeable with my greatness in this piddling manner to trade for trifles; and I esteem you a great werowance. Therefore lay me down all your commodities together, what I like I will take, and in recompense give you that I think fitting their value."

Captain Smith, being our interpreter, [and outwardly] regarding Newport as his father [but] knowing best the disposition of Powhatan, told us his intent was but to cheat us; yet Captain Newport thought to out-brave this savage in ostentation of greatness, and so to bewitch him with his bounty, as to have what he listed. But it so chanced, Powhatan having his desire, valued his corn at such a rate, as I think it . . . cheap[er] in Spain; for we had not four bushels for what we expected 20 hogsheads.

This bred some unkindness between our two captains, Newport seeking to please the humor of the insatiable savage, Smith to cause the savage to please him; but smothering his distaste to avoid the savages' suspicion, glanced in the eyes of Powhatan many trifles, who fixed his humor upon a few blue beads. A long time he importunately desired them, but Smith seemed so much the more to affect them, so that ere we departed, for a pound or two of blue beads, he brought over . . . [from the] king 200 or 300 bushels of corn, yet parted good friends. The like entertainment we found of Opechancanough, king of Pamunkey, whom also he in like manner fitted (at the like rates) with blue beads; and so we returned to the fort [on March 9, 1608].

Where this new supply being lodged with the rest, [something] accidentally fired the quarters, and so the town, which being but thatched with reeds the fire was so fierce as it burnt their pallisades (though 10 to 12 yards distant), with their arms, bedding, apparel, and much private provisions. Good Mr. Hunt, our preacher, lost all his library, and all that he had but the clothes on his back, yet none ever saw him repine at his loss. This happened in the winter, in that extreme frost, 1607 [-1608]. . . . Our ordinary [food] was but meal and water . . . whereby, with the extremity of the bitter cold air, more than half of us died, and took our deaths, in that piercing winter.

I cannot deny but both Scrivener and Smith did their best to amend what was amiss, but with the president went the major part [of the council], that their horns were too short. But the worst mischief was [with] our gold refiners, [who] with their golden promises made all men their slaves in hope of recompense. There was no talk, no hope, nor work, but dig gold, wash gold, refine gold, load gold.[21] Such a bruit of gold, as made one fellow desire to be buried in the sands, lest they should by their art make gold of his bones. . . . Were it that Captain Smith would not applaud all those golden inventions, because they admitted him not to the sight of their trials, nor golden consultations I know not: but I heard him question with Captain Martin and tell him, except he would show him a more substantial trial, he was not enamored with their dirty skill. . . .

The spring approaching, and the ship departed, Mr. Scrivener and Captain Smith divided betwixt them the rebuilding of our town, the repairing of our pallisades, the cutting down [of] trees, preparing our fields, planting our corn, and to rebuild our Church, and re-cover our storehouse. All men thus busy at their several labors, Mr. Nelson arrived with his lost *Phoenix* (lost, I say, for that all men deemed him lost), landing safely his men. So well he had managed his ill hap, causing the Indian isles to feed his company, that his victuals ([added] to what was left us before) was sufficient for half a year. He had nothing but he freely imparted it, which honest dealing (being a mariner) caused us [to] admire him. We would not have wished so much as he did for us.

Now to reload this ship with some good tidings, the president (it not standing with his dignity to leave the fort) gave orders to Captain Smith and Mr. Scrivener to discover and search the commodities of Monocans' country beyond the Falls. Sixty able men were allotted [as] their number, which within six days' exercise Smith had so well trained their arms and orders, that they little feared whom they should encounter. Yet so unseasonable was the time, and so opposite was Captain Martin to everything but only to freight his ship with his fantastical gold, as Captain Smith rather desired to reload her with cedar, which was a present dispatch, than either with dirt or the reports of an uncertain discovery. While their conclusion was resolving, this happened.

Conspiracies
by Captain John Smith

The next exploit was an Indian having stolen an axe, was so pursued by Mr. Scrivener and them next to him, as he threw it down; and flying, drew his bow at any that durst encounter him. Within four or five days after, Mr.

---

[21] There was no gold. The colonists convinced themselves, however, that the worthless dirt was full of it.

Scrivener and I, being a little [ways] from the fort, among the corn, [saw] two Indians, each with a cudgel and all newly painted with *Terrasigillata*, [who] came circling about me as though they would have clubbed me like a hare. I knew their faining love . . . towards me [was] not without a deadly hatred; but to prevent the worst, I, calling Mr. Scrivener, retired to the fort.

The Indians, seeing me suspect them, with good terms asked me for some of their men whom they would beat; and went with me into our fort. Finding one that lay ordinarily with us, only for a spy, they offered to beat him. I [irritated them] in persuading them to forebear, [whereupon] they offered to begin with me, being now four [in number]; for two others arrayed in like manner came in on the other side of the fort. Whereupon I caused [the men] to shut the ports[22] and apprehend them.

The president and the council, being presently acquainted [with the situation], remembering the first assault [on the settlement] . . . concluded to commit them to prison. . . . Eight more we seized at that present [moment]. An hour after came three or four other strangers extraordinarily fitted with arrows, skins, and shooting gloves; their jealousy and fear betrayed their bad intent, as also their suspicious departure.

The next day, [there] came first an Indian, then another, as ambassadors for their men. They desired to speak with me. Our discourse was, that what spades, shovels, swords, or tools they had stolen [they should] bring home; if not, the next day they [the prisoners] should hang. The next news was, they had taken two of our men [who were] ranging in the woods (which mischief no punishment will prevent but hanging): and these they would [return], should [we] redeem their own 16 or 18 [prisoners]; thus [they were] braving us to our doors. . . .

The confessions of Macanoe, who was the councillor of Paspahegh, first I, then Mr. Scrivener, upon several examinations [of the other prisoners] found all confirmed—that Paspahegh and Chickahominy did hate us, and intended some mischief; and who they were that took me; the names of them that stole our tools and swords; and that Powhatan received them; they all agreed. . . .

Powhatan, understanding [that] we detained certain savages, sent his daughter, a child of ten years old [actually thirteen]; who, not only for feature, countenance, and proportion, much exceeded any of the rest of his people, but for wit and spirit, the only *nonpariel* of his country. This he sent by his most trusted messenger, called Rawhunt, [who was] much exceeding in deformity of person, but of a subtle wit and crafty understanding. He, with a long circumstance, told me how well Powhatan loved and respected me; and . . . that I should not doubt . . . his kindness, he had sent his child, whom he most esteemed, to see me; [and] a deer and bread besides, for a present. . . .

[22] The fort was triangular, with gates in the center of each side.

After prayer, [I] gave them to Pocahontas, the king's daughter, in regard of her father's kindness in sending her. After having well fed them, as [we had] all the time of their imprisonment, we gave them their bows, arrows, and what else they had; and with much contentment, sent them packing. Pocahontas also we requited with such trifles as contented her.

THE NAME POCAHONTAS is all too familiar; yet her appearance here seems strangely late, and out of place. According to the standard myth, she should have arrived during Smith's imprisonment, to rescue him from certain death. Instead, she shows up in Jamestown to save fellow Native Americans. Smith himself later wrote that she had bravely intervened with her father Powhatan to prevent his execution. The accounts excerpted here, however, were written many years before Smith's later tale. Pocahontas clearly made a strong and positive impression upon him, but she probably played no part in his first encounter with her father.

Pocahontas did play a telling role in these events, however. As the other newly made Virginians abandoned themselves to the vain hunt for gold, Smith and the Indian "emperor" fought a duel of intrigue with startling ruthlessness. Powhatan tried to get at the valuable English metalware in two ways, by friendly trading and by laying traps; Smith sought to undo his plans with smiling lies and by torturing prisoners for information. Both were unwilling to risk open war; both were unwilling to risk alliance and trust. And into this volatile, cynical atmosphere came Pocahontas, all sincerity and friendship. The teenage girl apparently disarmed even Smith with her lack of guile, for she won the release of the prisoners after Opechancanough and others had failed.

As the struggle continued between Powhatan and Smith, between the Native American confederacy and the greedy, divided colony, Pocahontas would continue to play this unusual role on a practical and a symbolic plane. She would emerge as a trusted emissary between the two sides, and as an emblem of the alternatives to war. Over the years, those alternatives would loom up again and again in the colonists' (and Indians') minds. In the meantime, however, the Captain would have none of it. He was certain that only one thing could save sick, squabbling Jamestown in the shadow of Powhatan: utter ruthlessness, whether in diplomacy or in war. And Smith had plenty of it—enough to catapult himself into the presidency and Virginia into treachery and blood.

3

A WARRIOR AMONG WARRIORS

In those first desperate months, Captain John Smith and Samuel de Champlain could think of little else but Indians. War or friendship was the question—and the answer could well decide each settlement's survival. But apart from that rough similarity, the problems facing the two leaders could hardly have been more different.

When the English sailed up the river they called the James, to found the village they named (with an extraordinary lack of imagination) Jamestown, they traveled a dark passage to an utterly unknown shore. By chance, they placed themselves amidst a powerful, well-led Indian confederacy; had they been as few in number as the colonists who landed in New France, they might not have lasted a single year. On the other hand, the very smallness of Champlain's party betrays a salient fact: *he* knew where he was going. He had scouted the area before, and he remembered it as a scarcely inhabited no-man's-land. Perhaps a century earlier, a large settlement had existed on the site of Quebec; but something since had driven it out—a shift in climate, perhaps, the exhaustion of the soil,[23] or war.

Despite the strange emptiness of this St. Lawrence shore, it was not a land of harmony and peace; it was a land of deadly rivalries, and Champlain knew it. He immediately attracted the attention of powerful tribes (as he intended); they looked upon him as a source of highly valued, and lethal, European metalware—especially hatchets, knives, and muskets, along with such prosaic items as kettles. For decades these Indians had made the long trek from the interior to the harbor of Tadoussac, to trade furs for goods with fishermen and smugglers. But Champlain located his settlement farther upstream to intercept this traffic and control it; in turn, the Indians quickly came to value Quebec as a more convenient (and permanent) trading post.

But the energetic, devout, terribly earnest Champlain could never be satisfied as a glorified merchant. He thought of himself as an explorer first, a soldier next. Here, deep in the North American continent, he had a world to discover and strategic possibilities to exploit. The local Native Americans,

---

[23] The settled, agricultural tribes of the Northeast tended to move their villages every twenty years or so, as their corn fields grew unproductive.

on the other hand, saw him as a potentially potent ally in their wars—a new card to be played in the ancient game of bloodshed and retaliation.

The Indians Champlain met *loved* war, and they went at it with vigor. They cultivated a warrior culture that crossed tribal boundaries, in which prestige and power lay on the warpath. They carefully planned the killing of ancient enemies, and celebrated heartily when they succeeded. They often prosecuted war for reasons that seemed strange to the French: small parties would seek personal vengeance for the death of a loved one, and large groups would lay ambushes to obtain captives (some to torture, some to adopt as replacements for war dead). Yet they also fought for control of territory, for honor, to terrify the foe. The only reason their warfare seemed less deadly than that of the Europeans was their limited technology: stone- and bone-tipped arrows and wooden clubs made inefficient weapons. As they later obtained muskets from traders and colonists, however, the lethality of Indian-on-Indian warfare exploded.

The French and English called them savages, and savage they were—but no more so than the Europeans themselves. The difference really came down to separate customs of cruelty. Champlain could calmly give the order to strangle a dissident and mount his head on a pike—his priests could piously burn to death Jews and heretics—and still recoil at the way the Indians treated prisoners of war. There are no heroes of humanitarianism to be found here: all that separated the newcomers from the old was some metallurgy and a little chemistry.

Champlain began his own quest for allies by looking to his immediate neighbors. The nearest were the Montagnais, a nomadic tribe of hunters, and not reckoned a particularly powerful group. Some of these had come to his door, starving, during his first winter. Not far away, however, lived the more formidable Algonquins, who cultivated corn and lived in fixed, walled settlements of bark-covered cabins. Farther down the St. Lawrence came a still more powerful group of corn-growing Indians, a powerful nation dwelling in the triangle of land between what we now call Lakes Erie, Ontario, and Huron. This last lake, in fact, bears the name of this proud people: the Hurons. At the time of Champlain's arrival, the Hurons numbered at least 30,000.

For untold generations, these peoples had been in a loose alliance against their hated foes, the Iroquois. "Loose alliance" best describes their internal affairs as well: even the powerful Hurons were a rambling collection of villages, bound by language, custom, mutual identity, and blood. Cutting across other divisions was a clan structure. The Hurons shared this feature with the Iroquois—which is not surprising, since the two enemies were closely related.

As Champlain would soon discover, the Iroquois occupied their own vast stretch of land—from the Hudson valley in the east to the shores of Lakes Erie and Ontario in the west, from below the Mohawk valley in the south to the heights of the Adirondack Mountains in the north. Like the Powhatans, like the Hurons, they lived in a confederacy—but their political and social structure was unlike that of any other native people. In fact, according to Iroquois legend, they owed their unusual arrangement to an outcast Huron, a prophet named Deganawida.

Not many years before Champlain arrived on the St. Lawrence, the Huron Deganawida left his homeland with a vision of a great Tree of Peace, under which all people should gather in harmony. The Iroquois took up his dream, and established a family of five nations: the Seneca in the west (called "keepers of the western gate"); Cayuga, Onondaga ("keepers of the council fire"), and Oneida in the center; and the Mohawk ("keepers of the eastern gate") in the east. These five—soon dubbed "The Five Nations" by the Europeans—established peace among themselves and developed elaborate rituals that reinforced their shared identity and cooperation. Each of the five might follow its own policies—including war against outsiders—but all consulted with and informed the others.

The Iroquois confederacy cannot be fairly compared to European states. Its structure met the demands of people who existed in limited numbers in a large landscape, who had limited technology for travel and warfare—and who had limited tolerance for authority. Each of the Five Nations was split into clans, villages, and individual families—which were matrilineal, with a woman at the head.[24] Consensus and persuasion governed public policy (if their mutual actions can be called that); as historian Ian K. Steele notes, Iroquois unity has often been exaggerated.

And yet, when the Hurons, Algonquins, Montagnais, and other allied peoples looked south of the St. Lawrence, they saw a truly potent enemy. As Steele has also observed, it is telling that the Iroquois, unlike almost any other people, never needed allies outside their own league when they went to war. Linking hands with each other around the Tree of Peace, they had little but death and terror for those beyond its shade.

When Champlain approached his Indian neighbors about forging an alliance, there was only one direction they would take him: south, into the land of the easternmost, and perhaps the most ferocious, of the Five Nations—the Mohawk. His decision to join a war party against this dreaded foe seemed almost cavalier: his own narrative suggests that his primary motive was personal, to prove that he stood by his word. Yet the expedition proved to be a fateful one indeed, for it forged an undying enmity between fledgling New France and the Iroquois confederacy.

Many writers—most notably the great American historian Francis Parkman—have criticized Champlain's decision. The Five Nations occupied a

[24] The matrilineal nature of many tribes' family structures has often tempted writers to conjure up a feminist paradise. The reality was much murkier: women had a notable public role, but male war leaders exerted a great deal of authority.

strategic position, balanced between the St. Lawrence, the Great Lakes, and the Atlantic seaboard, controlling access to the mighty Hudson River. They also lived far enough inland to avoid a destructive war with any Europeans who might arrive by sea to the south. It seems a very foolish thing indeed for Champlain to have aroused the united hostility of perhaps 30,000 fierce Iroquois, when he had fewer than ten Frenchmen.

Yet he could hardly avoid an alliance with his neighbors. He might have alleviated the situation by not actively joining the hostilities, but he would have suffered the ire of the Iroquois at one time or another. And the mighty Hurons promised to be powerful allies indeed.

Most important of all, Champlain was a man of action. He longed to explore and to fight. On this first voyage from Quebec, he did plenty of both. His account provides fascinating insight into this critical moment: the discovery of natural wonders, including a great river (later called the Richelieu) and a vast lake—known as the Lake of the Iroquois, though Champlain thought it might better bear his own name. His was an epic (at one point almost mystical) journey into a strange land with strange, intricate customs. He also shows us a rare glimpse of what warfare was like before the Europeans—and their muskets—arrived on the scene. War would never be the same again. Nor would anything be the same, for this very old world was about to be changed by a new pattern of allies and enemies.

Allies Against the Iroquois
by Samuel de Champlain

On the 5th of June [1609], a shallop arrived at our settlement with Sieur des Marais, a son-in-law of Pont Gravé, bringing us the tidings that his father-in-law had arrived at Tadoussac on the 28th of May. This intelligence gave me much satisfaction, as we entertained hopes of assistance from him. Only eight out of the twenty-eight at first forming our company were remaining, and half of these were ailing. On the 7th of June, I set out from Quebec for Tadoussac, on some matters of business, and asked Sieur des Marais to stay in my place until my return, which he did.

Immediately upon my arrival, Pont Gravé and I had a conference in regard to some explorations which I was to make in the interior, where the savages had promised to guide us. We determined that I should go in a shallop with twenty men, and that Pont Gravé should stay at Tadoussac to arrange the affairs of our settlement; and this determination was carried out, he spending the winter there. This arrangement was especially desirable, since I was to return to France, according to the orders sent out by Sieur de Monts, in order to inform him of what I had done and the explorations I had made in the country.

After this decision, I set out at once from Tadoussac, and returned to Quebec, where I had a shallop fitted out with all that was necessary for making explorations in the country of the Iroquois, where I was to go with our allies, the Montagnais.

DEPARTURE FROM QUEBEC

With this purpose, I set out on the 18th of the month. Here the river begins to widen, in some places to the breadth of a league or a league and a half. The country becomes more and more beautiful. There are hills along the river in part, and in part it is a level country, with but few rocks. The river itself is dangerous in many places, in consequence of its banks and rocks. . . . The country is thickly covered with massive and lofty forests, of the same kind of trees as we have about our habitation. . . .

Pursuing our route, I met some two or three hundred savages, who were encamped in huts near a little island called St. Éloi. . . . We made a reconnaissance, and found that they were tribes of savages called Ochasteguins [Hurons] and Algonquins, on their way to Quebec to assist us in exploring the territory of the Iroquois, with whom they are in deadly hostility, sparing nothing belonging to their enemies.

After reconnoitering, I went on shore to see them, and inquired who their chief was. They told me there were two, one named Yroquet, and the other Ochasteguin, whom they pointed out to me. I went to their cabin, where they gave me a cordial reception, as is their custom. I proceeded to inform them of the object of my voyage, with which they were greatly pleased. After some talk, I withdrew. Some time after, they came to my shallop, and presented me with some pelts, exhibiting some tokens of pleasure. Then they returned to shore.

The next day, the two chiefs came to see me, when they remained some time without saying a word, meditating and smoking all the while. After due reflection, they began to harangue in a loud voice all their companions who were on the bank of the river, with their arms in their hands, and listening very attentively to what their chiefs said to them, which was as follows: That nearly ten moons ago, according to their mode of reckoning, the son of Yroquet had seen me, and that I had given him a good reception, and declared that Pont Gravé and I desired to assist them against their enemies, with whom they had for a long time been at warfare, on account of many cruel acts committed by them against their tribe, under color of friendship; that, having ever since longed for vengeance, they had solicited all the savages, whom I saw on the bank of the river, to come and make an alliance with us, and that their never having seen Christians also impelled them to come and visit us; that I should do with them and their companions as I wished; that they had no children with them, but men versed in war and full of courage, acquainted with the country and rivers in the land of the Iroquois; that now they entreated me to return to our settlement, that they might see our houses, and that, after three days, we should all together come back to engage in the war; that, as a token of firm friendship and joy, I should have muskets and harquebuses fired, at which they would be greatly pleased. This I did, when they uttered great cries of astonishment, especially those who had never heard nor seen the like.

After hearing them, I replied that, if they desired, I should be very glad to return to our settlement, to gratify them still more; and that they might conclude that I had no other purpose than to engage in the war, since we carried with us nothing but arms, and not merchandise for barter, as they had been given to understand; and that my only desire was to fulfill what I had promised them; and that, if I had known of any who had made evil reports to them, I should regard them as enemies more than they did themselves. They told me that they believed nothing of them, and that they never had heard anyone speak thus. But the contrary was the case; for there were some savages who told it to ours. I contented myself with waiting for an opportunity to show them in fact something more than they could have expected from me.

RETURN TO QUEBEC

The next day, we set out all together for our settlement, where they enjoyed themselves some five or six days, which were spent in dances and festivities, on account of their eagerness for us to engage in the war.

Pont Gravé came forthwith from Tadoussac with two little barks full of men, in compliance with a letter, in which I begged him to come as speedily as possible. The savages seeing him arrive rejoiced more than ever, inasmuch as I told them that he had given some of his men to assist them, and that perhaps we should go together.

On the 28th of the month [June 1609], we equipped some barks for assisting the savages. Pont Gravé embarked on one and I on the other, when we all set out together. The first of July, we arrived at St. Croix, distant fifteen leagues from Quebec, where Pont Gravé and I concluded that, for certain reasons, I should go with the savages and he to our settlement and to Tadoussac. This resolution being taken, I embarked in my shallop all that was necessary, together with Des Marais and La Routte, our pilot, and nine men.

I set out from St. Croix on the 3rd of July with all the savages. We passed the Trois Rivières, a very beautiful country, covered with a growth of fine trees. From this place to St. Croix is a distance of fifteen leagues. . . .

Thence we continued our course to the entrance of Lake St. Peter, where the country is exceedingly pleasant and level, and crossed the lake, in two, three, and four fathoms of water, which is some eight leagues long and four wide. . . . We went to the mouth of the River of the Iroquois [the Richelieu River], where we stayed two days, refreshing ourselves with good venison, birds, and fish, which the savages gave us.

Here sprang up among them some difference of opinion on the subject of the war, so that a portion only determined to go with me, while the others returned to their country with their wives and the merchandise which they had obtained by barter.

Setting out from the mouth of this river, which is some four hundred to five hundred paces broad, and very beautiful, running southward we arrived at a place in latitude 45°, and twenty-two or twenty-three leagues from the Trois Rivières. All this river from its mouth to the first fall, a distance of fifteen leagues, is very smooth, and bordered with woods, like all the other places before named, and of the same sorts. There are nine or ten fine islands before reaching the fall of the Iroquois, a league or a league and a half long and covered with numerous oaks and nut-trees. . . . There are here some meadows, but not inhabited by savages on account of the wars. . . .

As soon as we had reached the fall, Des Marais, La Routte, and I, with five men, went on shore to see whether we could pass this place; but we went some league and a half without seeing any prospect of being able to do so, finding only water running with great swiftness, and in all directions many stones, very dangerous, with but little water about them. The fall is perhaps six hundred paces broad. . . .

Having returned, and seeing the slight prospect there was of passing the fall with our shallop, I was much troubled. And it gave me especial dissatisfaction to go back without seeing a very large lake, filled with handsome islands, and with large tracts of fine land bordering on the lake, where their enemies live according to their representations. After duly thinking over the matter, I determined to go and fulfill my promise, and carry out my desire. Accordingly, I embarked with the savages in their canoes, taking with me two men, who went cheerfully. After making known my plan to Des Marais and others in the shallop, I requested the former to return to our settlement with the rest of our company giving them the assurance that, in a short time, by God's grace, I would return to them.

I proceeded forthwith to have a conference with the captains of the savages, and gave them to understand that they had told me the opposite of what my observations found to be the case at the fall; namely, that it was impossible to pass it with the shallop, but that this would not prevent me from assisting them as I had promised. This communication troubled them greatly; and they desired to change their determination, but I urged them not to do so, telling them that they ought to carry out their first plan, and that I, with two others, would go to the war with them in their canoes, in order to show them that, as for me, I would not break my word given to them, although alone; but that I was unwilling then to oblige any one of my companions to embark, and would only take with me those who had the inclination to go, of whom I had found two.

They were greatly pleased at what I had said to them, and at the determination which I had taken, promising as before to show me fine things.

ENCOUNTER WITH THE ENEMY

I set out accordingly from the fall of the Iroquois river on the 12th of July. All the savages set to carrying their canoes, arms, and baggage overland, some half a league, in order to pass by the violence and strength of the fall, which was speedily accomplished. Then they put them all in the water again, two men in each with the baggage; and they caused one of the men of each canoe to go by land some three leagues, the extent of the fall, which is not, however, so violent here as at the mouth, except in some places where rocks obstruct the river, which is not broader than three hundred or four hundred paces.

After we had passed the fall, which was attended with difficulty, all the savages, who had gone by land over a good path and level country, although there are a great many trees, re-embarked in their canoes. My men went also by land; but I went in a canoe. The savages made a review of their followers, finding that there were twenty-four canoes, with sixty men. After the review was completed, we continued our course to an island, three leagues long, filled with the finest pines I had ever seen. Here they went hunting, and captured some wild animals. Proceeding about three leagues farther on, we made a halt, in order to rest the coming night.

They all at once set to work, some to cut wood, and others to obtain the bark of trees for covering their cabins, for the sake of sheltering themselves, others to fell large trees for constructing a barricade on the river-bank around their cabins, which they do so quickly that in less than two hours so much is accomplished that five hundred of their enemies would find it very difficult to dislodge them without killing large numbers. They make no barricade on the river-bank, where their canoes are drawn up, in order that they may be able to embark, if the occasion requires.

After they were established in their cabins, they despatched three canoes, with nine good men, according to their custom in all their encampments, to reconnoiter for a distance of two or three leagues, to see if they can perceive anything, after which they return. They rest the entire night, depending upon the observation of these scouts, which is a very bad custom among them; for they are sometimes while sleeping surprised by their enemies, who slaughter them before they have time to get up and prepare for defense.

Noticing this, I remonstrated with them on the mistake they made, and told them they ought to keep watch, as they had seen us do every night, and have men on the lookout, in order to listen and see whether they perceived anything, and that they should not live in such a manner like beasts. They replied that they could not keep watch, and that they worked enough in the day-time in the chase, since, when engaged in war, they divide their troops into three parts: namely, a part for hunting scattered in several places; another to constitute the main body of their army, which is always under arms; and the third to act as *avant-coureurs*, to look out along the rivers, and observe whether they can see any mark or signal showing where their enemies or friends have passed. This they ascertain by certain marks which the chiefs of different tribes make known to each other; but, these not continuing always the same, they inform themselves from time to time of changes, by which means they ascertain whether they are enemies or friends who have passed.

The hunters never hunt in advance of the main body, or *avant-coureurs*, so as not to excite alarm or produce disorder, but in the rear and in the direction from which they do not anticipate their enemy. Thus they advance until they are within two or three days' march of their enemies, when they proceed by night stealthily and all in a body, except the *avant-coureurs*. By day, they withdraw into the interior of the woods, where they rest, without straying off, neither making any noise nor any fire, even for the sake of cooking, so as not to be noticed in case their enemies should by accident pass by. They make no fire, except in smoking, which amounts to almost nothing. They eat baked Indian meal, which they soak in water, when it becomes a kind of porridge. They provide themselves with such meal to meet their wants, when they are near their enemies, or when retreating after a charge, in which case they are not inclined to hunt, retreating immediately.

In all their encampments, they have their Pilotois, or Ostemoy, a class of persons who play the part of soothsayers, in whom these people have faith. One of these builds a cabin, surrounds it with small pieces of wood, and covers it with his robe: after it is built, he places himself inside, so as not to be seen at all, when he seizes and shakes one of the posts of his cabin, muttering some words between his teeth, by which he says he invokes the devil, who appears to him in the form of a stone, and tells them whether they will meet their enemies and kill many of them. This Pilotois lies prostrate on the ground, motionless, only speaking with the devil: on a sudden, he rises to his feet, talking and tormenting himself in such a manner that, although naked, he is all of a perspiration. All the people surround the cabin, seated on their buttocks, like apes. They frequently told me that the shaking of the cabin, which I saw, proceeded from the devil, who made it move, and not the man inside, although I could see the contrary. . . . They told me also that I should see fire come out from the top, which I did not see at all. These rogues counterfeit also their voice, so that it is heavy and clear, and speak in a language unknown to the other savages. And, when they represent it as broken, the savages think that the devil is speaking, and telling them what is to happen in their war, and what they must do. . . .

Now, after ascertaining from their soothsayers what is to be their fortune, the chiefs take sticks a foot long, and as many as there are soldiers. They take others, somewhat larger, to indicate the chiefs. Then they go into the wood, and seek out a level place, five or six feet square, where the chief, as sergeant-major, puts all the sticks in such order as seems to him best. Then he calls all his companions, who come all armed; and he indicates to them the rank and order they are to observe in battle with their enemies. All the savages watch carefully this proceeding, observing attentively the outline which their chief has made with the sticks. Then they go away, and set to placing themselves in such order as the sticks were in, when they mingle with each other, and return again to their proper order, which maneuver they repeat two or three times, and at all their encampments, without needing a sergeant to keep them in the proper order, which they are able to keep accurately without any confusion. This is their rule in war.

We set out on the next day, continuing our course in the river as far as the entrance of the lake. There are many pretty islands here, low, and containing very fine woods and meadows, with abundance of fowl and such animals of the chase as stags, fallow-deer, fawns, roe-bucks, bears, and others. . . . These regions, although they are pleasant, are not inhabited by any savages, on account of their wars; but they withdraw as far as possible from the rivers into the interior, in order not to be suddenly surprised.

The next day we entered the lake [Lake Champlain], which is of great extent, say eighty or a hundred leagues long, where I saw fine islands, ten, twelve, and fifteen leagues long, which were formerly inhabited by the savages, like the River of the Iroquois; but they have been abandoned since the wars of the savages with one another prevail. There are also many rivers falling into the lake, bordered by many fine trees of the same kinds as we have in France, and with many vines finer than any I have seen in any other place. . . .

Continuing our course over this lake on the western side, I noticed, while observing the country, some very high mountains on the eastern side,[25] on top of which there was snow. I made inquiry of the savages whether these localities were inhabited, when they told me that the Iroquois dwelt there, and that there were many beautiful valleys in these places, with plains productive in grain, such as I had eaten in this country, together with many kinds of fruit without limit. They said also that the lake extended near the mountains, some twenty-five leagues distant from us, as I judge. I saw, on the south, other mountains, no less high than the first, but without any snow [the Adirondacks]. The savages told me that these mountains were

[25] The Green Mountains of Vermont.

thickly settled, and that it was there we were to find their enemies; but that it was necessary to pass a fall in order to go there (which I afterwards saw), when we should enter another lake [Lake George], nine or ten leagues long. After reaching the end of the lake, we should have to go, they said, two leagues by land, and pass through a river [the Hudson] flowing into the sea. . . .

Now, as we began to approach within two or three days' journey of the abode of our enemies, we advanced only at night, resting during the day. But they did not fail to practice constantly their accustomed superstitions, in order to ascertain what was to be the result of their undertaking; and they often asked me if I had had a dream, and seen their enemies, to which I replied in the negative. Yet I did not cease to encourage them, and inspire in them hope. When night came, we set out on the journey until the next day, when we withdrew into the interior of the forest, and spent the rest of the day there. About ten or eleven o'clock, after taking a little walk about our encampment, I retired.

While sleeping, I dreamed that I saw our enemies, the Iroquois, drowning in the lake near a mountain, within sight. When I expressed a wish to help them, our allies, the savages, told me we must let them all die, and that they were of no importance. When I awoke, they did not fail to ask me, as usual, if I had had a dream. I told them that I had, in fact, had a dream. This, upon being related, gave them so much confidence that they did not doubt any longer that good was to happen to them.

When it was evening, we embarked in our canoes to continue our course; and, as we advanced very quietly and without making any noise, we met on the 29th of the month the Iroquois, about ten o'clock at evening, at the extremity of a cape which extends into the lake on the western bank. They had come to fight. We both began to utter loud cries, all getting their arms in readiness. We withdrew out on the water, and the Iroquois went on shore, where they drew up all their canoes close to each other and began to fell trees with poor axes, which they acquire in war sometimes, using also others of stone. Thus they barricaded themselves very well.

Our forces also passed the entire night, their canoes being drawn up close to each other, and fastened to poles, so that they might not get separated, and that they might be all in readiness to fight, if occasion required. We were out upon the water, within arrow range of the barricades.

When they were armed and in array, they despatched two canoes by themselves to the enemy to inquire if they wished to fight, to which the latter replied that they wanted nothing else: but they said that, at present, there was not much light, and that it would be necessary to wait for daylight, so as to be able to recognize each other; and that, as soon as the sun rose, they would offer us battle. This was agreed to by our side.

Meanwhile, the entire night was spent in dancing and singing, on both sides, with endless insults and other talk; as, how little courage we had, how feeble a resistance we should make against their arms, and that, when day came, we should realize it to our ruin. Ours also were not slow in retorting, telling them they would see such execution of arms as never before, together with an abundance of such talk as is not unusual in the siege of a town [in a European war].

After this singing, dancing, and bandying words on both sides to the fill, when day came, my companions and myself continued under cover, for fear that the enemy would see us. We arranged our arms in the best manner possible, being, however, separated, each in one of the canoes of the savage Montagnais. After arming ourselves with light armor, we each took an arquebus, and went on shore. I saw the enemy go out of their barricade, nearly two hundred in number, stout and robust in appearance. They came at a slow pace towards us, with a dignity and assurance which greatly delighted me, having three chiefs at their head.

Our men also advanced in the same order, telling me that those who had three large plumes were the chiefs, and that they had only these three, and that they could be distinguished by these plumes which were much larger than those of their companions, and that I should do what I could to kill them. I promised to do all in my power, and said that I was very sorry they could not understand me, so that I might give order and shape to their mode of attacking their enemies, and then we should, without doubt, defeat them all; but that this could not now be obviated, and that I should be very glad to show them my courage and good-will when we should engage in the fight.

As soon as we had landed, they began to run for some two hundred paces toward their enemies, who stood firmly, not having as yet noticed my companions, who went into the woods with some savages. Our men began to call me with loud cries; and, in order to give me a passage-way, they opened in two parts, and put me at their head, where I marched some twenty paces in advance of the rest, until I was within about thirty paces of the enemy, who at once noticed me, and halting, gazed at me, as I did also at them. When I saw them making a move to fire at us, I rested my musket against my cheek, and aimed directly at one of the three chiefs. With the same shot, two fell to the ground; and one of their men was so wounded that he died some time after. I had loaded my musket with four balls.[26]

When our side saw this shot so favorable for them, they began to raise such loud cries that one could not have heard it thunder. Meanwhile, the arrows flew on both sides. The Iroquois were greatly astonished that two men had been so quickly killed, although they were equipped with armor woven from cotton thread, and with wood which was proof against their arrows.

---

[26] Champlain's harquebus was a primitive device—basically an iron tube. It did not fire self-contained bullets; instead it took a charge of gunpowder, followed by a lead ball (or four), all packed down the barrel. At the breech, a fuse (or "match") was kept burning; the trigger would pull it down to ignite the gunpowder. Champlain's four balls undoubtedly scattered like a shotgun blast.

This caused great alarm among them. As I was loading again, one of my companions fired a shot from the woods, which astonished them anew to such a degree that, seeing their chiefs dead, they lost courage, and took to flight, abandoning their camp and fort, and fleeing into the woods, whither I pursued them, killing still more of them. Our savages also killed several of them, and took ten or twelve prisoners. The remainder escaped with the wounded. Fifteen or sixteen were wounded on our side with arrow-shots; but they were soon healed.

After gaining the victory, our men amused themselves by taking a great quantity of Indian corn and some meal from their enemies, also their armor, which they had left behind that they might run better. After feasting sumptuously, dancing and singing, we returned three hours after, with the prisoners.

RETURN FROM THE BATTLE

After going some eight leagues, toward evening they took one of the prisoners, to whom they made a harangue, enumerating the cruelties which he and his men had already practiced toward them without any mercy, and that, in like manner, he ought to make up his mind to receive as much. They commanded him to sing, if he had courage, which he did; but it was a very sad song.

Meanwhile, our men kindled a fire; and, when it was well burning, they each took a brand, and burned this poor creature gradually, so as to make him suffer greater torment. Sometimes they stopped, and threw water on his back. Then they tore out his nails, and applied fire to the extremities of his fingers and private member. Afterwards, they flayed the top of his head, and had a kind of gum poured all hot upon it; then they pierced his arms near the wrists, and, drawing up the sinews with sticks, they tore them out by force; but, seeing that they could not get them, they cut them.

This poor wretch uttered terrible cries, and it excited my pity to see him treated in this manner, and yet showing such firmness that one would have said, at times, that he suffered hardly any pain at all. I remonstrated with them, saying that we practiced no such cruelties, but killed them at once; and that, if they wished me to fire a musket-shot at him, I should be willing to do so. They refused, saying that he would not in that case suffer any pain. I went away from them, pained to see such cruelties as they practiced upon his body. When they saw that I was displeased, they called me, and told me to fire a musket shot at him. This I did without seeing it, and thus put an end, by a single shot, to all the torments he would have suffered, rather than see him tyrannized over.

After his death, they were not satisfied, but opened him, and threw his entrails into the lake. Then they cut off his head, arms, and legs, which they scattered in different directions; keeping the scalp, which they had flayed off, as they had done in the case of all the rest whom they had killed in the contest. They were guilty also of another monstrosity in taking his heart, cutting it into several pieces, and giving it to a brother of his to eat, as also to others of his companions, who were prisoners: they took it into their mouths, but would not swallow it. Some Algonquin savages, who were guarding them, made some of them spit it out, when they threw it into the water. This is the manner in which these people behave toward those whom they capture in war, for whom it would be better to die fighting, or to kill themselves on the spur of the moment, as many do, rather than fall into the hands of their enemies. After this execution, we set out on our return with the rest of the prisoners, who kept singing as they went along, with no better hopes for the future than he had had who was so wretchedly treated.[27]

Having arrived at the fall of the Iroquois, the Algonquins returned to their own country; so also the Ochasteguins [Hurons], with a part of the prisoners: well satisfied with the results of the war, and that I had accompanied them so readily. We separated accordingly with loud protestations of mutual friendship; and they asked me whether I would not like to go into their country, to assist them with continued fraternal relations; and I promised that I would do so.

I returned with the Montagnais. After informing myself from the prisoners in regard to their country, and of its probable extent, we packed up the baggage for the return, which was accomplished with such despatch that we went every day in their canoes twenty-five or thirty leagues, which was their usual rate of travelling. When we arrived at the mouth of the river of the Iroquois, some of the savages dreamed that their enemies were pursuing them. This dream led them to move their camp forthwith, although the night was very inclement on account of the wind and rain; and they went and passed the remainder of the night, from fear of their enemies, amid high reeds on Lake St. Peter. Two days after, we arrived at our settlement. . . .

After some days, I went to Quebec, whither some Algonquin savages came, expressing their regret at not being present at the defeat of their enemies, and presenting me with some furs, in consideration of my having gone there and assisted their friends.

Some days after they had set out for their country, distant about a hundred and twenty leagues from our settlement, I went to Tadoussac to see whether Pont Gravé had returned from Gaspé, whither he had gone. He did not arrive until the next day, when he told me that he had decided to return to France. We concluded to leave an upright man, Captain Pierre Chavin of Dieppe, to command at Quebec, until Sieur de Monts should arrange matters there.

[27] This passage does *not* exaggerate the ritual cruelty shown to prisoners; it was customary on both sides, and warriors who suffered it tried to show their bravery by refusing to succumb to the intense pain (as Champlain indicates).

RETURN TO FRANCE

After forming this resolution, we went to Quebec to establish him in authority, and leave him everything requisite and necessary for the settlement, together with fifteen men. Everything being arranged, we set out on the first day of September for Tadoussac, in order to fit out our vessel for returning to France.

We set out accordingly from the latter place on the 5th of the month [September]. . . . On the 8th [of October], we anchored at Conquet in lower Brittany. On Saturday the 10th, we set out from there, arriving at Honfleur on the 13th.

After disembarking, I did not wait long before taking post to go to Sieur de Monts, who was then at Fontainebleau, where His Majesty [Henry IV] was. Here I reported to him in detail all that had transpired in regard to the winter quarters and our new explorations, and my hopes for the future in view of the promises of the savages called Ochasteguins [Hurons], who are good Iroquois. The other Iroquois, their enemies, dwell more to the south. . . .[28]

I at once waited upon His Majesty, and gave him an account of my voyage, which afforded him pleasure and satisfaction. I had a girdle made of porcupine quills, very well worked, after the manner of the country where it was made, and which His Majesty thought very pretty. I had also two little birds, of the size of blackbirds and of a carnation color; also, the head of a fish caught in the great Lake of the Iroquois, having a very long snout and two or three rows of very sharp teeth. . . .

After I had concluded my interview with His Majesty, Sieur de Monts determined to go to Rouen to meet his associates, the Sieurs Collier and Le Gendre, merchants of Rouen, to consider what should be done the coming year. They resolved to continue the settlement, and finish the explorations up the great river St. Lawrence, in accordance with the promises of the Ochasteguins, made on the condition that we should assist them in their wars, as I had given them to understand. . . .

I provided myself with whatever was desirable and necessary for spending the winter at our settlement in Quebec. For this purpose I set out from Paris the last day of February following.

———

IN ONE EXPLOSIVE fight, this soldier of France revolutionized his allies' war with the Iroquois. Where once two or three enemy warriors might be killed in a successful skirmish, and another handful taken prisoner, the Hurons, Algonquins, and French now annihilated hostile war parties. Champlain won permanent status as a friend and a man of his word. And for

[28] The Hurons and Iroquois were closely related in culture and language.

a strange, fascinating moment, he entered fully into their mystical world, as he dreamed of drowning Iroquois. He derided their faith in dreams as superstition—yet he did not fail to record his own telling vision, and the unity it helped forge.

Unlike strife-torn, precarious Jamestown, Quebec now stood on firm foundations, thanks to Champlain's success in Native American diplomacy. But his victories came at a grave cost. The way south was barred permanently by Iroquois hatred. Thanks to the united front of the Five Nations, the lower frontier of New France would never push much more than a day's march below the St. Lawrence. The Iroquois stood destined to play a pivotal strategic role in the relations between the French colonists and whoever might appear on the seacoast to the south.

More and more, the fate of Quebec depended upon two forces: the Hurons and the crown. To the west, the mighty Huron confederacy provided the key to French power in North America—as essential allies against the Five Nations, as suppliers of furs, as guides to the wilderness of the interior. And Champlain's return trip to France reveals the close involvement of the monarch in the new colony: though his patron Henry IV died on an assassin's blade that same year, future kings would play a central role in making policy for Quebec.

Small but cohesive, prosperous but heavily armed, safely established but closely involved in Indian wars, the New France of 1610 already foreshadowed the patterns of a century and a half to come. On the banks of the St. Lawrence, Champlain had laid a permanent foundation for a future empire. Unknown to the squabbling Englishmen of Jamestown, an enemy was growing in North America, one that would still loom long after Powhatan became a half-forgotten ghost.

4

IN POWHATAN'S SHADOW

Captain John Smith was disgusted. Jamestown faced starvation, murderous disease, and persistent Indian attacks—yet the settlers behaved like a cross between squabbling small-town aldermen and a mutinous crew of pirates. Where cornfields needed planting and shelter needed building, the colonists chased the mirage of gold; where military discipline and subtle diplomacy were required, they preferred to whisper against their leaders and to bribe the natives.

When Smith confronted his disorganized, discontented comrades, he did not stand alone. His call for discipline, unity, and action found a receptive audience among a growing number of the settlers; already they had seen that Smith could back up his bold talk with brave deeds. So when the colonists gathered to select a new ruling council in September 1608, they asked their one-time prisoner to be their new president.

As the Captain—now President—saw it, he faced three problems: two internal, one external. First, order had to be established among the settlers; he solved this difficulty by imposing the equivalent of martial law. Second, they desperately lacked food. And third, the colony fell completely under the shadow of its powerful neighbor, the great Powhatan.

To Smith, the questions of provisions and Powhatan were one and the same. And to answer them both, he would pursue a policy that combined equal parts guile and brute force. This soldier of fortune had been schooled in some of the bitterest warfare in European history—including England's vicious struggle against the Irish—and he had learned additional lessons from his favorite author, Machiavelli. He would not hesitate at extreme measures.

But Smith faced a worthy foe. Long before the English ever arrived on American shores, Powhatan had proved himself to be truly a remarkable leader. Most Native American chiefs could only hope to achieve influence over their fellows—but Powhatan had seized something approaching sovereignty. His power stretched out over dozens of communities, as he constructed a sprawling confederacy centered on himself; wherever he went, his followers showed him a striking degree of reverence and obedience. Now he cast his eyes on this new people who had settled in the midst of his territory, seeing them both as potential subjects and as a dire threat.

So when Smith rose to predominance among the colonists, he became locked in a duel of intrigue and audacity with the great Powhatan. At times, the Englishman became entangled in his own lies. When he had been Powhatan's prisoner, for example, he fostered the idea that his own leader was Newport, the sea captain who had transported the colonists to Virginia. But then Newport returned with supplies and tried to fill this invented role, much to Smith's irritation. Newport brought orders from the Company in London to crown Powhatan as a vassal of King James I,[29] leading to a confusing three-way negotiation, as Newport puffed up his own importance, while Smith and Powhatan engaged in a battle of wits (offering rare insight into Indian diplomacy and Powhatan's shrewdness).

Powhatan hesitated at direct confrontation with the colony, choosing instead to apply indirect pressure. The settlers only slowly realized that all the villages around them owed their allegiance to Powhatan and followed his direction. They seemed to be independent at first, since each had its own leaders (one of the most important, Pamunkey, followed Opechancanough, Powhatan's powerful brother and heir). Playing on this ignorance of the structure of his confederacy, Powhatan urged the communities closest to Jamestown to deny them the food they desperately needed, while launching pinprick raids to test the colony's defenses and steal its tools.

This policy created dire problems for Smith, as disappearing food supplies caused rising dissension. Some of the settlers, in desperation, even deserted to the Indian villages, taking tools and weapons with them. But the colonists' new President met the challenge with whatever means were necessary. With cold, brutal logic, he developed a plan for keeping the Indians on the defensive, in part by forcing them to provide the colony with food. Simultaneously, he would pursue ties to Powhatan's enemies, the Monacans. And to carry out his schemes, he would lie, steal, kidnap, and murder.

The selections below follow those tense months, as the colonists struggled to survive in Powhatan's shadow. Once again, we see these events through the eyes of Smith's allies among the settlers—yet even from their opinionated perspective, we find a rich portrait of Powhatan's cunning, the colonists' dissension, and Smith's combination of bravery and ruthlessness. The new President did not hesitate to throw himself into the most dangerous situations—yet he always kept the colony's needs, and his own, clearly in view. Here is the stark reality of Captain John Smith, a man with the heart of a mercenary and a fierce determination to survive, a man who would force everyone in his path to bend to his will.

---

[29] Historian Ian K. Steele has suggested that Powhatan probably saw this coronation not as an act of submission to a king he had never seen, but as a presentation of gifts by new allies, in keeping with his own traditions.

President Smith
by Richard Wiffin, William Phettiplace, and Anas Todkill

The 10th of September, 1608, by the election of the Council and request of the company, Captain Smith received the letters patent, and took upon him the place of President, which till then by no means he would accept, though he were often importuned thereunto. [Smith now began to reorganize the colony.]

Now . . . the church was repaired, the storehouse re-covered; [and a storage] building prepared for the supply we expected. The fort reduced to the form of this figure [a triangle], the order of watch renewed, the squadrons (each setting of the watch) trained. The whole company every Saturday exercised in a field prepared for that purpose; the boats trimmed for trade, which in their journey encountered the second supply, that brought them back to discover the country of Monacan. . . .

As for the coronation of Powhatan, and his presents [that is, the presents to him] of basin, ewer, bed, clothes, and such costly novelties, they had been much better well spared than so ill spent, for we had his favor [previously] much better only for a poor piece of copper, till this stately kind of soliciting made him so much overvalue himself that he respected us as much as nothing at all. . . . But Captain Newport we only accounted the author [of the coronation plan], who to effect these projects had so gilded all our hopes with great promises. . . .

And Smith, to make clear . . . that the savages were not so desperate as was pretended by Captain Newport, and how willing he was to further them to effect their projects . . . undertook their message to Powhatan (to entreat him to come to Jamestown to receive his presents), accompanied only with Captain Waldo, M. Andrew Buckler, Edward Brinton, and Samuel Collier. With these four, he went overland against Werowacomoco, [and] passed the river of Pamunkey in the savages' canoes, Powhatan being 30 miles off, who was presently sent for. . . .

The next day came Powhatan [to Werowacomoco]. Smith delivered his message of the presents sent him, and redelivered him Namontack,[30] desiring him [to] come to his father Newport to accept those presents, and conclude their revenge against the Monacans.[31] Whereunto the subtle savage thus replied:

> If your king has sent me presents, I also am a king, and this [is] my
> land. Eight days I will stay to receive them. Your father is to come to

[30] Namontack was the man Powhatan had sent to live with the colonists.
[31] The Monacans were Powhatan's enemies. Smith, knowing this, had concocted a story that the colonists desired revenge against them. His actual purpose was to find and make contact with them, as possible allies against Powhatan.

me, not I to him, nor yet to your fort, neither will I bite at such a
bait. As for the Monacans, I can revenge my own injuries. . . . But
[as] for any salt water beyond the mountains, the relations you have
had from my people are false.

Whereupon he began to draw plots upon the ground, according to his discourse, of all those regions. Many other discourses they had (yet both desirous to give each other content[ment] in complimentary courtesies), and
so Captain Smith returned with this answer.

Upon this Captain Newport sent his presents by water, which is near
100 miles, [and] with 50 of the best shot [he] himself went by land, which
is but 12 miles, where he met with our three barges to transport him over.
All things being fit for the day of his coronation, the presents were brought,
his basin, ewer, bed, and furniture set up, his scarlet cloak and apparel (with
much ado) put on him (being persuaded by Namontack they would do him
no hurt).

But a foul trouble there was to make him kneel to receive his crown.
He, neither knowing the majesty nor meaning of a crown, nor bending of
the knee, endured so many persuasions, examples, and instructions, as tired
them all. At last, by leaning hard on his shoulders, he a little stooped, and
Newport put the crown on his head; when, by the warning of a pistol, the
boats were prepared with such a volley of shot, that the king started up in a
horrible fear, till he saw all was well. Then, remembering himself to con-
gratulate their kindness, he gave his old shoes and his mantle to Captain
Newport. But perceiving his [Newport's] purpose was to discover the
Monacans, he labored to divert his resolution, refusing to lend him either
men or guides more than Namontack. And so, after some complimentary
kindness on both sides, in requital of his presents, he presented Newport
with a heap of wheat [corn] ears, that might contain seven or eight bushels,
and as much more we bought, ready dressed, in the town, wherewith we returned to the fort.

The [newly arrived] ship, having unburdened herself of 70 persons,
with the first gentlewoman and woman servant that arrived in our colony,
Captain Newport with all the council, and 120 chosen men, set forward for
the discovery of [the] Monacan, leaving the President at the fort with 80
(such as they were) to reload the ship. Arriving at the falls, we marched by
land some 40 miles in two days and a half, and so returned down the same
path we went. Two towns we discovered of the Monacans, the people neither using us well nor ill, yet for our security we took one of their petty
werowances, and led him bound to conduct us the way. . . .

Coming to the falls, the savages fained [claimed] there were diverse
ships come into the bay to kill them at Jamestown. Trade they would not,
and find their corn we could not, for they had hid it in the woods; and being

thus deluded, we arrived at Jamestown half sick, all complaining and tired with toil, famine, and discontent, to have only but discovered our gilded hopes, and such fruitless certainties, as our President foretold us.

No sooner were we landed, but the President dispersed many as were able, some for glass, others for pitch, tar, and soap ashes,[32] leaving them with the fort to the Council's oversight. But 30 of us he conducted 5 miles from the fort to learn to make clapboard, cut down trees, and lie [fight] in woods. . . .

The President, returning from amongst the woods, seeing the time consumed and no provision gotten (and the ship lay idle, and would do nothing), presently embarked himself in the discovery barge, giving order to the Council to send Mr. Percy after him with the next barge that arrived at the fort. Two barges he had himself, and 20 men. But arriving at Chickahominy, [he found] that dogged nation was too well acquainted with our wants, refusing to trade with as much scorn and insolence as they could express. The President, perceiving it was Powhatan's policy to starve us, told them he came not so much for their corn, as to revenge his imprisonment, and the death of his men murdered by them.

And so, landing his men, and ready to charge them, they [the Indians] immediately fled. But then they sent their ambassadors, with corn, fish, fowl, or what they had, to make their peace. Their corn being that year bad, they complained extremely of their own wants, yet freighted our boats with 100 bushels of corn, and in like manner Mr. Percy's [barge], that not long after us arrived. They having done the best they could to content us, within four or five days we returned to Jamestown. . . .

THE PROCEEDINGS AND ACCIDENTS, WITH THE SECOND SUPPLY

Mr. Scrivener was sent with the barges and pinnace to Werowacomoco, where he found the savages more ready to fight than trade, but his vigilance was such as prevented their projects, and by the means of Namontack got three or four hogsheads of corn, and as much red paint, which was (then) esteemed an excellent dye.

Captain Newport, being dispatched with the trials of pitch, tar, glass, frankincense, and soap ashes, with [such] clapboard and wainscot [as] could be provided, met with Mr. Scrivener at Point Comfort, and so returned for England, leaving us in all 200, with those he brought us. . . .

Those poor . . . [conditions] so affrighted us all with famine, that the President provided for [a voyage to] Nansemond, taking with him Captain Winne and Mr. Scrivener (then returning from Captain Newport). These

---

[32] Smith argued that these products, more prosaic but far more obtainable than gold and silver, would be the true exports of Virginia.

people [had] also long denied him trade (excusing themselves to be so commanded by Powhatan), till we were constrained to begin with them [with force], and then they would rather sell us some, than we should take all. So loading our boats with 100 bushels, we parted friends, and came to Jamestown; at which time, there was a marriage between John Laydon and Anne Burrows, being the first marriage we had in Virginia.

Long he stayed not, but fitting himself and Captain Waldo with two barges, [he traveled to] Chawopo, Weanocke, and all parts there, [and] found neither corn nor savages, but all fled (being jealous of our intents) till we discovered the river and people of Appomattox, where we found little. . . .

The President, seeing that this procrastinating was no course [by which] to live, resolved with Captain Waldo (who he knew to be sure in time of need) to surprise Powhatan and all his provisions; but [was prevented by] the unwillingness of Captain Winne, and Mr. Scrivener. . . .

But the President, whom no persuasion could persuade to starve, [was] invited by Powhatan to come unto him, and if he would send him but men to build a house, bring him a grindstone, 50 swords, some pieces [muskets], a cock and a hen, with copper and beads, he would load his ship with corn. The President, not ignorant of his devices, yet unwilling to neglect any opportunity, presently sent three Dutchmen and two English (having no victuals to . . . [provide] them, all for want thereof being idle). . . .

To surprise Powhatan, to effect this project, he took order with Captain Waldo to second him, if need required. Scrivener he left [as] his substitute, and set forth with the pinnace, two barges, and six and forty men, which only were such as voluntarily offered themselves for this journey, the which . . . was very desperate. They all knowing Smith would not return empty [handed] howsoever, caused many of those that he had appointed to find excuses to stay behind.

CAPTAIN SMITH'S JOURNEY TO PAMUNKEY

The 29th of December, he set forward for Werowacomoco. . . . The company being victualed but for 3 or 4 days, lodged the first night at Weraskoyack's, where the President took sufficient provisions. This kind savage did his best to divert him from seeing Powhatan, but perceiving he could not prevail, he advised in this manner, "Captain Smith, you shall find Powhatan to use you kindly, but trust him not, and be sure he [will] have no opportunity to seize on your arms, for he has sent for you only to cut your throats."

The Captain thanked him for his good counsel, yet the better to try his love, desired guides to Chowanoke, for he would send a present to that king to bind him [as] his friend. . . . Then we departed thence, the President assuring the king [of] his perpetual love, and left with him Samuel Collier, his page, to learn the language. . . .

The 12th of January we arrived at Werowacomoco, where the river was frozen near half a mile from the shore. But to neglect no time, the President with his barge so far had approached, by breaking the ice, as the ebb left him amongst those oozy shoals; yet, rather than to lie there frozen to death, by his own example he taught them [his men] to march . . . through this muddy frozen ooze. . . .

Quartering in the next houses we found, we sent to Powhatan for provisions, who sent us plenty of bread, turkeys, and venison. The next day, having feasted us after his ordinary manner, he began to ask when we would be gone, faining he sent not for us, neither had he any corn, and his people much less, yet for 40 swords he would procure [for] us 40 bushels.

The President . . . asked him how it chanced [that] he became so forgetful; thereat, the king concluded the matter with a merry laughter, asking for our commodities, but none he liked without guns and swords, valuing a basket of corn more precious than a basket of copper, saying he could eat his corn, but not his copper.

Captain Smith, seeing the intent of this subtle savage, began to deal with him after this manner: "Powhatan, though I had many courses to have made my provision; yet believing your promises to supply my wants, I sent you my men [the Dutch craftsmen] for your building, neglecting my own. What your people had, you have engrossed, forbidding them our trade, and now you think by consuming the time, we shall consume [starve] for want, not having [the commodities] to fulfill your strange demands. As for swords and guns, I told you long ago I had none to spare. And you shall know, those I have can keep me from want; yet steal, or wrong you, I will not, nor dissolve that friendship we have mutually promised, except you constrain me by your bad usages."

The king having attentively listened to this discourse, promised that both he and his country would spare him what they could; the which within two days they would receive. Yet, Captain Smith (said the king), "Some doubt I have of your coming hither, that makes me not so kindly seek to relieve you as I would; for many do inform me, your coming is not for trade, but to invade my people and possess my country, who [therefore] dare not come to bring you corn, seeing you thus armed with your men. To cheer us of this fear, leave aboard [your ship] your weapons, for here they are needless, we being all friends and forever Powhatans.[33]

With many such discourses, they spent the day, quartering that night in the king's houses. The next day, he reviewed his building, which he little intended should proceed; for the Dutchmen finding his plenty, and knowing our want, and perceiving his preparation to surprise us, little thinking we

---

[33] As mentioned previously, his followers called themselves Powhatans.

could escape both him and famine, to obtain his favor revealed to him as much as they knew of our estates and projects, and how to prevent them. . . .

We wrangled out of the king 10 quarters of corn for a copper kettle; the which the President perceiving him much to affect, valued it at a much greater rate, but (in regard of his scarcity) he would accept of as much more the next year, or else the country of Monacan. The king, exceeding liberal of what he had not, yielded him Monacan. Wherewith each seeming well contented, Powhatan began to expostulate the difference between peace and war, after this manner:

"Captain Smith, you may understand that I, having seen the death of all my people thrice, and not one living of those three generations but myself, I know the difference of peace and war better than any in my country. But I am now old, and ere long must die. My brethren, namely Opichapam, Opechancanough, and Kekataugh, my two sisters, and their two daughters, are distinctly each other's successors.[34] I wish [well for] their experiences no less than mine, and your love to them, not less than mine to you; but this bruit [report] from Nansemond that you are come to destroy my country, so much affrighted my people as they dare not visit you. What will it avail you to take . . . [by force that which] you may quietly have with love, or to destroy them that provide you food? What can you get by war, when we can hide our provisions and fly to the woods, whereby you must famish, by wronging us your friends? And why are you thus jealous of our love, seeing us unarmed, and both do and are willing still to feed you with that you cannot get but by our labors?

"Think you I am so simple not to know it is better to eat good meat, lie well, and sleep quietly with my women and children, laugh, and be merry with you, have copper, hatchets, or what I want [in] being your friend—than be forced to fly from all, to lie cold in the woods, feed upon acorns and such trash, and be so hunted by you that I can neither rest, eat, nor sleep, but my tired men must watch, and if a twig but break, everyone cries, 'There comes Captain Smith'; then I must fly I know not whither, and thus with miserable fear and my miserable life, leaving my pleasures to such youths as you, which, through your rash unadvisedness, may quickly as miserably end, for want of that you never know how to find? Let this therefore assure you of our love, and every year our friendly trade shall furnish you with corn; and now also if you would come in friendly manner to see us, and not thus with your guns and swords, as to invade your foes."

To this subtle discourse, the President thus replied: "Seeing you will not lightly conceive of our words we strive to make you know our thoughts by our deeds. The vow I made you of my love, both myself and my men have kept. As for your promise, I find it every day violated by some of your sub-

---

[34] They observed matrilineal succession—first Powhatan's brothers would succeed him, then his sisters, then his sisters' children.

jects; yet we, finding your love and kindness, our custom is so far from being ungrateful, that for your sake only we have curbed our thirsting desire for revenge, [or] else had they known as well the cruelty we used to our enemies as our true love and courtesy to our friends. And I think your judgement sufficient to conceive, as well by the adventures we have undertaken, as by the advantage we have by our arms, of yours: that we intended you any hurt, long ere this we could have effected it. Your people coming at me at Jamestown are entertained with their bows and arrows without exception; we esteeming it with you as it is with us, to wear our arms as our apparel. As for the dangers of our enemies, in such wars consists our chief pleasure. For your riches we have no use. As for the hiding of your provision, or by your flying to the woods, we shall [not] so unadvisedly starve as you conclude; your friendly care in that behalf is needless, for we have a rule to find [what is] beyond your knowledge."

Many other discourses they had, till at last they began to trade. But the king, seeing his will would not be admitted as law, our guard dispersed, nor our men disarmed—he, sighing, breathed his mind once more, in this manner: "Captain Smith, I never used any of [the] werowances so kindly as yourself; yet from you I receive the least kindness of any.[35] Captain Newport gave me swords, copper, cloths, a bed, tools, or what I desired, ever taking what I offered him. And [he] would send away his guns when I entreated him. None do deny to lay at my feet, or do what I desire, but only you; of whom I can have nothing but what you regard not, and yet you will have whatsoever you demand. Captain Newport you call father, and so you call me; but I see, for all us both, you will do what you list, and we must both seek to content you. But if you intend [to be] so friendly as you say, send hence your arms that I may believe you; for you see the love I bear you does cause me thus nakedly to forget myself."

Smith (seeing this savage but trifled the time, to cut his throat) procured the savages to break the ice, that his boat might come to fetch both him and his corn; and gave order for his men to come ashore, to have surprised the king, with whom also he but trifled the time till his men landed. . . .

By this time, Powhatan, having knowledge [that] his men were ready, whilst the ice was breaking, his luggage, women, and children fled. And to avoid suspicion [he] left two or three of his women talking with the Captain, whilst he secretly fled, and his men as secretly beset the house. Which being at the instant discovered to Captain Smith; with his pistol, sword, and target [shield], he made such a passage amongst those naked devils that they fled before him, some one, way some another; so that without hurt he . . . [reached] the *corps du guard* [Smith's soldiers]. When they perceived him [Smith] so well escaped, and with his eight men (for he had no more with

---

[35] This sentence suggests that Powhatan saw Smith as a troublesome vassal.

him), to the uttermost of their skill they [the Indians] sought by excuses to dissemble the matter. And Powhatan, to excuse his flight and the sudden coming of this multitude, sent our Captain a great bracelet and a chain of pearls, by an ancient orator that bespoke us to this purpose (perceiving then from our pinnace, a barge, and men departing and coming unto us):

"Captain Smith, our werowance is fled, fearing your guns; and, knowing when the ice was broken there would come more men, sent those of his to guard his corn from the pilfering that might happen without your knowledge. Now though some be hurt by your misprison, yet he is your friend, and so will continue. And since the ice is open, he would have you send away your corn; and if you would have his company, send also your arms, which so affrighten his people that they dare not come to you, as he promised they should."

Now having provided baskets for our men to carry the corn, they kindly offered their services to guard our arms, that none should steal them. A great many they were, of goodly well appointed fellows, as grim as devils; yet the very sight of cocking our matches against them, and a few words, caused them to leave their bows and arrows to our guard, and bear down our corn on their own backs. . . . But our own barge, being left by the ebb, caused us to stay till the midnight tide carried us safe aboard [the pinnace]. . . .

HOW WE ESCAPED SURPRISING AT PAMUNKEY

We had no sooner set sail, but Powhatan returned, and sent Adam and Francis (two stout Dutchmen) to the fort; who fained [pretended] to Captain Winne that all things were well, and that Captain Smith had use for their arms; wherefore they requested new [weapons] (the which were given them). They told him their coming was for some extraordinary tools and shift of apparel. By this colorable excuse, they obtained six or seven more to their confederacy [the Powhatans], such expert thieves that presently furnished them with a great many swords, pike-heads, pieces, shot, powder, and such like. They had savages at hand ready to carry it away.

The next day, they returned unsuspected, to convey them . . . all things they could; for which service, they should live with Powhatan as his chief affected, free from those miseries that would happen to the colony. Samuel, their other consort, Powhatan kept for their pledge; whose diligence had provided him 300 of their kind of hatchets; the rest, 50 swords, eight pieces, and eight pikes. . . .

Within two or three days, we arrived at Pamunkey; the king [Opechancanough] as many days entertained us with feasting and much mirth. And the day he appointed to begin our trade, the President, with Mr. Percy, Mr. West, Mr. Russell, Mr. Beheathland, Mr. Powell, Mr. Crashaw, Mr. Ford, and some others, to the number of 15, went up to Opechancanough's house (near a quarter of a mile from the river); where we[36] found nothing but a lame fellow and a boy, and all the houses about, of all things abandoned. Not long we stayed here ere the king arrived, and after him, came diverse of his people loaded with bows and arrows. . . .

Our Captain began with him in this manner. "Opechancanough, the great love you profess with your tongue seems mere deceit by your actions. Last year, you kindly freighted our ship; but now you have invited me to starve with hunger. You know my want; and I, your plenty; of which, by some means, I must have part. Remember it is fit for kings to keep their promises. Here are my commodities, whereof take your choice; the rest I will proportion fit bargains for your people."

The king seemed kindly to accept this offer. . . . The barges and pinnace being committed to the charge of Mr. Phettiplace, the President, with his old 15, marched up to the king's house, where we found four or five men newly come with great baskets. Not long after came the king, who, with a strained cheerfulness, held us with discourse, [exclaiming] what pains he had taken to keep his promise, till Mr. Russell brought us in news that we were all betrayed, for at least 6 or 700 of well appointed Indians had environed the house and beset the fields. . . . Whereat, some of our company seeming dismayed with the thought of such a multitude, the Captain encouraged us. . . .

The time not permitting any argument, all vowed to execute whatsoever he attempted, or die. Whereupon the Captain, approaching the king, bespoke him in this manner: "I see, Opechancanough, your plot to murder me; but I fear it not. As yet your men and mine have done no harm. . . . Take therefore your arms; you see mine. My body shall be as naked as yours, the isle in your river is a fit place, if you be contented; and the conqueror of us two shall be Lord and Master over all our men. Otherwise draw all your men into the field; if you have not enough, take time to fetch more. And bring what number you will, so everyone bring a basket of corn, against all which I will stake the value in copper. You see I have but 15 men, and our game shall be, the conqueror take all."

The king, being guarded with 50 or 60 of his chief men, seemed kindly to appease Smith's suspicion of unkindness, by a great present at the door they entreated him to receive. This was to draw him without the door, where the present was guarded by at least 200 men, and 30 lying under a great tree that lay athwart as a barricade, each his arrow notched, ready to shoot. . . .

But, commanding Mr. Percy and Mr. West to make good the house, [Smith] took Mr. Powell and Mr. Beheathland to guard the door; and in such a rage, snatched the king by his vambrace,[37] in the midst of his men, with his pistol ready bent against his breast. Thus he led the trembling king, near dead with fear, amongst all his people . . . [and] all his men were easily

[36] Presumably one or all of the authors of this account went as well.
[37] The bracer, or leather covering, that protects the forearm when firing a bow.

entreated to cast down their arms, little dreaming any durst in that manner have used their king; who when, to escape himself, bestowed his presents in good sadness. And, having caused all his multitude to approach disarmed, the President argued with them to this effect:

> I see, you Pamunkeys, the great desire you have to cut my throat, and my long suffering [of] your injuries have emboldened you to this presumption. . . . But if you shoot but one arrow to shed one drop of blood of any of my men, or steal the least of these beads or copper I spurn before me with my foot; you shall see, I will not cease revenge, if once I begin, so long as I can hear where to find one of your nation that will not deny the name of Pamunkey. I am not now at Rawsenac, half drowned with mire, where you took me prisoner; yet then, for your keeping your promise, and your good usage, and saving my life, I so affect you, that your denials of your treachery do half persuade me to mistake myself. But if I be the mark you aim at, here I stand, shoot he that dare. You promised to freight my ship ere I departed; and so you shall, or I mean to load her with your dead carcasses. Yet if as friends you will come and trade, I once more promise not to trouble you, except you give me the first occasion.

Upon this, away went their bows and arrows; and men, women, and children brought in their commodities. . . . And whatsoever we gave them, they seemed well contented with it. . . .

Now so extremely Powhatan had threatened the death of his men, if they did not, by some means, kill Captain Smith . . . : yet . . . they were constrained, hating fighting almost as ill as hanging, such fear they had of bad success. The next morning, the sun had not long appeared, but the fields appeared covered with people and baskets to tempt us ashore. The President determined to keep aboard; but nothing was to be had without his presence, nor would they endure the sight of a gun. Then the President, seeing many depart and being unwilling to lose such a booty, so well contrived the pinnace and his barges with ambuscades, as only with Mr. Percy, Mr. West, and Mr. Russell armed, he went ashore. Others, unarmed, he appointed to receive what was brought.

The savages flocked before him in heaps, and (the bank serving as a trench for retreat) he drew them fair open to his ambuscades. For he, not being persuaded to go to visit their king [Opechancanough], the King came to visit him, with 2 or 300 men, in the form of two half-moons, with some 20 men and many women loaded with great painted baskets. But when they approached somewhat near us, their women and children fled. For when they had environed and beset the fields in this manner, they thought their purpose sure; yet so trembled with fear as they were scarce able to notch their arrows. Smith, standing with his three men ready bent, beholding them till they were within danger of our ambuscade; who, upon the word, discovered [revealed] themselves, he retiring to the bank: which the savages no sooner perceived, but away they fled, esteeming their heels . . . their best advantage. . . .

Men may think it strange there should be this stir for a little corn: but had it been gold, with more ease we might have got it; and had it wanted [been lacking], the whole colony had starved. We may be thought very patient to endure all those injuries. Yet only with fearing [frightening] them, we got what they had; whereas if we had taken revenge, then by their loss we should have lost ourselves. We searched also the countries of Youghtanund and Mattapamient, where the people imparted what little they had with such complaints and tears from women and children, as he had been too cruel a Christian that would not have been satisfied and moved with compassion. . . .

The main reason of our temporizing with the savages was to part friends, as we did, to give the less cause of suspicion to Powhatan to fly; by whom we now turned, with a purpose to have surprised him and his provisions. For effecting whereof, when we came against the town, the President sent Mr. Wiffin and Mr. Coe ashore, to discover and make way for his intended project. But they found that those damned Dutchmen had caused Powhatan to abandon his new house and Werowacomoco, and to carry away all his corn and provisions. And the people, they found, by their means, so ill affected, that had they not stood well upon their guard, they had hardly escaped with their lives.

So the President, finding his intention thus frustrated, and that there was nothing to be had, and therefore an unfit time to revenge their abuses, held on his course for Jamestown: we having in this journey (for 25 lbs. of copper, 50 lbs. of iron and beads) kept 40 men six weeks; and daily feasted with bread, corn, flesh, fish, and fowl. Every man having for his reward (and in consideration of his commodities) a month's provisions, no trade being allowed but for the store; and we delivered at Jamestown to the cape merchant 279 bushels of corn.

Smith's Reign
by Richard Pott and William Phettiplace

When the ships departed [in November 1608], all the provision of the store but that the President had gotten was so rotten with the last summer's rain, and eaten with rats and worms as the hogs would scarcely eat it; yet it was the soldiers' diet till our return. So that we found nothing done, but victuals spent, and the most part of our tools and a good part of our arms conveyed to the savages. But now, casting up the store and finding sufficient [food] till the next harvest, the fear of starving was abandoned; and the company divided into tens, fifteens, or as the business required. Four hours each day was spent in work, the rest in pastimes and merry exercise. But the untowardness of the greatest number caused the President to make a general assembly; and then he advised them as followeth.

> Countrymen, the long experience of our late miseries I hope is sufficient to persuade everyone to a present correction of himself; and think not that either my pains, or the adventurers' [investors'] purses, will ever maintain you in idleness and sloth. I speak not this to you all; for diverse of you, I know, deserve both honor and reward better than is yet here to be had; but the greater part must be more industrious, or starve. Howsoever you have been heretofore tolerated by the authority of the council from that I have often commanded you: yet seeing now the authority resteth wholly in myself,[38] you must obey this for a law, that he that will not work, shall not eat. . . .

He made also a table [notice board] as a public memorial of every man's deserts, to encourage the good and with shame to spur on the rest to amendment. By this, many became very industrious, yet more by severe punishment performed their business; for all were so tasked, that there was no excuse could prevail to deceive him. Yet the Dutchmen's consorts so closely still conveyed powder, shot, swords, and tools [to the Indian villages], that though we could find the defect, we could not find by whom it was occasioned, till it was too late. All this time, the Dutchmen remaining with Powhatan received them [the stolen goods], instructing the savages [in] their use. . . .

The President, fearing those bravadoes would but encourage the savages, began himself to try his conclusions; whereby six or seven savages were slain, as many made prisoners; [he] burnt their houses, took their boats with all their fishing wares, and planted them at Jamestown for his own use; and now resolved not to cease till he had revenged himself upon all that had injured him. . . .

From all parts with presents they desired peace; returning many stolen things which we neither demanded nor thought of. And after that, those that were taken stealing, both Powhatan and his people have sent them back to Jamestown to receive their punishment; and all the country became absolutely as free for us, as for themselves.

[38] Smith was essentially the last surviving member of the governing council.

THE STORE DEVOURED BY RATS

Now we so quietly followed our business that in three months, we made three or four last[39] of pitch, and tar, and soap ashes; produced a trial of glass; made a well in the fort of excellent sweet water, which till then was wanting; built some 20 houses; re-covered our church; provided nets and wares for fishing; and to stop the disorders of our disorderly thieves and the savages, built a blockhouse in the neck of our isle [peninsula], kept by a garrison, to entertain the savages' trade, and none to pass or repass, savages or Christian, without the President's order; 30 or 40 acres of ground, we digged and planted; of three sows, in one year increased 60 and odd pigs; and near 500 chickens brought up themselves, without having any meat [food] given them. But the hogs were transported to Hog Isle, where we also built a blockhouse with a garrison, to give us notice of any shipping; and for their exercise, they made clapboard, wainscot, and cut down trees against the ships' coming. . . .

In searching our casked corn, we found it half rotten, and the rest so consumed with the many thousand rats, increased first from the ships, that we knew not how to keep what little we had. This did drive us all to our wits' end, for there was nothing in the country but what nature afforded. . . .

But this want of corn occasioned the end of all our work, it being work sufficient to provide victuals. Sixty or eighty with Ensign Laxon were sent down the river to live upon oysters; and 20 with Lieutenant Percy to try for fishing at Point Comfort; but in six weeks, they could not agree once to cast out their net. Mr. West, with as many, went up to the falls; but nothing could be found but a few berries and acorns. Of that in the store, everyone had their equal proportion.

Till this present, by the hazard and endeavor of some 30 or 40, this whole number had ever been fed. We had more sturgeon than could be devoured by dog or man; of which, the industrious by drying and pounding, mingling with caviar, sorrel, and other wholesome herbs, would make bread and good meat. Others would gather as much tockwough roots in a day as would make them bread in a week. So that of those wild fruits, fish, and berries, these lived very well, in regard of such a diet.

But such was the most strange condition of some 150, that had they not been forced . . . to gather and prepare their victuals,[40] they would all have starved, and have eaten one another. . . . But . . . [Smith] caused the most part so well bestir themselves that of 200 men (except they were drowned), there died not past seven or eight. . . . Many were billeted among the savages, whereby we knew all their passages, fields, and habitations; how to gather and use their fruits as well as themselves. . . .

[39] A *last* of pitch and tar totals about fourteen barrels; twelve for ashes.
[40] Some colonists were gentry who considered physical labor beneath them.

By this you may see, for all those crosses, treacheries, and dissensions, how he [Captain Smith] wrestled and overcame (without bloodshed) all that happened; also what good was done, how few died, what food the country naturally affordeth; what small cause there is men should starve, or be murdered by the savages, that have the discretion to manage [with] this courage and industry.

The two first years, though by his adventures he had often brought the savages to tractable trade, yet you see how the [men who were] envious [of his] authority ever crossed him, and frustrated his best endeavors. Yet this wrought in him that experience and estimation among the savages, as otherwise it had been impossible he had ever effected that he did. Though the many miserable yet generous and worthy adventures he had long and oft endured as well in some parts of Africa and America, as in the most parts of Europe and Asia, by land or sea, had taught him much; yet, in this case, he was again to learn his lecture [lesson] by experience; which with thus much ado having obtained, it was his ill chance to end when he had but only learned how to begin.

THE ARRIVAL OF THE THIRD SUPPLY

To redress those jars and ill proceedings, the Council in England altered the government, and devolved the authority to the Lord De La Warr. Who for his deputy sent Sir Thomas Gates and Sir George Somers.[41] With nine ships and 500 persons, they set sail from England in May 1609. The Admiral [flagship], with 150 men, with the two knights and their new commission, their bills of loading with all manner of directions, and the most part of their provisions, arrived not.[42]

With the other seven, as captains, arrived Ratcliffe (whose right name was Sickelmore), Martin, and Archer: who as they had been troublesome at sea, began again to mar all ashore. For though, as is said, they were formerly deposed and sent for England, yet now returning again, graced by the title of *Captains of the Passengers,* seeing the admiral wanting [missing], and great probability of her loss, strengthened themselves with those new companies, so railing and exclaiming against Captain Smith, that they mortally hated him ere they ever see his face. . . . Happy had we been had they never arrived . . . for on earth was never more confusion or misery than their faction occasioned.

[41] This account slightly jumbles the actual chronology. De La Warr was named the second, not first, governor (though he was appointed to the post for life). Gates was named the first governor of Virginia. A veteran of the Dutch war of independence, he was one of the original members of the Virginia Company, and served as governor from 1609–10 and 1611–14.

[42] The ship *Sea Venture* was wrecked in Bermuda.

The President, seeing the desire those braves had to rule, seeing how his authority was so unexpectedly changed, would willingly have left all and have returned for England; but, seeing there was small hope this new commission would arrive, longer he would not suffer those factious spirits to proceed. It would be too tedious, too strange, and almost incredible, should I particularly relate the infinite dangers, plots, and practices he daily escaped among this factious crew; the chief whereof he quickly laid by the heels [threw into chains], till his leisure better served to do them justice. And to take away all occasions of further mischief, Mr. Percy had his request granted to return for England; and Mr. West with 120 men went to plant at the falls; Martin with near as many to Nansemond; and their due proportions of all provisions, according to their numbers.

Now the President's year being near expired, he made Martin president; who, knowing his own insufficiency and the company's scorn and conceit of his unworthiness, within three hours resigned it again to Captain Smith, and at Nansemond thus proceeded. The people [of Nansemond] being contributors used him kindly. Yet such was his jealous fear and cowardice, in the midst of his mirth, he did surprise this poor naked king, with his monuments, houses, and the isle he inhabited, and there fortified himself, but so apparently distracted with fear as emboldened the savages to assault him, kill his men, redeem their king, gather and carry away more than 1000 bushels of corn, he not once daring to intercept them. But he sent to the President, then at the falls, for 30 good shot, which from Jamestown immediately were sent him. But he so well employed them, as they did just nothing; but returned, complaining of his childishness. . . .

Master West, having seated his men at the falls, presently returned to revisit Jamestown. The President met him by the way, as he followed him to the falls; where he found this company so inconsiderately seated in a place not only subject to the river's inundation, but round environed with many intolerable inconveniences.

For remedy whereof, he sent presently to Powhatan to sell him [Smith] the place called Powhatan [Werowacomoco], promising to defend him against the Monacans, and these should be his conditions: With his people, to resign him the fort and houses and all that country for a proportion of copper. That all stealing offenders should be sent him, there to receive their punishment. That every house as a custom [a tax] should pay him a bushel of corn for an inch square of copper, and a proportion of *Pocones* as a yearly tribute to King James for their protection, as a duty; what else they could spare, to barter at their best discretion.

Both this excellent place and those good conditions did those furies [West and his men] refuse, condemning both him, his kind care, and authority. The worst they could to show their spite, they did. . . . But the worst was [done to] the poor savages. . . . That disorderly company so tormented those poor naked souls, by stealing their corn, robbing their gardens, beat ing them, breaking their houses, and keeping some prisoner, that they daily complained to Captain Smith [that] he had brought them for protectors worse enemies than the Monacans themselves. . . .

Seeing nothing would prevail with [the new arrivals], he [Smith] set sail for Jamestown. Now no sooner was the ship under sail, but the savages assaulted those 120 in their fort; finding some straggling abroad in the woods, they slew many, and so affrighted the rest as their [Indian] prisoners escaped; and they . . . retired with the swords and cloaks of those they had slain. But ere we had sailed a league, our ship grounding, gave us once more liberty to summon them [the dissidents] to a parley, where we found them all so strangely amazed with this poor simple assault as they submitted themselves upon any terms to the President's mercy; who presently put by the heels [put in irons] six or seven of the chief offenders. The rest he seated gallantly at Powhatan in their savage fort, [which] they built and prettily fortified with poles and barks of trees sufficient to have defended them from all the savages in Virginia, [along with] dry houses for lodgings, 300 acres of ground ready to plant.

But at that instant arrived Mr. West, whose good nature, with the persuasions and compassion of those mutinous prisoners, was so much abused, that to regain their old hopes, new . . . [dissensions] arose. For the rest, being possessed of all their victuals, ammunition, and everything, they grew to that height in their former factions, as there the President left them to their fortunes; they returning again to the open air at West Fort . . . and he to Jamestown with his best expedition. But this happened to him in that journey [in early September 1609].

Sleeping in his boat, for the ship was returned two days before, accidentally one fired his powder bag; which tore his flesh from his body and thighs nine or ten inches square, in a most pitiful manner. But to quench the tormenting fire, frying him in his clothes, he leaped overboard into the deep river, where ere they could recover him, he was near drowned. In this estate, without either surgeon or surgery, he was to go near 100 miles. Arriving at Jamestown . . . [he ordered] all things to be prepared for peace or war [and] to obtain provisions. . . .

So grievous were his wounds and so cruel his torment few expected he could live; nor was he able to follow his business, to regain what they had lost, suppress those factions, and range the countries for provisions as he intended; and well he knew in those affairs his own actions and presence were as requisite as his experience and directions, which now could not be. He presently went aboard [to go to England], resolving there to appoint them governors, and to take order for the mutineers and their confederates. Who seeing him gone, persuaded Master Percy to stay and be their President; and within less than an hour was this mutation [mutiny] begun and concluded. . . .

What shall I say? but thus we lost him that, in all his proceedings, made justice his first guide, and experience his second; ever hating baseness, sloth, pride, and indignity more than any dangers; that never allowed for himself [more] than his soldiers with him; that upon no danger, would send them where he would not lead them himself; that would never see us want what he either had, or could by any means get us; that would rather want than borrow, or starve than not pay; that loved actions more than words, and hated falsehood and cousinage worse than death; whose adventures were our lives, and whose losses our deaths. Leaving us thus [about October 4, 1609]. . . .

When the ships departed, Davis arrived in a small pinnace with some 16 proper men more; to those were added a company from Jamestown under the command of Captain Ratcliffe, to inhabit [a fort at] Point Comfort. Martin and Mr. West having lost their boats, and near half their men amongst the savages, were returned to Jamestown; for the savages no sooner understood of Captain Smith's loss, but they all revolted, and did murder and spoil all they could encounter. . . .

How they carried the business I know not, but Ratcliffe and his men were most slain by Powhatan; those that escaped returned near starved in the pinnace. And Mr. West, finding little better success, set sail for England. Now we all found the want of Captain Smith, yea his greatest maligners could then curse his loss. Now for corn, provisions, and contributions from the savages, we had nothing but mortal wounds with clubs and arrows. As for our hogs, hens, goats, sheep, horse, or what lived, our commanders and officers did daily consume them; some small proportions (sometimes) we tasted, till all was devoured. . . . Of 500, within six months after [from October 1609 to May 1610] there remained not many more than 60 most miserable and poor creatures. . . . Though we did live as is said, three years chiefly off what this good country naturally affordeth; yet now had we been in paradise itself (with those governors) it would not have been much better with us: yet was there some amongst us, who had they been the government, would surely have kept us from those extremities of miseries, that in 10 days more would have supplanted us all by death.[43]

But God, that would not it should be unplanted, sent Sir Thomas Gates and Sir George Somers, with 150 men, most happily preserved by the Bermudas to preserve us. Strange it is to say how miraculously they were preserved, in a leaking ship, in those extreme storms and tempests in such overgrown seas three days and three nights by bailing out water; and having given themselves to death. . . .

But when those noble knights [arriving May 23, 1610] did see our miseries (being strangers to the country) and could understand no more of the

---

[43] This winter was called "the starving time." Many died of hunger.

cause but by their conjecture of our clamors and complaints, of accusing or excusing one another: they embarked us with themselves, with the best means they could, and abandoning Jamestown, set sail for Virginia.

IN JUNE OF 1610, Powhatan won. After three years of squabbling, fighting, and stealing food, the colonists finally accepted defeat, packed their meager possessions, and joined the stunned members of Sir George Somers's relief expedition for the voyage back to England.

Powhatan realized early on that the Native Americans could not hope to defeat the English (with their swords, breastplates, and muskets) in open battle. Instead, he forged a subtler strategy, combining an embargo on food shipments, the use of defectors to steal tools and weapons, and bloody ambushes that picked off the colonists one by one. Yet Powhatan's victory could not be sealed until the departure of his ablest adversary, Captain John Smith. Only Smith had been able to enforce the iron discipline necessary to maintain the food supplies and defenses as Powhatan turned up the pressure on Jamestown. His furious raids for corn had kept the Indians off balance, while feeding the fractious colonists.

Yet Smith, as brutal as he was, remained a realist above all. Unlike most of his countrymen, he had experience with infidels and heathen (as the English saw them); he knew they had to be respected, especially in war. So he tried to preserve at least the possibility of peaceful relations. His corn raids, for example, were usually forced sales, rather than naked theft; by maintaining something of the appearance of normal trade, he left open a path to reconciliation. The new wave of Englishmen understood none of this; their pointless attacks on the Indians locked Powhatan into inalterable enmity (and exasperated the level-headed Smith). And they came at exactly the wrong time: now the colonists were dispersed into smaller settlements, which eased the supply burden but made defense far more difficult.

When a gunpowder explosion forced the Captain to return home, Powhatan launched all-out war. In the winter of 1609–10, the colonists endured "the starving time," a famine so desperate that the flesh of a dead comrade seemed like a logical meal. Any who wandered outside the colony's walls faced armed attack by furious warriors—some now armed with English weapons.

A technologically inferior enemy outfought them, outsmarted them, and outlasted them. In June 1610, they departed, leaving behind the land they so little understood, where they had come to search for nonexistent gold and the nonexistent Northwest Passage. The history of European expansion into North America, so often told as a tale of unbroken Indian defeats, had begun with a resounding Indian victory.

But Powhatan could little know that another wave of settlers was coming. He had triumphed in his own territory, where he knew the landscape, the people, the resources—but the next battle would be determined by decisions made far beyond his world, in a nation with far greater resources than he could ever imagine. The English were returning, this time to stay.

II

SERVANTS OF GOD

EMERGENCE OF THE
NORTHERN FRONTIER

5

PILGRIMS

Even as the colonists in Jamestown confronted the grim specter of starvation and murder, a small band of country folk in Nottinghamshire faced something rather more important: their eternal damnation. They were humble people, typical English farmers with little property; yet they lived largely in a world beyond this one. In their fields and villages, they saw the forces of good and evil, of God and Satan, locked in combat—and they feared the devil was winning. As they huddled together in their little fellowship, they saw no other choice than to flee, to wander the earth, to become refugees of this invisible war. They would be Pilgrims indeed.

The flight of the Pilgrims from England was only the most extreme sign of a greater conflict that gripped the people of England. This small congregation was not so unlike most other parishes on the island: this people felt their religion deep in their bones. The English believed, they *knew*, that the most minute errors of dogma and liturgy threatened their immortal souls. Though the Reformation in England had been launched by an act of King Henry VIII, it had swept the people; the souls of the English were so much dry wood for this consuming fire.

The problem, however, was that this popular faith was confined in the walls of an official church. There was only one legitimate denomination, the Church of England, and those who refused to partake suffered severe social and civil penalties. The church had inherited a governing structure (and much ritual) from Catholicism: parish priests, who followed bishops, who followed the Archbishop of Canterbury, who followed the King, who was Head of the Church. The people might believe one thing, but they must follow the rules dictated by the crown.

Despite the fervor of the English faithful, most were deeply loyal to their king, and almost all sought accommodation within the official church. Their hopes had been fostered by Queen Elizabeth I, who had firmly established Protestantism, but failed to clarify *what kind* of Protestantism would be taught by her bishops. Many of her subjects believed in a mildly reformed Catholicism: they liked the formality of Roman worship, the hierarchical structure of bishops and archbishops, though they hated Rome itself. They held that tradition was almost as important as the Bible in correct Christian doctrine.

A growing number opposed this view; they opposed it so ferociously that the traditionalists mocked them with the name "Puritans." The name may have been meant in jest, but it certainly fit, for they were determined to purify the faith. They devoutly followed the teachings of John Calvin, the great theologian of the city-state of Geneva. Calvin taught that scripture alone could be the basis of the Christian religion; anything not found in the Bible was suspect, and most likely an impediment to salvation, if not a guarantee of damnation. He also held that humanity was so corrupt, so vile, so fallen, that only God could choose to bestow salvation—to grant his grace; mere humans could never save themselves. Even faith in God came through an act of God's grace, not through one's own will.

This was Protestantism at the extreme—and people all across Europe found it extremely appealing. It swept much of France (where Calvinists were called Huguenots), the Netherlands, Bohemia, Scotland (where John Knox helped reform the official Church of Scotland), and now England. The Puritans raged against the Catholic forms that still held sway in the English church. The idea of priests as God's intermediaries offended them, and they saw no biblical justification for the rule of bishops.

The coronation of James I gave them hope for making a thorough sweep, but he quickly disappointed them. James believed firmly in royal supremacy in all areas of government—and the episcopal structure of the church was one extension of that supremacy. At the Hampton Court Conference in 1604, he flatly rejected the Puritan Millenary Petition, a plea for acceptance within the Church of England. In uncompromising terms, he equated the Puritan suspicion of church hierarchy with an attack upon the crown itself, declaring, "No bishop, no king."

Of all the Puritan dissidents in England, the congregation of Pilgrims in Scrooby, Nottinghamshire, were the purest, and offered the greatest dissent. They were certain that their immortal souls depended upon an uncompromising, completely biblical form of worship (as conceived by seventeenth-century English farmers, of course). After Hampton Court, they could see no hope on those shores; the forces of darkness ruled the church, and they would not be left alone to worship outside it. No, if they were to survive as God's free people, they must flee that country entirely, remove themselves from contact with evil.

In 1607, under the influence of their pastor John Robinson, this humble congregation began their migration, a migration that would eventually lead them to American shores. But before they could cross the Atlantic, they took themselves over the English Channel to the Netherlands—a small, prosperous country that had just emerged from decades of war with Spain. The Netherlands tolerated all forms of worship, and so they thought they might find refuge there. Where England offered persecution, however, the Dutch held out seduction, in the form of worldly prosperity in an interesting foreign land. For refugees of the spirit, it was almost as dire a threat as outright oppression.

In the pages that follow, William Bradford, one of the leaders of the Pilgrims (eventually the paramount leader), describes their journeys in the words of both a faithful Christian and an individual who struggled with the decisions that pressed upon his people. At each stage of their migrations, they debated, discussed, and, perhaps, shouted at one another—yet they managed to maintain their cohesion, their separateness, as they fled first to a foreign city and then a distant wilderness.

The Lord's Free People
by William Bradford

At the coming of King James into England, the new king found there established the reformed religion, according to the reformed religion of King Edward VI. Retaining, or keeping still, the spiritual estate of the Bishops, etc., after the old manner, much varying and differing from the reformed churches in Scotland, France and the Netherlands, Emden, Geneva, etc., whose churches [were] as it was in the Apostles' times.

So many therefore of those professors as saw the evil of these things, in these parts, and whose hearts the Lord had touched with heavenly zeal for his truth, they shook off this yoke of antichristian bondage, and as the Lord's free people, joined themselves (by a covenant of the Lord) into a church estate in the fellowship of the gospel. . . . And that it cost them something, this ensuing history will declare.

These people became two distinct bodies or churches, and in regard of distance of place did congregate severally; for they were of sundry towns and villages, some in Nottinghamshire, some of Lincolnshire, and some of Yorkshire, where they border nearest together. . . . They could not long continue in any peaceable condition, but were hunted and persecuted on every side, so as their former afflictions were but as flea-bitings in comparison [with] these which now came upon them. For some were taken and clapped up in prison, others had their houses beset and watched night and day, and hardly escaped their [the authorities'] hands; and the most were fain to flee and leave their houses and habitations, and the means of their livelihood. Yet these and many other sharper things which afterward befell them, were no other than they looked for, and therefore [they] were the better prepared to bear them by the assistance of God's grace and spirit.

Yet seeing themselves molested, and that there was no hope of their continuance there, by a joint consent they resolved to go into the Low

Countries, where they heard was freedom of religion for all men; and also how sundry from London and other parts of the land had been exiled and persecuted for the same cause, and were gone thither, and lived at Amsterdam, and in other places of the land. So after they had continued together about a year, and kept their meetings every Sabbath in one place or other, exercising the worship of God amongst themselves, notwithstanding all the diligence and malice of their adversaries, they seeing they could no longer continue in that condition, they resolved to get over into Holland as they could, which was in the year 1607 and 1608. . . .

OF THEIR DEPARTURE INTO HOLLAND

Being thus constrained to leave their native soil and country, their lands and livings, and all their friends and familiar acquaintances, it was much, and thought marvelous by many. But to go into a country they knew not (but by hearsay), where they must learn a new language, and get their livings they knew not how, it being a dear [expensive] place, and subject to the miseries of war,[1] it was by many thought an adventure almost desperate, a case intolerable, and a misery worse than death. Especially seeing they were not acquainted with [skilled] trades nor traffic [business], but had only been used to a plain country life and the innocent trade of husbandry.

But these things did not dismay them (though they did sometimes trouble them), for their desires were set on the ways of God, and to enjoy his ordinances; but they rested on his providence, and knew whom they had believed. Yet this was not all, for though they could not stay, yet were they not suffered to go, but the ports and havens were shut against them,[2] so as they were fain to seek secret means of conveyance, and to bribe and fee the mariners, and give extraordinary rates for their passages. And yet were they often times betrayed (many of them), and both they and their goods intercepted, and thereby put to great trouble and charge, of which I will give an instance or two, and omit the rest.

There was a large company of them purposed to get passage at Boston in Lincolnshire, and for that end had hired a ship wholely to themselves, and made [an] agreement with the master to be ready at a certain day, and take them and their goods in, at a convenient place, where they accordingly would all attend in readiness. So after long waiting, and large expenses . . . he came at length and took them in, in the night.

But when he had them and their goods aboard, he betrayed them, having beforehand plotted with the searchers and other officers so to do; who

---

[1] The Dutch had been fighting for independence from Spain since 1567; in 1607, the year before the Pilgrims' arrival, the two sides declared a truce.

[2] It was thought they were going to Virginia, which required a royal license.

took them, and put them into open boats, and rifled and ransacked them, searching them to their shirts for money, yea even the women further than became modesty; and then [the officers] carried them back into the town, and made them a spectacle and wonder to the multitude, which came flocking on all sides to behold them. Being thus first, by the catchpole officers, rifled and stripped of their money, books, and much other goods, they were presented to the magistrates, and messengers sent to inform the lords of the Council of them; and so they were committed to ward [jail]. Indeed the magistrates used them courteously, and showed them what favor they could, but could not deliver them till [the] order came from the Council table. But the issue was that after a month's imprisonment, the greatest part were dismissed and sent to the places from whence they came; but seven of the principal [Pilgrims] were still kept in prison, and bound over to the Assizes [a higher court]. . . .

But that I be not tedious in these things, I will omit the rest, though I might relate many other notable passages and troubles which they endured and underwent in these their wanderings and travels both at land and sea; but I hasten to other things. . . . And in the end, notwithstanding all these storms of opposition, they all got over at length, some at one time and some at another, and met together again according to their desires, with no small rejoicing.

OF THEIR SETTLING IN HOLLAND

Being now come into the Low Countries, they saw many goodly and fortified cities, strongly walled and guarded with troops of armed men. Also they heard a strange and uncouth language, and beheld the different manners and customs of the people, with their strange fashions and attires; all so far differing from that of their plain country villages (wherein they were bred, and had so long lived) as it seemed they were come into a new world.

But these were not the things they much looked on, or long took up their thoughts; for they had other work in hand, and another kind of war to wage and maintain. For though they saw fair and beautiful cities, flowing with abundance of all sorts of wealth and riches, yet it was not long before they saw the grim and grisly face of poverty coming upon them like an armed man, with whom they must buckle and encounter, and from whom they could not fly; but they were armed with faith and patience against him, and all his encounters; and though they were sometimes foiled, yet by God's assistance they prevailed and got the victory. . . .

THEIR REMOVAL TO LEIDEN

For these and some other reasons they removed to Leiden, a fair and beautiful city, and of a sweet situation, but made more famous by the university wherewith it is adorned, in which of late had been so many learned men. But wanting that traffic by sea which Amsterdam enjoys, it was not so beneficial for their outward means of living and estates. But being now here pitched they fell to such trades and employments as they best could, valuing peace and their spiritual comfort above any other riches whatsoever. And at length they came to raise a competent and comfortable living, but with hard and continual labor. . . .

After they had lived in this city about some 11 or 12 years (which is the more observable, being the whole time of the famous truce between that state and the Spaniards), and sundry of them were taken away by death, and many others began to be well stricken in years, the grave mistress Experience having taught them many things, those prudent governors with sundry of the sagest members began both deeply to apprehend their present dangers, and wisely to foresee the future, and think of timely remedy. In the agitation of their thoughts, and much discourse of things hereabout, at length they began to incline to this conclusion, of removal to some other place. Not out of any newfangledness, or other such giddy humor, by which men are oftentimes transported to their great hurt and danger, but for sundry weighty and solid reasons, some of the chief of which I will here briefly touch.

And first, they saw and found by experience the hardness of the place and country to be such, as few in comparison would come with them, and fewer that would bide it out, and continue with them. . . .

Secondly, they saw that though the people generally bore all these difficulties very cheerfully . . . within a few years more they would be in danger to scatter, by necessities pressing them, or sink under their burdens, or both. . . .

Lastly (and which was not least), a great hope and inward zeal they had of laying some good foundation, or at least to make some way thereunto, for the propagating and advancing the gospel of the kingdom of Christ in those remote parts of the world. . . . The place they had thoughts on was some of those vast and unpeopled countries of America, which are fruitful and fit for habitation, being devoid of all civil[ized] inhabitants, where there are only savage and brutish men, which range up and down, little otherwise than the wild beasts of the same.

This proposition being made public and coming to the scanning of all, it raised many variable opinions amongst men, and caused many fears and doubts amongst themselves. Some, from their reasons and hopes conceived, labored to stir up and encourage the rest to undertake and prosecute the same; others, again out of their fears, objected against it, and sought to divert [the congregation] from it, alleging many things, and those neither unreasonable nor unprobable. . . .

It was answered that all great and honorable actions are accompanied with great difficulties, and must be both enterprised and overcome with answerable courages. It was granted the dangers were great, but not desperate; the difficulties were many, but not invincible. . . . They lived here but as men in exile, and in a poor condition; and as great miseries might possibly befall them in this place, for the 12 years of truce were now out, and there was nothing but beating of drums and preparing for war, the events whereof are always uncertain. The Spaniard might prove as cruel as the savages of America, and the famine and pestilence as sore here as there, and their liberty less to look out for remedy.

After many other particular things answered and alleged on both sides, it was fully concluded by the major part to put this design into execution, and to prosecute it by the best means they could.

———

AFTER TEN YEARS and more in the cities of Holland, they felt themselves called away yet again—this time to "those vast and unpeopled countries of America." It was a grave decision for an entire congregation to make; they had settled themselves, reasonably prosperously so, in a country that tolerated their religion. They had taken up trades, made friends, established homes. The specter of war seems suspect as their motivation, for it was still a vague and distant threat.

What motivated them to flee was their very comfort in the Netherlands. In England, repression (mild as it was) had been the fire that forged their faith, that held them together in one tight-knit group. In their early years abroad, they were bound together as countrymen in a foreign land, with a foreign tongue. But time eroded their cohesion; as Bradford wrote, members died, moved away, and began to identify with the Dutch (who tolerated abominations, in the Pilgrims' eyes, alongside the true religion). It seemed that the devil, by switching tactics, was once again winning the war for their souls.

Trials and trouble had held their group together before, so they would go where there was all the trouble they could imagine: America. There they would find neither seduction nor persecution, but simply the difficulties of the natural world and "savage and brutish men." Such things merely endangered their lives, not their salvation.

The question of how to cross the Atlantic to this new promised land, however, drew them back into the problems of this mortal sphere: the voyage would cost money, and they had little. They had begun by applying for a patent for a settlement from the Virginia Company; however, the Company was in turmoil as Jamestown faced extinction. Fortunately, two other developments took place about the same time. First, Sir Fernando Gorges, a west country baronet, joined together with forty other aristocrats and wealthy men to organize the Council for New England. They would control the settlement of the northern part of the unclaimed shores of North America, much as the Virginia Company controlled the southern. Second, the Pilgrims were approached by a London businessman named Thomas Weston, who had a proposition for the sect.

After a decade in the business-minded Netherlands, the Pilgrims knew merchants, and they did not much like them. They despised their sharp dealing, their self-serving ways, their obsession with the rewards of this temporal world. Unfortunately, those were the qualities they needed just now. So when Weston proposed the formation of a joint stock company to fund a settlement in New England, the Pilgrims reluctantly agreed. With Weston's help, they would transfer their patent from the Virginia Company to Gorges's Council for New England. Weston and his London backers would provide money for the voyage, and the Pilgrims would repay them with furs and fish.

So began the European settlement of New England. The mission would be fraught with difficulties: squabbles with Weston, a leaking ship, a company that included a large number of non-Pilgrims, a lethal outbreak of disease. Yet it would also be a voyage blessed by astonishing good fortune—or by God's special providences, as Pilgrim leader William Bradford saw them. They would survive a perilous voyage intact, and later develop a very different relationship with their Indian neighbors than that of Jamestown with Powhatan. It was an experience that confirmed for every Pilgrim that they were indeed the elect of God.

A Special Providence of God
by William Bradford

And first after their humble prayers unto God for his direction and assistance, and a general conference held here about, they consulted what particular place to pitch upon, and prepare for. Some (and none of the meanest) had thoughts and were earnest for Guiana, or for some of those fertile places in those hot climates; others were for some parts of Virginia, where the English had already made entrance and beginning. . . .

But at length the conclusion was, to live as a distinct body by themselves, under the general government of Virginia; and by their friends to sue to his majesty that he would be pleased to grant them freedom of religion; and that this might be obtained, they were put in good hope by some great persons, of good rank and quality, that were made their friends. Whereupon two were chosen and sent in to England (at the charge of the rest) to solicit this matter, who found the Virginia Company very desirous to have them go thither, and willing to grant them a patent, with as ample privileges as they had, or could grant to any, and to give them the best furtherance they could. . . .

These things being long in agitation, and messengers passing too and again about them, after all their hopes they were long delayed by many rubs that fell in the way; for at the return of these messengers into England they found things far otherwise than they expected. For the Virginia Council was so disturbed with factions and quarrels amongst themselves, as no business could well go forward. . . .

About this time, whilst they were perplexed with the proceedings of the Virginia Company . . . , some Dutchmen made them fair offers about going with them. Also one Mr. Thomas Weston, a merchant of London, came to Leiden about the same time (who was well acquainted with some of them, and a furtherer of them in their former proceedings). . . . He and such merchants as were his friends (together with their own means) would set them forth; and they should make ready, and neither fear want of shipping nor money, for what they wanted should be provided. And, not so much for himself as for the satisfying of such friends as he should procure to adventure in this business, they were to draw such articles of agreement, and make such propositions, as might the better induce his friends to venture [their money].

Upon which (after the former conclusions) articles were drawn and agreed unto, and were shown unto him, and approved by him; and afterwards by their messenger (Mr. John Carver) sent into England, who, together with Robert Cushman, were to receive the moneys and make provision both for shipping and other things for the voyage. . . . About this time also they had heard, both by Mr. Weston and others, that sundry Honorable Lords had obtained a large grant from the king, for the more northerly parts of that country, derived out of the Virginia patent, and wholly secluded from their government, and to be called by another name, viz. New-England.[3] Unto which Mr. Weston, the chief of them, began to incline it was best for them to go, as for other reasons, so chiefly for the hope of present profit to be made by the fishing that was found in that country.[4]

But as in all businesses the acting part is the most difficult, especially where the work of many agents must concur, so it was found in this. For some of those that should have gone in England, fell off and would not go; other merchants and friends that had offered to adventure their moneys withdrew, and pretended many excuses. . . . Now another difficulty arose, for Mr. Weston and others that were for this course, either for their better advantage or rather for the drawing on of others, as they pretended, would

[3] This grant was the patent of the Council for New England, issued to a group of forty men, led by Sir Fernando Gorges, on November 3, 1620.

[4] This is a reference to the Grand Banks, off the coast of Newfoundland, which were already well known to European fishermen.

have some of those conditions altered that were first agreed on at Leiden. To which the two agents sent from Leiden (or at least one of them who is most charged with it) did consent; seeing else that all was like to be dashed, and the opportunity lost. . . .

OF THEIR DEPARTURE FROM LEIDEN

At length, after much travel and these debates, all things were got ready and provided. A small ship [the *Speedwell*] was bought and fitted in Holland, which was intended to serve to help to transport them, so to stay in the country and attend upon fishing and such other affairs as might be for the good and benefit of the colony when they came there. Another [the *Mayflower*] was hired at London, of burden about nine score [tons], and all other things got in readiness.

So being ready to depart, they had a day of solemn humiliation, their pastor taking his text from Ezra 8:21. *And there at the river, by Ahava, I proclaimed a fast, that we might humble ourselves before our God, and seek of him a right way for us, and for our children, and for all our substance*. Upon which he spent a good part of the day very profitably, and suitable to their present occasion. The rest of the time was spent in powering out prayers to the Lord with great fervence, mixed with abundance of tears.

And the time being come that they must depart, they were accompanied with most of their brethren out of the city, unto a town sundry miles off, called Delfshaven, where the ship lay ready to receive them. So they left that goodly and pleasant city, which had been their resting place near 12 years; but they knew they were pilgrims, and looked not much upon those things, but lift[ed] up their eyes to the heavens, their dearest country, and quieted their spirits. When they came to the place they found the ship and all things ready; and such of their friends as could not come with them followed after them, and sundry also came from Amsterdam to see them shipped and to take their leave of them.

That night was spent with little sleep by the most, but with friendly entertainment and Christian discourse and other real expressions of true Christian love. The next day, the wind being fair, they went aboard, and their friends with them, where truly doleful was the sight of that sad and mournful parting; to see what sighs and sobs and prayers did sound amongst them, what tears did gush from every eye, and pithy speeches pierced each heart; that sundry of the Dutch strangers that stood on the key [pier] as spectators could not refrain from tears. . . . But the tide (which stays for no man) calling them away, that they were thus loath to depart, their reverend pastor falling down on his knees (and they all with him), with watery cheeks commended them with most fervent prayers to the Lord and his blessing. And then with mutual embraces and many tears, they took their leaves one of another, which proved to be the last leave to many of them.

Thus hoisting sail [July 22, 1620], with a prosperous wind they came in short time to Southampton, where they found the bigger ship come from London, lying ready, with all the rest of their company. After a joyful welcome, and mutual congratulations, with other friendly entertainments, they fell to parley about their business, how to dispatch with the best expedition; as also with their agents about the alteration of the conditions. . . .

Mr. Weston, likewise, came up from London to see them dispatched and to have the conditions confirmed; but they refused, and answered him, that he knew right well that these were not according to the first agreement, neither could they yield to him without the consent of the rest that were behind. And indeed they had special charge when they came away, from the chief of those that were behind, not to do it. At which he was much offended, and told them they must look to stand on their own legs. So he returned in displeasure, and this was the first ground of discontent between them. And whereas there [was] wanted well near £100 to clear things at their going away, he would not take order to disburse a penny, but let them shift as they could. So they were forced to sell some of their provisions to stop this gap. . . .

All things being now ready, and every business dispatched, the company was called together, and this letter [from the Pilgrims' chief pastor, John Robinson, who stayed behind] read amongst them, which had good acceptation with all and fruit with many. Then they ordered and distributed their company for either ship, as they conceived for the best. And [they] chose a governor and two or three assistants for each ship, to order the people by the way, and to see the disposing of their provisions, and such like affairs. All of which was not only with the liking of the masters of the ships, but according to their desires. Which being done, they set sail from thence about the 5th of August; but what befell them further upon the coast of England will appear in the next chapter.

OF THE TROUBLE THAT BEFELL THEM ON THE COAST

Being thus put to sea they had not gone far, but Mr. Reinolds the master of the lesser ship complained that he found his ship so leaky that he durst not put further to sea till she was mended. So, the master of the bigger ship (called Mr. Jones) being consulted with, they both resolved to put into Dartmouth and have her there searched and mended, which accordingly was done, to their great charge and loss of time and a fair wind.

She was here thoroughly searched from stem to stern, some leaks were found and mended, and now it was conceived by the workmen and all that she was sufficient, and they might proceed without either fear or danger. So with good hopes from hence, they put to sea again, conceiving they should go comfortably on, not looking for any more lets [leaks] of this kind; but it fell out otherwise, for after they were gone to sea again above 100 leagues without the Land's End, holding company together all this while, the master of the small ship complained his ship was so leaky as he must bear up or sink at sea, for they could scarce free her with much pumping.

So they came to consultation again, and resolved both ships to bear back again and put into Plymouth, which accordingly was done. But no special leak could be found, but it was judged to be the general weakness of the ship, and that she would not prove sufficient for the voyage. Upon which it was resolved to dismiss her and part of the company, and proceed with the other ship. . . . So after they had took out such provisions as the other ship could well stow, and concluded both what number and what persons to send back, they made another sad parting, the one ship going back to London, and the other was to proceed on her voyage. . . .

And thus, like Gideon's army, this small number was divided as if the Lord by this work of his providence thought these few too many for the great work he had to do. . . .

HOW THEY PASSED THE SEA

These troubles being blown over, and now all being compact together in one ship, they put to sea again with a prosperous wind, which continued diverse days together, which was some encouragement unto them; yet according to the usual manner many were afflicted with sea-sickness. And I may not omit here a special work of God's providence. There was a proud and very profane young man, one of the seamen, of a lusty, able body, which made him the more haughty; he would always be condemning the poor people in their sickness, and cursing them daily with grievous execrations, and did not [fail] to tell them that he hoped to help cast half of them overboard before they came to their journey's end, and to make merry with what they had. And if he were by any gently reproved, he would curse and swear most bitterly. But it pleased God before they came half sea's over, to smite this young man with a grievous disease, of which he died in a desperate manner, and so was himself the first that was thrown overboard. . . .

But to omit other things (that I may be brief), after long beating at sea they fell with that land which is called Cape Cod; the which being made and certainly known to be it, they were not a little joyful. After some deliberation amongst themselves and with the master of the ship, they tacked about and resolved to stand for the southward (the wind and weather being fair) to find some place about the Hudson River for their habitation. But after they had sailed that course about half the day, they fell amongst dangerous shoals and roaring breakers, and . . . they resolved to bear up again for the

Cape, and thought themselves happy to get out of those dangers before night overtook them, as by God's providence they did. And the next day they got into the Cape harbor, where they rode in safety. . . .

Being thus arrived in a good harbor and brought safe to land, they fell upon their knees and blessed the God of heaven, who had brought them over the vast and furious ocean, and delivered them from all the perils and miseries thereof, again to set their feet on the firm and stable earth, their proper element. . . .

But here I cannot but stay and make a pause, and stand half amazed at this poor people's present condition; and so I think will the reader too, when he well considers the same. Being thus passed the vast ocean, and a sea of troubles before in their preparation (as may be remembered by that which went before), they had now no friends to welcome them, nor inns to entertain or refresh their weatherbeaten bodies, no houses or much less towns to repair to, to seek for succor. It is recorded in scripture, as a mercy to the apostle and his shipwrecked company, that the barbarians showed them no small kindness in refreshing them, but these savage barbarians, when they met with them (as after will appear) were readier to fill their sides full of arrows than otherwise. And for season it was winter, and they that know the winters of that country know them to be sharp and violent, and subject to cruel and fierce storms, dangerous to travel to known places, much more to search an unknown coast. Besides, what could they see but a hideous and desolate wilderness, full of wild beasts and wild men? And what multitudes there might be of them they knew not. . . .

What could now sustain them but the spirit of God and his grace? May not and ought not the children of these fathers rightly say: *Our fathers were Englishmen which came over this great ocean, and were ready to perish in this wilderness; but they cried unto the Lord, and he heard their voice, and looked on their adversity, etc. Let them therefore praise the Lord, because he is good, and his mercies endure forever.* . . .

SHOWING HOW THEY SOUGHT OUT A PLACE OF HABITATION

Being thus arrived at Cape Cod the 11th of November, and necessity calling them to look out a place for habitation (as well as the master's and mariner's importunity), they having brought a large shallop with them out of England, stowed in quarter in the ship, they now got her out and set their carpenters to work to trim her up; but being much bruised and shattered in the ship with foul weather, they saw she would be long in mending. Whereupon a few of them tendered themselves to go by land and discover those nearest places, whilst the shallop was in mending; and the rather because we went into that harbor there seemed to be an opening some two or three leagues off, which the master judged to be a river. It was conceived there might be some danger in the attempt, yet seeing them resolute, they were permitted to go, being 16 of them well armed, under the conduct [leadership] of Captain [Miles] Standish, having such instructions given them as was thought meet.

They set forth the 15th of November; and when they had marched the space of a mile by the sea side, they espied five or six persons with a dog coming towards them, who were savages; but they fled from them, and ran up into the woods; and the English followed them, partly to see if they could speak with them, and partly to discover if there might not be more of them lying in ambush. But the Indians, seeing themselves thus followed, they again forsook the woods, and ran away on the sands as hard as they could, so as they could not come near them, but followed them by the track of their feet sundry miles, and saw that they had come the same way. So, night coming on, they made their rendezvous and set out their sentinels, and rested in quiet that night; and the next morning followed their tracks till they headed [into] a great creek, and so left the sands and turned another way into the woods.

But they still followed them by guess, hoping to find their dwellings; but they soon lost both them and themselves, falling into such thickets as were ready to tear their clothes and armor in pieces, but were most distressed for want of drink. But at length they found water and refreshed themselves, being the first New-England water they drunk of, and was now in their great thirst as pleasant unto them as wine or beer had been in foretimes.

Afterwards they directed their course to come to the other shore, for they knew it was a neck of land they were to cross over, and so at length got to the sea-side, and marched to this supposed river, and by the way found a pond of clear fresh water, and shortly after a good quantity of clear ground where the Indians had formerly set corn, and some of their graves. And proceeding farther they saw new stubble where corn had been set the same year, also they found where lately a house had been, where some planks and a great kettle was remaining, and heaps of sand newly paddled with their hands, which they, digging up, found in them diverse fair Indian baskets filled with corn, and some in ears, fair and good, of diverse colors, which seemed to them a very goodly sight (having never seen any such before). . . .

So their limited time being expired, they returned to the ship, lest they should be in fear of their safety; and took with them part of the corn, and buried up the rest, and so like the men from Escholl carried with them of the fruits of the land, and showed their brethren; of which, and [of] their return, they were marvelously glad, and their hearts encouraged.

After this, the shallop being got ready, they set out again for the better discovery of this place, and the master of the ship desired to go himself, so there went some 30 men, but found it to be no harbor for ships but only for boats. There was also found two of their houses covered with mats, and sundry of their implements, but the people were run away and could not be seen; also there was found more of their corn, and of their beans of various colors. The corn and beans they brought away, purposing to give them full satisfaction when they should meet with any of them (as about some six months afterward they did, to their good content[ment]). And here is to be noted a special providence of God, and a great mercy to this poor people, that here they got seed to plant them corn the next year, or else they might have starved, for they had none. . . .

The month of November being spent in these affairs, and much foul weather falling in . . .

On the 15th of December they weighed anchor to go to the place they had discovered, and came within two leagues of it, but were fain to bear up again; but the 16th day the wind came fair, and they arrived safe in this harbor. And afterwards took better view of the place, and resolved where to pitch their dwelling; and on the 25th day began to erect the first house for common use to receive them and their goods.

The rest of this history (if God give me life, and opportunity) I shall, for brevity's sake, handle by way of annals, noting only the heads of principal things, and passages as they fell in order of time. . . .

THE REMAINDER OF ANNO 1620

I shall return back [to] a combination made by them before they came ashore, being the first foundation of their government in this place; occasioned partly by the discontented and mutinous speeches that some of the strangers [non-Pilgrims] amongst them had let fall from them in the ship: That when they came ashore they would use their own liberty; for none had power to command them, the patent they had being for Virginia and not for New England, which belonged to another government, with which the Virginia Company had nothing to do. And partly that such an act by them done (this their condition considered) might be as firm as any patent, and in some respects more sure.

The form was as followeth.

In the name of God, Amen. We whose names are underwritten, the loyal subjects of our dread sovereign Lord, King James, by the grace of God, of Great Britain, France,[5] and Ireland king, defender of the faith, etc., having undertaken, for the glory of God, and advancement of the Christian faith, and honor of our king and country, a voyage to plant the first colony in the northern part of Virginia, do by these presents solemnly and mutually in the presence of God, and of another, covenant and combine ourselves together into a civil

[5] The claim of kingship of France was a medieval relic dating back to before the Hundred Years' War, when the English king controlled much of France.

body politic, for our better ordering and preservation and furtherance of the ends foresaid; and by virtue hereof to enact, constitute,
and frame such just and equal laws, ordinances, acts, constitutions,
and offices, from time to time, as shall be thought most meet and
convenient for the general good of the colony, unto which we
promise all due submission and obedience. In witness whereof we
have hereunder subscribed our names at Cape Cod the 11th of November, in the year of the reign of our sovereign lord, King James,
of England, France, and Ireland the eighteenth, and of Scotland the
fifty-fourth. Anno: Dom. 1620.

After this they chose, or rather confirmed, Mr. John Carver (a man
godly and well approved amongst them) their governor for that year. And
after they had provided a place for their goods, their common store (which
were long in unloading for want of boats, foulness of winter weather, and
sickness of diverse), and begun some small cottages for their habitation, as
time would admit, they met and consulted of laws and orders, both for their
civil and military government, as the necessity of their condition did require,
and as cases did require.

In these hard and difficult beginnings they found some discontents and
murmurings arise amongst some, and mutinous speeches and carriages in
other; but they were soon quelled and overcome by the wisdom, patience,
and just and equal carriage of things by the governor and better part, which
clave faithfully together in the main. But that which was most sad and lamentable was, that in two or three months' time half of their company died,
especially in January and February, being the depth of winter, and wanting
houses and other comforts; being infected with the scurvy and other diseases, which the long voyage and their inaccommodate condition had
brought upon them; so as there died sometimes two or three a day, in the
foresaid time; that of 100 and odd persons, scarce 50 remained.

And of these in the time of most distress, there was but six or seven
sound persons, who, to their great commendations be it spoken, spared no
pains, night nor day, but with abundance of toil and hazard of their own
health, fetched them wood, made them fires, dressed them meat, made their
beds, washed their loathsome clothes, clothed and unclothed them; in a
word, did all the homely and necessary offices for them which dainty and
queasy stomachs cannot endure to hear named; and all this willingly and
cheerfully, without any grudging in the least, showing herein their true love
unto their friends and brethren. . . .

All this while the Indians came skulking about them, and would sometimes show themselves aloof off, but when any approached near them, they
would run away. And once they stole away their tools where they had been
at work, and were gone to dinner. But about the 16th of March a certain In-

dian came boldly amongst them, and spoke to them in broken English, which they could well understand, but marveled at it. At length they understood by discourse with him, that he was not of these parts, but belonged to the eastern parts, where some English ships came to fish, with whom he was acquainted, and could name sundry of them by their names, amongst whom he had got his language.

He became profitable to them in acquainting them with many things concerning the state of the country in the east parts where he lived, which was afterwards profitable unto them; as also of the people here, of their names, number, and strength; of their situation and distance from this place, and who was chief amongst them. His name was Samoset; he told them also of another Indian whose name was Squanto, a native of this place, who had been in England and could speak better English than himself.

Being, after some time of entertainment and gifts, dismissed, a while he came again, and five more with him, and they brought again all the tools that were stolen away before, and made way for the coming of their great Sachem, called Massasoit; who, about four or five days after, came with the chief of his friends and other attendants, with the aforesaid Squanto. With whom, after friendly entertainment, and some gifts given him, they made a peace with him (which now continued this 24 years) in these terms.

1. That neither he nor any of his, should injure or do hurt to any of their people.
2. That if any of his did any hurt to any of theirs, he should send the offender, that they might punish him.
3. That if anything were taken away from any of theirs, he should cause it to be restored; and they should do the like to his.
4. If any did unjustly war against him, they would aid him; if any did war against them, he should aid them.
5. He should send to his neighbors confederates, to certify them of this, that they might not wrong them, but might likewise [be] comprised in the conditions of peace.
6. That when their men came to them, they should leave their bows and arrows behind them.

After these things he returned to his place, called Sowams, some 40 miles from this place, but Squanto continued with them, and was their interpreter, and was a special instrument sent of God for their good beyond their expectation. He directed them how to set their corn, where to take fish and to procure other commodities, and was also their pilot to bring them to unknown places for their profit, and never left them till he died.

He was a native of this place [the abandoned village on the site of Plymouth], and scarce any left alive besides himself. He was carried away with diverse others by one Hunt,[6] a master of a ship, who thought to sell them for slaves in Spain; but he got away [after arriving in Spain, and left] for England, and was entertained by a merchant in London, and employed [in voyages] to Newfoundland and other parts, and lastly brought hither into these parts by one Mr. Dermer, a gentleman employed by Sir Fernando Gorges and others. . . .

ANNO 1621

They now began to dispatch the ship which brought them over, which lay till about this time, or the beginning of April. . . . Afterwards they (as many as were able) began to plant their corn, in which service Squanto stood them in great stead, showing them both the manner how to set it, and after how to dress and tend it. Also he told them except they got fish and set with it (in these old grounds)[7] it would come to nothing, and he showed them that in the middle of April they should have store enough [from] the brook, by which they began to build, and [he] taught them how to take it [fish], and where to get other provisions necessary for them; all which they found true by trial and experience. Some English seed they sew, as wheat and peas, but it came not to good, either by the badness of the seed, or the lateness of the season, or both, or some other defect.

In this month of April, whilst they were busy about their seed, their governor (Mr. John Carver) came out of the field very sick, it being a hot day. He complained greatly of his head, and lay down, and within a few hours his senses failed, so as he never spake more till he died, which was within a few days after. Whose death was much lamented, and caused great heaviness amongst them, as there was cause. He was buried in the best manner they could, with some volleys of shot by all that bore arms; and his wife, being a weak woman, died within five or six weeks after him.

Shortly after William Bradford [the author] was chosen governor in his stead, and being not yet recovered of his illness, in which he had been near the point of death, Isaak Allerton was chosen to be an assistant unto him, who, by renewed election every year, continued sundry years together. . . .

May 12th was the first marriage in this place, which, according to the

---

[6] Thomas Hunt was a captain of one of the ships in John Smith's expedition to New England in 1614; he enslaved about twenty Patuxet and seven Nauset Indians.

[7] As described, the Pilgrims arrived at the site of a recently occupied Indian village. The Indians tended to move their villages after they had exhausted the soil (roughly every twenty years); Squanto apparently indicated that they had planted these particular grounds for many years.

laudable custom of the Low Countries, in which they had lived, was thought most requisite to be performed by a magistrate, as being a civil thing, upon which many questions about inheritance do depend, with other things most proper to their cognizance, and most consonant to the scriptures. . . .

Having in some sort ordered their business at home, it was thought meet to send some abroad to see their new friend Massasoit, and to bestow upon him some gratuity to bind him the faster unto them; as also that hereby they might view the country, and see in what manner he lived, what strength he had about him, and how the ways were to his place, if at any time they should have occasion. So the 2nd of July they sent Mr. Edward Winslow and Mr. Hopkins, with the foresaid Squanto for their guide, who gave him a suit of clothes and a horseman's coat, with some other small things, which were kindly accepted; but they found but short commons, and came both weary and hungry home. For the Indians used then to have nothing so much corn as they have since the English have stored them with their hoes, and seen their industry in breaking up new grounds herewith.

They found his place to be 40 miles from hence, the soil good, and the people not many, being dead and abundantly wasted in the late great mortality which fell in all these parts about three years before the coming of the English, wherein thousands of them died, they not being able to bury one another; their skulls and bones were found in many places lying still above the ground, where their houses and dwellings had been; a very sad spectacle to behold. But they brought word that the Narragansetts lived but on the other side of that great bay [in Rhode Island], and were a strong people, and many in number, living compact together, and had not been at all touched with this wasting plague. . . .[8]

Thus their peace and acquaintance was pretty well established with the natives about them; and there was another Indian called Hobomok come to live amongst them, a proper lusty man, and a man of account for his valor and parts amongst the Indians, and continued very faithful and constant to the English till he died. . . .

They began now to gather in the small harvest they had, and to fit up their houses and dwellings against winter, being all well recovered in health and strength, and had all things in good plenty; for as some were thus employed abroad, others were exercising in fishing about cod, and bass, and other fish, of which they took good store, of which every family had their portion. All summer there was no want.

[8] This plague, which wiped out the village where the Pilgrims placed themselves, was probably smallpox, borne by English fishermen who crossed the Atlantic regularly, or by Captain John Smith's expedition of 1614.

HOW UNLIKE JAMESTOWN: this colony of the devout, perversely blessed by an epidemic that had wiped out their possible Indian rivals, yet determined to establish a just relationship with their neighbor Massasoit. These were a people who clung together, who did not plot murder against one another as did Champlain's first followers and Captain John Smith's rivals. And despite their own killing pestilence, they benefitted from astonishing good fortune. Who could have imagined that they would find an intact, abandoned village stocked with corn, or that out of the woods would walk a friendly warrior with fluent English, determined to act as their wilderness tutor and goodwill ambassador? The Pilgrims might have been far less faithful, and still have seen God's hand in everything.

In some ways, the importance of the Pilgrim voyage to Plymouth has been exaggerated in popular myth. The real establishment of New England came a decade later, when John Winthrop arrived farther up the bay with a thousand colonists; Plymouth would linger on for years with a scant population of a few hundred, only to be absorbed in time into the colony of Massachusetts. Even their historic governing document, the Mayflower Compact, has been derided by historians as an attempt to limit democracy, by excluding non-Pilgrims from the government.

Yet Plymouth was indeed significant—a clear turning point in the European invasion of North America. Quebec was created as both a royal outpost and a trading station, inhabited by a few soldiers who relied on alliances with their Native American neighbors. Similarly, Jamestown was for many years little more than a primitive fort, inhabited mostly by men, whose mission was to battle Powhatan and hunt for gold. In contrast, Plymouth was a true settlement: the colonists came over with intact families, determined simply to find a place to live, not to make a profit and leave. In addition, it was an organic effort, a spontaneous migration of people. In this sense, the Mayflower Compact was very important, for no matter how it limited the body politic, it was a groundbreaking act of self-government, such as would never be seen in Quebec.

The Pilgrims had shown the way. For the Puritans in England, there was now another strategy to follow in the invisible war of the faith, besides battling the king's bishops. There was an ancient world across the ocean, where the religious might create a new one all their own.

6

PURITANS

We know the face of John Winthrop. It has been preserved across the span of almost four centuries in a striking portrait that shows an expression both severe and commanding: high, arched eyebrows; a neatly trimmed beard, dark and pointed; large, observant eyes above a long, straight nose; and the dour yet fine clothing of a Puritan gentleman. This is the face of a substantial man, accustomed to the respect of others and the comforts of wealth. It is the face of a serious man, a careful man, a man who insists on order. It is the face of the father of New England.

In June 1630, John Winthrop arrived in America with a fleet of eleven ships and a thousand Puritans; in short order, he and his companions founded the colony of Massachusetts. It would be this settlement, not Plymouth, that would shape New England. Of course, they settled just a few dozen miles north of Pilgrim town, and their lives were founded upon virtually identical religious beliefs. But Winthrop and his expedition stood a world apart from those humble neighbors.

When the Pilgrims arrived in Cape Cod, they rode in one small, leaking ship—more of a boat, actually. Winthrop, on the other hand, sailed into Massachusetts Bay on the mighty *Arbella*. As historian David Hackett Fischer writes, she "was no ordinary emigrant vessel. She carried twenty-eight great guns and was the 'admiral' or flagship of an entire fleet." And the men and women she carried, he notes, "were also far from being ordinary passengers." A few were true nobility, including the Lady Arbella Fiennes, sister of the Earl of Lincoln; and many were wealthy and respected members of the gentry, including Winthrop himself.

And unlike the Pilgrim voyage, this expedition was extraordinarily well planned. The fleet carried a wealth of provisions, including entire herds of livestock. In addition, an advance party had been sent over two years before; when Winthrop's company arrived, they found an established community, well-scouted terrain, and preexisting (and peaceful) relations with the surrounding Indians.

This well-ordered voyage had been organized by the Company of Massachusetts Bay, which secured a patent from the crown on March 4, 1629. With Winthrop as a moving spirit, the venture had enlisted the support of a

number of influential gentlemen. And, thanks to Winthrop's foresight, it secured an unusual degree of independence. According to the charter, the
company was to be managed by a governor and a council (consisting of eighteen "assistants"), elected annually by the freemen of the company. The annual meeting of the council, called the general court, was to have the power
to make all necessary laws and regulations, consistent with those of England.
The charter, however, failed to designate where the general court should
meet. Taking advantage of this odd omission, Winthrop engineered the buy-
out of the non-Puritans in the company, ensuring that the colony would be
controlled from within Massachusetts itself.

This, then, was a voyage planned and executed with the skill of men
schooled in worldly ways, men with cunning and political sagacity—men
such as John Winthrop. Winthrop had drawn on his considerable wealth, his
connections at court, and his experience in commerce to make it a success.
The great question to be answered is, Why did he go? His portrait shows a
man more likely to be seen debating affairs of state than worrying about
corn supplies in a remote settlement. Why should a man with such a stake in
the world uproot his family and himself, cross a treacherous ocean, and settle in a distant wilderness?

The answer can be found in twenty years of history. For if the first few
years of James's reign had been enough to drive the humble Pilgrims out of
England, the next two decades pushed even such gentry as John Winthrop
beyond endurance.

The first problem that convulsed the kingdom was the crown itself.
After a bad start, James I had persisted in lecturing Parliament on the divine
right of kings; Parliament responded by appealing to its own ancient privileges. The Commons jealously guarded its power over taxation; the inflexible king thought it a gross indignity to have to beg for money each year.
After years of bitter disputes, James dismissed the Parliament of 1611, and
ruled largely without one for the next decade.

Without a Parliament, of course, James had to think of new ways to obtain funds. He began to auction off noble titles, along with commercial monopolies that were staggeringly unpopular. And to make matters worse, he
took a fancy to George Villiers (later dubbed the Duke of Buckingham), a
somewhat absurd fop who quickly concentrated power in his own hands. By
1619, Villiers was clearly the force behind the throne.

Villiers became the focus of popular discontent—so it was with great
dismay that the nation watched as he attached himself to James's son and
heir, Charles. The English, a vehemently anti-Spanish and anti-Catholic people, grew even more upset when Villiers took the crown prince on a trip to
Madrid to woo the princess of Spain.

In 1621, James finally needed more money than he could get without
Parliament, and so to Parliament he turned. Ten years of pent-up frustration
exploded when the Commons gathered. The members impeached royal of-

ficials, abolished the unpopular monopolies, and vigorously debated foreign policy. The furious James dismissed Parliament once again.

In 1625, Charles I succeeded his late, unhappy father, and inherited most of his problems. He clung to the detested Villiers and incensed his militantly Protestant subjects by marrying a Catholic princess, Henrietta Maria of France (the Madrid trip had gone badly). Thrown into war against Spain, and then France, he desperately needed money. In quick succession, he called and dismissed Parliaments—each of which feuded with him, as their predecessors had with his father. In 1628, he reluctantly granted the Petition of Right (which placed new limits on his power) in return for new taxes. Fortunately for Charles, Villiers was assassinated that year, but the next Parliament (in 1629) resulted in an explosive confrontation over the king's right to raise money, and over changes in the church.

And the church, of course, remained one of the most bitterly disputed subjects in England. Indeed, it was most likely this issue, even more than the dangerous tension between Parliament and the crown, that drove John Winthrop to seek that distant shore. By this time, Puritanism was no longer a subject for mockery; its doctrines had achieved both popularity and respectability, making it the faith of the realm. Charles, however, leaned toward a school of thought known as Arminianism. To Puritan England, this leaning was a threat to both body and soul.

Charles's marriage to a Catholic princess raised suspicions; his sponsorship of Arminianism sparked outright hatred. The doctrine was directly opposed to Calvinism: it held that humans could, indeed, voluntarily choose to accept or reject God. This alone drove Puritans into a rage; even worse, leading Arminians placed an emphasis on formal ritual, in a manner that struck Puritans as distinctly *Catholic*. Charles's favorite clergyman was the leading advocate of Arminianism, William Laud; he began to restore rituals and practices that had not been seen in English churches for a generation. Puritans despised Laud, but the king steadily promoted him, eventually making him Archbishop of Canterbury, second only to the king himself within the Church of England.

In 1630, then, even a Puritan gentleman with so much at stake in the world as John Winthrop began to think of removing himself to another country, one far from the cares and pollutions of this one. And so he founded his company, organized his voyage, and finally boarded the *Arbella*.

The passage that follows is taken from his journal; as Bradford did, he writes of himself in the third person, often referring to himself simply as "the governor." The view he presents, however, is distinctly first-person. No matter how well planned, the voyage faced numerous dangers, from both weather and Spanish privateers. No less important, in the Puritans' eyes, were the dangers within: the sins that so many fell into on their way to their New World. This was a voyage of the devout, determined to overcome the problems they had left behind. And so Winthrop and his fellows dealt with each such failing with unfailing severity.

A Well-Ordered Voyage
by John Winthrop

ANNO DOMINI 1630, MARCH 29, MONDAY.] Riding at the Cowes, near the Isle of Wight, in the *Arbella,* a ship of three hundred and fifty tons, whereof Captain Peter Milborne was master, being manned with fifty-two seamen, and twenty-eight pieces of ordnance (the wind coming to the N. by W. the evening before), in the morning there came aboard us Mr. [Matthew] Cradock, the late governor, and the masters of his two ships, Capt. John Lowe, master of the *Ambrose,* and Mr. Nicholas Hurlston, master of the *Jewel,* and Mr. Thomas Beecher, master of the *Talbot* (which was three ships rode then by us—the *Charles,* the *Mayflower,* the *William and Francis,* the *Hopewell,* the *Whale,* the *Success,* and the *Trial* being still at Hampton [Southampton] and not ready); when, upon conference, it was agreed that (in regard it was uncertain when the rest of the fleet would be ready) these four ships should consort together; the *Arbella* to be admiral, the *Talbot* vice-admiral, the *Ambrose* rear-admiral, and the *Jewel* a captain; and accordingly articles of consortship were drawn between the said captains and masters; whereupon Mr. Cradock took leave of us and our captain gave him a farewell with four or five shot.

About ten of the clock we weighed anchor and set sail, the wind at N., and came to an anchor again over against Yarmouth, and the *Talbot* weighed likewise, and came and anchored by us. Here we met with a ship of Hampton, called the *Plantation,* newly come from Virginia. Our captain saluted her, and she us again; and the master, one Mr. Graves, came on board our ship, and stayed with us about two or three hours, and in the meantime his ship came to anchor by us.

Tuesday, 30.]   In the morning, about ten of the clock, the wind being come to the W. with fair weather, we weighed and rode nearer Yarmouth.[9] When we came before the town, the castle put forth a flag; our captain saluted them, and they answered us again. . . .

Thursday, April 8.]   About six in the morning (the wind being E. and N. and fair weather) we weighed anchor and set sail, and before ten we gat through the Needles, having so little wind as we had much to do to stem the tide, so as the rest of our fleet (we being nine in all, whereof some were small ships, which were bound for Newfoundland) could not get out all then till the ebb. In the afternoon the wind came S. and W. and we were becalmed,

---

[9] These contrary winds stalled the expedition off Yarmouth.

so as being not able to get above three or four leagues from the Needles, our captain tacked about . . . and by daylight, Friday 9, we were come to Portland; but the other ships being not able to hold up with us, we were forced to spare our mainsail, and went on with a merry gale.

In the morning we descried from the top eight sail astern of us (whom Cap. Lowe told us he had seen at Dunnose in the evening). We supposing they might be Dunkirkers,[10] our captain caused the gunroom and gundeck to be cleared; all the hammocks were taken down, our ordnance loaded, and our powder-chests and fireworks made ready, and our landmen quartered among the seamen, and twenty-five of them appointed for muskets, and every man written down for his quarter.

The wind continued N. with fair weather, and afternoon it calmed, and we still saw those eight ships to stand towards us; having more wind than we, they came up apace, so as our captain and the masters of our consorts were more occasioned to think they might be Dunkirkers (for we were told at Yarmouth, that there were ten sail of them waiting for us); whereupon we all prepared to fight with them, and took down some cabins which were in the way of our ordnance, and out of every ship were thrown such bed matters as were subject to take fire, and we heaved out our long boats, and put up our waste cloths, and drew forth our men, and armed them with muskets and other weapons, and instruments for fireworks; and for an experiment our captain shot a ball of wild-fire fastened to an arrow out of a cross-bow, which burnt in the water a good time. The lady Arbella and the other women and children were removed into the lower deck, that they might be out of danger.

All things being thus fitted, we went to prayer upon the upper deck. It was much to see how cheerful and comfortable all the company appeared; not a woman or child that showed fear, though all did apprehend the danger to have been great . . . for there had been eight against four, and the least of the enemy's ships were reported to carry thirty brass pieces; but our trust was in the Lord of Hosts; and the courage of our captain, and his care and diligence, did much encourage us.

It was now about one of the clock, and the fleet seemed to be within a league of us; therefore our captain, because he would show he was not afraid of them, and that he might see the issue before night should overtake us, tacked about and stood to meet them, and when we came near we perceived them to be our friends—the *Little Neptune,* a ship of some twenty pieces of ordnance, and her two consorts, bound for the Straits; a ship of Flushing, and a Frenchman, and three other English ships bound for Canada and Newfoundland. So when we drew near, every ship (as they met) saluted each

[10] Dunkirk, a possession of Spain, was a major port for privateers and warships that raided English shipping.

other, and the musketeers discharged their small shot; and so (God be praised) our fear and danger was turned into mirth and friendly entertainment. Our danger being thus over, we espied two boats on fishing in the channel; so every of our four ships manned out a skiff, and we bought of them a great store of excellent fresh fish of diverse sorts.

Saturday, 10.] The wind at E. and by N. a handsome gale with fair weather. By seven in the morning we were come over against Plymouth. About noon the wind slacked, and we were come within sight of the Lizard, and towards night it grew very calm and a great fog, so as our ships made no way. . . .

This day two young men, falling at odds and fighting, contrary to the orders which we had published and set up in the ship, were adjudged to walk upon the deck till night with their hands bound behind them, which accordingly was executed; and another man, for using contemptuous speeches in our presence, was laid in bolts till he submitted himself, and promised open confession of his offense. . . .

About ten at night it cleared up with a fresh gale at N. and by W., so we stood on our course merrily. . . .

Thursday, 15.] About ten at night the wind grew so high, and rain withal, that we were forced to take in our topsail, and having lowered our mainsail and foresail, the storm was so great as it split our foresail and tore it in pieces, and a knot of the sea washed our tub overboard, wherein our fish was a-watering. The storm still grew, and it was dark with clouds (though otherwise moonlight) so as (though it was the *Jewel*'s turn to carry the light this night, yet) lest we should lose or go foul of one another, we hanged out a light upon our mizzen shrouds, and before midnight we lost sight of our vice-admiral.

Our captain, so soon as he had set the watch, at eight in the evening called his men, and told them he feared we should have a storm, and therefore commanded them to be ready upon the deck, if occasion should be; and himself was up and down the decks all times of the night.

Friday, 16.] About four in the morning the wind slacked a little, yet it continued a great storm still, and though in the afternoon it blew not much wind, yet the sea was so high as it tossed us more than before. . . .

All the time of the storm few of our people were sick (except the women, who kept under hatches), and there appeared no fear or dismayedness among them.

Saturday, 17.] The wind S. W. very stormy and boisterous. . . . This day the captain told me that our landmen were very nasty and slovenly, and that the gundeck, where they lodged, was so beastly and noisome with their victuals and beastliness, as would much endanger the health of the ship. Hereupon, after prayer, we took order, and appointed four men to see to it, and to keep that room clean for three days, and then four others should succeed them, and so forth on.

Monday, May 3.] We set two fighters in the bolts till night, with their hands bound behind them. A maid-servant in the ship, being stomach-sick, drank so much strong water that she was senseless, and had near killed herself. We observed it a common fault in our young people, that they gave themselves over to drink hot waters very immoderately. . . .

Tuesday, June 8.] The wind still W. and by S., fair weather, but close and cold. We stood N. N. W. with a stiff gale, and, about three in the afternoon, we had sight of land to the N. W. about ten leagues which we supposed was the Isles of Monhegan, but it proved Mount Mansell [Mount Desert Island]. Then we tacked and stood W. S. W. We had now fair sunshine weather, and so pleasant a sweet air as did much refresh us, and there came a smell off the shore like the smell of a garden. There came a wild pigeon into our ship, and another small land bird.

———

AFTER A LONG voyage—far more tedious than these brief excerpts of Winthrop's journal can suggest—the Puritans arrived, a thousand strong, off the New England shore. It had been an auspicious beginning, with few real problems, despite the gales and alarms they endured. On those alien shores waited more than 200 settlers, members of the advance parties dispatched over the previous two years; and the Indians were reasonably friendly, as they were divided among themselves and diminished by epidemics spread by earlier English visitors. All of Winthrop's careful planning would now pay a handsome return.

In accounting for the colonists' mortal needs, however, this English gentleman remembered their eternal souls—the concern that had launched them on this great journey. In a famous address delivered on the *Arbella,* he told his fellow Puritans, "Thus stands the cause between God and us: We are entered into Covenant." Like the ancient Israelites, they were to be a people whose temporal as well as spiritual states would be dedicated to the Lord. They would be a fire of Godliness in a world of darkness—"a city upon a hill," as Winthrop said.

In the passage that follows, Winthrop records the hectic first two years of the new colony. His early entries (many of which were edited from this selection) are brief and telegraphic; we sense that he was too absorbed in the work of laying out towns, clearing fields, and raising houses and barns to spend much time recording these events. The weeks pass swiftly; without warning, references to towns appear, where forests and Indian cornfields existed upon the colonists' arrival. Entry after entry records the arrival of ships (again, many deleted from this selection); a total of seventeen arrived in that first expansive year of settlement.

As the months pass by in this journal, however, questions of church and state begin to appear. Unlike the Pilgrims, they were not separatists; in England, they had obeyed the rule of the bishops, as much as they despised it.

Here, however, there were no bishops, and so the lay body of each congregation (as they formed in the new towns) selected its own ministers and governed its own membership. The Massachusetts Puritans were determined to restrict church membership (signified by access to the holy sacrament of Communion); they instituted a strict public examination of those who wished to be accepted as one of the "saints," requiring proof that they had received God's grace.

The question of who belonged to the church was not strictly religious— only full members of a congregation could vote for the assistants who ruled the colony. In Massachusetts, church and state were inextricably intertwined. As Governor Winthrop and the assistants began to enact laws for the colony, they used the civil power of government to enforce religious orthodoxy. They made church attendance mandatory, and imposed severe penalties for what they deemed errant opinions.

Despite such rigid restrictions on politics and speech, however, the government of Massachusetts represented a remarkable break with English tradition. The House of Commons might be a boisterous voice of the (wealthy, landowning) people, but it still answered to the hereditary office of the monarch; and it shared power with the House of Lords, whose membership was determined by the accident of birth. In Massachusetts, however, the governor and assistants were all elected; they might be gentlemen, men of high social status, but there was nothing about them that represented the hereditary nobility that touched all aspects of English government. They did not answer to the crown, but to free men.

On that fact rested Winthrop's aggravations and his greatness. He was an eminently practical man, a man accustomed to ordering things *just so,* to getting things done as they needed to be done. Accordingly, he swiftly set to work in the new colony, making up rules as he went along, anticipating the needs of the community, coping with questions of supplies, settlement, and Indian diplomacy. He did not wait for a consensus when something awaited action; if no one else moved his hand, then Winthrop stretched out his.

This utilitarian approach offended more than one important colonist; Winthrop, as they saw it, had no greater standing than anyone else. Such disputes were probably inevitable in a settlement founded on the consent of free men (and these men, after all, were people who could not get along in England). The opposition to Winthrop was championed by Thomas Dudley, who became the governor's bitter rival. Again and again in those early years, the cantankerous Dudley tested Winthrop's patience by challenging his authority *and* his motivation.

Such are the issues that dominate Winthrop's journal, once the first crops took root and the first houses arose. We also see glimpses of numerous aspects of life in Massachusetts: the trade with Virginia; questions of justice (including justice to the Indians); the enforcement of orthodoxy; and the blight of poverty. But poisonous political disputes absorbed more and more of his time. Before two years had passed, Winthrop would find a new metaphor for his conflict-ridden colony: not a city on a hill, but a battle between a mouse and a snake—between a poor, humble people (and governor) and the forces of darkness.

The Mouse and the Snake
by John Winthrop

Saturday, [June] 12.]   About four in the morning we were near our port. We shot off two pieces of ordnance, and sent our skiff to Mr. Peirce his ship (which lay in the harbor, and had been there days before). About an hour later, Mr. Allerton came aboard us in a shallop as he was sailing to Pemaquid. . . .[11]

After Mr. Peirce came aboard us, and returned to fetch Mr. Endecott, who came to us about two of the clock, and with him Mr. [Samuel] Skelton and Capt. Levett. We that were of the assistants, and some other gentlemen, and some of the women, and our captain, returned with them to Nahumkeck, where we supped with a good venison pasty and good beer, and at night we returned to our ship, but some of the women stayed behind. . . .

Thursday, 17.]   We went to Massachusetts,[12] to find out a place for our sitting down. We went up Mystic River about six miles. We lay at [Samuel] Maverick's, and returned home on Saturday. . . .

Thursday, July 1.]   The *Mayflower* and the *Whale* arrived safe in Charlestown[13] harbor. Their passengers were all in health, but most of their cattle dead (whereof a mare and a horse of mine). Some stone horses came over in good plight.

Friday, 2.]   The *Talbot* arrived there. She had lost fourteen passengers. My son, Henry Winthrop, was drowned at Salem. . . .

Thursday, 8.]   We kept a day of thanksgiving in all the plantations.

Thursday, August 18.]   Capt. Endecott and Gibson were married by the governor and Mr. [John] Wilson.

[11] William Peirce was a ship captain, and Isaac Allerton was from Plymouth. In addition, an advance party under John Endecott had arrived two years earlier to prepare the way for the Puritan migration. Endecott established himself at Naumkeag (called Nahumkeck by Winthrop), the site of the town of Salem.

[12] Winthrop here refers to the bay where Boston would soon be founded.

[13] Winthrop actually wrote "Charlton," a spelling used on Captain John Smith's map of New England. Smith named a number of sites along the New England coast, including Plymouth, on his explorations of 1614.

Saturday, 20.]   Monday we kept a court [that is, a general meeting of the company directors, or "assistants"].

Friday, 27.]   We of the congregation kept a fast, and chose Mr. Wilson our teacher, and Mr. Nowell an elder, and Mr. Gager and Mr. Aspinwall, deacons. We used imposition of hands, but with this protestation by all, that it was only as a sign of election and confirmation, not of any intent that Mr. Wilson should renounce his ministry he received in England. . . .[14]

September 30.]   About two in the morning, Mr. Isaac Johnson died; his wife, the Lady Arbella, of the house of Lincoln, being dead about one month before. He was a holy man, and wise, and died in sweet peace, leaving some part of his substance to the colony. . . .

Thomas Morton adjudged to be imprisoned, till he were sent into England, and his house burnt down, for his many injuries offered to the Indians, and other misdemeanors. Capt. Brook, master of the *Gift*, refused to carry him. . . .

Finch, of Watertown, had his wigwam burnt and all his goods. Billington executed at Plymouth for murdering one. Mr. Philipps, the minister of Watertown, and others, had their hay burnt. The wolves killed some swine at Saugus. A cow died at Plymouth, and a goat at Boston,[15] eating Indian corn. . . .

25.]   The governor, upon consideration of the inconveniences which had grown in England by drinking one to another, restrained it at his own table, and wished others to do the like, so as it grew, by little and little, to disuse. . . .

February 5.]   The ship *Lyon*, Mr. William Peirce, master, arrived at Nantasket. She brought Mr. [Roger] Williams (a godly minister) with his wife, Mr. Throgmorton, Perkins, Ogn, and others, with their wives and children, about twenty passengers, and about two hundred tons of goods. . . .

10.]   The frost brake up. . . . The poorer sort of people (who lay long in tents, etc.) were much afflicted with the scurvy, and many died, especially at Boston and Charlestown; but when this ship came and brought store of juice of lemons, many recovered speedily. It hath been always observed here, that such as fell into discontent, and lingered after their former conditions in England, fell into the scurvy and died. . . .

23.]   Chickatabot[16] came with his sannops [warriors] and squaws, and presented the governor with a hogshead of Indian corn. After they had all dined, and had each a small cup of sack and beer, and the men tobacco, he sent away all his men and women (although the governor would have stayed them, in regard of the rain and thunder). Himself and one squaw and one

[14] The Puritans were being careful to maintain their links to the Church of England. They would not yet completely separate, as had the Pilgrims at Plymouth.

[15] This is Winthrop's first use of the name "Boston."

[16] Chickatabot was sagamore of the Indians who lived on the Neponset River. This meeting reveals the beginning of a remarkable cultural intermingling.

sannop stayed all night, and, being in English clothes, the governor set him at his own table, where he behaved himself as soberly, etc., as an Englishman. The next day after dinner he returned home, the governor giving him cheese and peas and a mug and some other small things.

26.] John Sagamore[17] and James his brother, with diverse sannops, came to the governor to desire his letter for recovery of twenty beaver skins, which one Watts in England had forced him of. The governor entertained them kindly, and gave him his letter with directions to Mr. Downing in England, etc. . . .[18]

1631[19]

April 12.] At a court holden at Boston (upon information to the governor, that they of Salem had called Mr. [Roger] Williams to the office of a teacher), a letter was written from the court to Mr. Endecott to this effect: That whereas Mr. Williams had refused to join with the congregation at Boston, because they would not make a public declaration of their repentance for having communion with the churches of England, while they lived there; and, besides, had declared his opinion that the magistrate might not punish the breach of the Sabbath, nor any other offence, as it was a breach of the first table; therefore, they marveled that they [the congregation of Salem] would choose him without advising with the council; and withal desiring him, that they would forbear to proceed till they had conferred about it.

13.] Chickatabot came to the governor, and desired to buy some English clothes for himself. The governor told him, that English sagamores did not use to truck [trade]: but he called his tailor and gave him order to make him a suit of clothes; whereupon he gave the governor two large skins of coat beaver, and, after he and his men had dined, they departed, and said he would come again three days after for his suit.

14.] We began a court of guard upon the neck between Roxbury and Boston, whereupon should be always resident an officer and six men. An order was made last court, that no man should discharge a piece after sunset, except by occasion of alarm.

15.] Chickatabot came to the governor again, and he put him into a very good new suit from head to foot, and after he set meat before them; but

[17] John Sagamore held sway between the Charles and Mystic rivers. Within a year, the Puritans were already giving English names to prominent Indians.
[18] Emanuel Downing was Winthrop's brother-in-law, a man with a great deal of influence back in England. He later emigrated to Massachusetts.
[19] Until 1752, the English calendar marked March 25 as New Year's Day—hence the odd division of years here.

he would not eat till the governor had given thanks, and after meat he desired him to do the like, and so departed. . . .

16.]   There was an alarm given to all our towns in the night, by occasion of a piece which was shot off (but where could not be known), and the Indians having sent us word the day before, that the Mohawks were coming down against them and us.[20]

17.]   A general court at Boston.[21] The former governor [Winthrop himself] was chosen again, and all the freemen of the commons were sworn to this government. . . .

June 14.]   At a court, John Sagamore and Chickatabot being told at last court of some injuries that their men did to our cattle, and giving consent to make satisfaction, etc., now one of their men was complained of for shooting a pig, etc., for which Chickatabot was ordered to pay a small skin of beaver, which he presently paid. At this court one Philip Ratcliffe, a servant of Mr. Cradock, being convicted, *ore tenus,* of most foul, scandalous invectives against our churches and government, was censured to be whipped, lose his ears, and be banished from the plantation, which was presently executed. . . .

July 4.]   The governor built a bark at Mystick, which was launched this day, and called the *Blessing of the Bay.* . . .

13.]   Canonicus's son, the great sachem of Narragansett, came to the governor's house with John Sagamore. After they had dined, he gave the governor a skin, and the governor requited him with a fair pewter pot, which he took very thankfully, and stayed all night. . . .

21.]   The governor, and deputy, and Mr. Nowell, the elder of the congregation at Boston, went to Watertown to confer with Mr. Phillips, the pastor, and Mr. Brown, the elder of the congregation there, about an opinion which they had published, that the churches of Rome were true churches. The matter was debated before many of both congregations, and, by approbation of all the assembly, except three, was concluded an error. . . .

August 31.]   The governor's bark, called the *Blessing of the Bay,* being of thirty tons, went to sea.

September 6.]   At the last court, a young fellow was whipped for soliciting an Indian squaw to incontinency. Her husband and she complained of the wrong, and were present at the execution, and very well satisfied. At the same court, one Henry Linne was whipped and banished, for writing letters into England full of slander against our government and orders of our churches.

October 5.]   The *Blessing* went on a voyage to the eastward. . . .

---

[20] The power of the Iroquois caused fear and terror even here. The Mohawk were the easternmost of the Five Nations, and often sent war parties this far.

[21] The general court was the annual meeting of all the members of the Massachusetts Company.

November 2.] The ship *Lyon,* William Peirce master, arrived at Nantasket. There came in her the governor's wife, his eldest son and his wife, and others of his children, and Mr. [John] Eliot, a minister, and other families, being in all about sixty persons, who all arrived in good health, having been ten weeks at sea, and lost none of their company but two children, whereof one was the governor's daughter Ann, about one year and half old, who died about a week after they came to sea. . . .

February 17.] The governor and assistants called before them, at Boston, diverse of Watertown; the pastor and elder by letter, and the others by warrant. The occasion was, for that a warrant being sent to Watertown for levying of £8, part of a rate of £60, ordered for the fortifying of a new town [Newtown, later called Cambridge], the pastor and elder, etc., assembled the people and delivered their opinions that it was not safe to pay moneys after that sort, for fear of bringing themselves and their posterity into bondage.

Being come before the governor and council, after much debate, they acknowledged their fault, confessing freely that they were in an error, and made a retraction and submission under their hands, and were enjoined to read it in the assembly the next Lord's day. The ground of their error was, for that they took this government to be no other but as of a mayor and aldermen, who have not power to make laws or raise taxations without the people; but understanding that this government was rather in the nature of a parliament, and that no assistant could be chosen but by the freemen, who had power likewise to remove the assistants and put in others, and therefore at every general court (which was to be held once every year) they had free liberty to consider and propound anything concerning the same, and to declare their grievances, without being subject to question, or, etc., they were fully satisfied; and so their submission was accepted, and their offence pardoned. . . .

March 5.] The first court after winter. It was ordered that the courts (which before were every three weeks) should now be held the first Tuesday in every month. Commissioners [were] appointed to set out the bounds of the town. . . .

1632

April 3.] At a court at Boston, the deputy [governor], Mr. Dudley, went away before the court was ended, and then the secretary delivered the governor a letter from him, directed to the governor and assistants, wherein he declared a resignation of his deputyship and place of assistant; but it was not allowed. At this court an act was made expressing the governor's power, etc., and the office of the secretary and treasurer, etc. . . .

12.] The governor received letters from Plymouth, signifying that there had been a broil between their men at Sowamset and the Narragansett

Indians, who set upon the English house there to have taken Osamequin
[better known as Massasoit], the sagamore of Pokanoket [Wampanoag],
who was fled thither with all his people for refuge; and that Capt. Standish,
being gone thither to relieve the three English which were in the house, had
sent home in all haste for more men and other provisions, upon intelligence
that Canonicus, with a great army, was coming against them. Withal they
writ to our governor for some powder to be sent with all possible speed
(for it seemed they were unfurnished). Upon this the governor presently
despatched away the messenger with so much powder as he could carry, viz.,
twenty-seven pounds.

16.]   The messenger returned, and brought a letter from the governor, signifying that the Indians were retired from Sowams to fight with the
Pequots. . . .

A Dutch ship brought from Virginia two thousand bushels of corn,
which was sold at four shillings sixpence the bushel.

May 1.]   The governor and assistants met at Boston to consider for the
deputy [Dudley] his deserting his place. The points discussed were two. The
1st, upon what grounds he did it; 2nd, whether it was good or void. For
the 1st, his main reason was for public peace; because he must needs discharge his conscience in speaking freely, and he saw that bred disturbance,
etc. For the 2nd, it was maintained by all that he could not leave his place,
except by the same power which put him in; yet he would not be put from
his contrary opinion, nor would he be persuaded to continue till the general
court, which was to be the 9th of this month.

Another question fell out with him, about some bargains he had made
with some poor men, members of the same congregation, to whom he had
sold seven bushels and an half of corn to receive ten for it after harvest,
which the governor and some others held to be oppressing usury, and within
compass of the statute; but he persisted to maintain it to be lawful, and there
arose hot words about it, he telling the governor that if he had thought he
had sent for him to his house to give him such usage, he would not have come
there; and that he never knew any man of understanding of other opinion;
and that [if] the governor thought otherwise of it, it was his weakness.

The governor took notice of these speeches, and bore them with more
patience than he had done, upon a like occasion, at another time. Upon this
there arose another question, about his house. The governor having formerly
told him, that he did not well to bestow such cost about wainscotting and
adorning his house, in the beginning of a plantation, both in regard of the
necessity of public charges, and for example, etc., his answer now was, that
it was for the warmth of his house, and the charge was little, being but clap-
boards nailed to the wall in the form of a wainscot. These and other speeches
passed before dinner.

After dinner, the governor told them that he had heard, that the people
intended, at the next general court, to desire that the assistants might be

chosen anew every year, and that the governor might be chosen by the whole court, and not by the assistants only. Upon this, Mr. Ludlow grew into passion, and said that then we should have no government, but there would be an interim, wherein every man might do what he pleased, etc. This was answered and cleared in the judgment of the rest of the assistants, but he continued stiff in his opinion, and protested he would then return back into England. . . .

Thus the day was spent and no good done, which was the more uncomfortable to most of them, because they had commended this meeting to God in more earnest manner than ordinary at other meetings.

May 8.] A general court at Boston. Whereas it was (at our first meeting) agreed that the freemen should choose the assistants, and they the governor, the whole court agreed now that the governor and assistants should all be new chosen every year by the general court (the governor to be always chosen out of the assistants); and accordingly the old governor, John Winthrop, was chosen; accordingly all the rest as before. . . .

The deputy governor, Thomas Dudley, Esq., having submitted the validity of his resignation to the vote of the court, it was adjudged a nullity, and he accepted of his place again, and the governor and he being reconciled the day before, all things were carried very lovingly amongst all, etc., and the people carried themselves with much silence and modesty. . . .

June 13.] A day of Thanksgiving in all the plantations, by the public authority, for the good success of the king of Sweden and the Protestants of Germany against the emperor,[22] etc.; and for the safe arrival of all the ships, they having not lost one person, nor one sick among them. . . .

July 5.] At Watertown there was (in the view of diverse witnesses) a great combat between a mouse and a snake; and, after a long fight, the mouse prevailed and killed the snake. The pastor of Boston, Mr. Wilson, a very sincere, holy man, hearing of it, gave this interpretation: That the snake was the devil; the mouse was a poor contemptible people, which God had brought hither, which should overcome Satan here, and dispossess him of his kingdom. . . .

August 3.] The deputy, Mr. Thomas Dudley, being still discontented with the governor partly for that the governor had removed the frame of his house, which he had set up in Newtown, and partly for that he took too much authority upon him (as he conceived), renewed his complaints to Mr. Wilson and Mr. Welde, who acquainting the governor therewith, a meeting was agreed upon at Charlestown, where were present the governor and deputy, Mr. Nowell, Mr. Wilson, Mr. Welde, Mr. Maverick, and Mr. Warham.

[22] The Thirty Years' War was raging between the Catholic Holy Roman Emperor (of the Habsburg family) and the Protestant German princes, allied with King Gustavus Adolphus of Sweden. Gustavus had just won a great victory at Breitenfeld.

The conference being begun with calling upon the Lord, the deputy began—that howsoever he had some particular grievances, etc.; yet, seeing he was advised by those present, and diverse of the assistants, to be silent in them, he would let them pass, and so come first to complain of the breach of promise, both in the governor and others, in not building at Newtown.

The governor answered that he had performed the words of the promise; for he had a house up, and seven or eight servants abiding in it, by the day appointed; and for the removing of his house, he alleged that, seeing the rest of the assistants went not about to build, and that his neighbors of Boston had been discouraged from removing thither by Mr. Deputy himself, and thereupon had (under all their hands) petitioned him, that . . . he would not leave them; this was the occasion that he removed his house.

Upon these and other speeches to this purpose, the ministers went apart for one hour; then returning, they delivered their opinions, that the governor was in fault for removing of his house so suddenly, without conferring with the deputy and the rest of the assistants; but if the deputy were the occasion of discouraging Boston men from removing, it would excuse the governor a *tanto,* but not a *toto.* The governor, professing himself willing to submit his own opinion to the judgment of so many wise and godly friends, acknowledged himself faulty.

After dinner, the deputy proceeded in his complaint, yet with this protestation, that what he should charge the governor with, was in love and out of his care of the public, and that the things which he should produce were but for his own satisfaction, and not by way of accusation. Then demanded he of him the ground and limits of his authority, whether by the patent or otherwise.

The governor answered, that he was willing to stand to that which he propounded, and would challenge no greater authority than he might by the patent. The deputy replied, that then he had no more authority than every assistant (except the power to call courts, and precedency, for honor and order). The governor answered, he had more; for the patent, making him a governor, gave him whatsoever power belonged to a governor by common law or the statutes, and desired him to show wherein he had exceeded, etc.; and speaking this somewhat apprehensively, the deputy began to be in passion, and told the governor, that if he were so round [blunt], he would be round too.

The governor bade him be round, if he would. So the deputy rose up in great fury and passion, and the governor grew very hot also, so as they both fell into bitterness; but, by mediation of the mediators, they were soon pacified. Then the deputy proceeded to particulars, as followeth:

1st. By what authority the governor removed the ordnance and erected a fort at Boston? The governor answered, that the ordnance lying upon the beach in danger of spoiling, and having often complained of it in the court, and nothing done, with the help of diverse of the assistants, they were mounted upon their carriages, and removed where they might be of some use; and for the fort, it had been agreed, above a year before, that it should be erected there: and all this was done without a penny charged to the public.

2nd.   By what authority he lent twenty-eight pounds of powder to those of Plymouth? Governor answered, it was of his own powder, and upon their urgent distress, their own powder proving naught, when they were to send to the rescue of their men at Sowamsett.

3rd.   By what authority he had licensed Edward Johnson to sit down at Merrimack? Governor answered, that he had licensed him only to go forth on trading (as he had diverse others) as belonging to his place.

4th.   By what authority he had given them of Watertown leave to erect a weir [fish trap] upon Charles River, and had disposed of lands to diverse, etc.? The governor answered, the people of Watertown, falling very short of corn the last year, for want of fish, did complain, etc., and desired leave to erect a weir; and upon this the governor told them, that he could not give them leave, but they must seek it of the court; but because it would be long before the courts began again, and, if they deferred till then, the season might be lost, he wished them to do it, and there was no doubt but, being for so general a good, the court would allow it. . . . And for lands, he had disposed of none, otherwise than the deputy and other of the assistants had done—he had only given his consent, but referred them to the court, etc. . . .

5th.   By what authority he had given to Ratcliff and Grey (being banished men) to stay within our limits? Governor answered, he did it by that authority, which was granted him in court, viz., that, upon any sentence in criminal cases, the governor might, upon cause, stay the execution till the next court. Now the cause was that, being in the winter, they must otherwise have perished.

6th.   Why the fines were not levied? Governor answered, it belonged to the secretary and not to him . . . ; yet he confessed that it was his judgment that it were not fit, in the infancy of a commonwealth, to be too strict in levying fines, though severe in other punishments.

7th.   That when a cause had been voted by the rest of the court, the governor would bring new reasons, and move them to alter the sentence; which the governor justified, and all approved.

The deputy having made an end, the governor desired the mediators to consider, whether he had exceeded his authority or not, and how little cause the deputy had to charge him with it; for if he had made some slips, in two or three years' government, he ought rather to have covered them, seeing he could not be charged that he had taken advantage of his authority to oppress or wrong any man, or to benefit himself; but, for want of a public stock, had disbursed all common charges out of his own estate; whereas the deputy would never lay out one penny. . . .

Though the governor might justly have refused to answer these seven articles, wherewith the deputy had charged him, both for that he had no knowledge of them before (the meeting being only for the deputy [and] his personal grievances), and also for that the governor was not to give account of his actions to any but to the court; yet, out of his desire of the public peace, and to clear his reputation with those to whom the deputy had accused him, he was willing to give him satisfaction, to the end, that he might free him of such jealousy as he had conceived, that the governor intended to make himself popular, that he might gain absolute power, and bring all the assistants under his subjection; which was very improbable, seeing the governor had propounded in court an order established for limiting the governor's authority, and had himself drawn articles for that end, which had been approved and established by the whole court; neither could he justly be charged to have transgressed any of them.

So the meeting breaking up, without any other conclusion but the commending the success of it by prayer to the Lord, the governor brought the deputy onward of his way, and every man went to his own home. . . .

14.]   The governor's wife was delivered of a son, who was baptized by the name of William. The governor himself held the child to baptism, as others in the congregation did use. William signifies a common man. . . .

September 4.]   The ministers afterward, for the end of the difference between the governor and deputy, ordered that the governor should procure them a minister at Newtown, and contribute somewhat towards his maintenance for a time; or, if he could not, by the spring, effect that then to give the deputy, toward his charges in building there, twenty pounds. . . .

Notwithstanding the heat of contention which had been between the governor and deputy, yet they usually met about their affairs, and that without any appearance of any breach or discontent; and ever after kept peace and good correspondency together, in love and friendship. . . .

January 1.]   Mr. Edward Winslow chosen governor of Plymouth, Mr. Bradford having been governor about ten years, and by importunity gat off. . . .

17.]   The governor—having intelligence from the east that the French had bought the Scottish plantation near Cape Sable [in Nova Scotia], and that the fort and all the ammunition were delivered to them, and that the cardinal [Richelieu], having the managing thereof, had sent some companies already, and preparation was made to send many more the next year, and diverse priests and Jesuits among them—called the assistants to Boston, and the ministers and captains, and some of the chief men, to advise what was fit to be done for our safety, in regard of the French who were like to prove ill neighbors (being Papists).

At which meeting it was agreed, that a plantation and a fort should be begun at Nantasket partly to be some block in an enemy's way (though it could not bar his entrance), and especially to prevent an enemy from taking that passage from us; and also, that the fort begun at Boston should be finished—also, that a plantation should be begun at Agawam (being the best place in the land for tillage and cattle), lest an enemy, finding it void, should possess and take it from us.

WITHIN AND WITHOUT, dangers pressed upon Winthrop and his colony. Some problems he dealt with easily, such as the delicate relations with neighboring Indians; there he held the stronger hand, with technological superiority and greater numbers than any of those disease-wracked bands. There, too, he seemed disposed at first to deliver some justice to the Native Americans, provided they did not hinder the expansion of the settlement. On other questions, he sought compromise, as in the matter of taxation and representation; the dispute with Watertown forced him to accept that each town should send two representatives to the General Court, and that the governor as well as the assistants should be elected by the colony's freemen.

Dudley, unfortunately, could not be dismissed so easily. As Winthrop's terse prose suggests, their feud became a personal matter; the governor took offense at the snide suggestion that he wished to accumulate power, when he had spent so much time and money in the service of others. Despite the climactic confrontation, their duel was far from over.

Other problems had appeared on the horizon, meanwhile, promising to grow into nearly insurmountable conundrums. Roger Williams, for example, quickly emerged as a voice of the most radical of the religious; his message of total separation from the Church of England had great appeal for the Puritans of Massachusetts (after all, they had just put an ocean between themselves and the nearest bishop).

What concerned Winthrop most, however, were Jesuits and Frenchmen—the spiritual and mortal enemies of the English. Quebec might be two great rivers and a mountain range away, yet already it threatened to overthrow them all. In the Puritans' eyes, the serpent had entered the garden. At the very founding of New England, the colonists discovered a new mission: to destroy New France.

7

JESUITS

New France was destroyed. In January 1629, Samuel de Champlain reluctantly surrendered Quebec to Captain David Kirke, who had blockaded the St. Lawrence for the previous year with a squadron of English ships. Dangerously short of supplies, desperately short of men, Champlain sadly relinquished the colony he had spent twenty years in building—two decades of planning and administration, of lobbying the royal court, of explorations and war parties and diplomacy. All gone.

The fall of Quebec was merely one fruit of war between England and France. Despite this English victory, however, the contestants hardly made a fair match. Louis XIII reigned over a powerful, revived kingdom, bearing scant resemblance to the divided, war-weakened realm that had been seized by Henry IV. And to help rule it, Louis called upon one of the most remarkable men in French history—the famed Cardinal Richelieu. Richelieu's cunning and ruthlessness were formidable indeed, far greater than that of his opponents.

Across the channel, those opponents squabbled. The quarrelsome Charles I battled an even more quarrelsome Parliament over money and prerogative, when they should have been fighting the war. It was a war sparked, in large part, by Richelieu's well-considered plan for breaking the power of the Protestant Huguenots in France, who had their own independent fortress-city at La Rochelle; the Cardinal could not abide such a threat to the unity of the state, and he besieged the town. The English sent help to their fellow Calvinists, but the Commons provided little money, and Charles provided scant leadership. La Rochelle fell.

The capture of the Huguenot citadel marked the end of the war between England and France, but the news reached North America too late. When the aging Champlain arrived in his homeland, he learned that he had surrendered Quebec a full three months after a truce was declared. The surrender, he reasoned, should be invalid. But possession, as the saying goes, is nine-tenths of the law—and in the seventeenth century, it was usually everything. So Champlain lobbied the royal court once again, urging it to seek the restoration of New France in the extended peace negotiations with England. He had a difficult task: his tiny settlement along the St. Lawrence was about the least important thing in Richelieu's mind.

Fortunately for Champlain, it was unimportant to the English as well. In the Treaty of St. Germain-en-Laye, signed on March 29, 1632, the two parties agreed to restore the province of New France to the possession of King Louis XIII. For the last time, the tired warrior prepared for the voyage from Paris to Quebec—from the center of European civilization to the heart of the North American forest.

Once again, the sailor, soldier, explorer, diplomat, and governor Champlain would painstakingly lay the foundations for the empire he envisioned in the wilderness. To do so, he needed two things: settlers from France, and Indian allies. For the first, he would benefit from royal favor. Richelieu saw great possibilities for the little colony; if he never did spend much money on its development, at least he maintained a friendly attitude toward Champlain's life work. For the second, Champlain turned to a great unexploited resource: a mighty people he had long admired, and now wished to bind to New France in an eternal alliance.

Those people were the Hurons. At perhaps thirty thousand strong, they were one of the mightiest bodies of Native Americans, rivaling all Five Nations of the Iroquois. Living within the northernmost reaches of the corn-growing climate, they produced a great surplus of food, which they traded to their neighbors (and to Quebec). Situated within the triangle of land between Lakes Huron, Erie, and Ontario, they possessed a strategic region; and they used it, building up a great trading network that stretched from the deep interior to the seacoast (they began to accumulate European kettles and hatchets, for example, long before they first saw Champlain). And most important, for Champlain's purposes, they were a nation of deadly warriors—and implacable enemies of the Iroquois.

Champlain envisioned a mighty union between New France and the Hurons, combining European technology with Indian manpower and trade relations. These people were the key to his penetration of the interior of the continent—and to the destruction of the Five Nations, whose merciless war parties struck at Quebec as soon as the first Frenchmen returned. John Winthrop of New England would have recoiled in horror at such a plan—yet Champlain truly believed that the Hurons and French could become one people.

To create that alliance, he turned to the priests of the Society of Jesus, better known as the Jesuits. The order had been founded in 1540 by St. Ignatius of Loyola, who imparted a disciplined, military style to his followers, who became the shock troops of Catholicism's counterattack against the Reformation. With spiritual fervor and fierce realism, they evangelized the globe—always seeking to understand the cultures they met, the better to draw them into the church of Rome. Small wonder that John Winthrop and the Puritans trembled at word of the Jesuits' approach: they were as formidable an enemy in the war between Protestantism and Catholicism as the Huron warriors were in the wars with the Iroquois.

The Jesuits made the perfect conduit for Champlain's relations with the Hurons: they would eagerly learn their language and study their ways—even as they spread the French religion, mixing the two cultures and binding them together. And so, as we return with the French to the shores of the St. Lawrence, we follow the words of a Jesuit priest, Father Paul le Jeune, who carefully observed the resurrection of Quebec, the diplomacy with the Indians, and the beginnings of a decisive mission to the Hurons.

Return to New France
by Paul le Jeune

Having been notified . . . on the last day of March [1632] that I should embark as early as possible at Havre de Grace, to sail directly for New France, the joy and happiness that I felt in my soul was so great that I believe I have experienced nothing like it for twenty years, nor has any letter been so welcome. . . . I left Dieppe the next day, and, going to Rouen. . . . From Havre we went to Honfleur, and on Low Sunday, April 18, we set sail. . . .

On Thursday, June 3, we passed into the country through one of the most beautiful rivers in the world. The great island of Newfoundland intercepts it at its mouth, leaving two openings whereby it can empty into the sea, one to the north and the other to the south. We sailed in through the latter, which is about 13 or 14 leagues wide. Upon entering, you discover a gulf 150 leagues wide. . . . Ships come into this gulf on whaling expeditions. We have seen a great many fishing for cod. I saw here a number of seals, and our people killed some of them. In this great river, which is called the St. Lawrence, white porpoises are found, and nowhere else. . . .

On the 14th of June we cast anchor at Tadoussac. This is another bay or very small cove, near which there is another river named Saguenay, which empties into the great river of St. Lawrence. . . . As we were on our way to say the Holy Mass on the shore, one of our soldiers killed a great eagle near its eyrie. Its head and neck were entirely white. . . . We sojourned here from the 14th of June to the 3rd of July; that is to say, 19 days. . . . It was here that I saw savages for the first time. As soon as they saw our vessel, they lighted fires, and two of them came on board in a little canoe very neatly made of bark.

The next day a sagamore, with ten or twelve savages, came to see us. When I saw them enter our captain's room, where I happened to be, it seemed to me that I was looking at those maskers who run about in France at Carnival time. There were some whose noses were painted blue, the eyes, eyebrows, and cheeks painted black, and the rest of the face red; and these colors are bright and shining like those of our masks; others had black, red, and blue stripes drawn from ears to the mouth. Still others were entirely black, except the upper part of the brow and around the ears, and the end of the chin; so that it might have been truly said of them that they were masquerading. There were some who had only one black stripe, like a wide ribbon, drawn from one ear to the other, across the eyes, and three little stripes on the cheeks. Their natural color is like that of those French beggars who are half-roasted in the sun. . . . When we arrived at Tadoussac, the savages were coming back from a war against the Iroquois, and had taken nine of them; those of Quebec took six, and those of Tadoussac three. . . .

At length, on the 5th of July, which was Monday—two months and 18 days since the 18th of April, when we sailed—we reached the much desired port. We cast anchor in front of the fort, which the English held; we saw at the foot of this fort the poor settlement of Quebec all in ashes. The English, who come to this country to plunder and not to build up, not only burned a greater part of the detached buildings which Father Charles Lallement had had erected, but also all of that poor settlement of which nothing is to be seen but the ruins of its stone walls. This greatly inconveniences the French, who do not know where to lodge.

The next day Captain Thomas Ker was summoned, a man of French nationality, born at Dieppe, who had gone over to England, and who, with David and Louis Ker, his brothers, and one Jacques Michel, also born at Dieppe, all Huguenots, had thrown themselves upon this poor country, where they have done great damage and have prevented the doing of much good. This poor Jacques Michel, full of sadness at not having been rewarded as he desired by the English . . . also fell prey to conscience at having assisted these new Englishmen against his own countrymen, died suddenly, some time after the surrender of this country. He was buried at Tadoussac. I have learned here that the savages exhumed his body, and showed it every imaginable indignity, tore it to pieces, and gave it to their dogs; but such are the wages of traitors.

Monsieur Emergy de Caën had already sent a boat from Tadoussac with an extract from the Commissions and Letters Patent of the Kings of France and of England, by which the English captain was commanded to surrender the fort in eight days. Having seen the letter, he answered that they would obey when he had seen the original. It was therefore brought to him the day after our arrival. . . . The English dislodged, we again entered our little home. . . .

All considered, this country here is very fine. As soon as we had entered into our little home, the 13th of July [1632], we began to work and dig the earth, to sow purslane and turnips, and to plant lentils, and everything grew very well. . . .

On the 19th [of May, 1633], news was brought that an English vessel had entered Tadoussac a few days before; we did not know whether it was a trading vessel, or whether there was some trouble between France and England. Each one formed his own conjectures, and everyone was upon his guard. The following Sunday, day of Holy Trinity, having gone to say Holy Mass at the fort, I was told that, if we heard two cannon shots, we should promptly withdraw with our French people into the fortress. . . .

On the 22nd of the same month of May, we heard the sound of the cannon very early in the morning. In the uncertainty as to what was going on, Father de Noüe took our savage and started for Quebec; and he brought back without delay the news that Sieur de Champlain had arrived, and that Father Brébeuf was coming as fast as possible to our little house. We hastened to thank our Lord. In the meantime, behold, Father Brébeuf enters. God knows whether we received and embraced him with glad hearts. . . .

Having learned of the arrival of Monsieur de Champlain, I went to greet him. Arriving at the fort, I saw a squad of French soldiers, armed with pikes and muskets, who approached, beating their drums. As soon as they had entered, Monsieur de Caën gave the keys of the fort to Monsieur du Plessis Bochard, who delivered them the next day to Monsieur de Champlain, to take command of the ships according to the decree of Monseigneur the Cardinal [Richelieu]. I thanked Monsieur de Champlain as well as I could for the kindness shown by him to our Fathers, for it was very great, as Father Brébeuf has testified to me.

On the 24th of May, eighteen canoes of savages having descended to Quebec, Sieur de Champlain, suspecting that they might go on to the English, who had three vessels at Tadoussac and a bark far up the river, went into the cabins of these savages, and made to them a very suitable address through Sieur Olivier, the interpreter, who is an excellent man and well fitted for this country.

He said to them through the lips of this interpreter that the French had always loved and defended them, that he had assisted them in person in their wars; that he had greatly cherished the father of the captain to whom he was talking, who was killed at his side in a battle where he himself was wounded by an arrow; that he was a man of his word, and that notwithstanding the discomforts of the sea voyage, he had returned to see them again, as if they were his brothers. As they had expressed a wish that a French settlement should be made in their country to defend them against the incursions of their enemies, he contemplated granting this desire. . . .

Yet, notwithstanding the great obligations that they were under to the French, they had descended the river with the intention of going to see the thieves who came to pillage the French. He said they should consider well what they were doing; that these robbers were only birds of passage, while the French would remain in the country as it belonged to them. . . .

During this speech, the [Indian] captain and his men listened very attentively. He, among others, appeared to be in deep thought, drawing from his stomach from time to time this aspiration, while they were speaking to him, *hám! hám! hám!* as if approving the speech of the interpreter; which, when finished, this captain arose to answer, but with a keenness and delicacy of rhetoric that might have come out of the schools of Aristotle or Cicero. He won, in the beginning of this discourse, the good will of all of the French by his profound humility, which appeared with exceeding grace in his gestures and in his language. . . .

The conclusion was that Sieur de Champlain said to them: "When that great house shall be built,[23] then our young men will marry your daughters, and we shall be one people." They began to laugh, answering: "Thou always sayest something cheering to rejoice us. If that should happen, we would be very happy." Those who think that the savages have dull and heavy intellects will recognize by this speech that they are not so stupid as they might have been painted. . . .

On the last day of May, la Nasse, our savage, came to tell us that one of their men had dreamed that some Frenchmen would be killed. Now, either because the Devil had given them this sentiment, or that among all their dreams there is now and then one that happens perchance to be true, however that may be, on the 2nd day of June the Iroquois killed two of our Frenchmen and wounded four others, one of whom died shortly afterward.

This catastrophe happened in this way: A bark and a shallop were ascending the great river St. Lawrence; the latter went ahead, and, to hasten its speed, sailors went ashore to tow it with lines or cords. As they came to double [round] a point of land, thirty or forty Iroquois who were in ambush fell upon them with horrible cries; they killed the first two men encountered with blows from their hatchets, then discharged a storm of arrows so suddenly and unexpectedly that our Frenchmen did not know which way to turn, not having foreseen the attack. They even dared to try to board the shallop in their canoes; and, had it not been that a Frenchman took aim at them with his harquebus, and that the bark, which was so far away, speedily equipped a boat to come to the rescue, having heard the cries of the combat, it is probable that not one of them would have escaped. The Iroquois, seeing the harquebus, and the other boat coming to their help, fled, first skinning the heads of those whom they had killed and bearing away the scalps by the way of bravado. . . .

On the 27th of July, Louis de Saincte Foy, surnamed by the savages Amantacha[24] . . . came back to Sieur de Champlain, who had sent him to meet a great crowd of Hurons who were expected from day to day. Already a few canoes had arrived on different days, sometimes seven or eight, sometimes ten or twelve at a time; but at last, on the 28th of July, there arrived about one hundred and forty all at once, carrying easily five hundred Hurons—or 700, as some say—with their merchandise.

[23] The new settlement under discussion was at Three Rivers, or *Trois Rivières*, roughly halfway between Quebec and the future site of Montreal.

[24] Amantacha was a Huron boy who had spent several years in France, and now played an important role in relations between New France and that tribe.

The island savages and the Algonquins, two tribes on the route from the Hurons to Quebec, had tried to dissuade them from visiting the French, saying we would do them a bad turn on account of the death of one Brulé, whom they had killed; and that an Algonquin of the little nation, having killed a Frenchman, had been taken prisoner, and had been condemned to death; also that the same would be done to some Huron. Their design was to get all the merchandise from these Hurons at a very low price, in order afterwards to come themselves and trade it, with either the French or the English.

Louis Amantacha, meeting with them above, assured those of his tribe of the good feeling of the French toward them, declaring that they might put him to death if the French did not give them a very warm welcome. As to Brulé, who had been murdered, he was not looked upon as a Frenchman, because he had left his nation and gone over to the service of the English. In short, he convinced them so thoroughly, that six or seven hundred Hurons came to Quebec. . . .

On the 29th of the same month of July, having learned that the Hurons were to hold a council, when they would take some action concerning our Fathers who were destined for their country, Father Brébeuf and I went to see them. I found Louis Amantacha in their midst. I had an interview with them on some serious matters; and, passing from one subject to another, he told me that he was highly pleased because our Fathers were going to the help of his tribe. . . .

But let us speak of the council of his tribe. After it had assembled, Sieur de Champlain had us summoned. I have been told that Louis XI once held his council of war in the country, having for throne or chair only a piece of wood, or a fallen tree, that he happened to find in the midst of the field. This is the picture of the council of the Hurons, only they are seated a little lower still, that is to say, flat upon the ground, all pellmell without any order, unless it be that the people of one tribe or village are placed near those of another. While in France they are discussing precedence, and amusing themselves in offering a chair to one whom they would consider impertinent if he accepted it, here they will have held and concluded three councils among the savages, who, on the whole, do not cease to be very grave and serious in their rather long speeches.

There were about sixty men in their assembly, without counting the young men who were scattered here and there. Each one getting the best place he could find, a captain began his harangue, the substance of which was that the Huron tribe, the tribe [clan] of the Bear, and others, had met for the purpose of holding a council with the French. When this speech was finished, all the savages, as a sign of their approval, drew from the depths of their stomachs this aspiration, *ho, ho, ho,* raising the last syllable very high. . . . The same captain, continuing his speech, said that all these people were rejoiced at the return of Sieur de Champlain, and that they all came to warm themselves at his fire. The fuel they brought to the fire was two or three packages of beaver skins, which they gave him as a present. . . .

Thereupon Sieur de Champlain began to speak, and told them that he had always loved them, that he wished very much to have them as his brothers, and, having been sent in behalf of our great King to protect them, he would do it very willingly; that he had sent to meet them a bark and a shallop, and that the Iroquois had treacherously killed two or three of our men; that he did not lose heart on that account, that the French feared nothing, and that they cherished their friends very dearly. . . . He added that our Fathers were going to see them in their country, as a proof of the affection which we bore them, telling marvelous things in our favor.

"These are our Fathers," said he, "we love them more than our children or ourselves; they are held in very high esteem in France; it is neither hunger nor want that brings them to this country; they do not want to come to see you for your property or your furs. . . . If you love the French people, as you say you do, then love these Fathers; honor them, and they will teach you the way to Heaven. . . ."

The conclusion of the council was that Father Brébeuf told them, in their language, that we were going with them to live and to die in their country; that they would be our brothers, that hereafter we would be of their people. . . . All the savages, according to their custom, evinced their satisfaction by their profound aspiration: *ho, ho, ho, ho!* Then they surrounded Father Brébeuf, each one wanting to carry him in his boat. Some came to me and touched my hand, saying to each other: "See how much they look alike," speaking of the Father and me. . . .

On the 4th [of August], another council was held; I was present with Father Brébeuf, because the embarkation of our Fathers was to be talked over. . . .

At about ten or eleven o'clock that night, a one-eyed savage belonging to the island tribe, closely allied to the tribe of the prisoner, went among the cabins of all the savages crying out that they should be careful not to take any Frenchmen in their canoes, and that the relatives of the prisoner were on the watch along the river to kill the Frenchmen, if they could catch them during the passage. . . .

At eight or nine in the morning, Sieur de Champlain again assembled the captains of the Hurons, the island savages who had made this outcry, and the captain of the Montagnais. He asked the savage why he had aroused that opposition; he answered that the whole country was in a state of alarm, and that it would be lost if the French were embarked to be taken to the Hurons, for the relatives of the prisoner would not fail to kill some of the party and that thereupon war would be declared; that the Hurons even would be dragged into it; for, if they defended the French, they would be attacked, and that thus the whole country would be lost. . . .

The Hurons were asked if they still adhered to their wish to take us to their country. They answered that the river was not theirs, and that great caution must be observed in regard to those other tribes, if they were to pass by in security. . . .

Now Father Brébeuf, seeing the way closed for that year, addressed the Hurons, saying: "You are our brothers, we wish to go to your country to live and die with you; but, as the river is closed, we shall wait until the coming year, when all will be peaceable. It is you who will sustain the greater loss; because now, as I am beginning to be able to talk to you without an interpreter, I wish to teach you the way to heaven, and to reveal to you the great riches of the other life; but this misfortune deprives you of all these blessings." They replied that they were very sorry, and that a year would very soon pass. . . .

On the first of July [1634], Father Brébeuf and Father Daniel left in a bark to go to Trois Rivières, there to wait for the Hurons. This bark was destined to begin a new settlement in that quarter. Father Davost, who had come down from Tadoussac for the assistance of our French, followed our Fathers three days later. . . .

They waited for some time for the Hurons, who did not come down in so great numbers this year as usual; because the Iroquois, having been informed that five hundred men of this nation were moving toward their country to make war upon them, themselves went on ahead to the number of fifteen hundred, it is said; and, having surprised those who were to surprise them, they killed about two hundred of them, and took more than one hundred prisoners, Louis Amantacha being one of the number. They said his father was put to death, but the report is now that he escaped the hands of the enemy. We were told that these triumphant Iroquois sent some captains to the Hurons to treat for peace, retaining most of the prominent ones in their possession after having cruelly massacred the others.

This loss caused the Hurons to come in small bands, only seven canoes coming down at first. When Father Brébeuf heard of their arrival, he went to them, and did all he could to make them promise to receive him and his companions, and take them to their country. . . .

On the third of August, Monsieur de Champlain, having returned from Trois Rivières, where he had gone after the departure of our Fathers, told us that a French interpreter for the Algonquins had come from the Hurons and brought the tidings that Father Brébeuf was suffering greatly; that his savages were sick, and that he had to paddle continually to relieve them; that Father Daniel had died of starvation, or was in great danger of dying, because the savages who had taken him on board had left the usual route, where they had hidden their food. . . . God be praised for all. Those who die on the way to martyrdom are surely martyrs. . . .

On the fourth, Monsieur du Plessis came down from Trois Rivières. . . . He also told us that they were working with might and main in the place called the Trois Rivières; so, indeed, our French now have three settlements upon the great river Saint Lawrence—one at Quebec, newly fortified; another fifteen leagues farther up the river, on the Island of Saint Croix, where Monsieur de Champlain has had Fort Richelieu built; the third colony being established at Trois Rivières.

AS WORK WENT on at the new French settlements, the colonists feared for the fate of the tiny mission to the Hurons. It would be a treacherous voyage under any circumstances, stretching on for hundreds of miles, fraught with every sort of physical hardship. But this expedition faced particular dangers. The Iroquois, especially the westernmost Seneca, had taken to the warpath with deadly efficiency, dealing the large Huron war party a bitter defeat— and the missionaries could expect to find new ambushes along the way. The tribes between Quebec and the Huron heartland opposed direct contact between the French and this great nation, hoping to preserve their own role as middlemen in the fur trade. And disease struck everywhere—vile outbreaks of smallpox and other illnesses that spread farther and hit harder with every Huron convoy that paddled up the St. Lawrence and back.

Eventually, word came from the missionaries' own leader: Father Jean de Brébeuf, one of the most remarkable priests ever to wear the black robe of a seventeenth-century Jesuit.[25] A man of great strength and greater bravery, he had made a journey to the Hurons once before, and had begun to learn their language. He still had much to learn about their culture, but already he was known among them as someone to be respected. He admired his hosts in return—but he also proved a dogged (and effective) critic of their traditional beliefs.

The selection that follows offers a glimpse of life inside the Huron nation, as the Black Robes established themselves in New France's most important ally. It is a fascinating portrait, depicting a confident people with a rich, ancient culture, still largely untouched by the influence of European ways (sadly, there is only room here for a small excerpt of Brébeuf's engrossing relation). At the end of the Jesuits' harrowing trip, they found a worthy friend for the replanted colony of New France.

Mission to the Hurons
by Jean de Brébeuf

When last year, 1634, we arrived at the Trois Rivières, where the trading post was, we found ourselves in several difficulties and perplexities. For, on the one hand, there were only eleven Huron canoes to embark our ten addi-

[25] The Indians called the priests "black robes" after their clothing.

tional persons who were intending to go into their country. On the other hand, we were greatly in doubt whether any others would descend this year, considering the great loss they had experienced in war with the Iroquois, named *Sonontoerrhonons* [Senecas], last spring, and the fear they had of a new invasion. This placed us much in doubt whether we ought to take advantage of the opportunity which was presented, or wait for a better one.

At last, after full consideration, we resolved to try our fortune, judging that it was of vital importance to have a footing in the country in order to open the door which seemed firmly closed to the Faith. . . . I embarked with Father Antoine Daniel and one of our men; the two others were coming with the Algonquins. Monsieur du Plessis honored our departure with several volleys, to recommend us still more to the savages.

It was the seventh of July. Father Ambroise Davost embarked eight days later, with two others of our people. The rest followed eight days after, to take their part in the fatigues of a journey extremely wearisome, not only on account of its length and of the wretched fare to be had, but also on account of the circuits that have to be made in coming from Quebec to this place. . . . ; I believe that they amount to more than three hundred leagues. It is true the way is shorter by the Sault de St. Louis and the Lake of the Iroquois; but the fear of enemies, and the few conveniences to be met with, cause that route to be unfrequented.

Of two ordinary difficulties, the chief is that of the rapids and portages. . . . All the rivers of this country are full of them, and notably the St. Lawrence. . . . I kept count of the number of portages, and found that we carried our canoes thirty-five times, and dragged them [through dangerous rapids] at least fifty. I sometimes took a hand in helping my savages; but the bottom of the river is full of stones, so sharp that I could not walk long, being barefooted.

The second ordinary difficulty is in regard to provisions. Frequently one has to fast, if he misses the caches that were made when descending; and, even if they are found, one does not fail to have a good appetite after indulging in them; for the ordinary food is only a little Indian corn coarsely broken between two stones, and sometimes taken whole in pure water. It is no great treat. . . . Add to these difficulties that one must sleep on the bare earth, or on a hard rock, for the lack of space ten or twelve feet square on which to place a wretched hut; that one must endure continually the stench of the tired-out savages; and must walk in water, in mud, in the obscurity and entanglement of the forest, where the stings of an infinite number of mosquitoes and gnats are a serious annoyance. I say nothing of the long and wearisome silence to which one is reduced—I mean in the case of newcomers who have, for the time, no person in their company who speaks their own tongue, and who do not understand that of the savages. . . .

Father Davost, among others, was very badly treated. They stole from him much of his little outfit. They compelled him to throw away a little steel mill, and almost all our books, some linen, and a good part of the paper that we were taking, and of which we have great need. They deserted him at the island among the Algonquins, where he suffered in good earnest. When he reached the Hurons, he was so worn out and dejected that for a long time he could not get over it. . . .

Sometimes a word, or a dream, or a fancy, or even the smallest sense of inconvenience is enough to cause them to ill-treat, or set ashore, and I dare say murder one—as happened last year to a poor Algonquin, who was abandoned in a rapid by his own nephew; and, not a month ago, a poor young man, also an Algonquin, having fallen into the fire, was killed near our village by his own tribesmen for fear he might be an inconvenience in the canoe. What makes me believe they killed him is that it is the custom among them. . . .

I attribute, nevertheless, all these extraordinary difficulties to the sickness among our savages. For we know very well how sickness alters the disposition and the inclinations of even the most sociable. I know not at what price our French and the Montagnais will have become rid of it. I know, indeed, that the greater part of the Montagnais who were at the Trois Rivières when we embarked were sick, and that many of them died; and also that almost no one who returned by canoe from trading was not afflicted with this contagion. It has been so universal among the savages of our acquaintance that I do not know if one has escaped its attacks. All these poor people have been much inconvenienced by it, particularly during the autumn, as much in their fishing as in their harvesting. Many crops are lying beneath the snow; a large number of persons are dead; there are still some who have not recovered. . . .

I arrived among the Hurons on the fifth of August, the day of our Lady of the Snows, after being thirty days on the road in continual work, except one day of rest. . . . I set out to find the village, which fortunately I came up on at about three-quarters of a league. . . . As soon as I was perceived in the village, someone cried out, "Why, there is Echom come again" (that is the name they give me); and at once everyone came out to salute and welcome me, each calling me by name and saying, "What, Echom, my nephew, my brother, my cousin, have you then come again?" But without stopping, for night was approaching, I found a place to lodge; and, having rested a short time, I quickly set out with a volunteer band of young people to bring my slender baggage.

It was an hour after sunset when we returned to the village. I lodged with a man named *Aouandoié*, who is, or at least was, one of the richest of the Hurons. I did this on purpose, because another with smaller means might have been inconvenienced with the large number of Frenchmen whom I was expecting, and who had to be provided with food and shelter until we had gathered together, and our cabin was ready. You can lodge where you please; for this nation above all others is exceedingly hospitable toward all sorts of persons, even toward strangers; and you may remain as long as you please, being always well treated according to the fashion of the country. On going away, one acknowledges their hospitality by a *ho, ho, ho, outoécti,* or "many thanks!" at least among themselves; but from Frenchmen they expect some recompense, always at one's discretion. . . .

My host is one of the first in this virtue [of generosity]; and perhaps it is on this account that God has crowned him until now with temporal blessings, and has preserved him among all his fellow countrymen; for their village, named *Teandeouihata,* having been burned twice, each time his house alone has escaped the conflagration. Some attribute this to chance; for myself, I ascribe it to a nobler cause, and so I recall a fine trait, call it prudence or call it humanity, which he displayed on the occasion of the first conflagration. For jealousy having been kindled against him, and some wishing to destroy his cabin that the fire had spared, at once he caused a large cauldron to be hung, prepared a good feast, invited the whole village, and, having assembled them, delivered this harangue: "My brethren, I am very deeply grieved at the misfortune that has happened; but what can we do about it? It is over. For myself, I know not what I have done for Heaven, to be spared before all others. Now, in order to testify to you my deep grief and my desire to share in the common misfortune, I have two bins of corn" (they held at least one hundred to one hundred and twenty bushels); "I give one of them freely to the whole village." This action calmed their jealousy, and put an end to their wicked designs which they were already forming against him. It was a wise action, this losing a part to save the rest. . . .

Being at last all gathered together, we decided to dwell here at *Ihonatiria* [as the village was now called], and to build here our cabin. . . . I cannot better express the fashion of the Huron dwellings than to compare them to bowers or garden arbors—some of which, in place of branches and vegetation, are covered with cedar bark, some others with large pieces of ash, elm, fir, or spruce bark; and although the cedar bark is best, according to common opinion and usage, there is nevertheless, this inconvenience, that they are almost as susceptible to fire as matches. Hence arise many of the conflagrations of entire villages; and, without going farther this year, we have already seen in less than ten days two large ones entirely consumed, and another, that of Louis, partially burned. We have also once seen our own cabin on fire; but, thank God, we extinguished it immediately. . . . There are no different stories; there is no cellar, no chamber, no garret. It has neither window nor chimney, only a miserable hole in the top of the cabin, left to permit the smoke to escape. This is the way they built ours for us. . . .

They never cease coming to visit us from admiration, especially since we have put on two doors, made by a carpenter, and since our mill and our clock have been set to work. . . . As to the clock, a thousand things are said of it. They all think it is some living thing, for they cannot imagine how it sounds of itself; and when it is going to strike, they look to see if we are all there and if someone has not hidden, in order to shake it. They think it hears, especially when, for a joke, some one of our Frenchmen calls out at the last stroke of the hammer, "That's enough," and then it immediately becomes silent. They call it the Captain of the Day. When it strikes, they say it is speaking; and they ask when they come to see us how many times the Captain has already spoken. They ask us about its food; they remain a whole hour, and sometimes several, in order to be able to hear it speak. They used to ask at first what it said. We told them two things that they have remembered very well: one, that when it sounded four o'clock of the afternoon, during winter, it was saying, "Go out, go away that we may close the door," for immediately they arose, and went out. The other, that at midday, it said, *yo eiouahaoua,* that is, "Come, put on the kettle"; and this speech is better remembered than the other, for some of these spongers never fail to come at that hour, to get a share of our sagamité [corn meal]. . . .

It remains now to say something of the country, of the manners and customs of the Hurons. . . . The Huron country is not large, its greatest extent can be traversed in three or four days. Its situation is fine, the greater part of it consisting of plains. It is surrounded and intersected by a number of very beautiful lakes or rather seas, whence it comes that the one to the north and the northwest is called the "freshwater sea" [Lake Huron]. . . . It produces a quantity of very good Indian corn, and one may say that it is the granary of most of the Algonquins. There are twenty towns, which indicate about 30,000 souls speaking the same tongue, which is not difficult for one to master. It has distinction of genders, number, tense, person, moods; and, in short, it is very complete and very regular, contrary to the opinion of many. I am rejoiced to find that this language is common to some twelve other nations, all settled and numerous. . . . The Hurons are friends of all these people, except the *Sonontoerrhonons* [Senecas], *Onontaerrhonons* [Onondagas], *Oüioenrhonons* [Cayugas], *Onoiochrhonons* [Oneidas], and *Agnierrhonons* [Mohawks], all of whom we comprise under the name Iroquois. But they have already made peace with the *Sonontoerrhonons,* since they were defeated by them a year past in the spring. . . .

About the month of December, the snow began to lie on the ground, and the savages settled down in the village. For, during the whole summer and autumn, they are for the most part either in their rural cabins, taking care of their crops, or on the lake fishing, or trading; which makes it not a little inconvenient to instruct them. Seeing them, therefore, thus gathered together at the beginning of this year, we resolved to preach publicly to all, and to acquaint them with the reason of our coming to their country, which is not for their furs, but to declare to them the true God and his son, Jesus Christ, the universal savior of our souls. We gave instruction or catechism in our cabin, for we had as yet no other suitable church. . . . Finally, the whole is concluded [in a typical lesson] by the talk of the old men, who propound their difficulties, and sometimes make me listen in my turn to the statement of their belief. . . .

Our Hurons, as you see, are not so dull as one might think them. They seem to me to have rather good common sense, and I find them universally very docile. Nevertheless, some of them are obstinate, and attached to their superstitions and evil customs. These are principally the old people; for beyond these, who are not numerous, the rest know nothing of their own belief. We have two or three of this number in our village. I am often in conflict with them; and then I show them they are wrong, and make them contradict themselves, so that they frankly admit their ignorance, and the others ridicule them; still they will not yield, always falling back upon this, that their country is not like ours, that they have another god, another paradise, in a word, other customs.

They tell me how the woman, named *Eataentsic,* fell from heaven into the waters with which the earth was covered, and that little by little, the earth became bare. I ask them who created the heaven in which this woman could not stay, and they remain mute; as also when I press them to tell me who formed the earth, seeing that it was beneath the waters before the fall of this woman. One man asked me very cunningly, in this connection, where God was before the creation of the world. The reply was more easy for me, following St. Augustine, than the grasp of the question put to me was for them. Another good old man, having fallen sick, did not wish to hear of going to heaven, saying he desired to go where his ancestors were. . . .

Two things among others have aided us very much in the little we have been able to do here, by the grace of our Lord; the first is, as I have already said, the good health that God has granted us in the midst of sickness so general and so widespread. For our Hurons have thought that, if they believed in God and served him as we do, they would not die in so large numbers. The second is the temporal assistance we have rendered to the sick. . . .

They seek baptism almost entirely as an aid to health. We try to purify this intention, and to lead them to receive from the hand of God alike sickness and health, death and life; and teach them that the life-giving waters of holy baptism principally impart life to the soul, and not to the body. However, they have the opinion so deeply rooted that the baptized, especially the children, are no longer sickly, that soon they will have spread it abroad and published it everywhere. The result is that they are now bringing us children to baptize from two, three, yes, even seven leagues away. . . .

They have a faith in dreams which surpasses all belief. . . . They look upon their dreams as ordinances and irrevocable decrees, the execution of which is not permitted without crime to delay. A savage of our village dreamed this winter, in his first sleep, that he ought straightaway to make a feast; and immediately, night as it was, he arose and came and awakened us to borrow one of our kettles.

The dream is the oracle that all these poor people consult and listen to, the prophet which predicts to them future events, the Cassandra which warns them of misfortunes that threaten them, the usual physician in their sickness, the Asclepius and Galen of their whole country—the most absolute master they have. If a captain [chief] speaks one way and a dream another, the captain might shout his head off in vain—the dream is first obeyed. It is their Mercury in their journeys, their domestic economy in their families. The dream often presides in their councils; trade, fishing, and hunting are undertaken usually under its sanction, and almost as if only to satisfy it. They hold nothing so precious that they would not readily deprive themselves of it for the sake of a dream. . . . In a word, the dream does everything and is in truth the principal God of the Hurons. . . .

We have had this year two alarms, which resulted, thank God, in nothing worse than the fear aroused by the apprehension of enemies. . . . In other ways, however, these fears have not been useless, for besides the prayers and vows we made to turn aside the scourge, the pains each one took to prepare himself for death or slavery, and the opportunity we had to impress upon the savages the help they might expect from God—we were able to win for ourselves the regard and esteem of the people, and to make ourselves useful to them, as well by giving them iron arrowheads as by arranging to assist them in their forts, according to our power. In fact, we had four of our Frenchmen furnished with good harquebuses, who were ready to hasten to the first village where an attack should be made; and I resolved to accompany them, to assist them in spiritual matters. . . .

The Hurons have remained very friendly to us, on account of the promptitude we showed in assisting them. We have told them that henceforth they should make their forts square, and arrange their stakes in straight lines; and that, by means of four little towers at the four corners, four Frenchmen might easily with their arquebuses or muskets defend a whole village. They were greatly delighted with this advice, and have already begun to practice it at [the village the French called] La Rochelle, where they eagerly desire to have some of our Fathers. God employs all means to give an entrance to those who bear the Gospel.

"GOD EMPLOYS ALL means to give an entrance," Brébeuf writes—even if those means are the arts of war. Such things interested the Hurons above all else: they were a fierce people who cherished warrior values, who lived to scourge their enemies. And Brébeuf did not forget that their enemies were also the enemies of New France—the dreaded Five Nations.

And it was this enmity that drew the Jesuits into their most harrowing experience of Huron culture yet. The priests had already passed through remarkable events, many of which do not appear on these pages—notably the Feast of the Dead. Every ten to fifteen years, the people of the village would dig up their dead relatives (some no more than bones, others still rotting), dress them in the finest robes, and give them feasts, treating them as honored guests. Brébeuf, despite the deepest revulsion, made his rounds from house to house, sharing in the ritual. Then the people would strip off the flesh, throw the bones into a pit, and set them all on fire, amid the shrieks and howls of mourning. Even after this stunning spectacle, however, the Black Robes faced something far more disturbing.

In 1636, a Huron war party returned from battle with an Iroquois prisoner. The peace that followed the earlier Seneca victory had ended; this time, the Hurons had won a skirmish, and they brought the fruit of their triumph home. As was traditional, the prisoner was given to a leader who had suffered a loss at the hands of the enemy; it was up to him to decide how the captive should be treated. He could be adopted, for example, as a member of the family; the prisoner would, most likely, abide by such an act, and live and fight loyally as a Huron. Or the prisoner might be slowly tortured to death.

The reader should be aware that the passage that follows graphically depicts an extended scene of physical torture. It is all the more disturbing for the careful, observant detail provided by the writer, a Jesuit assistant to Father Brébeuf. It has been included in this book, however, for a number of important reasons. First, it provides an unvarnished look at this Native American culture, depicting a ritual which can be equated with European practices (as the Indians themselves do, in the pages that follow), but that cannot be glossed over or dismissed. Second, it makes clear the staggering hatred with which these warring nations tore at each other.

Last, and perhaps most important, it ironically reveals the shared culture of the Hurons and Five Nations. This prisoner was treated as he expected to be treated; indeed, as the Hurons point out, any Huron captive would be given the same reception in an Iroquois village. This ritual cruelty actually reveals the *respect* these enemies gave to one another. Note, as you read, that the prisoner was allowed to give a feast, as was traditional for those who were about to die. Note the way his captor spoke to him. Observe also how torture gave him an opportunity to show his bravery and endurance—to die like a warrior. The death depicted here was a brave one indeed, and the Hurons admired it. We can hardly help but shudder.

Torture
by François Joseph le Mercier

On the 2nd of September [1636], we learned that an Iroquois prisoner had been brought to the village of Onnentisati, and that they were preparing to put him to death. This savage was one of eight captured by them at the Lake of the Iroquois, where there were twenty-five or thirty of them fishing; the rest had saved themselves by flight. Not one, they say, would have escaped if our Hurons had not rushed on so precipitately. They brought back only seven, being content to carry off the head of the eighth one. . . .

When the prisoners had arrived in the country, the old men (to whom the young men on their return from war leave the disposition of the spoils) held another assembly, to take counsel among themselves as to the town where each individual prisoner should be burned and put to death, and the persons on whom they should be bestowed; for it is customary, when some notable personage has lost one of his relatives in war, to give him a present of some captive taken from the enemy, to dry his tears and partly assuage his grief.

Now the one who had been destined for this place was brought by the captain Enditsacone to the village of Onnentisati, where the war chiefs held a council and decided that this prisoner should be given to Saouandaouas-couay, who is one of the chief men of the country, in consideration of one of his nephews who had been captured by the Iroquois. This decision being made, he was taken to Arontaen, a village about two leagues distant from us.

At first, we were horrified at the thought of being present at this spectacle; but, having well considered all, we judged it wise to be there, not despairing of being able to win this soul for God. Charity causes us to overlook many considerations. Accordingly, we departed, the Father Superior [Brébeuf], Father Garnier, and I together.

We reached Arontaen a little while before the prisoner, and saw this poor wretch coming in the distance, singing in the midst of thirty or forty savages who were escorting him. He was dressed in a beautiful beaver robe and wore a string of porcelain beads around his neck, and another in the form of a crown around his head. A great crowd was present at his arrival. He was made to sit down at the entrance to the village, and there was a struggle as to who should make him sing.

I will say here that, up to the hour of his torment, we saw only acts of humanity exercised toward him; but he had already been quite roughly handled since his capture. One of his hands was badly bruised by a stone; and one finger was not cut off, but violently wrenched away. The thumb and forefinger of the other hand had been nearly taken off by a blow from the hatchet, and the only plaster he had was some leaves bound with bark. The joints of his arms were badly burned, and in one of them was a deep cut. . . .

Meanwhile, they brought him food from all sides—some bringing saga-mité, some squashes and fruits—and treated him only as a brother and a friend. From time to time he was commanded to sing, which he did with so much vigor and strength of voice that, considering his age, for he seemed to be more than fifty years old, we wondered how he could be equal to it—especially as he had hardly done anything else day and night since his capture, and especially since his arrival in their country. Meanwhile, a captain, raising his voice to the same tone used by those who make some proclamation in public places in France, addressed to him these words: "My nephew, you have good reason to sing, for no one is doing you any harm; behold yourself now among your kindred and friends."

Good God, what a compliment! All those who surrounded him, with their affected kindness and their fine words, were only so many butchers who showed him a smiling face only to treat him afterward with more cruelty.

In all the places through which he had passed he had been given something with which to make a feast; they did not fail here in this act of courtesy, for a dog was immediately put into the kettle, and before it was half cooked, he was brought into the cabin where the people were to gather for the banquet. . . . To see the treatment they accorded him, you might have thought he was the brother and relative of all those who were talking to him. His poor hands caused him great pain, and smarted so severely that he asked to go out of the cabin, to take a little air. His request was immediately granted. His hands were unwrapped, and they brought him some water to refresh them. They were half putrefied, and all swarming with worms, a stench arising from them that was almost insupportable. . . . Meanwhile, he did not cease singing at intervals, and they continued to give him something to eat, such as fruits or squashes.

Seeing that the hour of the feast was drawing near, we withdrew into the cabin where we had taken lodging. . . . We were greatly astonished and much rejoiced when we were told that he was coming to lodge with us. . . . The Father Superior found him so well disposed that he did not consider it advisable to postpone any longer his baptism. He was named Joseph. . . .

In the evening [of the next day] he made a feast, at which he sang and danced, according to the manner of the country, during a good part of the night. . . . The next morning, which was the 4th of September, the prisoner again confirmed his wish to die a Christian, and his desire to go to heaven, and he even promised the Father that he would remember to say, in his torments, "Jesus taïtenir," "Jesus, have pity on me." They were still waiting for the captain Saouandaouascouay, who had gone trading, to fix upon the day and the place for his torment; for this captive was entirely at his disposal. He arrived a little later. . . .

Saouandaouascouay looked at him pleasantly and treated him with incredible gentleness. This is a summary of the talk he had with him: "My nephew, you must know that when I first received news that you were at my disposal, I was wonderfully pleased, fancying that he whom I lost in war had been, as it were, brought back to life, and was returning to this country. At the same time I resolved to give you your life; I was already thinking of preparing you a place in my cabin, and thought that you would pass the rest of your days pleasantly with me. But now that I see you in this condition, your fingers gone and your hands half rotten, I change my mind, and I am sure that you yourself would now regret to live longer. I shall do you a greater kindness to tell you that you must prepare to die; is it not so? It is the Tohontaenras [the clan who injured him] who have treated you so ill, and who also cause your death. Come then, my nephew, be of good courage; prepare yourself for this evening, and do not allow yourself to be cast down through fear of the tortures."

Thereupon Joseph asked him, with a firm and confident mien, what would be the nature of his torment. To this Saouandaouascouay replied that he would die by fire. "That is well," said Joseph, "that is well." While this captain was conversing with him, a woman, the sister of the deceased, brought him some food, showing remarkable solicitude for him. . . . This captain often put his own pipe in the prisoner's mouth, wiped with his own hands the sweat that rolled down his face, and cooled him with a feather fan.

About noon he made his Astataion, that is, his farewell feast, according to the custom of those who are about to die. No special invitations were given, everyone being free to come; the people were there in crowds. Before the feast began, he walked through the middle of the cabin and said in a loud and confident voice, "My brothers, I am going to die; amuse yourselves boldly around me—I fear neither tortures nor death." He straightaway began to sing and dance through the whole length of the cabin; some of the others sang also and danced in their turn. Then food was given those who had plates, and those who had none watched the others eat. The feast over, he was taken back to Arontaen, to die there. . . .

Meanwhile the sun, which was fast declining, admonished us to withdraw to the place where this cruel tragedy was to be enacted. It was the cabin of one Atsan, who is the great war captain; therefore it is called "Otinontsiskiaj ondaon," meaning, "the house of the cut-off heads." It is there all the councils of war are held; as to the house where the affairs of the country, and those which relate only to the observance of order, are transacted, it is called "Endionrra ondaon," "house of the council." We took, then, a place where we could be near the victim, and say an encouraging word to him when the opportunity occurred.

Toward eight o'clock in the evening eleven fires were lighted along the cabin. . . . The people gathered immediately, the old men taking places above, upon a sort of platform which extends, on both sides, the entire length of the cabin. The young men were below, but were so crowded that they were almost piled upon one another, so that there was hardly a passage along the fires. Cries of joy resounded on all sides; each provided himself, one with a firebrand, another with a piece of bark, to burn the victim. Before he was brought in, Captain Aenons encouraged all to do their duty, representing to them the importance of this act, which was viewed, he said, by the sun and by the god of war. He ordered that at first they should burn only his legs, so that he might hold out until daybreak; also for that night they were not to go and amuse themselves in the woods.

He had hardly finished when the victim entered. . . . The cries redoubled at his arrival; he is made to sit down upon a mat, his hands are bound, then he rises and makes a tour of the cabin, singing and dancing; no one burns him at this time, but also this is the limit of his rest—one can hardly tell what he will endure up to the time when they cut off his head. He had no sooner returned to his place than the war captain took up his robe and said, "Oteiondi"—speaking of a captain—"will despoil him of the robe which I hold"; and he added, "The Ataconchronons [a certain clan] will cut off his head, which will be given to Ondessone, with one arm and the liver to make a feast." Behold his sentence thus pronounced.

After this, each one armed himself with a brand, or rather a piece of burning bark, and he began to walk, or rather run, around the fires; each one struggled to burn him as he passed. Meanwhile he shrieked like a lost soul; the whole crowd imitated his cries, or rather smothered them with horrible shouts. One must be there, to see a living picture of Hell. The whole cabin appeared as if on fire; and, athwart the flames and the dense smoke that issued therefrom, these barbarians—crowding one upon the other, howling at the top of their voices, with firebrands in their hands, their eyes flashing with rage and fury—seemed like so many demons who would give no respite to this poor man.

They often stopped him at the other end of the cabin, some of them taking his hands and breaking the bones thereof by sheer force; others pierced his ears with sticks which they left in them; others bound his wrists with cords which they tied roughly, pulling at each end of the cord with all their might. Did he make the round and pause to take a little breath, he was made to repose upon hot ashes and burning coals. . . . As for myself, I was reduced to such a degree that I could hardly nerve myself to look up to see what was going on. . . .

After he had reposed a short time upon the embers, they tried to make him arise as usual, but he did not stir; and one of these butchers having applied a brand to his loins, he was seized with a fainting fit, and would never have risen again if the young men had been permitted to have their way, for they had already begun to stir up the fire about him, as if to burn him. But the captains prevented them from going any farther, and ordered them to cease tormenting him, saying it was important that he should see the daylight. They had him lifted upon a mat, most of the fires were extinguished, and many of the people went away. . . .

At the end of an hour he began to revive a little, and to open his eyes; he was forthwith commanded to sing. He did this at first in a broken and, as it were, dying voice; but finally he sang so loud that he could be heard outside the cabin. The youth assembled again; they began to talk to him, they made him sit up—in a word, they began to act worse than before. For me to describe in detail all he endured during the rest of the night would be almost impossible; we suffered enough in forcing ourselves to see a part of it. Of the rest we judged from their talk; and the smoke issuing from his roasted flesh revealed to us something of which we could not have borne the sight.

One thing, in my opinion, greatly increased his consciousness of suffering—that anger and rage did not appear upon the faces of those who were tormenting him, but rather gentleness and humanity, their words expressing only raillery or tokens of friendship and good will. There was no strife as to who should burn him—each one took his turn; thus they gave themselves leisure to meditate some new device to make him feel the fire more keenly. They hardly burned him anywhere except in the legs, but these, to be sure, they reduced to a wretched state, the flesh being all in shreds. Some applied burning brands to them and did not withdraw them until he uttered loud cries; and, as soon as he ceased shrieking, they again began to burn him, repeating it seven or eight times—often reviving the fire, which they held close against the flesh, by blowing upon it. Others bound cords around him and then set them on fire, thus burning him slowly and causing him the keenest agony. There were some who made him put his feet on red-hot hatchets, and then pressed down on them. You could have heard the flesh hiss, and have seen the smoke which issued therefrom rise even to the roof of the cabin. They struck him with clubs upon the head, and passed small sticks through his ears; they broke the rest of his fingers; they stirred up the fire all around his feet. . . .

But, as I have said, what was most calculated in all this to plunge him into despair, was their raillery, and the compliments they paid him when they approached to burn him. This one said to him, "Here, uncle, I must burn you"; afterward this uncle found himself turned into a canoe. "Come," said he, "let me caulk and pitch my canoe, it is a beautiful new canoe which I lately traded for; I must stop all the water holes well," and meanwhile he was passing the brand all along his legs. Another one asked him, "Come, uncle, where do you prefer that I should burn you?" and this poor sufferer had to indicate some particular place. At this, another one came along and said, "For my part, I do not know anything about burning; it is a trade that I never practiced," and meantime his actions were more cruel than those of the others. In the midst of this heat, there were some who tried to make him believe that he was cold. "Ah, it is not right," said one, "that my uncle should be cold; I must warm you." Another one added, "Now as my uncle has kindly deigned to come and die among the Hurons, I must make him a present, I must give him a hatchet," and with that he jeeringly applied to his feet a red-hot hatchet.

Another one likewise made him a pair of stockings from old rags, which he afterwards set on fire; and often, after having made him utter loud cries, he asked him, "And now, uncle, have you had enough?" And when he replied, "Onna chouatan, onna," "Yes, nephew, it is enough, it is enough," these barbarians replied, "No, it is not enough," and continued to burn him at intervals, demanding of him every time if it was enough. They did not fail from time to time to give him something to eat, and to pour water into his mouth, to make him endure until morning; and you might have seen, at the same time, green ears of corn roasting at the fire and near them red-hot hatchets; and sometimes, almost at the same moment they were giving him the ears to eat, they were putting the hatchets upon his feet. If he refused to eat, "Indeed," said they, "do you think you are the master here?" and some added, "For my part, I believe you were the only captain in your country. But let us see, were you not very cruel to prisoners; now just tell us, did you not enjoy burning them? You did not think you were to be treated in the same way, but perhaps you thought you had killed all the Hurons?" . . .

One thing that consoled us was to see the patience with which he bore all this pain. In the midst of their taunts and jeers, not one abusive or impatient word escaped his lips. Let us add this, that God furnished to the Father Superior [Brébeuf] three or four excellent opportunities to preach his holy name to these barbarians, and to explain to them the Christian truths. . . . "Now now?" retorted some of them, "he is one of our enemies; and it matters not if he go to Hell and if he be forever burned." The Father replied very appropriately, that God was God of the Iroquois as well as that of the Hurons. . . . "But do you think," said another, "that for what you say here, and for what you do to this man, the Iroquois will treat you better if they come sometime to ravage our country?" . . .

"Why are you sorry," added someone, "that we tormented him?"

"I do not disapprove of your killing him, but of your treating him in that way."

"What then! What do you French people do? Do you not kill men?"

"Yes, indeed; we kill them, but not with this cruelty."

"What! Do you never burn any?"

"Not often," said the Father. . . .

All listened very attentively, except some young men, who said once or twice, "Come, we must interrupt him, there is too much talk," and they immediately began to torment the sufferer. He himself also entertained the company for a while, on the state of affairs in his country, and the death of some Hurons who had been taken in war. He did this easily, and with a countenance as composed as anyone there present would have showed. . . .

As soon as day began to dawn, they lighted fires outside the village, to display the excess of their cruelty to the sight of the sun. The victim was led thither. The Father Superior went to his side, to console him, and to confirm him in the willingness he had all the time to die a Christian. He recalled to his mind a shameful act he had been made to commit during his tortures— in which, all things rightly considered, there was but little probability of sin, at least not a grave sin—nevertheless, he had to ask God's pardon for it; and, after having instructed him briefly upon the remission of sins, he gave him conditional absolution, and left him with the hope of soon going to heaven.

Meanwhile, two of them took hold of him and made him mount a scaffold six or seven feet high; three or four of these barbarians followed him. They tied him to a tree which passes across it, but in such a way that he was free to turn around. There they began to burn him more cruelly than ever, leaving no part of his body to which fire was not applied at intervals. . . . They burned his eyes; they applied red-hot hatchets to his shoulders; they hung some around his neck, which they turned now upon his back, now upon his breast, according to the position he took in order to avoid the weight of this burden. If he attempted to sit or crouch down, someone thrust a brand from under the scaffolding which soon caused him to arise. . . .

So they harassed him upon all sides that they finally put him out of breath; they poured water into his mouth to strengthen his heart, and the captains called out to him that he should take a little breath. But he remained still, his mouth open, and almost motionless. Therefore, fearing that he would die otherwise than by the knife, one cut off a foot, another a hand, and almost at the same time a third severed the head from the shoulders, throwing it into the crowd, where someone caught it to carry it to the captain Ondessone, for whom it had been reserved, in order to make a feast therewith. As for the trunk, it remained at Arontaen, where a feast was made of it the same day. We commended his soul to God, and returned home to say Mass. On the way we encountered a savage who was carrying upon a skewer one of his half-roasted hands.

SUCH WERE THE ways of the Hurons and Iroquois, and such was their enmity. The scenes from this chapter could as well have been taken from a Seneca village, or a Mohawk, or an Algonquin; a vast culture zone spread across the northern tier of corn-growing Indian nations, uniting them in customs, language, and war.

By 1636, the northern frontier of European settlement had begun to emerge. The patterns of the next century, more or less, were largely set. Along the seacoast of Cape Cod, an independent collection of Puritan farmers were building a new version of old England, keeping their Indian neighbors at arm's length, at best. Along the St. Lawrence, a handful of Frenchmen, obedient to the crown, raised their outposts in the wilderness, stretching out to meet and unite with Algonquins and Hurons in a strategy of military alliance and cultural unification. And in the mountains between these mortal enemies lived yet another force, the Five Nations of Iroquois, who waged war in every direction.

But these were only a few of the communities that would shape the continent's destiny. The Dutch had also arrived in North America, and planted themselves along the banks of the Hudson—where they would further destabilize this volatile frontier. And there was still the matter of the very first English colony, Virginia. Like Champlain in Quebec, the settlers of Virginia had to replant themselves after a devastating defeat. But where the old soldier of France built his new house on a foundation of Indian alliances, the Virginians would root theirs in tobacco and blood.

III

IN THE LAND OF CANAAN

CONQUEST, CONSOLIDATION, ANNIHILATION

8

TOBACCO AND BLOOD

We have gone too far, too fast. In pursuing the history of Pilgrims and Puritans, of New France, the Hurons, and the Iroquois, we have passed by the bloody tale of Virginia. It is not a story we can afford to miss: in the battered stockade of Jamestown were the beginnings of the great history of Virginia, the province that would shape the American South and much of the continent's history. So we must return to where we left off—even before, in fact—to the moment when Captain John Smith left for England, badly burned and booted out of office.

If we have failed to keep to the chronological context in following Virginia's history, it is only because there is so much of it. The Pilgrims landed, made peace with their neighbors, planted their corn, and worried about repaying their debts. The Puritans landed, made peace with their neighbors, planted their corn, and worried about religious orthodoxy and local politics. But the Virginians—they reeled back and forth between the threats of starvation and destruction, alternately waging war and negotiating with their remarkable opponent, the aged Powhatan.

When Smith departed, so did the precarious balance he had worked out between the dangers of nature and Native Americans. Darkness descended on the colonists; it would take a miracle to save them from their much-deserved annihilation. Remarkably, a miracle they would have.

Smith never returned to his old realm (though he led a voyage of exploration in 1614 along the New England coast). He longed to go back, however; to bolster his claim that he alone could lead the colony, he published a book called *The Generall Historie of Virginia*. The volume was born out of a stroke of genius, when Smith decided to weave together eyewitness accounts with his own writing to provide a history of the colony; though the history that resulted is, needless to say, heavily biased toward the author, it still provides gripping insight into the years 1610 through 1622.

It is hard to describe those years except as a time of peril and adventure. It began with the starving time, when Powhatan sealed his grip on the dying settlement. It continued through the stunning, unexpected reestablishment of Jamestown, when the new governors imposed martial law to bring order out of chaos. It soared with new hope after peace was established—and after colonist John Rolfe discovered that smokeable tobacco thrived in Virginia soil. And it marched on despite the troubles of the Virginia Company back in London, which sent off governor after governor year after year as it drowned in near-bankrupt turmoil.

But the commentary can wait until later. First comes the story of early Virginia as told by the Virginians: beginning with famine, passing through (tobacco) smoke, and ending in blood.

The Generall Historie of Virginia
by Captain John Smith

OUT OF THE OBSERVATIONS OF WILLIAM SIMMONS

The savages no sooner understood Smith was gone, but they all revolted, and did spoil and murder all they encountered. . . . As for corn provision and contribution from the savages, we had nothing but mortal wounds from clubs and arrows. . . . By their cruelty, our governors' indiscretion, and the loss of our ships, of five hundred, within six months after Captain Smith's departure, there remained not past sixty men, women, and children, most miserable and poor creatures. And those were preserved for the most part by roots, herbs, acorns, walnuts, berries, now and then a little fish; they that had starch in these extremities made no small use of it; yea, even the very skins of our horses.

Nay, so great was our famine, that a savage we slew and buried, the poorer sort took him up again and [did] eat him; and so diverse one another boiled and stewed with roots and herbs. And one amongst the rest did kill his wife, powdered [salted] her, and had eaten part of her before it was known; for which he was executed, as he well deserved. Now whether she was better roasted, boiled, or carbonadoed, I know not; but of such a dish as powdered wife I never heard of.

This was that time, which still to this day we called the starving time; it were too vile to say, and scarce to be believed, what we endured; but the occasion was our own, for want of providence, industry, and government, and not the barrenness and defect of the country, as is generally supposed. . . . Yet had we been even in paradise itself with these governors, it would not have been much better with us. . . . In ten days more, [they] would have supplanted us all with death.

But God . . . [and the company] sent Sir Thomas Gates and Sir George Sommers with one hundred and fifty people most happily preserved by the Bermudas to preserve us [arriving on May 23, 1610]. . . . When these two noble knights did see our miseries, being but strangers in that country, and could understand no more of the cause, but by conjecture of our clamors and complaints, of accusing and excusing one another. They embarked us with themselves, and with the best means they could, and abandoned Jamestown, set sail for England. . . .

At noon they fell to the Isle of Hogs, and the next morning to Mulberry Point, at what time they descried the long boat of the Lord De la Warr; for God would not have it so abandoned. For this honorable Lord, then [the new] governor of the country, met them with three ships exceedingly well furnished with all necessaries fitting; who again returned them to the abandoned Jamestown.

THE GOVERNMENT DEVOLVED TO LORD DE LA WARR, BY WILLIAM BOX

His Lordship arrived the ninth of June 1610, accompanied with . . . diverse other gentlemen of sort; the tenth he came up with his fleet, went on shore, heard a sermon, read [aloud] his commission, and entered into consultation for the good of the colony; in which secret council we will a little leave them, that we may duly observe the revealed counsel of God. . . .

Never had any people more just cause to cast themselves at the very footstool of God, and to reverence his mercy, than this distressed colony; for if God had not sent Sir Thomas Gates from the Bermudas, within four days they had almost been famished. . . . If they had abandoned the fort any longer time, and had not so soon returned, questionless the Indians would have destroyed the fort, which had been the means of our safety amongst them and a terror. If they had set sail sooner, and had launched into the vast ocean, who would have promised they should have encountered the fleet of the Lord la Warr; especially when they made for Newfoundland, as intended, a course contrary to our navy approaching. If the Lord la Warr had not brought with him a year's provision, what comfort would those poor souls have received, to have been relanded to a second destruction? This was the arm of the Lord of Hosts, who would have his people pass the Red Sea and wilderness, and then to possess the land of Canaan. . . .

The Lord Governor, after mature deliberation, delivered some few words to the company, laying just blame upon them for their haughty vanities and sluggish idleness, earnestly entreating them to amend those desperate follies lest he should be compelled to draw the sword of justice and to cut off such delinquents . . . ; heartening them with relation of that store he had brought with him, constituting officers of all conditions to rule over them, allotting every man his particular place, to watch vigilantly, and work painfully.

This oration and direction being received with a general applause, you might shortly behold the idle and resty diseases of a divided multitude, by the unity and authority of this government, to be substantially cured. . . .

The houses which are built are as warm and defensive against wind and weather as if they were tiled and slated, being covered above with strong boards, and some matted round with Indian mats. Our forces are now such as are able to tame the fury and treachery of the savages; our forts assure the inhabitants and frustrate all assailants. . . .

The other comfort is that the Lord De la Warr hath built two new forts, the one called Fort Henry, the other Fort Charles, in honor of our most noble prince and his hopeful brother, upon a pleasant plain and near a little rivulet they call Southampton River. . . . And Sir Thomas Gates he sent for England [on July 15, 1610]. . . . Not long after, his Honor growing very sick, he returned for England the 28th of March. . . .

OUT OF MASTER HAMOR'S BOOK

Before Lord la Warr arrived in England, the Council and Company had dispatched away Sir Thomas Dale with three ships, men, and cattle, and all other provisions necessary for a year; all of which arrived well [on] the tenth of May, 1611. Where he found them growing again to their former state of penury, being so improvident as not to put corn in the ground for their bread, but trusted to the store, then furnished but with three months' provisions. His first care therefore was to employ all hands about setting [planting] of corn, at the two forts at Kecoughtan, Henry and Charles; whereby, the season then not fully past, though about the end of May, we had an indifferent crop of good corn.

This business taken order for, and the care and trust of it committed to his under-officers, to Jamestown he hastened, where most of the company were at their daily and usual work, bowling in the streets. These he employed about necessary work, as felling of timber, repairing their houses ready to fall on their heads, and providing pales [palisades], posts, and rails to impale his purposed new town, which by reason of his ignorance, being but newly arrived, with one hundred men he spent some time in viewing the River of Nansemond, in despite of the Indians then our enemies; then our own river to the falls, where upon a high land, environed with the main river, some twelve miles from the falls, by Arsahattock, he resolved to plant his new town.

It was no small trouble to reduce his people so timely to good order, being of so ill a condition, as may well witness his severity and strict imprinted book of articles, then needful with all extremity to be executed, now much mitigated. . . .

Now in England again, to second this noble knight, the Council and Company with all possible expedition prepared for Sir Thomas Gates six tall ships, with three hundred men, and one hundred kine and other cattle, with munition and all other manner of provision that could be thought needful; and about the first or second of August, 1611, arrived safely at Jamestown.

THE GOVERNMENT RETURNED AGAIN TO SIR THOMAS GATES, 1611

These worthy knights being met, after their welcoming salutations, Sir Thomas Dale acquainted him with what he had done, and what he intended; which design Sir Thomas Gates well approving, furnished him with three hundred and fifty men, such as himself made choice of. In the beginning of September, 1611, he set sail, and arrived where he intended to build his new town. Within ten or twelve days he had environed it with a pale [palisade], and in honor of our noble Prince Henry, called it Henrico. The next work he did was building at each corner of the town a high commanding watchhouse, a church, and storehouses; which finished, he began to think upon convenient houses for himself and men, which with all possible speed he could afford, he affected, to the great content of his company, and all the colony. . . .

But to conclude our peace, thus it happened. Captain Argall, having entered into a great acquaintance with Japazaws, an old friend of Captain Smith's, and so to all our nation ever since he discovered the country, heard by him there was Pocahontas, whom Captain Smith's relations entitleth the nonpareil of Virginia; and though she had been many times a preserver of him and the whole colony, yet till this accident she was never seen at Jamestown since his departure. . . . Thinking herself unknown, [she] was easily by her friend Japazaws persuaded to go abroad with him and his wife to see the ship; for Captain Argall had promised him a copper kettle to bring her but to him, promising no way to hurt her, but keep her till they could conclude a peace with her father. . . .

For though she had seen and been in many ships, yet he caused his wife to fain how desirous she was to see one, that he offered to beat her for her importunity, still she wept. But at last he told her, if Pocahontas would go with her, he was content. And thus they betrayed the poor innocent Pocahontas aboard, where they were all kindly feasted in the cabin. . . . The captain when he saw his time, persuaded Pocahontas to the gun room, faining to have some conference with Japazaws, which was only that she should not perceive he was anyway guilty of her captivity; so sending for her again, he told her before her friends, she must go with him, and compound peace betwixt her country and us, before she ever should see Powhatan. . . .

A messenger forthwith was sent to her father, that his daughter Pocahontas he loved so dearly he must ransom with our men,[1] swords, pieces, tools, etc., he treacherously had stolen. This unwelcome news much troubled Powhatan, because he loved both his daughter and our commodities well, yet it was three months after [in July 1613] ere he returned us any answer. Then by the persuasion of the council, he returned seven of our men,

[1] The English living with Powhatan were not prisoners; during and since the starving time, a number left the settlements to join the Indians—which incensed the English settlers who stayed behind.

with each of them an unserviceable musket, and sent us word that when we would deliver his daughter, he would make us satisfaction for all injuries done us, and give us five hundred bushels of corn, and forever be friends with us. That he sent, we received in part of payment, and returned him this answer: That his daughter should be well used, but we could not believe the rest of our arms were either lost or stolen from him, and therefore till he sent them, we would keep his daughter.

This answer, it seemed, much displeased him, for we heard no more from him for a long time after; when with Captain Argall's ship, and some other vessels belonging to the colony, Sir Thomas Dale with a hundred and fifty men well appointed went up into his own river [the York], to his chief habitation, with his daughter. With many scournfull bravadoes they affronted us, proudly demanding why we came thither. Our reply was, we had brought his daughter, and to receive the ransom for her that was promised, or to have it perforce. They nothing dismayed thereat, told us, we were welcome if we came to fight, for they had provided for us; but advised us, if we loved our lives, to retire, else they would use us as they had done Captain Ratcliffe. We told them, we would presently have a better answer; but we were no sooner within shot of the shore than they let fly their arrows among us in the ship.

Being thus justly provoked, we presently manned our boats, went on shore, burned all their houses, and spoiled all we could find. And so the next day proceeded higher up the river, where they demanded why we burnt their houses, and we, why they shot at us. They replied, it was some straggling savage, with many other excuses, they intended no hurt, but were our friends. We told them, we came not to hurt them, but visit them as friends also. Upon this we concluded a peace, and forthwith they dispatched messengers to Powhatan. . . .

Then we went higher, to a house of Powhatan's called Matchot [on the Pamunkey River], where we saw about four hundred men well appointed; here they dared us to come on shore, which we did; no show of fear they made at all, nor offered to resist our landing, but walking boldly up and down amongst us, demanded to confer with our captain, of his coming in that manner, and to have truce till they could but once more send to their king to know his pleasure, which if it were not agreeable to their expectations, then they would fight with us, and defend their own as they could. Which was but only defer the time, to carry away their provisions; yet we promised them truce till the next day at noon, and then if they would fight with us, they should know when we would begin by our drums and trumpets.

Upon this promise, two of Powhatan's sons came unto us to see their sister; at whose sight, seeing her well, though they heard to the contrary, they much rejoiced, promising they would persuade her father to redeem her, and forever to be friends with us. And upon this, the two brethren went aboard with us; and we sent Master John Rolfe and Master Sparkes to Powhatan, to acquaint him with the business; kindly they were entertained, but not admitted [to] the presence of Powhatan, but they spoke with Opechancanough, his brother and successor; he promised to do the best he could to Powhatan, all might be well. So, it being April and time to prepare our ground and set our corn, we returned to Jamestown, promising the forbearance of their performing their promise till the next harvest.

Long before this, Master John Rolfe, an honest gentleman and of good behavior, had been in love with Pocahontas, and she with him; which thing at that instant I made known to Sir Thomas Dale by a letter from him, wherein he entreated his advice, and she acquainted her brother with it, which resolution Sir Thomas Dale well approved. . . . This marriage came soon to the knowledge of Powhatan, a thing acceptable to him, as appeared by his sudden consent; for within ten days he sent Opachisco, an old uncle of hers, and two of his sons to see the manner of the marriage, and to do in that behalf what they were requested, for the confirmation thereof, as his deputy; which was accordingly done about the fifth of April [1614]. And ever since we have had friendly trade and commerce, as well with Powhatan himself as all his subjects. . . .

THE GOVERNMENT LEFT TO CAPTAIN YEARDLEY

Master George Yeardley now invested [as] Deputy Governor by Sir Thomas Dale, applied himself for the most part in planting tobacco, as the most present [likely] commodity they could devise for . . . present gain, so that every man betook himself to the best place he could for the purpose. Now though Sir Thomas Dale had caused an abundance of corn be planted, that every man had sufficient, yet . . . [the new colonists that] were sent us came so unfurnished, as quickly eased us of our superfluity. To relieve their necessities, he sent to the [Indians for corn]. . . .

This put all the rest of the savages in that fear, especially in regard of the great league we had with Opechancanough, that we followed our labors quietly, and in such security that diverse savages of other nations daily frequented us with what provisions they could get, and would guide our men on hunting, and oft hunt for us. Captain Yeardley had a savage or two so well trained up to their pieces, they were as expert as any of the English, and one he kept purposely to kill him fowl. There were diverse others had savages in like manner for their men. Thus we lived together, as if we had been one people, all the time Captain Yeardley stayed with us. . . . Captain Yeardley returned for England in the year 1617.

FROM THE WRITINGS OF CAPTAIN NATHANIEL POWELL,
WILLIAM CANTRILL, SERGEANT BOOTHE, EDWARD GURGANEY

During this time, the Lady Rebecca, alias Pocahontas, daughter to Powhatan, by the diligent care of Master John Rolfe her husband, and his
friends, was taught to speak such English as might be well understood; well
instructed in Christianity, as was become very formal and civil after our English manner. She also had by him a child which she loved most dearly, and
the treasurer and company took order both for the maintenance of her and
it; besides there were diverse persons of great rank and quality had been very
kind to her. And before she arrived at London, Captain Smith . . . made her
qualities known to the Queen's most excellent majesty and her court, and
writ a little book. . . .

Being about this time[2] preparing to sail for New England, I could not
stay to do her that service I desired, and she well deserved; but hearing she
was at Branford with diverse of my friends, I went to see her. After a modest salutation, without any word she turned about, obscured her face, as
not seeming well contented; and in that humor her husband, and diverse
others, we all let her two or three hours, repenting myself to have writ [as]
she could speak English.[3] But not long after, she began to talk, and remembered me well what courtesies she had done, saying, "You did
promise Powhatan what was yours should be his, and he the like to you.
You called him father, being in his land a stranger, and by the same reason
so must I do you." Which though I would have excused, I durst not allow
that title, because she was a king's daughter. With a set countenance she
said:

> Were you not afraid to come into my father's country, and caused
> fear in him and all his people (but me), and fear you here I should
> call you father; I tell you then I will, and you shall call me child,
> and so I will be for ever and ever your countryman. They did tell
> us always you were dead, and I knew no other till I came to Plym-
> outh [England]; yet Powhatan did command Uttamatomakkin to
> seek you and know the truth, because your countrymen will lie
> much.

This savage [Uttamatomakkin], one of Powhatan's council, being
amongst them held an understanding fellow, the king purposely sent him, as
they say, to number the people here, and inform him well what we were and
our state. Arriving at Plymouth, according to his directions, he got a long

---

[2] This and the next two paragraphs seem to have been written by Smith.
[3] It seems from this odd exchange that Smith addressed Pocahontas in her native language, which (striving to be English herself) she refused to speak.

stick, whereon by notches he did think to have kept the number of all the men he could see, but he was quickly weary of that task. . . .[4]

THE GOVERNMENT DEVOLVED TO CAPTAIN SAMUEL ARGALL, 1617
BY SAMUEL ARGALL AND JOHN ROLFE

The Treasurer [leader of the colony], council, and company, having well furnished Captain Samuel Argall, the Lady Pocahontas alias Rebecca, with her husband and others, [set sail] in the good ship called *George*. It pleased God at Gravesend to take this young lady to his mercy, where she made not more sorrow for her unexpected death, than joy to the beholders to hear and see her make so religious and godly an end. Her little child Thomas Rolfe therefore was left at Plymouth with Sir Lewis Stukly, that desired the keeping of it. . . .

In March they set sail, 1617, and in May he [Argall] arrived at Jamestown, where he was kindly entertained by Captain Yeardley and his company [who marched] in a martial order, whose right-hand file was led by an Indian. In Jamestown he found but five or six houses, the church [fallen] down, the palisades broken, the bridge in pieces, the well of fresh water spoiled; the storehouse they used for the church; the marketplace and streets, and all other spare places planted with tobacco. The savages [were] as frequent in their houses as themselves, whereby they were become expert in our arms, and had a great many in their custody and possession; the colony dispersed all about, planting tobacco.

Captain Argall, not liking these proceedings, altered them [to be] agreeable to his own mind, taking the best order he could for repairing those defects which did exceedingly trouble us. . . .

A RELATION BY MASTER JOHN ROLFE

Concerning the state of our new commonwealth, it is somewhat bettered, for we have sufficient to content ourselves, though not in such abundance as is vainly reported in England. Powhatan died this last April [1618], yet the Indians continue in peace. . . .

For to begin with the year of our Lord, 1619, there arrived a little pinnace privately from England about Easter for Captain Argall; who, taking order for his affairs, within four or five days returned in her, and left for his deputy, Captain Nathaniel Powell. On the eighteenth of April, which was but ten or twelve days after, arrived Sir George Yeardley [to serve as governor]. . . .

---

[4] After this the narrative seems to return to Smith's sources.

An industrious man not otherwise employed may well tend four acres of corn and 1,000 plants of tobacco; and where they say an acre will yield three or four barrels, we have ordinarily four or five, but of new ground six, seven, and eight . . . so that one man may provide corn for five, and apparel for two, by the profit of his tobacco. . . .

The 25th of June came in the *Triall* with corn and cattle all in safety, which took from us clearly all fear of famine; then our governor and council caused Burgesses to be chosen in all places, and met at a general assembly where all matters were debated [that were] thought expedient for the good of the colony. . . . About the last of August came in a Dutch man of war that sold us twenty niggers. . . .[5]

COLLECTED OUT OF THE COUNCIL'S LETTERS FOR VIRGINIA

The instructions and advertisements for this year [1621] were . . . much like the last; only whereas before they ever had a suspicion of Opechancanough, and all the rest of the savages, [and] they kept an eye over him more than any, but now they all write so confidently of their assured peace with the savages, [and that] there is now no more fear nor danger either of their power or treachery; so that every man planteth himself where he pleaseth, and followeth his business securely. . . .

THE MASSACRE UPON THE TWO AND TWENTIETH OF MARCH, BY MASTER JOHN PORY

[The new governor] Sir Francis Wyatt, at his arrival [in October 1621] . . . found the country settled in such a firm peace, as most men there thought sure and unviolable, not only in regard of their [the Indians'] promises, but of a necessity. The poor weak savages being every way bettered by us, and safely sheltered and defended, whereby we might freely follow our business. And such was the conceit of this conceited peace, as that there was seldom or never a sword, and seldomer a piece, except for a deer or fowl; by which assurances the most plantations were placed stragglingly and scatteringly, as a choice vein of rich ground invited them, and further from neighbors the better. The houses generally [were] open to the savages, who were always friendly fed at their tables, and lodged in their bed chambers; which made the way plain to . . . the conversion of the savages as they supposed.

Having occasion to send to Opechancanough about the middle of March, he used the messenger well, and told him he held the peace so firm, the sky should fall ere he dissolved it. Yet such was the treachery of those

[5] The Dutch ship brought the first African slaves to North America.

people, when they had contrived our destruction, even but two days before the massacre . . . they borrowed our boats to transport themselves over the river, to consult on the devilish murder that ensued, and of our utter extirpation. . . .

And as well on the Friday morning, that fatal day, being the two and twentieth of March, as also in the evening before, as at other times they came unarmed into our houses, with deer, turkeys, fish, fruits, and other provisions to sell us. Yea, in some places [they] sat down at breakfast with our people, whom immediately with their own tools they slew most barbarously, not sparing either age or sex, man, woman, or child; so sudden in their execution, that few or none discerned the weapon or blow that brought them to destruction. In which manner they slew many of our people at several works in the fields, well knowing in what places and quarters each of our men were, in regard of their familiarity with us. . . .

And by this means fell that fatal morning under bloody and barbarous hands of that perfidious and inhumane people, three hundred forty-seven men, women, and children; mostly by their own weapons. And not being content with their lives, they fell again upon the dead bodies, making as well as they could a fresh murder, defacing, dragging, and mangling their dead carcasses into many pieces, and carrying some parts away in derision, with base and brutish triumphs. Neither yet did these beasts spare those amongst the rest well known unto them, from whom they had daily received many benefits; but spitefully also massacred them without any remorse or pity. . . .

Almighty God[6] hath his great work in this tragedy, and will thereout draw honor and glory to his name, and a more flourishing estate and safety to themselves, and with more speed to convert the savage children to himself, since he so miraculously hath preserved the English; there being yet, God be praised, eleven parts of twelve remaining,[7] whose careless neglect of their own safeties seems to have been the greatest cause of their destructions. Yet you see, God by a converted savage that disclosed the plot saved the rest. . . .

The letters of Master George Sands, a worthy gentleman, and many others besides . . . brought us this unwelcome news, that hath been heard at large in public court, that the Indians and they lived as one nation; yet by a general combination in one day plotted to subvert the whole colony, and at one instant, though our several plantations were one hundred and forty miles upon [the James] River on both sides. But for the better understanding of all things, you must remember these wild, naked savages live not in great numbers together; but dispersed, commonly in thirty, forty, fifty, or sixty in a company. Some places have two hundred, few places more, but

---

[6] It seems that this and the next two paragraphs were written largely by Smith.

[7] Actually on March 22, 1622, the Indians killed 347 out of 1,240 colonists, leaving 893—far less than eleven out of every twelve.

many less; yet they had all warning given them from one another in all their habitations, though far asunder, to meet at the day and hour appointed for our destruction at all our several plantations. Some directed to one place, some to another, all to be done at the time appointed, which they did accordingly. Some entering their houses under color of trading, so took their advantage; others drawing us abroad under fair pretences; and the rest suddenly falling upon those that were at their labours. . . .

Thus have you heard the particulars of this massacre, which in those respects some will say be good for the plantation, because now we have just cause to destroy them [the Indians] by all means possible; but I think it had been much better had it never happened, for they have given us a hundred times as just occasions long ago to subject them. . . . The manner how to suppress them is so often related and approved, I omit it here. And you have twenty examples of the Spaniards, how they got the West Indies, and forced the treacherous and rebellious infidels to do all manner of drudgery work and slavery for them, themselves living like soldiers upon the fruits of their labors. This will make us circumspect, and be an example to posterity. . . . What growing state was there ever in the world which had not the like? Rome grew by oppression, and rose upon the backs of her enemies. . . .

This lamentable and so unexpected a disaster . . . drove them all to their wit's end. It was twenty or thirty days ere they could resolve what to do, but at last it was concluded, all the petty plantations should be abandoned, and drawn only to make good five or six places, where all their labors now for the most part must redound to the Lords of those lands where they were resident. Now for want of boats, it was impossible upon such a sudden to bring also their cattle and many other things, which with much time, charge, and labor they had then in possession with them; all which for the most part at their departure was burnt, ruined, or destroyed by the savages. . . .

Amongst the rest of the plantations all this summer little was done, but securing themselves and planting tobacco, which passes there as current silver, and by the oft turning and winding it, some grow rich, but many poor. Notwithstanding ten or twelve ships more hath arrived there since the massacre. . . .

To lull them the better in security, they sought no revenge till their corn was ripe, then they drew together three hundred of the best soldiers they could, that would leave their private business, and adventure themselves amongst the savages to surprise their corn, under the conduct of Sir George Yeardley, being embarked in convenient shipping, and all things necessary for the enterprise. They went first to Nansemond, where the people set fire on their own houses, and spoiled what they could, and then fled with what they could carry; so that the English did make no slaughter amongst them for revenge. Their corn fields being newly gathered, they surprised all they found, burnt the houses [that] remained unburnt, and so departed. . . .

Thence they sailed to Pamunkey, the chief seat of Opechancanough, the contriver of the massacre. The savages seemed exceeding fearful, promising to bring them Sara [Boys, a captive], and the rest of the English yet living, with all the arms, and what they had to restore, much desiring peace, and to give them any satisfaction they could. Many such devices they fained to procrastinate the time ten or twelve days, till they had got away their corn from all the other places up the river. . . .

At last, when they [the English] saw all those promises were but delusions, they seized on all the corn there was, set fire on their houses; and in following the savages that fled before them, some few of those naked devils [that] had that spirit, they lay in ambuscade, and as our men marched discharged some shot out of English pieces, and hurt some of them flying at their pleasures where they listed, burning their empty houses before them as they went, to make themselves sport. So they escaped, and Sir George returned with corn, where for our pains we had three bushels apiece. . . . Thus by this means the savages are like, as they report, to endure no small misery this winter, and that some of our men are returned to their former plantations.

———

IT WAS AS if Jamestown lay under a curse that bound Opechancanough to strike, despite prosperity, despite friendship, despite alliance. It was as if the soil of Virginia must be watered in blood. Indeed, the colony's cycle of treachery and murder would not end until Jamestown itself was destroyed, more than fifty years later.

But the true cycle of history here was one of pressure, repaid by slaughter, redeemed in fire. Each year, Powhatan's brother and heir had watched as the English flooded ashore. And there seemed to be no end: he had probably heard (and now believed) the report of Uttamatomakkin, who had been unable to number these remarkable, disturbing people in their home island. Meanwhile, past wars and present disease had reduced his people, until the Powhatans counted themselves a fraction of their old strength. Under these circumstances, the chief who had once felt Captain John Smith's pistol against his breastbone knew what to do: he would utterly destroy his enemies, with such terror that no more would come.

Opechancanough's plan came so close to success: the Indians killed a third of the colonists, and burned to the ground scores of plantations and settlements. Yet the English kept coming—this time, without mercy or restraint. In a wave of bloody raids, the men of Jamestown took their revenge, destroying the power of the Powhatans.

Among the hundreds of bodies that littered the fields of Virginia in that terrible year, there was one the Indians and the English knew equally well. His name was John Rolfe; he was the man who had fallen in love with Pocahontas, who had sealed the long peace between her father and Jamestown. He was the one who first planted smokeable tobacco in Virginia, and who first exported a batch in 1613. He was the one who began the great nicotine empire—perhaps the first time in history an economy rose purely on the export of an addictive drug.

John Rolfe, in his own quiet way, was as much the father of Virginia as John Winthrop was of New England. His initiative—and his rich profits—sparked the explosive growth of the colony. Exports of the leaf rose from 2,000 pounds in 1615 to 60,000 pounds four years later; and immigration climbed, as more than 3,700 walked off the ships to Virginia between 1619 and 1622 alone. Most were indentured servants, bound to work on tobacco plantations until their multiyear terms expired, or until they died. In Virginia's fever-ridden climate, these hard-worked souls usually died. But the tobacco craze went on, leading King James himself (always eager to lecture his subjects) to publish his *Counter Blaste to Tobacco*.

No sooner were the Indians beaten back, but the work of clearing and planting went on, as ship after ship landed servants and returned with cargoes of leaves. Powhatan's empire disintegrated as the kingdom of tobacco grew. Within fifteen years of its founding, Virginia had begun to acquire a society of great land-owning squires with pretensions to aristocracy; and beneath them, men and women who worked until death took them, or until they could be free to flee for the land around the edges of the great tobacco estates.

But there was one very significant change that resulted from Opechancanough's great blow: the crown swept away the Virginia Company, assuming direct rule of the colony through an appointed governor and a council. James I and his son Charles never managed to establish royal absolutism in troublesome England, where Parliament obstructed them; but Virginia would be their refuge, where the power of the prince would know few limits. Of course, there was that matter of the Burgesses, the popular assembly in Jamestown. It did not fit with the king's ideas of royal power (even though it was elected by a small minority of men). So the crown simply ignored its existence. Small, representative institutions in America were not something for the king to worry about.

9

PEQUOTS AND DISSIDENTS

In the first chapter of the book of Joshua, God commands the young prophet to carry out the unfulfilled mission of Moses: "Now therefore rise," He thunders, "go over this Jordan, thou, and all this people, unto the land which I do give to them, even to the children of Israel." Such was the mission that possessed John Winthrop in the raw settlement of Boston in 1633. Aristocratic though he was, in bearing if not in birth, he might hesitate to equate himself with Joshua (Winthrop, for example, would never lead an army, nor wish to). Yet he and all the Puritans of New England saw themselves as the new people of Israel—not in metaphor, but in fact. And this continent was to be their land of Canaan.

The book of Joshua also details precisely *how* the children of Israel took possession of that promised land. The scriptures summarize as follows: "So Joshua smote all the country of the hills, and of the south, and of the vale, and of the springs, and all their kings: he left none remaining, but utterly destroyed all that breathed, as the Lord God of Israel commanded." And along with external enemies, there was always the bad seed sown among them. Achor and his family, errant children of Israel, strayed against the Lord's command; we read, "And Joshua said, Why has thou troubled us? The Lord shall trouble thee this day. And all Israel stoned him with stones, and burned them with fire, after they had stoned them with stones."

Within five years of the founding of Massachusetts, John Winthrop could feel certain that the words of scripture described God's plan for his Puritans as much as it did the history of ancient Israel. During that brief span, he and his fellows waged one war of annihilation and another of purification, simultaneously battling some of the greatest external and internal threats the colony would ever face. These perils would drive the pious yet practical Winthrop to his wit's end: he would try fasting and prayer, lobbying and bargaining, political maneuvering and cold, hard edicts. In the end he would triumph, but the colony would be left shaken, divided, exhausted.

The external dangers hovered over the colony both to the south and the east. From across the Atlantic lurked the danger of a royal usurpation. King Charles I continued to tighten his pressure on the Puritans in England, as Archbishop William Laud enforced the new Arminian orthodoxy within the church. Laud also pressed Charles's plan to assert himself in New England, as he already had in Virginia. The Massachusetts charter came under attack; and to top it all off, Sir Fernando Gorges, of the Council for New England, sought to assert his own claims over what the Puritans had built.

Such threats were more potential than real, however. The most serious problem dwelled on North American shores, below the Puritan frontier. There the powerful tribe known as the Pequots sat astride the Connecticut River. They had only recently arrived in the area, and already they had made enemies of the Narragansetts, the nation that dominated the great bay west of Plymouth and south of Massachusetts. The Narragansetts had been careful to maintain courteous relations with the Puritans and Pilgrims alike, and sought to draw the English into this inter-Indian conflict. More important to the Boston government, however, were the Puritan colonists who had begun settlements on the Connecticut banks, and Saybrook, the new fort at the river's mouth, commanded by none other than John Winthrop, Jr. In the early 1630s, tensions between these self-styled children of Israel and these warlike Canaanites, the proud Pequots, rose toward an explosion.

Then there was the internal problem—or problems, for they were many. There was still the cantankerous Mr. Dudley, who argued that the practical Winthrop was too lenient in governing the colony. Dudley should not have worried: though the oft-protesting deputy soon became governor himself, Winthrop's turn would come again, and this time his patience would be tested by the greatest outbreak of political dissent in the colony's brief history.

First came Roger Williams, a man who impressed all with his holiness. In fact, he soon proved too holy for everyone. No one ever measured up to Mr. Williams's standards of unworldliness; what pushed the authorities over the edge, however (which never took very much in any case), was his argument that the settlers could not hold their lands from the king, but only from open agreements with the original inhabitants. This was a bit too reasonable for men such as Winthrop, who had granted themselves large holdings out of Indian lands— lands that would have been opened by force, if smallpox had not done the job.

Then there was Anne Hutchinson. We do not get a well-rounded portrait of this remarkable woman in Winthrop's journal; she lurks in the background, her passion and eloquence and force of mind evidenced by the ferocity of her adherents. She was a prophet, one well suited to this new Israel. These were a people who had thrown all away, who had risked their lives to cross an ocean to practice the purest form of worship they knew; small wonder that they eagerly listened to an even purer version, as taught in private rooms in Boston houses by the charismatic Mrs. Hutchinson. She even drew in young Henry Vane, who served as governor one year, and John Cotton, the second minister of the Boston congregation.

To have a woman teaching was bad enough; Winthrop might be practical, but he firmly believed in the sanctity of authority, which meant *male* authority. Even worse, Anne Hutchinson's teachings began to veer dangerously off the Christian page, even off the farthest Calvinist margins. The doctrine of God's grace began to twist into a secret knowledge which only she held—all else, even Winthrop's Puritanism, was a popish "gospel of works" that denied God's supremacy. Such teachings swept Boston, but the other towns looked on with growing hostility.

These were the threats that besieged New England, rising steadily to a crisis of dissension within and war without. The patient, practical Winthrop disappeared; now he emerged as an exasperated, authoritative leader, willing to engineer the seizure of power if necessary. To him and his many followers, the colony faced extinction, both temporal and spiritual. If they were truly to receive this promised land of Canaan, they must act as Joshua acted, and utterly destroy all that breathed.

Dissension and War
by John Winthrop

November 1633.] The ministers in the bay . . . did meet, once a fortnight, at one of their houses by course, where some question of moment was debated. Mr. Skelton, the pastor of Salem, and Mr. [Roger] Williams, who was removed from Plymouth thither (but not in any office, though he exercised [influence] by way of prophecy [preaching]), took some exception against it [the ministers' meeting], as fearing it might grow in time to a presbytery or superintendency, to the prejudice of the churches' liberties. But this fear was without cause; for they were all clear in that point, that no church or person can have power over another church; neither did they in their meetings exercise any such jurisdiction, etc.[8]

December 27.] The governor and assistants met at Boston, and took into consideration a treatise which Mr. Williams (then of Salem) had sent to them, and which he had formerly written to the governor and council of Plymouth, wherein, among other things, he disputes their right to the lands they possessed here, and concluded that, [in] claiming the king's grant, they could have no title, nor otherwise except [if] they compounded with the natives.

For this, taking advice with some of the most judicious ministers (who much condemned Mr. Williams's error and presumption), they gave order that he should be convented at the next court, to be censured, etc. . . .

January 21.] News came from Plymouth, that Capt. Stone, who this last summer went out of the bay . . . and so to Aquamenticus, where he took in Capt. Norton, putting in at the mouth of Connecticut, in his way to Vir-

[8] The Puritans viewed the source of all the (perceived) evils in the English church to be its system of government—a hierarchy of bishops, headed by the king. They viewed any network of clergy as the beginnings of an oppressive ruling body. This marks Williams's emergence as a dissident.

ginia, where the Pequots inhabit, was there cut off by them, with all his company, being eight [all told]. . . .

January 20.] Hall and two others, who went to Connecticut November 3, came now home, having lost themselves and endured much misery. They informed us that the smallpox was gone as far as any Indian plantation was known to the west, and much people dead of it, by reason whereof they could have no trade. . . .

January 24.] The governor and council met again at Boston, to consider . . . Mr. Williams's letter, etc., when, with the advice of [Boston ministers] Mr. Cotton and Mr. Wilson, and weighing his letter, and further considering of the aforesaid offensive passages in his book (which, being written in very obscure and implicative phrases, might well admit of doubtful interpretation), they found the matters not to be so evil as at first they seemed. Whereupon they agreed that, upon his retraction, etc., or taking an oath of allegiance to the king, etc., it should be passed over. . . .

1634[9]

April 1.] Notice being sent out of the general court to be held the 14th day of the third month, called May, the freemen deputed two of each town to meet and consider of such matters as they were to take order in at the same general court; who, having met, desired a sight of the patent, and, conceiving thereby that all their laws should be made at the general court [by all the freemen], repaired to the governor to advise with him about it, and about the abrogating of some orders formerly made, as for killing of swine in corn, etc.

He [Winthrop] told them that, when the patent was granted, the number of freemen was supposed to be (as in like corporations) so few, as they might well join in making laws; but now they were grown to so great a body, as it was not possible for them to make or execute laws, but they must choose others for that purpose. . . .

Yet this they might do at present, viz., they might, at the general court, make an order that, once in the year, a certain number should be appointed (upon summons from the governor) to revise all laws, etc., and to reform what they found amiss therein; but not to make any new laws, but refer their grievances to the court of assistants; and that no assessment should be laid upon the country without the consent of such a committee, nor any lands disposed of. . . .[10]

[9] As mentioned previously, the English calendar had March 25 as New Year's Day.

[10] This meeting was a key moment in the development of Massachusetts's representative government. Many commentators have pointed out, however, that "democracy" was a foul word to the Puritans; they pursued a government of the elect, those in the grace of God. And Governor Winthrop sought to restrain the devolution of lawmaking powers from the small council of assistants.

May 14.]   The court chose a new governor, viz., Thomas Dudley, Esq., the former deputy; and Mr. Ludlow was chosen deputy; and John Haynes, Esq., an assistant, and all the rest of the assistants chosen again.

At this court it was ordered that four general courts should be kept every year, and that the whole body of the freemen should be present only at the court of election of magistrates, etc., and that, at the other three, every town should send their deputies, who should assist in making laws, disposing lands, etc. . . .

September 18.]   At this court were many laws made against tobacco, and immodest fashions, and costly apparel, etc., as appears by the Records; and £600 raised towards fortifications and other charges, which were the more hastened because the *Griffin* and another ship now arriving with about two hundred passengers and one hundred cattle . . . there came over a copy of the commission granted to the two archbishops and ten others of the council [in England], to regulate all plantations [colonies], and power given them, or any five of them, to call in all patents, to make laws, to raise tithes and portions for ministers, to remove and punish governors, and to hear and determine all causes, and inflict all punishments, even death itself, etc.

This being advised from our friends [in England] to be intended specially for us, and that there were ships and soldiers provided, given out as for the carrying of the new governor, Capt. Woodhouse, to Virginia, but suspected to be against us, to compel us, by force, to receive a new governor, and the discipline of the church of England, and the laws of the commissioners—occasioned the magistrates and deputies to hasten our fortifications. . . .

November 6.]   There came to the deputy governor, about fourteen days since, a messenger from the Pequot sachem, to desire our friendship. He brought two bundles of sticks, whereby he signified how many beaver and otter skins he would give us for that end, and great store of wampompeage [wampum[11]] (about two bushels, by his description). He brought a small present with him, which the deputy received, and returned a moose coat of as good value, and withal told him that he must send persons of greater quality, and then our governor would treat with them.

And now there came two men, who brought another present of wampompeage. The deputy brought them to Boston, where most of the assistants were assembled, by occasion of the lecture, who, calling to them some of the ministers, grew to this treaty with them: That they were willing to have friendship, etc.; but because they had killed some Englishmen, viz., Captain Stone, etc., they must first deliver up those who were guilty of his death, etc. They answered that the sachem, who then lived, was slain by the

[11] The Indians highly valued wampum—belts of shells or beads strung together. It soon emerged as currency among both colonists and Native Americans.

Dutch, and all the men who were guilty, etc., were dead of the pox, except two, and that if they were worthy of death, they would move their sachem to have them delivered (for they had no commission to do it).

But they excused the fact. . . . This was related with such confidence and gravity as, having no means to contradict it, we were inclined to believe it. But, the governor not being present, we concluded nothing; but some of us went with them the next day to the governor.

The reason they desired so much our friendship was, because they were now in war with the Narragansetts, whom, till this year, they had kept under, and likewise with the Dutch, who had killed their old sachem and some other of their men, for that the Pequots had killed some Indians who came to trade with the Dutch at Connecticut;[12] and, by these occasions, they could not trade safely anywhere. Therefore they desired us to send a pinnace with cloth, and we should have all their trade. They offered us also all their right at Connecticut, and to further us what they could, if we would settle a plantation there.

When they came to the governor, they agreed, according to their former treaty, viz., to deliver us the two men who were guilty of Capt. Stone's death, when they would send for them; to yield up Connecticut; to give us four hundred fathom of wampompeage, and forty beaver, and thirty otter skins; and that we should presently send a pinnace with cloth to trade with them, and so should be at peace with them, and as friends to trade with them, but not to defend them, etc.

The next morning came, that two or three hundred of the Narragansetts were come to Cohann, viz., Neponsett, to kill the Pequot ambassadors, etc. . . . So we treated with them about the Pequots, and, at our request, they promised they should go and come to and from us in peace, and they were also content to enter further treaty of peace with them; and in all things showed themselves very ready to gratify us. So the Pequots returned home, and the Narragansetts departed well satisfied. . . . The agreement they made with us was put in writing, and the two ambassadors set to their marks—one a bow with an arrow in it, and the other a hand.

November 27.]   The assistants met at the governor's. . . . It was . . . informed, that Mr. Williams of Salem had broken his promise to us, in teaching publicly against the king's patent, and our great sin in claiming right thereby to this country, etc., and for usual terming of the churches of England antichristian. We granted summons to him for his appearance at the next court. . . .

January 19.]   All the ministers, except Mr. [Nathaniel] Ward of Ipswich, met at Boston, being requested by the governor and assistants, to consider of these two cases: 1. What we ought to do, if a general governor

[12] The Dutch maintained a trading post on the Connecticut River, at the present site of Hartford.

should be sent out of England? 2. Whether it be lawful for us to carry the cross in our banners? In the first case, they all agreed that, if a general governor were sent, we ought not to accept him, but defend our lawful possessions (if we were able); otherwise to avoid or protract. For the matter of the cross, they were so divided, and so deferred it to another meeting. . . .

1635

May 6.]   A general court was held at Newtown, where John Haynes, Esq., was chosen governor, Richard Bellingham, Esq., deputy governor, and Mr. Hough and Mr. Dummer chosen assistants to the former; and Mr. Ludlow, the late deputy, was left out of the magistracy. . . .

July 8.]   At the general court, Mr. Williams of Salem was summoned, and did appear. It was laid to his charge, that, being under question before the magistracy and the churches for diverse dangerous opinions. . . . The said opinions were adjudged by all, magistrates and ministers (who desired to be present), to be erroneous, and very dangerous, and the calling of him to office, at that time, was judged a great contempt of authority. So, in fine, time was given to him and the church of Salem to consider of these things till the next general court, and then either to give satisfaction to the court, or else to expect the sentence. . . .

July 12.]   Salem men had preferred a petition, at the last general court, for some land in Marblehead Neck, which they did challenge as belonging to their town; but, because they had chosen Mr. Williams their teacher, while he stood under question of authority, and so offered contempt to the magistrates, etc., their petition was refused till, etc. . . .

October.]   At this general court, Mr. Williams, the teacher of Salem, was again convented, and all the ministers in the bay being desired to be present, he was charged with the said two letters—that to the churches, complaining of the magistrates for injustice, extreme oppression, etc., and the other to his own church, to persuade them to renounce communion with all the churches in the bay, as full of antichristian pollution, etc. He justified both these letters, and maintained all his opinions; and, being offered further conference or disputation, and a month's respite, he chose to dispute presently. So Mr. Hooker was appointed to dispute with him, but could not reduce him from any of his errors.

So, the next morning, the court sentenced him to depart out of our jurisdiction within six weeks, all the ministers, save one, approving the sentence; and his own church had him under question for the same cause. And he, at his return home, refused communion with his own church, who openly disclaimed his errors, and wrote an humble submission to the magistrates, acknowledging their fault in joining with Mr. Williams in that letter to the churches against them, etc.

October 15.]   About sixty men, women, and little children went by land toward Connecticut with their cows, horses, and swine, and, after a tedious and difficult journey, arrived safe there. . . .

November 3.]   Mr. Winthrop, Jr., the governor appointed by the lords for Connecticut, sent a bark of thirty tons, and about twenty men, with all needful provisions, to take possession of the mouth of Connecticut. . . .[13]

January 11.]   The governor and assistants met at Boston to consider about Mr. Williams, for that they were credibly informed that, notwithstanding the injunction laid upon him (upon the liberty to stay till the spring) not to go about to draw others to his opinions, he did use to entertain company in his house, and to preach to them, even of such points as he had been censured for; and it was agreed to send him into England by a ship then ready to depart. The reason was, because he had drawn above twenty persons to his opinion, and they were intended to erect a plantation about the Narragansett Bay, from whence the infection would easily spread into these churches. . . . But, when they came at his house, they found he had been gone three days before; but whither they could not learn. . . .[14]

January 18.]   Mr. Vane and Mr. Peter, finding some distraction in the commonwealth, arising from some difference in judgment, and withal some alienation of affection among the magistrates and some other persons of quality, that hereby factions began to grow among the people, some adhering more to the old governor, Mr. Winthrop [the writer], and others to the late governor, Mr. Dudley—the former carrying matters with more lenity, and the latter with more severity—they procured a meeting, at Boston, of the governor [John Haynes], deputy, Mr. Cotton, Mr. Hooker, Mr. Wilson, and there was present Mr. Winthrop, Mr. Dudley, and themselves; where, after the Lord had been sought, Mr. Vane declared the occasion of this meeting (as is before noted), and the fruit aimed at, viz., a more firm and friendly uniting of minds, etc., especially of the said Mr. Dudley and Mr. Winthrop. . . .

Whereupon the governor, Mr. Haynes, spake to this effect: that Mr. Winthrop and himself had been always in good terms, etc.; therefore he was loath to give any offence to him. . . . Then he spake of one or two passages, wherein he conceived that [he] dealt too remissly in point of justice; to which Mr. Winthrop answered, that his speeches and carriage had been in part mistaken; but withal professed, that it was his judgment, that in the in-

[13] The ways of the government of Massachusetts did not sit well with many Puritans, who made their way to new lands in Connecticut. They even secured a patent from the crown for this colony. Winthrop outmaneuvered them, however, and had his own son (John Jr.) appointed governor. The younger Winthrop seated himself at a fort at Saybrook, at the mouth of the Connecticut River.

[14] Winthrop himself had warned Williams of the order to send him back to England, where he would surely have landed in prison. Winthrop admired Williams's inflexible dedication to godliness. He suggested to the young dissident that he go to live among the Narragansett, and start a new colony—Rhode Island.

fancy of plantation, justice should be administered with more lenity than in a settled state, because people were then more apt to transgress, partly of ignorance of new laws and orders, partly through oppression of business and other straits; but, if it might be made clear to him that it was an error, he would be ready to take up a stricter course.

Then the ministers were desired to consider the question by the next morning, and to set down a rule in the case. The next morning, they delivered their several reasons, which all sorted to this conclusion, that strict discipline, both in criminal offenses and in martial affairs, was more needful in plantations than in a settled state, as tending to the honor and safety of the gospel. Where upon Mr. Winthrop acknowledged that he was convinced, that he had failed in overmuch lenity and remissness, and would endeavor (by God's assistance) to take a more strict course hereafter. . . .

1636

May 25.]   The last winter Capt. Mason died. He was the chief mover in all the attempts [in England] against us, and was to have sent the general governor, and for this end was providing shipping; but the Lord, in mercy, taking him away, all the business fell on sleep, so as the ships came and brought what and whom they would, without any question or control. . . .

July 20.]   John Gallop, with one man more, and two little boys, coming from Connecticut in a bark of twenty tons, intending to put in at Long Island to trade, and being at the mouth of the harbor, were forced by a sudden change of wind to bear up for Block Island, or Fisher's Island, lying before Narragansett, where they espied a small pinnace, which, drawing near unto, they found to be Mr. Oldham's (an old planter, and a member of the Watertown congregation, who had been long out a trading, having with him only two English boys and two Indians of Narragansett).

So they hailed him, but had no answer; and the deck was full of Indians (fourteen in all) and a canoe was gone from her full of Indians and goods. Whereupon they suspected they had killed John Oldham. . . . [After a chase,] there being now but four left in her, they boarded her; whereupon one Indian came up and yielded; him they bound and put into [the] hold. Then another yielded, whom they bound. But John Gallop, being well acquainted with their skill to untie themselves, if two of them be together, and having no place to keep them asunder, threw him bound into [the] sea; and, looking about, they found John Oldham under an old seine, stark naked, his head cleft to the brains, and his hand and legs cut as if they had been cutting them off, and yet warm. So they put him into the sea; but could not get to the other two Indians, who were in a little room underneath, with their swords. So they took the goods which were left, and the sails, etc., and towed the boat away. . . .

July 26.]   The two Indians which were with Mr. Oldham, and one other, came from Canonicus, the chief sachem of Narragansett, with a letter from Mr. [Roger] Williams to the governor, to certify [to] him what had befallen Mr. Oldham, and how grievously they were afflicted, and that Miantunnomoh was gone with sixteen canoes and two hundred men to take revenge, etc.

But, upon examination of the Indian who was brought prisoner to us, we found that all the sachems of the Narragansett, except Canonicus and Miantunnomoh, were the contrivers of Mr. Oldham's death; and the occasion was, because he went to make peace and trade with the Pequots last year, as is before related. . . .

But the governor wrote back to Mr. Williams to let the Narragansetts know, that we expected they should send us the two boys, and take revenge upon the islanders; and withal gave Mr. Williams a caution to look to himself, if we should have occasion to make war upon the Narragansetts, for Block Island was under them. . . .

July 30.]   Mr. Oldham's two boys were sent home by one of Miantunnomoh his men, with a letter from Mr. Williams, signifying that Miantunnomoh had caused the sachem of Niantic to send to Block Island for them; and that he had near one hundred fathom of wampum and other goods of Mr. Oldham's, which should be reserved for us; and that three of the seven which were drowned were sachems; and one of the two, which were hired by the sachem of Niantic, was dead also. So we wrote back to have the rest of those, which were accessory, to be sent to us, and the rest of the goods, and that he should tell Canonicus and Miantunnomoh, that we held them innocent; but that six other under-sachems were guilty, etc.

August 8.]   Lieutenant Edward Gibbons, and John Higginson, with Cutshamekin, the sagamore of Massachusetts, were sent to Canonicus to treat with him about the murder of John Oldham. [On August] 13 they returned, being very well accepted, and good success in their business. They observed in the sachem much state, great command over his men, and marvelous wisdom in his answers and the carriage of the whole treaty, clearing himself and his neighbors of the murder, and offering assistance for revenge of it, yet upon very safe and wary conditions.

August 25.]   The governor and council, having lately assembled the rest of the magistrates and ministers to advise with them about doing justice upon the Indians for the death of Mr. Oldham, and all agreeing that it should be attempted with expedition, did this day send forth ninety men, distributed to four commanders—Capt. John Underhill, Capt. Nathaniel Turner, Ensign Jenyson, and Ensign Davenport; and over them all, as general, John Endecott, Esq., one of the assistants, was sent.

They were embarked in three pinnaces, and carried two shallops and two Indians with them. They had commission to put to death the men of Block Island, but to spare the women and children, and to bring them away, and to take possession of the island; and thence to go to the Pequots to demand the murderers of Capt. Stone and other English, and one thousand fathom of wampum for damages, etc., and some of their children as hostages, which if they should refuse, they were to obtain it by force. No man was impressed for this service, but all went voluntaries.

August 24.][15]   John Endecott, Esq., and four captains under him, with twenty men apiece, set sail. They arrived at Block Island the last [day] of the same [month]. The wind blowing hard at N.E. there went so great a surf, as they had much to do to land; and about forty Indians were ready upon shore to entertain them with their arrows, which they shot oft at our men; but, being armed [armored] with corslets, they had no hurt, only one was lightly hurt upon his neck, and another near his foot. So soon as one man leaped on shore, they all fled.

The island is about ten miles long, and four broad, full of small hills, and all overgrown with brushwood of oak—no good timber in it—so as they could not march but in one file and in the narrow paths. There were two plantations, three miles in sunder, and about sixty wigwams—some very large and fair—and above two hundred acres of corn, some gathered and laid on heaps, the rest standing. When they had spent two days in searching the island, and could not find the Indians, they burnt their wigwams, and all their mats, and some corn, and staved seven canoes, and departed. They could not tell what men they killed, but some were wounded and carried away by their fellows.

Thence they went to the mouth of the Connecticut, where they lay wind-bound four days, and taking thence twenty men and two shallops, they sailed to the Pequot harbor, where an Indian came to them in a canoe, and demanded what they were, and what they would have. The general told him he came from the governor of Massachusetts to speak with their sachems. He [the Indian] told them, Sassacus [chief sachem of the Pequots] was gone to Long Island. Then he bade him go tell the other sachem, etc. So he departed; and in the meantime our men landed. . . .

Then the messenger returned, and the Indians began to gather about our men till there were about three hundred of them; and some four hours passed while the messenger went to and fro, bringing still excuses for the sachems' not coming. At last the general told the messenger, and the rest of the Indians near, the particulars of his commission, and sent him to tell the sachem that if he would not come to him, nor yield to those demands, he would fight with them. The messenger told him, that the sachem would meet him, if our men would lay down their arms, as his men should do their bows, etc.

When the general saw they did but dally, to gain time, he bade them be gone, and shift for themselves; for they had dared the English to come fight

[15] This entry has been left out of chronological sequence, as in the original.

with them, and now they were come for that purpose. Thereupon they all withdrew. Some of our men would have made a shot at them, but the general would not suffer them; but when they were gone out of musket shot, he marched after them, supposing they would have stood to it awhile, as they did to the Dutch. But they all fled, and shot at our men from the thickets and rocks, but did us no harm. Two of them our men killed, and hurt others.

So they marched up to their town, and burnt all their wigwams and mats, but their corn being standing, they could not spoil it. At night they returned to their vessels, and the next day they went ashore on the west side of the river, and burnt all their wigwams, and spoiled their canoes; and so set sail, and came to the Narragansett, where they landed their men, and, the 14th of September, they came all safe to Boston, which was a marvelous providence of God, that not a hair fell from the head of any of them, nor any sick or feeble person among them. . . .

The Narragansett men told us after, that thirteen of the Pequots were killed, and forty wounded; and but one of Block Island killed. . . . Canonicus sent word of some English, whom the Pequots had killed at Saybrook; and Mr. Williams wrote that the Pequots and Narragansetts were at truce, and that Miantunnomoh told him that the Pequots had labored to persuade them that the English were minded to destroy all Indians. Whereupon we sent for Miantunnomoh to come to us. . . .

October.] After Mr. Endecott and our men were departed from the Pequot, the twenty men of Saybrook lay wind-bound there, and went to fetch some of the Indians' corn; and having fetched every man one sackful to their boat, they returned for more, and having loaded themselves, the Indians set upon them. So they laid down their corn and gave fire upon them, and the Indians shot arrows at them. . . .

So they continued the most part of the afternoon. Our men killed some, as they supposed, and hurt others; and they shot only one of ours. . . .

About two days after, five men of Saybrook went up the river about four miles, to fetch hay in a meadow on [the] Pequot side. The grass was so high as some Pequots, being hid in it, set upon our men, and one, that had hay on his back, they took; the others fled to their boat, one of them having five arrows in him (but yet recovered). . . .

About fourteen days after, six of Saybrook, being sent to keep the house in their cornfield, about two miles from the fort, three of them went forth on fowling (which the lieutenant had strictly forbidden them). Two had pieces, and the third only a sword. Suddenly about one hundred Indians came out of the cover, and set upon them. He who had the sword brake through them (and received only two shot, not dangerous), and escaped to the house, which was not a bow shot off, and persuaded the other two to follow him; but they stood still till the Indians came and took them, and carried them away with their pieces. Soon after they burnt down the said house, and some outhouses and haystacks within bow shot of the fort, and killed a cow, and shot diverse others. . . .

October 21.] The governor of Plymouth wrote to the deputy [Winthrop himself], that we had occasioned the war, etc., by provoking the Pequots. . . . The deputy took it ill (as there was reason), and returned answer accordingly. . . .

One Mrs. [Anne] Hutchinson, a member of the church of Boston, a woman of a ready wit and bold spirit, brought over [from England] with her two dangerous errors: 1. That the person of the Holy Ghost dwells in a justified person. 2. That no sanctification can help to evidence to us our justification.[16] From these two grew many branches. . . . There joined with her in these opinions a brother of hers, one Mr. Wheelwright, a silenced minister sometimes in England.

October 25.] The other ministers in the bay, hearing of these things, came to Boston at the time of a general court, and entered conference in private with them, to the end they might know the certainty of these things; that if need were, they might write to the church of Boston about them, to prevent (if it were possible) the dangers, which seemed hereby to hang over that and the rest of the churches. At this conference, Mr. Cotton was present, and gave satisfaction to them, so as he agreed with them all in the point of sanctification, and so did Mr. Wheelwright; so as they all did hold, that sanctification did help evidence justification. . . .

December.] Mr. Wilson [the chief minister in Boston] made a very sad speech of the condition of the churches, and the inevitable danger of separation, if these differences and alienations among brethren were not speedily remedied; and laid the blame upon these new opinions risen up amongst us. . . .

The speech of Mr. Wilson was taken very ill by Mr. Cotton and others of the same [Boston] church, so as he and diverse of them went to admonish him. But Mr. Wilson and some others could see no breach of rule, seeing he was called by the court about the same matter with the rest of the elders, and exhorted to deliver their minds freely and faithfully, both for discovering the danger and the means to help. . . . The next day Mr. Wilson preached, notwithstanding, and the Lord so assisted him, as gave great satisfaction, and the governor himself gave public witness to him. . . .

Upon these public occasions, other opinions brake out publicly in the church of Boston—as that the Holy Ghost dwelt in a believer as he is in heaven; that a man is justified before he believes; that faith is no cause for justification. And others spread more secretly—as that the letter of the scrip-

[16] In plain English, Hutchinson argued that nothing could outwardly indicate whether a person had been selected by God for salvation. This was a revolutionary idea, since the churches had a rigorous examination to decide just that before accepting a new member (and only full members of congregations could vote). The natural question was: Who *could* tell if God had saved someone?

ture holds forth nothing but a covenant of works; and that the covenant of grace was the spirit of the scripture, which was known only to believers; and that this covenant of works was given by Moses in the ten commandments; that there was a seed (viz., Abraham's carnal seed) went along in this, and there was a spirit and life in it, by virtue whereof a man might attain to any sanctification in gifts and graces, and might have spiritual and continual communion with Jesus Christ, and yet be damned. After, it was granted, that faith was before justification, but it was only passive, an empty vessel, etc.; but in conclusion, the ground of all was found to be assurance by immediate revelation.

All the congregation of Boston, except four or five, closed with these opinions, or the most of them; but one of the brethren [Winthrop himself] wrote against them, and bore witness to the truth; together with the pastor, and very few others joined with them. . . .

February 22.][17]   The lieutenant of Saybrook, at the mouth of Connecticut, going out with nine men armed with swords and pieces, they startled three [Pequot] Indians, whom they pursued till they were brought into an ambush of fifty, who came upon them, and slew four of their men, and had they not drawn their swords and retired, they had all been slain. The Indians were so hardy as they came up close to them, notwithstanding their pieces.

January 20.]   A general fast was kept in all the churches. The occasion was, the miserable estate of the [Protestant] churches in Germany; the calamities upon our native country [the rise of Arminianism in England], the bishops making havoc in the churches, putting down the faithful ministers, and advancing popish ceremonies and doctrines . . . ; the dangers of those at Connecticut, and of ourselves also, by the Indians; and the dissensions in our churches.

The differences in the said points of religion increased more and more, and the ministers of both sides (there being only Mr. Cotton of one party) did publicly declare their judgments in some of them, so as all men's mouths were full of them.

March 9.]   The general court began. When any matter about these new opinions was mentioned, the court was divided; yet the greater number [most from outside of Boston] far were sound. . . .

The ministers, being called to give advice about the authority of the court in things concerning the churches, etc., did all agree of these two things: 1. That no member of the court ought to be publicly questioned by a church for any speech in the court, without license of the court. . . . The second thing was, that, in all such heresies or errors of any church members as are manifest and dangerous to the state, the court may proceed without tarrying for the church; but if the opinions be doubtful, etc., they are first to refer them to the church, etc. . . .

[17] This entry is chronologically misplaced in the original.

Mr. Wheelwright, one of the members of Boston, preaching at the last fast, inveighed against all that walked in a covenant of works, as he described it to be, viz., such as maintain sanctification as an evidence of justification, etc., and called them antichrists, and stirred up the people against them with much bitterness and vehemency. For this he was called into the court, and his sermon being produced, he justified it, and confessed he did mean all that walk in such a way.

Whereupon the elders of the rest of the churches were called, and asked whether they, in their ministry, did walk in such a way [as Wheelwright condemned]. They all acknowledged they did. So, after much debate, the court adjudged him guilty of sedition, and also of contempt, for that the court had appointed the fast as a means of reconciliation of the differences, etc., and he purposely set himself to kindle and increase them. . . .

Much heat of contention was this court between the opposite parties; so as it was moved, that the next court might be kept at Newtown. The governor [Henry Vane] refused to put it to the vote; the deputy was loath to do it, except the court would require him, because he dwelt in Boston, etc. So the court put it to Mr. Endecott. . . .

1637

April 1.]   Those of Connecticut returned answer to our public letters, wherein they showed themselves unsatisfied about our former expedition against the Pequots, and their expectations of a further prosecution of the war, to which they offered to send men. . . .

April 10.]   Capt. Underhill was sent to Saybrook with twenty men to keep the fort, both in respect of the Indians and especially of the Dutch, who, by their speeches and supplies out of Holland, gave cause of suspicion that they had some design upon it. The men were sent at the charge of the gentlemen of Saybrook, and lent by order of the council here, for fear any advantage should be taken by the adverse party, through the weakness of the place. . . .

May 17.]   Our court of elections was at Newtown. . . . Mr. Winthrop [the writer] was chosen governor; Mr. Dudley deputy, and Mr. Endecott of the standing council; and Mr. Israel Stoughton and Mr. Richard Saltonstall were called in to be assistants; and Mr. Vane, Mr. Coddington, and Mr. Dummer (being all of that [Anne Hutchinson's] faction) were left quite out. There was great danger of a tumult that day; for those of that side grew into fierce speeches, and some laid hands on others; but seeing themselves too weak, they grew quiet. They expected great advantage that day, because the remote towns were allowed to come in by proxy; but it fell out, that there were enough beside. But if it had been otherwise, they must have put in their deputies, as other towns had done, for all matters beside elections.

Boston, having deferred to choose deputies till the election was passed, went home that night, and the next morning they sent Mr. Vane, the late governor, and Mr. Coddington and Mr. Hoffe [all members of the Hutchinson faction] for their deputies; but the court, being grieved at it, found a means to send them home again, for that two of the freemen of Boston had not notice of the election. So they went all home, and the next morning they returned the same gentlemen again upon a new choice; and the court not finding how they might reject them, they were admitted.

Upon the election of the new governor [Winthrop himself], the sergeants, who had attended the old governor to the court (being all Boston men, where the new governor also dwelt), laid down their halberds and went home; and whereas they had been wont to attend the former governor to and from the meetings on the Lord's days, they gave over now, so as the new governor was fain to use his own servants to carry two halberds before him; whereas the former governor had never less than four. . . .

At the court Mr. Wheelwright, according as he was enjoined, did appear; but, because a general day of humiliation was appointed, and it was agreed, that all the churches should choose certain men to meet and confer about the differences, the court gave him respite to the next session . . . to bethink himself, that, retracting and reforming his error, etc., the court might show him favor, which otherwise he must not expect. His answer was, that if he had committed a sedition, then he ought to be put to death; and if we did mean to proceed against him, he meant to appeal to the king's court; for he could retract nothing. . . .

The intent of the court in deferring the sentence was that, being thus provoked by their tumultuous course, and diverse insolent speeches, which some of that party had uttered in the court, and having now power enough to have crushed them, their [the court's] moderation and desire of reconciliation might appear to all.

Having received intelligence from Miantunnomoh that the Pequots had sent their women and children to an island for their safety, we presently sent away forty men by land to the Narragansetts, and there to take in Miantunnomoh (and he offered to send sixteen men with ours), and so, in the night, to set upon them. We also provided to send one hundred and sixty more after them to prosecute the war; and Mr. Stoughton, one of the magistrates, was sent with them, and Mr. Wilson, the pastor of Boston. . . .

May 24.]   By letters from Mr. Williams we were certified (which the next day was confirmed by some who came from Saybrook), that Capt. Mason was come to Saybrook with eighty English and one hundred Indians; and that the Indians had gone out there, and met with seven Pequots; five they killed; one they took alive, whom the English put to torture; and set all their heads upon the fort. The reason was, because they had tortured such of our men as they took alive. . . .

May 25.]   Our English from Connecticut, with their Indians, and many of the Narragansetts, marched in the night to a fort of the Pequots at Mystic, and, besetting the same about break of the day, after two hours' fight they took it (by firing it), and slew therein two chief sachems, and one hundred and fifty fighting men, and about one hundred and fifty old men, women, and children, with the loss of two English, whereof but one was killed by the enemy. Diverse of the Indian friends were hurt by the English, because they had not some mark to distinguish them from the Pequots, as some of them had. . . .

Presently upon this came news from the Narragansetts, that all the English, and two hundred of the Indians, were cut off in their retreat, for want of powder and victuals. Three days after, this was confirmed by a post from Plymouth, with such probable circumstances, as it was generally believed. But, three days after, Mr. Williams, having gone to the Narragansetts to discover the truth, found them mourning, as being confident of it; but that night some came from the army, and assured them all was well, and that all the Pequots were fled, and had forsaken their forts. The general defeat of the Pequots at Mystic happened the day after our general fast. . . .

June 15.] There was a day of thanksgiving kept in all the churches for the victory obtained against the Pequots, and for other mercies.

June 26.] We had news of a commission granted in England to diverse gentlemen here for the governing of New England, etc.; but instead thereof we received a commission from Sir Fernando Gorges[18] to govern his province of New Somersetshire, which is from Cape Elizabeth to Sagadahoc [including all of New England] and withal to oversee his servants and private affairs; which was observed as a matter of no good discretion, but passed in silence. . . . As also for that it did not appear to us what authority he had to grant such a commission. As for the commission from the king, we received only a copy of it.

July 5.] Capt. Stoughton and his company, having pursued the Pequots beyond Connecticut, and missing of them, returned to Pequot River, where they were advertised that one hundred of them were newly come back to a place twelve miles off. So they marched thither by night, and surprised them all. They put to death twenty-two men, and reserved two sachems, hoping by them to get Sassacus [the foremost leader of the Pequots] (which they promised). All the rest were women and children, of whom they gave the Narragansetts thirty, and our Massachusetts Indians three, and the rest they sent hither. . . .

July 6.] There were sent to Boston forty-eight [Pequot] women and children. There were eighty taken, as before is expressed. These were disposed of to particular persons in the country. Some of them ran away and were brought again by the Indians our neighbors, and those we branded on the shoulder.

[18] The Council for New England granted Gorges this territory in February 1635.

July 12.]   Here came over a brother of Mrs. Hutchinson, and some other of Mr. Wheelwright's friends, whom the governor thought not fit to allow, as others, to sit down among us, without some trial of them. Therefore, to save others from the danger of the law in receiving of them, he allowed them for four months. This was taken very ill by those of the other party, and many hot speeches given forth about it, and about their removal, etc.

July 13.]   Mr. Stoughton, with about eighty of the English, whereof Mr. Ludlow, Capt. Mason, and [another] of Connecticut, were part, sailed to the west in pursuit of Sassacus, etc. At Quinepiack [now New Haven], they killed six, and took two. At a head of land a little short they beheaded two sachems; whereupon they called the place Sachem's Head. About this time they had given a Pequot his life to go find out Sassacus. He went, and found him not far off; but Sassacus, suspecting him, intended to kill him, which the fellow perceiving, escaped in the night, and came to the English. Whereupon Sassacus and Mononotto, their two chief sachems, and some twenty more, fled to the Mohawks.

But eight of their stoutest men, and two hundred others, women and children, were at a place within twenty or thirty miles of the Dutch, whither our men marched, and, being guided by a divine providence, came upon them, where they had twenty wigwams, hard by a most hideous swamp, so thick with bushes and quagmiry, as men could hardly crowd into it. Into this swamp they were all gotten.

Lieut. Davenport and two or three more, that entered the swamp, were dangerously wounded by Indian arrows, and with much difficulty were fetched out. Then our men surrounded the swamp, being a mile about, and shot at the Indians, and they at them, from three of the clock in the afternoon till they desired to parley, and offered to yield, and life was offered to all that had not shed English blood.

So they began to come forth, now some and then some, till about two hundred women and children were come out, and amongst them the sachem of that place, and thus they kept us two hours, till night was come on, and then the men told us they would fight it out; and so they did all the night, coming up behind the bushes very near our men, and shot many arrows into their hats, sleeves, and stocks, yet (which was a very miracle) not one of ours was wounded. When it was near morning, it grew very dark, so as such of them as were left crept out at one place and escaped, being (as was judged) not above twenty at most, and those like to be wounded; for in the pursuit they found some of them dead of their wounds.

Here our men got some booty of kettles, trays, wampum, etc., and the women and children were divided, and sent some to Connecticut, and some to the Massachusetts. The sachem of the place, having yielded, had his life, and his wife and children, etc. The women, which were brought home, reported that we had slain in all thirteen sachems, and that there were thirteen more left. We had now slain and taken, in all, about seven hundred. . . .

August 5.] Mr. Hooker and Mr. Stone came, with Mr. Wilson, from Connecticut by Providence [Roger Williams's new town on Narragansett Bay]; and, the same day, Mr. Ludlow, Mr. Pincheon, and about twelve more, came the ordinary way by land, and brought with them a part of the skin and lock of hair [the scalp] of Sassacus and his brother, and five other Pequot sachems, who, being fled to the Mohawks for shelter, with their wampum, being to the value of five hundred pounds, were by them [the Mohawks] surprised and slain, with twenty of their best men. Mononotto was also taken, but escaped wounded. They brought news also of diverse other Pequots, which had been slain by other Indians, and their heads brought to the English; so that now there had been slain and taken between eight and nine hundred. . . .

August 31.] Mr. Eaton, and some others of Mr. Davenport's company, went to view Quinepiack, with intent to begin a plantation there. . . . Some of the magistrates and ministers of Connecticut being here, there was a day of meeting appointed to agree upon some articles of confederation, and notice was given to Plymouth, that they might join in it (but their warning was so short as they could not come). This was concluded after. . . .

August 30.][19] The synod, called the assembly, began at Newtown. There were all the teaching elders about the country, and some new come out of England, not yet to be called to any place here, as Mr. Davenport, etc.

The assembly began with prayer, made by Mr. Shepherd, the pastor of Newtown. Then the erroneous opinions, which were spread in the country, were read (being eighty in all); next the unwholesome expressions; then the scriptures abused. Then they chose two moderators for the next day, viz., Mr. Buckly and Mr. Hooker, and these were continued in that place all the time of the assembly. There were about eighty opinions, some blasphemous, others erroneous, and all unsafe, condemned by the whole assembly. . . . Upon this some of Boston departed from the assembly, and came no more. . . .

September.] The last day of the assembly other questions were debated and resolved:

1. That though women might meet (some few together) to pray and edify one another; yet such a set assembly (as was then in practice at Boston), where sixty or more did meet every week, and one woman [Mrs. Hutchinson] (in a prophetical way, by resolving questions of doctrine, and expounding scripture) took upon her the whole exercise, was agreed to be disorderly, and without rule.

2. Though a private member might ask a question publicly, after a sermon, for information; yet this ought to be very wisely and sparingly done,

[19] This entry is out of chronological order in the original.

and that with leave of the elders; but questions of reference (then in use), whereby the doctrines delivered were reproved, and the elders reproached, and that with bitterness, etc., was utterly condemned.

3.   That a person, refusing to come to the assembly to abide the censure of the church, might be proceeded against, though absent; yet it was held better, that the magistrates' help were called for, to compel him to be present.

4.   That a member, differing from the rest of the church in any opinion which was not fundamental, ought not for that to forsake the ordinances there. . . .

September 22.]   The assembly brake up. . . .

November 1.]   There was great hope that the late general assembly would have had some good effect in pacifying the troubles and dissensions about matters of religion; but it fell out otherwise. For though Mr. Wheelwright and those of his party had been clearly confuted and confounded in the assembly, yet they persisted in their opinions, and were as busy in nourishing contentions (the principal of them) as before. Whereupon the general court, being assembled in the 2nd [day] of the 9th month [November] . . . agreed to send away some of the principal [dissenters]. . . .

Then the court sent for Mr. Wheelwright, and he persisting to justify his sermon, and his whole practice and opinions, and refusing to leave either the place or his public exercisings, he was disfranchised and banished. . . .

The court also sent for Mrs. Hutchinson, and charged her with diverse matters, as her keeping two public lectures every week in her house, whereto sixty or eighty persons did usually resort, and for reproaching most of the ministers (viz., all except Mr. Cotton) for not preaching a covenant of free grace, and that they had not the seal of the spirit, nor were able ministers of the New Testament; which were clearly proved against her, though she sought to shift it off.

And, after many speeches to and fro, at last she was so full as she could not contain, but vented her revelations; amongst which was this one, that she had it revealed to her, that she should come into New England, and should here be persecuted, and that God would ruin us and our posterity, and the whole state, for the same. So the court proceeded and banished her; but, because it was winter, they committed her to a private house, where she was well provided, and her own friends and the elders permitted to go to her, but none else.

The court also called Capt. Underhill, and some five or six more of the principal, whose hands were to be the said petition; and because they stood to justify it, they were disfranchised, and such as had public places were put from them.

The court also ordered that the rest who had subscribed the petition (and would not acknowledge their fault, and which near twenty of them did), and some others who had been chief stirrers in these contentions, etc., should be disarmed. This troubled some of them very much, especially because they were to bring them in themselves; but at last, when they saw no remedy, they obeyed. . . .

After this, many of the church of Boston, being highly offended with the governor for this proceeding, were earnest with the elders to have him called to account for it; but they were not forward in it, and himself, understanding their intent, thought fit to prevent such a public disorder, and so took occasion to speak to the congregation. . . .

March 22.] After she [Hutchinson] was excommunicated, her spirits, which seemed before to be somewhat dejected, revived again, and she gloried in her sufferings, saying that it was the greatest happiness, next to Christ, that ever befell her. Indeed, it was a happy day to the churches of Christ here, and to many poor souls, who had been seduced by her, who, by what they heard and saw that day, were (through the grace of God) brought off quite from her errors, and settled again in the truth.

At this time the good providence of God so disposed diverse of the congregation (being the chief men of the party, her husband being one) were gone to Narragansett [Rhode Island] to seek out a new place for plantation, and taking liking of one in [the] Plymouth patent, they went thither to have it granted them; but the magistrates there, knowing their spirit, gave them a denial, but consented they might buy of the Indians an island in the Narragansett Bay.

───────

NO CITY OF Canaan suffered greater retribution at the hands of Joshua than what the Pequots received from the Puritans. The war had been provoked by Massachusetts Bay—but it was the colonists of Connecticut who suffered Pequot wrath. The tribe's war parties scourged the new settlements along the river and laid siege to Fort Saybrook. And so the Puritans of Connecticut took matters into their own hands: they landed a mixed force, including Indian allies, on the coast beyond the fortified Pequot town at Mystic. Then they surrounded the village, burned it down, and utterly destroyed everything that breathed.

The Pequots received no mercy: they were hunted down, slain, and sold into slavery; Winthrop carefully noted the mounting death toll. The Puritan dissidents suffered equal severity, though without the bloodshed. The less passionate malcontents founded the new colony of Connecticut; Roger Williams fled to Narragansett Bay, where he began the unrecognized colony of Rhode Island; and the exiled Anne Hutchinson and her followers soon joined him.

But how, we may ask, could the Puritans of Massachusetts be roused to such repression by such obscure points of doctrine? After all, these were the years when representative government took shape in the bay colony, when Winthrop was criticized for being too lenient, when the ministers of the church were explicitly excluded from civil matters. How could such reasoned consideration of public opinion, such emphasis on consent, coexist with this intolerance of mere opinions?

The answers lie in the remarkable homogeneity of the colonists. The Great Migration from England to Massachusetts in the 1630s—a movement of some 80,000 people within an eleven-year span—originated in one particular area of England. Historian David Hackett Fisher has shown that 60 percent of the immigrants came from just nine eastern counties; they came mostly from the middle strata of society, and shared customs, culture, speech, and outlook.[20] Without an aristocracy, none of these middling sorts sought to establish a government founded on hierarchy (something they loathed within the Church of England); and with such social uniformity, the authorities need not fear any danger in rule by consent. Indeed, Winthrop saw that consultation and compromise were in the best interests of the government, and the colony itself.

But Roger Williams—and especially Anne Hutchinson—did pose such a danger, upsetting the balance of shared values and beliefs. As the congregations outside of Boston saw it, the purity of the faith had to be preserved. But as Winthrop saw it, to preserve a government without hierarchy—the rule of the saints—then a society without divisions must be maintained. There would be no room in Israel for the worshipers of idols.

---

[20] See David Hackett Fisher's magisterial *Albion's Seed: Four British Folkways in America* (New York: Oxford University Press, 1989), an exhaustive study of the four main British culture groups that shaped society in colonial America.

10

THE HURON APOCALYPSE

When the last refugee Pequots fled the wrath of the Puritans, they ran straight into the arms of a power even more deadly, if possible, than the New England militia. They were the Mohawks, a people whose very name was a synonym for terror. They were not the largest of the Five Nations of Iroquois, but they were certainly the most ferocious in war. Almost casually, the Mohawks removed the heads of the Pequot sachems and dispatched them to Boston, with Iroquois compliments. Then they turned their attentions northward.

The Five Nations had hated the French ever since Champlain joined that war party of destiny in 1608. But Champlain followed his acts of war with skilled diplomacy, uniting the enemies of the Iroquois into a solid front under his auspices. In 1624, this coalition signed a grand peace—more of a truce, actually—that halted the bloodshed. But the ceasefire proved more useful to the Iroquois than to New France and its allies. The Five Nations were now allowed a breathing space, as they suffered devastating losses from disease.

The Mohawks gained a particular advantage after the arrival of the Dutch at Fort Orange (now the city of Albany, New York). With their northern frontier secure, thanks to the truce, they waged a bitter war against the Mahican tribe from 1624 through 1628 to gain access to this Dutch outpost. In the end, the defeated Mahicans withdrew east of the Hudson River, leaving the Mohawks with a monopoly on trade with Fort Orange. Though the Dutch backed the Mahicans at first, they now dealt with their new customers—the only customers they would be allowed to have. For rich supplies of Mohawk furs, they sold hoes, kettles, knives, and hatchets—as well as wampum, the belts of shells and beads that formed the universal currency of colonial trade. And, gradually, they began to sell the Mohawks what the Indians most desired: muskets, gunpowder, and lead.

As the Iroquois expanded their trade network, they also grappled with the vicious smallpox epidemics of the 1630s, which caused a sudden collapse of their population. Tribe after tribe in the northeast failed to cope with this demographic disaster—but the Five Nations found a way to rebuild their strength through war. As was seen so graphically in earlier chapters, both the Five Nations and Hurons often tortured prisoners to death; but now the Iroquois began to adopt most prisoners as members of their own nations. So strong was the bond of common custom that the captives accepted their fate and fought loyally as members of this great confederacy.

During these rebuilding years, the Five Nations cast their eyes across the St. Lawrence, across the Great Lakes, to the lands of their mortal enemies, the Hurons. The Iroquois and Hurons had always been rivals; now the issues of commerce and demographics threw them into the final war of their long history of hatred. First came trade: as the Mohawks sold furs to the Dutch, beaver stocks dwindled rapidly in the eastern part of the continent. The animals still abounded in streams and rivers to the west— but this supply was controlled by the Hurons, who possessed a sprawling trade network with the Native Americans in the interior.

After Champlain returned to New France in 1633, the Mohawks resumed their raids north: they attacked settlements, and set ambushes for Huron canoe convoys along that great trade artery, the St. Lawrence. The French struggled to respond after the death of their leader Champlain in 1635. Finally, they called a peace conference at the new town of Montreal in 1645, using Iroquois rituals to frame the negotiations. Some of the Five Nations, however, sought a more permanent solution. As Ian K. Steele writes, "Seneca and Mohawk began recruiting their fellow Iroquois for war, not to capture the Huron trading network, but to destroy it."

In the four years that followed the Montreal conference, the Seneca and Mohawk tribes accelerated their offensive, sending massive armies (for Native American warfare) into Huron and French territory. In 1648, their warriors even slaughtered a Huron diplomatic mission to the Onondaga. The mighty nation of the Hurons now shook with the blows of large, daring, deep-ranging expeditions, heavily equipped with Dutch firearms. And with each success, the Iroquois eased their second crisis—population. They began to adopt Huron captives by the hundreds.

The Hurons acquired their own muskets from their French allies, but the supply was controlled by the Jesuit missionaries who largely shaped their relations. In their quest to convert this great nation, the Jesuits insisted that only *baptized* Hurons should be given firearms. It was a tactic that sped up the process of conversion, but it may have slowed the race for survival. And it would be a desperate race indeed—not only for the Hurons, but for the Jesuits themselves.

Onslaught
by Paul Ragueneau

Last summer, in the past year, 1648, the Iroquois, enemies of the Hurons, took from them [the Hurons] two frontier villages, from which most of the defenders had gone forth—some for the chase, others for purposes of war, in which they could meet no success. These two frontier places composed the mission which we named for St. Joseph; the principal of these villages contained about 400 families, where the faith had long sustained itself with luster . . . through the indefatigable labors of Father Antoine Daniel, one of the earliest missionaries in these regions.

Hardly had the Father ended Mass, and the Christians—who, according to their custom, had filled the church after the rising of the sun—were still continuing their devotions there, when the cry arose, "To arms! and repel the enemy!"—who, having come unexpectedly, had made his approaches by night. Some hastened to the combat, others to flight; there is naught but alarm and terror everywhere. The Father, among the first to rush where he sees the danger greatest, encourages his people to a brave defense. . . .

Meanwhile, the enemy continued his attacks more furiously than ever. . . . When the Father saw that the Iroquois were becoming masters of the place, he—instead of taking flight with those who were inviting him to escape in their company—forgetting himself, remembered some old men and sick people whom he had long ago prepared for baptism. He goes through the cabins, and proceeds to fill them with his zeal—the infidels themselves presenting their children in crowds, in order to make Christians of them.

Meanwhile the enemy, already victorious, had set everything on fire, and the blood of even the women and children irritated their fury. The Father, wishing to die in his church, finds it full of Christians, and of Catechumens who ask him for baptism. . . . He baptizes some, gives absolution to others, and consoles them all with the sweetest hope of the saints—hardly other words on his lips than these: "My brothers, today we shall be in heaven."

The enemy was warned that the Christians had betaken themselves, in very great number, into the church, and it was the easiest and richest prey that they could have hoped for. He [the Iroquois] hastens thither, with barbarous howls and stunning yells. At the noise of these approaches, "Flee, my brothers," said the Father to his new Christians. . . .

At the same time, he goes out in the direction whence come the enemy, who stop in astonishment to see one man alone come to meet them, and even recoil backward, as if he bore upon his face the terrible and frightful appearance of a whole company. Finally—having come to their senses a little and being astonished at themselves—they incite one another; they surround him on all sides, and cover him with arrows, until, having inflicted upon him a mortal wound from an harquebus shot, which pierced him through and through in the very middle of his breast, he fell. . . .

The fire meanwhile was consuming the cabins; and when it had spread as far as the church, the Father was cast into it, at the height of the flames, which soon made of him a whole burnt offering. . . . While the enemy delayed around the pastor of that church, his poor scattered flock had at least more leisure to escape; and many, in fact, betook themselves to a place of safety—indebted for their lives to the death of their Father. . . . A part of those who had escaped from the capture and burning of that Mission of Saint Joseph came to take refuge near our house of Saint Marie. The number of those who had been killed or taken captive was probably about seven hundred souls, mostly women and children. . . .

IN THE WINTER OF THE SAME YEAR, 1648

The victorious return of the Huron fleet [which defeated a Mohawk ambush], which had gone down to Trois Rivières in the spring, and the aid received (four of our Fathers and a score of Frenchmen, who fortunately arrived here at the beginning of the month of September) was an act of God's love over these peoples, and the salvation of many souls whom he wished to prepare for heaven. . . .

OF THE CAPTURE OF THE VILLAGES OF THE MISSION OF ST. IGNACE

The 16th day of March of the present year, 1649, marked the beginning of our misfortunes—if, however, that may be a misfortune which no doubt has been the salvation of many of God's elect.

The Iroquois, enemies of the Hurons, to the number of a thousand men, well furnished with weapons—and mostly firearms, which they obtain from the Dutch, their allies—arrived by night at the frontier of this country, without our knowledge of their approach; although they had started from their country in the autumn, hunting in the forests throughout the winter, and had made over the snow nearly two hundred leagues of a very difficult road, in order to come and surprise us.

They reconnoitered by night the condition of the first place upon which they had designs—which was surrounded by a stockade of pine-trees, from fifteen to sixteen feet in height, and with a deep ditch, wherewith nature had strongly fortified this place on three sides—there remaining only a little space which was weaker than the others. It was at that point that the enemy made a breach at daybreak, but so secretly and promptly that he was master of the place before people had put themselves on the defensive—all being then in a deep sleep. Thus the village was taken, almost without striking a blow, there having been only ten Iroquois killed. Part of the Hurons—men, women, and children—were massacred then and there; the others were made captives, and reserved for cruelties more terrible than death. Three men alone escaped, almost naked, across the snows. . . .

The enemy does not stop there; he follows up his victory, and before sunrise he appears in arms to attack the village of Saint Louis, which was fortified with a fairly good stockade. Most of the women and the children had just gone from it, upon hearing the news which had arrived regarding the approach of the Iroquois. The people of most courage, about eighty persons, being resolved to defend themselves well, repulsed with courage the first and second assault, having killed among the enemy some thirty of their most venturesome men, besides many wounded. But, finally number has the advantage—the Iroquois having undermined with blows of their hatchets the palisades of stakes, and having made a passage for themselves through considerable breaches.

Toward nine o'clock in the morning, we perceived from our house at Saint Marie the fire which was consuming the cabins of that village, where the enemy, having entered victoriously, had reduced everything to desolation—casting into the midst of the flames the old men, the sick, the children who had not been able to escape, and all those who, being too severely wounded, could not have followed them into captivity. At the sight of those flames, and by the color of the smoke which issued from them, we understood sufficiently what was happening—this village of Saint Louis not being farther distant from us than one league. Two Christians, who escaped from the fire, arrived almost at the same time, and gave us assurance of it.

In this village of Saint Louis were at that time two of our Fathers—Father Jean de Brébeuf and Father Gabriel Lalemant, who had charge of five closely neighboring villages; these formed but one of the eleven missions . . . ; we named it the Mission of St. Ignace. . . .

All this band of Christians fell, mostly alive, in the hands of the enemy; and with them, our two Fathers, pastors of that church. They were not killed on the spot; God was reserving them for much nobler crowns; of which we will speak hereafter.

Martyrdom
by Christophe Regnaut

This is what these savages told us of the taking of the village of St. Ignace, and about the Fathers Jean de Brébeuf and Gabriel Lalemant: "The Iroquois came, to the number of twelve hundred men; took our village and seized Father Brébeuf and his companion; and set fire to all the huts. They proceeded to vent their rage on those two fathers; for they took them both and stripped them entirely naked, and fastened each to a post. They tied both of their hands together. They tore the nails from their fingers. They beat them with a shower of blows from cudgels, on the shoulders, the loins, the belly, the legs, and the face—there being no part of their bodies which did not endure this torment."

The savages told us further that although Father de Brébeuf was overwhelmed with the weight of these blows, he did not cease continually to speak of God, and to encourage all the new Christians who were captives like himself to suffer well, that they might die well.

While the good Father was thus encouraging these good people, a wretched Huron renegade—who had remained a captive of the Iroquois, and whom Father de Brébeuf had formerly instructed and baptized—hearing him speak of paradise and holy baptism, was irritated, and said to him, "Echom," that is Father de Brébeuf's name in Huron, "thou sayest that baptism and the sufferings of this life lead straight to paradise; thou wilt go soon, for I am going to baptize thee, and to make thee suffer well, in order to go the sooner to thy paradise." The barbarian, having said that, took a kettle full of boiling water, which he poured over his body three different times, in derision of holy baptism. And each time he baptized him in this manner, the barbarian said to him, with bitter sarcasm, "Go to heaven, for thou art well baptized."

After that, they made him suffer several other torments. The first was to make the hatchets red hot, and to apply them to the loins and under the armpits. They made a collar of these red-hot hatchets, and put it on the neck of this good father. This is the fashion in which I have seen the collar made for other prisoners: They make six hatchets red hot, take a large twig of green wood, pass the six hatchets over the large end of the twig, take the two ends together, and then put it over the neck of the sufferer. I have seen no torment which more moved me to compassion than that. For you see a man, bound naked to a post, who, having this collar on his neck, cannot tell what posture to take. For, if he leans forward, those above his shoulders weigh the more on him; if he leans back, those on his stomach make him suffer the same torment; if he keep erect, without leaning to one side or the other, the burning hatchets, applied equally on both sides, give him a double torture.

After that, they put on him a belt of bark, full of pitch and resin, and set fire to it, which roasted his whole body. During all these torments, Father de Brébeuf endured like a rock, insensible to fire and flames, which astonished all the bloodthirsty wretches who tormented him. His zeal was so great that he preached continually to the infidels, to try to convert them. His executioners were enraged against him for constantly speaking to them of God and of their conversion. To prevent him from speaking more, they cut off his tongue, and both his upper and lower lips. After that, they set themselves to strip the flesh from his legs, thighs, and arms, to the very bone; and then they put it to roast before his eyes, in order to eat it.

When they tormented him in this manner, those wretches derided him, saying, "Thou seest plainly that we treat thee as a friend, since we shall be the cause of thy eternal happiness; thank us, then, for these good offices which we render thee—for, the more thou shalt suffer, the more will thy God reward thee."

Those butchers, seeing that the good Father began to grow weak, made him sit down on the ground; and one of them, taking a knife, cut off the skin covering his skull. Another one of those barbarians, seeing that the good Father would soon die, made an opening in the upper part of his chest, and tore out his heart, which he roasted and ate. Others came to drink his blood, still warm, which they drank with both hands—saying that Father de Brébeuf had been very courageous to endure so much pain as they had given him, and that, by drinking his blood, they would become courageous like him.

Annihilation
by Paul Ragueneau

The Iroquois having dealt their blow, and wholly reduced to fire the village of Saint Louis, retraced their steps into that of Saint Ignace, where they had left a good garrison, that it might be for them a sure retreat in case of misfortune, and that the victuals which they had found there might serve them as refreshments and provisions for their return.

On the evening of the same day, they sent scouts to reconnoiter the condition of our house at Saint Marie. Their report having been made in the council of war, the decision was adopted to come and attack us the next morning—promising themselves a victory which would be more glorious to them than all the successes of their arms in the past. We were in a good state of defense, and saw not one of our Frenchmen who was not resolved to sell his life very dear. . . .

Meanwhile, a part of the Hurons, who are called Atinniaoentent (that is to say, the nation [clan] of those who wear a bear on their coat of arms), having armed in haste, were at hand the next morning, the 17th of March, about three hundred warriors—who, while awaiting a more powerful help, secreted themselves in the ways of approach, intending to surprise some portion of the enemy.

About two hundred Iroquois, having detached themselves from their main body in order to get the start and proceed to the attack of our house, encountered some advance guards of that Huron troop. The latter straightaway took flight after some skirmishing, and were eagerly pursued until within sight of our fort—many having been killed while they were in disorder in the midst of the snows. But the more courageous of the Hurons, having stood firm against those who joined combat with them, had some advantage on their side, and constrained the Iroquois to take refuge within the palisades of the village of Saint Louis—which had not been burned, but only the cabins. These Iroquois were forced into that palisade, and about thirty of them were taken captives.

The main body of the enemy, having heard of the defeat of their men, came to attack our people in the very midst of their victory. Our men were the choicest Christians of the village of La Conception, and some others of the village of La Magdelaine. Their courage was not depressed, although they were only about one hundred and fifty. They proceeded to prayers, and sustained the assault of a place which, having been so recently captured and recaptured, was no longer adequate for defense. The shock was furious on both sides—our people having made many sallies, notwithstanding their small number, and having often constrained the enemy to give way. But (the combat having continued quite far into the night) as not more than a score of Christians, mostly wounded, were left, the victory remained wholly in the hands of the infidels. It had, however, cost them very dear, as their chief had been seriously wounded, and they had lost nearly a hundred men on the spot, of their best and most courageous.

All night the French were in arms, waiting to see at our gates this victorious enemy. We redoubled our devotions, in which were our strongest hopes, since help could only come from heaven. . . . The whole day passed in a profound silence on both sides—the country being in terror and in the expectation of some new misfortune.

On the nineteenth, the day of the great Saint Joseph, a sudden panic fell upon the hostile camp—some withdrawing in disorder, and others thinking only of flight. Their captains were constrained to yield to the terror which had seized them; they precipitated in their retreat, driving forth in haste a part of their captives, who were burdened above their strength, like packhorses, with the spoils which the victors were carrying off—their captors reserving for some other occasion the matter of their death.

As for the other captives who were left to them, destined to die on the spot, they attached them to stakes fastened in the earth, which they had arranged in various cabins. To these, on leaving the village, they set fire on all sides—taking pleasure, at their departure, in feasting upon the frightful cries which these poor victims uttered in the midst of those flames, where children were broiling beside their mothers; where a husband saw his wife roasting near him. . . .

MEANS OF HELPING THESE PEOPLES

In consequence of the losses incurred, a part of the country of the Hurons is seen to be in desolation; fifteen villages have been abandoned, the people of each scattering where they could in the woods and forests, on the lakes and rivers, and among the islands most unknown to the enemy. Others have taken refuge in the neighboring nations more capable of sustaining the stress of war. . . .

What increases the public misery is that famine has been prevalent this year in all these regions, more than it had been in fifty years—most of the people not having wherewith to live, and being constrained either to eat acorns, or else to go and seek in the woods some wild roots. With these they sustain a wretched life—still too happy not to have fallen into the hands of an enemy a thousand times more cruel than the wild beasts, and than all the famines in the world. . . .

Since the above writing, most of the Huron villages, which had become scattered, have conceived the desire to reunite in the Island of St. Joseph [modern-day Christian Island in Lake Huron]; and twelve of the most considerable captains have come to entreat us, in the name of all this poor desolate people, that we should have pity on their misery. They said that, without us, they saw themselves the prey of the enemy; that, with us, they esteemed themselves too strong not to defend themselves with courage; that we must have compassion on their widows, and on the poor Christian children; that those who remained infidels were all resolved to embrace our faith; and that we would make that island an Island of Christians. . . .

In a word, their eloquence . . . conquered us. We could not doubt that God had chosen to speak to us by their lips. . . . Our design is, therefore, to transfer the entire body of our forces, and this house of Saint Marie, to the Island of St. Joseph, which will be at once the center of our missions, and the bulwark of these countries. We have need more than ever of the prayers of France. . . .

OF THE REMOVAL TO THE ISLAND OF ST. JOSEPH

In consequence of the bloody victories obtained by the Iroquois over our Hurons at the commencement of the spring of last year, 1649, and of the more than inhuman acts of barbarity practiced toward their prisoners of war, and the cruel torments pitilessly inflicted on Father Jean de Brébeuf and Father Gabriel Lalemant, pastors of this truly suffering church—terror having fallen upon the neighboring villages, which were dreading a similar misfortune—all the inhabitants dispersed.

These poor, distressed people forsook their lands, houses, and villages, and all that in the world was dearest to them, in order to escape the cruelty of an enemy whom they feared more than a thousand deaths, and more than all that remained before their eyes—calculated as that was to strike terror into hearts already wretched. . . .

But on each of us lay the necessity of bidding farewell to that old home of Saint Marie—to its structures which, though plain, seemed to the eyes of our poor savages master works of art; and to its cultivated lands, which were promising us an abundant harvest. That spot must be foresaken, which I may call our second fatherland, our home of innocent delights, since it had been the cradle of this Christian church; since it was the temple of God, and the home of the servants of Jesus Christ. Moreover, for fear that our enemies, only too wicked, should profane the sacred place, and derive from it an advantage, we ourselves set fire to it, and beheld burn before our eyes, in less than one hour, our work of nine or ten years.

It was between five and six o'clock on the evening of the 14th of June that a part of our number embarked in a small vessel we had built. I, in company with most of the others, trusted myself to some logs, fifty or sixty feet in length, which we had felled in the woods, and dragged into the water, binding all together, in order to fashion for ourselves a sort of raft that should float on that faithless element—just as, in former days, we had seen in France floating timbers transported down the streams. We voyaged all night upon our great lake, by dint of arms and oars; and, the weather being favorable, we landed without mishap after a few days upon an island where the Hurons were awaiting us, and which was the spot we had fixed upon for making a general reunion, that we might make of it a Christian island.

God, doubtless, led us on this journey; for even while we coasted along those deserted lands, the enemy was in the field, and on the following day delivered his blow upon some Christian families whom he surprised, during their sleep, along the road which we had followed; some were massacred on the spot, others led away captive. The Hurons who were awaiting us on that island, called the Island of St. Joseph, had sown their Indian corn; but the summer droughts had been so excessive that they lost hope of their harvest, unless heaven should afford them some favoring showers. On our arrival, they besought us to obtain this favor for them; and our prayers were granted that very day, although previously there had been no appearance of rain.

These grand forests, which since the creation of the world had not been felled by the hand of any man, received us as guests; while the ground furnished to us, without digging, the stone and cement we needed for fortifying ourselves against our enemies. In consequence, thank God, we found ourselves very well protected, having built a small fort according to military rules; which, therefore, could be easily defended, and would fear neither the fire, the undermining, nor the escalade of the Iroquois. Moreover, we set to work to fortify the village of the Hurons, which was adjacent to our place of abode. We erected for them bastions, which defended its approaches—intending to put at their disposal the strength, the arms, and the courage of our Frenchmen. . . .

OF THE MISSION OF ST. JOSEPH

This island to which we had transferred the house of Saint Marie, being called by the name of Saint Joseph, patron of these regions, the savages who had removed there constituted the mission bearing the same name. The Huron village comprised over a hundred cabins, one of which might contain eight or ten families—making, say, sixty or eighty persons. Besides this village, in the country here and there were a few more distant cabins. . . .

The famine here has been very severe. Not that the lands which had been sown would not have returned with interest what we desired—indeed, more than a hundredfold—that which had been entrusted to them; but for the reason that there was hardly one family in ten which had been able to apply itself to the labor needed to cultivate a field of Indian corn in a place which, when they came to it, was but a thick forest, unprepared in any way for tillage.

The greater number of these poor people, exiles in their own country, had passed the whole summer, a part also of the autumn, living in the woods on roots and wild fruit; or taking, here and there, in the lakes and rivers, a few small fish, which aided rather in postponing for a little time their death, than in satisfying the needs of life. Winter having set in, covering the ground with three or four feet of snow and freezing all the lakes and rivers, that entire multitude of people who had crowded near us found themselves in immediate need, and in the extremity of their misery not having laid in nor being able to store any provisions.

Then it was that we were compelled to behold dying skeletons eking out a miserable life, feeding even on the excrements and refuse of nature. The acorn was to them, for the most part, what the choices viands are in France. Even carrion dug up, the remains of foxes and dogs, excited no horror. And they even devoured one another, but this in secret. . . .

OF THE DEVASTATION OF THE COUNTRY OF THE HURONS

We had all passed the winter in the extremities of a famine which prevailed over all these regions, and everywhere carried off large numbers of Christians, never ceasing to extend its ravages, and casting despair on every side. Hunger is an inexorable tyrant; one who never says, "It is enough"; who never grants a truce; who devours all that is given him; and, should we fail to pay him, repays himself in human blood, and rends our bowels. . . .

But, when spring came, the Iroquois were still more cruel to us, and it is they who have indeed blasted all our hopes. It is they who have transformed into an abode of horror—into a land of blood and carnage, into a theater of cruelty, and into a sepulchre of bodies stripped of their flesh by the exhaustions of a long famine—a country of plenty, a land of holiness, a place no longer barbarous, since the blood shed for the love of it had made all its people Christians.

Our poor famished Hurons were compelled to part from us at the commencement of the month of March, to go in search of acorns on the summits of the mountains, which were divesting themselves of their snow; or to repair to certain fishing grounds in places more open to the southern sun, where the ice melted sooner. They hoped to find, in those remote places, some little alleviation from famine, which was rendering their existence a living death. . . . Before going away, they confessed, redoubling their devotions in proportion as their miseries increased. Many received holy communion as preparation for death. . . . They split up into bands, so that, if some fell into the hands of the enemy, others might escape.

The great lake which surrounded our Island of St. Joseph was, at that time, nothing but a bed of ice two or three feet in thickness. Hardly had these good Christians left our sight than the ice melted under their feet; some were drowned in the depths, and found there their grave; others, more fortunate, extricated themselves, though benumbed with a deadly cold. . . .

Our poor starvelings were just beginning to enjoy the benefits of their fishery, which they found abundant enough; but their joy was to savor more of heaven than of earth. On the day of the Annunciation, the 25th of March, a war party of Iroquois—who had marched over nearly two hundred leagues of country, across ice and snow, crossing mountains and forests full of terrors—surprised, one nightfall, our Christians' camp, and perpetrated in it a cruel butchery.

It seemed as if heaven directed their [the Iroquois party's] every step, and as if they had an angel for a guide; for they divided their forces so successfully as to discover, in less than two days, every party of our Christians who had scattered hither and thither. These were separated by six, seven, or eight leagues—one hundred in one place, fifty in another; there were even some solitary families who had strayed into less well-known places, and away from all beaten track. Strange circumstance! Of all that scattered people, but a single man escaped, who came to bring us the news. . . .

My pen can no longer express the fury of the Iroquois in these encounters; it shrinks from the repeated portrayal of such scenes of cruelty—to which our eyes cannot become familiarized any more than our feelings, which are never dulled to the violence of all these torments which rage suggests. Our sole consolation is this, that these horrible inflictions end with our lives; and that God will crown them with a happiness that has no end.

Since then, misfortunes have crowded upon us. . . . Hunger, it is said, drives the wolves from the woods; our starving Hurons were likewise compelled to leave a village where only horror abounded. This was toward the end of Lent. Alas! these poor Christians would have been only too happy had they had anything from which to fast, as even acorns and water. On Easter day, we had a general communion for them. The next day, they parted from us, leaving in our care all their little property—the greater number publicly declaring that they made us their heirs, perceiving clearly that their death was not far away, and that they carried it within.

Indeed, but a few days had slipped by when news reached us of the misfortune we had anticipated. That poor scattered band fell into the snares of our enemies, the Iroquois. Some were slain on the spot; others dragged away captive; women and children were burned; some few escaped from the midst of the flames, which struck dismay and terror into every heart.

Eight days later, a similar misfortune assailed yet another band. Whithersoever they go, massacres await them. Famine follows them everywhere . . . and to fill up the measure of misery without hope, they learned that two powerful war parties were on the way, who were coming to exterminate them; that the first designed to make havoc of their fields, to pluck up their Indian corn, and to lay waste the country; while the second party was to cut down everything that might have escaped the fury of the first. Despair reigns everywhere.

At the height of these alarms, two old captains came to see me privately, and addressed me thus: "My brother," they said to me, "thine eyes deceive thee when thou lookest on us; thou believest that thou seest living men, while we are but specters, the souls of the departed. The ground thou treadest on is about to open under us, to swallow us up, together with thyself, that we might be in the place where we ought to be, among the dead.

"It is needful that thou shouldst know, my brother, that this night, in council, we have resolved upon leaving this island. The greater number intend to take refuge within the forest, and live alone; and as no one in the world will know where they are, the enemy cannot have knowledge of them. . . . Some speak boldly of taking their wives and children, and throwing themselves into the arms of the enemy—among whom they have a great number of relatives who wish for them,[21] and counsel them to make their escape as soon as possible from a desolated country, if they do not wish to perish beneath its ruins. . . .

"My brother, take courage," added these captains. "Thou alone canst bestow upon us life, if thou wilt strike a daring blow. Choose a place where thou mayst be able to reassemble us, and prevent this dispersion. Cast thine eyes toward Quebec, and transport thither the remnants of this ruined nation. Do not wait until famine and war have slain the last of us. Thou bear-

---

[21] To rebuild their numbers, reduced by smallpox epidemics, the Iroquois now kept most of their captives alive, adopting them as part of their own people.

est us in thy hands in thy heart. More than ten thousand of us have been snatched away by death. If thou delay longer, not one will remain. . . . If thou listen to our wishes, we will build a church under the shelter of the fort at Quebec. . . ."

God had spoken to us by the lips of these captains; for the truth was apparent that the entire Huron country was but a land of horror and a region of massacres. . . . But if we could conduct them to the shelter of a French fort at Montreal, Trois Rivières, or Quebec, it would be, we thought, their only place of refuge. . . .

It was not without tears that we left a country which possessed our hearts and engaged our hopes; and which, even now reddened with the glorious blood of our brethren, promised us a like happiness, and opened to us the way to heaven, and the gate of paradise. . . . Amid these regrets, the thought was consoling that we were to take away with us poor Christian families numbering about three hundred souls—sad remains of a nation formerly so numerous, which calamities have assailed at a time when they were most faithful to God. . . .

By roads which covered a distance of about three hundred leagues we marched, upon our guard as in an enemy's country—there not being any spot where the Iroquois is not to be feared, and where we did not see traces of his cruelty, or signs of his treachery. On one side we surveyed districts which, not ten years ago, I reckoned to contain eight or ten thousand men. For all that, there remains not one of them. Going beyond, we coasted along shores but lately reddened with the blood of our Christians. On another side you might have seen the trail, quite recent, of those who had been taken captive. A little farther on were but the shells of cabins abandoned to the fury of the enemy—those who had dwelt in them having fled into the forest, and condemned themselves to a life which is but perpetual banishment. . . .

Midway in our journey, we had an alarm that was thrilling enough. A band of about forty Frenchmen, and a few Hurons, who had wintered at Quebec, and who were ascending this great river, noticed the tracks of some of our scouts, which they took to be those of the enemy. At the same time, our vanguard had also noticed the footprints of those who had just discovered us. Both having retraced their steps, each side prepared itself for battle; but on drawing near, our fears were soon changed to joy. These Frenchmen whom we met had effected, but a very few days ago, the capture of some Iroquois, who had intended to surprise them. . . . The company which had met us, having been apprised of the overthrow of the whole Huron nation, determined to retrace their steps; so we pursued our way.

Alas, that those wretched Iroquois should have caused such desolation in all these regions! When I ascended the great river, only thirteen years ago, I had seen it bordered with large numbers of people of the Algonquin tongue, who knew no God. These, in the midst of their unbelief, looked upon themselves as the gods of the earth, for the reason that nothing was lacking to them in the richness of their fisheries, their hunting grounds, and the trade which they carried on with allied nations; add to which, they were the terror of their enemies. Since they have embraced the faith, and adored the cross of Jesus Christ, he has given them, as their lot, a portion of that cross— verily a heavy one, having made them a prey to miseries, torments, and cruel deaths; in a word, they are a people wiped off the face of the earth.

"A PEOPLE WIPED off the face of the earth." So it was for the once-mighty Hurons, the pillar of French power in North America. With baptism had come fire; with missionaries had come pestilence; with gunpowder had come annihilation. "Archeologically and anthropologically," historian Ian Steele writes, "the Huron can be regarded as exterminated in 1649." Their once-vast territory was a wasteland, a landscape of abandoned cornfields, burned villages, mutilated bodies.

A few survived: some joined the Erie and Neutral nations, though these would be destroyed as well by the Iroquois before 1654. Some joined the Petun, forming a new tribe called the Wyandot. A few hundred made the trek to Quebec, where they formed a settlement at Lorette; others settled at Detroit; both these small groups kept the Huron name. The largest number to survive, ironically, were the thousands adopted into the Five Nations. Indeed, at least one Iroquois village consisted entirely of captured Hurons— who, in accordance with their common culture, accepted their fate and lived as loyal Iroquois. So it was that the Five Nations rebuilt their numbers, as other tribes fell before the smallpox plague.

For New France, the Huron apocalypse was an unspeakable catastrophe. Over the next fifteen years, Mohawk raids would ravage the sparsely settled colony. Parties of warriors scourged its riverside settlements; they even attacked the towns of Montreal, Trois Rivières, and Quebec itself in 1651 and 1652. In 1661, the Five Nations killed thirty-eight settlers and captured sixty-one, slaying twenty-one in Quebec alone. No other European settlement depended so on Native American alliances—and no other faced so great a crisis. With the annihilation of the Huron nation, the colony of New France trembled on the edge of extinction.

11

NEW NETHERLANDS, NEW YORK

When the Powhatan confederacy collided with the English at Jamestown, they endured first pressure, then a devastating defeat. When the Pequots challenged the expanding Puritan settlements in Connecticut, they suffered virtual extinction. But the Five Nations of the Iroquois actually grew in power after the European arrival. They dispersed nation after nation of their Native American enemies. They destroyed the mighty Huron. They even threatened to overrun New France itself. The reasons for this record were many: skillful tactics, brave warriors, close internal cooperation, a key geographical location, effective strategies for coping with disease and other crises. And then there were their partners, the Dutch.

The story told so far of European settlement has been incomplete. We have followed the tobacco empire of Virginia, the fur-trading center of Quebec, the Pilgrim and Puritan farmers of New England. But starting as early as 1614, the merchants of the Netherlands began a permanent Dutch presence along the Hudson River. That presence would grow into the colony of New Netherlands—a settlement that decisively shifted the balance of Native American power, of intercolonial relations, and eventually the culture of the English colonies themselves.

Like the Iroquois, the Netherlands went against the tide of history. In an age when European kings were expanding their power (or trying to, in the case of the Stuarts, England's royal family), the Dutch broke away from Spanish rule to form a republic—fighting a war of independence that lasted from 1572 to 1609. The seven provinces of the Netherlands (one of which, Holland, lent its name as the popular designation for the country) sat on the swampy soil of lands reclaimed from the sea—they were Low Countries indeed, protected from the tides by the legendary dikes. But it was the sea that carried them to greatness.

On land, the Dutch just barely managed to hold their own against the Spanish armies of Philip II—but on the waves, their fleets of warships won victory after victory against their foes. Even more important, however, were the merchant craft that went out from the ports of the Netherlands. This was a nation of traders who quickly rose to dominate the commerce of Europe. Dutch hulls carried Europe's cargoes; Dutch workshops fashioned raw materials into finished goods, to be shipped out again; and Dutch businessmen created institutional innovations, establishing banks and powerful joint-stock companies. As the Pilgrims learned, these were a people who pursued private gain above all else, and chased profit wherever it might be found; they even traded with the Spanish enemy during their desperate war for independence.

In 1614, a group of Dutch merchants built Fort Nassau on the Hudson River, at the present-day location of Albany. There they traded with the local Mahican Indians for furs. In the early 1620s, one of the mightiest of those joint-stock corporations, the Dutch West India Company, took over the post, rebuilding it as Fort Orange (named after the family that had long provided leadership for the republic of the Netherlands). The Company also established a settlement on Manhattan, a strategically located island at the mouth of the Hudson River.

So began New Netherlands, a colony run from first to last by the West India Company, under the very loose control of the Dutch government. The first selection that follows is not from an eyewitness, but rather a writer who made a point of gathering the news about the colony from his home in Amsterdam. He provides, nevertheless, a relatively accurate contemporary account of its early years. He reveals the mechanism behind the colony's founding, and the pivotal Mohawk–Mahican war over access to the post of Fort Orange. The Dutch, hoping to keep their trade options open, backed the losing side; they later learned to do as they were told by their Native American partners.

The Dutch New World
by Nicolaes van Wassanaer

Numerous voyages realize so much profit for adventurers, that they discover other countries, which are afterwards settled and planted with people. Virginia, a country lying in 42½ degrees, is one of these. . . . The Lords States General, observing the great abundance of their people as well as their desire to occupy other lands, have allowed the West India Company to settle that same country. . . .

This country, now called New Netherlands, is usually reached in seven or eight weeks from here [Amsterdam]. . . . It is worthy of remark that, with so many tribes [in New Netherlands], there is so great a diversity of language. They vary frequently not over five or six leagues; forthwith comes another language; if they meet they can hardly understand one another. . . .

A ship was fitted out under a commission from the West India Company, and freighted with families, to plant a colony among this people. But to go forward safely, it is first of all necessary that they be placed in a good defensive position and well provided with forts and arms, since the Spaniard, who claims all the country, will never allow anyone to gain a possession there. . . .

APRIL 1624

The West India company being chartered to navigate these rivers, did not neglect to do so, but equipped in the spring [of 1624] a vessel . . . called the *Nieu Nederlandt,* whereof Cornelius Jacobsz May of Hoorn was skipper, with a company of 30 families, mostly Walloons, to plant a colony there. . . .

The ship sailed up to the Maykans [Mahicans], 44 leagues, and they built and completed a fort named Orange, with four bastions, on an island, called by them Castle Island. They forthwith put the spade in the ground and began to plant. . . . Regarding this colony, it has already a prosperous beginning; and the hope is that it will not fall through provided it be zealously sustained. . . .

NOVEMBER 1626

In our preceding discourse mention was made of New Netherlands and its colony planted by the West India Company, situated in Virginia on the river called by the French Montaigne, and by us Mauritius [the Hudson], and that some families were sent thither out of Holland, now increased to two hundred souls; and afterwards some ships, one with horses, the other with cows, and the third with hay; two months afterwards a fly-boat was equipped carrying sheep, hogs, wagons, and all other implements of husbandry.

The colony is now established on the Manhates [Manhattan], where a fort has been staked out by Master Kryn Frederycks, an engineer.[22] It is planned to be of large dimensions. . . . The counting house there is kept in a stone building, thatched with reed; the other houses are of the bark of trees. Each has his own house. The Director and *Koopman* (secretary) live together; there are thirty ordinary houses on the east side of the river, which runs nearly north and south. The Honorable Peter Minuit is director there at present. . . . François Molemaecker is busy building a horse-mill, over which shall be constructed a spacious room sufficient to accommodate a large congregation, and then a tower is to be erected where the bells brought from Puerto Rico will be hung. . . .[23]

Everyone there who fills no public office is busy about his own affairs.

[22] Peter Minuit arrived as Director General of New Netherlands on May 4, 1626, and bought the island of Manhattan for sixty guilders worth of trade goods. The secretary, Isaac de Rasieres, arrived on July 27.

[23] The Dutch Admiral Boudewyn Hendricks sacked the city of San Juan in October 1625, and the bells were brought to New Amsterdam as spoils of war.

Men work there as in Holland: one trades, upwards, southwards, and northwards; another builds houses; the third farms. Each farmer has his own farmstead on the land purchased by the Company, which also owns the cows; but the milk remains to the profit of the farmer. He sells it to those of the people who receive their wages for work every week. The houses of the Hollanders now stand outside the fort, but when that is completed, they will all repair within, so as to garrison it and be secure from sudden attack. . . .

At Fort Orange, the most northerly point at which the Hollanders traded, no more than fifteen or sixteen men will remain; the remainder will come down [to Manhattan]. Right opposite is the fort of the Maykans [Mahicans], which they built against their enemies, the Maquaes [Mohawks], a powerful people.

It happened this year that the Maykans, going to war with the Maquaes, requested to be assisted by the commander of Fort Orange and six others. Commander Krieckebeeck went up with them; a league from the fort they met the Maquaes who fell so boldly upon them with a discharge of arrows, that they were forced to fly, and many were killed, among whom were the commander and three of his men. Among the latter was Tymen Bouwensz, whom they devoured, after having roasted him. The rest they burnt. The commander was buried with the other two by his side. Three escaped: two Portuguese and a Hollander from Hoorn. One of the Portuguese was wounded by an arrow in the back whilst swimming. The Indians carried a leg and an arm home to be divided among their families, as a sign that they had conquered their enemies.

Some days after the worthy Pieter Barentsz, who usually was sent upwards and along the coast with the sloops, visited them [the Mohawks]. They wished to excuse their act, on the plea that they had never set themselves against the whites, and asked the reason why the latter had meddled with them; otherwise, they would not have shot them.[24]

There being no commander, Pieter Barentsen assumed the command of Fort Orange by order of Director Minuit. There were eight families there, and ten or twelve seamen in the Company's service. The families were to leave there this year—the fort to remain garrisoned by sixteen men, without women—in order to strengthen the colony near the Manhates [tribe], who are becoming more and more accustomed to the strangers. . . .

OCTOBER 1628

The government over the people of New Netherlands continued on the 19th of August of this year in the aforesaid Minuit, successor to Verhulst.

[24] The whole point of the war the Mohawks were waging against the Mahicans was to gain access to trade with Fort Orange; they were dismayed to see the Dutch fight against them, and sought to smooth things over. Note that these Iroquois were able to defeat the Europeans, even though they had no firearms.

He went thither from Holland on January 9, Anno 1626, and took up his residence in the midst of a nation called Manhates, building a fort there to be called [New] Amsterdam, having four bastions and faced outside with stone, as the ramparts crumbled away like sand, and are now to be more substantial. The population consists of two hundred and seventy souls, including men, women, and children. They remained as yet without [outside] the fort, in no fear, as the natives live peaceably with them. . . .

There are now no families at Fort Orange, situated higher up the river among the Maykans. They have all been brought down. Five and twenty persons, traders, remain there. Bastiaen Jansz Crol is vice-director there, who has remained there since the year 1626, when the others came down. . . .

Beyond the South [Delaware] River . . . Englishmen are settled, freemen, but planted there by merchants on condition that they deliver as much tobacco to their masters as is agreed on; the remainder is their own. Considerable trade is carried on with them, and many ships come thither out of England. On the north side are the English Brownists [Pilgrims] who maintain themselves very well and are much resorted to, supporting their reputation bravely with the natives, whom they do not fear, having acted strictly with these from the first, and so continuing.

In the beginning of this year, war broke out [again] between the Maykans near Fort Orange and the Maquaes, but these beat and captured the Maykans and drove off the remainder, who have settled towards the north by the Fresh [Connecticut] River, so called; where they begin again to cultivate the soil, and thus the war has come to an end.

MARCH 1630

After the Right Honorable Directors of the chartered West India Company in the United Netherlands had provided everything for the defense of New Netherlands and put everything there in good order, they, taking into consideration the advantages of said place . . . [had] sent some free emigrants thither with all sorts of cattle and implements necessary for agriculture, so that in the year 1628 there already resided on the Island of the Manhates two hundred and seventy souls. . . . But as the land, being extensive and in many places full of weeds and wild growth, could not be properly cultivated in consequence of the scantiness of the population, the said Directors of the West India Company, to better people their lands, and to bring the country to produce more abundantly, resolved to grant diverse privileges, freedoms, and exemptions to all patroons, masters, or individuals who should plant any colonies and cattle in New Netherlands . . . to afford better encouragement and infuse greater zeal into whosoever should be inclined to reside and plant his colony in New Netherlands.

THE WEST INDIA Company faced something of a quandary in its new colony: it needed to populate New Netherlands, but it wished to spend little or no money doing so. The solution it arrived at seems a rather odd one for the most commercial people in Europe: it decided to sell patroonships— virtual feudal realms to be ruled at the discretion of the purchasers (and to be settled at their expense). This jumble of private enterprise, sovereign power, and medieval trappings reflected the status of the colony itself, which was virtually a Company fiefdom run as a commercial enterprise.

One of the men who decided to become a patroon was David de Vries, an oceangoing merchant with a great deal of experience in sailing up and down American shores. In the account that follows, de Vries reveals the central role played by the Dutch in seaborne trade: they controlled much of the commerce in tobacco, for instance, despite the English near-monopoly on production. After making a small fortune in trade, he decided to settle in New Netherlands, a colony wracked by disputes—by traditional Dutch sharp dealing—and devoted to profit above all else. He also reveals the rising tensions with the English colonists in Connecticut and on Long Island, territories the Dutch claimed for themselves.

Following de Vries's account is a letter from Isaac Jogues, a Jesuit missionary whom the Dutch freed from captivity among the Iroquois. The priest's description of New Netherlands suggests his bewilderment and dismay at this strange colony—so unlike the military/diplomatic center of New France or the devout farming towns of New England. Trade, religion, settlement, even language—nothing seemed unified and orderly in this colony. How indeed could it survive?

Englishmen and Patroons
by David de Vries

The 17th [of May, 1635, de Vries's ship] came before the harbor of the English Virginias. . . . We arrived about four o'clock in the afternoon before the fort called Point Comfort. . . . I landed here all the English whom I had rescued [from a Spanish attack on Tortuga], and endeavored to obtain some provisions in order to sail to New Netherlands, and to make my ship tight, as it was extremely leaky, which I could not do in the English Virginias.

As it was out of season to trade for tobacco, I let all of my cargo lie here, and gave directions to trade when the crop of tobacco should be ripe, and I would return again when the unhealthy season should be over, that is towards September—for June, July, and half of August are very unhealthy there for those who have not lived there a year. The English die there at this season very fast, but one who has been there over a year they say is seasoned; that is, he is accustomed to the land. . . .

The 28th, after I had provided myself again with everything, we weighed anchor, and sailed for New Netherlands, where we arrived safe behind the point towards the evening of the 30th.

The 1st of June I went ashore with a boat to Fort Amsterdam, where I found Wouter van Twiller governor, as before. Asked him if he would let me hire some carpenters, in order to repair my ship, which was very leaky; if not, I would sail to New [England]. He promised me assistance. I then sent my boat back, in order to let my ship come in, which was five leagues from here, and sent also a young man aboard who might pilot her in. . . . We prepared to empty the ship, in order to get at the leak, and unloaded her and hauled her upon the strand. . . . We spent here the unhealthy season of the English Virginias—June, July, and August.

The 1st of September, we were lying ready to go to the English Virginias, to see whether we could obtain our dues from the rescued English, whom I had brought from the Tortugas, and for the goods left there. . . . The 10th we arrived at Point Comfort, before the English fort. . . . We sailed up the river eight leagues, to Blank Point, and found there thirty-six large ships— all of them English ships of twenty to twenty-four guns—for the purpose of loading with tobacco. Fifteen of the captains were dead, in consequence of their coming too early in the unhealthy season, and not having been before in the country.

The 1st of October I began to sail up and down the river to my customers, in order to collect my debts; but found that little tobacco had been made, and that there had been this year great mortality among the people, and large quantities of goods brought into the country by the English; and that there were great frauds among the English, who had not paid each other for the tobacco, and that half the ships of their own nation were not laden; so that I consider, in regard to this trade, that he who wishes to trade here must keep a house here, and continue all the year, that he may be prepared when the tobacco comes from the field to seize it, if he would obtain any of his debts. It is thus the English do among themselves; so that there is not trade for us, unless there be an overplus of tobacco, or few English ships.

After I had spent the winter here, I was compelled to return, as did almost all the ships, without tobacco, and to let my debts stand. I determined to go off again, and sold some beaver to the English. . . .

ANNO 1638

The 25th of September I joined a [West India] Company's ship, freighted by them, and in which were some persons in my service. On the same day, we weighed anchor and set sail. . . . [On the 27th of December the ship arrived at New Amsterdam.] We quickly sailed to the fort, where there was great rejoicing, inasmuch as they were not expecting any ship at that time of year. Found there a commander, named Willem Kieft. . . . Going ashore, I was made welcome by the commander, who invited me to his house.

ANNO 1639

The 5th of January I sent my people to Staten Island to begin to plant a colony there and build. The 4th of June I started north in a yacht to the Fresh [Connecticut] River, where the West India Company has a small fort called the House of Hope. . . . The 9th arrived with the yacht at the House of Hope, where one Gysbert van Dyck commanded with fourteen or fifteen soldiers. This redoubt stands upon the plain on the margin of the river; and alongside it runs a creek toward a high woodland, out of which comes a waterfall, which makes this creek, and where the English, in spite of us, have begun to build up a small town [Hartford], and have built a fine church and over a hundred houses. The commander had given me orders to make a protest against them, as they were using our own land, which we bought from the savages. Some of our soldiers had forbidden them to put the plow into it; but they had opposed them, and had cudgelled some of the Company's soldiers.

Going there, I was invited by the English governor [John Haynes] to dine. When sitting at the table, I told him that it was wrong to take by force the Company's land, which it had bought and paid for. He answered that the lands were lying idle; that, though we had been there many years, we had done scarcely anything; that it was a sin to let such rich land, which produced such fine corn, lie uncultivated; and that they had already built three towns upon this river, in a fine country. There are many salmon up this river.

These English live soberly, drink only three times at a meal, and whoever drinks himself drunk they tie to a post and whip him, as they do thieves in Holland. . . . These people give out that they are Israelites, and that we at our colony are Egyptians, and that the English in the Virginias are also Egyptians. I frequently told the governor that it would be impossible for them to keep the people so strict, seeing they had come from so luxurious a country as England.

The 14th took leave of the House of Hope. . . . Towards evening [of the 16th] reached the Minates [Manhattan], before Fort Amsterdam. . . .

The 10th of February I began to make a plantation a league and a half or two leagues above the fort, as there was there a fine location, and full thirty-one *morgens* [about sixty acres] of maize land, where there were no trees to remove; and hay land lying all together, sufficient for two hundred cattle, which is a great commodity there. I went there to live, half on account of the pleasure of it, as it was all situated along the river. I leased out the plantation of Staten Island, as no people had been sent me from Holland, as was promised me in the contract which I had made with Frederick de Vries, a director of the West India Company. . . .

The 1st of December, I began to take hold of Vriessendael [as he called this plantation], as it was a fine place, situated along the river, under a mountain . . . but the evil of it was that, though I earnestly took hold of the place, I was not seconded by my partner, according to our agreement, who was Frederick de Vries, a director of the Company, and who thought that colonies could be built up without men or means; as his idea was that Godyn, Kiliaen van Rensselaer, Bloemaert, and Jan de Laet had established their colonies [patroonships] with the means of the company, which had brought there all the cattle and the farmers. When the work began to progress, these persons were directors of the Company and commissioners of New Netherlands, and helped themselves by the cunning tricks of merchants; and the Company . . . bestowed not a thought upon their best trading post, at Fort Orange, whether people were making farms there or not. But these fellows, especially Rensselaer, who was accustomed to refine pearls and diamonds, succeeded in taking it from the other managers—their partners. Michael Pauw, discovering that they had appropriated the land at Fort Orange to themselves, immediately had the land below, opposite Fort Amsterdam, where the Indians are compelled to cross to the fort with their beavers, registered for himself, and called it Pavonia.

[Upon] the Company seeing afterwards that they were affected, much contention and jealousy arose among them, because they who undertook to plant colonies with their own money should have taken the property of the Company. Thus was the country kept down by these disputes, so that it was not settled; for at that time there were friends enough who would have peopled the country by patroonships, but they were always prevented by the contention of the managers. . . .

ANNO 1642

As I was daily with Commander Kieft, generally dining with him when I went to the fort, he told me that he had now a fine inn built of stone, in order to accommodate the English who daily passed with their vessels from New England to Virginia, from whom he suffered great annoyance, and who might now lodge in the tavern.

I replied that it happened well for the travellers, but there was great want of a church, and that it was a scandal to us when the English passed there, and saw only a mean barn in which we preached; that the first thing the English in New England built, after their dwellings, was a fine church, and we ought to do so, too, as the West India Company was deemed to be a principal means of upholding the Reformed Religion against the tyranny of Spain, and had excellent material therefore—namely fine oak-wood, good mountain stone, and good lime burnt of oyster shells, much better than our lime in Holland.

He then inquired who would undertake the work. I answered, the lovers of the Reformed Religion, of whom there were enough. He then said that I must be one of them, as I proposed it, and must give a hundred guilders. I told him that I was satisfied, and that he must be the first to give, as he was commander, and then we chose Jochem Pietersz. Kuyter, a devout person of the Reformed Religion, who had good workmen who would quickly provide a good lot of timber, and also chose [Jan Jansen] Damen, because he lived close by the fort.

And so we four, as church wardens, were the ones to undertake the work of building the church. The commander was to give several thousand guilders on behalf of the Company, and we should see whether the rest would be subscribed by the community. The church should be built in the fort, to guard against any surprise by the savages. Thus were the walls of the church speedily begun to be laid up with quarry stone, and to be covered by the English carpenters with overlapping shingles cleft from oak.

The Land of Eighteen Languages
by Isaac Jogues

New Holland, which the Dutch call in Latin *Novum Balgium*—in their own language, *Nieuw Nederland,* that is to say, New Low Countries—is situated between Virginia and New England. . . . The channel [of the Hudson River] is deep, fit for the largest ships, which ascend to Manhattes Island, which is seven leagues in circuit, and on which there is a fort to serve as the commencement of a town to be built there, and to be called New Amsterdam.

The fort, which is at the point of the island . . . is called Fort Amsterdam; it has four regular bastions, mounted with several pieces of artillery. All these bastions and the curtains were, in 1643, but mounds, most of which had been crumbled away, so that one entered the fort on all sides. There were no ditches. The garrison of the said fort, and another which they had built farther up against the incursions of the savages, their enemies, there were sixty soldiers. They were beginning to face the gates and bastions with stone. Within the fort there was a pretty large stone church, the house of the Governor, whom they call Director General, quite neatly made of brick, the storehouses, and barracks.

On the island of Manhattes, and in its environs, there may well be four or five hundred men of different sects and nations. The Director General told me that there were men of eighteen different languages; they are scattered here and there on the river, above and below, as the beauty and convenience of the spot has invited each to settle. Some mechanics, however, who ply their trade are ranged under the fort; all the others are exposed to the incursions of the natives, who in the year 1643, when I was there, actually killed some two score Hollanders, and burnt many houses and barns full of wheat. . . .

No religion is publicly exercised but the Calvinist, and orders are to admit none but Calvinists, but this is not observed. For besides the Calvinists there are in the colony Catholics, English Puritans, Lutherans, Anabaptists, here called Mennonites, etc. When anyone comes to settle in the country, they lend him horses, cows, etc.; they give him provisions, all which he returns as soon as he is at ease; and as to the land, after ten years he pays to the West India Company the tenth of the produce which he reaps.

This country is bounded on the New England side by a river which they call the Fresh [Connecticut] River, which serves as a boundary between them and the English. The English, however, come very near to them, choosing to hold lands under the Hollanders, who ask nothing, rather than depend upon the English Milords [sic], who exact rents, and would fain be absolute. On the other side, towards Virginia, its limits are the river which they call the South [Delaware] River, on which there is also a Dutch settlement, but the Swedes have one at the mouth extremely well supplied with cannons and men [Fort Nya Elfsborg]. It is believed that these Swedes are maintained by some Amsterdam merchants, who are not satisfied that the West India Company should alone enjoy all the commerce of these parts. . . .

Ascending the [Hudson] river to the 43rd degree, you meet the second settlement, which the tide reaches but does not pass. Ships of a hundred and a hundred and twenty tons can come up to it. There are two things in this settlement (which is called Rensselaerwick, as if to say, settlement of Rensselaers, who is a rich Amsterdam merchant)—first, a miserable little fort called Fort Orange, built of logs, with four or five pieces of Breteuil cannon, and as many pedereros [small cannons]. This has been reserved and is maintained by the West India Company. . . .

Secondly, a colony sent here by this Rensselaers, who is the patroon. This colony is composed of about a hundred persons, who reside in some twenty-five or thirty houses built along the river, as each found most convenient. In the principal house lives the patroon's agent; the minister has his apart, in which service is performed. There is also a kind of bailiff here, whom they call the seneschal [schout] who administers justice. All their houses are merely boards and thatched, with no mason work except the chimneys. The forest furnishing many large pines, they make boards by means of their mills, which they have here for the purpose.

They found some pieces of ground all ready, which the savages had formerly cleared, and in which they sow wheat and oats for beer, and for their horses, of which they have great numbers. There is little land fit for tillage, being hemmed in by the hills, which are poor soil. This obliges them to separate, and they already occupy two or three leagues of country. Trade is free to all; this gives the Indians things cheap, each of the Hollanders outbidding his neighbor, and being satisfied provided he can gain some little profit.

IN 1664, PETER STUYVESANT boarded a ship in the harbor of New Amsterdam and set sail for the Netherlands. It was undoubtedly the greatest moment of disappointment in his disappointment-filled life. He was the governor of New Netherlands—the last governor—and he had just surrendered to an English fleet.

Stuyvesant, however, was not one to take defeat lightly. Upon his return to his mother country, he wrote a bitter letter to his superiors, the directors of the West India Company. He wrote with testy self-righteousness, addressing the directors as "your Illustrious High Mightinesses" so often, that the sarcasm quickly became unmistakable. The fall of the colony, he told them, was their fault, not his. It was also the fault of those treacherous colonists he had ruled.

There was some truth in Stuyvesant's complaint. After his arrival in New Amsterdam, shortly after the departure of Father Jogues, he succeeded in raising the colony to the height of its power as a province of the Netherlands. The population grew, and grew wealthier. Their allies, the Iroquois (especially the Mohawks), battled the French to the edge of complete defeat, and crushed the Susquehannocks to the south. And in 1655, Stuyvesant captured the rival colony of New Sweden.

In the 1660s, however, fate ran the other way. Mohawk raiding parties suffered repulses at the hands of the Mahican, Ottawa, Susquehannock, and Delaware nations. Regular army troops from France arrived in Quebec, in preparation for a major offensive against the Five Nations. Within New Netherlands, Stuyvesant suffered persistent intrigues from the Board of Nine, the (somewhat) representative council he had formed to better rule the colony. And war broke out between the two old allies, England and the Netherlands.

In 1664, Stuyvesant was caught between two fires: the colonial forces of Connecticut (allied with English settlers in Dutch Long Island) and the royal fleet commanded by King Charles II's brother, James, the Duke of York (more on Charles and his brother in the next chapter). The penurious West India Company had left him with few arms, and fewer soldiers. The mutinous merchants of New Amsterdam left him with almost no support—especially when the English promised that all the Dutch settlers would keep their property and their rights. Stuyvesant had to admit defeat—but he could still shirk the blame.

Surrender
by Peter Stuyvesant

Whilst I, your Illustrious High Mightinesses' humble servant, was still in New Netherlands, I was informed . . . that the unfortunate loss and reduction of New Netherlands were . . . spoken of and judged in this country by many variously, and by most people not consistently with the truth, according to the appetite and leaning of each. Therefore your Illustrious High Mightinesses' servant, sustained by the tranquility of an upright and loyal heart, was moved to abandon all, even his most beloved wife, to inform you . . . of the true state of the case. . . .

I dare not interrupt your Illustrious High Mightinesses' most important business by a lengthy narrative of the poor condition in which I found New Netherlands on my assuming its government [in May 1647]. The open country was stripped of inhabitants to such a degree that, with the exception of the three English villages of Heemstede, New Flushing, and Gravesend, there were not fifty . . . plantations on it, and the whole province could not muster 250, at most 300 men capable of bearing arms. Which was caused, first (in default of a settlement of the boundary, so repeatedly requested) by the troublesome neighbors of New England, who numbered full fifty to our one [actually 25,000 to 1,500], continually encroaching on lands within established bounds, possessed and cultivated in fact by your Illustrious High Mightinesses' subjects.

Secondly, by the exceedingly detrimental, land-destroying, and people-expelling wars with the cruel barbarians, which endured two years before my arrival there, whereby many subjects who possessed means were necessitated to depart, others to retreat under the crumbling fortress of New Amsterdam, which, on my arrival, I found resembling more a molehill than a fortress, without gates, the walls and bastions trodden under foot by men and cattle.

Less dare I, to avoid self-glorification, encumber your [time] . . . with the trouble, care, solicitude, and continual zeal with which I have endeavored to promote the increase of population, agriculture, and commerce; the flourishing condition whereunto they were brought—not through any wisdom of mine, but through God's special blessing, and which might have been more flourishing if your formerly dutiful, now afflicted, inhabitants . . . [had been] protected and remained protected by a suitable garrison, as necessity demanded, against the deplorable and tragic massacres by the barbarians, whereby (in addition to ten private murders) we were plunged three times into perilous wars, through want of sufficient garrisons; especially had they, on the supplicatory remonstrances of the people and our own . . . entreaties, which must be considered almost innumerable, had been helped with the long sought-for settlement of the boundary, or in default thereof had they been seconded with the oft-besought reinforcements of men and ships against the continual troubles, threats, encroachments, and invasions of the English neighbors and government of Hartford colony [Connecticut], our too powerful enemies.

That assistance, nevertheless, appears to have been retarded so long (wherefore and by what unpropitious circumstances the Honorable Directors best know) that our abovementioned too-powerful neighbors and enemies found themselves reinforced by four royal ships, crammed full with an extraordinary amount of men and warlike stores. Our ancient enemies throughout the whole of Long Island, both from the east end and from the villages belonging to us, united with them, hemmed us by water and by land, and cut off all supplies. Powder and provisions failing, and no relief nor reinforcement being expected, we were necessitated to come to terms with the enemy, not through neglect of duty or cowardice, as many, more from passion than knowledge of the facts, have decided, but in consequence of the absolute impossibility to defend the fort, much less the city of New Amsterdam, and still less the country. As you, Illustrious, High, and Mighty, in your more profound and more discreet wisdom, will be able to judge from the following:

First, in regard to want of powder: The annexed account shows what had been received during the last four years and what was left over, from which it appears that . . . there were not 600 pounds good and fit for muskets; the remainder damaged by age, so that when used for artillery, the cannon required a double charge or weight. If necessary and you, Illustrious, High, and Mighty, demand it, the truth hereof can be sought from the gunner . . . [who had said when the English attacked]: "What can my lord do? He knows well that there is no powder, and that the most of it is good for nothing. There is powder enough to do harm to the enemy, but 'tis no good; were I to commence firing in the morning, I should have all used up by noon."

What efforts we have employed to receive this and some other reinforcements and assistance may appear from the two copies of the letters sent to the colony of Renselaerswyck [*sic*] and the village of Beverwyck, marked No. A; whose answers intimate that we could not be assisted by either one or the other, because of the difficulties into which they had just then fallen with the northern Indians, owing to the killing of three or four Christians and some cows. . . .

Provisions were likewise so few and scarce in the city, in consequence of the approaching harvest, for the inhabitants are not in the habit of laying up more provisions than they have need of, that about eight days after the surrender of the place, there was not in the city of New Amsterdam enough of provisions, beef, pork, and peas, to be obtained for the transportation of the military, about ninety strong, and the new grain had to be thrashed.

In addition to the want of the abovementioned necessaries, and many other minor articles, a general discontent and unwillingness to assist in defending the place became manifest among the people; which unwillingness was occasioned and caused in no small degree, first among the people living out of the city, and next among the burghers, by the attempts and encroachments experienced at the hands of the English in the preceding year, 1663. [Which were,] first, through John Talcot's reducing Eastdorp [Westchester], situated on the mainland, not two leagues from New Amsterdam, by order and commission of the government of Hartford; next, through Captain Co's later invasion and subjugation of all the English villages and plantations on Long Island, which were under oath and obedience to you, Illustrious, High, and Mighty, and the Honorable Company, with an armed troop of about 150 to 160 of John Schott's horse and foot. . . .

Owing to the very serious war with the Esopus Indians and their confederates, in consequence of a third deplorable massacre perpetrated there on the good inhabitants, we could not at the time do anything against such violent attempts and encroachments, except to protest against them. . . .

This dissatisfaction and unwillingness [to fight] on the part of the burgher and farmer were called forth by the abovementioned and other frequently bruited threats, by the hostile invasions and encroachments that had been experienced and the inability to oppose them for want of power and reinforcements; but mainly by the sending of proclamations and open letters containing promises, in the [English] King's name, to burgher and farmer, of free and peaceable possession of their property, unobstructed trade and navigation, not only to the King's dominions, but also to the Netherlands with their own ships and people.

Besides the abovementioned reasons for dissatisfaction and unwillingness, the former as well as the ruling burgomasters and schepens, and principal citizens, complained that their . . . remonstrances, letters, and petitions . . . had not been deemed worthy of any answer; [so they were reduced to] publicly declaring, "If the Honorable Company give themselves so little concern about the safety of the country and its inhabitants as not to be willing to send a ship of war to its succor in such pressing necessity, nor even a letter of advice as to what we may depend on and what succor we have to expect, we are utterly powerless, and, therefore, not bound to defend the city, to imperil our lives, property, wives, and children without hope of any succor or relief, and to lose all after two or three days' resistance."

———

THE NEW NETHERLANDS were captured and transformed into an English crown colony; the Duke of York cast about for a new name, and decided he liked the sound of New York. He liked it so much, he applied it to the city of New Amsterdam as well as the colony of New Netherlands. Yet the colony would remain an anomaly in the English New World. Despite many Puritan settlers, New York would never be a part of New England. For one thing, it was connected to the crown as neither Massachusetts Bay, Plymouth, Connecticut, nor Rhode Island (see chapter 13), would ever be. It had been conquered, not spontaneously founded by English subjects, and the royal family would always exert a great deal of control.

What would distinguish New York most, however, was the lasting cultural influence of the Dutch. This profit-minded people remained after the conquest, secure in their possessions, and formed much of the elite of the colony for generations to come. With their merchant culture, their continuing ties to the fur-selling Iroquois, and the strategic trading position of the city of New York, the Dutch placed an abiding commercial stamp on the settlement. So, too, would their worldly, accommodating ways persist: this land of eighteen languages would continue to be a cosmopolitan center—the English colonies' doorway on both the European world and the world of the interior, accessible through the vital Hudson corridor. Stuyvesant may have lost his dominion, but he and his compatriots left their mark for centuries to come.

IV

DESPERATE MEASURES

LATE-SEVENTEENTH-CENTURY TURMOIL

12

BACON'S REBELLION

Historians are often so full of knowledge, they have little room for wisdom. In the mountain of details they accumulate through the study of colonial society, government, commerce, diplomacy, and culture, they frequently neglect the role of the individual. Sometimes, especially at the very beginnings of the colonies, a single soul clearly stands out: Champlain, for instance, who did so much to create and define New France; and Winthrop, who helped establish the institutions and outlook of New England. In both cases, of course, these men rode the waves of deeper historical forces—but they clearly turned the course of events with human intention, planning, and will.

When we move beyond those precarious beginnings, however, the importance of the solitary being does seem to diminish. Captain John Smith may have personally guaranteed the survival of Virginia—but who could play such a role twenty, thirty, or forty—let alone fifty—years later? When we last visited this tobacco dominion in the 1620s, it seemed solidly established: its government reordered as a crown colony; its economy based on a popular, highly addictive drug; its Indian enemies defeated; its labor force supplied by waves of indentured servants. Could any man shift the direction of such an enterprise?

The answer, as might be guessed, is yes—with the aid of those deeper historical forces, of course. "No less than New England," writes historian David Hackett Fischer, "the colony of Virginia was the conscious creation of human will and purpose. In that process, Sir William Berkeley played the leading role, laboring through his long years in office to build an ideal society which was the expression of his own values." Reigning as governor from 1642 through 1676, Berkeley recreated the society and government of Virginia in the image of an idealized England—and, in his final, catastrophic failure, inadvertently sparked the final changes that would later mark all of the American South.

When Berkeley arrived in Jamestown in late 1641, he personally embodied the values of his beloved king, Charles I. He was born in 1606, as Fischer writes, "to a powerful West Country family which had been seated since the eleventh century at Berkeley Castle in Gloucestershire." He was, in short, a nobleman, exuding hierarchy and privilege from his long, thick

215

strands of curly hair down to the expensive sword he wore at his side. He had been educated at Oxford, knighted on the field of battle, and richly rewarded as a fawning sycophant of the king (who still longed for his assassinated favorite, the Duke of Buckingham). Berkeley was also a loyal member of the Church of England, content with the ritualistic liturgy of Archbishop Laud that the Puritans so detested.

When King Charles dispatched his friend to rule Virginia, he faced a mounting crisis at home. The Scots had risen against him; desperate for money and support, he called Parliament after a decade of ruling without it. In the newly elected House of Commons, pent-up fury at his various innovations (in both the church and in arbitrary taxation) exploded. Still might Charles have defused the tension—but he was far too imbued in the royal absolutism taught by his father to bend to the winds of this political hurricane. Irresistible force met immovable object—and, unexpected to all, civil war erupted.

Wars—especially civil wars—tend to take on a life of their own, following unpredictable turns in the quest for victory. So it was in the English Civil War. At first, Parliament declared that its goal was to free the king from the grasp of evil advisers; in the end, it put Charles on trial and beheaded him in 1649, leading to a Commonwealth without a monarch. At first, Parliament tried to fight with locally raised militia; in the end, it formed the New Model Army, eventually headed by Oliver Cromwell—which became an independent force, deposing Parliament and placing Cromwell in power. At first, Parliament sought to reform the Church of England; in the end, the church was destroyed, replaced with a toleration of all Protestant sects (leading to an explosion of new forms of worship, such as the Baptist, Quaker, and Unitarian faiths, though a New England–style Congregationalism predominated).

Charles's son and heir, Charles II, fled across the water to the continent; he later returned to Scotland in 1651. Defeated by Cromwell—a better general with a better army—the son took flight again. Left behind were his supporters—notably much of the nobility, who detested the mere gentry (even *merchants*) who now held sway in Cromwell's England, and who eyed the aristocracy suspiciously. The world had turned upside down. As one Royalist wrote, "When we meet, it is but to consult to what foreign plantation we shall fly." For the Puritans, the reverse was true; the Great Migration to New England not only stopped—it went in reverse, as rejoicing separatists saw the millennium arriving in their homeland.

This new England, then, made a fertile recruiting ground for Governor Berkeley, as he sought to remake the old England on North American shores—only making it even better than before. He urged the great houses of Royalists—known, in the Civil War, as Cavaliers—to come to Virginia, where they could preside over a society that would fawn on them hand and foot, where they could have estates to rival those they had known in the British isles.

After Cromwell's death in 1658, the lack of an equally strong successor led to the sudden restoration of the Stuart monarchy. In 1660, Charles II returned in triumph to London (restoring Berkeley to the governorship of Virginia, which he had briefly lost during Cromwell's rule). Yet Berkeley continued to successfully recruit noblemen for his colony. Younger sons of great houses found Virginia particularly attractive, because they could not inherit the family lands in England. The fortunes to be made from tobacco, the enormity of the estates to be had, and the Royalist, Cavalier society Berkeley had erected all drew them in. In thirty-five years, Berkeley rebuilt his dominion, raising the colony's population from 8,000 to more than 40,000.

In 1674, the aged Governor Berkeley could look about his colony with smug satisfaction. He had created his ideal society of nobility and indentured servants. He had immensely enriched himself, often through outright corruption (but a gentleman and an officer, he thought, was entitled to bend the rules). So it was with a complacent heart that he welcomed a dashing new aristocrat to his realm, the young Nathaniel Bacon. Though Bacon was only twenty-seven, Berkeley named him to the council, the appointed body that ruled together with the elected House of Burgesses. He undoubtedly aided the young man in obtaining an estate for himself.

One year later, Berkeley would regret the day he met that man. The gentlemanly Bacon turned out to be the embodiment of youthful rebellion—and restive Virginia, this Cavalier paradise, teemed with reasons to rebel. First were the Indians: though Virginia's neighbors were, for the most part, at peace (even allied) with the English, the colonists on the frontier seethed with almost unreasoning fear and resentment of those well-armed communities of Native Americans.

Second was the polarized nature of Virginian society. Though generations of historians have debated the social forces behind the outbreak of rebellion, there can be little doubt that the presence of large numbers of completely disfranchised indentured servants (often worked literally to death), and the impoverished souls who survived their terms of servitude, heated the pot of this colony's mix. The vast estates that Berkeley and his fellow Cavaliers granted themselves often left the newly released servants with nothing but marginal land to farm, or distant homesteads along that volatile Indian frontier.

Finally, there was the corrupt, authoritarian style of Berkeley's government. In his own small way, he recreated many of the reasons for rebellion that his lord and benefactor, Charles I, had given the English before 1642. Both men believed in the rule of the elite, in supreme executive authority, in hierarchical society, in princely perks: even in a world that largely accepted such beliefs, they created dangerous friction.

The selection that follows (written by one of the great planters who ruled Virginia) describes how those frictions turned a frontier skirmish into an outright rebellion. After thirty-five years of careful nurturing, Berkeley's Virginia was about to turn on its leader—and itself. Staggering acts of revolt and destruction would sweep the landscape, sending the governor scurrying for refuge on the Eastern Shore. In the end, as with his own king Charles II, it would take an act of God to return the appointed prince to his desolate capital.

The Beginning, Progress, and Conclusion of Bacon's Rebellion
by Thomas Mathew

About the year 1675, appeared three prodigies in that country, which, from the attending disasters, were looked upon as ominous presages. The one was a large comet every evening for a week. . . . Another was flights of pigeons, in breadth nigh a quarter of the mid-hemisphere, and of their length was no visible end; whose weights brake down the limbs of large trees whereon these rested at nights. . . . This sight put the old planters under the more portentous apprehensions, because the like was seen (as they said) in the year 1640, when the Indians committed the last massacre, but not after, until that present year 1675. . . . The third strange appearance was swarms of flies about an inch long, and big as the top of a man's little finger, rising out of spigot holes in the earth. . . .

My dwelling was in Northumberland, the lowest county on the Potomac River, Stafford being the upmost; where having also a plantation, servants, cattle, etc., my overseer there had agreed with one Robert Hen to come thither, and be my herdsman, who then lived ten miles above it. But on a Sabbath day morning in the summer Anno 1675, people on their way to church saw this Hen lying 'thwart his threshold, and an Indian without the door, both chopped on their heads, arms, and other parts, as if done with Indian hatchets. The Indian was dead, but Hen, when asked who did that? answered "Doegs Doegs,"[1] and soon died. Then a boy came out from under a bed, where he had hid himself, and told them Indians had come at break of day and done these murders.

From this Englishman's blood did (by degrees) arise Bacon's Rebellion with the following mischiefs which overspread all Virginia and twice endangered Maryland, as by the ensuing account is evident.

Of this horrid action, Col. [George] Mason, who commanded the militia regiment of foot, and Capt. [George] Brent, [commander of] the troop

[1] An Indian tribe living in Maryland.

of horse in that county (both dwelling six or eight miles downwards), having speedy notice, raised 30 or more men, and pursued those Indians 20 miles up and 4 miles over that river into Maryland, where landing at dawn of day, they found two small paths. Each leader with his party took a separate path and in less than a furlong, either found a cabin, which they silently surrounded.

Capt. Brent went to the Doegs' cabin (as it proved to be), who speaking the Indian tongue called to have a *Matchacomicha Weewhip*, i.e. a council, called presently such being the usual manner with the Indians. The king came trembling forth, and would have fled, when Capt. Brent, catching hold of his twisted lock (which was all the hair he wore) told him he was come for the murderer of Robert Hen. The king pleaded ignorance and slipped loose, whom Brent shot dead with his pistol. The Indians shot two or three guns out of the cabin; the English shot into it; the Indians thronged out the door and fled. The English shot as many as they could, so that they killed ten, as Capt. Brent told me, and brought away the king's son. . . .

The noise of this shooting awakened the Indians in the cabin which Col. Mason had encompassed, who likewise rushed out and fled, of whom his company (supposing from that noise of shooting Brent's party to be engaged) shot (as the Col. informed me) fourteen before an Indian came, who with both hands shook him (friendly) by one arm, saying, *Susquehanougs Netoughs,* i.e. Susquehannock friends, and fled. Whereupon he ran amongst his men, crying out, "For the Lord's sake shoot no more, these are our friends the Susquehannocks."

This unhappy scene ended. . . . The Susquehannocks were newly driven from their habitations at the head of Chesapeake Bay by the Seneca Indians, down to the head of Potomac, where they sought protection under the Piscataway Indians, who had a fort near the head of that river and also were our friends.

After this unfortunate exploit of Mason and Brent, one or two being killed in Stafford, boats of war were equipped to prevent excursions over the river, and at the same time murders being (likewise) committed in Maryland, by whom not known, on either side of the river, both countries raised their quotas of a thousand men, upon whose coming before the fort [Piscataway, where the Susquehannocks had taken refuge], the Indians sent out four of their great men, who asked the reason of that hostile appearance. What they said more or offered, I do not remember to have heard; but our two commanders caused them to be (instantly) slain, after which the Indians made an obstinate resistance, shooting many of our men, and making frequent, fierce, and bloody sallies. And when they were called to, or offered parley, gave no other answer than, "Where are our four *Cockarouses,* i.e. great men?"

At the end of six weeks, marched out seventy-five Indians with their women, children, etc., who (by moonlight) passed our guards, hallowing and firing at them without opposition, leaving three or four decrepits in the fort. The next morning the English followed, but could not or (for fear of ambuscades) would not overtake these desperate fugitives. . . .

The walls of this fort were high banks of earth, with flankers having many loopholes, and a ditch round all, and without [outside] this, a row of tall trees fastened three foot deep in the earth, their bodies from five to eight inches diameter, wattled six inches apart to shoot through the tops twisted together, and also artificially wrought, as our men could make no breach to storm it, nor (being lowland) could they undermine it by reason of water— neither had they cannon to batter it, so that 'twas not taken, until famine drove the Indians out of it.

These escaped Indians (forsaking Maryland) took their route over the head of that river, and thence over the heads of Rappahannock and York rivers, killing whom they found of the upmost plantations, until they came to the head of the James River, where (with [Nathaniel] Bacon and others), they slew Bacon's overseer whom he much loved, and one of his servants, whose blood he vowed to revenge if possible.

In these frightful times the most exposed small families withdrew into houses of better numbers, which we fortified with palisades and redoubts. Neighbors in bodies joined their labors from each plantation to others alternately, taking their arms into the fields, setting sentinels. No man stirred out of door unarmed. Indians were (ever and anon) espied, three, four, five, or six in a party lurking throughout the whole land, yet (what was remarkable) I rarely heard of any houses burnt, tho' abundance was forsaken, nor ever of any corn or tobacco cut up, or any other injury done, besides murders. . . .

Frequent complaints of bloodsheds were sent to Sir William Berkeley (then governor) from the heads of the rivers, which were as often answered with promises of assistance. These at the heads of James and York rivers (having now [the] most people destroyed by the Indians' flight thither from Potomac) grew impatient at the many slaughters of their neighbors, and rose for their own defence; who, choosing Mr. Bacon for their leader, sent often times to the governor, humbly beseeching a commission to go against those Indians at their own charge, which his Honor as often promised but did not send. The mysteries of these delays were wondered at, and which I never heard any could penetrate into, other than the effects of his passion, and a new (not to be mentioned) occasion of avarice, to both which, he was (by the common vogue) more than a little addicted.

Whatever were the popular surmises and murmurings, viz.: "That no bullets would pierce beaver skins. Rebels' forfeitures would be loyal inheritances, etc."

During these protractions . . . 300 men, taking Mr. Bacon for their commander, met, and concerted together the danger of going without a commission on the one part, and the continual murders of their neighbors on the other part (not knowing whose or how many of their own turns might be next), and came to this resolution, viz.: To prepare themselves with necessaries for a march, but interim to send again for a commission, which if could or could not be obtained by a certain day, they would proceed, commission or no commission.

This day lapsing and no commission come, they marched into the wilderness in quest of these Indians; after whom [the militia] the governor sent his proclamation, denouncing all [as] rebels who should not return within a limited day. Whereupon all estates obeyed; but Mr. Bacon and fifty-seven men proceeded until their provisions were near spent, without finding enemies, when coming nigh a fort of friend Indians, on the other side of a branch of James River, they desired relief, offering payment; which these Indians kindly promised to help them with on the morrow, but put them off with promises until the third day.

So as having then eaten their last morsels, they could not return, but must have starved in the way homeward, and now 'twas suspected, these Indians had received private messages from the governor and those to be the causes of these delusive procrastinations. Whereupon the English waded shoulder deep thro' that branch [of the James] to the fort palisades, still entreating and tendering pay for victuals. But that evening a shot from the place they left on the other side of that branch killed one of Mr. Bacon's men, which made them believe those in the fort had sent for other Indians to come behind them and cut them off.

Hereupon they fired the palisades, stormed and burnt the fort and cabins, and (with the loss of three English) slew 150 Indians.[2] The circumstances of this expedition Mr. Bacon entertained me with, at his own chamber, on a visit I made him, the occasion whereof is hereafter mentioned.

From thence they returned home, where writs were come up to elect members for an assembly, when Mr. Bacon was unanimously chosen for one; who, coming down the river, was commanded by a ship with guns to come on board; where waited Major Hone the high sheriff of Jamestown ready to seize him, by whom he was carried down to the governor, and by him received with a surprising civility, in the following words: "Mr. Bacon, have you forgot to be a gentleman?" "No, may it please your honor," answered Mr. Bacon. "Then," replied the governor, "I'll take your parole"; and gave him his liberty.[3]

In March 1676, writs came up to Stafford to choose their two members for an assembly to meet in May; when Col. Mason, Capt. Brent, and other gentlemen of that county invited me to stand [as] a candidate; a matter I little dreamt of, having never had inclinations to tamper in the precarious intrigues of government; and my hands being full of my own business. They

[2] This village, of the small Occaneechee tribe, probably did feed Bacon's men; they also joined the English in raids on the Susquehannocks. Bacon, however, launched this attack on them anyway, possibly in a dispute over beaver furs.

[3] Bacon showed up in Jamestown in a sloop with fifty armed supporters. Berkeley captured him with a trick, then (to diffuse political tensions) pardoned him and promised him a military commission.

pressed several cogent arguments . . . and so Col. Mason and myself were elected without objection. He at [a] time convenient went on horseback; I took my sloop; and the morning I arrived at Jamestown after a week's voyage, was welcomed with the strange acclamations of "All's over, Bacon is taken," having not heard at home of these southern commotions, other than rumors like idle tales, of one Bacon risen up in rebellion, nobody knew for what, concerning the Indians.

The next forenoon, the assembly being met in a chamber over the general court and our speaker chosen, the governor sent for us down, where his Honor [Governor Berkeley] with a pathetic emphasis made a short and abrupt speech wherein were these words: "If they [the Indians] had killed my grandfather and grandmother, my father and mother and all my friends, yet if they had come to treat of peace, they ought to have gone in peace," and sat down. The two chief commanders at the forementioned siege, who slew the four Indian great men, being present and part of our assembly [were insulted by this].

The governor stood up again and said, "If there be joy in the presence of the angels over one sinner that repenteth, there is joy now, for we have a penitent sinner come before us, called Mr. Bacon." Then did Mr. Bacon upon one knee at the bar deliver a sheet of paper confessing his crimes, and begging pardon of God, the King, and the governor, whereto (after a short pause), he answered, "God forgive you, I forgive you," thrice repeating the same words. When Col. [William] Cole (one of the council) said, "And all that were with him," twenty or more persons being then in irons who were taken coming down in the same and other vessels with Mr. Bacon.

About a minute after this, the governor, starting up from his chair a third time, said, "Mr. Bacon! If you will live civilly but till next quarter court," (doubling the words), "but till next quarter court, I'll promise to restore you again to your place there," pointing with his hand to Mr. Bacon's seat, he having been of the council before these troubles, tho' he had been a very short time in Virginia, but was deposed by the foresaid proclamation. And in the afternoon, passing by the court door in my way up to our chamber, I saw Mr. Bacon on his quondam seat with the governor and council, which seemed a marvelous indulgence to one whom he had so lately proscribed as a rebel.

The governor had directed us to consider of means for security from the Indians' insults, and to defray the charge, etc., advising us to beware of two rogues amongst us, namely Lawrence and Drummond, both dwelling at Jamestown and who were not at the Piscataway siege.[4] But at our entrance

---

[4] Richard Lawrence and William Drummond became leading men in the coming rebellion. The governor's early warning about them suggests that they were already fomenting dissent against his leadership.

upon business, some gentlemen took this opportunity to endeavor the redressing of several grievances the country then labored under. Motions were made for inspecting the public revenues, the collectors' accounts, etc., and so far as was proceeded to name part of a committee . . . when we were interrupted by pressing messages from the governor to meddle with nothing, until the Indian business was dispatched. . . .

Whilst some days passed in settling the quotas of men, arms, and ammunition, provisions, etc., each county was to furnish, one morning early a bruit ran about the town, "Bacon is fled, Bacon is fled." Whereupon I went straight to Mr. Lawrence. . . . Now shaking his head, [he] said [of the governor], "Old treacherous villain," and that his house was searched that morning at daybreak, but Bacon was escaped into the country, having intimation that the governor's generosity in pardoning him and his followers and restoring him to his seat on the council were no other than previous wheedles to amuse him and his adherents, and to circumvent them by strategem, foreasmuch as the taking Mr. Bacon again into the council was first to keep him out of the assembly; and in the next place the governor knew the country people were hastening down with dreadful threatenings to double prevent all wrongs [that] should be done to Mr. Bacon or his men, or whosoever should have had the least hand in them. . . .

In three or four days after this escape, upon news that Mr. Bacon was thirty miles up the river at the head of four hundred men, the governor sent to parts adjacent, on both sides of the James River, for the militia and all the men [who] could be gotten to come and defend the town [Jamestown]. Expresses came almost hourly of the [Bacon's] army's approaches, who in less than four days after the first account of them, at two of the clock entered the town, without being withstood, and formed a body upon the green, not a flight shot from the end of the statehouse, of horse and foot, as well regular as veteran troops, who forthwith possessed themselves of all the avenues, disarming all in town, and coming thither in boats or by land.

In half an hour after this the drum beat for the House to meet, and in less than an hour more Mr. Bacon came with a file of fusileers[5] on either hand near the corner of the statehouse where the governor and council went forth to meet him. We saw from the window the governor open his breast, and Bacon strutting betwixt his two files of men with his left arm akimbo, flinging his right arm every way; both like men distracted. And if in this moment of fury, that enraged multitude had fallen upon the governor and council, we of the assembly expected the same immediate fate. I stepped down and amongst the crowd of spectators found the seamen of my sloop, who prayed me not to stir from them; when in two minutes, the governor walked towards his private apartment, a quoit's cast distant at the other end

---

[5] A fusil was a lightweight flintlock musket, and was distinguished from the standard, heavier musket.

of the statehouse, the gentlemen of the council following him. And after them walked Mr. Bacon with outrageous postures of his head, arms, body, and legs, often tossing his hand from his sword to his hat; and after him came a detachment of fusileers (muskets not being there in use), who with their cocks bent presented their fusils at a window of the assembly chamber filled with faces, repeating with menacing voices, "We will have it, We will have it," half a minute. . . .

In this hubub a servant of mine got so nigh as to hear the governor's words, and also followed Mr. Bacon and heard what he said, who came to me and told me that when the governor opened his breast he said, "Here! Shoot me, 'fore God, fair mark, shoot," often rehearsing the same, without any other words. Whereto Mr. Bacon answered, "No, may it please your Honor, we will not hurt a hair of your head, nor of any other man's. We are come for a commission to save our lives from the Indians, which you have so often promised, and now we will have it before we go."

But when Mr. Bacon followed the governor and council with the fore-mentioned impetuous (like delirious) actions whil'st that party presented their fusils at the window full of faces, he said, "Damn my blood, I'll kill the governor, council, assembly, and all, and then I'll sheath my sword in my own heart's blood." And afterwards 'twas said Bacon had given a signal to his men who presented their fusils at those gazing out at the window, that if he should draw his sword, they were on sight of it to fire and slay us. So near was the massacre of us all that very minute, had Bacon, in that paroxism of frenetic fury, but drawn his sword. . . .

In an hour or more after these violent concussions, Mr. Bacon came up to our chamber and desired a commission from us to go against the Indians. Our speaker sat silent, when one Mr. Blayton, a neighbor to Mr. Bacon and elected with him a member of assembly for the same county (who therefore durst speak to him), made answer, " 'Twas not in our province, or power, nor of any other save the King's viceregent, our governor"; he pressed hard nigh half an hour's harangue on preserving our lives from the Indians, inspecting the public revenues, the exorbitant taxes, and redressing the grievances and calamities of that deplorable country. Whereto having no other answer, he went away dissatisfied.

Next day there was a rumor the governor and council had agreed Mr. Bacon should have a commission to go [as] general of the forces we were then raising. . . .

Col. [Nicholas] Spencer, being my neighbor and intimate friend and a prevalent member in the council, I prayed him to entreat the governor [that] we might be dissolved, for that was my first and should be my last going astray from my wonted sphere of merchandise and my other private concernments, into the dark and slippery meanders of court embarrassments. He told me the governor had not (then) determined his intention, but he would move his Honor about it, and in two or three days we were dissolved, which I was most heartily glad of, because of my getting loose again from being hampered amongst those pernicious entanglements in the labyrinths and snares of state ambiguities. . . .

Many members being met one evening [June 25] nigh sunset, to take our leaves of each other in order the next day to return homewards, came General Bacon with his hand full of unfolded papers, and overlooking us round, walking into the room said, "Which of these gentlemen shall I en treat to write a few words for me." Where everyone looking aside as not willing to meddle, Mr. Lawrence pointed to me, saying, "That gentleman writes very well." Which I endeavoring to excuse, Mr. Bacon came stooping to the ground and said, "Pray sir, do me the honor to write a line for me."

This surprising accostment shocked me into a melancholy consternation, dreading upon one hand that Stafford County would fee [pay] the smart of his resentment should I refuse him . . . and on the other hand fearing the governor's displeasure, who I knew would soon hear of it. What seemed most prudent at this hazardous dilemma was to obviate the present impending peril; so Mr. Bacon made me sit the whole night by him filling up those papers, which I then saw were blank commissions signed by the governor, inserting such names and writing other matters as he dictated. . . .

I went home to Potomac, where reports were afterwards various. We had account that General Bacon was marched with a thousand men into the forest to seek the enemy Indians,[6] and in a few days after our next news was that the governor had summoned together the militia of Gloucester and Middlesex counties to the number of twelve hundred men, and proposed to them to follow and suppress that rebel Bacon. Whereupon arose a murmuring before his face, "Bacon Bacon Bacon," and all walked out of the field, muttering as they went, "Bacon Bacon Bacon," leaving the governor and those that came with him to themselves, who being thus abandoned wafted over Chesapeake Bay thirty miles to Accomac, where are two counties of Virginia.

Mr. Bacon, hearing this, came back part of the way, and sent out parties of horse patrolling through every county, carrying away prisoners; all whom he distrusted, might [lest] any more molest his Indian prosecution, yet giving liberty to such as pledged him their oaths to return home and live quiet. The copies or contents of which oaths I never saw, but heard were very strict, tho' little observed.

About this time a spy was detected, pretending himself a deserter who had twice or thrice come and gone from party to party, and was by council of war sentenced to death; after which Bacon declared openly to him, that if any one man in the army would speak a word to save him, he should not suffer, which no man appearing to do, he was executed. Upon this manifesta-

---

[6] Bacon actually attacked the Pamunkey, who were now friendly. He wiped out these last remnants of Powhatan's once-great realm in the Dragon Swamp.

tion of clemency Bacon was applauded for [a] merciful man, not willing to spill Christian blood, nor indeed was it said that he put any other man to death in cold blood, or plunder any house.

Nigh the same time came Major Langston with his troop of horse and quartered two nights at my house, who (after nigh compliments from the general) told me I was desired to accept the lieutenancy for preserving the peace in the five northern counties betwixt Potomac and Rappahannock rivers. I humbly thanked his Honor, excusing myself; as I had done before on that invitation of the like nature at Jamestown, but did hear he was mightily offended at my evasions and threatened to remember me.

The governor made a second attempt [at] coming over from Accomac, with what men he could procure, in sloops and boats, forty miles up the river to Jamestown. Which Bacon hearing of, came again down from his forest pursuit, and finding a bank not a flight shot long, cast up athwart the neck of the peninsula there in Jamestown. He stormed it, and took the town, in which attack were twelve men slain and wounded. But the governor with most of his followers fled back down the river in their vessels.

Here, resting a few days, they [Bacon's men] concerted the burning of the town; wherein Mr. Lawrence and Mr. Drummond, owning the two best houses save one, set fire each to his own house, which example the soldiers following laid the whole town (with church and statehouse) in ashes, saying, "The rogues should harbor no more there."

On these reiterated molestations, Bacon calls a convention at Middle Plantation [later site of Williamsburg], fifteen miles from Jamestown, in the month of August 1676, where an oath with one or more proclamations were formed, and writs by him issued for an assembly. The oaths or writs I never saw, but one proclamation commanded all men in the land on pain of death to join him, and retire into the wilderness upon the arrival of the forces expected from England, and oppose them until they should propose or accept to treat of an accommodation, which we who lived comfortably could not have undergone. So as the whole land must have become an Aceldama if God's exceeding mercy had not timely removed him.[7]

During these tumults in Virginia a second danger menaced Maryland, by an insurrection in that province complaining of their heavy taxes, etc. Where two or three of the leading malcontents (men otherwise of laudable characters) were put to death, which stifled the further spreading of that flame. . . .

Mr. Bacon now returns from his last expedition sick of a flux, without finding any enemy Indians, having not gone far by reason of the vexations behind him, nor had he one dry day in all his marches to and fro in the forest, whilst the plantations (not fifty miles distant) had a summer so dry as

[7] "Aceldama," or "field of blood," is a reference to the field where Judas committed suicide (Acts 1:19).

stinted the Indian corn and tobacco, etc. Which the people ascribed to the *Pawawings,* i.e. the sorceries of the Indians. In a while Bacon dies [on October 18], and was succeeded by his Lieutenant General Ingram, who had one Wakelet next in command under him, [with whom he] whereupon hastened over the governor [Berkeley] to York River, and with him they articled for themselves and whom else they could, and so submitted and were pardoned, exempting those nominated and otherwise proscribed, in a proclamation of indemnity, the principal of which were Lawrence and Drummond. . . .

In a few days Mr. Drummond was brought in, and the governor being on board a ship came immediately to shore and complimented him with the comical sarcasm of a low bend, saying, "Mr. Drummond! You are very welcome. I am more glad to see you than any man in Virginia, Mr. Drummond; you shall be hanged in half an hour." Who answered, "What your Honor please." And as soon as a council of war could meet, his sentence be dispatched, and a gibbet erected (which took up near two hours), he was executed. . . .

The last account of Mr. Lawrence was from an uppermost plantation, whence he and four other desperadoes with horses, pistols, etc., marched away in a snow ankle deep, who were thought to have cast themselves into a branch of some river, rather than be treated like Drummond. Bacon's body was so made away, as his bones were never found to be exposed on a gibbet as was purposed, stones being laid in his coffin. Supposed to be done by Lawrence.

Near this time arrived a small fleet with a regiment from England. Sir John Berry, admiral; Col. Herbert Jeffreys, commander of the land forces; and Col. Moryson, who had one year been a former governor there; all three joined in commission with or to Sir William Berkeley. Soon after when a general court and also an assembly were held, where some of our former assembly (with so many others) were put to death, diverse whereof were persons of honest reputations and handsome estates, as that assembly petitioned the governor to spill no more blood; and [assemblyman] Mr. Presley, at his coming home, told me he believed the governor would have hanged half the country, if they had let him alone. . . .

The governor went in the fleet to London (whether by command from his Majesty or spontaneous I did not hear), leaving Col. Jeffreys in his place. And by next shipping came back a person who waited on his Honor in his voyage, and until his death, from whom a report was whispered about, that the King did say, "That old fool has hanged more men in that naked country, than I have done for the murder of my father." Whereof the governor hearing died soon after without having seen his Majesty; which shuts up this tragedy.

BERKELEY DEPARTED VIRGINIA, never to return to the society he had done so much to create. But his departure heralded a new turning point in colonial history. The lords of Virginia now believed that indentured servants posed too great a danger: they looked forward to the end of their service with poisonous anticipation; upon their release, they looked on their poverty with evil resentment; and they armed themselves with Virginia's too-numerous muskets. In the ashes of Jamestown, the Cavaliers decided that indentured servitude had to end. Perhaps, they mused, African slavery would be a much better idea.

13

KING PHILIP'S WAR

The year that revolt ravaged Virginia, a different sort of darkness descended upon New England. Like Bacon's Rebellion, it was a bitter conflict named for a remarkable leader; and like Bacon's Rebellion, it would largely sputter out with that leader's death. But King Philip's War, compared to Virginia's revolt, was as the recent Fire of London next to an autumn bonfire. It rained death and destruction upon New England as had never happened before, and never would again.

This devastating war would emerge, perversely enough, from a background of peace and cooperation. When the Pilgrims arrived inside Cape Cod, they were lucky to land near the Wampanoag, a tribe led by the practical Massasoit. The two people established a remarkable partnership in trade and defense. Native Americans and English settlers lived almost side by side; they exchanged land, furs, corn, kettles, and wampum; eventually the Indians even bought muskets, gunpowder, and lead. The Wampanoag enjoyed a very un-Pequot experience—more along the lines of the Huron and Algonquin alliance with New France.

But the New Englanders put pressure on their Indian neighbors. Their population swelled: on top of the Great Migration of the 1630s, the Puritans and Pilgrims increased through extremely large families. Their numbers *doubled* with each generation. And these settlers enjoyed a social and cultural cohesion the Indians would never know. As David Hackett Fischer has shown, they were held together by more than their mere Englishness—they had emerged from the same group of eastern counties, with its own particular folkways.

So too in politics, for the colonies of Massachusetts Bay, Plymouth, and Connecticut had bound themselves together in the United Colonies of New England. Rhode Island was something of an exception to this unity: founded by the dissident Roger Williams, it only gained official status as a colony during Oliver Cromwell's rule, which looked favorably on its religious toleration.

This expansion inevitably created friction with the Native Americans— and by the 1670s, the will for accommodation on both sides had withered away. The New Englanders faced their own political pressure from the

229

mother country: they had conspicuously supported the anti-Royalist forces
in the Civil War—but Cromwell was dead, and King Charles II had been restored to the throne. Closer to home, Charles's brother and heir, James,
Duke of York, had conquered New Netherlands and ruled it as the renamed
colony of New York; and James was hated as a well-known Catholic. The
New Englanders were actually relieved when the Dutch briefly recaptured
the province in 1674, though the Duke soon retook it. That war with the
Netherlands was a relief in another sense as well: it interrupted the work of
a royal commission Charles had named to investigate Massachusetts Bay.
Times were grim for the New England colonists, and they were in no mood
for compromise.

Nor were the Native Americans any more eager to find the middle
ground. The accommodating Massasoit had long since passed on, as had his
son and successor Wamsutta; now his second son, Metacom (also called
Metacomet), ruled the tribe as chief sachem. Plymouth and the Wampanoag
remained closely intertwined (Metacom, for example, accepted the name
Philip), but the English hunger for land pressed upon the Native Americans,
leading Philip and his people to mutter darkly.

In 1667, Plymouth established the town of Swansea, only four miles
from Philip's own village. In 1671, the sachem threatened the town with
armed warriors. The Plymouth authorities responded sharply to Philip's defiance, forcing him to sign a treaty that required the surrender of his
firearms. His appeals to Massachusetts Bay did him no good, for a meeting
of the United Colonies confirmed the agreement, and fined him £100 for
raising the specter of war.

The English had pushed things too far: they treated him not as the king
they said he was, but as a truant child. But Philip was not without resources
of his own. Recent shifts in Native American diplomacy had improved his
position. The neighboring Narragansetts were now close friends, if not exactly allies; once linked to the Mohawk, the Narragansetts saw those ties fall
off as the Iroquois nation concentrated its attentions on Fort Orange (now
Albany). And Philip paid his fine with a land sale—using the rest of the proceeds to buy more muskets and powder.

Certainly Philip prepared for war—but it is unlikely that he planned to
start one. He knew how badly outnumbered his people were, and how divided the Native American nations were in the face of the United Colonies.
But he faced pressure from his own followers; he was no all-powerful ruler
in the manner of Powhatan. At the very least, he had to show that he was
willing and ready to fight.

Not all of the English, however, were as unyielding as the Plymouth and
Massachusetts authorities. Certain leading men of Rhode Island actively
sought peace. Their colony, after all, sat in the midst of what would be the
battle zone: they were surrounded by Narragansett and Wampanoag villages,
including Philip's chief settlement on the Mount Hope peninsula. And

Rhode Island had been founded by Roger Williams, who believed in treating Indians with decency and dignity.

In 1674, a bloody incident brought tensions to a head. Rumors of war ran wild after a converted Indian warrior was found murdered. To head off the impending violence, a man named John Easton joined a party of Rhode Islanders who went to negotiate with Philip. Unfortunately, their efforts failed to secure the peace; but Easton's reasonably objective account provides insight into Philip's complaints—and into the depth of fear and frustration that convinced both sides that only war would solve their dilemma.

A Relacion of the Indyan Warre
by John Easton

In the winter in the year 1674, an Indian was found dead; and by a coroner['s] inquest of Plymouth colony judged murdered. . . . The dead Indian was called Sassamon, and a Christian that could read and write. . . .

The report came that the three Indians had confessed and accused Philip so as to [have] employ[ed] them, and that the English would hang Philip. So the Indians were afraid, and reported that the English had flattered them (or by threats) to belie Philip that they might kill him to have his land. . . . So Philip kept his men in arms.

Plymouth governor [Josias Winslow] required him to disband his men, and informed him his jealousy was false. Philip answered he would do no harm, and thanked the governor for his information. The three Indians were hung, [but] to the last denied the fact; but one broke the halter, as it was reported then, desire[d] to be saved, and so was a little while then. [He] confessed they three had done the fact, and then he was hanged; and it was reported Sassamon, before his death, had informed [the English] of the Indian plot, and that if the Indians knew it they would kill him, and that the heathen might destroy the English for their wickedness as God had permitted the heathen to destroy the Israelites of old.

So the English were afraid and Philip was afraid and both increased in arms; but for forty years' time reports and jealousies of war had been very frequent, that we did not think that now a war was breaking forth. But about a week before it did we had cause to think it would; then to endeavor to prevent it, we sent a man to Philip that if he would come to [Trip's] ferry we would come over to speak with him. About four miles we had to come thither. . . .

He called his council and agreed to come to us; [he] came himself, unarmed, and about forty of his men, armed. Then five of us went over. Three were magistrates. We sat very friendly together. We told him our business was to endeavor that they might not reserve [intend] or do wrong. They said that that was well; they had done no wrong; the English had wronged them. We said we knew the English said the Indians wronged them, and the Indians said the English wronged them, but our desire was the quarrel might rightly be decided in the best way, and not as dogs decide their quarrels.

The Indians owned that fighting was the worst way; then they propounded how right might take place; we said by arbitration. They said all English agreed against them; and so by arbitration they had had much wrong, many square miles of land so taken from them, for the English would have English arbitrators. . . . We said they might choose an Indian king, and the English might choose the governor of New York, that neither had cause to say either were parties in the difference. They said they had not heard of that way, and said we honestly spoke; so we were persuaded [that] if that way had been tendered they would have accepted.

We did endeavor not to hear their complaints, [and] said it was not convenient for us now. . . . But Philip charged it to be dishonesty in us to put off the hearing of the complaints; therefore we consented to hear them. They said they had been the first in doing good to the English, and the English the first in doing wrong; [he] said when the English first came, their king's [Philip's] father was as a great man and the English as a little child. He constrained other Indians from wronging the English, and gave them corn, and showed them how to plant, and was free to do them any good and had let them have a hundred times more land than now the king had for his own people. . . .

And another grievance was if twenty of their honest Indians testified that an Englishman had done them wrong, it was as nothing; but if one of their worst Indians testified against any Indian or their king when it pleased the English, that was sufficient. Another grievance was, when their kings sold land, the English would say it was more than they agreed to, and a writing must be proof against all them, and some of their kings had done wrong to sell so much. He left his people none; and some being given to drunkness, the English made them drunk, and then cheated them in bargains. But now their kings were forewarned not to part with land for nothing in comparison to the value thereof. . . .

Another grievance: the English cattle and horses still increased that when they [the Indians] removed thirty miles from where English had anything to do, they could not keep their corn from being spoiled. They never being used to fence, and thought when the English bought land of them that they would have kept their cattle upon their own land. Another grievance: the English were so eager to sell the Indians liquors that most of the Indians spent all in drunkness. . . .

We knew before these were their grand complaints, but then we only endeavored to persuade that all complaints might be righted without war. . . . We endeavored [to convince them] that, however, they should lay down their arms, for the English were too strong for them. They said the English should do to them as they did when they were too strong for the English.

So we departed without any discourtesies; and suddenly had [a] letter from Plymouth['s] governor, [that] they intended in arms to conform [subdue] Philip . . . and in a week's time after we had been with the Indians the war thus begun.

———————

WAR, NOT TALK, would rule the day: this conclusion seems to have dominated the councils of Boston, Plymouth, Hartford, and Philip's Mount Hope. Philip's young warriors would not abide the indignities any longer; already they struck out on raids on encroaching English homesteads. The New Englanders would not tolerate this latest insult to their authority. They might not be able to overturn Charles II in London, but they could strike out against this other king, so dangerously close to home. Easton and his fellow diplomats went home discouraged, as the governors of Massachusetts and Plymouth called out the militia.

One of the men who answered the call of duty was Benjamin Church, a Plymouth-born man in his mid-thirties who was equally at home with Indians and English. Like his father, he was a carpenter—yet somewhere along the line, he acquired extraordinary tracking and fighting skills. In short, he was a frontiersman, as comfortable on the boundary between cultures as he was in the woods and swamps. The governor thought him an obvious choice to lead a militia company.

Church's abilities were not matched by his fellow officers, let alone the rank and file. In the passage that follows (written, like Bradford's and Winthrop's journals, in the third person), Church recalls the excruciating frustration of working with men who refused to fight the Indians effectively: that is, with small tracking parties, with patient traps; in short, as the Indians themselves fought. Instead, they slogged heavily into Mount Hope peninsula as Philip's forces sniped at them, ambushed them, and then skipped nimbly away. Even Church's own efforts would be sabotaged by the unprofessionalism of this citizen militia.

The commanders of the colonies' forces did not much like Church's advice. Philip's men, however, would strike again and again, with ever growing effectiveness. So the colonists decided to take revenge on the helpless—driving this colonial warrior home in disgust.

———————

Entertaining Passages
by Benjamin Church

In the year 1674, Benjamin Church of Duxbury, being providentially at Plymouth in the time of the court, fell into acquaintance with Capt. John Almy of Rhode Island. Capt. Almy with great importunity invited him to ride with him, and view that part of Plymouth Colony that lay next to Rhode Island, known then by their Indian names of *Pocasset* and *Seconet*. Among other arguments to persuade him, he told him the soil was very rich, and the situation pleasant. Persuades him by all means to purchase of the company some of the court grant rights. He accepted the invitation, views the country, and was pleased with it; makes a purchase, settled a farm, found the gentlemen of the Island very civil and obliging. And being himself a person of uncommon activity and industry, he soon erected two buildings upon his farm, and gained a good acquaintance with the natives; got much into their favor, and was in little time in great esteem among them.

The next spring advancing, while Mr. Church was diligently settling his new farm . . . Behold! The rumor of a war between the English and the natives gave a check to his projects. . . . Philip, according to his promise to his people, permitted them to march out of the neck [of the Mount Hope peninsula, where they lived] . . . when they plundered the nearest houses that the inhabitants had deserted [on the rumor of war]; but as yet offered no violence to the people, at least none were killed. However, the alarm was given by their numbers, and hostile equipage, and by the prey they made of what they could find in the foresaken houses.

An express came the same day to the governor, who immediately gave orders to the captains of the towns to march the greatest part of their companies [of militia], and to rendezvous at Taunton on Monday night, where Major [William] Bradford[8] was to receive them, and dispose them under Capt. (now made Major) [James] Cudworth of Scituate. The governor desired Mr. Church to give them his company, and to use his interest in their behalf with the gentlemen of Rhode Island. He complied with it, and they marched the next day.

Major Bradford desired Mr. Church, with a commanded party consisting of English and some friend Indians, to march in the front at some distance from the main body. Their orders were to keep so far before, as not [to] be in sight of the army. And so they did, for by the way, they killed a deer [on Tuesday, June 22, 1675], fleeced, roasted, and ate the most of him before the army came up with them.

But the Plymouth forces soon arrived at Swansea, and were posted at Major Brown's and Major Miles's garrisons chiefly; and were there soon

---

[8] William Bradford was the second son of the former governor of Plymouth, and second only to Miles Standish as the leading soldier of the colony.

joined with those that came from Massachusetts, who had entered into a confederacy with their Plymouth brethren against the insidious heathen.

The enemy, who began their hostilities with plundering and destroying cattle, did not long content themselves with that game. They thirsted for English blood, and they soon broached it; killing two men in the way not far from Mr. Miles's garrison. And soon after, eight more at Mattapoisett, upon whose bodies they exercised more than brutish barbarities. . . . The enemy, flushed with these exploits, grew yet bolder, and skulking everywhere in the bushes, shot at all passengers, and killed many that ventured abroad. They came so near as to shoot down two sentinels at Mr. Miles's garrison, under the very noses of our forces.

These provocations drew out the resentments of some of Capt. Prentice's troop, who desired they might have liberty to go out and seek the enemy in their own quarters. Quartermasters Gill and Belcher commanded the parties drawn out, who earnestly desired Mr. Church's company. They provided him with a horse and furniture [saddle] (his own being out of the way); he readily complied with their desires, and was soon mounted.

This party was no sooner over Miles's bridge, but were fired upon by an ambuscade of about a dozen Indians, as they were afterwards discovered to be. When they drew off, the pilot [guide] was mortally wounded; Mr. Belcher received a shot in his knee, and his horse was killed under him; Mr. Gill was struck with a musket-ball on the side of his belly, but being clad with a buff coat and some thickness of paper under it, it never broke his skin. The troopers were surprised to see both their commanders wounded, and wheeled off. But Mr. Church persuaded, at length stormed and stamped, and told them 'twas a shame to run, and leave a wounded man there to be a prey to the barbarous enemy. For the pilot yet sat on his horse, though so mazed [dazed] with the shot, as not to have sense to guide him.

Mr. Gill seconded him, and offered, though much disabled, to assist in bringing him off. Mr. Church asked a stranger who gave them his company in that action, if he would go with him and fetch the wounded man. He readily consented; they with Mr. Gill went, but the wounded man fainted and fell off his horse before they came to him. But Mr. Church and the stranger dismounted, took up the man dead, and laid him before Mr. Gill on his horse.

Mr. Church told the other two, if they would take care of the dead man, he would go and fetch his horse back, which was going . . . toward the enemy. But . . . he saw the enemy run to the right, into the neck [Mount Hope peninsula]. He brought back the horse, and called earnestly and repeatedly to the army to come over and fight the enemy. And while he stood calling and persuading, the skulking enemy returned to their old stand, and all discharged their guns at him at one clap, though every shot missed him; yet one of the army on the other side of the river received one of the balls in his foot. Mr. Church now began (no succor coming to him) to think it time to retreat, saying, *The Lord have mercy on us,* if such a handful of Indians shall thus dare such an army!

Upon this 'twas immediately resolved, and orders were given, to march down into the neck; and having passed the bridge . . . the direction [from the commander] was to extend both wings, which being not well headed by those that remained in the center, some of them mistook their friends for their enemies, and made a fire upon them on the right wing, and wounded that noble heroic youth Ensign Savage in the thigh; but it happily proved but a flesh wound.

They marched until they came to the narrow of the neck . . . where they took down the heads of eight Englishmen that were killed at the head of Mattapoisett Neck, and set upon poles, after the barbarous manner of those savages. There Philip had staved all his drums, and conveyed his canoes to the east side of Mattapoisett River [later called Lee's River]. Hence it was concluded by those that were acquainted with the motions of those people, that they had quitted the neck. Mr. Church told 'em that Philip was doubtless gone over to Pocasset side, to engage those Indians in rebellion with him; which they soon found to be true.

The enemy were not really beaten out of Mount Hope neck, though 'twas true they fled from thence; yet it was before any pursued them. 'Twas but to strengthen themselves, and to gain a more advantageous post. However, some, and not a few, pleased themselves with the fancy of a mighty conquest.

A grand council was held, and a resolve passed to build a fort there to maintain the first ground they had gained, by the Indians leaving it to them. And to speak the truth, it must be said that as they gained not that field by their sword, nor by their bow; so 'twas rather their fear than their courage that obliged them to set up the marks of their conquest. Mr. Church looked upon it, and talk[ed] of it with contempt, and urged hard the pursuing of the enemy on Pocasset side. . . .

The council adjourned themselves from Mount Hope to Rehoboth, where Mr. Treasurer [Constant] Southworth, being weary of his charge as Commissary General (provision being scarce and difficult to be obtained for the army that now lay still to cover the people from nobody, while they were building a fort for nothing) retired, and the power and trouble of that post was left with Mr. Church, who still urged the commanding officers to move over to Pocasset side to pursue the enemy and kill Philip, which would in his opinion be more probable to keep possession of the neck, than to tarry to build a fort. He was still restless on that side of the river. . . .

And Captain Fuller also urged the same, until at length there came further order concerning the fort. And with all, an order for Capt. Fuller with six files to cross the river to the side so much insisted on, and to try if he could get speech with any of the Pocasset or Seconet Indians, and that Mr. Church should go [as] his second. Upon the captain's receiving his orders, he asked Mr. Church whether he was willing to engage in this enterprise: to whom 'twas indeed too agreeable to be declined, tho' he thought the enterprise was hazardous enough for them to have more men assigned to them. Captain Fuller told him that for his own part he was grown ancient and heavy, he feared the travel and fatigue would be too much for him. But Mr. Church urged him, and told him he would cheerfully excuse him his hardship and travel, and take that part to himself, if he might but go; for he had rather do anything in the world than stay there to build the fort.

Then they drew out the number assigned them and marched the same night to the ferry, and were transported to Rhode Island, from whence the next night they got passage over to Pocasset side in Rhode Island boats, and concluded there to dispose themselves in two ambushes before day, hoping to surprise some of the enemy by their falling into one or other of their ambushments. But Capt. Fuller's party, being troubled with the epidemical plague of lust after tobacco, must needs strike fire to smoke it; and thereby discovered themselves to a party of the enemy coming up to them, who immediately fled with great precipitation.

This ambuscade drew off about break of day, perceiving they were discovered. The other continued in their post until the time assigned them, and the light and heat of the sun rendered their station both insignificant and troublesome, and then returned unto the place of rendezvous, where they were acquainted with the other party's disappointment, and the occasion of it. . . .

Soon after this [July 15, 1675] was Philip's headquarters visited by some English forces; but Philip and his gang had the very fortune to escape. . . . They took into a swamp and their pursuers were commanded back. After this, Dartmouth's distresses required succor, [the] greater part of the town being laid desolate, and many of the inhabitants killed.

The most of Plymouth forces were ordered thither; and coming to Russel's garrison on Apponegansett [River], they met with a number of the enemy that had surrendered themselves prisoners on terms promised by Capt. [Samuel] Eells of the garrison; and Ralph Earl had persuaded them (by a friend Indian he had employed) to come in. And had their promises to the Indians been kept, and the Indians fairly treated, 'tis probable that most if not all the Indians in those parts had soon followed the example of those that had now surrendered themselves; which would have been a good step towards finishing the war.

But in spite of all that Capt. Eells, Church, and Earl could say, argue, plead, or beg, somebody else that had more power in their hands improved it; and without any regard to the promises made them on their surrendering themselves, they were carried away to Plymouth, there sold, and transported out of the country; being about eight score persons. An action so hateful to Mr. Church, that he opposed it to the loss of the goodwill and respect of some that before were his good friends.

But while these things were acting at Dartmouth, Philip made his escape, leaving his country, fled over the Taunton River, and Rehoboth [Seekonk] plain, and at Pawtuxet [Blackstone] River. . . . And now another fort was built at Pocasset, that proved as troublesome and chargeable [expensive] as that at Mount Hope; and the remainder of the summer was improved in providing for the forts and forces there maintained, while our enemies fled some hundreds of miles into the country, near as far as Albany.

PHILIP WAS FREE. Indeed, he was victorious. Though driven with all his people into wandering the deep woods that fringed the New England settlements, he and his warriors struck back hard, ambushing militia detachments and raiding English towns. The soldiers were reduced to enslaving the helpless who had surrendered.

Not content with these mishaps, the rulers of the United Colonies were about to grant another important gift to the Wampanoag: they were about to attack their own allies, the Narragansetts, driving them into an alliance with Philip. As English losses mounted, the colonists grew more and more uncompromising. They knew some Narragansett warriors had joined with the Wampanoag; they knew that some suffering Wampanoag, Pocasset, and Seconet Indians had found refuge with their Narragansett neighbors. Such relationships were inevitable in a Native American society that granted wide latitude to its individual members (so unlike the Puritans' stern moral guardianship). Yet the colonial governments decided to hold the Narragansetts, as a people, responsible for such incidents. The outcome could only be war—or rather, a drastic expansion of the existing war.

In the passages that follow, both John Easton and Benjamin Church offer their perspectives on this dangerous new stage of the conflict. Easton bitterly regretted the stance taken against these friends and neighbors of Rhode Island. The Indians did their best to appease the English; but even Easton himself, it seems, misjudged the lust for revenge of his countrymen. Benjamin Church, on the other hand, plunged into the attack on the Narragansetts with wholehearted vigor. He might detest the enslavement of surrendered Indians; he might throw up his hands in frustration at the militia commanders; but he wanted to be at the forefront of the fighting. And the fighting against the Narragansetts would be fierce, for the tribe had just constructed a formidable fort deep in the wilds known as the Great Swamp.

The Indians Have Cause to Think Me Deceitful
by John Easton

After hunting Philip from all seashores . . . they could not tell what was become of him. . . . After the English army, without our consent or informing us, came into our colony [and] brought the Narragansett Indians . . . articles of agreement . . . about 150 Indians came into a Plymouth garrison voluntarily. Plymouth . . . sold all for slaves (but about six of them), to be carried out of the country. It is true that the Indians generally are very barbarous people, but in this war I have not heard of their tormenting any, but that the English army caught an old Indian and tormented him. . . .

As Philip fled, the foresaid queen [of the Seconet] got to the Narragansetts and as many of her men as she could get, but one part of the Narragansetts' agreement to Boston was to kill or deliver as many as they could of Philip's people; therefore [the] Boston men demanded the foresaid queen and others. . . . For which the Indians . . . made many excuses, as that the queen was none of them, and some others were but sojourners with Philip because [they had been] removed by the English having got their land, and were of their kindred, which we know is true. Not but we think they did shelter many they should not, and that they did know some of their men did assist Philip; but according to their barbarous rules they accounted . . . no wrong, or they could not help it.

But some enemies' heads they did send in, and told us they were informed that however when winter came they might be sure the English would be their enemies, and so they stood doubtful for about five months. The English were jealous [suspicious] that there was a general plot of all Indians against [the] English, and the Indians were in like manner jealous of the English. I think it was general that they were unwilling to be wronged, and that the Indians do judge the English partial against them. . . .

When winter was come we had a letter from Boston of the United commissioners that they were resolved to reduce the Narragansetts to conformity, not to be troubled with them anymore, and desired some help of boats and otherwise, if we saw cause, and that we should keep secret concerning it. Our governor sent them word we were satisfied Narragansetts were treacherous, and had aided Philip, and as we had assisted to relieve their army before, so we should be ready to assist them still, and advised that terms might be tendered. . . .

We [were] not in the least expecting they would have begun the war, and not before [the Narragansetts] proclaimed it . . . , I having often informed the Indians that the Englishmen would not be beginning a war, otherwise it was brutish to do so. I am sorry so the Indians have cause to think me deceitful, for the English thus began the war with the Narragansetts [on September 9, 1675].

We having sent off our island many Indians, and informed them if they kept by the water sides and did not meddle, that however the English would do them no harm, although it was not safe for us to let them live there. The army first take [*sic*] all those [under Rhode Island's protection as] prisoners, then fell upon Indian houses, burned them, and killed some men. The war [began] without proclamation. . . . They sold the Indians that they had taken as aforesaid for slaves. . . .

And now the English army is out to seek after the Indians; but it is mostly likely that such most able to do mischief will escape, and the women and children and impotent may be destroyed, and so the most able will have the less encumbrance to do mischief.

But I am confident it would be best for English and Indians that a peace were made upon honest terms, for each to have a due propriety and to enjoy it without oppression or usurpation by one to the other. But the English dare not trust the Indians' promises, neither the Indians to the English promises, and each have great cause therefore.

Assault on the Narragansetts
by Benjamin Church

And now strong suspicions began to arise of the Narragansett Indians, that they were ill affected, and designed mischief; and so the event soon discovered. The next winter they began their hostilities upon the English. The United Colonies then agreed to send an army to suppress them, Governor [Josias] Winslow to command the army. He, undertaking the expedition, invited Mr. Church to command a company in the expedition; which he declined, craving excuse from taking commission, [though] he promised to wait upon him as a reformado [aide-de-camp] thro' the expedition. . . .

Upon the general's request he went thence the nearest way over the ferries, with Major [Richard] Smith to his garrison in the Narragansett country, to prepare and provide for the coming of General Winslow; who marched round thro' the country with his army, proposing by night to surprise Pumham (a certain Narragansett sachem) and his town [of Shawomet]. But being aware of the approach of our army, [they] made their escape into the deserts [swamps]. . . .

Their next move was to a swamp which the Indians had fortified with a fort.[9] Mr. Church rode in the general's guard when the bloody engagement began; but being impatient of being out of the heat of the action, importu-

[9] This was a new fortified village on an island in the Great Swamp. The works were elaborate, with palisades, firing platforms, blockhouses, and abatis (tangles of brush to slow down attackers). The English assaulted the fort on December 19, 1675, focusing their attack on a gap in the still-incomplete palisades.

nately begged leave of the general that he might run down to the assistance of his friends. The general yielded to his request, provided he could rally some hands to go with him.

Thirty men immediately drew out and followed him. They entered the swamp and passed over the log that was the passage into the fort [through the palisades], where they saw many men and several valiant captains lie slain. Mr. Church, spying Capt. [Joseph] Gardiner of Salem amidst the wigwams in the east end of the fort, made towards him; but on a sudden, while they were looking each other in the face, Capt. Gardiner settled down. Mr. Church stepped to him, and seeing the blood run down his cheek, lifted his cap, and calling him by his name; he looked up in his face, but spoke not a word, being mortally shot thro' the head; and observing his wound, Mr. Church found the ball entered his head on the side that was next the upland, where the English entered the swamp.

Upon which, having ordered some care to be taken of the captain, he dispatched information to the general that the best and forwardest of his army that hazarded their lives to enter the fort, upon the muzzles of the enemies' guns, were shot in their backs, and killed by them that lay behind.

Mr. Church with his small company hastened out of the fort (that the English were now possessed of) to get a shot at the Indians that were in the swamp, and kept firing upon them. He soon met with a broad bloody track, where the enemy had fled with their wounded men. Following hard in the track, he soon spied one of the enemy, who clapped his gun across his breast, made towards Mr. Church, and beckoned to him with his hand. Mr. Church immediately commanded no man to hurt him, hoping by him to have gained some intelligence of the enemy, that he might be of advantage. But it unhappily fell out that a fellow that had lagged behind, coming up, shot down the Indian, to Mr. Church's great grief and disappointment.

But immediately they heard a great shout of the enemy, which seemed to be behind them, or between them and the fort; and discovered them [the Narragansetts] running from tree to tree to gain advantages of firing upon the English that were in the fort. Mr. Church's great difficulty now was how to discover [reveal] himself to his friends in the fort, using several inventions, till at length [he] gained an opportunity to call to and inform a sergeant in the fort that he was there, and might be exposed to their shots, unless they observed it.

By this time he discovered a number of the enemy almost within shot of him, making towards the fort. Mr. Church and his company were favored by a heap of brush that was between them and the enemy, and prevented their being discovered to them. Mr. Church had given his men their particular orders for firing upon the enemy; and as they were rising up to make their shot, the aforementioned sergeant in the fort called out to them, *for God's sake not to fire,* for he believed they were some of them their friend Indians. They clapped down again, but were soon sensible of the sergeant's mistake.

The enemy got to the top of the tree, the body whereof the sergeant stood upon, and there clapped down out of sight of the fort; but all this while never discovered Mr. Church, who observed them to keep gathering unto that place, until there seemed to be a formidable black heap of them. *Now brave boys* (said Mr. Church to his men), *if we mind our hits, we may have a brave shot, and let our sign for firing on them be their rising up to fire into the fort.* It was not long before the Indians, rising up as one body, designing to pour a volley into the fort, when our Mr. Church nimbly started up and gave them such a round of volley, and an unexpected clap on their backs, that they who escaped with their lives were so surprised, that they scampered, they knew not whither themselves.

About a dozen of them ran right over the log into the fort, and took into a sort of a hovel that was built with poles, after the manner of a corn crib. Mr. Church's men, having their cartridges fixed, were soon ready to obey his order, which was immediately to charge and run on upon the hovel, and overset it, calling as he run on to some that were in the fort to assist him in oversetting it. They no sooner came to face the enemy's shelter, but Mr. Church discovered that one of them had found a hole to point his gun through, right at him; but however encouraged his company, and ran right on, till he was struck with three bullets, one in his thigh, which was near half of it cut off as it glanced on the joint of the hip bone; another through the gatherings of his breeches and drawers, with a small flesh wound; a third pierced his pocket, and wounded a pair of mittens. . . .

But however he made shift to keep on his legs, and nimbly discharged his gun at them that wounded him. Being disenabled now to go a step, his men would have carried him off; but he forbid their touching of him until they had perfected their project of oversetting the enemy's shelter. . . . And by this time the English people in the fort had begun to set fire to the wigwams and houses in the fort, which Mr. Church labored hard to prevent. They told him, *They had orders from the General to burn them. . . .*

And burning up all the houses and provisions in the fort, the army returned the same night in the storm and cold. And I suppose that everyone who is acquainted with the circumstances of that night's march deeply laments the miseries that attended them, especially the wounded and dying men. . . . Some of the enemy that were then in the fort have since informed us that near a third of the Indians belonging to all that Narragansett country were killed by the English, and by the cold that night, and they fled out of the fort so hastily that they carried nothing with them. . . . Mr. Church was moved with the other wounded men over to Rhode Island, where in about a month's time he was in some good measure recovered of his wounds, and the fever that attended them.

THE MILITIA CAPTURED the Narragansett stronghold, but at a bitter price. At least seventy New England soldiers died; another 150 were wounded. Church was one of the lucky ones: though his deep wound was infected (as we can tell by his fever), he survived, unlike most men in his condition. As he relates, the army suffered a long, desperate march home, only to be disbanded in February 1676.[10]

The Narragansett had suffered heavily in the assault on the fort: losses among the warriors probably equalled those of the soldiers, in addition to the deaths of between 300 and 1,000 women and children. The survivors fled to join Philip, now in winter camp among the Mahicans,[11] carrying their arms and gunpowder.

As the militiamen dispersed to their homes, those homes came under ferocious attack. The Wampanoag and Narragansetts became refugee armies, legions of the persecuted and dispossessed, filled with the fury and fanaticism that might be expected of those who had seen their villages destroyed and families murdered. As John Easton feared, they became the scourge of God, punishing the Puritans for their sins. Specifically, they launched a sweeping winter offensive against New England border towns—now almost helpless after the disbanding of the cumbersome colonial army. They would show no mercy: they would follow the New England example, and disregard distinctions between combatants and civilians.

The first town they struck in this new wave of attacks was Lancaster, Massachusetts. When the Narragansett war party arrived outside the settlement in the early hours of February 10, 1676, fifty large families slept peacefully in their houses. By the end of the day, not one person would remain. It was only one of twelve towns that would be utterly destroyed by Indian raids; half of the rest would suffer serious damage. Defeat after scalding defeat would wrack New England, in bitter repayment for the unprovoked attack on the Narragansetts; the colonial war effort would virtually collapse.

One witness, and victim, of New England's darkest hour was Mary Rowlandson, a loving wife, a devout churchgoer, and a talented writer. She was one of the few to survive the raid on Lancaster; she was carried away by the Indians, and later traded to King Philip's Wampanoag. When she finally got home again, she wrote an astonishing account of her experiences—the first, and one of the best, of a new genre in American literature, the captivity narrative.

[10] The reader should remember that, according to the English calendar then in use, 1675 continued until March 24. The editor's narrative features modern usage, as here, but the dates in the historical selections have been left as written.

[11] Philip attempted to open an alliance with the Mohawks, but was rebuffed; they had passed on their partnership from the Dutch to the conquering English. So the Wampanoag took refuge with the enemies of the Mohawks, the Mahicans.

The excerpt below follows Rowlandson's capture and subsequent wanderings with the refugee Native Americans, and highlights the course of the war. It also sheds fascinating light on the Indians and their relationship with the colonists. Half a century of living side by side created a hybrid culture: they wore the English clothes Rowlandson made and paid her in English currency. Philip even called his council of sachems the "General Court," in imitation of colonial government. Here, too, are the powwows before battle, and the dances in celebration of victory.

Rowlandson's account also sheds light on other key aspects of the war. King Philip, for example, had only limited sway over his warriors. And despite their victories, the Native Americans would suffer shortages of everything from tobacco to gunpowder to food. As the months dragged on, they eagerly put their captives up for sale, desperate for the supplies they could only get from the English themselves.

What Desolations He Has Made in the Earth
by Mary Rowlandson

On the tenth of February 1675, came the Indians with great numbers upon Lancaster. Their first coming was about sun-rising; hearing the noise of some guns, we looked out. Several houses were burning, and the smoke ascending to heaven. . . .

At length they came and beset our own house, and quickly it was the dolefullest day that ever mine eyes saw. The house stood upon the edge of a hill; some of the Indians got behind the hill, others into the barn, and others behind anything that could shelter them; from all which places they shot against the house, so that the bullets seemed to fly like hail. And they quickly wounded one man among us, then another, then a third. About two hours (according to my observation, in that amazing time) they had been about the house before they prevailed to fire it (which they did with flax and hemp, which they brought out of the barn). . . .

Now is the dreadful hour come, that I have often heard of (in time of war, as it was in the case of others) but now mine eyes see it. Some in our house were fighting for our lives, others wallowing in their blood, the house on fire over our heads, and the bloody heathen ready to knock us on the head if we stirred out. Now might we hear mothers and children crying out for themselves, and one another, Lord, what shall we do? Then I took my children (and one of my sister, hers) to go forth and leave the house; but as soon as we came to the door and appeared, the Indians shot so thick that the bullets rattled against the house, as if one had taken an handful of stones and threw them, so that we were fain to give back. . . . But out we must go, the fire increasing, and coming along behind us, roaring, and the Indians gaping before us with their guns, spears, and hatchets to devour us.

No sooner were we out of the house, but my brother-in-law (being before wounded in defending the house, in or near the throat) fell down dead, whereat the Indians scornfully shouted and hallowed, and were presently upon him, stripping off his clothes. The bullets flying thick, one went through my side, and the same (as would seem) through the bowels and hand of my dear child in my arms. One of my elder sister's children, named William, had then his leg broken; which the Indians perceiving, they knocked him on [his] head.

Thus were we butchered by those merciless heathen, standing amazed, with blood running down to our heels. My eldest sister, being yet in the house, and seeing those woeful sights, the infidels hailing mothers one way, and children the other, and some wallowing in their blood; and her elder son telling her that her son William was dead, and myself was wounded; she said, And Lord let me die with them, which was no sooner said, but she was struck with a bullet, and fell down dead over the threshold. I hope she is reaping the fruit of her good labors, being faithful to the service of God in her place. . . .

But to return: the Indians laid hold of us, pulling me one way, and the children another, and said, Come go along with us. I told them they would kill me; they answered, If I were willing to go along with them, they would not hurt me.

Oh the doleful sight that now was to behold at this house! *Come, behold the works of the Lord, what desolations he has made in the Earth.*[12] Of thirty-seven persons who were in this one house, none escaped either present death or a bitter captivity, save only one, who might say as he, Job 1:15, *And I only am escaped alone to tell the news.* There were twelve killed, some shot, some stabbed with their spears, some knocked down with their hatchets. When we are in prosperity, oh the little that we think of such dreadful sights, and to see our dear friends and relations lie bleeding out their heart blood upon the ground. There was one who was chopped into the head with a hatchet, and stripped naked, and yet was crawling up and down. It is a solemn sight to see so many Christians lying in their blood, some here, and some there, like a company of sheep torn by wolves. . . .

I had often before this said that if the Indians should come, I should choose rather to be killed by them than taken alive; but when it came to the trial my mind changed. Their glittering weapons so daunted my spirit, that I chose rather to go along with those (as I may say) ravenous beasts, than that moment to end my days. . . .

[12] Psalms 46:8.

THE FIRST REMOVE

Now away we must go with those barbarous creatures, with our bodies wounded and bleeding, and our hearts no less than our bodies. About a mile we went that night, up upon a hill within sight of the town, where they intended to lodge. There was hard by a vacant house (deserted by the English before, for fear of the Indians). I asked them whether I might not lodge in the house that night, to which they answered, What, will you love Englishmen still?

This was the dolefullest night that ever my eyes saw. Oh the roaring, and singing and dancing, and yelling of those black creatures in the night, which made the place a lively resemblance of hell. And as miserable was the waste that was there made, of horses, cattle, sheep, swine, calves, lambs, roasting pigs, and fowl (which they had plundered in the town), some roasting, some lying and burning, and some boiling to feed our merciless enemies; who were joyful enough though we were disconsolate.

To add to the dolefullness of the former day, and the dismalness of the present night, my thoughts ran upon my losses and sad bereaved condition. All was gone, my husband gone (at least separated from me, being in the bay [in Boston]; and to add to my grief, the Indians told me they would kill him as he came homeward), my children gone, my relations and friends gone, our house and home and all our comforts within door, and without, all was gone (except my life); and I knew not but the next moment that might go too. There remained nothing to me but one poor wounded babe. . . .

THE SECOND REMOVE

But now, the next morning, I must turn my back upon the town, and travel with them into the vast and desolate wilderness, I knew not whither. . . . One of the Indians carried my poor wounded babe upon a horse; it went moaning all along, I shall die, I shall die. I went on foot after it, with sorrow that cannot be expressed. At length I took it off the horse, and carried it in my arms till my strength failed, and I fell down with it. Then they set me upon a horse with my wounded child in my lap. . . .

After this it quickly began to snow, and when night came on, they stopped; and now I must sit in the snow, by a little fire, and a few boughs behind me, with my sick child in my lap, calling much for water, being now (through the wound) fallen into a violent fever. My own wound also growing so stiff, that I could scarce sit down or rise up. . . .

THE THIRD REMOVE

The next day was the Sabbath. I then remembered how careless I had been in God's holy time, how many Sabbaths I had lost and misspent, and how evilly I had walked in God's sight; which lay so close unto my spirit, that it was easy for me to see how righteous it was with God to cut off the thread of my life, and cast me out of his presence forever. Yet the Lord still showed mercy to me, and upheld me; and as he wounded me with one hand, so he healed me with the other. . . .

I sat much alone with a poor, wounded child in my lap, which moaned night and day, having nothing to revive the body or cheer the spirits of her; but instead of that sometimes one Indian would come and tell me one hour, that Your master will knock your child in the head, and then a second, and then a third, Your master will quickly knock your child in the head.

This was the comfort I had from them, miserable comforters are ye all, as he [Job] said. Thus nine days I sat upon my knees with my babe in my lap, till my flesh was raw again; my child being even ready to depart this sorrowful world, they bade me carry it out to another wigwam (I suppose because they would not be troubled with such spectacles). Whither I went with a very heavy heart, and down I sat with the picture of death in my lap. About two hours in the night, my sweet babe like a lamb departed this life, on February 18, 1675. It being about six years, five months old. It was nine days from the first wounding. . . .

In the morning, when they understood that my child was dead, they sent for me home to my master's wigwam (by my master in this writing, must be understood Quinnapin, who was a sagamore, and married King Philip's wife's sister . . . ; I was sold to him by another Narragansett Indian, who took me when first I came out of the garrison). I went to take up my dead child in my arms to carry it with me, but they bid me let it alone; there was no resisting, but go I must and leave it. When I had been at my master's wigwam, I took the first opportunity I could get to go look after my dead child; when I came I asked them what they had done with it. Then they told me it was upon the hill; then they went and showed me where it was, where I saw the ground was newly digged, and there they told me they had buried it. There I left that child in the wilderness, and must commit it, and myself also, in this wilderness condition to him who is above all.

God having taken away this dear child, I went to see my daughter Mary, who was at this same Indian town, at a wigwam not very far off, though we had very little liberty or opportunity to see one another. She was about ten years old, and taken from the door at first by a praying Indian, and afterward sold for a gun. When I came in sight, she would fall a'weeping; at which they were provoked, and would not let me come near her, but bade me be gone; which was a heart-cutting word to me. I had one child dead, another in the wilderness, I knew not where, the third they would not let me come near to. . . .

As I was going up and down mourning and lamenting my condition, my son came to me, and asked me how I did. I had not seen him before, since the destruction of the town, and I knew not where he was, till I was informed by himself that he was amongst a smaller parcel of Indians, whose place was about six miles off. With tears in his eyes, he asked me whether his sister Sarah was dead; and told me he had seen his sister Mary; and prayed me, that I would not be troubled in reference to himself.

The occasion of his coming to see me at this time was this: There was, as I said, about six miles from us, a small plantation of Indians, where it seems he had been during his captivity; and at this time, there were some forces of the Indians gathered out of our company, and some also from them (among whom was my son's master) to go to assault and burn Medfield.[13] In this time of the absence of his master, his dame brought him to see me. . . .

The next day, viz. to this, the Indians returned from Medfield, all the company, for those that belonged to the other small company came through the town that now we were at. But before they came to us, Oh! The outrageous roaring and hooping that there was. They began their din about a mile before they came to us. By their noise and hooping they signified how many they had destroyed (which was at that time twenty-three). Those that were with us at home were gathered together as soon as they heard the hooping, and every time that the other went over their number, these at home gave a shout, and the very Earth rung again. And thus they continued till those that had been upon the expedition were come up to the sagamore's wigwam; and then, Oh, the hideous insulting and triumphing that there was over some Englishmen's scalps that they had taken (as their manner is) and brought with them. . . .

THE FOURTH REMOVE

And now I must part with that little company I had. Here I parted from my daughter Mary (whom I never saw again till I saw her in Dorchester, returned from captivity), and from four little cousins and neighbors, some of which I never saw afterward; the Lord only knows the end of them. . . . But to return to my own journey: We traveled about half a day or little more, and came to a desolate place in the wilderness, where there were no wigwams or inhabitants before. . . .

---

[13] Medfield was attacked on February 21, 1676 (according to the modern calendar). About fifty houses were burned.

THE FIFTH REMOVE

The occasion (as I thought) of their moving at this time was the English army, it being near and following them. For they went as if they had gone for their lives, for some considerable way, and then they made a stop, and chose some of their stoutest men, and sent them back to hold the English army in play while the rest escaped. And then, like Jehu, they marched on furiously, with their old, and with their young; some carried their old decrepit mothers, some carried one, and some another. . . .

I was at this time knitting a pair of white cotton stockings for my mistress; and had not yet wrought upon a Sabbath day. When the Sabbath came they bade me go to work; I told them it was the Sabbath day, and desired them to let me rest, and told them I would do as much more tomorrow; to which they answered me, they would break my face. . . .

On Monday they set their wigwams on fire, and away they went. On that very day came the English army after them to this river, and saw the smoke of their wigwams, and yet this river put a stop to them. God did not give them courage or activity to go over after us; we were not ready for so great a mercy as victory and deliverance. . . .

THE EIGHTH REMOVE

On the morrow morning we must go over the river, i.e. Connecticut, to meet with King Philip. . . . In this travel up the river, about noon the company made a stop and sat down; some to eat, and others to rest them. As I sat amongst them, my son Joseph unexpectedly came to me. We asked of each other's welfare, bemoaning our doleful condition, and the change that had come upon us. . . . But to return.

We traveled on till night; and in the morning, we must go over the river to Philip's crew. When I was in the canoe, I could not but be amazed at the numerous crew of pagans that were on the bank on the other side. When I came ashore, they gathered all about me, I sitting alone in the midst. I observed they asked one another questions, and laughed, and rejoiced over their gains and victories. Then my heart began to fail, and I fell a'weeping which was the first time in my remembrance, that I wept before them. . . . But now I may saw, as Psalm 137:1, *By the rivers of Babylon, there we sat down; yea, we wept when we remembered Zion.*

There was one of them asked me, why I wept; I could hardly tell what to say. Yet I answered, they would kill me. No, said he, none will hurt you. Then came one of them and gave me two spoonfulls of meal to comfort me, and another gave me half a pint of peas; which was more worth than many bushels at another time.

Then I went to see King Philip. He bade me come in and sit down, and asked me whether I would smoke it (a usual compliment nowadays amongst saints and sinners), but this no way suited me. . . .

Now the Indians gather their forces to go against Northampton; overnight one went about yelling and hooting to give notice of the design. Where upon they fell to boiling ground-nuts, and parching of corn (as many as had it) for their provision; and in the morning away they went. During my abode in this place, Philip spake to me to make a shirt for his boy, which I did, for which he gave me a shilling.[14] I offered the money to my master, but he bade me keep it. And with it I bought a piece of horse flesh. Afterwards he asked me to make a cap for his boy, for which he invited me to dinner. I went, and he gave me a pancake, about as big as two fingers; it was made of parched wheat, beaten, and fried in bear's grease; but I thought I never tasted pleasanter meat in my life. . . .

The Indians, returning from Northampton, brought with them some horses and sheep, and other things which they had taken.[15] I desired them, that they would carry me to Albany,[16] upon one of those horses, and sell me for powder; for so they had sometimes discoursed. I was utterly hopeless of getting home on foot. . . .

THE NINTH REMOVE

But instead of going either to Albany or homeward, we must go five miles up the river, and then go over it. Here we abode for a while. . . . This was about the time that their great captain, Naananto, was killed in the Narragansett country. . . .[17]

THE NINETEENTH REMOVE

Then came Tom and Peter, with the second letter from the [Massachusetts] council about the captives.[18] Though they were Indians, I gat them by the

---

[14] This shilling jumps out as evidence of the Indian-colonial economic links. Rowlandson goes on to reveal the food shortages that plagued the warring Indians.

[15] Northampton was attacked on March 14, 1676 (according to the modern calendar). The town was surrounded by palisades, however, and the Indians failed to penetrate the defenses.

[16] The Dutch traders often sold arms and ammunition even to Indians at war with the English colonists, though this trade had recently been stopped.

[17] Naananto, also known as Canonchet, was a leading Narragansett warrior. His death on April 3, 1676, was a severe blow.

[18] Tom Dublet Nepanet and Peter Conway Tatatiquinea were "praying Indians"—Christian converts—who were conducting negotiations for the release of the prisoners. This was their second visit, roughly April 12, 1676.

hand, and burst out into tears. My heart was so full that I could not speak to them; but recovering myself, I asked them how my husband did, and all my friends and acquaintances. They said, they are all very well but melancholy. They brought me two biscuits, and a pound of tobacco. The tobacco I quickly gave away. . . .

When the letter was come, the sagamores met to consult about the captives, and called me to them to enquire how much my husband would give to redeem me. When I came, I sat down among them, as I was wont to do, as their manner is. Then they bade me stand up, and said, they were the General Court. They bid me speak what I thought he would give. Not knowing that all we had was destroyed by the Indians, I was in a great strait: I thought if I should speak of but a little, it would be slighted, and hinder the matter; if of a great sum, I knew not where it would be procured. Yet at a venture, I said twenty pounds, yet desired them to take less. But they would not hear of that, but sent that message to Boston, that for twenty pounds I should be redeemed. It was a praying Indian that wrote their letter for them. . . .

There was another praying Indian, so wicked and cruel as to wear a string about his neck, strung with Christian fingers. Another praying Indian, when they went to the Sudbury fight, went with them, and his squaw also with him, with her papoose at her back. Before they went to that fight, they got a company together to *Powow*. . . . And they went out not so rejoicing, but they came home with as great a victory. For they said they had killed two captains and almost an hundred men. One Englishman they brought along with them; and he said, it was too true, for they had made some sad work at Sudbury, as indeed it proved. . . .[19]

THE TWENTIETH REMOVE

It was their usual manner to remove, when they had done any mischief, lest they should be found out; and so they did at this time. We went about three or four miles, and there they built a great wigwam, big enough to hold an hundred Indians, which they did in preparation to a great day of dancing. They would say now amongst themselves, that the Governor would be so angry for his loss at Sudbury, that he would send no more about the captives, which made me grieve and tremble. . . .

On a Sabbath day, the sun being about an hour high in the afternoon, came Mr. John Hoar (the Council permitting him) together with the two forementioned Indians, Tom and Peter, with their third letter from the Council. . . .

I begged them to let me see the Englishman, but they would not. But

[19] On April 18, Captain Samuel Wadsworth of Milton and Captain Samuel Brocklebank of Rowley were ambushed and killed, along with thirty of their men.

there was I, fain to sit their pleasure. When they had talked their fill with him, they suffered me to go to him. We asked each other of our welfare, and how my husband did, and all my friends. He told me they were all well, and would be glad to see me. . . .

I asked them whether I should go home with Mr. Hoar? They answered no, one and another of them; and it being night, we lay down with that answer. . . . At night I asked them again, if I should go home? They all as one said No, except my husband would come for me. When we were lain down, my master went out of the wigwam, and by and by sent in an Indian called James the Printer, who told Mr. Hoar that my master would let me go home tomorrow, if he would let him have one pint of liquors. Then Mr. Hoar called his own Indians, Tom and Peter, and bid them go and see whether he would promise it before them three; and if he would, he should have it; which he did, and he had it.

Then Philip, smelling the business, called me to him, and asked me what I would give him, to tell me some good news, and speak a good word for me. I told him, I could not tell what to give him. I would anything I had, and asked him what he would have? He said, two coats and twenty shillings in money, and half a bushel of seed corn, and some tobacco. I thanked him for his love; but I knew the good news as well as the crafty fox. . . .

On Tuesday morning they called their General Court (as they call it) to consult and determine whether I should go home or no. And they all as one man did seemingly consent to it, that I should go home; except Philip, who would not come among them. . . . They assented to it, and seemed much to rejoice in it. . . .

So I took my leave of them, and in coming along my heart melted into tears, more than all the while I was with them, and I was almost swallowed up with the thoughts that ever I should go home again. About the sun going down, Mr. Hoar, myself, and the two Indians came to Lancaster, and a solemn sight it was to me. There had I lived many comfortable years amongst my relations and neighbors, and now not one Christian to be seen, nor one house left standing. We went on to a farm house that was yet standing, where we lay all night; and a comfortable lodging we had, though nothing but straw to lie on. The Lord preserved us in safety that night, and raised us up again in the morning, and carried us along, that before noon we came to Concord.

Now was I full of joy, and yet not without sorrow: joy to see such a lovely sight, so many Christians together, and some of them my neighbors. There I met with my brother, and my brother-in-law, who asked me if I knew where his wife was? Poor heart! He had helped to bury her, and knew it not; she being shot down by the house was partly burnt. . . .

Yet I was not without sorrow, to think how many were looking and longing, and my own children amongst the rest, to enjoy that deliverance that I had now received, and I did not know whether ever I should see them again. Being recruited with food and rainment, we went to Boston that day, where I met with my dear husband, but the thoughts of our dear children, one being dead, and the others we could not tell where, abated our comfort each to other. . . .

We kept enquiring and listening to hear concerning them, but not certain news as yet. About this time the council had ordered a day of public Thanksgiving [June 29, 1676]; though I thought I had still cause of mourning, and being unsettled in our minds, we thought we would ride toward the eastward, to see if we could hear anything concerning our children. As we were riding along (God is the wise disposer of things) between Ipswich and Rowley, we met Mr. William Hubbard, who told us that our son Joseph was come into Major [Richard] Waldron's, and another with him, which was my sister's son. . . . On Monday we came to Charlestown, where we heard that the Governor of Rhode Island [William Coddington] had sent over for our daughter, to take care of her, and brought her to his own house. . . .

Before I knew what affliction meant, I was ready sometimes to wish for it. When I lived in prosperity, having the comforts of the world about me, my relations by me, my heart cheerful, and taking little care for anything; and yet seeing many, whom I preferred before myself, under many trials and afflictions, in sickness, weakness, poverty, losses, crosses, and cares of the world, I should be sometimes jealous lest I should have my portion in this life. . . . But now I see the Lord had his time to scourge and chasten me. The portion of some is to have their afflictions by drops, now one drop and then another; but the dregs of the cup, the wine of astonishment, like a sweeping rain that leaveth no food, did the Lord prepare to be my portion. Affliction I wanted, and affliction I had, full measure (I thought) pressed down and running over. . . . The Lord hath shown me the vanity of these outward things.

———

THE SUMMER OF 1676 brought joy and redemption—and sad reflection—into the life of Mary Rowlandson; but it heralded despair for the Wampanoag and Narragansetts. In a few short months, their sweeping victories had turned sour. In fact, their very success was a cause of their desperation.

In the attacks that destroyed Lancaster and so many other towns, the Indians created a vast no-man's-land, an uninhabited zone of desolation. The English retreated into their larger settlements; their militia companies even feared to pursue retreating raiding parties. But this cut off the refugee Native Americans from supplies they desperately needed. They had lived in close connection with the English; now they depended on English goods. Some things they could supply for themselves: they possessed forges, for example, to keep at least some of their muskets in working order. But they could not make their own gunpowder; nor could they stay in one place long enough to grow corn, and their raids provided them with less and less as the English retreated or lost what they had. As Ian Steele writes, the field of Indian victories "had become a foodless barrier."

Hunger, from the sachems' point of view, was a strategic problem; but it created tactical conundrums as well. The great encampments, such as Mary Rowlandson had seen, were forced to break up so smaller bands could disperse to seek food. As they did so, they became vulnerable to small parties of Mohegans (allies of New England, not to be confused with the Mahicans), and of those colonists daring enough to march out and fight.

In August 1676, one such party of colonists and allied Indians marched out against their enemies—and it should be no surprise that it was led by the indomitable Benjamin Church. Church benefitted greatly from the food crisis that gripped the Wampanoag and Narragansett refugees; yet his own fighting skills led him to the greatest prize of all: King Philip himself. In the passage that follows, Church recalls (in vivid, believable detail) how he trapped the Wampanoag leader—nowhere else than where the war began, in the Mount Hope peninsula.

To Have the Rogue's Head
by Benjamin Church

Capt. Church being now at Plymouth again, weary and worn, would have gone home to his wife and family, but the government being solicitous to engage him in the service until Philip was slain, and promising him satisfaction and redress for some mistreatment he had met with, he fixes for another expedition.

He had soon volunteers enough to make up the company he desired, and marched thro' the woods, until he came to Pocasset. And not seeing nor hearing of any of the enemy, they went over the ferry to Rhode Island to refresh themselves. The captain with about half a dozen in his company took horse and rid about eight miles down the island, to Mr. Sanford's, where he had left his wife; who no sooner saw him but fainted with the surprise.

And by that time she was a little revived, they spied two horsemen coming at a great pace. Capt. Church told his company that those men (by their riding) came with tidings. When they came up they proved to be Maj. Sanford and Capt. Golding; who immediately asked Capt. Church, What would he give to hear some news of Philip? He replied, That was what he wanted. They told him they had rid hard with some hopes of overtaking him, and were now come on purpose to inform him, that there was just now tidings from Mount Hope. An Indian came down from thence (where Philip's camp now was) . . . he reported that he was fled from Philip, *who* (said he) *has killed my brother just before I came away, for giving some advice that displeased him.* And said, he was fled for fear of meeting with the same his brother had met with. He told them also, that Philip was in Mount Hope neck.

Capt. Church thanked them for their good news, and said, he hoped by tomorrow morning to have the rogue's head. The horses that he and his company came on standing at the door (for they had not been unsaddled), his wife must content herself with a short visit, when such game was ahead; they immediately mounted, let spurs to their horses, and away. The two gentlemen that brought him the tidings told him they would gladly wait upon him to see the event of his expedition. He thanked them, and told them he should be as fond of their company as any men's; and (in short) they went with him.

And they were soon at Trip's Ferry (with Capt. Church's company) where the deserter was; who was a fellow of good sense, and told his story handsomely. He offered Capt. Church to pilot him to Philip, and to help to kill him, that he might revenge his brother's death. [And] told him, that Philip was now upon a little spot of upland that was in the south end of the mirey swamp just at the foot of the Mount, which was a spot of ground that Capt. Church was well acquainted with.

By the time they were got over the ferry, and came near the ground, half the night was spent. The Captain commands a halt, and bringing the company together, he asked Maj. Sanford and Capt. Golding's advice, what method was best to take in making the onset; but they, declining [the] giving of any advice, telling him that his great experience and success forbid their taking upon them to give advice. Then Capt. Church offered Capt. Golding, that he should have the honor (if he would please accept it) to beat up Philip's headquarters. He accepted the offer, and had his allotted number drawn out to him, and the pilot.

Capt. Church's instructions to him were to be very careful in his approach to the enemy, and be sure not to show himself until by daylight they might see and discern their own men from the enemy. Told him also, that his custom in the like cases was to creep with his company on their bellies, until they came as near as they could; and that as soon as the enemy discovered them they would cry out; and that was the word for his men to fire and fall on. [Church] directed him when the enemy should start and take into the swamp, they should pursue with speed, every man shouting and making what noise they could; for he would give orders to his ambuscade to fire on any that should come silently.

Capt. Church, knowing it was Philip's custom to be foremost in the flight, went down to the swamp and gave Capt. [John] Williams of Scituate the command of the right wing of the ambush, and placed an Englishman and an Indian together behind such shelters of trees, etc., that he could find, and took care to place them at such distance as none might pass undiscovered between them. . . . But it being somewhat further thro' the swamp than he was aware of, he wanted [lacked] men to make up his ambuscade. Having placed what men he had, he took Maj. Sanford by the hand, said, *Sir, I have so placed them that 'tis scarce possible that Philip should escape them.*

The same moment a shot whistled over their heads, and then the noise of a gun towards Philip's camp. Capt. Church at first thought it might be some gun fired by accident; but before he could speak, a whole volley followed, which was earlier than he expected. One of Philip's gang going forth to ease himself, when he had done, looked round him, and Capt. Golding thought the Indian looked right at him (tho' probably 'twas but his conceit); so fired at him, and upon his firing, the whole company that were with him fired upon the enemy's shelter before the Indians had time to rise from their sleep, and so overshot them.

But their shelter was open on that side next the swamp, built so on purpose for the convenience of flight on occasion. They were soon in the swamp and Philip the foremost; who, starting at the first gun, threw his Petunk [pouch or shot bag] and powderhorn over his head, catched up his gun, and ran as fast as he could scamper, without any more clothes than his small breeches and stockings, and ran directly upon two [men] of Capt. Church's ambush.

They let him come fair within shot, and the Englishman's gun missing fire, he bid the Indian fire away; and he did so to purpose, sent one musket bullet thro' his heart, and another not above two inches from it. He fell upon his face in the mud and water with his gun under him.

By this time the enemy perceived they were waylaid on the east side of the swamp, [and] tacked short about. One of the enemy who seemed to be a great surly old fellow, hallowed with a loud voice, and often called out, *iootash, iootash* (fight, fight). Captain Church called to his Indian Peter and asked him, who that was that called so? He answered, it was the old Annowan, Philip's great captain, calling on his soldiers to stand to it and fight stoutly.

Now the enemy, finding that place of the swamp which was not ambushed, many of them made their escape in the English tracks. The man that had shot down Philip ran with all speed to Capt. Church, and informed him of his exploit, who commanded him to be silent about it, and let no man more know about it, until they had drove the swamp clean. But when they had drove the swamp thro' and found the enemy had escaped, or at least the most of them, and the sun now up, and the dew gone, that they could not so easily track them, the whole company met together at the place where the enemy's night shelter was. And then Capt. Church gave them the news of Philip's death; upon which the whole army gave three loud huzzas.

Capt. Church ordered his body to be pulled out of the mire on to the upland, so some of Capt. Church's Indians took hold of him by his stockings, and some by his small breeches (being otherwise naked), and drew him thro' the mud unto the upland, and a doleful, great, naked, dirty beast he looked like. Capt. Church then said, that foreasmuch as he had caused many an Englishman's body to lie unburied and rot above ground, that not one of his bones should be buried. And calling his old Indian executioner, bid him behead and quarter him.

Accordingly, he came with his hatchet and stood over him, but before he struck he made a small speech, directing it to Philip and said, *He had been a very great man, and had made many a man afraid of him, but so big as he was he would now chop off his ass for him;* and so went to work, and did as he was ordered. Philip having one very remarkable hand . . . occasioned by the splitting of a pistol in it formerly; Capt. Church gave the head and that hand to Alderman, the Indian who shot him, to show such gentlemen as would bestow gratuities upon him; and accordingly he got many a penny by it.

———

A LONG, BLOODY year after the first shots were fired, the colonists removed the head of Metacom, King Philip, chief sachem of the Wampanoag. It had been a year unlike any other in the history of New England, a year that changed everything.

The Narragansetts and Wampanoag were disrupted, dispersed, devastated. Men, women, and children had died in battle, starved to death, fled to other tribes, or were carried into slavery; the survivors fled into New France's sphere of influence. As a result, the war permanently altered settlement patterns in New England: instead of colonist and Native American living side by side, now there would always be a wilderness frontier between English and Indians.

Twelve colonial towns had been utterly wiped out; half of the rest suffered damage. One out of fifteen men of military age had been killed—including eight percent of Plymouth's adult male population (which markedly evened the sex ratio). The colonial governments reeled with debt. Dead cattle littered the countryside; burned and abandoned cornfields sat desolate. The frontier of settlement had been pushed back, not to be reached again for decades to come.

In the midst of this suffering, this truly biblical suffering, the ruling councils of New England suffered another shock—this one delivered from across the ocean. England's third war with the Dutch had ended; the cherished project of Charles II could now proceed. The king would finally inquire into those self-governing colonists who had so actively supported the overthrow of his father.

In 1675, Charles created a body of councilors he called the Lords of Trade. Their special mission was to investigate New England—to see how it could be brought into line with the sort of government that ruled Virginia and New York, where a governor appointed by the king held sway. So it was that Winthrop's children passed through one kind of peril, only to land in another.

14

TERRORS OF THE INVISIBLE WORLD

It is time to tell the story of the Salem witch trials. To do so, we must leap fifteen years beyond the events of the last chapter, and more than a decade past the chapter to come. The jump is necessary, however, if we are to understand how this tragedy came about. The trials of Salem have taken on a life of their own in American memory, emerging as a mythic saga, more metaphor than reality. So we must return them to their proper place in the current of history, and see them in light of the fifteen torrential, terrible years that led up to the first accusation of sorcery.

When the Indians fled New England, God fled with them. So it must have seemed to this, the third generation of English colonists. The torment of King Philip's War left the northern colonies battered, impoverished, their bravest men dead, their newest towns destroyed, their faith in God's grace badly shaken. And yet, in many ways, the worst was yet to come.

The terrors of war immediately gave way to the perils of politics. New England—especially the colony of Massachusetts Bay—now stood in the way of the long-term goal of England's Stuart monarchs: the centralization of power in the king's hands. As related at the end of the previous chapter, Charles II formed the Lords of Trade in the 1670s to look into colonial affairs; the Lords dispatched a special envoy, Edward Randolph, to investigate the government of Massachusetts. This mission was repugnant enough to the self-governing New Englanders; even worse, Randolph also came to enforce the hated Navigation Acts.

The Navigation Acts aimed at a goal that most Englishmen (in England) could agree upon: to harness the colonial economy more firmly to that of the mother country. Indeed, the various acts spanned both Cromwell's unroyal rule and the restored reign of Charles II. But to the colonists, they were onerous: They required that all trade be carried in English ships (thus excluding the Dutch, once so active in the export of tobacco), and that colonial imports and exports be routed through England or its dependencies. The most recent act, passed in 1673, imposed customs duties on colonial trade, and allowed for royal commissioners to collect them.

Randolph received a cold welcome in Massachusetts, where the people hated both the Stuart monarchy and the Navigation laws. After all, they had always been a tribe of oceangoing merchants (John Winthrop himself had built a trading ship immediately upon arriving in the bay). They did not appreciate being checked up on, as if they were errant children (which is how the crown actually saw them). They obstructed Randolph at every turn. The royal investigator soon departed in frustration, only to come back in 1681 as a customs collector.

Randolph's return created a crisis in Massachusetts that most colonists tried to ignore. All around them, the storm of the House of Stuart gathered force. To the west they faced James, the Duke of York, who ruled New York; this Catholic prince appointed a Catholic governor there, and refused to allow an elected assembly. To the north, the crown declared New Hampshire a royal colony. And now Randolph landed in their very midst, where he made trouble. If there was ever a dogged champion of the crown's rights, it was this persistent official. He prosecuted ship after ship for violating the Navigation Acts; yet each case went before the colony's courts, which would release the vessel and bill Randolph for the costs. Yet he went on in the face of this resistance, until he had prosecuted thirty-four merchant craft—each one released, each case a charge against his purse.

Meanwhile, he painstakingly catalogued the colony's offenses against the throne. The government of Massachusetts harassed every faith but the official Congregational church—the colonists even persecuted the king's own Church of England, and executed Quakers, members of a radical new faith. The colonists left Charles's name out of official documents, and refused the oath of loyalty.

Charles II never earned a reputation for activity; he honored the Stuart family goal of building royal power, but he never put much energy into it. He rather preferred the aspects of kingship that involved self-indulgence, rather than affairs of state. Yet Randolph's reports of the pigheaded, insulting obstinacy of Massachusetts moved him to action. For Charles, this obstructionism formed part of a larger crisis: the resistance in England to allowing his brother James to take the throne upon his death. Charles lacked a son of his own, so the Duke of York was his official heir. But James was a Catholic. What's more, he was a cunning, energetic Catholic, which meant he not only enraged the antipapal English, but frightened them as well.

As opposition to James's succession brewed in the House of Commons in 1680, Charles struck with uncharacteristic speed. He dissolved Parliament and began redrawing the boroughs (the ancient electoral districts) by royal decree, with the goal of obtaining a more pliant assembly at the next election. The crown applied this thinking to North America as well; though the colonies did not send members to Parliament, Randolph's reports showed that they posed a challenge to the throne.

After long legal proceedings, the Court of King's Bench ruled October 1684 that the charter of Massachusetts Bay was invalid. The crown could now take direct control. Before the colonists could recover from their shock, Charles died; in February 1685, the Duke of York became King James II. With tremendous personal force, James swiftly moved to concentrate power in his own hands. He aimed at the sort of royal supremacy enjoyed by his close friend, Louis XIV of France.

Back in Massachusetts, Winthrop's legacy disintegrated with appalling speed before James's sweeping assault. The very colony itself disappeared: James amalgamated it with Plymouth, Rhode Island, Connecticut, New Hampshire, and Maine (and eventually New York) into the Dominion of New England. Short of instituting Catholicism, the Dominion represented an overthrow of everything the Puritans had built. It would have a royal governor and no elected assembly. It disestablished the Congregational church, imposing Christian freedom of conscience, with a preference for the Church of England. In 1686, the king named Sir Edmund Andros to the governorship; Andros (who had governed James's province of New York a decade earlier) arrived in Boston with a frigate and a garrison of troops. In a symbolic assertion of the new order, Andros held an Anglican church service in the high tabernacle of Congregationalism, the Old South Meeting House.

Only a decade had passed since King Philip had ravaged the borders of New England; but that Indian sachem could only strike the periphery—the English king had seized its heart. God seemed to spurn these late-generation Puritans with his toe. Andros's sheriffs, not local justices, now appointed juries; Admiralty courts now judged violations of the Navigation Acts; men who protested the taxes Andros levied landed in jail.

One small sign raised the hopes of these late-generation Puritans: James suspended the Test and Corporation Acts. These laws imposed civil penalties on Catholics and dissenters (Protestants who did not adhere to the Church of England). James suspended the acts to allow his Catholic friends to hold office; he was already putting pressure on leading nobles to convert to the church of Rome. The New England Congregationalists saw the suspension, mistakenly, as a friendly gesture toward themselves. With completely misplaced optimism, they sent their leading clergyman, Increase Mather, to plead their case in London.

After a decade of neglect, it seemed that God began to smile on New England once more. Increase Mather's visit to the capital happily coincided with a sudden turn of events known as the Glorious Revolution. It seems that the English detested their king's Catholicism as much as the colonists hated his centralizing ways. Their only hope was the fact that James had no son, and his daughter (and heir) Mary was a Protestant married to William of Orange, Stadtholder (head of state) in the Calvinist Netherlands. But in early 1688, the illusion of a Protestant succession to the aging James evaporated when his (second) wife gave birth to a boy. With no options left, several leading figures in England wrote to William of Orange, promising him and his wife the joint throne if only he would rescue them.

Before 1688 ended, William had landed in England and swept James across the water to Ireland with scarcely a fight. William pursued, and decisively defeated the Catholic ex-king at the Battle of the Boyne (still celebrated by Ulster's Protestants). A delighted Parliament confirmed the new king as William III; in turn, he agreed to sweeping reforms that bound the crown to act within the law.

Such was the dramatic scene that greeted Increase Mather as he stepped onto English shores. Equally unexpected was Mather's own transformation: this pious, provincial minister quickly proved himself a master of the lobby, as he pestered Whigs, placated Tories, and pleaded with the new king and queen. He deftly undermined Governor Andros, ensuring that no orders or information would flow from London to Boston during those critical few months. Back in Massachusetts, leaders of the old order took full advantage: they swiftly and bloodlessly overthrew Andros, and promptly declared their loyalty to William and Mary.

Both the gamble in New England and the negotiations in London paid off. Elsewhere in the realm, William III left most of James's (Protestant) officials in place; but in New England, he erased the Dominion and restored the old colonies. With some changes, of course, especially in Massachusetts Bay. That colony received a new charter: it was amalgamated with sparsely populated Plymouth, and would now have a royal governor. In addition, it was no longer allowed to prefer the Congregational church and persecute other (Protestant) denominations. But the colony kept its elected assembly; the governor's council was to be elected by that assembly; the colonists' land titles were confirmed; and the old rights of the towns were restored. Massachusetts even regained its former control of Maine.

All in all, New England came off quite well in the Glorious Revolution; much better than New York, where a revolt known as Leisler's Rebellion led to bloodshed and, eventually, the execution of the ringleaders. But an ominous sense of God's grim judgment still hung over these Puritan grandchildren. The Navigation Acts were still on the books; Parliament even urged the crown to enforce them more energetically. And war haunted the colony again, as the Abenaki to the north emerged as New England's lasting Native American enemies. Fighting began in 1688, and continued to plague frontier settlements.

Then came open war with New France, the start of seventy years of virtually constant hostilities. The spark came from Europe, where William III drew his new country into the battle his old one was waging against Louis XIV. In New England, the fight began under the direction of Sir William Phips, the new governor of Massachusetts. In 1690, Phips led an expedition (funded by the colony) that captured Port Royal, a port in French Acadia (present-day Nova Scotia). He followed up with an intercolonial invasion of the Canadian heartland: his thirty-two vessels were to thrust down the St. Lawrence to Quebec, in coordination with an overland advance from New York. But the New Yorkers failed to show up. Phips had to retreat, empty-handed and missing many of his men, who fell victim to disease.

This was the world that surrounded the town of Salem, Massachusetts, in 1692. Many adults, from the ages of perhaps twenty through thirty-five, had lived their entire lives under a cloud of bloodshed and strife, of divine judgment and temporal uncertainty. The elders, who remembered the time before the troubles, could only feel a sense of loss, perhaps a feeling that the world itself was approaching its end. They had endured two Indian wars—one still raging—and another with New France, where the New Englanders had just been defeated. They had seen their economy wracked by new taxes, new duties, new restrictions, while their very rights to their land had been thrown into question. They had endured not one but two political revolutions—and who knew what might come next?

At the same time, they were still a terribly devout people, as committed to the idea of God's absolute grace, to the idea of humanity's absolute depravity, as the first generation had ever been. Their pulpits rang with calls for repentance, with warnings that their troubles were God's retribution for their sins.

In February 1692, both the niece and the daughter of Salem's minister Samuel Parris went into wild convulsions; the doctor, reasonably enough, diagnosed it as the result of witchcraft. Parris suspected his slave Tituba, a woman knowledgeable in the ways of African and Caribbean Indian charms and folklore. Tituba confessed to avoid execution, and began to spin a wild tale that horrified the credulous Puritans of Salem.

The crisis soon spread. More girls began to throw fits; they put the blame on a number of prominent women in the community. When the husbands of the accused defended their wives, they came under suspicion as well. The charges went farther afield, taking in the prominent clergyman George Burroughs, the former minister of Salem who had since moved away. Events took on a higher profile when Governor (and recently defeated admiral) Sir William Phips appointed a court to hear the accusations and try the defendants. The prominent Boston minister Cotton Mather (son of Increase Mather) arrived to aid in the examination of the accused. Some of those indicted confessed (evading death by doing so), accusing others to gain credibility. Charges of witchcraft soon spread to other towns as well; by autumn, well over a hundred were indicted, fifty had confessed, twenty-six were convicted, and nineteen executed.

Historians have offered any number of reasons to explain the trials. Many of their theories are plausible and thought-provoking; the selections that follow offer points to support a variety of explanations. Paul Boyer and Stephen Nissenbaum, for instance, have examined the factionalism that divided the area, rooted in social tensions between the farmers of Salem Village and the more prosperous merchant community of Salem town. Recently scholars have focused their attentions on Tituba, the slave who was the initial center of the accusations. Elaine Breslaw convincingly argues that she was a South American Arawak, brought to New England via Barbados with African prisoners. When accused, she told a story (using elements of her own ancestral culture) that adroitly played on Puritan fears, theology, and popular beliefs; on social tensions; and on Indian ideas of the demonic that had been incorporated into New England culture.

Yet social tensions and multicultural influences are insufficient to explain this craze. We must keep in mind the way that fears and rumor can spread through society like a grass fire on a dry prairie; by repetition, the wildest claims take on a social force of their own, burning on, impervious to reason. And the initial thrust of the accusations was on Satanic plots against Salem's children; experience shows that fears for the most helpless tend to override all else.[20] The general tensions and fears of the age now found a specific focus: the defense of the young against the Devil.

The following two selections offer opposing perspectives on this remarkable tragedy. The first comes from minister Cotton Mather, a believer—indeed, a moving hand—in the charges of witchcraft. He relates the story of two of the cases, including one against minister George Burroughs. Note the features of the trial: the fits, the supposed calming touch, the supposed out-of-body specter (or "shape") the witch would use to torment others, the ever-present book of damnation (never to be found, of course). Note also the old tensions and personal enmities that emerged.

The second comes from a skeptic, Thomas Brattle. He wrote this critique as a letter to a friend in England, probably in hopes that it would be published. His review of the charges and trials strikes home, and shows that many in Massachusetts realized that this madness had gone too far.

The Wonders of the Invisible World
by Cotton Mather

I have indeed set myself to countermine the whole plot of the Devil against New England, in every branch of it, as far as one of my darkness [poor understanding] can comprehend such a work of Darkness. . . . But while I am doing these things, I have been driven a little to do something likewise for myself; I mean, by taking off the false reports and hard censures about my opinion in these matters. . . .

[20] In a striking echo of the Salem trials, the 1980s saw an explosion of trials for ritual Satanic child abuse. Though an FBI study found no evidence to support even a single case, dozens of people were tried (and convicted) for conducting demonic rituals, usually solely on the testimony of children under the age of five.

But I shall no longer detain my reader from his expected entertainment, in a brief account of the trials which have passed upon some of the malefactors lately executed at Salem, for the witchcrafts whereof they stood convicted. For my own part, I was not present at any of them;[21] nor ever had I any personal prejudice at the persons thus brought upon the stage; much less at the surviving relations of those persons, with and for whom I would be as hearty a mourner as any man living in the world: The Lord comfort them!

But having received a command [from the governor] to do so, I can do no other than shortly relate the chief matters of fact, which occurred in the trials of some that were executed, in an abridgment collected out of the court papers, on this occasion put into my hands. You are to take the truth, just as it was; the truth will hurt no good man. . . .

THE TRIAL OF G.B. AT A COURT OF OYER AND TERMINER HELD IN SALEM, 1692

Glad I should have been, if I had never known the name of this man;[22] or never had this occasion to mention so much as the first letters of his name. But the government requiring some account of his trial to be inserted in this book, it becomes me with all obedience to submit unto the order.

I. This G.B. was indicted for witchcrafts, and in the prosecution of the charge against him, he was accused by five or six of the bewitched, as the author of their miseries; he was accused by eight of the confessing witches,[23] as being an head actor at some of their hellish rendezvouses, and one who had the promise of being a king in Satan's kingdom, now going to be erected. . . .

II. The court . . . now heard the testimonies of several persons, who were most notoriously bewitched, and every day tortured by invisible hands, and these all now charged the specters of G.B. to have a share in their torments. At the examination of this G.B., the bewitched people were grievously harassed with preternatural mischiefs, which could not possibly be dissembled; and they still ascribed it unto the endeavors of G.B. to kill them.

And now upon his trial, one of the bewitched persons testified, that in her agonies a little black-haired man came to her, saying his name was B., and bidding her set her hand unto a book which he showed her; and bragging that he was a conjurer, above the ordinary rank of witches; that he often persecuted her with the offer of that book, saying, She should be well, and

---

[21] Mather is thought to have been present at the pretrial interrogations.

[22] "G.B." refers to Rev. George Burroughs. Of all the victims of the Salem trials, he had the highest public profile. A Harvard graduate, he had preached in Maine. In 1680 he became a pastor at Salem, and he moved back to Maine in 1683.

[23] Mather is not proceeding chronologically in his account; others had been accused before George Burroughs; some had evaded execution by confessing.

need fear nobody, if she would but sign it; but he inflicted cruel pains and hurts upon her, because of her denying so to do. The testimony of the other sufferers concurred with these. . . .

One of them, falling into a kind of trance, afterwards affirmed that G.B. had carried her into a very high mountain, where he showed her mighty and glorious kingdoms, and said he would give them all to her, if she would write in his book; but she told him, they were none of his to give, and refused the motions, enduring of much misery for that refusal.

It cost the court a wonderful deal of trouble, to hear the testimonies of the sufferers; for when they were going to give in their depositions, they would for a long time be taken with fits, that made them incapable of saying anything. The Chief Judge asked the prisoner, who he thought hindered these witnesses from giving their testimonies? And he answered, he supposed it was the Devil. That honorable person then replied, how comes the Devil so loathe to have any testimony born against you? Which cast him into a very great confusion. . . .

Now God had been pleased so to leave this G.B. that he had ensnared himself by several instances, which he had formerly given of a preternatural strength, and which were now produced against him. He was a very puny man; yet he had often done things beyond the strength of a giant. . . . Yea, there were two testimonies that G.B. with only putting the forefinger of his right hand into the muzzle of an heavy gun, a fowling piece of about six or seven foot barrel, did lift up the gun, and hold it out at arm's end. . . .

Faltering, faulty, unconstant, and contrary answers upon judicial and deliberate examination are counted some unlucky symptoms of guilt, in all crimes, especially in witchcraft. Now there never was a prisoner more eminent for them than G.B., both at his examination and on his trial. . . . He gave in a paper to the jury, wherein, altho' he had many times before granted not only that there are witches, but also that the present sufferings of the country are the effect of horrible witchcrafts; yet he now goes to evince it, that there neither are, nor ever were witches that, having made a compact with the Devil, can send a devil to torment other people at a distance. . . .

The jury brought him in guilty. But when he came to die, he utterly denied the fact, whereof he had been convicted.[24]

THE TRIAL OF BRIDGET BISHOP, ALIAS OLIVER, AT THE COURT OF OYER AND TERMINER HELD AT SALEM, JUNE 2, 1692

She was indicted[25] for bewitching several persons in the neighborhood. The

[24] Burroughs was executed on August 19, 1692. Mather observed and approved.

[25] Bridget Bishop was the first to be tried. She had lived for many years in Salem and owned property there, though she now ran a tavern in Salem Village.

indictment being drawn up, according to the form in such cases usual. And pleading not guilty, there were brought in several persons who had long undergone many kinds of miseries, which were preternaturally inflicted and generally ascribed unto an horrible witchcraft.

There was little occasion [need] to prove the witchcraft, it being evident and notorious to all beholders. Now to fix the witchcraft on the prisoner at the bar, the first thing used was the testimony of the bewitched; whereof several testified that the shape of the prisoner did oftentimes very grievously pinch them, choke them, bite them, and afflict them; urging them to write their names in a book, which the said specter called, Ours. One of them did further testify, that it was the shape of this prisoner, with another, which one day took her from her wheel, and carrying her to the riverside, threatened to drown her, if she did not sign to the book mentioned; which she refused. . . .

II. It was testified that the examination of the prisoner before the magistrates, the bewitched were extremely tortured. If she did but cast her eyes on them, they were presently struck down; and this in such a manner as there could be no collusion in the business. But upon the touch of her hand upon them, when they lay in their swoons, they would immediately revive; and not upon the touch of anyone else's. Moreover, upon some special actions of her body, as the shaking of her head, or the turning of her eyes, they presently and painfully fell into the like postures. . . .

III. There was testimony likewise brought in, that a man striking once at the place where a bewitched person said the shape of this Bishop stood, the bewitched cried out that he had tore her coat, in the place then particularly specified; and the woman's coat was found to be torn in that very place.

IV. One Deliverance Hobbs, who had confessed her being a witch, was now tormented by the spectres for her confession. . . . And she affirmed, that this Bishop was at a General Meeting of the witches, in a field at Salem Village, and there partook of a diabolical sacrament in bread and wine then administered!

V. To render it further unquestionable that this prisoner at the bar was the person truly charged in *this* witchcraft, there were produced many evidences of *other* witchcrafts, by her perpetrated. . . .

VI. Samuel Gray testified that about fourteen years ago, he waked on a night, and saw the room where he lay full of light; and that he then saw plainly a woman between the cradle and the bedside, which looked upon him. He rose, and it vanished; tho' he found the doors all fast. Looking out the entry door, he saw the same woman, in the same garb again; and said, In God's name, what do you come for? He went to bed, and had the same woman again assaulting him. The child in the cradle gave a great screech, and the woman disappeared. . . . He knew not Bishop, nor her name; but when he saw her after this, he knew by her countenance, and apparel, and all the circumstances, that it was the apparition of this Bishop which had thus troubled him.

VII. John Bly and his wife testified that he bought a sow of Edward Bishop, the husband of the prisoner; and was to pay the price agreed unto another person. This prisoner, being angry that she was thus hindered from fingering the money, quarrelled with Bly. Soon after which, the sow was taken with strange fits, jumping, leaping, and knocking her head against the fence; she seemed blind and deaf, and would neither cat [mate] nor be sucked. Whereupon a neighbor said, she believed the creature was Overlooked; and sundry other circumstances concurred, which made the deponents believe that Bishop had bewitched it. . . .

IX. Samuel Shattock testified, that in the year 1680, this Bridget Bishop often came to his house upon such frivolous and foolish errands, that they suspected she came indeed with a purpose of mischief. Presently whereupon his eldest child, which was of as promising health and sense as any child of its age, began to droop exceedingly; and oftener that Bishop came to the house, the worse grew the child. . . .

About seven or eight years after, there came a stranger to Shattock's house, who seeing the child, said, "This poor child is bewitched; and you have a neighbor not far off, who is a witch." He added, "Your neighbor has had a falling out with your wife; and she said in her heart, your wife is a proud woman, and she would bring down her pride in this child." He then remembered, that Bishop had parted from his wife on muttering and menacing terms, a little before the child was taken ill.

The abovesaid stranger would needs carry the bewitched boy with him to Bishop's house, on pretence of buying a pot of cider. The woman entertained him in furious manner; and flew also upon the boy, scratching his face till the blood came; and saying, "Thou rogue, what, dost thou bring this fellow here to plague me?" Now it seems the man had said, before he went, that he would fetch the blood of *her*. Ever after the boy was followed with grievous fits, which the doctors themselves generally ascribed unto witchcraft; and wherein he would be thrown still into the fire or the water, if he were not constantly looked after; and it was verily believed that Bishop was the cause of it. . . .

XIII. One thing that made against the prisoner was her being evidently conficted of gross lying in the court, several times, while she was making her plea. But besides this, a jury of women found a preternatural teat upon her body; but upon a second search, within three or four hours, there was no such thing to be seen. There was also an account of other people whom this woman had afflicted. And there might have been many more, if they had been enquired for. But there was no need of them. . . .

Having thus far done the service imposed upon me, I will further pursue it, by relating a few of those matchless curiosities with which the witchcraft now upon us has entertained us. And I shall report nothing but with good authority, and what I would invite all my readers to examine, while 'tis yet fresh and new. . . .

In all the witchcraft which now grievously vexes us, I know not whether anything be more unaccountable than the trick which the witches have to render themselves and their tools invisible. . . . But I will not speak too plainly, lest I should unawares poison some of my readers. . . . This much I will say: the notion of procuring invisibility by any natural expedient yet known is, I believe, a mere Plinyism. How far it may be obtained by a magical sacrament is best known to the dangerous knaves that have tried it. But our witches do seem to have got the knack; and this is one of the things that make me think witchcraft will not be fully understood, until the day when there shall be not one witch in the world.

An Hellish Design
by Thomas Brattle

I would sooner bite my fingers' ends than willingly cast dirt on authority, or any way offer reproach to it. . . . However, sir, I never thought judges infallible; but reckoned that they, as well as private men, might err; and that when they were guilty of erring, standers by, who possibly had not half their judgment, might, notwithstanding, be able to detect and behold their errors. And furthermore, when errors of that nature are thus detected and observed, I never thought it an interfering with dutifullness and subjection for one man to communicate his thoughts to another thereabout. . . . I am very open to communicate my thoughts unto you, and in plain terms tell you what my opinion is of the Salem proceedings.

First, as to the method which the Salem justices do take in their examinations, it is truly this: A warrant being issued out to apprehend the persons that are charged and complained of by the afflicted children (as they are called), said persons are brought before the justices (the afflicted being present). The justices ask the apprehended why they afflict these poor children; to which the apprehended answer, they do not afflict them. The justices order the apprehended to look upon the said children, which accordingly they do; and at the time of that look (I dare not say by that look, as the Salem gentlemen do) the afflicted are cast into a fit. The apprehended are then blinded [blindfolded], and ordered to touch the afflicted; and at that touch, tho' not by the touch (as above) the afflicted ordinarily do come out of their fits. The afflicted persons then declare and affirm, that the apprehended have afflicted them; upon which the apprehended persons, tho' of never so good repute, are forthwith committed to prison, on suspicion for witchcraft. . . .

I suppose his Honor never made the experiment whether there was not as much virtue in his own hand . . . to cure by a touch. I know a man that will venture two to one with any Salemite whatever, that let the matter be duly managed, and the afflicted person shall come out of her fit upon the touch of the most religious hand in Salem. It is worthily noted by some, that at some times the afflicted will not presently come out of their fits upon the touch of the suspected; and then, forsooth, they are ordered by the justices to grasp hard, harder yet, etc., insomuch that at length the afflicted come out of their fits. . . .

I cannot but condemn this method of the justices, of making this touch of the hand a rule to discover witchcraft, because I am fully persuaded that it is sorcery, and a superstitious method, and that which we have no rule for, either from reason or religion. . . .

I would fain know of these Salem gentlemen, but as yet could never know, how it comes about that if these apprehended persons are witches, and, by a look of the eye, do cast the afflicted into their fits by poisoning them, how it comes about, I say, that by a look of their eye, they do not cast others into fits, and poison others by their looks. . . .

But let this pass with the S.G. [Salem gentlemen] for never so plain and natural a demonstration; yet certain it is, that the reasonable part of the world, when acquainted herewith, will laugh at the demonstration [of witchcraft], and conclude that the said S.G. are actually possessed, at least with ignorance and folly. . . .

Secondly, with respect to the confessors (as they are improperly called) or such as confess themselves to be witches . . . there are now about fifty of them in prison; many of which I have again and again seen and heard; and I cannot but tell you, that my faith is strong concerning them, that they are deluded, imposed upon, and under the influence of some evil spirit; and therefore unfit to be evidences either against themselves, or anyone else. . . .

These confessors (as they are called) do very often contradict themselves, as inconsistently as is usual for any crazed, distempered person to do. This the S.G. do see and take notice of; and even the judges themselves have, at some times, taken these confessors in flat lies or contradictions, even in the courts. By reason of which, one would have thought that the judges would have frowned upon the said confessors, discarded them, and not minded one tittle of anything they said; but instead thereof (as sure as we are men) the judges vindicate these confessors, and salve their contradictions by proclaiming that the Devil takes away their memory, and imposes upon their brain. . . .

But now, if in the judges' account these confessors are under the influence of the Devil, and their brains are affected and imposed upon by the Devil, so that they are not their own men, why then should these judges, or any other men, make such account of, and set so much by, the words of these confessors, as they do? . . . But now, if it be thus granted that the Devil is able to represent false ideas (to speak vulgarly) to the imaginations of the confessors, what man of sense will regard the confessions, or any of the words, of these confessors?

The great cry of many of our neighbors now is, What, will you not believe the confessors? Will you not believe men and women who confess that they have signed to the Devil's book? That they were baptized by the Devil; and that they were at the mock sacrament once and again? What! will you not believe that this witchcraft, and that such and such men are witches, altho' the confessors do own and assert it? Thus, I say, many of our good neighbors do argue; but methinks they might soon be convinced that there is nothing at all in these arguings, if they would but duly consider of the premises. . . .

Now, for the proof of the said sorcery and witchcraft, the prisoner at the bar pleading not guilty.

1.   The afflicted persons are brought into court; and after much patience and pains taken with them, do take their oaths that the prisoner at the bar did afflict them. . . .

2.   The confessors do declare what they know of the said prisoner; and some of the confessors are allowed to give their oaths; a thing which I believe was never heard of in this world, that such as confess themselves to be witches, to have renounced God and Christ and all that is sacred, should yet be allowed and ordered to swear by the name of the great God! . . .

3.   Whoever can be an evidence against the prisoner at the bar is ordered to come into court. . . .

4.   They are searched by a jury; and as to some of them, the jury is brought in, that such or such a place there was a preternatural excrescence. And I wonder what person there is, whether man or woman, of whom it cannot be said but that, in some part of their body or other, there is a preternatural excrescence. The term is a very general and inclusive term.

Some of the S.G. are very forward to censure and condemn the poor prisoner at the bar, because he sheds not tears. But such betray great ignorance in the nature of passion, and as great heedlessness as to common passages of a man's life. Some there are who never shed tears; others there are that ordinarily shed tears upon light occasions, and yet for their lives cannot shed a tear when the deepest sorrow is upon their hearts; and who is there that knows not these things? . . .

As to the late executions, I shall only tell you, that in the opinion of many unprejudiced, considerate, and considerable spectators, some of the condemned went out of the world not only with as great protestations, but also with as good shows of innocency, as men could do.

They protested their innocency as in the presence of the great God, whom forthwith they were to appear before. They wished, and declared their wish, that their blood might be the last innocent blood shed upon that account. With great affection, they entreated Mr. C.M. [Cotton Mather] to pray with them; they prayed that God would discover what witchcrafts were among us; they forgave their accusers; they spake without reflection on jury and judges, for bringing them in guilty, and condemning them; they prayed earnestly for pardon for all other sins, and for an interest in the precious blood of our dear Redeemer; and seemed to be very sincere, upright, and sensible of their circumstances on all accounts. . . . But they were executed, and so I leave them. . . .

I know there are several worthy gentlemen in Salem who account this practice [the trials] as an abomination, have trembled to see the methods of this nature which others have used, and have declared themselves to think the practice to be very evil and corrupt; but all avails little with the abbetors of the said practice. . . .

I cannot but admire [be amazed] that these afflicted persons should be so much countenanced and encouraged in their accusations as they are. . . . It is worthy of our deepest consideration, that in the conclusion (after multitudes have been imprisoned, and many have been put to death) these afflicted persons should own that all was a mere fancy and delusion of the Devil's . . . ; if, I say, in after times this be acknowledged by them, how can the justices, judges, or anyone else concerned in these matters, look back upon these things without the greatest of sorrow and grief imaginable? I confess to you, it makes me tremble when I seriously consider of this thing. . . .

But altho' the Chief Judge, and some of the other judges, be very zealous in these proceedings, yet this you may take for a truth, that there are several about the Bay [in Massachusetts], men for understanding, judgment, and piety inferior to few (if any) in N.E. [New England] that do utterly condemn the said proceedings, and do freely deliver their judgment in the case to be this, *viz.*, that these methods will utterly ruin and undo poor N.E. . . .

I am very apt to think, that did you know the circumstances of the said confessors, you would not be swayed thereby, any otherwise than to be confirmed that all is perfect Devilism, and an Hellish design to ruin and destroy this poor land. . . . What will be the issue of these troubles, God only knows; I am afraid ages will not wear off that reproach and those stains which these things will leave behind them upon our land.

BEFORE THE MADNESS had ended, the accused included the wives of the most prominent men of the colony: those of magistrate Dudley Bradstreet, minister John Hale, and even of Governor Phips himself. The entire affair had spun out of control, and murmurings such as those Thomas Brattle refers to now broke out into open resistance. Even the judge of the special court declared his regret. The next year, 1693, the court announced it would hear no further charges. Nineteen innocent dead were enough. Eventually, in 1711, the survivors received payment in compensation for the persecution.

When Massachusetts finally passed out of the trials of witchcraft, it emerged from the last of its great crises. For almost twenty years, it had been tormented, even threatened with destruction. Whole towns had been annihilated in war; age-old rights, even the government itself, had been eradicated by the crown; and the devil himself had stalked the quiet streets of the colony's towns (though as witch or as magistrate, the colonists could not agree).

At the end, an acceptable settlement ended the political crisis. They lost some of what their ancestors had built, but the bulk of it now rested on a firm foundation. The danger of extinction by the sword ended as well: though New England was now locked in a virtually permanent state of war with the Abenaki and New France, its survival would never be threatened. And the devil quietly retreated from the countryside, the plague of witchcraft never to be heard of again.

V

EXPANSION

FROM OUTPOSTS TO EMPIRES

15

LA SALLE IN THE WILDERNESS

As New England faced the perils of enemy Indians and royal envoys, New France stood reborn. When we last looked at Quebec, in 1661, it was a small, besieged village, its inhabitants cowering in their houses for fear of Mohawk raiders; by the end of the century, its power would span the continent, stretching in a vast arc around the English colonies to the mouth of the Mississippi River. For the second time in its brief history, Champlain's struggling seedling would surge back from the point of death—growing into a mighty imperial tree that overshadowed England's children.

The year 1661 was the critical one in New France's survival: the moment of its greatest danger, and the beginning of its rebirth. Without any effort on the part of the frightened French, the war with the Iroquois suddenly, unexpectedly slackened. The Senecas, Onondagas, and Cayugas found themselves bogged down in a bitter war with the Susquehannocks to the south (the same tribe that befriended Virginia, only to suffer Nathaniel Bacon's attacks); so they opened peace negotiations with Quebec, leading to a settlement. Even the intransigent Mohawks made fewer assaults after that bloody year, thanks to another smallpox outbreak and military setbacks in their wars with the Mahicans (to the east) and the Ottawas (to the west).

The future of New France, however, changed course thanks to another event, one far across the Atlantic. An energetic young king took control of the French government; unlike his predecessors, he would personally direct the affairs of state, applying his boundless enthusiasm and ambition to the expansion of his power and glory. His name was Louis XIV, and he soon earned the title "Sun King" by making France the burning light of Europe.

Louis XIV might rule without a prime minister, but he did have a minister for economic affairs—and a very able one at that. Jean-Baptiste Colbert quickly took on the task of reforming France's backward economy; he imposed a system of manufacturing subsidies, protective tariffs, and strict regulations on goods and prices, and began comprehensive internal improvements (such as the construction of an extensive road network). Colbert impressed the young king, who made him minister of naval affairs as well; with typical energy, this humble son of a draper established shipyards, began building a mighty navy, and expanded the merchant fleet. He also reorganized colonial affairs, beginning with that ragged, underpopulated, besieged settlement, New France.

Colbert moved swiftly to calm the colony's troubled waters. He took control from the Company of New France, instituting the sort of strict royal authority that James II would later try to impose in New England. He set up a governor-general in Quebec, assisted by an intendant. When things were at their best, the intendant would operate as a prime minister for the governor-general, taking care of administrative details; at the worst, he would be a sort of political commissar, keeping a watchful eye on his nominal superior. Colbert also instituted subordinate governors in Acadia (modern-day Nova Scotia), Montreal, and Trois Rivières.

In 1665, the new governor-general, Daniel de Rémy de Courcelle, arrived in Quebec. And he came with something the colonists had never seen before: 1,200 soldiers of the Carignan-Salières regiment, one of the best units in the French army (the troops also carried the revolutionary new flintlock muskets, destined to give them an edge over even firearm-equipped Indian warriors). As historian Ian Steele has written, these troops "transformed the military balance immediately and temporarily increased the little colony's population of 3,035 by nearly 40 percent. They also permanently imprinted a military tone" to life in New France.

The smallpox-ravaged Mohawks saw Quebec switch suddenly from victim to tormentor. The French regulars quickly built three forts in the main Iroquois invasion corridor, along Lake Champlain and the Richelieu River, which slowed Five Nations raiding parties. Then they struck south in a series of offensives—each more effective than the last. In late 1666, French soldiers, Algonquin allies, and Canadian militia wiped out four major, fortified Mohawk towns, destroying enormous stores of food; though the Iroquois slipped safely away, they suffered a severe blow nonetheless. Within a year, the Mohawks joined the rest of the Five Nations in making peace with resurgent French.

In the royal army, New France found a replacement for their lost Huron allies; though alliances with Indian neighbors would always be crucial to the colony's survival, the pillar of its existence would now be regular troops. The military would be a prime source of immigrants as well; following the example of ancient Rome, the government convinced many of the discharged soldiers of the Carignan-Salières regiment to settle permanently in New France; they were followed by hundreds more retired troops from France itself. These ex-soldiers formed the backbone of an effective citizen militia, which also comprised much of the administrative network of the colony, reinforcing its military, authoritarian character. To further assist the defense of this colony, Colbert created the *troupes de la marine:* regular troops recruited in France specifically for colonial duty.

Royal control and regular troops may have haunted New England, but they reenergized New France. The population tripled in the twenty years after Colbert's reforms began, reaching almost 11,000 in 1685. And the economy flourished as well: the agreements with the Five Nations began sixteen years of peace, allowing the French themselves to rebuild the Huron fur-trading network. Canadian traders ranged deep along the St. Lawrence–Great Lakes waterway, closed for so long by Iroquois war parties. They were encouraged by Governor-General Frontenac (short for Louis de Baude, comte de Frontenac), an ambitious aristocrat who ruled New France from 1672–82 and 1689–98. Frontenac was expansionistic, self-promoting, and greedy: though the government-owned Compagnie de l'Occident had a monopoly on the fur trade, the governor took a cut from the widespread smuggling.

Frontenac soon took on a remarkable partner in his empire-building, moneymaking endeavors: a young nobleman named René-Robert Cavelier de La Salle. In 1673, the governor granted the thirty-year-old La Salle command of the fort of Cataraqui, a strategic post located where Lake Ontario ends and the St. Lawrence begins. Showing a flair for politics, La Salle renamed it Fort Frontenac. Within two years, the royal court granted him a patent of nobility and feudal overlordship of his new post. But the supremely energetic La Salle soon looked farther afield.

In 1678, an Italian soldier of fortune named Henri de Tonty found himself at the court of Louis XIV, in search of a job. There he met the charismatic La Salle, who had come in search of royal backing for an ambitious exploration of the interior of North America. The two got along well, and the brusque Tonty immediately became La Salle's loyal subordinate. Together they set out on an epic journey, one that would open a path to the heart of North America, and extend French power more than two thousand miles into the interior.

In the selection that follows, Tonty describes his travels, fights, and explorations in clipped, no-nonsense prose. He reveals the intense hardships of their incredible treks, as they went back and forth between new posts they built in the interior and their base at Fort Frontenac. He details the treacherous art of Indian diplomacy—an art he grew more skilled in as time went on—and the individualistic, even treasonous bent of their own men. Tonty experienced wonders in America: a journey to the mouth of the Mississippi, the building of a network of Indian alliances, the start of a new war against the Iroquois, an invasion of the Seneca homeland, and finally the tragic death of La Salle himself.

La Salle's Discoveries
by Henri de Tonty

After having been eight years in the French service, by land and by sea, and having had a hand shot off in Sicily by a grenade, I resolved to return to France to solicit employment. At that time the late M. Cavelier de La Salle came to court, a man of great intelligence and merit, who sought to obtain leave from the court to explore the Gulf of Mexico by traversing the countries of North America. Having obtained of the King the permission he desired through the favor of the late M. Colbert and M. de Seignelai, the late Monseigneur the Prince of Conti,[1] who was acquainted with him and who honored me with his favor, sent me to ask him to be allowed to accompany him in his long journeys, to which he very willingly assented.

We sailed from Rochelle on the 14th of July, 1678, and arrived at Quebec on the 15th of September following. We recruited there for some days, and after having taken leave of M. the Count de Frontenac, governor general of the country, ascended the St. Lawrence as far as Fort Frontenac, 120 leagues from Quebec, on the banks of the Lake of Frontenac [Lake Ontario], which is about 300 leagues around. And after staying there four days, we embarked in a boat of forty tons to cross this lake, and on Christmas day we found ourselves opposite a village called Tsonnontauan [a Seneca village near the Genesee River], to which M. de La Salle sent some canoes to procure Indian corn for our subsistence.[2] From thence we sailed towards Niagara, intending to look for a suitable place above the falls where a boat might be built. . . .

The boat in which we came was lost on the coast through the obstinacy of the pilot, whom M. de La Salle ordered to bring it ashore. The crew and the things in it were saved. M. de La Salle determined to return to Fort Frontenac over the ice, and I remained in command at Niagara with a [Franciscan] Recollect Father [Louis Hennepin] and thirty men. The bark was completed in the spring. M. de La Salle joined us with two other Recollect Fathers and several men to aid in bringing this bark up, on account of the rapids, which I was not able to ascend on account of the weakness of my crew.

He directed me to wait for him at the extremity of Lake Erie, at a place called Detroit, 120 leagues from Niagara, to join there some Frenchmen whom he had sent off the last autumn. I went in advance in a bark canoe, and when we were near Detroit the ship came up. We got into it, and continued our voyage as far as Michilimackinac,[3] where we arrived at the end of August, having crossed two lakes [Huron and Erie] larger than that of Frontenac [Lake Ontario].

We remained there for some days to rest ourselves, and as M. de La Salle intended to go to the [Indian nation of the] Illinois, he sent me to the Sault Sainte-Marie, where Lake Superior discharges itself into Lake Huron, to

[1] Conti was not only a great, influential noble, he was the king's son-in-law.

[2] As mentioned previously, a comprehensive but uneasy peace had been declared between New France and the Five Nations of Iroquois. A league equaled roughly 2.8 miles.

[3] Michilimackinac was a post at the northernmost tip of the Michigan peninsula. It had been founded in 1670 by Jacques Marquette, a Jesuit explorer.

look for some of his men who had deserted, and himself set sail on the Lake of the Illinois [Lake Michigan]. . . . M. de La Salle sent his ship back to Niagara to fetch the things he wanted, and, embarking in a canoe, continued his voyage to the Miami River [now the St. Joseph, in southern Michigan]. There he commenced building a house [fort].

In the meantime I came up with the deserters, and kept on my way to within thirty leagues of the Miami River, where I was obliged to leave my men in order to hunt, our provisions failing us. I then went on to join M. de La Salle. . . . As soon as I arrived we ascended twenty-five leagues, as far as the portage,[4] where the men whom I had left behind joined us. We made the portage, which is about two leagues in length, and came to the source of the Illinois River. We embarked there and descended the river for 100 leagues. When we arrived at the village of the savages [the Illinois], they were absent hunting, and as we had no provisions we opened some caches of Indian corn.

During this journey some of our Frenchmen, fatigued, determined to leave us, but that night was so cold that their plan was broken up. We continued our route, in order to join the savages, and found them thirty leagues below the village. When they saw us they thought we were Iroquois, and therefore put themselves on the defensive and made their women run into the woods; but when they recognized us, the women with their children were called back, and the calumet[5] was danced to M. de La Salle and me, in order to mark their desire to live in peace with us. We gave them some merchandise for the corn which we had taken in their village.

This was on the 3rd of January, 1680. It was necessary to fortify ourselves for the winter. Applying ourselves to it, we made a fort which was called Crèvecoeur. Part of our people deserted, and they even put poison into our kettle. M. de La Salle was poisoned, but he was saved by some antidote a friend had given him in France. The desertion of these men gave us less annoyance than the effect which it had on the minds of the savages, for the enemies of M. de La Salle had spread a report among the Illinois that we were friends of the Iroquois, who were their greatest enemies. The effect this produced will be seen hereafter.

M. de La Salle commenced building a boat to descend the river. He sent a Recollect Father [Hennepin] with the Sieur [Michel] Accault to explore the nation of the Sioux, 400 leagues from the Illinois, toward the north, on the Mississippi River, a river that runs not less than 800 leagues to the sea without rapids, and having determined to go himself by land to Fort Frontenac, because he had heard nothing of the bark which he had sent to Niagara. He gave me command of this place, and left us on the 22nd of March with five men. . . .

[4] This portage from the St. Joseph to the Kankakee River was located above the present city of South Bend, Indiana.

[5] The calumet was a ceremony performed to seal a peace or an alliance.

Whilst I was [briefly] absent all my men deserted. They took away everything that was finest and most valuable, and left me with two Recollects and five Frenchmen, newly arrived from France, stripped of everything and at the mercy of the savages. All that I could do was to draw up an authentic account of the affair and send it to M. de La Salle. He lay in wait for them [the deserters] on Lake Frontenac, took some of them, and killed the others. After this he returned towards the Illinois. As for his bark, it has never been heard of.

In the meantime, the Illinois were greatly alarmed at seeing a party of 600 Iroquois.[6] It was then near the month of September. The desertion of our men and the journey of M. de La Salle to Fort Frontenac made the savages suspect that we were betraying them. They severely reproached me respecting the arrival of their enemies. As I was recently come from France and was not then acquainted with their manners, this embarrassed me and determined me to go to the enemy with necklaces [wampum] to tell them that I was surprised they had come to make war upon a nation dependent on the Governor of New France; and that M. de La Salle, whom he [the governor] esteemed, governed these peoples.

An Illinois accompanied me, and we separated ourselves from the body of the Illinois, who were 400 in number, and were already fighting with the enemy. When I was within gun-shot, the Iroquois fired a great volley at us, which compelled me to tell the Illinois to retire. He did so. When I had come up to them, these wretches seized me, took the necklace from my hand, and one of them, reaching through the crowd, plunged a knife into my breast, wounding a rib near the heart. However, having recognized me, they carried me into the midst of their camp and asked me what I came for. I gave them to understand that the Illinois were under the protection of the King of France and of the governor of that country, and that I was surprised that they wished to break with the French, and to postpone peace.

All this time skirmishing was going on on both sides, and a warrior came to give notice to the chief that their left wing was giving way, and that they had recognized some Frenchmen among the Illinois, who were shooting at them. On this they were greatly irritated against me and held a council regarding what they should do with me. There was a man behind me with a knife in his hand, who every now and then lifted up my hair.

They were divided in opinion. Tegancouti, chief of the Tsonnontouan [Senecas], wished positively to have me burnt. Agonstot, chief of the Onantagués [Onondagas], as a friend of M. de La Salle, wished to have me set at liberty. He carried his point. They agreed that, in order the better to deceive the Illinois, they should give me a necklace of porcelain beads to show to

6 The appearance of this large Iroquois force hundreds of miles from the Five Nations homeland shows the deep extension of their power after the extinction of the Hurons. They now challenged the French for control of the Ohio Valley.

them that they were also children of the Governor, and that they all ought to unite and make a good peace.

They sent me to deliver their message to the Illinois. I had much difficulty in reaching them on account of the great quantity of blood I had lost, both from my wound and from my mouth [presumably from being beaten]. On my way I met the Fathers Gabriel de La Ribourde and Zénoble Membré, who were coming to look after me. They expressed their joy that these barbarians had not put me to death. We went together to the Illinois, to whom I reported the sentiments of the Iroquois, adding, however, that they must not altogether trust them. They retired within their village, but seeing the Iroquois present themselves always in battle array, they felt obliged to rejoin their wives and children, three leagues off. They left us there: namely, the two Recollect Fathers, the three Frenchmen, and myself.

The Iroquois made a fort in the village and left us in a cabin at some distance from their fort. Two days later, the Illinois appearing on the hills near the Iroquois, the Iroquois thought that we had some conference together, which led them to bring us inside their fort. They pressed me to go and find the Illinois and induce them to come and make a treaty of peace. They gave me one of their own nation as a hostage. I went with Father Zénoble. The Iroquois [hostage] remained with the Illinois, and one of the latter came with me.

When we got to the fort, instead of mending matters he [the Illinois] spoilt them entirely by saying to the enemy that they had in all only 400 men, and that the rest of their young men were gone to war, and that if the Iroquois really wished to make peace with them they were ready to give them a quantity of beaver skins and some slaves which they had. The Iroquois called to me and loaded me with reproaches; they told me that I was a liar to have said that the Illinois had 1,200 warriors, and several tribes of allies who had given them assistance. Where were the sixty Frenchmen who, I had told them, were at the village? I had much difficulty in getting out of the scrape.

The same evening they sent back the Illinois to tell his nation to come the next day to within half a league of the fort, and that they would there conclude the peace, which in fact was done at noon. The Illinois, having come to the meeting place, the Iroquois gave them presents of necklaces and merchandise. The first necklace signified[7] that the Governor of New France was not angry at their having come to molest their brothers; the second was addressed to M. de La Salle with the same meaning; and by the third, accompanied with merchandise, they bound themselves by oath to a strict alliance, that hereafter they should live as brothers.

They then separated, and the Illinois believed, after these presents, in

[7] In Iroquois peace negotiations, each belt of wampum symbolized a point agreed to by the two parties

the sincerity of the peace, which induced them to come several times into the fort of their enemies; where, some Illinois chiefs having asked me what I thought, I told them they had everything to fear, that there was among these barbarians no good faith, and that I knew that they were making canoes of elm bark and that consequently they were intending to pursue them, and that they should take advantage of the time and retire to some distant nation, for they were most assuredly betrayed.

The eighth day after their arrival, on the 10th of September, they called me and Father Zénoble to council; and having made us sit down, they placed six packets of beaver skins before us, and, addressing me, they said that the two first packets were to inform M. de Frontenac that they would not eat his children and that he should not be angry at what they had done; the third was to serve as a plaster for my wound; the fourth was oil to rub on my own and the Recollect Father's limbs, on account of the journeys we had taken; the fifth, that the sun was bright; the sixth, that we should depart the next day for the French settlements.

I asked them when they would go away themselves. Murmurs arose among them. Some of them answered me that they would eat some of the Illinois before they went away; upon which I kicked away their presents, saying that there was no use making presents to me, I would have none of them, since they designed to eat the children of the governor. An Abenaki who was with them, and who spoke French, told me that the men were irritated, and the chiefs rising drove me from the council.

We went to our cabin, where we passed the night on our guard, resolved to kill some of them before they should kill us; for we thought that we should not live out the night. However, at daybreak they directed us to depart, which we did.[8] After making some five leagues in the canoe, we landed to dry some peltries, which were wet. While we were repairing our canoe, Father Gabriel told me he was going aside to pray. I advised him not to go away, because we were surrounded by enemies. He went about 1,000 paces off and was taken by forty savages of the nation called Kickapoos, who carried him away and broke his head. Finding that he did not return, I went to look for him with one of my men. Having discovered his trail, I found it cut by several others, which joined and ended at last in one. . . .

The next day we recrossed the river to look for our equipment, and after waiting till noon we embarked and reached the Lake of the Illinois by short journeys, always hoping to meet with the good Father. After having sailed on this lake till All Saints' Day, we were wrecked, twenty leagues from the village of the Potawatomis. Our provisions failing us, I left a man to take care of our things and went off by land, but, as I had a fever constantly on me, and my legs were swollen, we did not arrive at the village of the Potawatomis

[8] After this bold talk, the Frenchmen were obliged to flee for their lives. But the diplomatic point (that the Illinois would not be abandoned) had been made.

till St. Martin's Day [November 14]. During this time we lived on nothing but wild garlic, which we were obliged to grub up under the snow. When we arrived we found no savages; they had gone to their winter quarters. So we were obliged to go into their wilds, where we obtained hardly as much as two handfuls of Indian corn a day and some frozen gourds, which we piled up in a cabin at the water's side. . . .

When I left this place in the spring for Michilimackinac, we had hardly recovered from the miseries which we had suffered from hunger and cold. . . . We reached Michilimackinac about Corpus Christi [June 5] in 1681. M. de La Salle arrived some time afterwards, on his way to seek us at the Illinois, with M. [Guillaume] de La Forest. He was very glad to see us again, and notwithstanding all reverses, we made new preparations to continue the exploration which we had undertaken. I therefore embarked with him for Fort Frontenac, to bring things that we should need for the expedition. . . .

When we came to the Miami River [after going to Frontenac and back], I assembled some Frenchmen and savages for the exploration, and M. de La Salle joined us in December. We went in canoes to the River Chicago, where there is a portage which joins that of the Illinois. The rivers being frozen, we made sledges and dragged our baggage to a point thirty leagues below the village of the Illinois, and there, finding the navigation open, we arrived at the end of January at the River Mississippi [February 6, 1682]. . . .

We descended this river and found, six leagues below, on the right, a great river, which comes from the west [the Missouri]. We slept at its mouth. The next day we went on to the village of the Tamarois [a branch of the Illinois tribe], six leagues off on the left. There was no one there, all the people being at their winter quarters in the woods. We made our marks to inform the savages that we had passed, and continued our route as far as the River Ouabache [Ohio], which is eighty leagues from that of the Illinois. It comes from the east and is more than 500 leagues in length. It is by this river that the Iroquois advance to make war against the nations of the south.

Continuing our voyage, we came to a place, about sixty miles from there [near the present city of Memphis], which was named Fort Prudhomme, because one of our men of that name lost himself there when out hunting, and was nine days in the woods without food. As they were looking for him they fell in with two Chickasaw savages, whose village was three days' journey from there, in the lands along the Mississippi. They have 2,000 warriors, the greatest number of whom have flat heads, which is considered a beauty among them, the women taking pains to flatten the heads of their children by means of a cushion which they put on their foreheads and bind with a band. . . .

M. de La Salle sent back one of them with presents to his village, so that, if they had taken [the man] Prudhomme, they might send him back; but we found him on the tenth day, and as the Chickasaws did not return, we continued our route as far as the village of Capa, eighty leagues off. We arrived there in foggy weather, and as we heard the beating of the drum we crossed to the other side of the river, where in less than half an hour we made a fort. These savages, having been informed of our coming down the river, came in their canoes to look for us. We made them land, and sent two Frenchmen as hostages to their village. Their chief visited us with the calumet,[9] and we went to visit them. They regaled us for five days with the best they had, and after having danced the calumet to M. de La Salle, they conducted us to the village of Tonengan, of their nation, eight leagues from Capa. They received us in the same manner, and from thence they went with us to Toriman, two leagues farther on, where we met with the same reception.

It should be remarked that these villages, with another called Osotouy, which is six leagues to the right descending the river, are commonly called Arkansas. The first three villages are situated on the great river. M. de La Salle erected the arms of the king there. They have cabins made with the bark of cedar; they have no worship, adoring all sorts of animals. Their country is very beautiful. . . . They gave us guides to conduct us to their allies, the Taensas [allies of the Natchez], sixty leagues distant.

The first day we began to see and kill alligators, which are numerous, and from fifteen to twenty feet long. When we arrived opposite to the village of the Taensas, M. de La Salle ordered me to go to it and inform the chief of his arrival. I went with our guides. We had to carry a bark canoe for ten arpents [roughly a third of a mile], and to launch it on a small lake on which their village was placed. I was surprised to find their cabins made of mud and covered with cane mats. The cabin of the chief was forty feet square, the wall about ten feet high and a foot thick, and the roof, which was of a dome shape, about fifteen feet high.

I was not less surprised when, on entering, I saw the chief seated on a camp bed, with three of his wives at his side, surrounded by more than sixty old men, clothed in large white cloaks, which are made by the women out of the bark of the mulberry tree, and are tolerably well worked. The women were clothed in the same manner, and every time the chief spoke to them, before answering him, they howled and cried out several times—"Oh! Oh! Oh!"—to show their respect for him, for their chiefs are held in as much consideration as our kings. No one drinks out of the chief's cup, nor eats out of his dishes; no one passes before him; when he walks they clean the path before him. When he dies they sacrifice his principal wife, his principal house-steward, and a hundred men of the nation, to accompany him into the other world.

They have a form of worship, and adore the sun. They have a temple opposite the house of the chief, and similar to it, except that three eagles are

[9] In this case, a peace pipe, used in the calumet ceremony.

placed on this temple who look towards the rising sun. . . . When I wished to see what was inside, the old men prevented me, giving me to understand that their God was there; but I have since learnt that it is the place where they keep all their treasure, such as fine pearls which they fish up in the neighborhood, and European merchandise.

At the last quarter of each moon all the cabins make an offering of a dish of the best food they have, which is placed at the door of the temple. The old men take care to carry it away and make a good feast of it with their families. Every spring they make a clearing, which they name "the field of the spirit," where all the men work to the sound of the drum. In the autumn the Indian corn of this field is harvested with ceremony and stored in magazines until the moon of June in the following year, when all the village assemble, and invite their neighbors to the feast to eat it. . . .

Let us return to the chief. When I was in his cabin he told me with a smiling countenance the pleasure he felt at the arrival of the French. I saw that one of his wives wore a pearl necklace. I presented her with ten yards of blue glass beads in exchange for it. She made some difficulty, but the chief having told her to let me have it, she did so. I carried it to M. de La Salle, giving him an account of all that I had seen and told him that the chief intended to visit him the next day—which he did. He would not have done this for savages, but the hope of obtaining some merchandise induced him to act thus.[10]

He came the next day to our cabins, to the sound of the drum and the music of the women, who had embarked in wooden canoes. The savages of the river use no other boats than these. M. de La Salle received him with much politeness, and gave him some presents; they gave us, in return, plenty of provisions and some of their robes. The chief returned well satisfied. We stayed during the day, which was the 21st of March. . . .

We left on the 22nd, and slept on an island ten leagues from there. The next day we saw a canoe. M. de La Salle ordered me to chase it, which I did, and when I was just on the point of taking it, more than 100 men appeared on the banks of the river, with bows bent, to defend their people. M. de La Salle shouted to me to come back, which I did. We went on and encamped opposite them. Afterwards, M. de La Salle expressing to me a wish to meet them peacefully, I offered to carry to them the calumet. I embarked, and crossed to the other side. At first they joined their hands, as a sign that they wished to be friends; I, who had but one hand, told our men to do the same thing.

I made the chief men among them cross over to M. de La Salle, who accompanied them to their village, three leagues inland, and passed the night with some of his men. The next day he returned with the chief of the vil-

---

[10] These were very likely the first Europeans this village had seen, yet they knew of—and had acquired—European goods through trade with other Indians.

lage where he had slept, who was a brother of the great chief of the
Natchez; he conducted us to his brother's village, situated on the hillside
near the river, six leagues distance. We were very well received there. This nation counts more than 3,000 warriors. These men cultivate the ground as
well as hunt, and they fish as well as the Taensa, and their customs are the
same. We departed thence on Good Friday, and after a voyage of twenty
leagues, encamped at the mouth of a large river, which comes in from the
west [the Red River]. We continued our journey, and crossed a great canal,
which went towards the sea on the right.

Thirty leagues further on we saw some fishermen on the bank of the
river, and sent to reconnoiter them. It was the village of the Quinipissa [a
Choctaw tribe], who let fly arrows upon our scouts, who retired in consequence, as ordered. As M. de La Salle did not wish to fight against any nation, he made us embark. Twelve leagues from this village, on the left, we
found that of the Tangipahoa. Not a week before, this village had been totally destroyed. Dead bodies were lying on one another and the cabins were
burnt. We proceeded on our course, and after going forty leagues, arrived at
the sea on the 7th of April. . . .

Provisions failing, we were obliged to leave sooner than we wished, in
order to seek provisions in the neighboring villages. We did not know how
to get anything from the Quinipissa, who had received us badly as we went
down the river. We lived on potatoes until six leagues from their village,
when we saw smoke. M. de La Salle went to reconnoiter at night. Our people reported that they had seen some women. We went there at daybreak
and, taking four of their women, encamped on the other bank, opposite
their village.

One of the women was sent with merchandise, to show this tribe that
we had no evil design against them and wished for their alliance and for provisions. She made her report. One of them came immediately and invited us
to encamp on the other bank, which we did. We sent back the three other
women, keeping, however, constant guard. They brought us some provisions in the evening, and the next morning, at daybreak, the scoundrels
attacked us.

We vigorously repulsed them, and by ten o'clock had smashed their
canoes, and, but for the fear of using up our ammunition for the future, we
should have attacked their village. We left in the evening in order to reach
the village of the Natchez, where we had left a quantity of grain as we passed
down.

When we arrived there the chief came out to meet us. M. de La Salle
made them a present of the scalps we had taken from the Quinipissa. They
had already heard the news, for they had resolved to betray and kill us. We
went up to their village armed, and, as we saw no women there, we had no
doubt of their having some evil design. In a moment we were surrounded
by more than 1,500 men. They brought us something to eat, and we ate

with our guns in our hands. As they are afraid of firearms, they did not dare to attack us. The chief of the nation begged M. de La Salle to go away, as his young men had not much sense, which we very willingly did—the game not being equal, we having only fifty men, French and savages. We then went on to the Taensa, and then to the Arkansas, where we were very well received.

From thence we came to Fort Prudhomme, where M. de La Salle fell dangerously ill, which obliged him to send me forward, with five others, to arrange his affairs at Michilimackinac. In passing toward the Ouabache [Ohio], I found four Iroquois, who told us that there were 100 men of their nation coming on after them. This gave us some alarm, for there is no pleasure in meeting warriors on one's road, especially when they have been unsuccessful. I left them and at about twenty leagues from the Tamarois, we saw smoke. I ordered our people to prepare their arms, and we resolved to advance, expecting to meet Iroquois.

When we were near the smoke, we saw some canoes, which made us think that they could only be Illinois or Tamarois. They were in fact the latter. As soon as they saw us, they came out of the wood in great numbers to attack us, taking us for Iroquois. I presented the calumet to them. They laid down their arms and conducted us to their village without doing us any harm. The chiefs held a council, and, taking us for Iroquois, had already resolved to burn us; and, but for some Illinois who were among them, we should have fared ill. They let us proceed.

We arrived about the end of June [1682] at the River Chicago, and, by the middle of July, at Michilimackinac. M. de La Salle, having recovered, joined us in September. Resolving to go to France, he ordered me to go and collect together the French who were on the River Miami to construct the Fort of St. Louis in the Illinois. I left with this design, and when I arrived at the place, M. de La Salle, having changed his mind, joined me. They set to work at the fort, and it was finished in March, 1683.[11]

During the winter I gave all the nations notice of what we had done to defend them from the Iroquois, at whose hands they had lost 700 people in the preceding years. They approved of our good intentions, and established themselves, to the number of 300 lodges, at the Fort—Illinois and Miamis and Chaouanons.

M. de La Salle departed for France in the month of September, leaving me to command the fort. He met on his way the Chevalier de Bogis, whom M. de La Barre [the new governor of New France] had sent with letters ordering M. de La Salle to Quebec. He had no trouble in getting him to make the journey, as he found him on the road. M. de La Salle wrote to me to receive M. de Bogis well, which I did.

The winter passed, and on the 20th of March, 1684, being informed

---

[11] Fort St. Louis des Illinois was located near the present town of La Salle in the state of Illinois—near the bend in the Illinois River. It became a major outpost of French power and influence, greatly affecting Indian trade and interrelations.

that the Iroquois were about to attack us, we prepared to receive them well, and dispatched a canoe to M. de La Durantaye, governor of Michilimackinac, to ask him for assistance in case the enemy should hold out against us a long time. The savages appeared on the 21st. We repulsed them with loss. After six days' siege they retired with some slaves which they had made in the neighborhood, who afterwards escaped and came back to the fort.

M. de La Durantaye, with Father [Claude] Daloy, a Jesuit, arrived at the fort with about sixty Frenchmen, whom they are bringing to our assistance, and, more particularly, to inform me of the orders of M. de La Barre to leave the place, and that M. de Bogis was in possession of a place [the command] belonging to M. de La Salle. I obeyed orders, and went to Montreal, and thence to Quebec, where M. de La Forest, who had accompanied M. de La Salle to France, returned by order of M. de La Salle with a letter de cachet, by which M. de La Barre was directed to deliver up to M. de La Forest the lands belonging to Sieur de La Salle, and which were occupied by others to his prejudice.[12]

As he brought me news that M. de La Salle was sailing by way of the islands [the West Indies] to find the mouth of the Mississippi, and had at court obtained a [military] company for me, and sent me orders to go and command at Fort St. Louis, as captain of foot, and governor, we took our measures together, and formed a company [corporation] of 20,000 livres to maintain the fort.

M. de La Forest went away in the autumn for Fort Frontenac, and I began my journey to the Illinois. Being stopped by the ice, however, I was obliged to halt at Montreal, where I passed the winter. M. de La Forest arrived there in the spring. We took new measures. He embarked for Fort Frontenac, and I for the Illinois, where I arrived in June [1685]. M. le Chevalier de Bogis retired, according to the orders that I brought him from M. de La Barre.

The Miamis having seriously defeated the Illinois, it cost us 1,000 dollars in presents to reconcile these two nations, which I did not accomplish without great trouble. In the autumn I embarked for Michilimackinac, in order to obtain news of M. de La Salle. I heard that M. le Marquis de Denonville had succeeded M. de La Barre [as governor]; and by a letter which he did me the honor to write to me, he expressed his wish to see me, that we might take measures for the war against the Iroquois, and informed me that M. de La Salle was engaged in seeking the mouth of the Mississippi in the Gulf of Mexico. This made me resolve to go in search of him and aid him, with a number of Canadians that I should take to him, and as soon as

12 This paragraph abbreviates the torturous political struggle that followed the removal of Frontenac as governor of New France in 1682. His successor, La Barre, took a dim view of all who had held positions of authority under Frontenac—especially La Salle, who fought back with his connections at the French court.

I should have found him, to return to execute the orders of M. de Denonville.

I embarked, therefore, for the Illinois on St. Andrew's Day [November 30, 1685], but, being stopped by the ice, I was obliged to leave my canoe and proceed by land . . . with thirty Frenchmen and five Illinois and Chaouanons for the sea, which I reached in Holy Week [1686]. . . . [Not having found La Salle], I decided to return the way I came. . . . When we were at Arkansas, ten of the Frenchmen who accompanied me asked for settlements on the River Arkansas, on a seigniory [feudal fief] that M. de La Salle had given me on our first voyage.[13] I granted the request to some of them. They remained there and built a house surrounded with stakes. The rest accompanied me to the Illinois. . . . I arrived there on St. John's Day [June 24, 1686]. I made two chiefs of the Illinois embark with me in my canoe, to go and receive the orders of M. de Denonville, and we arrived at Montreal by the end of July.

I left that place at the beginning of September to return to the Illinois. I came there in December, and I directly sent some Frenchmen to our savage allies to declare war against the Iroquois, inviting them to assemble in good season at the fort. They did so in the month of April, 1687. The Sieur de La Forest was already gone in a canoe with thirty Frenchmen, and he was to wait for me at Detroit till the end of May. I gave our savages a dog feast,[14] and after having declared to them the will of the King and of the Governor of New France, I set out on April 17 with sixteen Frenchmen and a guide to the Miami nation. . . .

After 200 leagues of journey by land, we came on the 19th of May to Fort Detroit. We there made some canoes of elm wood. I sent one of them to Fort St. Joseph [in what is now southwest Michigan, on the St. Joseph River], which was at the harbor of Detroit, thirty leagues from where we were, to give Sieur Dulud, the commander of this fort, information of my arrival.

The Sieur de Beauvais de Tilly, his lieutenant, joined me, and afterwards the Sieur de La Forest, and then the Sieurs de La Durantaye and Dulud. I made the French and the savages line up along the road, and, after the Sieur de La Durantaye saluted us, we returned the salute. They had with them 300 English [and Iroquois], whom they had taken on Lake Huron, who had come there to trade. It was the Sieur de La Durantaye who commanded the party that captured them.[15]

[13] The government granted such feudal domains to encourage settlement.

[14] This dog feast is a sign of Tonty's knowledge of Indian customs. For centuries before the introduction of the horse, the dog was essentially the only domesticated animal in North America; cooking and eating it in this ritual feast was a solemn act, of the greatest symbolic importance.

[15] The French reacted angrily to these English attempts to penetrate their rich fur trade with the interior of the continent, conducted along the Great Lakes.

We made more canoes, and coasted along Lake Erie to Niagara, where we made a fort below the portage to wait there for news. On our way we took thirty more Englishmen, who were going to Michilimackinac, commanded by Major [Patrick] Macgregory, who was bringing back some Huron and Ottawa slaves taken by the Iroquois. Had it not been for these two strokes of good luck, our affairs would have turned out badly, as we were at war with the Iroquois and the English. From the great quantity of brandy and merchandise which they had with them, [they] would have gained over our allies, and thus we should have had all the savages and the English upon us at once.

I sent the Sieur de La Forest to inform M. the Marquis de Denonville of everything. He was at Fort Frontenac, and he joined us at Fort des Sables. . . .[16] The Potawatomis, Hurons, and Ottawas joined us there, and built some canoes. There was an Iroquois slave among the Hurons. Because of some foolish words he spoke of the French I proposed to have him put to death. They paid no attention to my proposal, and twelve leagues on our march, he ran away and gave our enemies information of our approach, and of the marks which our savages bore, which did us great harm in the ambuscade, as will be seen.

On the 10th [of July] we arrived at the marsh of Fort des Sables, and the army from below arrived at the same time. I received orders to take possession of a certain position, which I did with my company and savages. We then set about building a fort. On the 11th I went with fifty men to reconnoiter the road, three leagues from camp. On the 12th the fort was finished, and we set off for the [Seneca] village.

On the 13th, half a league from the clearing, we found an ambuscade. My company, who were the advance guard, forced it. We lost there seven men, of whom my lieutenant was one, and two of my people. We were occupied for seven days in cutting the corn of four villages.[17] We returned to Fort des Sables, then embarked, and went to build a [permanent] fort at Niagara. . . .

We crossed Lake Erie . . . and went on from there in company with the Reverend Father Gravier as far as Michilimackinac, and thence on to Fort St. Louis. . . . On the 7th of September [1687], one named Couture brought to me two Arkansas, who danced the calumet to me, and informed me of the death of M. de La Salle. . . .

M. de La Salle having landed [on the Gulf coast] beyond the Mississippi, on the side toward Mexico, about eighty leagues from the mouth of the river, and having lost his vessels on the coast, saved a part of the cargo, and began to march along the seashore, in search of the Mississippi. Meet-

[16] This was a temporary post in what is now northern New York. The French gathered their forces and allies at this point for an offensive into Seneca Iroquois territory, which Tonty describes in the following paragraphs.

[17] The Seneca ambush of the French forces took a great toll; Tonty's company was only one unit of many that suffered losses. The Iroquois warriors then faded away with their families, leaving their villages and fields to French torches.

ing with many obstacles to his plans on account of the bad roads, he resolved to go to the Illinois by land. So he loaded several horses to carry what was necessary. The Recollect Father Anastase; M. Cavelier, the priest, his [La Salle's] brother; M. Cavelier, his nephew; M. de Moranget, his relative [nephew]; MM. du Haut and Lanquetot;[18] and several Frenchmen accompanied him, with a Chaouanon savage.

When three days' journey from the Natchez, finding himself short of provisions, he sent M. de Moranget, his servant, and the Chaouanon to hunt in a small wood with orders to return in the evening. When they had killed some buffaloes, they stopped to dry the meat. [When they did not return,] M. de La Salle was uneasy, so he asked the Frenchmen who among them would go and look for them.

Du Haut and Lanquetot had for a long time determined to kill M. de La Salle, because, during the journey he had made along the seacoast, he had compelled the brother of Lanquetot, who was unable to keep up, to return to camp, and as he was returning alone he was massacred by the savages. This caused Lanquetot to swear that he would never forgive his brother's death. And, as in long journeys there are always many discontented persons in a company, he easily found partisans. He offered therefore, with them, to search for M. de Moranget, in order to have an opportunity to execute their design.

Having found the men, he told them that M. de La Salle was uneasy about them; but, they declaring that they could not set off till the next day, it was agreed to sleep there. After supper they arranged the order of the watch, that it should begin with M. de Moranget; after him was to follow the servant of M. de La Salle, and then the Chaouanon. After they had kept their watch and were asleep, the others massacred them, as [they were] persons attached to M. de La Salle.

Towards daybreak they heard the reports of pistols, which were fired as signals by M. de La Salle, who was coming with the Recollect Father in search of them. The wretches, suspecting that it was he, lay in wait for him, placing M. du Haut's servant in front. When M. de La Salle came near, he asked where M. de Moranget was. The servant, [insolently] keeping on his hat, answered that he was behind. As M. de La Salle advanced to remind him of his duty, he received three balls in his head, and fell down dead (March 19, 1687).

I do not know whether the Recollect Father could do anything, but it is agreed that he was frightened, and, thinking that he also was to be killed, threw himself on his knees before the murderers, and begged for a quarter of an hour to prepare his soul. They replied that they were willing to spare his life. They went together to where M. Cavelier was, and, as they advanced, shouted, "Down with your arms." M. Cavelier, on hearing the noise, came forward, and, when told of the death of his brother, threw himself on his

---

[18] Lanquetot (whose name is also spelled Liotot) was the expedition's surgeon.

knees before the murderers, making the same request that had been made by the Recollect Father. They granted him his life. He asked to go and bury the body of his brother, but they refused.

Such was the end of one of the greatest men of this age, a man of admirable spirit, and capable of undertaking all sorts of explorations. This murder much grieved the three Natchez whom M. de La Salle had found hunting, and who had accompanied him to the village. After the murderers had committed this crime, they seized all the baggage of the deceased, and the rest of the Frenchmen continued their journey to the village of the Natchez, where they found two Frenchmen domesticated among the savages, who had deserted in M. de La Salle's time.

After staying some days in this village, the savages proposed to them to go to war against the Quanouatino, to which the Frenchmen agreed, lest the savages should ill-treat them. As they were ready to set off for war, an English buccaneer, whom M. de La Salle had always liked, begged of the murderers that, as the savages were soon going to war, they would give him and his comrades some shirts. They flatly refused, which offended the Englishman, and he could not help expressing this to his comrades. They agreed together to make a second demand, and if refused, to revenge the death of M. de La Salle.

This they did some days afterwards. The Englishman, taking two pistols in his belt, accompanied by a Frenchman with a gun, went deliberately to the cabin of the murderers, whom they found outside shooting with bows and arrows. Lanquetot bade them good day, and asked how they were. They answered that they were pretty well, that as for his party it was not necessary to ask how they did, as they were always eating turkeys and good venison. Then the Englishman asked if they would not give some ammunition and shirts, as they had taken possession of everything. They replied that M. de La Salle was their debtor, and that what they had taken was theirs. "You will not, then?" said the Englishman. "No," replied they. On which the Englishman said to one of them, "You are a wretch; you murdered my master," and, firing his pistol, killed him [Lanquetot] on the spot.

Du Haut tried to get into his cabin, but the other Frenchman shot him also with a pistol, in the loins, which threw him on the ground. M. Cavelier and Father Anastase ran to his assistance. Du Haut had hardly time to confess himself, for the Father had but just given him absolution when he was finished by another pistol shot at the request of the savages, who could not endure that he should live after having killed their chief.

LA SALLE WAS DEAD, but his legacy would endure for generations. His explorations and skillful network-building secured the great fur trade for New France and built a string of alliances that could successfully challenge the power of the Five Nations.

And the Five Nations, not the English, remained the most pressing con-

cern of the government in Quebec. The Iroquois occupied a strategic location in the highlands along the Great Lakes–St. Lawrence trade route; and
though they were far less numerous than the roughly 200,000 English
colonists, they were a people dedicated to war. As Tonty's account illustrates,
large Five Nations war parties penetrated almost a thousand miles into the
heart of the Illinois country; they persistently threatened to break the tenu-
ous links that held New France to its western Indian allies (and fur suppliers). Hence the fury of the French at the large parties of Iroquois and
English traders, captured on their way to Michilimackinac.

Tonty took part in one of the greatest efforts of the French to deal with
the Five Nations threat: Governor Denonville's offensive of 1687. With
eight hundred regular troops, a thousand militiamen, and almost a thousand
Native American warriors, Denonville smashed into the Seneca homeland,
destroying villages and food supplies. He followed up by establishing Fort
Niagara, on the southern shore of Lake Ontario. The Five Nations fought
back, besieging both Niagara and Frontenac; meanwhile a smallpox epidemic
ravaged New France (showing how the sword of disease cut both ways). In
1688, the two sides finally agreed to another truce.

Colbert never liked the idea of a sprawling colony in North America,
with its head at Quebec and its tail on the Mississippi River. It would be in-
defensible, easily broken by a determined attack. Yet the demand for furs and
allies caused New France to stretch out, as it were, on its own. A few adventurers, led by La Salle, shifted the course of empires; they helped realign the
relations of numerous Native American peoples—though the Iroquois were
still able to battle them to a standstill.

New France would never have more than a small fraction of the population of the English colonies, yet it rose to be their potent rival. In every respect, it represented a polar opposite of the multitude of settlements below
the St. Lawrence: it was united, authoritarian, Catholic (of course), and mil-
itaristic. It also followed a very different path in its relations with Native
Americans. Both the English and the French sought alliances with various
Indian nations, but the government in Quebec welcomed Indian settlements
in the midst of the colony, while the English drove them beyond the frontier line. The Jesuits sought to convert their "savage" neighbors, while English ministers abandoned that idea in the wake of King Philip's War. And
every Quebec governor would speak of intermarrying the French and Indians, to make one people; nothing could have horrified the English more.

Such were the two distinctive paths taken by the Europeans as they col-
onized North America. In 1688, no one could tell which path would prevail.

16

PROPRIETORS IN THE COLONIES

Even as France centralized power in Quebec, King Charles II of England took a remarkable step in the opposite direction: he began auctioning off his sovereign authority in North America. What he actually put on the block were sparsely settled lands, to be transformed into colonies at the buyers' expense, and under their complete control. The king saw it as an easy way to settle debts or raise cash, while painlessly expanding his realm. Prospective purchasers saw the promise of vast estates and enormous riches (such as those earned in Virginia's tobacco trade), along with the immaterial reward of ruling burgeoning little countries as absolute monarchs. In fact, these men would be more than monarchs: they would be proprietors.

The idea of the proprietary colony actually began during the reign of Charles I. In 1632, he granted the territory of Maryland to Lord Baltimore, a friend and Catholic nobleman.[19] With absolute authority in his new realm, Baltimore created a refuge for his fellow Catholics, who suffered unceasing persecution in perennially Pope-hating England. The colony endured numerous rebellions at the hands of its large number of Protestant subjects (eventually Baltimore's descendants converted, sparing themselves further trouble); but the family remained in power, for the most part, until the American Revolution.

The social turmoil that resulted from England's bloody Civil War, however, threw all hierarchical, hereditary institutions in doubt, including proprietorships. The English aristocrats fled in large numbers to Governor William Berkeley's Virginia—but they knew better than to apply for their own petty tyrannies from stone-faced Oliver Cromwell. Only with the Stuart Restoration in 1660 did they once again think of building personal empires on American shores.

The first new petitioners for a proprietary colony came from places founded, fittingly enough, on indentured servitude and slave labor: Virginia and the English West Indies—specifically, Barbados. Governor Berkeley was one: as he surveyed his realm in the 1660s, he saw that the best lands had already been claimed by rich planters (including himself). But he knew that a

---

[19] The legality of this grant derived from a medieval device for securing England's vulnerable borders—something known as the Durham palatinate.

number of humbler Virginians had migrated south to Albemarle Sound, on the coast of what is now North Carolina. A vast stretch of unclaimed coastline reached from that point to Spanish Florida. This region also attracted the attention of two sugar planters from Barbados, Sir John Colleton and Anthony Ashley Cooper, whose island estates already suffered from exhausted soil.

These three men (together with Berkeley's brother, John Lord Berkeley) decided to secure a proprietorship for this region. To get political pull and financial capital, they approached four of the leading figures in London: Edward Hyde, Earl of Clarendon (the king's chief minister); George Monck, Duke of Albemarle (the military commander most responsible for restoring the Stuart monarchy); and two close friends of Charles's brother James, the Earl of Craven and Sir George Carteret. Once this powerful group united, they faced few problems in securing a grant from the king. In 1663, Charles II declared them "absolute proprietors" of the area between Virginia and Spanish Florida, with the right to make laws, wage war, and dispose of the lands. They called their lands Carolina.

From the start, the proprietors' efforts at settlement focused on the southern half of this colony, known as Clarendon (the northern district, called Albemarle, absorbed a spontaneous stream of migrants from Virginia). In 1670 and 1671, they sent two groups of Barbadians, who brought slaves with them. These English West Indians would soon be joined by French Huguenots, migrants from New York, and members of two sects that emerged from the religious ferment of the Civil War, Baptists and Quakers.

The two selections that follow describe this growing colony in its early years, from the 1670s through the 1690s, focusing in particular upon Clarendon (later known as South Carolina). The first provides an enthusiastic endorsement of the place—a sort of real estate broker's brochure. But the second reveals the growing problems facing this settlement—problems that would shape its troubled future.

In those first few decades, the colonists depended on the fur trade to survive. This region was largely untapped in that respect; while overtrapping in the north had forced New France to look deep into the continent, the Carolinians could obtain handsome quantities of fur from powerful Indian nations that lived nearby. The Westo tribe supplied them at first; after a vicious inter-Indian war dispersed these people, the English turned to the Yamasee and the Creek (who were divided into Upper and Lower branches).

As the colonists built up their fur-trading network, however, imperial rivalries complicated the situation. War loomed again and again with Spanish Florida, which boasted a powerful fortress at St. Augustine. To the west, the Frenchman Pierre Le Moyne d'Iberville followed in La Salle's footsteps, founding the colony of Louisiana around the end of the century (he established Biloxi in 1699 and Mobile in 1700). The French allied with the Choctaw nation, and the Spanish with the Apalachee, establishing several

Catholic missions among them. Creek wars against these tribes, often sparked by disputes over the fur trade, served English purposes; indeed, the Creek sold their prisoners of war as slaves to Carolina, heavily supplementing the growing number of captives brought over from Africa.

In this volatile, frontier environment, war emerged as one of the greatest weaknesses of the proprietors' government. Even though a plantation economy began to supplement the commerce in fur (especially after the introduction of rice in 1693), the fur and slave trade kept the colony entangled in a web of Indian and intercolonial wars. No one felt safe. Soon the proprietors' governors would feel a little insecure as well, in the face of so much hostility among the settlers.

There is one more thing to note about the second selection: it was written by none other than Edward Randolph, the dogged customs inspector who did so much to bring down the government of Massachusetts and erect the Dominion of New England. By the time he wrote the report that follows, James II had been overthrown by William III and his wife Mary; yet Randolph landed on his feet with a new appointment. And his pugnacity serves us well, for he provides a sharp portrait of this colony, only a few years before proprietary government collapsed.

An Account of the Province of Carolina
by Samuel Wilson

This province of Carolina was in the year 1663 granted by letters patent in propriety of His Most Gracious Majesty [to the Lords Proprietors]. . . . By the care and endeavors of the said Lords Proprietors, and at their very great charge, two colonies have been settled in this province, the one at Albemarle in the most northerly part, the other at Ashley River [called Clarendon]. . . .

Albemarle bordering on Virginia, and only exceeding it in health, fertility, and mildness of winter, is in the growths, productions, and other things much of the same nature with it; wherefore I shall not trouble the reader with a particular description of that part, but apply myself principally to discourse of the colony at Ashley River, which being many degrees more southward than Virginia, differs much from it in the nature of its climate and productions.

Ashley River was first settled in April 1670, the Lords Proprietors having at their sole charge sent out three vessels, with a considerable number of men, eighteen months' victuals, with clothes, tools, ammunition, and what else was thought necessary for a new settlement, and continued at this charge to supply the colony for diverse years after, until the inhabitants were able by their own industry to live of themselves; in which condition they have been for diverse years past. . . .

Ashley River, about seven miles in from the sea, divides itself into two branches; the southernmost retaining the name of Ashley River, the north branch is called Cooper River. In May 1680 the Lords Proprietors sent their orders to the government there, appointing the port town for these two rivers to be built on the point of land that divides them, and to be called Charles Town [later Charleston], since which time about an hundred houses are there built, and more are building daily by the persons of all sorts that come there to inhabit from the more northern English colonies, and the sugar islands, England, and Ireland.

And many persons who went to Carolina [as indentured] servants, being industrious since they came out of their times with their masters, at whose charge they were transported, have gotten good stocks of cattle, and servants of their own, have here also built houses, and exercise their trades. And many that went thither in that condition, are worth several hundreds of pounds, and live in a very plentiful condition, and their estates still increasing. And land is become of that value near the town, that it is sold for twenty shillings per acre, though pillaged of all its valuable timber, and not cleared of the rest; and land that is cleared and fitted for planting, and fenced, is let for ten shillings per annum the acre, though twenty miles distant from the town, and six men will in six weeks' time, fell, clear, fence in, and fit for planting six acres of land.

At this town, in November 1680, there rode at one time sixteen sail of vessels (some of which were upwards of 200 tons) that came from diverse parts of the King's dominions to trade there, which great concourse of shipping will undoubtedly in a short time make it a considerable town. . . .

Negroes by reason of the mildness of the winter thrive and stand much better than in any of the more northern colonies, and require less clothes, which is a great charge saved. . . .

With the Indians the English have a perfect friendship, they being both useful to one another. And care is taken by the Lords Proprietors, that no injustice shall be done them. . . . The Indians have been always so engaged in wars, one town or village against another (their government being usually of no greater extent), that they have not suffered any increase of people, there having been several nations in a manner quite extirpated by wars amongst themselves since the English settled at Ashley River. This keeps them so thin of people, and so divided, that the English have not the least apprehensions of danger from them; the English being already too strong for all the Indians within five hundred miles of them.

Spaniards, Settlers, and Slaves
by Edward Randolph

After a dangerous voyage at sea, I landed at Charles Town, in the province of So. Carolina, and soon after my arrival [1698], I administered the oath to Mr. Jos. Blake, one of the proprietors and governor of this province. . . .

There are but few settled inhabitants in this province. The Lords have taken up vast tracts of land for their own use, as in Colleton County and other places, where the land is most commodious for settlement, which prevents peopling the place, and makes them less capable to preserve themselves. As to their civil government, 'tis different from what I have met with in other proprieties. Their militia is not above 1,500 soldiers white men, but have thro' the province generally four negroes to one white man, and not above 1,100 families, English and French.

Their chief town is Charles Town, and the seat of government in this province, where the governor, council, and triennial parliament set, and their courts are holden, being above a league distance from the entrance to their harbor mouth. . . .

In the year 1686, one hundred Spaniards, with Negroes and Indians, landed at Edisto (50 miles to the southward of Charles Town), and broke open the house of Mr. Joseph Morton, then governor of this province, and carried away Mr. [Edward] Bowell, his brother-in-law, prisoner, who was found murdered two or three days after. They carried away all his money and plate, and 13 slaves, to the value of £1,500 sterling, and their plunder to St. Augustine. . . .

About the same time they robbed Mr. Grimball's house, the secretary of the province, and carried away to the value of over £1,500 sterling. They also fell upon a settlement of Scotchmen at Port Royal, where there was not above 25 men in health to oppose them. The Spaniards burnt down their houses, destroyed and carried away all that they had, because (as the Spaniards pretended) they were settled upon their land, and had they at any time a superior force, they would also destroy this town built upon Ashley and Cooper rivers. . . .

The inhabitants complained of the wrong done them by the Spaniards to the Lords Proprietors, and humbly prayed them (as I have been truly informed) to represent it to His Majesty. But they, not hearing from the Lords Proprietors, fitted out two vessels with 400 stout men, well armed, and resolved to take St. Augustine. But Jas. Colleton came in that time from Barbados with a commission to be governor, and threatened to hang them if they proceeded; whereupon they went on shore very unwillingly. The Spaniards, hearing the English were coming upon them for the damages, they left their town and castle, and fled into the woods to secure themselves.

The truth is, as I have been credibly informed, there was a design on foot to carry on a trade with the Spaniards.

I find the inhabitants greatly alarmed upon the news that the French continue their resolution to make a settling at Mississippi River, from [which] they may come overland to the head of Ashley River without opposition. 'Tis not known yet what care the Lords Proprietors intend to take for their preservation. Some ingenious gentlemen of this province (not of the council) have lately told me the deputies have talked of making an address to the Lords Proprietors for relief. But 'tis apparent that all the time of this French War they never sent them one barrel of powder or a pound of lead to help them.

They concluded they have no reason to depend upon them for assistance, and are resolved to forsake this country betimes, if they find the French are settled at Mississippi, or if upon the death of the King of Spain these countries fall into the hands of the French, as inevitably they will (if not timely prevented) and return their families to England or some other place where they may find safety or protection. It was one of the first questions asked by several of the chief men at my arrival, whether His Majesty will please allow them half pay for two or three years at furthest, that afterwards they will maintain themselves and families (if they have any) in making pitch and tar and planting of Indian corn. His Majesty will thereby have so many men seasoned to the country ready for service upon all occasions. . . .

I heard one of the council (a great Indian trader [James Moore], and has been 600 miles up in the country west from Charles Town) discourse that the only way to discover the Mississippi is from this province by land. He is willing to undertake it if His Majesty will please to pay the charge. . . .

The great improvement made in this province is wholly owing to the industry and labor of the inhabitants. They have applied themselves to make such commodities as might increase the revenue of the crown, as cotton, wool, ginger, indigo, etc. But finding them not to answer the end [of making a profit], they are set upon making pitch, tar, and turpentine, and planting rice, and can send over great quantities yearly, if they had encouragement from England to make it, having about 5,000 slaves to be employed in that service, upon occasion. . . .

The season for making those commodities in this province being six months longer than in Virginia and more northern plantations, a planter can make more tar in any one year here with 50 slaves than they can do with double the number in those places, their slaves here living at very easy rates and with few clothes.

SUCH EASY PROSPERITY awaited the wealthy few in the midst of so much turmoil. The writers above point out the means of obtaining riches in

Carolina: take a party of slaves, give them the bare minimum necessary for life, and work them brutally in rice plantations during the long growing season. Though the fur trade still had plenty of life in it, these methods and products promised a long future.

Meanwhile, war burst across the colony again. It was sparked in part by the War of the Spanish Succession: in 1700 the king of Spain died without an heir, so the aging Louis XIV tried to place his grandson on the throne in Madrid. William III rallied Europe once more to battle France and prevent this dangerous union. But the war in Carolina had a more immediate cause: the imperial ambitions of the Upper and Lower Creek, and the trade in Indian furs and slaves.

In 1702, Governor James Moore (the same trader mentioned by Randolph) led an attack on Spanish St. Augustine. The mission—paid for by the nervous colonists, not the proprietors—failed badly. But the English allies, the Creek, carried out a successful assault on the Apalachee, allies of Spain. Indeed, it would be the Indians, and not English soldiers, who would save Charlestown from Spanish wrath. In 1704, Moore went to the Creek as a private citizen to join a vast offensive against the Apalachee. More than 1,000 warriors and a handful of colonists destroyed the Spanish missions and burned Apalachee villages. The Creek then crushed a counterattack led by Spanish troops. Moore returned home with 1,000 slaves.

Creek fury prevented Spanish revenge for Moore's attack on St. Augustine. Indian alliances, however, shifted rapidly. The Creek had also waged war against the Louisiana-allied Choctaw; but in 1712, they made a lasting peace with the French. The Creek then encouraged the Yamasee—a tribe suffering under the machinations of English traders—to take revenge for Carolina's many wrongs. In 1715, the Yamasee launched a coordinated offensive against the colony. In one swift blow, they killed all the English traders among them and swept down on the settlements.

The Yamasee War was the Carolina equivalent of King Philip's War, only worse. The English hastily abandoned perhaps half of the cultivated farmland. Out of a population of 5,500 Europeans (along with 8,700 slaves), more than 400 died in ruthlessly effective Yamasee attacks. Meanwhile, the proprietors did little or nothing: they had seen virtually no return on their sizeable investment in the colony, and they did not feel inclined to pour more money down this (besieged) hole. In the end, the colony was saved not by force of arms, but by adroit diplomacy; though the fighting dragged on for years, the sudden defection of the Creek and the Cherokee (another powerful tribe) drastically reduced the force of the attacks.

The Yamasee War effectively destroyed proprietary government in what would soon be called South Carolina (a similar war with the Tuscaroras ravaged Albemarle—North Carolina—in 1711 and 1712). A bloodless revolt by colonists in 1719 overthrew the governor in Clarendon; the crown soon endorsed the action, appointing a royal governor in 1720 (having already sent one to Albemarle). The Board of Trade—the body established by William III to oversee the colonies—began buying out the proprietors' shares, a process completed by 1729. North and South Carolina now emerged as separate, royal provinces.

But proprietary government would not vanish from American shores. Lord Baltimore's heirs managed to survive in Maryland. And there was one more proprietorship destined to last—a land as blessed with peace, prosperity, and toleration as Carolina was burdened by war, dissension, and slavery. The name of this remarkable colony was Pennsylvania; and the name of its remarkable founder was William Penn.

The Puritan belief in the grace of God would find strong evidence in Penn's life, for he was surely blessed. His father, like the Duke of Albemarle (a proprietor of Carolina), had been an effective naval commander under Cromwell's government; like the Duke of Albemarle, he had switched sides after Cromwell's death, and escorted Charles II back to England; and like the Duke of Albemarle, he received vast estates as a reward. Charles and his brother James took a liking to the admiral's son as well; the youthful Penn became something of a court favorite. But where the admiral was a stern realist, his son William lost himself in an ineffable whiff of a vision, an otherworldly burst of insight. He became a Quaker.

The Quaker church (as the Society of Friends was popularly known) began with the vision of George Fox, a humble Englishman. The year of Fox's vision was significant: it was 1647, when England shook with rebellion against Charles I. Though the Civil War had been started by respectable gentlemen in defense of conservative ideals, events soon took on a force of their own, uncorking radical new political and religious beliefs. Dozens of new faiths originated in the Interregnum, as those kingless years came to be called—and some of those faiths lasted, including the Unitarians, Baptists, and George Fox's Quakers.

Compared to the drastic simplicity of Fox's faith, Puritanism was ornate, Latin-and-vestments Catholicism. His vision had revealed to him the ultimate truth, that God is within each person; next to that truth, nothing else mattered, not liturgy, not scripture, not even the Holy Trinity itself. He and his followers trembled with the spirit of this inner light (hence the nickname); they began to live, as far as they could, without distractions or obstructions. They wore humble black clothes; they abhorred violence; they even refused to swear oaths in court, for that would imply that they lied at other times. This was a faith purer than Puritanism—so the Puritans tried to purge it. In Massachusetts, Quakerism became a hanging offense.

Fox's vision swept up thousands of humbly born English: tradesmen, domestic servants, artisans, shopkeepers. The church extended particularly strong roots in the north Midlands, especially the counties of Cheshire, Lancashire, Yorkshire, Derbyshire, and Nottinghamshire. They suffered terrible persecution, for royalist Anglicans disliked them just as much as Cromwellian Puritans. But in William Penn, they found a convert who could offer them protection: specifically, he could buy them a haven in America.[20]

Penn's first venture, taken together with a group of eleven Quaker merchants, was in West New Jersey, a sparsely populated area along the Delaware River. The number of investors in this first proprietary effort, however, hampered its success. So he decided to strike out on his own by acquiring rights to the lands west of the Delaware, between Maryland and New York.

Charles II happily agreed to the idea, for he owed the Penn family quite a debt, both in capital and in services. In 1681, he chartered a new province for young William, granting him sweeping proprietary control. With grant in hand, Penn moved swiftly to establish his colony. In England he recruited a new group of investors, the Free Society of Traders; like his former partners, they were Friends (as Quakers are more properly called), and they received extensive concessions from the proprietor in return for their efforts and investment. The Society began recruiting migrants and acquiring ships; in 1682 and 1683, they sent more than 50 shiploads of settlers to the new colony of Pennsylvania. Before 1715, at least 23,000 colonists would arrive in the Delaware Valley—most of them Friends.

Penn crossed the Atlantic as well; when he arrived, he made a point of meeting and negotiating with the Native Americans who inhabited his proprietorship, especially the nation of the Delaware. Unlike so many English in America, he treated the Indians as fellow human beings, in keeping with the teachings of George Fox. Penn refused to accept his new fief purely on the grant of King Charles II; instead, he arranged to purchase his lands, at reasonably fair prices, from the native inhabitants. With this act, he set Pennsylvania on a sharply different path from those taken elsewhere. Peace and fair dealing would be the colony's watchwords (if not always followed); and unlike the Dutch in New Netherlands, the Quakers would not pit Indian neighbors against Indian foes.

Two selections follow, each presenting a first-person view of the new proprietary colony. The first is from Penn himself. It is the work of an enthusiastic entrepreneur, and a terribly earnest one. He wrote this description in an attempt to recruit new settlers; yet he strays, interestingly, into a long digression about the native inhabitants, revealing his own fascination with their ways, and his extensive personal dealings with them. Finally, almost reluctantly, he proceeds with his account of the new colony—including the many European nationalities to be found there: English, Dutch, Finns, and Swedes.

And Germans. In founding his refuge for Friends, Penn extended his protection to all, creating the most tolerant environment in North America.

[20] The finest single source of social, cultural, and demographic information on the Quaker migrants to America is David Hackett Fischer's *Albion's Seed*.

As a result, members of numerous sects, churches, and nationalities flocked to the banks of the Delaware, to live and prosper under the government of this unusual proprietor. The Germans were among the most important (known to later generations as the "Pennsylvania Dutch," from a corruption of the German word for German, *Deutsch*). They belonged to a half dozen or so Protestant churches: they were Moravians, Mennonites, Amish, and more. They built cohesive, consolidated communities—and they thrived, attracting yet more immigrants to Pennsylvania.

It is from the writings of one particularly important German immigrant, Francis Daniel Pastorius, that we take the second selection below. This humble, diligent religious leader helped found the German presence in Pennsylvania; the short excerpt that follows provides insight into the reasons for and means of this migration, shedding light on why so many non-English chose to live in this "holy experiment," as Penn called it. It would soon be the most diverse of all the colonies.

The Propriety of Pennsylvania
by William Penn

For the Province, the general condition of it take as followeth:

I. The country itself in its soil, air, water, seasons, and produce both natural and artificial is not to be despised. The land containeth diverse sorts of earth . . . God in his wisdom having ordered it so, that the advantages of the country are divided, the backlands being generally three to one richer than those that lie by navigable waters. . . .

VI. Of living creatures: fish, fowl, and beasts of the woods, here are diverse sorts, some for food and profit, and some for profit only. . . . The creatures for profit only by skin or fur, and that are natural to these parts, are the wild cat, panther, otter, wolf, fox, fisher, minx, muskrat; and of the water, the whale for oil, of which we have good store; and two companies of whalers, whose boats are built, will soon begin their work, which hath the appearance of a considerable improvement. To say nothing of our reasonable hopes of good cod in the bay. . . .

XI. The *Natives* I shall consider in their persons, language, manners, religion, and government, with my sense of their original. For their persons, they are generally tall, straight, well-built, and of singular proportion; they treat strong and clever, and mostly walk with a lofty chin. Of complexion, black, but by design, as the gypsies in England: They grease themselves with bear's fat clarified, and using no defense against sun or weather, their skins must needs be swarthy. Their eye is little and black, not unlike a straight-looked Jew; the thick lip and flat nose, so frequent with the East Indians and

Blacks, are not common to them; for I have seen as comely European-like faces among them of both, as on your side of the sea; and truly an Italian complexion hath not much more of the white, and the noses of several of them have as much of the Roman.

XII. Their language is lofty, yet narrow, but like the Hebrew; in signification full, like short-hand in writing; one word serveth in the place of three, and the rest are supplied by the understanding of the hearer. Imperfect in their tenses, wanting in their moods, participles, adverbs, conjunctions, interjections: I have made it my business to understand it, that I might not want an interpreter on any occasion. And I must say, that I know not a language spoken in Europe that hath words of more sweetness and greatness, in accent and emphasis, than theirs. . . .

VXI. Their diet is maize, or Indian corn, diverse ways prepared: sometimes roasted in the ashes, sometimes beaten and boiled with water, which they call *Homine*. They also make cakes, not unpleasant to eat. They likewise eat several sorts of beans and peas that are good nourishment. . . .

XVIII. They are great concealers of their own resentments; brought to it, I believe, by the revenge that hath been practiced among them; in either of these, they are not exceeded by the Italians. . . .

XIX. But in liberality they excell; nothing is too good for their friend. Give them a fine gun, coat, or any other thing, it may pass twenty hands, before it sticks. Light of heart, strong affections, but soon spent; the most merry creatures that live, feast and dance perpetually. They never have much, nor want much: wealth circulateth like the blood, all parts partake; and though none shall want what another hath, yet exact observers of property.

Some kings have sold, others presented me with several parcels of land; the pay or presents I made them were not hoarded by the particular owners, but the neighboring kings and their clans being present when the goods were brought out, the parties chiefly concerned consulted, what and to whom they should be give them? To every king then, by the hands of a person for that work appointed, is a proportion sent, so sorted and folded, and with that gravity, that is admirable. Then that king sub-divideth it in like manner among his dependents, they hardly leaving themselves an equal share with one of their subjects; and be it on such occasions, at festivals, or at their common meals, the kings distribute, and to themselves last. . . .

Since the European came into these parts, they are grown great lovers of strong liquors, rum especially, and for it exchange the richest of their skins and furs. If they are heated with liquors, they are restless till they have enough to sleep. That is their cry, Some more, and I will go to sleep; but when drunk, one of the most wretchedest spectacles in the world.

XX. In sickness, impatient to be cured, and for it give anything, especially for their children, to whom they are extremely natural [i.e., to whom they show natural affection]. They drink at those times a *Teran* or decoction of some roots in spring water; and if they eat any flesh, it must be of the female of any creature. If they die, they bury them with their apparel, be they men or women, and the nearest kin fling in something precious with them, as a token of their love. Their mourning is blacking of their face, which they continue for a year. . . .

XXII. Their government is by kings, which they call *Sachema,* and those by succession, but always of the mother's side. For instance, the children of him that is now king, will not succeed, but his brother by the mother, or the children of his sister, whose sons (and after them the children of her daughters) will reign; for no woman inherits. The reason they render for this way of descent is that their issue may not be spurious. . . .

XIII. Every king hath his council, and that consists of all the old and wise men of his nation. . . . 'Tis admirable to consider, how powerful the kings are, and yet how they move by the breath of their people. I have had occasion to be in council with them upon treaties for land, and to adjust the terms of trade.

Their order is thus: The king sits in the middle of an half moon, and hath his council, the old and wise on each hand; behind them, or at a little distance, sit the younger fry, in the same figure. Having consulted and resolved their business, the king ordered one of them to speak to me; he stood up, came to me, and in the name of his king saluted me, then took me by the hand, and told me that he was ordered by his king to speak to me, and that now it was not he, but the king that spoke, because what he should say was the king's mind. He first prayed me to excuse them that they had not complied with me the last time; he feared, there might be some fault in the interpreter, being neither Indian nor English. Besides, it was the Indian custom to deliberate, and take up much time in council, before they resolve; and that if the young people or owners of the land had been as ready as he, I had not met with so much delay.

Having thus introduced the matter, he fell to the bounds of the land they had agreed to dispose of, and the price (which [land] now is little and dear, that which would have bought twenty miles, not buying now two). During this time that this person spoke, not a man of them was observed to whisper or smile; the old, grave, the young, reverent in their deportment; they do speak little, but fervently, and with elegancy. I have never seen more natural sagacity, considering them without help (I was a'going to say, the spoil) of tradition; and he will deserve the name of wise, that outwits them in any treaty about a thing they understand.

When the purchase was agreed, great promises passed between us of kindness and good neighborhood, and that the Indians and English must live in love, as long as the sun gave light. Which done, another made a speech to the Indians, in the name of all the *Sachamakers* or kings, first to tell them what was done; next, to charge and command them, to love the Christians, and particularly to live in peace with me, and the people under my government; that many governors had been in the river, but that no governor had come himself to live and stay here before; and having now such a one that had treated them well, they should never do him or his any wrong. At every sentence of which they shouted, and said Amen, in their way. . . .

XXV. We have agreed, that in all differences between us, six of each side shall end the matter. Don't abuse them, but let them have justice, and you will win them. The worst is that they are the worse for the Christians, who have propagated their vices, and yielded them tradition for ill, and not for good things. . . .

XXVI. For their original, I am ready to believe them of the Jewish race, I mean, of the stock of the Ten [lost] Tribes. . . . So much for the natives; next the old planters will be considered in this relation, before I come to our colony. . . .

XXVII. The first planters in these parts were Dutch, and soon after them the Swedes and Finns. The Dutch applied themselves to traffic [trade], the Swedes and Finns to husbandry. There were some disputes between them some years, the Dutch looking upon them as intruders upon their purchase and possession, which was finally ended in the surrender made by. . . . the Swedes' governor, to Peter Stuyvesant, governor for the States of Holland, *Anno* 1655.

XXVIII. The Dutch inhabit mostly those parts of the province that lie upon or near to the bay, and the Swedes the freshes of the river Delaware. There is no need of giving any description of them, who are better known there than here; but they are a plain, strong, industrious people, yet have made no great progress in culture or propagation of fruit trees, as if they desired rather to have enough, than plenty or traffic. But I presume the Indians made them the more careless, by furnishing them with the means of profit, to wit, skins and furs, for rum and such strong liquors.

They kindly received me, as well as the English, who were few, before the people concerned with me came among them. I must needs commend their respect to authority, and kind behavior to the English. . . .

XXXI. Our people are mostly settled upon the upper rivers, which are pleasant and sweet, and generally bounded with good land. The planted part of the province and territories is cast into six counties: Philadelphia, Buckingham [Bucks], Chester, New Castle, Kent, and Sussex, maintaining about four thousand souls. The General Assemblies have been held, and with such concord and dispatch that they sat but three weeks, and at least seventy laws were passed without one dissent in any material thing. But of this more hereafter, being yet raw and new in our gear.

However, I cannot forget their singular respect to me in this infancy of things, who by their own private expenses so early considered mine for the public, as to present me with an impost upon certain goods imported and exported; which after my acknowledgments of their affection, I did as freely remit to the province and traders to it. And for the well government of the said counties, courts of justice are established in every county, with proper officers, as justices, sheriffs, clerks, constables, etc., which courts are held every two months. But to prevent lawsuits, there are three peace-makers chosen by every county court, in the nature of common arbitrators, to hear and end differences betwixt man and man; and spring and fall there is an orphan's court in each county, to inspect and regulate the affairs of orphans and widows.

XXXII. Philadelphia, the expectation of those that are concerned in this province, is at last laid out to the great content of those here, that are in any way interested therein. The situation is a neck of land, and lieth between two navigable rivers, Delaware and Schuykill, whereby it hath two fronts upon the water, each a mile, and two from river to river. . . . It is advanced within less than a year to about four score houses and cottages, such as they are, where merchants and handicrafts are following their vocations as fast as they can, while the countrymen are close at their farms. . . .

I bless God, I am fully satisfied with the country and entertainment I can get in it; for I find that particular content which hath always attended me, where God in his providence hath made it my place and service to reside. You cannot imagine my station can be at present free of more than ordinary business, and as such, I must say, it is a troublesome work.[21] But the method things are putting in will facilitate the charge, and give an easier motion to the administration of affairs.

A Place for Germans
by Francis Daniel Pastorius

On October 24, 1685, I, Francis Daniel Pastorius, with the good will of the governor, laid out another new city, of the name of Germantown, or Germanopolis, at a distance of two hours' walk from Philadelphia, where there are a good black fertile soil, and many fresh wholesome springs of water, many oak, walnut, and chestnut trees, and also good pasturage for cattle. The first settlement consisted of only twelve families of forty-one persons, the greater part High German mechanics and weavers, because I had ascertained that linen cloth would be indispensable.

I made the main street of this city sixty feet wide, and the side streets forty; the space, or ground-plot, for each house and garden was as much as three acres of land, but for my own dwelling twice as much. Before this, I had also built a little house in Philadelphia, thirty feet long and fifteen wide. Because of the scarcity of glass the windows were of oiled paper. Over the house door I had written:

Parva Domus, sed amica Bonis, procul este profani[22]

[21] This comment cuts against the extremely positive tone, providing an honest note of dismay at the growing difficulties of governing this fractious colony.

[22] "A little house, but a friend to the good; remain at a distance, ye profane."

Whereat our governor [Penn], when he visited me, burst into laughter, and encouraged me to keep on building.

I have also acquired for my High German Company fifteen thousand acres of land in one piece, upon the condition that, within a year, they shall actually place thirty households thereon; and for this reason, that we High Germans may maintain a separate little province, and thus feel more secure from all oppression.

It would, therefore, be a very good thing if the European associates should at once send more persons over here, for the common advantage of the Company; for only the day before yesterday, the governor said to me that the zeal of the High Germans in building pleased him very much, and that he preferred them to the English, and would grant them special privileges. . . .

The native savages have their own little kings. We Christians acknowledge William Penn as ruler of the country, to whom this land was granted and ceded for his own by King Charles II, and the Christian inhabitants were instructed to give him personal allegiance. But this wise and God-fearing ruler did not, upon his arrival, wish to accept this inheritance of the heathen thus for nothing, but he gave presents to the native inhabitants and their appointed kings, and compensated them, and thus bought from them one piece of land after another, so that they withdrew even further into the wilderness. Penn, however, had bought all the land which he occupied by just right of purchase, and from him I bought at the start, in London, thirty thousand acres for my German Company.

And notwithstanding that the aforesaid William Penn belongs to the sect of Tremblers, or Quakers, yet he constrains no one to any religion, but leaves to each nation freedom of belief.

SUCH A HAPPY beginning—so unlike the birth of South Carolina, which came into the world adorned by blood and chains. With an instant metropolis, a flood of immigrants, and rapidly growing prosperity, Penn's Pennsylvania resembled Winthrop's Massachusetts, only better. There would be no Pequot War here, and certainly no repression of religious dissent. Yet both slavery and blood (actually, cries for blood) would dog this rising province. Certain Quaker merchants avidly took part in the buying and selling of human beings, provoking an outcry among other, more principled Friends (and by Pastorius).

And Penn engaged in a long and difficult struggle with his colonial subjects over money, rights, and the form of government. Though he was forced to return to England in 1684 to settle a border dispute with Lord Baltimore, he sent back across the Atlantic one Frame of Government after another—finally settling on a simple Charter of Privileges in 1701 that established a unique unicameral assembly. He also gave up on three rebellious counties that had been included (against the inhabitants' wishes) in his proprietorship; in 1702, he allowed them to split off and form the colony of Delaware. But his proprietorship lived on, even after his death in 1718.

Despite the stinging nettles of political bickering and the thorns of Delaware's resentments, Pennsylvania emerged into the eighteenth century as the proverbial keystone of the coastal arc of colonies. Penn's holy experiment would pay off, as his province grew into a treasure house of population, prosperity, and diversity.

17

FRANKLIN IN THE CITIES

As the eighteenth century began, the American empires ruled by Paris and London had expanded just about as far as they ever would. New France, for instance, now stretched in a vast arc from Quebec to Fort St. Louis in the Illinois country to the new territory of Louisiana on the Gulf of Mexico. The British[23] colonies would grow a little more yet—Georgia would begin to blossom in the 1730s, and a new influx of immigrants from Ulster and northern Britain would push into the Appalachian hill country—but the essential outline of settlement was set. The next frontier of expansion would be internal: in the colonies' fledgling cities.

The British colonies would always remain heavily agricultural and rural—eighty to ninety percent of the population, depending on the region. Yet urban centers quickly took on central importance in American life. The colonists were, after all, a people who had traveled across the ocean from their homelands and now lived hard by that ocean in a relatively thin coastal strip. The seaports made natural hubs of politics and economics, connecting the circles of rural counties to the axle of trade and official communication with Britain. Within a number of colonies important towns sprang up almost immediately—Boston, New Amsterdam, Charlestown (later Charleston), and Philadelphia, to name a few.

Avocation and opportunity pulled many colonists into the burgeoning towns. Artisans and shopkeepers made up a significant part of the immigration to North America, and they plied their trades better on streets than on country lanes. Shipbuilding, fishing, whaling, and oceangoing trade flourished early on (men active in shipping had naturally been a part of the transatlantic migration). Beginning with John Winthrop's own vessel, Boston quickly became a major seaport, followed by New York and Philadelphia.

Of course, "major" is a relative term. In 1690, out of a total colonial population of perhaps 250,000, Boston could boast only 6,000 inhabitants; New York, 4,700; and Philadelphia, 2,200. After 1720, Boston stagnated as the newer cities (especially Philadelphia) continued to grow; by 1750, the

---

[23] From this point on, we will speak of *Britain* rather than England. In 1707, Parliament passed the Act of Union, formally joining Scotland and England.

British colonists numbered 1.2 million—but Boston's population was only 16,000, while Philadelphia reached 20,000, and would soon pass 40,000. The business of most people continued to be farming—and in a society that equated land ownership with social status, the vast expanse of the rural landscape beckoned.

Despite the allure of the land, commerce eventually flourished. Gradually the simple barter trade of early settlers fell away; the European market economy, such as it was, infiltrated the everyday lives of colonists. The simplest aspects of capitalism, however, cannot be taken for granted at this time: for example, there was a constant shortage of currency (which meant coins, supposedly containing their face value in gold or silver). Northern colonists made do first with Indian wampum, then with whatever coins they could get—even Dutch thalers and Spanish pieces of eight. Virginians used "commodity money": they set the prices of most goods and services in terms of tobacco. The shortage of money punished trade, which was also strictly regulated by British mercantilist policies. Fortunately, the Americans were aided by a tidy profit in their commerce with the West Indian colonies, but even this influx of gold and silver could not meet the demands of a growing population.

This was a turbulent time, in urban economics as much as on the frontier—a time when a few men accumulated vast fortunes (with opportunities largely denied women). Some did so through political power and connections; others were thrown back on the traditional resources of blind luck, shrewd judgment, and guts. And one man who had plenty of them all (including political connections) was Benjamin Franklin.

Perhaps no one in the colonial era is better known to us than Franklin—not even George Washington, Thomas Jefferson, or any of the other Founding Fathers. The reason for this is the centuries-long popularity of Franklin's remarkable *Autobiography*. It records, with charming candor, his rise from humble origins to his exalted status as one of the wealthiest and most influential men in America. It became required reading for generations of children, which annoyed Mark Twain to no end. "The subject of this memoir was of a vicious disposition," Twain wrote. "His simplest acts, also, were contrived with a view to their being held up for the emulation of boys forever—boys who might otherwise have been happy. . . . With a malevolence which is without parallel in history, he would work all day and then sit up nights and let on to be studying algebra by the light of a smouldering fire, so that all other boys might have to do that also or else have Benjamin Franklin thrown up to them."

Twain actually makes an important point for our purposes here: Franklin was not a typical colonist. He achieved a degree of upward mobility that was, almost by definition, extremely rare. With that in mind, however, we can appreciate his account for what it tells us about the society around him as he moved up the twisting ladder of success. He sheds light on urban trades, on education, on the system of apprenticeship, on the gritty reality of shops and small businesses. Franklin's words also reveal the expectations that his family and friends had for his life and theirs, highlighting the rather humble goals they hoped to meet. And he takes us on a personal journey that parallels the larger shift in population and prosperity, as he travels from stagnant Boston to flourishing Philadelphia.

From Apprentice to Public Man
by Benjamin Franklin

Josiah, my father, married young, and carried his wife with three children unto New England, about 1682. . . . By the same wife he had four children more born there, and by a second wife ten more, in all 17, of which I remember 13 sitting at one time at his table, who all grew up to be men and women, and married. I was the youngest son [born in 1706], and the younger child but two, and was born in Boston, N. England. My mother, the second wife, was Abiah Folger, a daughter of Peter Folger, one of the first settlers of new England. . . .

My elder brothers were all put apprentices to different trades. I was put to the grammar school at eight years of age, my father intending to devote me as the tithe of his sons to the service of the Church [of England]. My early readiness in learning to read (which must have been very early, as I do not remember when I could not read) and the opinion of all his friends that I should certainly make a good scholar, encouraged him in this purpose of his. My uncle Benjamin too approved of it, and proposed to give me all his shorthand volumes of sermons, I suppose as a stock to set up with, if I would learn his character [shorthand].

I continued however at the grammar school not quite one year, tho' in that time I had risen gradually from the middle of the class of that year to be the head of it, and farther was removed into the next class above it, in order to go with that into the third at the end of the year. But my father in the meantime, from a view of the expense of a college education which, having so large a family, he could not well afford, and the mean living many so educated men were afterwards able to obtain, reasons that he gave to his friends in my hearing, altered his first intention, took me from the grammar school, and sent me to a school for writing and arithmetic kept by a then famous man, Mr. Geo. Brownell. . . . Under him I acquired fair writing pretty soon, but I failed in the arithmetic, and made no progress in it.

At ten years old, I was taken home to assist my father in his business, which was that of a tallow chandler and soap boiler. A business he was not bred to, but had assumed on his arrival in New England and on finding his dying trade would not maintain his family, being in little request. Accordingly I was employed in cutting wick for the candles, filling the dipping mold, and the molds for the cast candles, attending the shop, going of errands, etc.

I disliked the trade and had a strong inclination for the sea; but my father declared against it. However, living near the water, I was much in and about it, learned early to swim well, and to manage boats, and when in a boat or canoe with other boys I was commonly allowed to govern, especially in any case of difficulty; and upon other occasions I was generally a leader among the boys, and sometimes led them into scrapes. . . .

To return. I continued thus employed in my father's business for two years, that is till I was 12 years old; and my brother John, who was bred to that business, having left my father, married and set up for himself at Rhode Island. There was all appearance that I was destined to supply his place and be a tallow chandler. But my dislike to the trade continuing, my father was under apprehensions that if he did not find one for me more agreeable, I should break away and get to sea, as his son Josiah had done to his great vexation. He therefore sometimes took me to walk with him, and see joiners, bricklayers, turners, braziers, etc., at their work, that he might observe my inclination, and endeavor to fix it on some trade or other on land. . . .

From a child I was fond of reading, and all the little money that came into my hands was ever laid out in books. Pleased with the Pilgrim's Progress, my first collection was of John Bunyan's works, in separate little volumes. I afterwards sold them to enable me to buy R. Burton's Historical Collections; they were small Chapmen's Books, and cheap, 40 or 50 in all. . . . This bookish inclination at length determined my father to make me a printer, tho' he had already one son (James) of that profession.

In 1717 my brother James returned from England with a press and letters to set up his business in Boston. I liked it much better than that of my father, but still had a hankering for the sea. To prevent the apprehended effect of such an inclination, my father was impatient to have me bound to my brother. I stood out some time, but at last was persuaded and signed the indentures, when I was yet but 12 years old. I was to serve as an apprentice till I was 21 years of age, only I was to be allowed journeyman's wages during the last year.

In a little time I made great proficiency in the business, and became a useful hand to my brother. I now had access to better books. An acquaintance with the apprentices of booksellers enabled me sometimes to borrow a small one, which I was careful to return soon and clean. Often I sat up in my room reading the greatest part of the night, when the book was borrowed in the evening and to be returned early in the morning, lest it should be missed or wanted. . . .

My brother had in 1720 or 21 begun to print a newspaper. It was the second that appeared in America, and was called *The New England Courant*. The only one before it was *The Boston News Letter*. I remember his being dissuaded by some of his friends from the undertaking, as not likely to succeed, one newspaper being in their judgment enough for America. . . . He went on, however, with the undertaking, and after having worked in composing the types and printing off the sheets I was employed to carry the papers thro' the streets to meet customers.

He had some ingenious men among his friends who amused themselves by writing little pieces for this paper, which gained it credit, and made it more in demand; and these gentlemen often visited us. Hearing their conversations, and their accounts of the approbation their papers were received with, I was excited to try my hand among them. But being still a boy, and suspecting that my brother would object to printing anything of mine in his paper if he knew it to be mine, I contrived to disguise my hand, and writing an anonymous paper I put it in at night under the door of the printing house.

It was found in the morning and communicated to his writing friends when they called in as usual. They read it, commented on it in my hearing, and I had the exquisite pleasure of finding it met with their approbation, and that in their different guesses at the author, none were named but men of some character among us for learning and ingenuity. I suppose now that I was rather lucky in my judges, and that perhaps they were not really so very good ones as I then esteemed them.

Encouraged however by this, I wrote and conveyed in the same way to the press several more papers, which were equally approved, and I kept my secret till my small fund of sense for such performances was pretty well exhausted, and then I discovered [revealed] it; when I began to be considered a little more by my brother's acquaintances, and in a manner that did not quite please him, as he thought, probably with reason, that it tended to make me too vain.

And perhaps this might be one occasion of the differences that we frequently had about this time. Tho' a brother, he considered himself as my master, and me as his apprentice; and accordingly expected the same services from me as he would from another; while I thought he demeaned me too much in some he required of me, who from a brother expected more indulgence. Our disputes were often brought before our father, and I fancy I was either generally in the right, or else a better pleader, because the judgment was generally in my favor. But my brother was passionate and had often beaten me, which I took extremely amiss; and thinking my apprenticeship very tedious, I was constantly wishing for some opportunity of shortening it, which at length offered in a manner unexpected.[24]

One of the pieces in our newspaper, on some political point which I have now forgotten, gave offense to the Assembly. He [Franklin's brother]

[24] [Original author's footnote] I fancy his harsh and tyrannical treatment of me, might be a means of impressing me with that aversion to arbitrary power that has stuck to me thro' my whole life.

was taken up, censured, and imprisoned for a month by the Speaker's Warrant, I suppose because he would not discover his author. I too was taken up and examined before the Council; but tho' I did not give them any satisfaction, they contented themselves with admonishing me, and dismissed me; considering me perhaps as an apprentice, who was bound to keep his master's secrets.

During my brother's confinement, which I resented a good deal, notwithstanding our private differences, I had the management of the paper, and I made bold to give our rulers some rubs with it, which my brother took very kindly, while others began to consider me in an unfavorable light, as a young genius that had a turn for libelling and satire. My brother's discharge was accompanied with an order of the House (a very odd one) *that James Franklin should no longer print the paper called the New England Courant.*

There was a consideration held in our printing house among his friends what he should do in this case. Some proposed to evade the order by changing the name of the paper, but my brother, seeing the inconveniences in that, it was finally concluded on as a better way, to let it be printed for the future under the name of *Benjamin Franklin.* And to avoid the censure of the Assembly that might fall on him, as still printing it by his apprentice, the contrivance was that my old indenture should be returned to me with a full discharge on the back of it, to be shown on occasion; but to secure to him the benefit of my service I was to sign new indentures for the remainder of the term, which were to be kept private.

A very flimsy scheme it was, but however, it was immediately executed, and the paper went on accordingly under my name for several months. At length a fresh difference arising between my brother and me, I took upon me to assert my freedom, presuming that he would not venture to produce the new indentures. It was not fair in me to take this advantage, and this I therefore reckon one of the first errata of my life. But the unfairness of it weighed little with me. . . .

When he found I would leave him, he took care to prevent my getting employment in any other printing house of the town, by going round and speaking to every master, who accordingly refused to give me work. I then thought of going to New York as the nearest place where there was a printer; and I was rather inclined to leave Boston, when I reflected that I had already made myself a little obnoxious to the governing party; and from the arbitrary proceedings of the Assembly in my brother's case it was likely I might if I stayed soon bring myself into scrapes; and farther that my indiscreet disputations about religion begun to make me pointed at with horror by good people, as an infidel or atheist.

I determined on the point; but my father now siding with my brother, I was sensible that if I attempted to go openly, men would be used to prevent me. My friend Collins therefore undertook to manage a little for me. He agreed with the captain of a New York sloop for my passage, under the

notion of my being a young acquaintance of his that had got a naughty girl
with child. . . . So I sold some of my books to raise a little money, was taken
on board privately, and as we had a fair wind in three days I found myself in
New York, near 300 miles from home, a boy of but 17, without the least
recommendation to or knowledge of any person in the place, and with very
little money in my pocket. . . .

I offered my service to the printer of the place, old Mr. William Bradford (who had been the first printer in Pennsylvania, but removed from
thence upon the quarrel of [Governor] George Keith). He could give me no
employment, having little to do, and help enough already. But, says he, my
son at Philadelphia has lately lost his principal hand, Aquila Rose, by death.
If you go thither I believe he may employ you. . . .

[I] arrived there [in Philadelphia] about 8 or 9 o'clock, on the Sunday
morning, and landed at the Market Street wharf. . . . I was in my working
dress, my best clothes being to come round by sea. I was dirty from my journey; my pockets were stuffed out with shirts and stockings; I knew no soul,
nor where to look for lodging. I was fatigued with travelling, rowing, and
want of rest. I was very hungry, and my whole stock of cash consisted of a
Dutch dollar and about a shilling in copper. The latter I gave the people of
the boat for my passage, who at first refused it on account of my rowing; but
I insisted on their taking it, a man being sometimes more generous when he
has but a little money than when he has plenty, perhaps thro' fear of being
thought to have but little.

Then I walked up the street, gazing about, till near the Market House
I met a boy with bread. I had made many a meal on bread, and inquiring
where he got it, I went immediately to the baker's he directed me to in Second Street; and asked for biscuit, intending such as we had in Boston, but
they it seems were not made in Philadelphia. Then I asked for a three-penny
loaf, and was told they had none such; so not considering or knowing the
difference of money and the greater cheapness nor the names of his bread,
I bad him give me three penny worth of any sort. He gave me accordingly
three great puffy rolls. I was surprised at the quantity, but took it, and having no room in my pockets, walked off, with a roll under each arm, and eating the other. . . .

Thus refreshed I walked again up the street, which by this time had
many clean dressed people in it who were all walking the same way. I joined
them, and thereby was led into the great Meeting House of the Quakers
near the Market. I sat down among them, and after looking round a while
and hearing nothing said, being very drowsy thro' labor and want of rest the
preceding night, I fell fast asleep, and continued so till the meeting broke up,
when one was kind enough to rouse me. This was therefore the first house I
was in or slept in, in Philadelphia. . . .

[The next morning, after spending the night in an inn,] I made myself
as tidy as I could and went to Andrew Bradford the printer's. I found in the

shop the old man his father, whom I had seen in New York, and who travelling on horseback had got to Philadelphia before me. He introduced me to his son, who received me civilly, gave me a breakfast, but told me he did not at present want a hand, being lately supplied with one. But there was another printer in town lately set up, one Keimer, who perhaps might employ me. If not, I should be welcome to lodge at his house, and he would give me a little work to do now and then till fuller business should offer.

The old gentleman said he would go with me to the new printer. And when we found him, Neighbor, says Bradford, I have brought to see you a young man of your business, perhaps you may want such a one. He asked me a few questions, put a composing stick in my hand to see how I worked, and then said he would employ me soon, tho' he had just then nothing for me to do. . . .

These two printers I found poorly qualified for their business. Bradford had not been bred to it, and was very illiterate; and Keimer, tho' something of a scholar, was a mere composer, knowing nothing of presswork. . . . He did not like me lodging at Bradford's while I worked with him. He had a house indeed, but without furniture, so he could not lodge me. But he got me a lodging at Mr. Read's . . . who was the owner of his house. And my chest and clothes being come by this time, I made a rather more respectable appearance in the eyes of Miss Read [Read's daughter] than I had done when she first happened to see me eating my roll in the street.

I began now to have some acquaintance among the young people of the town, that were lovers of reading, with whom I spent my evenings very pleasantly. And gaining money by my industry and frugality, I lived very agreeably, forgetting Boston as much as I could. . . .

I had a brother-in-law, Robert Holmes, master of a sloop that traded between Boston and Delaware. He being at New Castle 40 miles below Philadelphia, heard there of me and wrote me a letter, mentioning the concern of my friends in Boston at my abrupt departure, and assuring me of their good will to me. . . . I wrote an answer to his letter, thanked him for his advice, but stated my reasons for quitting Boston fully, and in such a light as to convince him I was not so wrong as he apprehended.

Sir William Keith, governor of the province, was then at New Castle, and Capt. Holmes happening to be in company with him when my letter came to hand, spoke to him of me, and showed him the letter. The governor read it, and seemed surprised when he was told my age. He said I appeared to be a young man of promising parts, and therefore should be encouraged. The printers at Philadelphia were wretched ones, and if I would set up there, he made no doubt I should succeed; for his part, he would procure me the public business [government printing contracts], and do me every other service in his power.

This my brother-in-law afterwards told me in Boston. But I knew as yet nothing of it; when one day Keimer and I being at work together near the window, we saw the Governor and another gentleman (which proved to be Col. French, of New Castle) finely dressed, come directly across the street to our house, and heard them at the door. Keimer ran down immediately, thinking it a visit to him. But the Governor inquired for me, came up, and with a condescension and politeness I had been quite unused to, made me many compliments, desired to be acquainted with me, blamed me kindly for not having made myself known to him when I first came to the place, and would have me away with him to the tavern where he was going with Col. French to taste as he said some excellent Madeira.

I was not a little surprised, and Keimer stared like a pig poisoned. I went however with the Governor and Col. French to a tavern the corner of Third Street, and over the Madeira he proposed my setting up my business, laid before me the probabilities of success, and both he and Col. French assured me I should have their interest and influence in procuring the public business of both governments.[25] On my doubting whether my father would assist me in it, Sir William said he would give me a letter to him, in which he would state the advantages, and he did not doubt of prevailing with him. So it was concluded I should return to Boston in the first vessel with the Governor's letter recommending me to my father. . . .

My unexpected appearance surprised the family; all were however very glad to see me and made me welcome, except my brother. I went to see him at his printing house; I was better dressed than ever while in his service, having a genteel new suit from head to foot, a watch, and my pockets lined with near five pounds sterling in silver. He received me not very frankly, looked me all over, and turned to his work again. The journeymen were inquisitive where I had been, what sort of country it was, and how I liked it? I praised it much, and the happy life I led in it. . . .

This visit of mine offended him extremely. For when my mother some time after spoke to him of reconciliation, and of her wishes to see us on good terms together, and that we might live for the future as brothers, he said I insulted him in such a manner before his people that he could never forget or forgive it. In this however he was mistaken.

My father received the Governor's letter with some apparent surprise; but said little of it to me for some days; when Capt. Holmes returning, he showed it to him, and asked if he knew Keith, and what kind of man he was; adding his opinion that he must be of small discretion, to think of setting a boy up in business who wanted yet three years of being at man's estate. Holmes said what he could in favor of the project; but my father was clear in the impropriety of it, and at last gave a flat denial to it. . . .

We returned to Philadelphia. . . . Sir William, on reading his [Franklin's father's] letter, said he was too prudent. There was great difference in persons, and discretion did not always accompany years, nor was youth always

[25] Keith was governor of both Pennsylvania and Delaware.

without it. And since he will not set you up, says he, I will do it myself. Give me an inventory of the things necessary to be had from England, and I will send for them. You shall repay me when you are able; I am resolved to have a good printer here, and I am sure you must succeed.

This was spoken with such an appearance of cordiality that I had not the least doubt of his meaning what he said. . . . Had it been known that I depended on the Governor, probably some friend that knew him better would have advised me not to rely on him, as I afterwards heard it as his own character to be liberal of promises which he never meant to keep. Yet unsolicited as he was by me, how could I think his generous offers insincere? I believed him one of the best men in the world.

I presented him with an inventory of a little printing house, amounting by my computation to be about £100 sterling. He liked it, but asked me if my being on the spot in England to choose the types and see that everything was good of the kind, might not be of some advantage. . . . But it would be some months before the *Annis* [the ship to be taken to England] sailed, so I continued working with Keimer. . . .

I made some courtship during this time to Miss Read. I had a great respect and affection for her, and had some reason to believe she had the same for me; but as I was about to take a long voyage, and we were both very young, only a little above 18, it was thought most prudent by her mother to prevent our going too far at present, as a marriage if it was to take place would be more convenient after my return, when I should be as I expected set up in my business. Perhaps too she thought my expectations not so well founded as I imagined them to be. . . .

The Governor, seeming to like my company, had me frequently to his house; and his setting me up was always mentioned as a fixed thing. I was to take with me letters recommendatory to a number of his friends, besides the letter of credit to furnish me with the necessary money for purchasing the press and types, paper, etc. For these letters I was appointed to call at different times, when they were to be ready, but a future time was still named. Thus we went on till the ship whose departure too had been several times postponed was on the point of sailing. Then when I called to take my leave and receive the letters, his secretary, Dr. Bard, came out to me and said the Governor was extremely busy in his writing, but would be down at New Castle before the ship, and there the letters would be delivered to me. . . . [Franklin boarded the ship and sailed for England.]

When we came into the channel, the captain . . . gave me an opportunity of examining the bag for the Governor's letters. I found none upon which my name was put, as under my care. I picked out six or seven that by the handwriting I thought might be the promised letters, especially as one of them was directed to Basket, the King's printer, and another to some stationer.

We arrived in London the 24th of December, 1724. I waited upon the stationer who came first in my way, delivering the letter as from Gov. Keith. I didn't know such a person, says he; but opening the letter, O, this is from Riddlesden; I have lately found him to be a complete rascal, and I will have nothing to do with him, nor receive any letters from him. So putting the letters into my hand, he turned on his heel and left me to serve some customer. I was surprised to find these were not the Governor's letters. And after recollecting and comparing circumstances, I began to doubt his sincerity.

I found my friend Denham, and opened the whole affair to him. . . . He laughed at the notion of the Governor's giving me a letter of credit, having as he said no credit to give. On my expressing some concern about what I should do, he advised me to endeavor getting some employment in the way of my business. Among the printers here, says he, you will improve yourself; and when you return to America, you will set up to greater advantage. . . .

Thus I spent about 18 months in London. Most part of the time, I worked hard at my business, and spent but little upon myself except in seeing plays and in books. . . . We sailed from Gravesend on the 23rd of July, 1726. . . . We landed in Philadelphia the 11th of October, where I found sundry alterations. Keith was no longer governor, being superseded by Major Gordon. I met him walking the streets as a common citizen. He seemed a little ashamed at seeing me, but passed without saying anything. I should have been as much ashamed at seeing Miss Read, had not her friends, despairing with reason of my return, after the receipt of my letter, persuaded her to marry another, one Rogers, a potter, which was done in my absence. With him, however, she was never happy, and soon parted from him, refusing to cohabit with him, or bear his name, it being now said that he had another wife. . . . Keimer had got a better house, a shop well supplied with stationery, plenty of new types, a number of hands tho' none good, and seemed to have a great deal of business. . . .

My brother-in-law Holmes, being now at Philadelphia, advised my return to my business. And Keimer tempted me with an offer of large wages by the year to come and take the management of his printing house, that he might better attend his stationer's shop. I had heard a bad character of him in London, from his wife and her friends, and was not fond of having any more to do with him. I tried for farther employment as a merchant's clerk; but not readily meeting with any, I closed again with Keimer. . . .

Our printing house often wanted sorts [duplicate type], and there was no letter founder in America. I had seen types cast at James's in London, but without much attention to the manner; however, I now contrived a mold, made use of the letters we had, as puncheons, struck the matrices in lead, and thus supplied in a pretty tolerable way all deficiencies. I also engraved several things on occasion. I made the ink, I was warehouseman, and everything, in short quite a factotum.

But however serviceable I might be, I found that my services became every day of less importance, as other hands improved in the business. And when Keimer paid my second quarter's wages, he let me know that he felt them too heavy, and thought I should make an abatement. He grew by degrees less civil, and put on more of the master, frequently found fault, and was captious and seemed ready for an outbreaking. I went on nevertheless with a good deal of patience, thinking that his incumbered circumstances were partly the cause.

At length a trifle snapped our contention. For a great noise happening near the courthouse, I put my head out of the window to see what was the matter. Keimer being in the street looked up and saw me, called out to me in a loud voice and angry tone to mind my business, adding some reproachful words that nettled me the more for their publicity; and all the neighbors who were looking out on the same occasion being witnesses to how I was treated. He came up immediately into the printing house, continued the quarrel, high words passed on both sides, he gave me the quarter's warning we had stipulated, expressing a wish that he had not obliged to so long a warning. I told him his wish was unnecessary for I would leave him that instant; and so taking my hat walked out of doors; desiring Meredith [a friend and coworker] whom I saw below to take care of some things I left, and bring them to my lodging.

Meredith came accordingly in the evening, when we talked my affair over. . . . He then let me know that his father had a high opinion of me, and from some discourse that had passed between them, he was sure he would advance money to set us up, if I would enter into partnership with him. My time, says he, will be out with Keimer in the spring. By that time we may have our press and types in from London. I am sensible I am no workman. If you like, your skill in the business be set against the stock I furnish, and we will share the profits equally. The proposal was agreeable, and I consented. . . .

But I. . . . remained idle a few days, when Keimer, on a prospect of being employed to print some paper money[26] in New Jersey, which would require various cuts and various types that I only could supply, and apprehending Bradford might engage me and get the job from him, sent me a very civil message, that old friends should not part for a few words, the effect of sudden passion, and wishing me to return. . . . So I returned, and we went on more smoothly than for some time before. The New Jersey job was obtained. I contrived a copper-plate press for it, the first that had been seen in the country. I cut several ornaments and checks for the bills. We went together to Burlington, where I executed the whole to satisfaction, and he re-

[26] Paper money did not function as legal tender currency, as it now does. It was issued more in the form of securities, backed by such things as real estate mortgages; as such, it had to be redeemed eventually with interest. But most colonies found it to be an essential supplement to scarce silver and gold.

ceived so large a sum for the work as to be enabled thereby to keep his head much longer above water. . . .

We had not long returned to Philadelphia, before the new types arrived from London. We settled with Keimer, and left him by his consent before he heard of it. We found a house to hire near the market, and took it. To lessen the rent (which was then but £24 a year tho' I have since known it let for 70) we took in Thomas Godfrey, a glazier, and his family, who were to pay a considerable part of it to us, and we to board with them.

We had scarce opened our letters and put our press in order, before George House, an acquaintance of mine, brought a countryman to us, whom he had met in the street inquiring for a printer. All our cash was now expended in the variety of particulars we had been obliged to procure and this countryman's five shillings being our first fruits, and coming so seasonably, gave me more pleasure than any crown I have since earned; and from the gratitude I felt toward House, has made me often more ready than perhaps I should otherwise have been to assist young beginners. . . .

Our first papers made quite a different appearance from any before in the province, a better type and better printed. But some spirited remarks of my writing on the dispute then going between the Governor Burnet and the Massachusetts Assembly, struck the principal people, occasioned the paper and the manager of it to be much talked of, and in a few weeks brought them all to be our subscribers. Their example was followed by many, and our number went on growing continually.

This was one of the first good effects of my having learned a little to scribble. Another was that the leading men, seeing a newspaper now in the hands of one who could also handle a pen, thought it convenient to oblige and encourage me. Bradford still printed the votes and laws and other public business. He had printed an address of the House to the Governor in a coarse blundering manner; we reprinted it elegantly and correctly, and sent one to every member. They were sensible of the difference, it strengthened the hands of our friends in the House, and they voted us their printers for the year ensuing. . . .

About this time there was a cry among the people for more paper money, only £15,000 being extant in the province and that soon to be sunk [redeemed with interest]. The wealthy inhabitants opposed any addition, being against all paper currency, from an apprehension that it would depreciate as it had done in New England to the prejudice of all creditors. We had discussed this point in our Junto [Franklin's discussion club], where I was on the side of an addition, being much persuaded that the first small sum struck in 1723 had done much good by increasing the trade, employment, and number of inhabitants in the province, since I now saw all the old houses inhabited, and many new ones building, where as I remembered well, that when I first walked about the streets of Philadelphia, eating my roll, I saw most of the houses in Walnut Street between Second and Front Streets with bills on their doors, to be let. . . . which made me then think the inhabitants of the city were one after another deserting it.

Our debates possessed me so fully of the subject, that I wrote and printed an anonymous pamphlet on it, entitled, *The Nature and Necessity of a Paper Currency*. It was well received by the common people in general; but the rich men disliked it, for it increased and strengthened the clamor for more money; and they having not writers among them that were able to answer it, their opposition slackened, and the point was carried by majority in the House. My friends there, who conceived I had been of some service, thought fit to reward me by employing me in printing the money, a very profitable job, and a great help to me. . . .

Having turned my thoughts to marriage, I looked round me, and made overtures of acquaintances in other places, but soon found that the business of a printer being generally thought a poor one, I was not to expect money with a wife unless with such a one as I should not otherwise think agreeable. In the meantime, that hard-to-be-governed passion of youth had hurried me frequently into intrigues with low women that fell in my way, which were attended with some expense and great inconvenience, besides a continual risk to my health by a distemper [syphilis] which of all things I dreaded, tho' by great good luck I escaped it. . . .

I pitied poor Miss Read's unfortunate situation, who was generally dejected, seldom cheerful, and avoided company. I considered my giddiness and inconstancy when in London as a great degree the cause of her unhappiness; though the mother was good enough to think the fault more her own than mine, as she had prevented our marrying before I went thither, and persuaded the other match in my absence. Our mutual affection was revived, but there were now great objections to our union. That match was indeed looked upon as invalid, a preceding wife being said to be living in England; but this could not be easily proved, because of the distance. . . . We ventured, however, over all these difficulties, and I took her to wife Sept. 1, 1730. . . .

And I now set on foot my first project of a public nature, that for a subscription library. I drew up the proposal, got them put into form by our great scrivener Brockden, and by the help of my friends in the Junto, procured fifty subscribers. . . . We afterwards obtained a charter, the company being increased to 100. This was the mother of all the North American subscription libraries now so numerous. It is become a great thing itself, and continually increasing. These libraries have improved the general conversation of the Americans, made the common tradesmen and farmers as intelligent as most gentlemen from other countries, and perhaps have contributed in some degree to the stand so generally made throughout the colonies in defense of their privileges. . . .

In 1732 I first printed my almanac, under the name of *Richard Saunders;* it was continued by me about 25 years, commonly called *Poor Richard's* almanac. I endeavored to make it both entertaining and useful, and it accordingly came to be in such demand that I reaped considerable profit from it, vending annually near ten thousand. . . .

After ten years' absence from Boston, and having become more easy in my circumstances, I made a journey thither to visit my relations, which I could not sooner well afford. In returning I called at Newport, to see my brother then settled there with his printing house. Our former differences were forgotten, and our meeting was very cordial and affectionate. He was fast declining in his health, and requested of me that in case of his death, which he apprehended not far distant, I would take home his son, then but ten years of age, and bring him up to the printing business. This I accordingly performed, sending him a few years to school before I took him into the office. . . .

In 1736 I lost one of my sons, a fine boy of four years old, by the small pox taken in the common way. I long regretted bitterly and still regret that I had not given it to him by inoculation; this I mention for the sake of parents, who omit that operation on the supposition that they should never forgive themselves if a child died under it. . . .

My first promotion was my being chosen in 1736 clerk of the General Assembly. The choice was made that year without opposition. . . . Besides the pay for immediate service as clerk, the place gave me a better opportunity of keeping up an interest among the members, which secured to me the business of printing the votes, laws, paper money, and other occasional jobs for the public, that on the whole were very profitable. . . .

In 1737, Col. Spotswood, late Governor of Virginia, and then Postmaster General, being dissatisfied with the conduct of his deputy at Philadelphia, respecting some negligence in rendering and inexactitude of his accounts, took from him the commission and offered it to me. I accepted it readily, and found it of great advantage; for tho' the salary was small, it facilitated the correspondence that improved my newspaper, increased the number demanded, as well as the advertisements to be inserted, so that it came to afford me a very considerable income. . . . I began now to turn my thoughts a little to public affairs. . . .

My business was now continually augmenting, and my circumstances growing daily, my newspaper having become very profitable, as being for a time the only one in this and the neighboring provinces. I experienced too the truth of the observation, that *after getting the first hundred pound, it is more easy to get the second:* money itself being of a prolific nature.

FRANKLIN GOT HIS hundred pounds—and the next, and the next. Indeed, rising on his quick wit, his remarkable luck, and his shrewd use of political connections, he became one of the wealthiest men in American history. But his story provides something more than the pleasure of watching his rise to riches and influence. It offers a social core sample, to borrow a term from geology: it reveals fascinating details about every level of society as he moved up through the strata. Life was not easy in the colonies; but there were opportunities, lands, and comforts unavailable to most Europeans. Franklin as everyman? Not quite—but he tells us a story that probably could not be told across the Atlantic.

———

VI

BY THE RIVERS OF BABYLON

AMERICAN CAPTIVITIES

18

RETURN TO ZION

In October 1703, three years before Benjamin Franklin's birth, a fascinating episode began in the city of Montreal. The Governor-General of New France, Pierre de Rigaud, the Marquis de Vaudreuil, called his military officers together and sketched out plans for a raid on Massachusetts. The mission would be significant enough in its own right: for one thing, it would renew hostilities with New England. But this attack also began a remarkable story, one that gives us a close look at the mingling cultures of the northern frontier and at a little-known commerce in slaves—Puritan slaves.

At the time, Vaudreuil's colony stood at the height of its power. Since 1680, it had waged a furious war against the once-invincible Iroquois. Tonty's account in chapter 15 describes how Five Nations warriors had challenged New France deep in the continent; with the Hurons destroyed, they raided far down the Great Lakes and the Ohio River, even into the Illinois country. Tonty also took part in the ferocious counterattack: the French not only reclaimed the old Huron domain, they swept the Iroquois out of the Ohio valley and launched a bold offensive into the heart of Seneca territory. They pushed the military frontier into the Five Nations homeland by planting forts on Lake Champlain, as well as on the southern shores of the Great Lakes, at Detroit and Niagara.

Though the Iroquois fought back, the introduction of regular army troops from Europe gave New France the advantage. During the 1690s, they burned Mohawk, Onondaga, and Oneida towns; and they recruited war parties from the western tribes of Ojibwa, Ottawa, and Potawatomi. By 1700, historian Ian Steele writes, the much-reduced Iroquois had lost perhaps half of their 2,150 warriors.

In July 1701, the envoys of the Five Nations made a sad trek to Montreal to negotiate a peace—a peace that could be little more than a surrender. They arrived at the greatest Indian diplomatic conference in American history: in addition to French and Iroquois representatives, more than a thousand members of thirty-one tribes allied to New France attended the meeting. The long warfare between Canada and the Iroquois came to an end; the new French forts would remain in place; and the Five Nations promised strict neutrality in the wars between the European colonies.

In many respects, the Iroquois came off quite well in the "Great Peace," as the settlement came to be known. For one thing, they retained their homeland (despite the encroaching forts around the periphery); for another, they were not forced to turn against their friends, the English. Unknown to the French, the Five Nations shrewdly cultivated the British by granting them sovereignty over the Great Lakes region—a district they had already lost in the war with New France. But neutrality would suit them well, keeping them out of the constant intercolonial wars and allowing them to turn their undivided attention to their Indian rivals to the south (especially the Cherokees and Catawbas).

But for all of the Five Nations' shrewdness and luck, New France unquestionably won a major victory in the Great Peace of 1701. First, they forever ended the attacks of their most determined foes—but left those foes in place as a buffer against the much more populous British colonies to the south. Indeed, complete annihilation of the Iroquois would have been a catastrophic blunder; it would have cleared the way for a sweeping advance of British settlement. Second, the French sealed an alliance with a vast network of western tribes (especially the Ojibwa, Illinois, Potawatomi, and Ottawa). These nations supplemented the colony's eastern Native American allies, particularly the Abenakis and the Huron community at Lorette (one of the last remnants of that lost nation).

The French also derived a tremendous benefit from one particular aspect of the Great Peace—a loophole, of sorts, that would attract the attention of Governor-General Vaudreuil in October 1703. The agreement on Five Nations neutrality did not apply to a group of Mohawks known as the Kahnawake.[1] The Kahnawake were just as ferocious as their Iroquois brothers—but they were firm allies of New France.

The origins of the Kahnawake can be found in 1667, when Jesuit missionaries began to make inroads among the Mohawks; they were aided by the sympathies of the numerous former Hurons who had been captured and adopted by the Iroquois. The priests established a mission, called La Prairie, on the southern banks of the St. Lawrence, across from Montreal. The location of the village was attractive: decades of war had prevented anyone from settling the region, leaving its soil rich and its wild game abundant. During years of truce, some Mohawks visited; some stayed. More came, and more stayed.

The community developed its own distinctive culture, mixing a cup of Catholicism with a gallon of traditional Iroquois ways. The purity of life taught by the Jesuits appealed to many Mohawks, who witnessed so much

[1] As with most names in colonial history, "Kahnawake" has multiple spellings. Ian K. Steele prefers "Caughnawaga," which is more accurate for the pronunciation of the last consonant. I choose to follow John Demos, author of *The Unredeemed Captive: A Family Story from Early America* (New York: Knopf, 1994). Demos's book is the single most important source for this chapter.

strife and destruction in the late 1600s. Historian John Demos writes that a saying grew up among them: "I am off to La Prairie," meaning the speaker had determined to give up alcohol and promiscuity (which was rarely accomplished beyond the watchful eyes of a priest). As the village grew larger, it moved to find untapped soil for its cornfields (in the traditional Iroquois manner); every ten years or so, it edged west, changing its name each time. One of those names stuck, and these people—the "French Mohawks" to New Englanders, and "our brethren at Canada" to mainstream Mohawks—named themselves after it: Kahnawake.

The Kahnawake provided Governor-General Vaudreuil with nagging problems. They embodied the inability of colonial governments to neatly define boundaries and zones of influence. Though the Kahnawake had left the English-friendly Five Nations behind, though they attended mass and lived in the shadow of Montreal, they maintained close ties to their Mohawk relatives to the south. Through them they conducted an illicit trade in furs with the English at Albany; since the French now controlled the beaver-rich west, only the Kahnawake could supply New York traders with pelts. This commerce, of course, was illegal, but the French government never figured out how to shut it down.

As Vaudreuil met with his military subordinates in October 1703, however, he set the problems with the Kahnawake aside and focused on their strengths. Together with the Hurons of Lorette and the Abenakis of St. Francis (another Jesuit mission), these Mohawks supplied New France with brave, experienced, Catholic warriors. They proved themselves essential in the fighting that raged along the colonial frontier—warfare marked not by conventional battles and sieges, but by daring raids on settlements and woodland ambushes of enemy detachments. And a fresh round of bloodshed had just erupted: encouraged by New France, Abenaki warriors had recently struck at towns in Maine and New Hampshire. British colonial forces (led by the aging Colonel Benjamin Church, of King Philip's War fame) counterattacked, burning several Abenaki villages. Now the Abenakis wanted revenge; the Hurons and Kahnawake wanted glory and booty; and the governor of New France knew just how to satisfy them all.

Vaudreuil decided to launch an attack on Deerfield, a small Massachusetts village on the Connecticut River, on what was then the New England frontier. The raiding party would consist of Hurons from Lorette, Abenakis from St. Francis, and Kahnawake Mohawks (perhaps 200 Indians in all), along with almost fifty French soldiers; it would be led by an enterprising young officer named Jean-Baptiste Hertel de Rouville.

We cannot be sure why Vaudreuil targeted Deerfield, but John Demos convincingly argues that he wanted his men to capture its most prominent resident: Rev. John Williams, one of the most important clergymen in Massachusetts. At the time, the Boston jail held a valuable French prisoner, a very effective privateer known as Captain Baptiste. Vaudreuil needed Baptiste to contest British control of colonial waters—and a captive Williams would make an ideal exchange.

In early 1704, the raiding party gathered for the long winter trek through the mountains to the distant village of Deerfield. The soldiers no doubt fretted about their mission: their assigned target, Rev. Williams, might not be present when they struck—or he might be killed in the attack. The Indian warriors, on the other hand, could hardly care less about European diplomacy and prisoner exchanges. They had plenty of other targets waiting for them in Deerfield: for them, this would be a slave raid, a mission to capture as many marketable English as possible. Some they might adopt into their own families (especially the children); others, particularly those with useful skills, they would sell to the Canadians. And down in Deerfield itself, Rev. Williams no doubt preached to his congregation the age-old sermon of New England Puritans, that they were the new nation of Israel. Little did he realize how right he was—for he and much of his flock would soon be carried into Babylonian captivity.

Into a Strange Land
by John Williams

On Tuesday, the 29th of February, 1703-4,[2] not long before the break of day, the enemy came in like a flood upon us, our watch being unfaithful. . . . They came to my house in the beginning of the onset, and by their violent endeavors to break open doors and windows with axes and hatchets, awaked me out of sleep; on which I leaped out of bed, and, running towards the door, perceived the enemy making their entrance into the house. I called to awaken two soldiers in the chamber, and returning toward my bedside for my arms, the enemy immediately broke into the room, I judge to the number of twenty, with painted faces and hideous acclamations.

I reached up my hands to the bedtester for my pistol, uttering a short petition to God for everlasting mercies for me and mine, on account of the merits of our glorified Redeemer; expecting a present passage through the valley of the shadow of death. . . . Taking down my pistol, I cocked it and put it to the breast of the first Indian who came up; but my pistol missing fire, I was seized by three Indians, who disarmed me, and bound me naked, as I was in my shirt, and so I stood for near the space of an hour. Binding me, they told me they would carry me to Quebec.

My pistol missing fire was the occasion of my life's being preserved; since which I have also found it profitable to be crossed in my own will. The

---

[2] By the modern calendar, this was 1704. Williams's odd rendering suggests that he is aware that the English were unusual in starting the new year on March 25.

judgment of God did not long slumber against one of the three which took me, who was a captain, for by sunrising he received a mortal shot from my next neighbor's house; who opposed so great a number of French and Indians as three hundred, and yet were no more than seven in an ungarrisoned house.

I cannot relate the distressing care I had for my dear wife, who had laid in [delivered] but a few weeks before; and for my poor children, family, and Christian neighbors. The enemy fell to rifling the house, and entered in great numbers into every room. . . . The enemies who entered the house were all of them Indians and Macquas [Mohawks], insulted over me a while, holding up hatchets over my head, threatening to burn all I had; but yet God, beyond expectation, made us in a great measure to be pitied, for though some were so cruel and barbarous as to take and carry to the door two of my children and murder them, as also a negro woman; yet they gave me liberty to put on my clothes, keeping me bound with a cord on one arm, till I put on my clothes to the other; and then changing my cord, they let me dress myself, and then pinioned me again. [They] gave liberty to my dear wife to dress herself and our remaining children.

About sun an hour high, we were all carried out of the house for a march, and saw many of the houses of my neighbors in flames, perceiving the whole fort [village], one house excepted, to be taken. Who can tell what sorrows pierced our souls, when we saw ourselves carried away from God's sanctuary, to go into a strange land, exposed to so many trials; the journey being at least three hundred miles we were to travel; the snow up to the knees, and we never inured to such hardships and fatigues; the place we were being carried to, a Popish country.

Upon my parting from the town, they fired my house and barn. We were carried over the river, to the foot of the mountain, about a mile from my house, where we found a great number of our Christian neighbors, men, women, and children, to the number of an hundred. . . . When we came to the foot of the mountain, they took away our shoes, and gave us in the room of them Indian shoes, to prepare us for our travel.

Whilst we were there, the English beat out a company that remained in the town, and pursued them to the river, killing and wounding many of them, but the body of the army being alarmed, they repulsed those few English that pursued them. I am not able to give you an account of the number of the enemy slain, but I observed after this fight no great, insulting mirth, as I expected; and saw many wounded persons, and for several days together they buried of their party, and one of the chief note among the Macquas. The Governor of Canada [later] told me his army had that success with the loss of but eleven men: three Frenchmen, one of which was the lieutenant of the army, five Macquas, and three Indians. But after my arrival at Quebec, I spake with an Englishman who was taken in the last war, and of their religion; who told me, they lost above forty, and that many were wounded. . . .

After this, we went up to the mountain, and saw the smoke of the fires in the town, and beheld the awful desolations of Deerfield. And before we marched any farther, they killed a sucking child belonging to one of the English.[3] There were slain by the enemy of the inhabitants of Deerfield, to the number of thirty-eight, besides nine of the neighboring towns. We travelled not far the first day; God made the heathen so as to pity our children, that though they had several wounded persons of their own to carry upon their shoulders, for thirty miles, before they came to the river,[4] yet they carried our children, incapable of travelling, in their arms, and upon their shoulders.

When we came to our first lodging place, the first night, they dug away the snow, and made some wigwams, cut down small branches of the spruce-tree to lie down on, and gave the prisoners somewhat to eat; but we had but little appetite. I was pinioned and bound down that night, and so I was every night whilst I was with the army. Some of the enemy who brought drink with them from the town fell to drinking, and in their drunken fit they killed my negro man, the only dead person I either saw at the town, or in the way.

In the night an Englishman made his escape; in the morning (March 1), I was called for, and ordered by the general to tell the English that if any more made their escape, they would burn the rest of the prisoners. He that took me was unwilling to let me speak with any of the prisoners, as we marched; but on the morning of the second day, he being appointed to guard the rear, I was put into the hands of my other master, who permitted me to speak to my wife, when I overtook her, and to walk with her to help her in her journey. . . .

My wife told me her strength of body began to fail, and that I must expect to part with her; saying, she hoped God would preserve my life, and the life of some, if not of all our children with us; and commended me, under God, the care of them. . . . We soon made a halt, in which time my chief surviving master [captor] came up, upon which I was put upon marching with the foremost, and so made my last farewell of my dear wife, the desire of my eyes, and companion in many mercies and afflictions. Upon our separation from each other, we asked for each other grace sufficient for what God should call us to. . . .

I was made to wade over a small river, and so were all the English, the water above knee deep, the stream very swift; and after that to travel up a small mountain; my strength was almost spent, before I came to the top of

[3] Infants were often murdered by raiding parties, who feared the children's cries might alert any enemies who followed them. And as Williams notes, the counterattack cost the French and Indians dearly, making them worry about pursuit.

[4] This was the Connecticut River. Even though Deerfield was situated on the west bank of the Connecticut, the raiding party swung west for some distance before returning to the river's banks on its journey north.

it. No sooner had I overcome the difficulty of that ascent, but I was permitted to sit down, and be unburdened of my pack. I sat pitying those who were behind, and entreated my master to let me go down and help my wife; but he refused, and would not let me stir from him. I asked each of the prisoners (as they passed by me) after her, and heard that, passing through the above-said river, she fell down, and was plunged over head and ears into the water; after which she travelled not far, for at the foot of that mountain, the cruel and bloodthirsty savage who took her slew her with his hatchet at one stroke, the tidings of which were very awful.

And yet such was the hard-heartedness of the adversary, that my tears were reckoned to me as a reproach. My loss and the loss of my children was great; our hearts were so filled with sorrow, that nothing but the comfortable hopes of her being taken away, in mercy to herself, from the evils we were to see, feel, and suffer under. . . . could have kept us from sinking under at that time. . . . We were again called upon to march, with a far heavier burden on my spirits than on my back. . . .

In our march they killed a sucking infant of one of my neighbors; and before night a girl of about eleven years of age. . . . When we came to our lodging place, an Indian captain from the eastward [a Huron from Lorette] spake to my master about killing me, and taking off my scalp. I lifted up my heart to God, to implore his grace and mercy in such a time of need; and afterwards I told my master, if he intended to kill me, I desired he would let me know of it; assuring him that my death, after a promise of quarter, would bring the guilt of blood upon him. He told me he would not kill me. We laid down and slept, for God sustained and kept us.[5]

In the morning (March 2), we were all called before the chief sachems of the Macquas and Indians, that a more equal distribution might be made of the prisoners among them. At my going from the wigwam, my best clothing was taken from me. As I came nigh the place appointed, some of the captives met me, and told me they thought the enemies were going to burn some of us, for they had peeled off the bark from several trees, and acted very strangely.[6] To whom I replied, they could act nothing against us, but as they were permitted of God, and I was persuaded he would prevent such severities. When we came to the wigwam appointed, several of the captives were taken from their former masters, and put into the hands of others; but I was sent again to my two masters who brought me from my house.

[5] Demos writes that relatives of the Huron chief who had died at Deerfield wanted to commit a revenge killing—to murder a captive of equal rank. These warriors went to Williams's captor, a noted chief named Thaovenhosen, and demanded that the minister be the selected victim.

[6] At this meeting, the demand for Williams's death by the Hurons came to a head. Thaovenhosen then made an eloquent speech, declaring that he, too, was related to the dead chief, laying claim to (a living) Williams as his own compensation for the death.

In the fourth day's march (Friday, March 3), the enemy killed another of my neighbors, who, being near the time of travail, was wearied with her journey. When we came to the great river [the Connecticut], the enemy took sleighs to draw their wounded, several of our children, and their packs, and marched a great pace. I traveled many hours in water up to the ankles. . . .

On Saturday (March 4), the journey was long and tedious; we travelled with such speed that four women were tired, and then slain by them who led them captive. On the Sabbath day (March 5), we rested, and I was permitted to pray, and to preach to the captives. . . .

The next day (Wednesday, March 8), we were made to scatter one from another into smaller companies; and one of my children was carried with Indians belonging to the eastern parts. At night my master came to me, with my pistol in his hand, and put it to my breast, and said, "Now I will kill you, for," he said, "you would have killed me with it if you could." But by the grace of God, I was not much daunted, and whatever his intention might be, God prevented my death.

The next day (Thursday, March 9), I was again permitted to pray with that company of captives with me, and we were allowed to sing a psalm together. After which, I was taken from all the company of the English, excepting two children of my neighbors, one of which, a girl of four years of age, was killed by her Macqua master the next morning (Friday, March 10); the snow being so deep when we left the river, that he could not carry the child and his pack too. . . .

My youngest daughter, aged seven years, was carried all the journey, and looked after with a great deal of tenderness. My youngest son, aged four years, was wonderfully preserved from death; for though they that carried him or drawed him on sleighs were tired with their journeys, yet their savage, cruel tempers were so overruled by God that they did not kill him, but in their pity he was spared, and others would take care of him; so that four times on the journey he was thus preserved, till at last he arrived in Montreal, where a French gentleman, pitying the child, redeemed it out of the hands of the heathen.

My son Samuel and my eldest daughter were pitied so as to be drawn on sleighs when unable to travel; and though they suffered very much through scarcity of food and tedious journeys, they were carried through to Montreal. And my son Stephen, about eleven years of age, wonderfully preserved from death in the famine whereof three English persons died, and after eight months brought into Chambly.[7]

My master returned on the evening of the Sabbath (March 12), and told me he had killed five moose. The next day (Monday, March 13), we were removed to the place where he killed them. We tarried there three days,

[7] Chambly was a fortified village on the Richelieu River east of Montreal.

till we had roasted and dried the meat. My master made me a pair of snow-shoes; "For," said he, "you cannot possibly travel without, the snow being knee-deep." We parted from thence heavy laden. I travelled, with a burden on my back, with snow-shoes, twenty-five miles the first day of wearing them; and again the next day till afternoon, and then we came to the French river [the Winooski, above Lake Champlain].

My master at this place took away my pack, and drew the whole load on the ice; but my bones seemed to be misplaced, and I was unable to travel with any speed. My feet were very sore, and each night I wrung blood out of my stockings when I pulled them off. My shins also were very sore, being cut with crusty snow in time of my travelling without snow-shoes. But finding some dry oak leaves by the river banks, I put them to my shins, and in once applying them they were healed. And here my master was very kind to me—would always give me the best he had to eat. . . . My master also gave me a piece of a Bible; never disturbed me in reading the scriptures, or in praying to God.

My march on the French river was very sore, for, fearing a thaw, we travelled a very great pace. My feet were so bruised, and my joints so distorted by my travelling in snow-shoes, that I thought it impossible to hold out. One morning a little before break of day my master came and awaked me out of sleep, saying, "Arise, pray to God, and eat your breakfast, for we must go a great way today." After prayer, I arose from my knees, but my feet were so tender, swollen, bruised, and full of pain, that I could scarce stand upon them without holding by the wigwam. And when the Indians said, "You must run today," I answered that I could not run. My master pointed out his hatchet, and said to me, "Then I must dash out your brains and take off your scalp." I said, "I suppose, then, you will do so, for I am not able to travel with speed."

He sent me away alone, on the ice. About sun half an hour high he overtook me, for I had gone very slowly, not thinking it possible to travel five miles. When he came up, he called me to run; I told him I could go no faster. He passed by without saying one word more; so that sometimes I scarce saw anything of him for an hour together. I travelled from about break of day till dark, never so much as sat down at noon to eat warm victuals—eating frozen meat, which I had in my coat pocket, as I travelled. We went that day two of their days' journey as they came down. I judge we went forty or forty-five miles that day. . . .

Once we entered the lake [Champlain], the ice was rough and uneven, which was very grevious to my feet, that could scarce bear to be set down on the smooth ice on the river. . . .

We went a day's journey from the lake, to a small company of Indians who were hunting. . . . After our stay there, and undergoing difficulties in cutting wood, and suffering by lousiness [lice], having lousy old clothes of soldiers put upon me when they stripped me of mine, to sell to the French soldiers in the army, we again began a march for Chambly. . . . After another day's travel, we came to a river [the Richelieu] where the ice was thawed. We made a canoe of elm bark in one day; and arrived on a Saturday [April 15] near noon at Chambly, a small village where is a garrison and fort of French soldiers.

AT CHAMBLY

This village is about fifteen miles [east] from Montreal. The French were very kind to me. A gentleman of the place took me into his house and to his table, and lodged me at night on a good feather-bed. The inhabitants and officers were very obliging to me the little time I stayed with them, and promised to write a letter to the Governor-in-Chief to inform him of my passing down the river. Here I saw a girl taken from our town, and a young man, who informed me that the greatest part of the captives were come in, and that two of my children were at Montreal; that many of the captives had been in, three weeks before my arrival. . . .

As we passed along the river towards Sorel [a town on the St. Lawrence], we went into a house where was an English woman of our town, who had been left among the French in order to [speed] her conveyance to the Indian fort. The French were very kind to her and myself, and gave us the best provision they had; and she embarked with us to go down to St. Francis fort. . . .

When we came to the St. Francis River we found some difficulty by reason of the ice. . . . The next morning we met with such a great quantity of ice, that we were forced to leave our canoe and travel on land. We went to a French officer's house, who took us into a private room, out of the sight of the Indians, and treated us very courteously. That night we arrived at the fort called St. Francis; where we found several poor [English] children who had been taken from the eastward the summer before; a sight very affecting, they being in habit much like Indians, and in manners very much symbolizing with them.

At this fort lived two Jesuits, one of which was made Superior of the Jesuits at Quebec. One of these Jesuits met me at the fort gate, and asked me to go into the church and give God thanks for preserving my life. I told him I would do that in some other place. When the bell rang for evening prayers, he that took me bid me go, but I refused. The Jesuit came to our wigwam and prayed a short prayer, and invited me to sup with them, and justified the Indians in what they did against us, rehearsing some things done by [the English] Major Walden above thirty years ago, and how justly God retaliated them in the last war, and inveighed against us for beginning this war with the Indians, and said we had before the last winter and in the winter before been very barbarous and cruel in burning and killing Indians.

I told them that the Indians, in a very perfidious manner, had committed murders on many of our inhabitants after signing articles of peace; and as to what they spake of cruelties, they were undoubtedly falsehoods, for I well knew the English were not approvers of any inhumanity or barbarity towards enemies. . . .

The next morning the bell rang for mass. My master bid me go to church. I refused. He threatened me, and went away in a rage. At noon the Jesuit sent for me to dine with them, for I ate at their table all the time I was at the fort; and after dinner they told me the Indians would not allow any of their captives staying in their wigwams whilst they were at church, and were resolved by force and violence to bring us all to church if we would not go without.

I told them it was highly unreasonable to impose upon those who were of a contrary religion, and to force us to be present at such a service as we abhorred, was nothing becoming Christianity. They replied, they were savages, and would not hearken to reason, but would have their wills. Said also, if they were in New England themselves, they would go into their churches and see their ways of worship. . . .

The next mass, my master bid me go to church. I objected; he rose and forcibly pulled me by my head and shoulders out of the wigwam to the church, which was nigh the door. So I went in and sat down behind the door; and there saw a great confusion, instead of any Gospel order. For one of the Jesuits was at the altar saying mass in a tongue unknown to the savages, and the other, between the altar and the door, saying and singing prayers among the Indians at the same time. . . . At our going out we smiled at their devotion so managed, which was offensive to them, for they said we made a derision of their worship. . . .

After a few days the Governor de Vaudreuil, Governor-in-Chief, sent down two men with letters to the Jesuits, desiring them to order my being sent up to him at Montreal, upon which one of the Jesuits went with my two masters, and took me along with them, as also two more from Deerfield, a man and his daughter about seven years of age. . . .

AT MONTREAL

When I came to Montreal, which was eight weeks after my captivity, the Governor, de Vaudreuil, redeemed me out of the hands of the Indians, gave me good clothing, took me to his table, gave me the use of a very good chamber; and was, in all respects relating to my outward man, courteous and charitable to admiration. At my first entering his house, he sent for my two children who were in the city, that I might see them; and promised to do what he could to get all my children and neighbors out of the hands of the savages. My change of diet, after the difficulties of my journeys, caused an alteration in my body: I was physicked, and blooded [bled], and very tenderly taken care of in my sickness.

The Governor redeemed my eldest daughter out of the hands of the Indians; and she was carefully tended in the hospital, until she was well of her lameness; and by the Governor provided for respectfully, during her stay in the country. My youngest child was redeemed by a gentlewoman in the city, as the Indians passed by. After the Indians had been at their fort, and discoursed with the priests, they came back and offered to the gentlewoman a man for the child, alleging that the child could not be profitable to her, but the man would, for he was a weaver, and his service would much advance the design she had of making cloth; but God overruled so far, that this temptation to the woman prevailed not for an exchange. . . .[8]

The Governor gave orders to certain officers to get the rest of my children out of the hands of the Indians, and as many of my neighbors as they could. After six weeks, a merchant of the city obtained my eldest son, that was taken, to live with him. He took a great deal of pains to persuade the savages to part with him. An Indian . . . from Cowass brought word of my son Stephen's being near that place; some money was put into his hands for his redemption. . . . But the Indian proved unfaithful, and I never saw my child till a year after.

The Governor ordered a priest to go along with me to see my youngest daughter [Eunice] among the Macquas [the Kahnawake Mohawks], and endeavor for her ransom. I went with him; he was very courteous to me, and from his parish, which was near the Macqua fort, he wrote a letter to the Jesuit, to desire him to send my child to see me, and to speak with them that took her to come also. But the Jesuit wrote back a letter, that I should not be permitted to speak with or see my child, and if I came my labor would be lost; and that the Macquas would as soon part with their hearts as my child.

At my return to the city, I with a heavy heart carried the Jesuit's letter to the Governor, who, when he read it, was very angry, and endeavored to comfort me, assuring me that I should see her, and speak with her. . . . After some days, he went with me in his own person to the fort. When we came thither, he discoursed with the Jesuits. After which my child was brought to the chamber where I was. I was told I might speak with her, but should not be permitted to speak to any other English person there.

My child was about seven years old; I discoursed with her near an hour; she could read very well, and had not forgotten her catechism; and was very desirous to be redeemed out of the hands of the Macquas. . . . I told her, she must pray to God for his grace every day. She said, she did as she was able, and God helped her. "But," says she, "they force me to say some prayers in Latin, and I don't understand one word of them; I hope it won't

[8] This incident reveals the extent of the trade in captives from New England; the offer was a serious one, and the woman no doubt seriously considered it.

do me any harm." I told her she must be careful she did not forget her catechism and the scriptures she had learnt by heart. . . . I saw her once a few days after in the city, but had not many minutes of time with her; what time I had I improved to give her the best advice I could.

The governor labored much for her redemption. At last he had the promise of it, in case he would procure for them an Indian girl in her stead. Accordingly, he sent up the river some hundred of leagues for one, and when offered by the Governor it was refused. He offered them an hundred pieces of eight for her redemption, but it was refused. His lady went over to have begged her from them, but all in vain. She is there still, and has forgotten to speak English. . . .

After my return to the city, I was very melancholy, for I could not be permitted to so much as pray with the English who dwelt in the same house; and the English who came to see me were most of them put back by the guard at the door, and not suffered to come and speak with me. Sometimes the guard was so strict, that I could scarce go aside on necessary occasions without a repulse; and whenever I went out into the city (a favor the Governor never refused when I asked it of him) there were spies to watch me and observe whether I spake to the English. . . .

At my first coming to Montreal, the Governor told me I should be sent home as soon as Captain Baptiste was returned, and not before; and that I was taken in order to [secure] his redemption. The Governor sought by all means to divert me from my melancholy sorrows, and always showed a willingness for my seeing my children. . . . But within a little time I had orders to go down to Quebec. . . .

[Before leaving], the Superior of the priests said to me, "Do not flatter yourself in hopes of a short captivity, for," said he, "there are two young princes contending for the kingdom of Spain"; and for a third, that care was taken of his establishment on the English throne.[9] And [he] boasted what they would do in Europe; and that we must expect, not only in Europe, but in New England, the establishment of Popery.

I said, "Glory not; God can make great changes in a little time, and revive his own interest, and yet save his poor, afflicted people." Said he, "The time for miracles is past; and in the time of the last war the King of France was as it were against all the world, and yet did very great things. But now the kingdom of Spain is for him, and the Duke of Bavaria, and the Duke of Savoy," etc.; and spake in a lofty manner of great things to be done by them, and having the world, as I may say, in subjection to them.

[9] A reference to the War of the Spanish Succession. War had begun in North America (called by the English colonists Queen Anne's War), independent of events in Europe. But Britain was now caught up in a massive struggle to stop Louis XIV from putting his grandson on the throne of Spain, where the king had died without an heir. Also, the French tried to put the Catholic Stuarts back in power in England. The wars in Europe and North America were related, but not one and the same.

I was sent down to Quebec in company with Governor [Claude] de Ramezay, Governor of Montreal, and the Superior of the Jesuits, and ordered to live with one of the Council; from whom I received many favors, for seven weeks. He told me it was the priests' doing to send me down before the Governor came down; and that if I went much to see the English, or they came much to visit me, I should yet certainly be sent away, where I should have no conversation with the English.

AT QUEBEC

After coming down to Quebec, I was invited to dine with the Jesuits; and to my face they were civil enough. . . . From this day forward God gave them to hear sorrowful tidings from Europe;[10] that a war had been commenced against the Duke of Savoy [a French ally], and so their enemies increased; that their bishop was taken, and two millions of wealth with him. News every year more distressing and impoverishing to them; and the Duke of Bavaria so far from being Emperor that he was dispossessed of his dukedom; and France so far from being strengthened by Spain, that the kingdom of Spain was like to be an occasioning of weakening and impoverishing their own kingdom; they themselves so reporting.

And their great army going against New England turned back ashamed; and they were discouraged and disheartened, and every year very exercising fears and cares as to the savages who lived up the river. Before the return of that army, they told me we were [to be] led up and down and sold by the heathen as sheep for the slaughter, and they could not devise what they should do with us, we should be so many prisoners when the army returned. . . .

On the 21st of October, 1704, I received some letters from New England, with an account that many of our neighbors escaped out of the desolations in the fort, and that my dear wife was decently buried, and that my eldest son, who was absent in our desolation, was sent to college and provided for; which occasioned thanksgiving to God in the midst of our afflictions, and caused prayers even in Canada to be going daily up to heaven for a blessing on our benefactors showing such kindness to the desolate and afflicted. . . .

Not long after came Captain [John] Livingston and Mr. [John] Sheldon, with letters from his excellency our Governor [Joseph Dudley, governor of Massachusetts] to the Governor of Canada, about the exchange of prisoners, which gave a revival to many and raised expectation of a return.

[10] Under the leadership of Britain's highly skilled general, the Duke of Marlborough, the anti-French alliance won a series of striking victories in the Low Countries and against Bavaria, which was allied to France.

These visits from New England to Canada so often greatly strengthened many who were ready to faint, and gave some check to the designs of the Papists to gain proselytes. But God's time of deliverance was not yet come. . . .

I implored Captain de Beauville, who had always been very friendly, to intercede with the Governor for the return of my eldest daughter, and for his purchasing my son Stephen from the Indians at St. Francis Fort, and for liberty to go and see my children and neighbors at Montreal. Divine Providence appeared to the moderating of my afflictions, in that five English persons of our town were permitted to return with Captain Livingston, among whom were my eldest daughter. And my son Stephen was redeemed and sent to live with me. He was almost quite naked, and very poor. He had suffered very much among the Indians. . . .

In August, Mr. [William] Dudley and Captain [Samuel] Vetch arrived, and great encouragements were given as to an exchange in the spring of the year; and some few again were sent home, amongst whom I obtained leave to send my son Stephen. . . . The priests, after Mr. Dudley's going from Canada, were ready to think their time was short for gaining English proselytes, and doubled their vigilance and wiles to gain over persons to their persuasion. . . .

We were almost out of hopes of being returned before winter, the season proving so cold the latter end of September, and were praying to God to prepare our hearts with an holy submission to his holy will, to glorify his holy name in a way of passive obedience, in the winter. . . . In the beginning of last June, the Superior of the priests came to the parish where I was, and told me he saw I wanted my friend, Captain de Beauville, and that I was ragged. But, says he, "Your obstinacy against our religion discourages us from providing better clothes." I told him, "It was better going in a ragged coat, than with a ragged conscience." . . .

When they were promising themselves another winter to draw away the English to Popery, news came that an English brigantine was coming, and that the honorable Capt. Samuel Appleton, Esq., was coming [as] ambassador, to fetch off the captives, and Capt. John Bonner was with him. I cannot tell you how the clergy and others labored to stop many of the prisoners. To some liberty, to some money, and yearly pensions were offered, if they would stay. . . .

We have reason to bless God, who has wrought deliverance for so many; and yet pray to God for a door of escape to be opened for the great number yet behind, not much short of an hundred; many of which are children, and of these not a few among the savages, and having forgot the English tongue, will be lost, and turn savages in a little time, unless something extraordinary prevent. . . .

We came away from Quebec, October 25, [1706]; and by contrary winds, and a great storm, we were retarded, and then driven back nigh the city, and had a great deliverance from a shipwreck, the vessel striking twice upon a rock in that storm. But through God's goodness, we all arrived in safety at Boston, November 21; the number of captives, fifty-seven, two of which were my children. I have yet a daughter of ten years of age, and many neighbors, whose case bespeaks your compassion and prayers to God, to gather them, being outcasts ready to perish.

At our arrival at Boston, we found the kindness of the Lord in a wonderful manner, in opening the hearts of many to bless God and for us; wonderfully to give us supplies in our needy state. We are under obligation to praise God.

———

AS WILLIAMS RETURNED to the land he called Zion, his fellow colonists plotted their revenge for the destruction of Deerfield. As the Jesuits told him, a massive war wracked the states of Europe; under the Duke of Marlborough, British and allied troops performed remarkable feats of arms, forcing the aging King Louis XIV onto the defensive. But here in North America, the hostilities had a life of their own, as French, New Englanders, and Indians angled for advantage.

The colonists' main target was Port Royal, the most important town of Acadia (modern-day Nova Scotia). In 1707 Massachusetts launched two separate attacks, but failed to capture it. They appealed to London for assistance, but the far more intense warfare on the continent demanded all of Britain's military resources. Finally, in 1710, a squadron of the Royal Navy captured Port Royal, and with it most of Acadia.

By now the colonists had convinced Queen Anne's government that Quebec itself had to fall. In 1711, London dispatched a mighty fleet—forty-six ships with over 5,000 troops—to sail up the St. Lawrence, in coordination with a column of more than 2,000 militia that ascended the Lake Champlain corridor from New York. This was precisely the sort of war that Governor-General Vaudreuil could not win: a battle of numbers and equipment, fought by conventional forces. He could do little against this massive force but pray for a miracle.

A miracle is exactly what happened next. As the mighty British fleet sailed into the Canadian river, heavy fog and a succession of storms left nine ships smashed on the rocks, killing almost a thousand men. The fleet pulled back. New France was saved.

In 1713, the Peace of Utrecht settled both the War of the Spanish Succession and the largely unrelated conflict across the Atlantic. The French gave up Newfoundland and well-populated Acadia—now renamed Nova Scotia—though they kept Cape Breton Island, where, in 1720, they began to build a powerful naval base named Louisburg.[11] But in Europe, the aged

———

[11] The British allowed the Acadians to remain, though they refused to swear loyalty to their new masters. Finally, in 1755, the British deported the Acadians en masse; many ended up in French Louisiana—where Acadians became Cajuns.

Louis XIV won the essential point: his grandson would rule Spain. As Ian Steele writes, "New France paid Louis XIV's debts at the bargaining table in Utrecht." Two years later, the great king died.

Meanwhile, other changes swept America. Real peace between New France and New England finally arrived—and it would stay, for the most part, until King George's War in 1744 (though numerous bloody skirmishes and troubles would dog the intervening years). The way was clear on both sides for the sort of internal growth described by Franklin in the last chapter. Indian relations shifted decisively as well. When the Carolinians defeated the Tuscarora in 1713, the remnants of that tribe migrated to the upper reaches of the Delaware River, where they joined the Iroquois. From now on, the Five Nations would be the Six Nations.

As for John Williams, his daughter Eunice never returned from captivity. She never wanted to: born to Puritan parents, she became a Catholic and a Mohawk, unable to speak English any longer. She became known as A'ongote, an accepted part of the ethnic and cultural stew that was Kahnawake. For her, Kahnawake *was* Zion.[12]

---

[12] Eunice Williams—now A'ongote, meaning "she has been planted as a person"—married a Kahnawake warrior named Arosen and had at least three children. Her father John Williams died in 1729. Her brother Stephen tried repeatedly to convince her to return; finally, in 1740, she journeyed south for a reunion. She paid four visits to her New England family, the last in 1761, but she refused to stay. As a devout Catholic, she reportedly feared for her soul if she moved back to Protestant New England—and she could no longer speak English. Stephen died at age 89 in 1782; Eunice died in 1785, also 89 years old.

19

DIASPORA

Young Eunice Williams found herself carried off as a prisoner to Kahnawake—but in Kahnawake, she found love, acceptance, and freedom. She
had endured a harrowing capture and a vicious journey to Canada (a journey that killed many, including her own mother); once there, her masters
took away her language, religion, even her name. But in her new identity
as A'ongote, Mohawk woman, she became a full member of her captors'
community.

We know what her father thought of all this: John Williams could not
grasp that her acceptance of her new homeland brought her full release from
bondage. He would always think of her as an "outcast ready to perish."
Sadly, the trek to Kahnawake killed another person who might have provided
a more interesting perspective on Eunice's fate. He certainly would have seen
things rather differently from Eunice's father; he might even have given John
Williams pause before denouncing the Indians and declaring, "The English
were not approvers of any inhumanity." This person was, of course, John
Williams's unnamed "negro man."

Captivity and slavery, as we have seen, marked virtually all of the cultures of North America: Carolinians bought Indian slaves from Indian allies;
Pilgrims and Puritans sold their prisoners of war; Mohawks and Abenakis
plundered the towns of New England for captives, to be marketed in
Canada. But this commerce paled before a far larger, far more robust traffic
in human beings: the African slave trade. In the late seventeenth century, the
massive importation of captive Africans, bought and sold as human chattel,
drastically shifted colonial demographics. It introduced a new race of people
who, unlike all the other North American captives, existed purely as a slave
labor force. It created a hereditary class of people in bondage, something
unknown on the continent before that time.

For generations, historians have wrestled with the question of how this
distinctive, terrible trade came about. They have uncovered thousands of details, leading to a thousand disputes—but the basic outlines can be sketched
without debate. In the 1600s, African slavery gradually spread northward
from Brazil, where the Portuguese introduced it to replace their earlier reliance on captive Indians (who could easily escape to friendly peoples in the

wilderness beyond the European settlements). The Dutch emerged as the pioneering middlemen in this grim commerce; as we saw in the chapter on New Netherlands, they handled much of the early intercolonial and transatlantic trade. In the 1630s, they extended generous terms and credit to the English colonies in the West Indies, such as Barbados. Within the span of a decade, Africans became the basis of the islands' labor force.

In the 1660s, the Barbados system of African slavery spread to South Carolina, carried by the many immigrants from the island. It took particularly strong root after the introduction of rice as a cash crop; many of the captive Africans already knew how to cultivate the plant, which brought large profits as an export commodity. Slaves soon outnumbered Europeans in the young colony.

The Carolina example (following the Barbados example, following the Brazil example) found a receptive audience in Virginia in the 1680s. The cavaliers of Virginia had been hesitant to buy many Africans, at first because indentured servants were cheaper, then because the Navigation Acts excluded the slave-trading Dutch. But the bloody events of Bacon's Rebellion made believers out of the great tobacco planters. In a relatively brief span of time, Africans replaced indentured servants. Almost as swiftly, the colony's government clarified their legal status: they would be permanent, hereditary slaves.

Olaudah Equiano was one young man who found himself carried from Africa to Virginia. His journey would be far longer, far harder, and far more lasting than the one endured by John Williams and his family. It began deep in Africa, where the farthest tendrils of this intercontinental trade in human beings reached his inland village. It carried him across the landscape, as he was sold by one master to another. It threw him into European hands, and onto a European ship. It landed him in a slave market in the West Indies, and finally on a tobacco plantation in North America. There is little more that need be said about Equiano's account: it is both accurate enough and moving enough on its own.

Slavery
by Olaudah Equiano

That part of Africa, known by the name of Guinea, to which the trade for slaves is carried on, extends along the coast about 3,400 miles, from Senegal to Angola, and includes a variety of kingdoms. Of these the most considerable is the kingdom of Benin, both as to extent and wealth, the richness and cultivation of the soil, the power of its king, and the number and wealth of the inhabitants. It is situated nearly under the [equator] line, and extends along the coast about 170 miles, but runs back into the interior part of Africa to a distance hitherto I believe unexplored by any traveler; and seems only terminated at length by the empire of Abyssinia, nearly 1,500 miles from its beginning.

The kingdom is divided into many provinces or districts; in one of the most remote and fertile of which I was born, in the year 1745, in a charming fruitful vale named Essaka. The distance of this province from the capital of Benin and the sea coast must be very considerable, for I had never heard of white men or Europeans, nor of the sea; and our subjection to the king of Benin was little more than nominal, for every transaction of the government, as far as my slender observation extended, was conducted by the chiefs or elders of the place.

My father was one of those elders or chiefs I have spoken of, and was styled Embrenché; a term, as I remember, importing the highest distinction, and signifying in our language a mark of grandeur. This mark is conferred on the person entitled to it by cutting the skin across the top of the forehead, and drawing it down to the eyebrows; and, while it is in this situation, applying a warm hand and rubbing it until it shrinks up into a thick weal across the lower part of the forehead. Most of the judges and senators were thus marked. My father had long borne it; I had seen it conferred on one of my brothers; and I was also destined to receive it by my parents.

These Embrenché, or chief men, decided disputes and punished crimes; for which purpose they always assembled together. The proceedings were generally short; and in most cases the law of retaliation prevailed. . . .

We are almost a nation of dancers, musicians, and poets. Thus every great event, such as a triumphant return from battle, or other cause of public rejoicing, is celebrated in public dances, which are accompanied with songs and music suited to the occasion. The assembly is separated into four divisions, which dance either apart or in succession, and each with a character peculiar to itself. The first division contains the married men, who in their dances frequently exhibit feats of arms, and the representation of a battle. To these succeed the married women, who dance in the second division. The young men occupy the third; and the maidens the fourth. Each represents some interesting scene of real life, such as a great achievement, domestic employment, a pathetic story, or some rural sport. . . .

Our land is uncommonly rich and fruitful, and produces all kinds of vegetables in great abundance. . . . All our industry is exerted to improve those blessings of nature. Agriculture is our chief employment; and everyone, even the children and women, are engaged in it. Thus we are all habituated to labor from our earliest years. . . .

Our tillage is in a large plain or common, some hours walk from our dwellings, and all the neighbors resort thither as a body. . . . This common is oftimes the theater of war, and therefore when our people go out to till their land, they not only go in a body, but generally take their arms with them, for fear of surprise. And when they apprehend an invasion they guard the avenues to their dwellings by driving sticks into the ground, which are so sharp as to pierce the foot, and generally are dipped in poison.

From what I can recollect of these battles, they appear to have been the eruptions of one little state or district on the other, to obtain prisoners or booty. Perhaps they were incited to this by those traders who brought the European goods I mentioned amongst us. Such mode of obtaining slaves in Africa is common, and I believe more are procured this way, and by kidnapping, than any other. When a trader wants slaves, he applies to a chief for them, and tempts him with his wares. It is not extraordinary, if on this occasion he yields to the temptation with as little firmness, and accepts the price of his fellow creature's liberty with as little reluctance, as the enlightened merchant. Accordingly, he falls on his neighbors, and a desperate battle ensues. If he prevails, and takes prisoners, he gratifies his avarice by selling them. . . .

We have firearms, bows and arrows, broad two-edged swords and javelins; we have shields also, which cover a man from head to foot. All are taught the use of weapons. Even our women are warriors, and march boldly out to fight along with the men. Our whole district is a kind of militia; on a certain signal given, such as the firing of a gun at night, they all rise in arms and rush upon their enemy. . . .

We practiced circumcision like the Jews, and made offerings and feasts on that occasion in the same manner they did. Like them also, our children were named for some event, some circumstance, or fancied foreboding at the time of their birth. I was named *Olaudah,* which, in our language, signifies vicissitude, or fortunate also; one favored, and having a loud voice and well spoken. . . .

I have before remarked, that the natives of this part of Africa are extremely cleanly. This necessary habit of decency was with us a part of religion, and therefore we had many purifications and washings. . . .

THE AUTHOR'S BIRTH AND PARENTAGE—HIS BEING KIDNAPPED

I hope the reader will not think I have trespassed on his patience in introducing myself to him with some account of the manners and customs of my country. They have been implanted in me with great care, and made an impression on my mind which time could not erase, and which all the adversity and variety of fortune I have since experienced served only to rivet and record. . . .

My father, besides many slaves, had a numerous family, of which seven lived to grow up, including myself and a sister, who was the only daughter. As I was the youngest of the sons, I became, of course, the greatest favorite with my mother, and was always with her; and she used to take particular pains to form my mind. I was trained up from my earliest years in the arts of agriculture and war; my daily exercise was shooting and throwing javelins; and my mother adorned me with emblems, after the manner of our greatest warriors. In this way I grew up till I was turned the age of eleven, when an end was put to my happiness in the following manner.

Generally, when the grown people in the neighborhood were gone far in the fields to labor, the children assembled together in some of the neighbors' premises to play; and commonly some of us used to get up a tree to look for any assailant, or kidnapper, that might come upon us. For they sometimes took those opportunities of our parents' absence to attack and carry off as many as they could seize.

One day, as I was watching at the top of a tree in our yard, I saw one of those people come into the yard of our next neighbor but one, to kidnap, there being many stout people in it. Immediately on this I gave the alarm of the rogue, and he was surrounded by the stoutest of them, who entangled him with cords, so that he could not escape till some of the grown people came and secured him. But, alas! ere long it was my fate to be thus attacked, and to be carried off, when none of our grown people were nigh.

One day, when all our people were gone out to their works as usual, and only I and my dear sister were left to mind the house, two men and a woman got over our walls, and in a moment seized us both; and, without giving us time to cry out, or to make resistance, they stopped our mouths, tied our hands, and ran off with us into the nearest wood, and continued to carry us as far as they could, till night came on, when we reached a small house, where the robbers halted for refreshment, and spent the night.

We were then unbound, but were unable to take any food; and, being quite overpowered by fatigue and grief, our only relief was some sleep, which allayed our misfortune for a short time. The next morning we left the house, and continued travelling all the day. For a long time we had kept to the woods, but at last we came into a road which I believed I knew. I now had some hopes of being delivered, for we had advanced but a little way before I discovered some people at a distance, on which I began to cry out for their assistance; but my cries had no other effect than to make them tie me faster, and stop my mouth, and then they put me into a large sack. They also stopped my sister's mouth, and tied her hands. And in this manner we proceeded till we were out of the sight of these people.

When we went to rest the following night they offered us some victuals, but we refused them; and the only comfort we had was in being in one another's arms all that night, and bathing each other in our tears. But, alas! we were soon deprived of even the smallest comfort of weeping together. The next day proved a day of greater sorrow than I had yet experienced; for my sister and I were then separated, while we lay clasped in each other's arms. It was in vain that we besought them not to part us: she was torn from me, and immediately carried away, while I was left in a state of distraction not to be described. I cried and grieved continually; and for several days I did not eat anything but what they forced into my mouth.

At length, after many days travelling, during which I had often changed masters, I got into the hands of a chieftain, in a very pleasant country. This man had two wives and some children, and they all used me extremely well, and did all they could to comfort me; particularly the first wife, who was something like my mother. Although I was a great many days journey from my father's house, yet these people spoke exactly the same language with us. This first master of mine, as I may call him, was a smith, and my principal employment was working his bellows, which were the same kind as I had seen in my vicinity. . . . I believe it was gold he worked, for it was of a lovely, bright yellow color, and was worn by the women on their wrists and ankles.

I was there I suppose about a month, and they at last used to trust me some little distance from the house. This liberty I used in embracing every opportunity to inquire the way to my own home. . . . I had also remarked where the sun rose in the morning, and set in the evening, as I had travelled along; and I had observed that my father's house was towards the rising of the sun. I was therefore determined to seize the first opportunity for making my escape, and to shape my course for that quarter; for I was quite oppressed and weighed down by grief after my mother and friends. . . .

While I was projecting my escape one day, an unlucky event happened, which quite disconcerted my plan, and put an end to my hopes. I used to be sometimes employed in assisting an elderly woman slave to cook and take care of the poultry; and one morning, while I was feeding some chickens, I happened to toss a small pebble at one of them, which hit it on the middle, and directly killed it. The old slave, having soon after missed the chicken, inquired after it; and on my relating the accident (for I told her the truth, because my mother would never suffer me to tell a lie) she flew into a violent passion, threatened that I should suffer for it; and, my master being out, she immediately went and told her mistress what I had done.

This alarmed me very much, and I expected an instant correction, which to me was uncommonly dreadful; for I had seldom been beaten at home. I therefore resolved to fly; and accordingly I ran into the thicket that was hard by, and hid myself in the bushes. Soon afterwards my mistress and the slave returned, and, not seeing me, they searched all the house; but, not finding me, and I not making answer when they called to me, they thought I had run away, and the whole neighborhood was raised in pursuit of me. . . .

The neighbors continued the whole day looking for me, and several times many of them came within a few yards of the place where I lay hid. I expected every moment, when I heard a rustling among the trees, to be found out, and punished by my master; but they never discovered me, though they were often so near that I even heard their conjectures as they were looking about for me; and now I learned from them, that any attempt to return home would be hopeless. Most of them supposed I had fled towards home; but the distance was so great, and the way so intricate, that they thought I could never reach it, and that I should be lost in the woods.

When I heard this I was seized with a violent panic, and abandoned myself to despair. Night too began to approach, and aggravated all my fears. I had before entertained hopes of getting home, and I had determined when it should be dark to make the attempt; but I was now convinced it was fruitless, and I began to consider that, if possibly I could escape all other animals, I could not those of the human kind; and that, not knowing the way, I must perish in the woods. . . .

I at length quitted the thicket, very faint and hungry, for I had not eaten or drank anything all the day, and crept to my master's kitchen, from whence I set out at first, and which was an open shed, and laid myself down in the ashes, with an anxious wish for death to relieve me from all my pains. I was scarcely awake in the morning when the old woman slave, who was the first up, came to light the fire, and saw me in the fireplace. She was very much surprised to see me, and could scarcely believe her own eyes. She now promised to intercede for me, and went for her master, who soon after came, and having slightly reprimanded me, ordered me to be taken care of, and not ill-treated.

Soon after this, my master's only daughter and child by his first wife sickened and died, which affected him so much that for some time he was almost frantic, and really would have killed himself had he not been watched and prevented. However, in a small time afterwards he recovered, and I was again sold. . . .

I had been travelling for a considerable time, when one evening, to my great surprise, whom should I see brought to the house where I was but my dear sister. As soon as she saw me she gave a loud shriek, and ran into my arms. I was quite overpowered; neither of us could speak, but, for a considerable time, clung to each other in mutual embraces, unable to do anything but weep. Our meeting affected all who saw us. . . . When these people knew we were brother and sister, they indulged us to be together. . . .

But even this small comfort was soon to have an end; for scarcely had that fatal morning appeared, when she was again torn from me forever! I was now more miserable, if possible, than before. . . .

Yes, thou dear partner of all my childish sports! Thou sharer of my joys and sorrows! Happy should I have ever esteemed myself to encounter every misery for you, and to procure your freedom by the sacrifice of my own. Though you were early forced from my arms, your image has been always riveted in my heart, from which neither time nor fortune have been able to remove it. So that, while the thoughts of your sufferings have damped my prosperity, they have mingled with adversity, and increased its bitterness. To that heaven which protects the weak from the strong, I commit the care of your innocence and virtues, if they have not already received their full reward; and if your youth and delicacy have not long since fallen victims to the violence of the African trader, the pestilential stench of a Guinea ship, the seasoning of the European colonies, or the lash and lust of a brutal and unrelenting overseer.

I did not long remain after my sister. I was again sold, and carried through a number of places. . . . Thus I continued to travel, sometimes by land, sometimes by water, through different countries, and various nations, till, at the end of six or seven months after I had been kidnapped, I arrived at the seacoast. It would be tedious and uninteresting to relate all the incidents which befell me during this journey, and which I have not yet forgotten; of the various hands I passed through, and the manners and customs of all the different people among whom I lived. . . .

The first object which saluted my eyes when I arrived on the coast was the sea, and a slave-ship, which was then riding at anchor and waiting for its cargo. These filled me with astonishment, which was soon converted into terror, which I am yet at a loss to describe, nor the tense feelings of my mind. When I was carried on board I was immediately handled, and tossed up, to see if I were sound, by some of the crew; and I was now persuaded that I had gotten into a world of bad spirits, and that they were going to kill me.

Their complexions too differing so much from ours, their long hair, and the language they spoke, which was very different from any I had ever heard, united to confirm me in this belief. Indeed, such were the horrors of my views and fears at that moment that, if ten thousand worlds had been my own, I would have freely parted with them all to have exchanged my condition with that of the meanest slave of my own country. When I looked round the ship too, and saw the large furnace of copper boiling, and a multitude of black people of every description chained together, every one of their countenances expressing dejection and sorrow, I no longer doubted of my fate, and, quite overpowered with horror and anguish, I fell motionless on the deck and fainted.

When I recovered a little, I found some black people about me, who I believed were some of those who brought me on board, and had been receiving their pay; they talked to me in order to cheer me, but all in vain. I asked them if we were not to be eaten by those white men with horrible looks, red faces, and long hair? They told me I was not; and one of the crew brought me a small portion of spirituous liquor in a wine glass; but, being afraid of him, I would not take it out of his hand. One of the blacks therefore took it from him and gave it to me, and I took a little down my palate, which, instead of reviving me, as they thought it would, threw me into the greatest consternation at the strange feeling it produced, having never tasted any such liquor before. Soon after this, the blacks who brought me on board were off, and left me abandoned to despair.

I now saw myself deprived of every chance of returning to my native country, or even the least glimpse of hope of gaining the shore, which I now considered friendly; and I even wished for my former slavery in preference to my present situation, which was filled with horrors of every kind, still heightened by my ignorance of what I was to undergo. I was not long suffered to indulge my grief; I was soon put down under the decks, and there I received such a salutation in my nostrils as I had never experienced in my life; so that with the loathsomeness of the stench, and crying together, I became so sick and low that I was not able to eat, nor had I the least desire to taste anything.

I now wished for the last friend, Death, to relieve me; but soon, to my grief, two of the white men offered me eatables; and, on my refusing to eat, one of them held me fast by the hands, and laid me across, I think, the windlass, and tied my feet, while the other flogged me severely. I had never experienced anything of this kind before; and although, not being used to the water, I naturally feared that element the first time I saw it; yet, nevertheless, could I have got over the nettings, I would have jumped over the side, but I could not; and, besides, the crew used to watch us very closely who were not chained down to the decks, lest we should leap into the water. And I have seen some of these poor African prisoners most severely cut for attempting to do so, and hourly whipped for not eating. This was indeed the case with myself.

In a little time after, amongst the poor chained men, I found some of my own nation, which in a small degree gave ease to my mind. I inquired of these what was to be done with us? They gave me to understand we were to be carried to these white men's country to work for them. I then was a little revived, and thought, if it were no worse than working, my situation was not so desperate; but still I feared I should be put to death. The white people looked and acted, as I thought, in so savage a manner; for I had never seen among my people such instances of brutal cruelty; and this not only shown towards us blacks, but also to some of the whites themselves. One white man in particular I saw, when we were permitted to be on deck, flogged so unmercifully with a large rope near the foremast, that he died in consequence of it; and they tossed him over the side as they would have done a brute. This made me fear these people the more; and I expected nothing less than to be treated in the same manner.

I could not help expressing my fears and apprehensions to some of my countrymen. I asked them if these people had no country, but lived in this hollow place the ship? They told me they did not, but came from a distant one. "Then," said I, "how comes it in all our country we never heard of them?" They told me, because they lived so very far off. I then asked where were their women? Had they any like themselves? I was told they had. "And why," said I, "do we not see them?" They answered, because they were left behind. I asked how the vessel could go? They told me they could not tell; but that there were cloths put upon the masts by the help of the ropes I saw, and then the vessel went on; and the white men had some spell or magic they put in the water when they liked in order to stop the vessel.

I was exceedingly amazed at this account, and really thought they were spirits. I therefore wished much to be from them, for I expected they would sacrifice me; but my wishes were vain, for we were so quartered that it was impossible for any of us to make our escape. . . .

The stench of the hold when we were on the coast was so intolerably loathsome, that it was dangerous to remain there for any time, and some of us had been permitted to stay on the deck for the fresh air; but now that the whole ship's cargo were confined together, it became absolutely pestilential. The closeness of the place, and the heat of the climate, added to the number in the ship, which was so crowded that each had scarcely room to turn himself, almost suffocated us. This produced copious perspirations, so that the air soon became unfit for respiration, from a variety of loathsome smells, and brought on a sickness among the slaves, of which many died, thus falling victims to the improvident avarice, as I may call it, of their purchasers. This wretched situation was again aggravated by the galling of the chains, now become insupportable; and the filth of the necessary tubs, into which the children fell, and were almost suffocated. The shrieks of the women, and the groans of the dying, rendered the whole a scene of horror almost inconceivable. Happily for myself I was soon reduced so low that it was thought necessary to keep me almost always on deck; and from my extreme youth I was not put in fetters. . . .

Every circumstance I met with served only to render my state more painful, and heighten my apprehensions, and my opinion of the cruelty of the whites. One day they had taken a number of fishes; and when they had killed and satisfied themselves with as many as they thought fit, to our astonishment who were on the deck, rather than give any of them to us to eat, as we expected, they tossed the remaining fish into the sea again, although we begged and prayed for some as well as we could, but in vain; and some of my countrymen, being pressed by hunger, took an opportunity, when they thought no one saw them, of trying to get a little privately; but they were discovered, and the attempt procured them some very severe floggings.

One day, when we had a smooth sea, and moderate wind, two of my wearied countrymen, who were chained together (I was near them at the time), preferring death to such a life of misery, somehow made it through the nettings, and jumped into the sea; immediately another quite dejected fellow, who, on account of his illness, was suffered to be out of irons, also followed their example; and I believe many more would very soon have done the same, if they had not been prevented by the ship's crew, who were instantly alarmed. Those of us that were the most active were, in a moment, put down under the deck; and there was such a noise and confusion among the people of the ship as I never heard before, to stop her, and get the boat out to go after the slaves. However, two of the wretches were drowned, but they got the other, and afterwards flogged him unmercifully, for thus attempting to prefer death to slavery.

In this manner we continued to undergo more hardships than I can now relate; hardships which are inseparable from this accursed trade. . . .

At last we came in sight of the island of Barbados, at which the whites on board gave a great shout, and made many signs of joy to us. We did not know what to think of this; but as the vessel drew nearer we plainly saw the harbor, and other ships of different kinds and sizes; and we soon anchored amongst them off Bridge Town. Many merchants and planters now came on board, though it was in the evening. They put us in separate parcels, and examined us attentively. They also made us jump, and pointed to the land, signifying we were to go there.

We thought by this we should be eaten by these ugly men, as they appeared to us; and, when soon after we were all put down under the deck again, there was much dread and trembling among us, and nothing but bitter cries to be heard all the night from these apprehensions, insomuch that at last the white people got some old slaves from the land to pacify us. They told us we were not to be eaten, but to work, and were soon to go on land, where we should see many of our country people. This report eased us much; and sure enough, soon after we were landed, there came to us Africans of all languages.

We were conducted immediately to the merchant's yard, where we were all pent up together like so many sheep in a fold, without regard to sex or age. As every object was new to me, everything I saw filled me with surprise. What struck me first was that the houses were built with bricks, in storeys, and in every other respect different from those I have seen in Africa. But I was still more astonished on seeing people on horseback. I did not know what this could mean; and indeed I thought these people were full of nothing but magical arts. While I was in this astonishment, one of my fellow prisoners spoke to a countryman of his about the horses, who said they were the same kind they had in their country. I understood them, though they were from a distant part of Africa, and I thought it odd I had not seen any horses there; but afterwards, when I came to converse with different Africans, I found they had many horses amongst them, and much larger than those I then saw.

We were not many days in the merchant's custody before we were sold after their usual manner, which is this: On a signal given (as the beat of a drum), the buyers rush at once into the yard where the slaves are confined, and make choice of that parcel they like best. The noise and clamor with which this is attended, and the eagerness visible in the countenances of the buyers, serve not a little to increase the apprehensions of the terrified Africans, who may well be supposed to consider them as the ministers of that destruction to which they think themselves devoted. In this manner, without scruple, are relations and friends separated, most of them never to see each other again. I remember in the vessel in which I was brought over, in the men's apartment, were several brothers, who, in the sale, were sold in different lots; and it was very moving on this occasion to see and hear their cries at parting. O, ye nominal Christians! Might not an African ask you, Learned you this from your God? . . .

THE AUTHOR IS CARRIED TO VIRGINIA

I now totally lost the small remains of comfort I had enjoyed in conversing with my countrymen; the women too, who used to wash and take care of me, were all gone different ways, and I never saw one of them afterwards.

I stayed in this island for a few days; I believe it could not be above a fortnight; when I and some few more slaves, that were not saleable amongst the rest, from very much fretting, were shipped off in a sloop for North America. On the passage we were better treated than when we were coming from Africa, and we had plenty of rice and fat pork.

We were landed up a river a good way from the sea, about Virginia country, where we saw few or none of our native Africans, and not one soul who could speak to me. I was a few weeks weeding grass, and gathering stones in a plantation; and at last all my companions were distributed different ways, and only myself was left. I was now exceedingly miserable, and thought myself worse off than any of the rest of my companions; for they could talk to each other, but I had no person to speak to that I could understand.

In this state I was constantly grieving and pining, and wishing for death, rather than anything else. While I was in this plantation, the gentleman to whom I supposed the estate belonged, being unwell, I was one day sent to his dwelling house to fan him. When I came into the room where he was, I was very much affrighted at some things I saw, and the more so as I had seen a black woman slave as I came through the house, who was cooking the dinner, and the poor creature was cruelly loaded with various kinds of iron machines. She had one particularly on her head, which locked her mouth so fast that she could scarcely speak; and could not eat nor drink. I was much astonished and shocked at this contrivance, which I afterwards learned was called the iron muzzle.

Soon after I had a fan put into my hand, to fan the gentleman while he slept; and so I did indeed with great fear. While he was fast asleep I indulged myself a great deal in looking about the room, which to me appeared very fine and curious. The first object that engaged my attention was a watch which hung on the chimney, and was going. I was quite surprised at the noise it made, and was afraid it would tell the gentleman anything I might do amiss; and when I immediately after observed a picture hanging in the room, which appeared constantly to look at me, I was still more affrighted, having never seen such things as these before. . . .

In this state of anxiety I remained till my master awoke, when I was dismissed out of the room, to my no small satisfaction and relief, for I thought that these people were all made of wonders. . . .

I had been some time in this miserable, forlorn, and much dejected state, without having anyone to talk to, which made my life a burden, when the kind and unknown hand of the Creator (who in very deed leads the blind in a way they know not) now began to appear, to my comfort; for one day the captain of a merchant ship, called the *Industrious Bee,* came on some business to my master's house. This gentleman, whose name was Michael Henry Pascal, was a lieutenant in the royal navy, but now commanded this merchant ship, which was somewhere in the confines of the county many miles off. While he was at my master's house it happened that he saw me, and liked me so well that he made a purchase of me. . . . It was about the beginning of the spring of 1757 when I arrived in England, and I was near twelve years of age at that time.

LIKE EUNICE WILLIAMS, Olaudah Equiano found himself carried by violence into a strange land, where his language, culture, religion, and countrymen were denied him. But unlike Eunice Williams, he would never be accepted as a member of this new society, no matter what tongue he spoke, faith he held, or name he assumed. The laws of Virginia, and the prejudices of the English, marked him as something other than human (in European eyes): he was destined for a permanent state of servitude.

The horrors of slavery are well known; certainly they do not need repetition here. But the comparison with the captivity of Eunice Williams shows that African slavery differed markedly from the various kinds of bondage that marked the New World. This was a hereditary state, a state defined by race. This was something unique, and uniquely terrible.

For all he had been through, Olaudah Equiano would be far luckier than most of his fellow Africans who crossed the Atlantic with him. He now crossed the ocean once more; instead of laboring and dying in the fields of Virginia, he would serve a British sea captain. He would learn to read and write, he would wear decent—occasionally fine—clothing. Eventually, he would be able to buy his own freedom, and to write his remarkable memoirs. But Equiano's second trip across the Atlantic would soon be followed by a return voyage. This time, he would sail with a mighty fleet—one that would join the final, climactic war between Britain and France for control of North America.

VII

CONQUEST

20

BRITAIN REBUKED

The fourth of July may well have been the worst day of George Washington's life. The year was 1754; Washington was a 22-year-old colonel in the Virginia militia; and already he had suffered the most humiliating defeat of his career. The day before, deep in the Appalachian mountains, he had surrendered a humble pile of logs (honored with the equally humble name Fort Necessity) to French forces; along with the fort went himself and more than 150 troops. The young Virginian endured little more than wounded pride, for he was soon released to fight again—but that embarrassing surrender sparked a massive war that would shake two world empires and change the face of North America forever.

Washington's surrender of Fort Necessity brought to a head decades of rising tensions between New France and the British colonies. Since 1713 the two sides had been maneuvering for strategic territory. They had even waged open war, as recently as the 1740s in fact, but with little effect. In the early 1750s, however, the friction between their imperial ambitions lit an unquenchable firestorm over the rich valley of the Ohio River.

In 1749, New France had declared sovereignty over the valley as an extension of its claims to the Great Lakes region and the Mississippi River basin. In 1752, the French drove out English traders who had made inroads among the Indians north of the Ohio, between the Appalachians and the Illinois country. In 1753, more than a thousand Canadian troops enforced these claims by constructing a series of posts south of Lake Erie: forts Machault, Le Boeuf, and the keystone, Presqu'ile.

All of this drove the great planters of Virginia to distraction. For generations, the central and southern colonies had kept out of the wars with New France. But now younger sons of the wealthy cavaliers (such as George Washington) cast their eyes across the mountains, where they might claim new estates for themselves. They formed the Ohio Company, which received a grant of more than 500,000 acres from the British king (not, of course, from the Indians). But when they tried to take control of the land they held on paper, they now saw French troops, French forts, and Native Americans allied with Quebec. The solution to this problem seemed obvious. drive them out. In 1753, Virginia Governor Robert Dinwiddie received permission from London to eject the encroaching enemy.

All of which led to Colonel George Washington's march into the wilderness with his little band of men. He had gone once before, to warn the French to depart. When he returned in 1754, he planned to fortify the strategic forks of the Ohio River (the modern-day site of Pittsburgh). The march began well enough: he ambushed a Canadian patrol, killing its commander (to the outrage of France) along with a few others. But the enemy had already arrived at the Ohio forks, where they had built Fort Duquesne; the French garrison pursued the impertinent young colonel to his improvised Fort Necessity, leaving him with no alternative but to give up.

The trivial battle that resulted in Washington's embarrassment, however, captured the attention of London. "All of North America will be lost if these practices are tolerated," fumed the Duke of Newcastle, the leader of the British government.[1] In previous decades, the skirmish might not even have been reported; but now, as Newcastle's outburst demonstrates, the British saw a continentwide empire at stake. New France might hold only 55,000 inhabitants of European descent, yet it seemed to have the upper hand in the struggle with the million-strong English colonists. It held the Great Lakes, it had forged alliances with most western Native American tribes, it had seized the Ohio valley—and now it attacked a British fortification (humble and temporary though it was) in peacetime.

The top officials in King George II's government agreed that the encroaching French had to be driven back—preferably without sparking a major European war. The Duke of Cumberland, the king's son and captain-general of the army, proposed the dispatch of two regiments of regular troops under the command of an esteemed officer from his personal unit, the Coldstream Guards. The fellow could pursue a measured campaign, designed to win concessions from the French, by attacking a succession of the infringing forts, one by one, with negotiations in between. The other members of the government quickly agreed, and the young general and his men soon set sail. That officer's name was Edward Braddock.

Cumberland's ideas, however, came under attack from the Earl of Halifax, the president of the Lords Commissioners for Trade and Plantations. Halifax argued in favor of a four-pronged offensive in 1755, aimed at the key fortifications on the military frontiers of New France. Halifax's bold plan carried the day; the government soon issued revised orders to Braddock.

According to the new strategy, Braddock himself would lead a column of regular troops over the mountains against Fort Duquesne. This would open the way to a complete conquest of the Ohio valley. The second column, composed of Americans and some Iroquois volunteers, would assault

[1] Quoted in Ian K. Steele, *Betrayals: Fort William Henry and the "Massacre"* (New York: Oxford University Press, 1990), p. 28—a key account of this campaign.

Fort Niagara, which controlled the Great Lakes waterway. A third force of Iroquois and colonial militia would march against Fort St. Frederic, the fortress that dominated strategic Lake Champlain. Finally, a fourth unit of New Englanders would go after Fort Beauséjour, which controlled the neck of land connecting Nova Scotia to the Canadian mainland.

Halifax's plan reveals the new importance of North America in London's global outlook. As much as British gentlemen might sniff at the continent as a wilderness, it now held a sizeable proportion of King George II's subjects—colonial affairs no longer seemed insignificant. Gone were the days when American wars would be fought solely by colonial volunteers, commanded by part-time colonial officers, under the pay of colonial legislatures. Now veteran regiments of the regular army, officers from the finest families, and silver from the British treasury would all flow across the Atlantic to advance the king's interests.

What we need to remember as we follow this impending war, however, is the fact that everything in America tended to blend. European officers, whether British or French, would command combined columns of both regular troops and colonial militia; their operations would interweave formal tactics and sieges with guerrilla methods; their units almost always marched with numerous Native American allies. And the cooperation of colonial governments and leaders would prove essential to military success.

One of those leaders was an influential Philadelphia politician and businessman named Benjamin Franklin. During the many years of warfare before 1754, Franklin had argued vainly in the Pennsylvania assembly for measures to support the struggle against New France. But pacifist Quakers dominated the colony's government; they refused out of principle to pay for arms, soldiers, and fortifications. Not coincidentally, their idealistic stance also saved the people of Pennsylvania a good amount of money. And non-Quakers could well ask, why should they pay for wars against Canada? The fighting always took place far to the north, in New York and New England. Franklin could only shake his head at such shortsightedness.

Some aspects of this situation (especially the role of the Quakers) were specific to Pennsylvania. In other respects, however, such debates over defense reflected the politics of the American colonies in general. A number of different forces influenced military policy: the crown, with its imperial ambitions; the colonial governors (almost all appointed by the king), who often served as military commanders; and the elected legislatures, where a mix of interests competed for precedence. In New England, war against the French enemy aroused a great deal of popular enthusiasm; the colonists themselves paid for numerous offensives against Canada. In Pennsylvania, Maryland, Virginia, and the Carolinas—each far from the disputed frontier—such costly endeavors seemed irrelevant.

Washington's surrender in 1754 turned this situation upside down. The French had invaded the Ohio valley, the promised land to Pennsylvania traders and Virginia land speculators. These two large colonies suddenly took an interest in colonial defense. And just as suddenly, Franklin went from political irritant to intercolonial envoy; the year that Fort Necessity fell, he traveled to Albany to attend a remarkable conference of representatives from most of the American provinces. Even as the crown laid grand plans for a war in North America, its transatlantic subjects began to shape their own policies for the battle against New France.

Talk as they might, however, the colonists soon discovered that London would have the final say: it had the troops and the money. As Franklin and his fellows sketched out their schemes for defense, General Edward Braddock arrived in Virginia with his two regiments of regular troops. The imperial plan for a four-pronged offensive proceeded inexorably. Orders went out to colonial governors to organize units of American volunteers; envoys went out to recruit Indian auxiliaries (especially among the Six Nations of the Iroquois, who remained friendly, if officially neutral). Influential colonists rounded up transportation, equipment, and supplies for the gathering troops (both American militia and regular army).

The main offensive would be Braddock's own thrust to Fort Duquesne—and the man Braddock most relied on for logistical support was Benjamin Franklin. The famous printer took the measure of this aristocratic British officer, and wrote up opinions of him that have influenced us to this day. He found the general to be arrogant, dismissive of Americans and Indians, and unappreciative of the difficulties of a wilderness campaign. Franklin saw him as a man comfortable with the formal drill of European battlefields, but unprepared for the raids and ambushes that marked American warfare.

Such views may be accurate, but they are certainly incomplete. First of all, the formal tactics of European warfare made a good deal of sense. British and French regulars marched and fought in dense lines because they wielded notoriously inaccurate smoothbore muskets: the only way they could hit anything was to fire in massed volleys. The highly accurate rifle existed, but could not be used on the regular battlefield because it took too long to load (the bullet fit the barrel so tightly, a ramrod and mallet were required to drive it down to the firing chamber). Even colorful, showy uniforms made sense—they allowed commanders to identify their own units in the confusion of battle.

Second, European armies knew about irregular warfare. The French especially had experience in partisan fighting, in the use of raids and ambushes. Their generals published books on the subject, and incorporated light troops into their regular units. The British lagged behind in this respect, but an officer of Braddock's status knew about such tactics and the dangers they posed. Finally, Braddock and his fellow professionals brought organizational and logistical skills that are often overlooked by armchair strategists. The accumulation and movement of food, ammunition, clothing, shoes, and all the materiel of war would become more difficult, and more important, as the armies fighting in North America grew bigger.

Braddock, however, *was* arrogant and aristocratic—weaknesses that could not make up for any amount of professional skill and experience. He set off on his march across the mountains with both colonial volunteers and regular troops, confident that his regulars would carry the day against the mere Canadians and Indians who stood in his way. At his side rode young Colonel Washington, full of admiration for this professional officer who embodied everything he wanted to be. Braddock would soon have the chance to prove his superiority, and that of his men.

A Plan of Union, a Plan of Attack
by Benjamin Franklin

My being many years in the Assembly, the majority of which were constantly Quakers, gave me frequent opportunities of seeing the embarrassment given them by their principle against war, whenever application was made to them by the order of the Crown to grant aids for military purposes. They were unwilling to offend Government on the one hand, by a direct refusal, and their friends the body of Quakers on the other, by a compliance contrary to their principles. Hence a variety of evasions to avoid complying, and modes of disguising the compliance when it became unavoidable.

The common mode at last was to grant money under the phrase of its being *for the King's use,* and never to inquire how it was applied. But if the demand was not directly from the Crown, that phrase was found not so proper, and some other thing was to be invented. As when powder was wanting (I think it was for the garrison at Louisburg) and the government of New England solicited a grant of some from Pennsylvania, which was much urged on the House by Governor Thomas, they could not grant money to buy powder, because that was an ingredient of war, but they voted an aid to New England, of three thousand pounds, to be put into the hands of the Governor, and appropriated it for the purchasing of bread, flour, wheat, *or some other grain.* . . . He replied, "I shall take the money, for I understand very well their meaning; *other grain* is gunpowder"; which he accordingly bought, and they never objected to it. . . .

In 1754, war with France being again apprehended, a Congress of Commissioners from the different colonies was by an order of the Lords of Trade to be assembled at Albany, there to confer with the chiefs of the Six Nations, concerning our means of defending both their country and ours. Governor Hamilton, having received this order, acquainted the House with it, requesting they would furnish proper presents for the Indians to be given on this occasion, and naming the Speaker (Mr. Norris) and myself to join Mr. Thomas Penn and Mr. Secretary Peters as commissioners to act for Pennsylvania. The House approved the nomination, and provided the goods for the present, tho' they did not much like treating out of the province, and we met the other commissioners and met at Albany about the middle of June.

On our way thither, I projected and drew up a plan for the union of all the colonies, under one government so far as might be necessary for defense, and other important general purposes. As we passed thro' New York, I had there shown my project to Mr. James Alexander and Mr. Kennedy, two gentlemen of great knowledge in public affairs, and being fortified by their approbation I ventured to lay it before the Congress. It then appeared that several of the commissioners had formed plans of the same kind.

A previous question was first taken whether a Union should be established, which passed in the affirmative unanimously. A committee was then appointed, one member from each colony, to consider the several plans and report. Mine happened to be preferred, and with a few amendments was accordingly reported. By this plan, the general government was to be administered by a President General, appointed and supported [paid] by the Crown, and a Grand Council to be chosen by the representatives of the people of the several colonies met in their respective assemblies. Debates upon it in Congress went on daily hand in hand with the Indian business. Many objections and difficulties were started, but at length they were all overcome, and the plan was unanimously agreed to, and copies ordered to be transmitted to the Board of Trade and to the assemblies of the several provinces.

Its fate was singular. The assemblies did not adopt it as they all thought there was too much *prerogative* in it; and in England it was judged to have too much of the *democratic*. The Board of Trade therefore did not approve it; nor recommend it for the approbation of His Majesty. But another scheme was formed (supposed better to answer the same purpose) whereby the governors of the provinces with some members of their respective councils were to meet and order the raising of troops, building of forts, etc., etc., to draw upon the Treasury of Great Britain for the expense, which was afterwards to be refunded by an act of Parliament laying a tax on America. . . .

Being the winter following in Boston, I had much conversation with Governor Shirley [of Massachusetts] upon both the plans. Part of what passed between us on the occasion may also be seen among those [Franklin's other] papers. The different and contrary reasons of dislike to my plan makes me suspect that it was really the true medium; and I am still of the opinion it would have been happy for both sides of the water if it had been adopted. The colonies so united would have been sufficiently strong to have defended themselves; there would then have been no need of troops from England; of course the subsequent pretense for taxing America, and the bloody contest it occasioned, would have been avoided. But such mistakes are not new; history is full of errors of states and princes. . . .

The British government, not choosing to permit the Union of the Colonies as proposed at Albany, and to trust that Union with their defense, lest they should thereby grow too strong militarily, and feel their own strength, suspicions and jealousies at this time being entertained of them; sent over General Braddock with two regiments of regular English troops for that purpose.

He landed at Alexandria in Virginia, and thence marched to Frederic Town in Maryland, where he halted for carriages. Our Assembly apprehending, from some information, that he conceived violent prejudices against them, as averse to the service, wished me to wait upon him, not as from them, but as Postmaster General, under the guise of proposing to settle with him the mode of conducting with most celerity and certainty the dispatches between him and the governments of the several provinces, with whom he must necessarily have continual correspondence, and of which they proposed to pay the expense.

My son accompanied me on this journey. We found the General at Frederic Town, waiting impatiently for the return of those he had sent thro' the back parts of Maryland and Virginia to collect wagons. I stayed with him several days, dined with him daily, and had full opportunity of removing all his prejudices, by the information of what the Assembly had before his arrival actually done and were still willing to do to facilitate his operations.

When I was about to depart, the returns of wagons to be obtained were brought in, by which it appeared that they amounted only to twenty-five, and not all of those were in serviceable condition. The General and all the officers were surprised, declared the expedition at an end, being impossible, and exclaimed against the ministers for ignorantly landing them in a country destitute of the means of conveying their stores, baggage, etc., not less than 150 wagons being necessary. I happened to say, I thought it a pity they had not landed in Pennsylvania, as in that great country almost every farmer had his wagon. The General eagerly laid hold of my words, and said, "Then you, sir, who are a man of interest [wealth and influence] here, can probably secure them for us; and I beg you will undertake it."

I asked what terms were to be offered the owners of the wagons; and I was desired to put on paper the terms that appeared to me necessary. This I did, and they were agreed to, and a commission and instructions accordingly prepared immediately. . . .

I received of the General about £800 to be disbursed in advance money to the wagon owners, etc.; but that sum being insufficient, I advanced upwards of £200 more, and in two weeks, the 150 wagons with 259 carrying horses were on their march for the camp. . . . The General too was highly satisfied with my conduct in procuring him the wagons, etc., and readily paid my account of disbursements; thanking me repeatedly and requesting my farther assistance in sending provisions after him. I undertook this also, and was busily employed in it till we heard of his defeat, advancing for the service, of my own money, upwards of £1,000 sterling, of which I sent him an account. It came to his hands luckily for me a few days before the battle, and he returned me immediately an order on the paymaster for the round sum of £1,000, leaving the remainder to the next account. I consider this payment as good luck, having never been able to obtain the remainder. . . .

This General was I think a brave man, and might probably have made a figure as a good officer in some European war. But he had too much self-confidence, too high an opinion of the validity of regular troops, and too mean a one of both Americans and Indians. . . .

In conversation one day, he was giving me some account of his intended progress. "After taking Fort Duquesne," says he, "I am to proceed to Niagara; and having taken that, to Frontenac, if the season will allow time; and I suppose it will, for Duquesne can hardly detain me above three or four days; and then I see nothing that can obstruct my march to Niagara."

Having before revolved in my mind the long line his army must take in their march, by a very narrow road to be cut for them thro' the woods and bushes; and also what I had read of a former defeat of 1,500 French who had invaded the Iroquois country, I had conceived some doubts and some fears for the event of the campaign. But I ventured only to say, To be sure, sir, if you arrive well before Duquesne, with these fine troops so well provided with artillery, that place, not yet completely fortified, and as we hear with no very strong garrison, can probably make but a short resistance. The only danger I apprehend of obstruction to your march, is from ambuscades of Indians, who by constant practice are dextrous in laying and executing them. And the slender line, near four miles long, which your army must make, may expose it to be attacked by surprise in its flanks, and to be cut like a thread into several pieces, which from their distance cannot come up in time to support each other.

He smiled at my ignorance, and replied, "These savages may indeed be a formidable enemy to your raw American militia; but upon the King's regular and disciplined troops, sir, it is impossible they should make any impression." I was conscious of an impropriety in my disputing with a military man in matters of his profession and said no more.

The enemy, however, did not take the advantage of his army which I apprehended its long line of march exposed it to, but let it advance without interruption till within nine miles of the place; and then when more in a body (for it had just passed a river where the front had halted till all were come over) and in a more open part of the woods than any it had passed, attacked its advanced guard, by a heavy fire from behind trees and bushes; which was the first intelligence the General had of an enemy's being near him.

This guard being disordered, the General hurried the troops up to their assistance, which was done in great confusion thro' wagons, baggage, and cattle; and presently the fire came upon their flank. The officers being on horseback were more easily distinguished, picked out as marks, and fell very fast; and the soldiers were crowded together in a huddle, having or hearing no orders, and standing to be shot at till two thirds of them were killed, and then being seized with a panic the whole fled with precipitation. The wagoners each took a horse out of his team, and scampered; their example was immediately followed by others, so that all the wagons, provisions, artillery, and stores were left to the enemy.

The General being wounded[2] was brought off with difficulty; his secretary Mr. Shirley was killed by his side; and out of 86 officers, 63 were killed or wounded, and 714 men killed out of 1,100. These 1,100 had been picked men, from the whole army, the rest had been left behind with Colonel Dunbar, who was to follow with the heavier part of the stores, provisions, and baggage. The flyers, being not pursued, arrived at Dunbar's camp, and the panic they brought with them instantly seized him and all his people. And tho' he had now above 1,000 men, and the enemy who had beaten Braddock did not at most exceed 400, Indians and French together, instead of proceeding and endeavoring to recover some of the lost honor, he ordered all the stores, ammunition, etc., to be destroyed, that he might have more horses to assist his flight towards the settlements, and less lumber to remove.

He was there met with requests from the governors of Virginia, Maryland, and Pennsylvania, that he would post his troops on the frontiers so as to afford some protection to the inhabitants; but he continued his hasty march thro' all the country, not thinking himself safe till he arrived at Philadelphia, where the inhabitants could protect him. This whole transaction gave us Americans the first suspicion that our exalted ideas of the prowess of British regulars had not been well founded. . . .

The secretary's papers with all the General's orders, instructions, and correspondence falling into the enemy's hands, they selected and translated into French a number of the articles, which they printed to prove the hostile intentions of the British Court before the declaration of war.

———

BRADDOCK'S CRUSHING DEFEAT shocked both the British government and the American colonists. One of the most promising officers in the army, at the head of two veteran regiments, had been crushed by a smaller band of Canadians and Indians. The disaster would have been worse had it not been for the bravery and skill of Colonel Washington, who had helped rally the shattered troops.[3]

This decisive battle overshadowed all else in 1755—yet Braddock's thrust was only one part of the British offensive. The strategists in London called for simultaneous attacks on the four primary links in Canada's defen-

[2] Braddock died of his wounds.

[3] Braddock's defeat marked the start of what the Americans called the French and Indian War—known to the Europeans (eventually) as the Seven Years' War.

sive chain: Fort Duquesne (Braddock's target), Fort Niagara (controlling the Great Lakes waterway), Fort St. Frederic (on Lake Champlain), and Fort Beauséjour (on the isthmus between the mainland and Nova Scotia). Only the attack on Beauséjour succeeded: it fell to an assault by New England volunteers. The move against Niagara stalled quickly: the troops never left their staging area in northern New York. The French also withstood the Lake Champlain offensive—but events on this front soon took on a life of their own, which would direct the strategy of both sides for the next two years.

Just as Fort Duquesne dominated access to the Ohio valley, Fort St. Frederic controlled the only practical overland route to the Canadian heartland. Between the Adirondack and White Mountains, a string of waterways offered a north–south corridor of invasion: just above the Hudson River came Lake St. Sacrement, then the long Lake Champlain, followed by the Richelieu River. Fort St. Frederic stood on a strategic site (known to the British as Crown Point), where it could prevent any large force from passing up Lake Champlain. In addition, the fort served as a staging point for attacks on New York and New England, and as a base for patrols that inhibited Six Nations warriors from raiding New France. It also damped down the illicit fur trade conducted among the Kahnawake, the Mohawks, and the merchants of Albany. Everyone in the northern colonies—from royal governors to traders to the Iroquois—wanted to destroy Fort St. Frederic.

As Braddock marched into the mountains with his two regiments of regulars in 1755, a very different force moved toward Lake Champlain. Composed of colonial militia and recruits from the Six Nations, it came under the command of Sir William Johnson, one of the most remarkable men in New York history. Johnson handled New York's relations with the Iroquois, who greatly respected him (the Six Nations declared him a sachem, with the name Chief Much Business). As he moved north from Fort Edward (a post on the northern bend of the Hudson River), he cut a road through sixteen miles of woods to the southern shore of Lake St. Sacrement—which Johnson renamed Lake George. There he intended to collect his men and supplies for an assault on Fort St. Frederic, just one short portage away on Lake Champlain.

Unfortunately for Johnson, he faced a potent enemy: Baron Dieskau, in command of a mixed force of regular French troops, the Canadian regulars called *troupes de la marine*, Canadian militiamen, Hurons, Abenakis, and Kahnawake Mohawks. Dieskau had just arrived from France, but he was steeped in the ways of irregular warfare. He quickly launched a brilliant plan to trap the British forces. First he sent troops through the woods to threaten Fort Edward; when Johnson turned his men around and marched back to protect it, Dieskau ambushed them on the narrow wilderness road. The colonial troops retreated north to the shores of Lake George, pursued by the triumphant French soldiers, Canadians, and Indians.

Dieskau had won a magnificent victory, yet he promptly soiled his achievement by launching headlong attacks on the regrouped British forces. Cannon fire tore apart his regulars as they dashed in tight columns at the desperate colonial militia. In the end, Johnson's men shattered the Canadian army and captured Dieskau himself. Even so, the French commander had achieved his strategic aims: he had stopped Johnson's attack and saved Fort St. Frederic.

Unable and unwilling to continue his march north, Johnson began to build a fort on the site of his battle with Dieskau. The offensive would eventually resume, he knew; these works would provide it with an advanced base. Throughout the winter of 1755–56, British troops constructed an extremely powerful fortress here on the southern shore of Lake George. The French also constructed a new fort (called Fort Carillon) at the portage between Lakes George and Champlain, but it was the new British base that would dominate the strategic thinking on both sides in the coming year. The English dubbed it Fort William Henry.

As British troops and American militiamen erected Fort William Henry, two men arrived in Quebec from France. Though completely different from one another in outlook and upbringing, they would jointly shape the remaining years of war—a war that had begun so well for New France. The first to arrive was the new governor-general, Pierre-François de Rigaud, Marquis de Vaudreuil de Cavagnial (known simply as Vaudreuil). Even in the long chain of remarkable Canadian governors, Vaudreuil stood out: the first to be born in New France, and the first whose father had also served as governor (the previous Vaudreuil had ordered the capture of John Williams fifty years before). Already he had served quite capably as governor of Louisiana; now his skills were needed to save the province of his birth.

Vaudreuil exuded confidence, even arrogance, with every footstep. He was proud to be a Canadian, and he never tired of reminding his French army officers of what his provincials had accomplished. He also had a keen understanding of the irregular warfare that worked so well in the American forests. Indian warriors were important assets to this governor, and raids on poorly defended settlements were shrewd tactics. As he pored over the map of North America, he combined his self-assurance and his guerrilla instincts to shape his own offensive for 1756–57.

Vaudreuil's counterattack would prove just as comprehensive as the British scheme for the year before—and far shrewder. He would combine Canadian woodsmen, Native American allies, and regular French troops to force the more numerous British onto the defensive. He selected three targets: first, the Pennsylvania and Virginia frontier, to be raided by Indian warriors with support from Fort Duquesne. Second, Fort Oswego, the vulnerable British outpost on Lake Ontario (and the only interruption in New France's control of the Great Lakes coastline). And third, that new British bastion, Fort William Henry.

The first part of Vaudreuil's plan went better than he could have dreamed. Canada's Indian allies needed little encouragement to swoop down on Pennsylvania and Virginia frontier settlements. They terrorized the backcountry, preventing these two large colonies from aiding more vulnerable New York and New England. The second and third phases of Vaudreuil's offensive, however, would be carried out by his new military commander, General Louis-Joseph de Montcalm.

General Montcalm would have recognized Braddock as a kindred soul. Each of them represented the best a European regular army of the 1750s could produce: a professional yet aristocratic officer, technically skilled and personally brave. Montcalm shared Braddock's condescension toward these colonials and Indians, who (it seemed to them) thought war was a matter of running around the woods for a while, then going home. Montcalm's cold arrogance grew all the colder after he met Vaudreuil. This Canadian-born buffoon of a governor, the general thought, knew nothing of strategy, of real campaigns—yet he prattled on about his brave provincials and sketched out plans best left to the professionals.

Of course, Montcalm was not Braddock. For one thing, Montcalm managed to stay alive just a bit longer. For another, he silently acknowledged the soundness of Vaudreuil's offensive strategy, and even tried to claim credit for it when it succeeded. Finally, Montcalm allowed his condescension to thaw long enough to recognize the importance of irregular warfare in North America. In his campaigns, he would (perhaps grudgingly) blend his regular troops with Indians and Canadian militia, making use of the strengths of each.

Montcalm won his first success by carrying out the second part of Vaudreuil's plan for 1756, the capture of Fort Oswego. The general even tried to improve upon it: he intended to drag out the siege of the post long enough to draw away British forces that were now collecting at Fort William Henry for a thrust up Lake Champlain. In other words, he would both capture Oswego and save Fort St. Frederic in one blow. This thoughtful touch came to nothing when Oswego fell instantly, obviating the need on the British side to send a relief force. Montcalm accepted the surrender, then hurried east to command the forces gathering at St. Frederic.

The British intended to go over to the offensive in 1756 as well, but a number of problems forestalled their plans. First, the short-term colonial militiamen melted away, and new units had to be recruited. Second, the British government changed military commanders. Governor William Shirley of Massachusetts had succeeded Braddock, but his political enemies got the best of him. It took the better part of the year for his replacement—or replacements, really—to arrive. First came General Daniel Webb; then came his superior, Major General James Abercromby; and finally the new overall commander, Lord Loudon.

In 1757, the attention of both sides became fixed on Fort William Henry. The French had won in the west, from the Pennsylvania and Virginia frontier to the Great Lakes. Nor could the British penetrate in the east as long as the French fortress port of Louisburg controlled the mouth of the St. Lawrence. The only route available from the English colonies to Canada was through Lake Champlain. Meanwhile, both sides rushed reinforcements to North America—but the British command of the sea now began to tell: Montcalm received only 1,800 new troops, while more than 8,000 regulars set sail from English ports. And the Canadian harvest had failed in 1756, leaving New France dependent on food shipments from Europe—across an ocean patrolled by British ships.

The French had to strike fast to relieve the pressure. As much as Montcalm might grumble about Vaudreuil's arrogance and incompetence, the governor's plan was a sound one: Fort William Henry had to be destroyed to forestall an invasion of Canada. To carry out this plan, as Ian Steele writes, "Vaudreuil assembled an astonishing multicultural army in the summer of 1757." More than 1,000 Indian warriors flocked to the French standard from as far away as 1,500 miles: they had heard about the easy victory at Oswego, about the prisoners and plunder gathered in its ruins. Ottawa, Ojibwa, Menominee, Potawatomi, Winnebago, Fox, Sauk, Miami, and Delaware joined traditional French allies such as the Kahnawake, Abenaki, and Hurons of Lorette. In addition, Montcalm assembled more than 3,000 regular soldiers and *troupes de la marine*, along with more than 2,500 Canadian militia. As the summer began, the general moved south with this remarkable force.

His opponent was General Daniel Webb, the commander of this sector. Webb could boast a number of strengths: Fort William Henry was a powerful fortress with a number of cannon; its garrison now included experienced regulars as well as militia; and William Henry's commander was the veteran Lieutenant Colonel George Monro. And the fortress sat just sixteen miles down a good road from Fort Edward; Webb himself remained at Edward, where he was in a good position to reinforce and supply Monro as needed. But Webb was a notoriously timid man.

In July 1757, as Montcalm moved south, a Jesuit priest named Pierre Roubaud accompanied the Catholic Abenaki Indians in his army. Roubaud proved to be a keen observer of this dramatic campaign. It must have seemed a desperate adventure: the bulk of French forces were gathered together for one determined thrust, a gamble that they could destroy the principal base for a British invasion of Canada. The British had more men, shorter supply lines, and solid fortifications. And Montcalm struggled to hold together his diverse army; the Indian allies who accompanied him were crucial to his success, yet they did not like taking orders. They had come for plunder and prisoners, not to accomplish strategic objectives. This conflict of interest would plague the French commander all through the campaign, as Roubaud shows—right up to its tragic end.

A Tragic Victory
by Pierre Roubaud

I set out on the 12th of July [1757] from Saint Francis—the principal village of the Abenaki mission—to go to Montreal; the purpose of my journey was simply to bring to the Monsieur the Marquis de Vaudreuil a deputation of twenty Abenakis. . . . When I arrived at Montreal—a day and a half distant from my mission—I thought myself at the end of my journey; but Providence ordered otherwise.

An expedition was projected against the enemy; and, on account of the state of feeling among the savage tribes, the greatest success was expected. The Abenakis were to be of the party; and, as all the Christian savages are accompanied by their missionaries, who are eager to furnish them the aid suitable to their office, the Abenakis could be sure that I would not abandon them at so critical a moment. . . .

Two days afterward, I embarked on the great river Saint Lawrence in company with two gentlemen from Saint Sulpice. One was Monsieur Picquet, missionary of the Iroquois from La Galette; and the other was Monsieur Mathavet, missionary of the Nipissings from the lake of the two mountains. My Abenakis were encamped at Saint Jean, one of the colony's forts distant from Montreal a day's journey. My arrival surprised them; they had not been informed of my coming. Hardly had they perceived me when they made the woods and the neighboring mountains resound with the report of my approach. . . .

Toward evening, the kindness of an officer obtained for me an opportunity to witness one of those savage military spectacles which many people admire, as being fitted to arouse in the most cowardly hearts that martial ardor which makes veritable warriors; as for me, I have never seen in them anything but a comic farce, capable of making anyone burst into laughter who was not on his guard.

I am speaking of a war feast. Imagine a large assembly of savages, decorated with every ornament most fitted to disfigure, in European eyes, their physiognomies. Vermillion, white, green, yellow, and black made from soot or scrapings of the pots—on a single savage face are seen united all these different colors, methodically applied by the aid of a little tallow which serves as an ointment. This is the paint that is used on these grand occasions to adorn not only the face, but also the head—which is almost wholly shaved, excepting a little lock reserved on the top for the purpose of attaching to it feathers of birds, or a few pieces of porcelain, or some other similar gewgaw. Each part of the head has its distinct ornaments: the nose has its ring; there are also rings for the ears, which are pierced at an early age, and so greatly elongated by the weight with which they have been overloaded that they swing and beat against the shoulders. . . .

Now imagine an assembly of people thus decorated, and arranged in rows. In the midst are placed large kettles, filled with meat cooked and cut into pieces, so as to be more readily distributed to the spectators. After a respectful silence, which indicates the importance of the meeting, certain captains appointed by the various tribes that are present at the feast begin to chant in succession. . . .

When the assembly has been organized, the orator of the tribe begins to speak, and solemnly addresses the guests. The panegyric of the king, the eulogy of the French nation, the arguments that prove the lawfulness of the war, the motives of glory and of religion, all of these are fitted to tempt the young men to press on with joy to battle; this is the substance of that sort of address, which ordinarily bears no mark of savage barbarism. I have more than once heard addresses which would not have been disavowed by our finest minds in France. . . .

When the speech is finished, they proceed to name the captains who are to command the party. As soon as one is named, he rises from his place and proceeds to seize the head of one of the animals which are to make the principal part of the feast. He raises it high enough to be seen by the whole assembly, crying aloud: *Behold the head of the enemy.* Shouts of joy and applause are then raised on every side, and announce the satisfaction of the assembly. The captain, with the head of the animal still in his hand, goes through the lines singing his war song, in which he exerts all his force in boastings and insulting defiance of the enemy. . . . As he passes in review before the savages, these latter answer his chant by hollow cries, broken, drawn from the pit of the stomach, and accompanied by such ridiculous motions of the body that you must be familiar with them in order to witness them with composure. . . .

This first warrior is followed by others, who greatly protract the meeting—especially when it is a question of forming large parties, because with this kind of ceremony the enlistments are made. At last, the feast comes to an end with the distribution and consumption of the food.

Such was the war feast that was given to our savages, and such the ceremony that was observed. The Algonquins, the Abenakis, the Nipissings, and the Amenecis were at this feast. In the meantime, the more serious cares were demanding our presence elsewhere; we arose, and each missionary, followed by his neophytes, went to close the day with the usual prayers. A part of the night was spent in making the final preparations for our departure, which was fixed for the next day. . . .

The tediousness of the way was alleviated by the privilege that I had every day of celebrating the holy sacrifice of the Mass—sometimes on an island, sometimes on the bank of a river, but always in a spot sufficiently open to favor the devotion of our little army. It was no slight consolation to the ministers of the Lord to hear his praises sung in as many different tongues as there were tribes assembled. . . . We crossed Lake Champlain, where the dexterity of the savages in fishing furnished us with a very interesting spectacle. Placed in front of the canoe, standing, with spear in hand, they hurled it with marvelous skill, and drew out large sturgeons. . . .

Finally, after six days' travel, we came to Fort Vaudreuil, formerly [actually still] named Carillon, which had been assigned as the general rendezvous of our troops. Hardly had we begun to distinguish the summit of the fortifications before our savages drew up for battle, each tribe under its own standard. Two hundred canoes placed in this fine order formed a sight that messieurs the French officers, who had flocked to the shore, did not deem unworthy of attention.

As soon as I had landed I hastened to pay my respects to Monsieur the Marquis de Montcalm, whom I had had the honor to know in Paris. The regard with which he honors our missionaries was known to me. He received me with an affability which indicated the goodness and generosity of his heart. The Abenakis, less for the sake of conforming to ceremony than for satisfying their inclinations and their respect, lost no time in appearing before their General. . . .

After having taken leave of Monseiur de Montcalm, I repaired to the quarters of the Abenakis. I sent word to the orator to call together at once his tribesmen, and announce to them that, before going in a few days to attack the English fort, I expected from their religion that they should prepare themselves for this perilous undertaking every step fitted to assure its success before God. . . .

These were the occupations to which I devoted myself during our stay in the vicinity of Fort Vaudreuil [Fort Carillon]. It was not long; at the end of the third day we received orders to join the French army, encamped a league higher up, near the portage—that is to say, near the place where a great fall of water would oblige us to transport by land to Lake Saint Sacrement [Lake George] the munitions necessary for the siege. Preparations were being made for the departure when they were stopped by a sight that attracted all eyes.

We saw appearing in the distance, in one of the inlets of the river, a little fleet of savage canoes which by their order and decorations announced a victory. It was Monsieur Marin—a Canadian officer of great merit—who was returning glorious and triumphant from the expedition with which he had been charged. At the head of a body of about two hundred savages, he had been detached to scour the country about Fort Edward;[4] he had the courage with a small flying camp to attack the outer entrenchments, and the good fortune to carry a chief part of them. The savages had only time to cut off thirty-five scalps from the two hundred men whom they had killed; their victory was not stained with a single drop of their own blood and did not cost

---

[4] The writer consistently refers to Fort Edward as "Lydis" in the original; it has been changed to Edward throughout to avoid confusion.

them a single man. The enemy, numbering three thousand men, sought in vain to have revenge by pursuing them in their retreat, but it was made without the slightest loss.[5]

They were engaged in counting the number of barbarous trophies—that is to say, the English scalps—with which the canoes were decorated, when we perceived in another part of the river a French bark, which was bringing to us five Englishmen, bound, and accompanied by some Ottawas, whose prisoners they were. The sight of these unfortunate captives brought joy and gladness to the hearts of the spectators; but for the most part it was a ferocious and barbarous joy which manifested itself by frightful yells, and by acts very sad to humane men.

A thousand savages—drawn from thirty-six tribes united under the French flag—were present and lining the bank. In an instant, without any apparent consultation, I saw them run with extreme haste to the neighboring woods. I did not know what was to be the result of such a sudden and unexpected retreat; but I very soon understood. A moment after, I saw these furious men return, armed with clubs which they were preparing in order to give these unfortunate Englishmen the most cruel reception. I could not control my feelings at the sight of these cruel preparations. . . . Without stopping to deliberate I went to meet these ferocious brutes in the hope of calming them; but alas! what could my feeble voice do but utter some sounds that the tumult, the diversity of tongues, still more the ferocity of hearts, rendered unintelligible? At least the most bitter reproaches were not spared to a few Abenakis who chanced to come in my way. . . .

The French officer who was commanding the bark had perceived the commotion which was being made on the shore; touched with that commiseration so natural to an upright man at the sight of the unfortunate, he endeavored to infuse it into the hearts of the Ottawas, masters of the prisoners. He worked on their feelings so skillfully that he succeeded in rendering them sensitive, and interested them favorably in the cause of the wretched men. They took this cause up with an ardor which could not fail to succeed.

Hardly was the barge near enough to the shore for a voice to be heard when an Ottawa began to speak fiercely, and exclaimed in a menacing tone: *These prisoners belong to me; I wish you to respect me by respecting what belongs to me; let us have no ill treatment, of which the whole odium would fall upon my head.* A hundred French officers could have spoken in the same tone, but their speech would have resulted only in drawing contempt upon themselves, and an increase of blows upon their captives; but a savage fears his fellow savage, and fears him only. Their slightest disputes lead to death; therefore they

[5] Roubaud repeats a faulty version of Marin's raid—a camp rumor that inflated a successful little skirmish with a small British party into a full-scale assault on Fort Edward. A handful of scalps were taken, then cut in two or three by Indians who wanted a share in the glory, thus inflating Roubaud's count.

seldom engage in them. Accordingly, the wishes of the Ottawa were respected as soon as announced; the prisoners were landed without tumult and
led to the fort; not the slightest shout attended them.

At first they were separated; they underwent interrogation, in which it
was unnecessary to use artifice in order to win from them the explanations
that were desired. Their fright, from which they had not wholly recovered,
loosened their tongues, and gave them a volubility which apparently would
not have been the case otherwise. . . .

I went to hasten the embarking of my people; it was done forthwith.
The passage was not long; two hours sufficed to complete it. The tent of
Monsieur the Chevalier de Lévis was placed at the entrance of the camp. I
took the liberty of paying my respects to this dignitary whose name an-
nounces his merit, and whose name even is his least title to respect. The conversation turned upon the act which had decided the fate of the five
Englishmen whose perilous adventure I have just related. I was very far from
knowing the circumstances; they are somewhat surprising. Listen to them.

Monsieur de Corbiere, a French officer serving in the colonial troops,
had been commanded the previous night to go to cruise on Lake Saint Sacrement [Lake George]. His company numbered about fifty Frenchmen, and a
little more than three hundred savages. At the first peep of day he discovered a body of three hundred English, who had also been detached to cruise
in about fifteen barges [whaleboats]. The form of these boats—high on the
sides, and strongly built, when contrasted with our frail canoes—counterbal-
anced sufficiently and more the slight superiority that we might have had in
the way of numbers.

Nevertheless, our men did not hesitate to begin the combat; the enemy
at first appeared to accept the defiance readily, but that temper did not last
long. The French and savages, who could reasonably base the hope of victory only on the boarding that their number encourages—and who, besides,
risked everything in fighting at a distance—began to draw closer to the
enemy, notwithstanding the activity of their firing. The enemy no sooner saw
themselves pursued than fear made them drop their arms.[6]

It was no longer a contest; it was nothing more than a defeat. Of all
ways, doubtless, the least honorable—but, what is more, the most dangerous—was to gain the beach. It was on this that they decided. In an instant,
we saw them moving with haste to the shore; some of them, in order to
reach it sooner, began to swim, flattering themselves with being able to escape to the shelter of the woods—an ill-planned undertaking, the folly of
which they continually had to lament. Whatever be the speed which the increased efforts of rowers can give to boats that the science and skill of the
workman have made capable of swiftness, it does not approach, by a great

---

[6] The French and Indians executed a waterborne ambush, surrounding the English whaleboats with their more numerous canoes.

deal, the fleetness of a bark canoe; this glides—or, rather, it flies—over the water with the rapidity of an arrow. Therefore the first English were soon overtaken.

In the first heat of the combat all were massacred without mercy; all were cut to pieces. Those who had already gained the woods did not meet a better fate. The woods are the element of the savages; they run through them with a swiftness of a deer. The enemy were overtaken there and cut to pieces. In the meantime, the Ottawas, seeing that they were no longer dealing with warriors, but with a people who allowed themselves to be slaughtered without resistance, decided to take prisoners. The number of these amounted to a hundred and fifty-seven; that of the dead, to a hundred and thirty-one; only twelve were fortunate enough to escape captivity and death. The barges, the equipments, the stores—everything was taken and pillaged. . . . Such a complete success was purchased at the price of one single savage wounded, whose wrist was put out of joint by a shot. . . .

As for their prisoners, the greater part are still groaning in the chains of Monsieur the Chevalier de Lévis. I saw them go by in squads escorted by their victors—who, barbarian-like, engrossed with their triumph, showed little inclination to alleviate the defeat of the vanquished. In the space of a league, which I was obliged to make in order to rejoin my Abenakis, I met several little companies of these captives. More than one savage stopped me on the way to parade his captives before me, and to enjoy, in passing, my commendation. . . . These prisoners were presented to me in a very wretched state, their eyes bathed in tears, their faces covered with perspiration and even with blood, and with ropes around their necks; at this sight feelings of compassion and humanity certainly had a right over my heart. . . .

My tent had been placed in the midst of the Ottawas' camp. The first object that appeared to my eyes on arriving there was a large fire; and the stakes of wood set in the ground betokened a feast. There was one indeed. But, oh, heavens! what a feast! The remains of an English body, more than half stripped of the skin and flesh. I perceived a moment after these inhuman creatures eating, with a famished avidity, this human flesh; I saw them taking large spoonfuls of this detestable broth, without being able to satiate themselves. . . . The saddest thing was that they had placed near them about ten Englishmen, to be spectators of their infamous repast.

The Ottawa resembles the Abenaki; I believed that by mildly expostulating with these monsters of inhumanity I should gain some influence over them. But I flattered myself. A young man began to speak, and said to me in bad French: *Thou have French taste; me savage, this meat good for me.* He accompanied his remark by offering to me a piece of this English roast. I made no response to his argument, which was worthy of a barbarian; as to his offer, you may easily imagine with what horror I rejected it. . . .

An appetite for liquor is the favorite passion, the universal weakness of all the savage tribes; and unfortunately there are only too many hands eager to pour liquor out for them, in spite of divine and human laws. . . . I was somewhat distant from my people; I was separated from them by a little wood. I could not think of passing through it at night, to go to see if good order were reigning in their camp, without being exposed to some sinister adventure, not only on the part of the Iroquois attached to the English army—who, at the very entrance of the camp, a few days before, had torn off the scalp of one of our grenadiers—but also on the part of our own idolaters, on whom experience had taught me that we could not depend. . . .

At last the moment so much desired arrived. Monsieur the Chevalier de Lévis, at the head of three thousand men, had made the journey by land, on Friday the 29th of July, so that he might protect the descent of the army that was to go by water. . . . The departure of his body had preceded our own by a few days. It was on Sunday that we embarked with the savages alone, who at that time had a body of perhaps 1,200 men, the rest having gone by land. We had hardly made four or five leagues on the lake before we observed painful signs of our late victory: these were the abandoned English barges, which, after having floated a long time at the will of the winds and waves, had at last run aground on the beach. But the most striking spectacle was a somewhat large number of English bodies stretched out along the shore, or scattered here and there in the woods. Some were cut into pieces, and nearly all were mutilated in the most frightful manner. What a terrible scourge war appeared to me! . . .

The next day, about four o'clock in the afternoon, Monsieur de Montcalm arrived with the rest of the army. We were obliged to continue our way, notwithstanding a deluge of rain that drenched us. We marched nearly the whole night, until we distinguished the camp of Monsieur de Lévis by three fires, placed triangularly on the top of a mountain. We halted at this place, where a general council was held, after which the land troops began anew to march toward Fort William Henry,[7] only four leagues distant.

It was not until noon that we again entered our canoes. We paddled slowly, in order to give the boats loaded with artillery time to follow us. They were far from being able to do it. By evening we were more than a full league ahead. However, as we had come to a bay, the point of which we could not double without wholly exposing ourselves to the enemy, we decided to spend the night there, while waiting for new orders. It was marked by an unimportant fight, which was the prelude to the siege.

About eleven o'clock [in the evening] two barges, which had left the fort, appeared on the lake. They were sailing with a confidence and composure which they soon gave up. One of my neighbors, who was watching over the general safety, descried them at a considerable distance. The news was

---

[7] Roubaud refers consistently to Fort William Henry as "Fort George." To erase any confusion, the name has been corrected in this text.

carried to all the savages, and preparations for receiving them were concluded with admirable activity and silence. . . . Four hundred boats or canoes, which for two days had covered the surface of Lake Saint Sacrement,
made too great a show to have escaped the watchful and clear-sighted eyes
of an enemy. Holding this opinion, I had difficulty in persuading myself that
two barges would have the temerity, I do not say to measure themselves with
such superior forces, but to appear before them; I was arguing, and it was
only necessary to open my eyes.

One of my friends, a witness of everything, warned me again, in a tone
too serious for me not to yield, that I was out of place. He was right. All the
missionaries were together on a somewhat large boat. A tent had been put
on this . . . [which] made a sort of shadow that was easily discovered by the
light of the stars. Eager to inquire into it, the English steered directly toward
us. To take such a course and to run to death was almost the same thing.
Few, in truth, would have escaped it, if fortunately for them, a slight circumstance had not betrayed us a few moments too soon.

A sheep belonging to our people began to bleat; at this cry, which disclosed the ambush, the enemy faced about, steered for the opposite shore,
and plied their oars that they might escape under cover of the darkness and
the woods. This maneuver being immediately understood, what was to be
done? Twelve hundred savages began to move, and flew in pursuit of them,
with yells as terrifying by their duration as by their number.

Nevertheless, both sides seemed at first to respect each other; not a single gunshot was fired. The aggressors, not having had time to form themselves, were fearful of shooting each other; and, besides, they wished to take
prisoners. The fugitives were using their arms to advantage in accelerating
their flight. They had nearly reached their point when the savages, who perceived that their prey was escaping them, fired. The English, pressed too
closely by some canoes in advance, were obliged to answer it. Very soon a
gloomy silence followed all this uproar. . . .

I hastened to rejoin our people, in order to cede my place to Monsieur
Mathavet, the missionary of the Nipissing Tribe. I was arriving by water
when Monsieur de Montcalm—who, at the report of musketry, had landed
a little above—came through the woods; he learned that I had come with
news from the place, and applied to me that he might better understand the
affair; my Abenakis, whom I recalled, gave him a short report of the combat. The darkness of the night did not permit us to learn the number of the
enemy's dead; their barges had been seized and three men had been taken
prisoners. The rest were wandering at random in the woods. Monsieur de
Montcalm, delighted with these details, retired that he might with his accustomed prudence consider the operations of the next day.

[The next day,] the bay in which we had anchored resounded on all
sides with noises of war. Everyone was in motion and action. Our artillery,
which consisted of thirty-two guns and five mortars, put on platforms which

had been laid on boats fastened together, took the lead. In passing the tongue of land which concealed us from the sight of the enemy, we took care to salute the fort by firing a volley—which was, to begin with, but mere ceremony, but which announced more serious volleys. The rest of the little fleet followed, but slowly.

Already a body of savages had established their camp in the rear of Fort William Henry, on the way to Fort Edward, in order to cut off all communication between the two English forts. The force of Monsieur the Chevalier de Lévis occupied the defiles of the mountains, which led to the place chosen for our landing. Favored by such wise measures, our descent was made without opposition to a good half-league below the fort.

The enemy had too many affairs of their own to undertake throwing obstacles in our way. They were expecting anything rather than a siege; but I hardly know from what cause their confidence sprang. The vicinity of the fort was occupied by a multitude of tents, which at our arrival were still standing. We observed there a number of barracks, well fitted to favor the besiegers. The enemy were obliged to clear the outworks, to take down the tents, and burn the barracks; these movements could not be made without their being exposed to many volleys on the part of the savages, who are always ready to avail themselves of advantages that are given to them. Their fire would have been more active and deadly if another object had not attracted part of their attention. Herds of cattle and horses, which the enemy had not had time to put in safety, were roving on the lowlands situated in the neighborhood of the fort. The savages at once gave their whole attention to chasing these animals; a hundred and fifty oxen killed or taken, and fifty horses, were the first fruits of this little war; but this was only one of the precursors and preparations of the siege.

Fort William Henry was a square flanked by four bastions; the curtains had fraises [lines of sharpened sticks], the ditches were dug to the depth of eighteen or twenty feet, and the scarp and counter scarp [sides of the ditches] were embanked with moving sand. The walls were formed of large pine trees, filled in with the earthwork, and sustained by extremely heavy stakes. . . . Four or five hundred men defended the fort, with the aid of nineteen guns—two of which were of thirty-six [pounds], the others of less caliber—and with four or five mortars.

The place was not protected by any other outwork than a fortified rock [hill] faced with palisades secured by heaps of stones. The garrison consisted of seventeen hundred men, and continually relieved that of the fort. The chief defense of this entrenchment was its position, which overlooked the surrounding country, and which was accessible to artillery only on the side of the fort, as mountains and swamps skirted the different avenues leading to it.

Such was Fort William Henry, according to the information which I gained on the spot after the surrender of the place; it was not possible to invest it and entirely block all the ways to it. Six thousand Frenchmen or Canadians and seventeen hundred savages, who formed our whole force, were not sufficient for the immense amount of ground that would have been necessary to encircle in order to succeed in this; hardly would twenty thousand men have been able to do it. Accordingly, the enemy always possessed a back door by which they could slip into the woods—which could have served them as an advantageous resource if they had not had the savages in front; but a person rarely escapes from their hands in this way. Besides, the quarters of the savages were placed on the Fort Edward road—so close to the neighborhood of the woods, and where they were so often on the scout, that it would have indeed been risking life to seek an asylum in that direction.

At a short distance were quartered the Canadians, holding the summit of the mountains, and always in condition to assist the savages. Lastly the regular troops who came from France—to whom properly belonged the hardships of the siege—occupied the edge of the wood, very near the ground where the trenches were to be opened; then followed the reserve, composed of sufficient troops to protect it from every attack.

These arrangements having been made, Monsieur the Marquis de Montcalm sent to the enemy some propositions, which would have spared them much blood and many tears had they been accepted. The summons was couched in very nearly the following words, and was addressed to Monsieur Monro,[8] commandant of the fort in the name of His Brittanic Majesty. *Sir: I have come with troops sufficient to carry the place you hold, and to cut off all aid which might come to you from elsewhere. I number among my soldiers a crowd of savage tribes, whom the least shedding of blood might exasperate to the point of rooting out in them forever all feelings of moderation and clemency. Love of humanity urges me to summon you to yield at a time when it will not be impossible for me to make them agree to terms honorable for you and advantageous for all. I have, etc. Signed, Montcalm.*

The bearer of the letter was Monsieur Fontbrane, aide-de-camp of Monsieur de Lévis. He was received by messieurs the English officers, several of whom were his acquaintances, with a politeness and consideration from which the laws of honor excuse no person when he makes war like an honest man. But this favorable reception decided nothing as to the surrender of the fort, as was shown by the answer. Here it is: *Monsieur the General Montcalm: I am especially obliged to you for the kind offers that you make me, but I cannot accept them. I am little afraid of barbarity; besides, I have under my orders soldiers who are determined, like myself, to die or to conquer. I have,* etc. *Signed, Monro.* The haughtiness of this answer was very soon proclaimed by the noise of a volley from the enemy's artillery.

We were far from being in condition to reply immediately. Before we

[8] Roubaud consistently referred to Lieutenant Colonel George Monro, commander of Fort William Henry, as "Moreau." It has been corrected throughout.

were able to plant a battery it was necessary to drag our guns for a full half-league over rocks and through the forests. Thanks to the voracity of the savages, we could not have for this work the aid of any of our beasts of burden; being weary, as they said, of salt meat, they had not scrupled to seize these animals and feast on them, some days previously, without considering anything but their own appetite. . . . During all this commotion I was staying near the hospital, where I hoped to be within call so that I might perform the duties of my office for the dying and for the dead. . . .

There were other people whose fate was also to be pitied. Every day, savage activity and bravery multiplied the prisoners—that is to say, the wretched. It was not possible for the enemy to take a step beyond the fort without being exposed either to captivity or to death, so alert were the savages. You may judge of it by this single account. An English woman ventured to go to gather vegetables in a kitchen garden almost adjoining the trenches. Her boldness cost her dear; a savage concealed in a bed of cabbages perceived her, and with his gun killed her on the spot. The enemy had not opportunity of coming to take away her body; the victor, still concealed, kept guard all day long, and took off her scalp.

In the meantime, all the savage tribes were very weary of the silence of our "great muskets"—it is thus that they designate our cannon. They were anxious [to be] no longer alone to bear the brunt of the war. In order, therefore, to satisfy them, it was necessary to hasten the work of the entrenchments, and plant our first battery. The first time it was fired, there were cries of joy, and all the mountains resounded with the uproar. It was not necessary during the whole course of the siege to make great efforts to be aware of the success of our artillery; the shouts of the savages every moment brought news of it to all the quarters. . . .

I rejoined my Abenakis, with the purpose of not separating myself from them again in the whole course of the campaign. No other remarkable event took place for some days, unless it were the cheerful alacrity and the activity with which the work on the entrenchments was advanced.

The second battery was in place in two days. This was a new holiday which the savages celebrated in military fashion. They were continually around our gunners, whose dexterity they admired. But their admiration was neither inactive nor fruitless. They wished to try everything, so as to make themselves more useful. They aspired to become gunners, and one of their number distinguished himself; after having himself pointed his gun, he shot accurately in the reentrant angle that had been assigned to him for a mark. But he refused to repeat it, notwithstanding the solicitations of the French—alleging as his reason for his refusal that, having attained in his very first attempt that degree of perfection to which he could aspire, he ought not to hazard his fame by a second trial.

But the cause of their chief astonishment was those several zigzags which, forming the different branches of a trench, are so many covered ways, very useful for protecting the besiegers against the guns of the besieged. They examined with an eager curiosity the manner in which our French grenadiers proceeded to give to this sort of work the perfection it required. Having been taught by their eyes, they very soon tried their hands at the practical part.

Armed with shovels and pickaxes, they were seen making a covered way to the fortified rock, the attack on which had fallen to their lot. They pushed it forward so well that they were very soon within gunshot. Monsieur de Villiers, brother of Monsieur de Jumonville[9]—an officer whose mere name is a eulogy—improved these advances by coming, at the head of a body of Canadians, to attack the outer entrenchments. The action was sharp, disputed for a long time, and deadly for the enemy. They were driven from their first position, and it is to be presumed that the great entrenchments would have been carried that very day if their capture could have decided the surrender of the fort. Every day was marked by some splendid act on the part of the French, the Canadians, and the savages.

In the meantime, the enemy were continually sustained by the hope of a speedy aid. A little event that happened at this time ought indeed to have diminished their confidence. Our scouts met in the woods three messengers coming from Fort Edward; they killed the first, took the second, and the third escaped by his swiftness in running. They seized a letter put into a hollow ball and so well concealed on the body of the dead man that it would have escaped the scrutiny of any other than that of a military man who knows this sort of stratagem of war.

The letter was signed by the commandant of Fort Edward and was addressed to the commandant of Fort William Henry. It contained in substance the deposition of a Canadian taken prisoner [by the British] on the first night of our arrival. According to his declaration, our army numbered eleven thousand men, and the corps of our savages two thousand; and our artillery was most formidable. There was a mistake in this reckoning. Our forces were in this letter exaggerated far beyond the truth.

The error was not, however, to be attributed to fraud and deceit. . . . Before this war, the most numerous armies of Canada had scarcely exceeded eight hundred men; surprise and astonishment would magnify objects to eyes unaccustomed to seeing large ones. In the course of this campaign, I have been witness of much greater mistakes of this kind. The commandant of Edward concluded his letter by telling his colleague that the interest of the King his master not permitting him to dismantle his fort, the other would be better to capitulate, and procure as advantageous conditions as possible.

Monsieur de Montcalm did not think that he could put this letter to

---

[9] Jumonville had been killed by Washington's men in the skirmish that started the war.

better use than to forward it as addressed, by the very messenger who had fallen living into our hands. He received from the English officer thanks, accompanied by the modest request that he would continue to him for a long time the same civilities. Such a compliment either partook of the nature of trifling, or it promised a long resistance. The actual state of the fort did not indicate this: part of its batteries dismounted and out of service, through the success of our own; the fear prevalent among the besieged, who were now retained as soldiers only by the means of a liberal supply of rum; and, lastly, the frequent desertions—all these tokens announced its approaching fall. . . .

Finally, on the morrow—the eve of Saint Lawrence's day and the seventh day after our arrival—the entrenchments having been pushed forward so far as the gardens, we prepared to plant our third and last battery. The proximity of the fort led us to hope that in three or four days we should be able to make a general assault, by means of a suitable breach; but the enemy spared us the trouble and the danger; they hoisted a French flag, and asked to capitulate.

We are near the surrender of the fort and the bloody catastrophe which followed. . . . I shall relate only facts of such incontestable publicity and authenticity that I could, without fear of being contradicted, support them by the testimony of even messieurs the English officers, who were the witnesses and victims of them.

Monsieur the Marquis de Montcalm thought that he ought, before consenting to any terms, to take the opinion of all the savage tribes, in order to appease them by this condescension and to render the treaty inviolable by their consent. He assembled all the chiefs, to whom he communicated the conditions of capitulation, which granted to the enemy the right of going out of the fort with all the honors of war; and imposed on them with the obligation of not serving against His Most Christian Majesty [of France] for eighteen months, that of restoring liberty to all Canadians taken in this war.

All these articles were universally approved: stamped with the seal of general approbation, the treaty was signed by the generals of the two crowns. Accordingly the French army, in order of battle, advanced to the fort to take possession of it in the name of His Most Christian Majesty; while the English troops, ranged in good order, went out to take refuge until the next day in the entrenchments. Their march was not marked by any contravention of the law of nations; but the savages lost no time in violating it.

During the military ceremony which accompanied taking possession, crowds of them had penetrated into the fort through gun embrasures, that they might proceed to pillage what we had agreed to give up to them, but they were not content with pillaging. A few sick soldiers had remained in the casemates, their condition not permitting them to follow their fellow countrymen in the honorable retreat accorded to their valor. These were the victims upon whom they pitilessly rushed, and whom they sacrificed to their cruelty. I was a witness of this spectacle. I saw one of these barbarians come out of the casemates into which nothing less than an insatiable avidity for blood could make anyone enter, so insupportable was the stench which exhaled from them. He carried in his hand a human head, from which trickled streams of blood, and which he displayed as the most splendid prize that he could have secured.

This was only a very faint prelude to the cruel tragedy of the next day. At the very dawn of day, the savages reassembled about the entrenchments. They began by asking the English for goods, provisions—in a word, for all the riches that their greedy eyes could see; but these demands were made in a tone that foretold a blow with a spear as the price of refusal. The English dispossessed and despoiled themselves, and reduced themselves to nothing, that they might buy at least life by this general renunciation. . . . They [the Indians] were not on this account less inclined to proceed to the harshest extremes.

The body of four hundred men of the French troops, selected to protect the line of retreat of the enemy, arrived, and drew up in a line on both sides. The English began to defile. Woe to all those who brought up the rear, or to stragglers whom indisposition or any other cause separated however little from the troop. They were so many dead whose bodies very soon strewed the ground and covered the enclosure of the entrenchments. This butchery, which in the beginning was the work of only a few savages, was the signal which made nearly all of them so many ferocious beasts. They struck, right and left, heavy blows of the hatchet on those who fell into their hands. However, the massacre was not of long continuance, or so great as such fury gave us cause to fear; the number of men killed was hardly more than forty or fifty. The patience of the English, who were content to bend the head under the sword of their executioners, suddenly appeased the weapon, but did not bring the tormenters to reason and equity. Continually uttering loud cries, these began to take them prisoners.

In the midst of this I arrived. No, I do not believe that anyone can be a man and be insensible in such sorrowful circumstances. The son torn from the arms of the father, the daughter snatched from the bosom of the mother, the husband separated from the wife; officers stripped even to their shirts, without regard for their rank or for decency; a crowd of unfortunate people who were running at random, some toward the woods, some toward the French tents—these toward the fort, others to every place that seemed to promise an asylum; such were the pitiable objects that were presented to my sight.

Nevertheless, the French were not inactive and insensible spectators of the catastrophe. Monsieur the Chevalier de Lévis was running wherever the tumult appeared the most violent, endeavoring to stop it, with a courage inspired by the kindness so natural to his illustrious blood. A thousand times he faced death—which, notwithstanding his birth and his virtues, he would not have escaped if a special providence had not watched over his life and had not restrained the savage arms already raised to strike him. The French officers and the Canadians imitated his example, with a zeal worthy of the humanity which has always characterized the nation; but the main part of our troops, occupied in guarding our batteries and the fort, was, on account of the distance, unable to give them aid.

Of what help could four hundred men be against the fifteen hundred furious savages who were not distinguishing us from the enemy? One of our sergeants, who had strongly opposed their violence, was thrown to the ground by a blow from a spear. One of our French officers, in reward for the same zeal, received a severe wound which brought him to the gate of death; besides, in this time of alarm people did not know in what direction to turn. . . .

Monsieur de Montcalm—who was not apprised of the affair for some time, on account of the distance to his tent—came at the first notice to the place of the uproar, with a celerity which showed the goodness and nobility of his heart. He seemed to be in several places at once, he would reappear, he was everywhere; he used prayers, menaces, promises; he tried everything, and at last resorted to force. . . .

In the meantime, the tumult was continually increasing, when happily someone thought of calling out to the English, who formed a large body, to hasten their march. This forced march had its effect; the savages—partly through the futility of their pursuit, partly satisfied with their captures—retired; the few who remained were easily dispersed. The English continued their way in peace to Fort Edward, where they arrived—numbering, at first, only three or four hundred. I do not know the number of those who, having gained the woods, were fortunate enough to reach the fort by the help of a cannon which our people took care to fire, for several days, in order to guide them.

The remainder of the garrison, whoever had not perished by the sword, neither were they groaning under the weight of chains. Many of them had found safety in the French tents, or in the fort, whither I repaired, after the disorder had been once quieted. A crowd of women came and with tears and groans surrounded me, threw themselves at my feet; they kissed the hem of my robe, uttering from time to time lamentable cries that pierced my heart. It was not in my power to dry up the source of their tears; they asked the return of their sons, their daughters, their husbands, whose capture they were deploring. . . .

A French officer informed me that a Huron, at that very time in his camp, was in possession of an infant six months old, whose death was certain if I did not immediately go to its rescue. I did not hesitate. I ran in haste to the tent of the savage, in whose arms I perceived the innocent victim, who was tenderly kissing the hands of its captor and playing with some porcelain necklaces that adorned him. . . . He understood me at once: *Here,* said he to me very civilly, *dost thou see this infant? I have not stolen it; I found it deserted in a hedge; thou wishest it, but though shalt not have it.* . . . I believed the death-sentence already pronounced, when I perceived that the man was consulting in Huron with his companions; for until then the conversation had been held in French, which he understood. This conference made a ray of hope dawn on my eyes; this hope was not deceived. The result was that the infant belonged to me, if I would hand over to him an enemy's scalp. The proposition did not embarrass me: *It will soon be seen,* I replied to him on rising, *if thou art a man of honor.*

I set out in haste for the camp of the Abenakis. I asked the first one I met if he were the possessor of any scalp, and if he would do me the favor of giving it to me. I had every reason to rejoice at his readiness to oblige me; he untied his bag, and gave me my choice. Supplied with one of those barbarous trophies, I carried it in triumph, followed by a crowd of French and Canadians eager to know the outcome of the adventure. Joy lent me wings; in a moment I was with my Huron. "Here," said I on meeting him, "here is thy payment." *Thou art right,* he answered me, *it is indeed an English scalp, for it is red.* In reality it is this color which more commonly designates the English colonists of these districts. *Well then! Here is the infant. Take it away; it belongs to thee.*

I did not give him time to withdraw from the agreement. I immediately took into my hands the little unfortunate creature. . . . I reached the fort; at the cries of the little one, all the women came to me in haste. Each one hoped to find the object of her maternal tenderness. They examined it eagerly; but neither the eyes nor the heart of any one of them recognized in it her son. They withdrew apart, to give anew free vent to their groaning and lamentation. . . .

One of them agreed. . . . [to care for the child] if I would answer for her life and that of her husband, to be responsible for their maintenance, and have them taken to Boston by way of Montreal. I immediately accepted the proposal. . . . I was preparing to leave the fort when the father of the infant was found; he had been wounded by the explosion of a shell, and was unable to help himself; he could only acquiesce with pleasure in the arrangements that I had made for the safety of his son. . . .

Such were the circumstances of the unfortunate expedition which dishonored the bravery that the savages had displayed throughout the course of the siege, and which have made even their services burdensome to us. . . . The news of that fatal deed, having spread abroad through the English colonies, produced in them such grief and dread that one single savage actually dared to carry his temerity so far as to go to carry away captives almost at the gates of Orange [Albany], without having been disturbed either in his expedition or in his retreat. Therefore the enemy planned no undertaking against us at the time which followed the capture of the fort.

Nevertheless, nothing was more critical for us than the situation in which the French army then was. The savages, with the exception of the

Abenakis and Nipissings, had disappeared on the very day of their wretched expedition; twelve hundred men were occupied in demolishing the fort; and nearly a thousand were employed in transporting the immense supplies of food and ammunition that we had seized. Hardly a handful of men remained to cope with the enemy, if they had assumed the offensive. Their tranquillity gave us the opportunity of accomplishing our work. Fort William Henry has been destroyed and razed to the ground and the ruins consumed by fire. It was only during the burning that we comprehended the greatness of the enemy's loss. Casemates and secret underground passages were found filled with dead bodies, which for several days furnished fresh fuel for the activity of the flames. As for our loss, it consisted of twenty-one dead—three of whom were savages—and about twenty-five wounded; that was all.

IF ONLY FRANCE could have switched navies with Britain, it would have won the war when Fort William Henry fell. Everywhere in North America it stood victorious. Though its Canadian population numbered only 55,000, it had fenced the 1.2 million English subjects into a narrow strip along the Atlantic coast. In the west, it had blocked all advances over the Appalachians, thanks to its bases at Forts Duquesne and Niagara and its many Indian allies. In the east, it drove off an assault on Louisburg, carried out that same year by Lord Loudon. And in the critical Lake Champlain corridor, General Montcalm destroyed Britain's most important fortress—the staging area for any northward advance.

In this grim year, the British and their colonists focused their outrage on the massacre of prisoners that followed the surrender of Fort William Henry. Had not Montcalm promised to let the captured men go free? Had he not given his word of honor that they could leave unmolested, with a simple promise not to fight again in North America? Then the general must be a scoundrel, a villain, and the French all ruthless savages.

Of course, as Roubaud's account shows, the French army tried very hard to restrain their Indian allies. The fault lies not with any dark plot or sinister intentions, but in a clash of irreconcilable martial ethics. Throughout this book, we have seen the ferocity—the traditional, ritual ferocity—of many Native Americans toward their enemies. We have seen that they went to war for captives, plunder, and glory. They did not go on the warpath for strategic considerations—certainly not those warriors who had canoed a thousand miles to join Montcalm, descending the Great Lakes from modern-day Manitoba, Minnesota, Wisconsin, and Michigan. As Ian Steele has argued, these men found European honors of war incomprehensible, even dangerous.

A bitter irony lies hidden in the colonists' outrage at the massacre. From the days of Captain John Smith and John Winthrop, English immigrants had waged war against the Indians without any sort of civilized restraint. The burning of villages, wholesale slaughter, and slave auctions of the survivors sum up their methods. The idea of honors of war had been introduced only recently by European regular armies; they came from a culture that had taken a different path from that of the colonists since they first left Europe. Braddock, Montcalm, Webb, Monro: they belonged to the eighteenth century; in many ways, both Canadians and Americans belonged to the seventeenth, one of the darkest in European history.

Meanwhile, the third year of war ended as a third year of defeat for Britain in North America. Vaudreuil's offensive had succeeded brilliantly on all fronts. The English despair, even hysteria, can best be imagined. Montcalm burned Fort William Henry because he lacked the manpower to hold it, let alone advance farther; yet the governors and assemblies of New York and New England convinced themselves that he would promptly capture Fort Edward, march to the Hudson, and descend to the Atlantic. Meanwhile Indian raids plagued the Appalachian frontier, ruling out any aid for the north from Pennsylvania, Maryland, and Virginia. And Louisburg stood defiant against Britain's fleet. If France could have seized control of the sea, it could have completely sealed off America and dictated terms. But Britannia still ruled the waves—so there was hope for the English yet, if they had the will to fight on.

21

THE FALL OF NEW FRANCE

God seemed to have a habit of saving New France. In 1690 and 1711 (to name two examples) superior English forces had held Quebec in their grasp, only to be driven away by storms, smallpox, and misfortune. The Almighty might well take such steps again. But as 1758 began, the colony's leaders knew they must follow the Jesuit dictum: to trust in God, but act as if all depended on themselves alone.

When Governor-General Vaudreuil, General Montcalm, and Montcalm's chief of staff, Louis Antoine de Bougainville, gathered to discuss the strategic situation, they realized that self-reliance was their only option. War had now spread to Europe; French troops were tied down across the Atlantic, leaving none to spare for Canada; and French ports suffered a tight blockade by Britain's large and efficient fleet. The colony would have neither reinforcements nor badly needed supplies—and New France still suffered the effects of the bad harvest of 1756. Even the Indians faded away: Montcalm's vast force of 1,000 warriors quickly dispersed to their distant homes, content with their plunder.

Though the population of the British colonies still despaired, though the people of Canada still exulted, the leaders on both sides knew that 1758 would change the war drastically. A new politician dominated the British government: William Pitt, an irascible and extremely energetic administrator. Pitt moved swiftly to bring his nation's power to bear on New France. He removed Lord Loudon as overall commander in North America, replacing him with Major General James Abercromby. He dispatched 11,000 regular troops, and recruited an equal number of Americans into the British army (forming the Royal American regiment, among others). The army also organized units of colonial rangers, who took the place of Six Nations scouts who had deserted after the fall of Fort William Henry (they now saw the British as the losing side). Convoy after convoy crossed the Atlantic, transporting Pitt's new forces to American shores.[10]

Pitt ordered a three-pronged offensive against New France—essentially a repeat of Braddock's failed attack. This time, however, many of the regu-

[10] Pitt could afford to send troops to North America because the fighting on the European continent was being shouldered by his allies, the Prussians, under the command of Frederick II—the brilliant soldier-king remembered as "the Great."

lar troops had experience in woodland fighting; they were also far more numerous, better supplied, and better supported by both London and the colonial governments. In the west, Brigadier General John Forbes would march against Fort Duquesne—taking a shorter route than Braddock's, this time through Pennsylvania. In the east, an extremely powerful fleet would carry assault troops under Major General Jeffrey Amherst to attack the fortress port of Louisburg. And in the north, Major General Abercromby himself would lead an offensive against Fort Carillon—the French works on Lake Champlain, at the portage to Lake George.

In these foreboding times, the cautious, professional Montcalm began to supplant Vaudreuil in New France's military planning. The governor-general's daring offensive of the two previous years had succeeded beyond anyone's wildest dreams—but the British had command of the sea, bringing thousands of reinforcements, which limited their options to the simple idea of holding on. Who knew? If they husbanded their resources, fought hard enough, and held out long enough, perhaps a miracle would once again save New France. Given time, a victory in Europe and a well-negotiated peace settlement might preserve Paris's New World empire.

As Montcalm made his calculations, he decided to concentrate his forces to meet one of the three attacks he knew would come in 1758. At Fort Duquesne, he left a handful of men under François-Marie Le Marchand de Ligneris to fend for themselves. At Louisburg, he trusted to strong defensive works and the few warships that had escaped Britain's tight blockade of French ports. He himself took command of the remaining troops, which he gathered at Fort Carillon—the target of Abercromby's offensive.

Here, on the shores of Lake Champlain, the two supreme commanders would face each other in battle. Here British numbers would meet French valor and skill. Here the two sides would engage in a race—Abercromby to break through to the St. Lawrence, and Montcalm to hold him off until reinforcements arrived under the daring and talented Chevalier François-Gaston Lévis.

Fortunately, one of the most important officers at Carillon also wrote about it in a journal. Bougainville, Montcalm's chief of staff, kept a close record of those dramatic events: a conventional battle in the midst of the wilderness, where New France gambled everything on victory.

The Enemy Repulsed
by Louis Antoine de Bougainville

JULY 1, 1758:   The Marquis de Montcalm went this morning . . . to reconnoiter the surroundings of Fort Carillon in order to select a battlefield and the place for an entrenched camp. We lack manpower, and perhaps time is also lacking. Our situation is critical. Action and audacity are our sole resources.

Council with a dozen Ottawas who wanted to return to Montreal and from there to Michilimackinac. With breechclouts, mitasses, shirts, guns, the Marquis de Montcalm has held them. They have promised to do him the favor of [forming] a war party and waiting until other Indians come. Great good fortune that they are willing to stay. This evening there arrived a convoy bringing thirty thousand rations, that is to say provisions for seven or eight days for our present number. . . .

JULY 2:   It has been decided to occupy the heights which dominate Carillon with an entrenched camp, with redoubts and abatis.[11] . . . But to carry out these works strong arms are needed, as well as the arrival of the colony troops, and time granted us by the enemy. All that can be done at the moment, and which is being done, is to lay out the works and get the troops at the falls and the portage to make as many fascines and palisades as their camp duties will permit. The third battalion of Berry, which is in the fort, can furnish only eighty to ninety workers. How to do it with so few people? . . .

JULY 3:   M. de Raymond, captain of [*troupes de*] *la marine,* arrived with 118 men, 80 Canadians, the rest soldiers of *la marine.* M. Mercier also arrived to take command of the artillery. He brought letters from the Marquis de Vaudreuil which announced the arrival of powerful reinforcements and of the detachment of the Chevalier de Lévis. . . .

The King having judged it proper to employ me in America as "*aide-maréchal des logis*" [chief of staff] of his troops, under orders of the Marquis de Montcalm, the Marshal de Bell-Isle has sent him the commission. . . .

JULY 4:   Duties, guards, and patrols as usual. Our position, very risky, obliges us to [take] the greatest precautions. . . .

This evening there departed, under orders of Sieur de Langy, a detachment of about 150 men, 104 of them volunteers from our battalions [of regular troops], 25 Canadians, and a score of Indians. . . . His orders are to go and observe the location, the number, and the movements of the enemy at the end of the Lake St. Sacrement [Lake George] and to make prisoners if possible. . . .

JULY 5:   Arrival of three captains of the colony [militia and *troupes de la marine*] with 150 Canadians and soldiers of *la marine.* . . . The first part of Chevalier de Lévis's division should reach St. Jean today. They assured us that the promised aid will join us.

At five o'clock in the evening Sieur de Langy's detachment returned,

---

[11] Abatis was a tangle of brush, often with sharpened sticks, spread in front of a defensive position to slow down an attacking enemy. Carillon sat on a point, with Lake Champlain to the east and the river connecting it with Lake George to the southwest.

having seen on the lake a great [body] of enemy barges which could only be what it was, the advance guard of their army, led by Colonel Bradstreet and Major Rogers.

Orders [given] at once to the troops at the falls [on the river between the two lakes] that at a general call by drum beat, they should spend the night in bivouac and should commence to clear away the equipment. . . .

JULY 6:   The troops under arms; enemy barges seen on the move around four o'clock in the morning; sending back the equipment of the battalions at the falls and their bateaux [boats] to Carillon; orders to Sieur de Pontleroy and Desandrouins to mark out immediately the abatis defenses on the heights [as] determined the first of this month; to Sieur de Trécesson to put the third battalion of Berry to work there with the flags.

Sieur Germain returns to camp after having fired at those barges which passed within range of him. Bernard's volunteers fall back also after having fired a few times. The enemy started to disembark at Contrecoeur's camp around nine o'clock. Sieur de Bourlamaque retreated in good order and without losing a single man, although in the presence of the enemy. He joined up with the Marquis de Montcalm, and the five reunited battalions crossed the River of the Falls, destroying the bridge, and with the [battalions] of La Sarre and Languedoc, took up battle position on the heights situated opposite and on the left [north] of this river. . . .

This same evening a party of the enemy's regular troops and their light troops came to occupy the two banks of the Falls River extending as far as the Bernetz River and took up defensive positions there. General Abercromby with all the militia occupied Contrecoeur's camp, the portage, and took up positions there.

JULY 7:   The army was all busy working on the abatis outlined the previous evening by the third battalion of Berry. It was covered by the grenadier companies and the volunteers. Even the officers, ax in hand, set the example, and the flags were planted on the works. It [the line] had been, as we have said, traced the evening before on the heights, about 650 troises [paces] in advance of Fort Carillon.

The left rested on a steep slope eighty troises from the Falls River, the summit crowned with an abatis. This abatis flanked a gap behind which we were going to place six cannon to cover it as well as the river. The right also rested on a height whose slope was not so steep as that on the left. The plain, between this height and the St. Frederic River, was flanked by a branch of our entrenchments on the right, and should have been [covered] by a battery of four guns which was finished only after the action of the eighth. Moreover, the cannon of the fort were directed on this plain as well as on the landing place they could use on our left. The center followed the sinuosities of the ground holding to the high ground, and all parts gave each other flanking [support]. There were, to be sure, several places there, as well as on the right, subject to enemy cross fire; but this was because they did not give us time enough to raise traverses. These kinds of defensive works were made of tree trunks, lying one on top of the other, and having in front overturned trees whose cut and sharpened branches gave the effect of *chevaux-de-frise* [barriers of criss-crossing sharpened sticks]. The army worked with such ardor that the line was in a defensible state the same evening.

Between six and eight in the evening the light companies of our troops detached with the Chevalier de Lévis reached camp. They had been most diligent, advancing day and night despite contrary winds to join their comrades, whom they knew were about to be attacked; they were received by our little army with the same joy as were Caesar's legions by those Roman cohorts blockaded with Cicero by a multitude of Gauls. The Chevalier de Lévis arrived in the course of the night.

All day long our volunteers exchanged shots with the enemy's light troops. General Abercromby himself, with a large party of militia and the rest of the regulars, advanced as far as the falls. . . .

The army slept in the open along the entrenchments.

JULY 8:   They beat to arms at daybreak so that all the soldiers could know their posts for the defense of the works . . . which was nearly the same as that where they had worked. . . . The Chevalier de Lévis was charged with the right, Sieur de Bourlamaque with the left, and the Marquis de Montcalm remained in the center to be within range of all parts. This disposition determined and understood, the troops immediately went back to work; part were busy perfecting the abatis, the rest at constructing the two batteries mentioned before and a redoubt intended to protect the right.

This morning Colonel [Sir William] Johnson arrived at the enemy army with 300 Choctaws, Delawares, and Iroquois, and Captain Jacob with 150 more. Around ten o'clock we saw them as well as a few light troops on the mountain which is opposite Carillon, the other side of the River of the Falls. They let off a great fusillade which did not interrupt our work at all; we amused ourselves by not replying.

Half an hour after noon the English army advanced on us. The grenadier companies, the volunteers, and the advanced guards fired, fell back in good order, and re-entered the lines without losing a single man. At the same moment, at an agreed signal, all the troops were under arms at their posts.

The left was first attacked by two columns, one of which tried to outflank the defenses and found itself under fire of La Sarre,[12] the other directed its efforts on a salient between Languedoc and Berry. The center, where Royal Roussillon was, was attacked at almost the same time by a third column, and a fourth carried its attack toward the right between Béarn and La Reine. These different columns were intermingled with their light troops

12 La Sarre, Languedoc, Berry, Royal Roussillon, Béarn, and La Reine were all regular army units.

and better marksmen who, protected by trees, delivered a most murderous fire on us.

At the start of the affair a few of the enemy's barges and pontoons advanced down the River of the Falls. Bernard's and Duprat's volunteers, posted in this area, received them in fine style; Sieur de Poulhariez, at the head of the company of grenadiers and of a light company of Royal Roussillon also appeared there and, the cannon of the fort having smashed two of these barges, they withdrew and did not appear again during the action.

The different attacks, almost all afternoon and almost everywhere, were made with the greatest of vigor.

As the Canadians and colony troops were not attacked at all, they, from the defenses which sheltered them, directed their fire against the column which attacked our right and which a few times came within range. . . . This column, composed of English grenadiers and Scottish Highlanders, returned unceasingly to the attack, without becoming discouraged or broken, and several times got themselves killed within fifteen paces of our abatis. Chevalier de Lévis twice ordered the Canadians and the *troupes de la marine* to make sorties and take them in the flank.

Around five o'clock the column which had spiritedly attacked Royal Roussillon, threw itself against the salient defended by the Guyenne regiment and by the left of Béarn. The column which had attacked La Reine and Béarn with the greatest fury threw itself there again with the result that this attack threatened danger. Chevalier de Lévis went there with a few troops from the right, at which the enemy was only shooting [and not advancing]. The Marquis de Montcalm also ran there with a few reserve troops and the enemy met a resistance which finally cooled their ardor.

The left withstood the fire of the two columns which tried to penetrate this area, in which their supply depot was. M. de Bourlamaque had been dangerously wounded there around four o'clock and Sieurs de Senezergues and de Privat, lieutenant colonels of La Sarre and Languedoc, made up for his absence and continued to give the best of orders. The Marquis de Montcalm went there several times and was attentive to getting reinforcements there at all moments of crisis. For, throughout the entire affair, the grenadiers and light companies of the reserve always ran to the most threatened places. Around six o'clock the two columns on the right gave up the attack on Guyenne and came to make another attempt at the center against Royal Roussillon and Berry and finally a last effort on the left.

At seven o'clock the enemy thought only of retreat, covered by the fire of the light troops, which was kept up until dark.

During this action our abatis caught fire outside several times, but it was put out at once, the soldiers courageously passing over the back of it to stop the progress [of the flames]. . . .

We even thought that they [the British] would try next day to take their revenge, and consequently we worked all night to secure defilade against the neighboring heights by traverses, to perfect the abatis of the Canadians, and to finish the batteries on the right and left commenced in the morning.

JULY 9: The day was devoted to the same work and to burying our dead and those the enemy had left on the field of battle. Our companies of volunteers went out, advanced up to the falls, and reported that the enemy had abandoned the posts at the falls and even at the portage.

JULY 10: At break of day the Marquis de Montcalm detached the Chevalier de Lévis with the eight grenadier companies, the volunteers, and some fifty Canadians to find out what had become of the enemy army.

The Chevalier de Lévis advanced to beyond the portage. He everywhere found signs of a hurried flight. The English have since told me that the affair got underway before the dispositions were entirely completed, that hurry had occasioned a sort of disorder, augmented subsequently by the death of a great number of officers. . . .

Wounded, provisions, abandoned equipment, shoes left in miry places, remains of barges and burned pontoons: incontestable proof of the great loss our enemy had suffered. . . . The greatest part of the Indians, especially those of the Five Nations [*sic*], remained as spectators at the tail of the columns. They doubtless awaited the outcome of a combat which the English believed could not be doubtful. . . . Justice is due them [the English] that they attacked us with the greatest of determination. It is not common that defenses are attacked for seven hours and almost without any respite.

This victory which, for the moment, has saved Canada, is due to the sagacity of the dispositions, to the good maneuvers of our generals before and during the action, and to the unbelievable valor of our troops. All the officers of the army have so conducted themselves that each of them deserves a personal eulogy. We had forty-four officers and nearly four hundred men killed or wounded [compared to British losses of 1,610 killed, wounded, or missing]. . . .

JULY 29: Certain people are talking a lot of going home.[13] They never made war [that is, conventional war] in Canada before 1755. They never had gone into camp. To leave Montreal with a party, to go through the woods, to take a few scalps, to return at full speed once the blow was struck, that is what they called war, a campaign, a success, victory.

They assembled [once before] in a body of [Canadian troops and Indians], and the object of this army was to destroy the Foxes [an anti-French tribe]. It is the first and only campaign of the Marquis de Vaudreuil. It is where he educated himself in the difficult arts of Mars. The success was brilliant and instructive. They took an old man whom they tied to a stake and

---

[13] The remainder of this selection is devoted to Bougainville's bitterness toward Canadians, and especially the Canadian-born Governor-General Vaudreuil. Bougainville shared Montcalm's prejudice against the provincials and their irregular mode of warfare.

who, according to what I have often heard the governor general tell, made very comical faces while they were burning him. The Marquis de V. still laughed at the memory of it. . . .

Now war is established here on the European basis. Projects for the campaign, for armies, for artillery, for sieges, for battles. It no longer is a matter of making a raid, but of conquering or being conquered. What a revolution! What a change! One would believe that the people of this country, astonished at the novelty of these objects, would ask some time to accustom themselves to it, some more time to reflect on what they have seen, still more to efface their first ideas [now] become false ideas, dangerous, prejudiced from infancy, and still much more time to learn [proper] principles, to draw conjectures, to put themselves to the school of experience. On the contrary, townsmen, bankers, merchants, officers, bishops, parish priests, Jesuits, all plan this [war], speak of it, discuss it, pronounce on it. Everyone is a Turenne or a Folard.[14]

Great misfortune for this country: it will perish, victim of its prejudices, of its blind confidence, of the stupidity or of the roguery of its chiefs.

A GLORIOUS VICTORY against a foe four times as numerous—yet Bougainville and his master Montcalm nursed their bitterness toward Vaudreuil and the Canadian cabal they imagined was hindering them. For the third time, French forces had stopped a British offensive up Lake Champlain, saving New France—yet the two officers saw a greater achievement in their newfound supremacy in Quebec's councils of war.

Bougainville was right: war *was* established there on a European basis. The fight for Fort Carillon showed that: it featured little of the scouting and none of the ambushes that marked, for instance, the campaign against Fort William Henry. Two conventional armies transported themselves through the woods to smash headlong against one another in a textbook battle. Montcalm handled his men very well—but credit must also go to General Abercromby's unimaginative, straight-ahead assault against a far smaller foe in hastily erected fortifications.

Abercromby's dunderheadedness has been the delight of generations of American historians, who seized it (together with Braddock's defeat) as proof that European methods did not apply to American conditions. But such arguments are empty and meaningless. Forts played a crucial role in frontier warfare, as bases for attack and refuges in defeat; even Indians took advantage of friendly fortifications. The best way to capture forts was with cannons and a large number of men, preferably trained, professional troops with a sophisticated logistical system. The adjustment to North American conditions demanded flexibility and imagination, a blending of irregular and

[14] Both the men named were noted French soldiers and strategists.

regular warfare. As much as Montcalm complained of his Indians and Canadians, he relied on their skills, and he used them well. Braddock and Abercromby did not, and they met defeat.

Bougainville's sour tone after this resounding victory can be explained by something more than the petty bickering between the regular army and Canadian chauvinists: as decisive as Carillon proved to be, it could not stop the enemy advance. In 1755, the annihilation of Braddock stunned the British; in 1756, the capture of Oswego sent them reeling; in 1757, the destruction of Fort William Henry stopped all their plans cold. But in 1758, Pitt's leadership kept the offensive rolling.

Even as Abercromby scrambled south with his troops, he dispatched Lieutenant Colonel John Bradstreet with 3,600 men (mostly Americans) to destroy Fort Frontenac. Moving with remarkable secrecy, Bradstreet surprised this strategic post, capturing and burning it—along with great stores of supplies and boats. This blow proved critically important for Brigadier General John Forbes's attack on Fort Duquesne. Like Braddock, Forbes built a long road through the wilderness—but this general understood the problems of woodland warfare. He lined it with stockades, and laid it out across the shortest, most easily defended path. When he finally arrived at Duquesne (193 miles from his starting point), he found the post in ashes: the French had abandoned it, since their badly needed supplies had been destroyed by Bradstreet at Fort Frontenac.

The advance on Fort Duquesne and the construction of Forbes's strategic road into the Ohio valley led to another victory in the west in 1758. At the town of Easton, more than 500 representatives of fifteen tribes met Pennsylvania Governor William Denny, Governor Francis Bernard of New Jersey, and a representative of the British army. In exchange for adjusting land claims and an English promise to stay out of the Ohio country, the tribes agreed to stop their raids on the Pennsylvania, Maryland, and Virginia frontier. British arms and American diplomacy had suddenly sheared off a vast region claimed by New France—tearing away its most important allies.

Finally, there was the easternmost of the British attacks planned for 1758: the assault on Louisburg. This powerful fortress dominated the entrance to the St. Lawrence River; it had been a major concern to the British ever since the French began constructing it in the 1720s. Most recently it had survived Loudon's expedition in 1757, thanks to a well-placed French naval squadron. But Pitt had put truly global forces into play in this decisive year; a massive fleet gathered in English waters, one strong enough to overcome any amount of opposition at Louisburg. And the blockade of the French coast had tightened, keeping Paris's ships of the line and transports locked in port.

The selections that follow offer us two eyewitness accounts of this clash of empires. The first belongs to none other than Olaudah Equiano—the young African of Benin who had found himself carried away into slavery, hauled across the Atlantic, then sent off to England to be a naval officer's servant. Equiano's words offer a personal perspective on the Royal Navy and this particular operation; they also reveal the imperial scope and scale of this expedition to New France, showing how much the world had changed since a few hundred Europeans crossed the Atlantic in the seventeenth century.

On the way to Louisburg, Equiano met a dashing young army officer who commanded many of the troops embarked on the ships. He was Brigadier General James Wolfe. Wolfe would prove himself in the Louisburg operation, leading to an even greater mission—the capture of Quebec itself.

Immediately following Equiano's account comes the journal of Bougainville, Montcalm's advisor, assistant, and chief of staff. Even as the British busied themselves with the attack on all-but-impregnable Louisburg, Montcalm prepared the defenses of Quebec. He paid particular attention to the northern banks of the St. Lawrence River. By careful fortification and deft deployment of his troops, he believed, he could forestall any landings above or below the city. Meanwhile, he gathered all available men around the citadel. As 1758 passed away and 1759 began, Bougainville would be at the heart of the action—up until the final, climactic moment.

The Fleet Sails
by Olaudah Equiano

I remained [in Guernsey] till the summer of the year 1757, when my master, being appointed first lieutenant of His Majesty's Ship the *Roebuck,* sent for Dick and me, and his old mate. On this we all left Guernsey, and set out for England in a sloop bound for London.

As we were coming up towards the Nore,[15] where the *Roebuck* lay, a man of war's boat came alongside to press our people [into the service]; on which each man ran to hide himself. I was very much frightened at this, though I did not know what it meant, or what to think or do. However, I went and hid myself also under a hencoop. Immediately the press gang came on board with their swords drawn, and searched all about, pulled the people out by force, and put them into the boat. At last I was found out also; the man that found me held me up by the heels while they all made their sport of me. I was roaring and crying out all the time most lustily; but at last the mate, who was my conductor, seeing this, came to my assistance, and did all he could to pacify me; but all to very little purpose, till I had seen the boat go off. Soon afterwards we came to the Nore, where the *Roebuck* lay; and, to our great joy, my master came on board to us, and brought us to the ship.

[15] This was the Royal Navy's assembly point in the mouth of the Thames.

I was amazed indeed to see the quantity of men and the guns. However, my surprise began to diminish as my knowledge increased; and I ceased to feel the apprehensions and alarms which had taken such strong possession of me when I first came among the Europeans, and for some time after. I began now to pass to an opposite extreme; I was so far from being afraid of anything new which I saw, that after I had been some time in this ship, I even began to long for an engagement. My griefs too, which in young minds are not perpetual, were now wearing away; and I soon enjoyed myself pretty well, and felt tolerably easy in my present situation. There was a number of boys on board, which still made it more agreeable; for we were always together, and a great part of our time was spent in play.

I remained in this ship a considerable time, during which we made several cruises, and visited a variety of places. . . . All this time we had never come to an engagement, though we were frequently cruising off the coast of France, during which we chased many vessels, and took in all seventeen prizes. I had been learning many of the maneuvers of the ship during our cruise, and I was several times made to fire the guns. . . .

My master . . . got an appointment to be sixth lieutenant of the *Namur,* which was then at Spithead, fitting up for Vice-Admiral [Edward] Boscawen, who was going with a large fleet on an expedition against Louisburg. . . . There was a very great fleet of men of war of every description assembled together for this expedition, and I was in hopes soon to have an opportunity of being gratified with a sea fight.

All things being now in readiness, this mighty fleet (for there was also Admiral Cornish's fleet in company, destined for the East Indies) at last weighed anchor, and sailed. The two fleets continued in company for several days, and then parted; Admiral Cornish, in the *Lenox,* having first saluted our Admiral in the *Namur,* which he returned. We then steered for America. . . .

We . . . proceeded for America, which we soon made, and got into a very commodious harbor called St. George, in Halifax, where we had fish in great plenty, and all other fresh provisions. We were here joined by different men of war and transport ships with soldiers; after which, our fleet being increased to a prodigious number of ships of all kinds, we sailed for Cape Breton in Nova Scotia. We had the good and gallant General Wolfe on board our ship, whose affability made him highly esteemed and beloved by all the men. He often honored me, as well as other boys, with marks of his notice; and saved me once a flogging for fighting with a young gentleman.

We arrived at Cape Breton in the summer of 1758; and here the soldiers were to be landed, in order to make an attack upon Louisburg. My master had some part in superintending the landing; and here I was in a small measure gratified in seeing an encounter between our men and the enemy. The French were posted on the shore to receive us, and disputed our landing for a long time; but at last they were driven from their trenches, and a complete landing was effected. Our troops pursued them as far as the town of Louisburg.

In this action many were killed on both sides. One thing remarkable I saw this day: A lieutenant of the *Princess Amelia,* who, as well as my master, superintended the landing, was giving the word of command, and while his mouth was open, a musket ball went through it, and passed out his cheek. I had that day in my hand the scalp of an Indian king who was killed in the engagement; the scalp had been taken off by an Highlander. I saw this king's ornaments too, which were very curious, and made of feathers.

Our land forces laid siege to the town of Louisburg, while the French men of war were blocked up in the harbor by the fleet, the batteries at the time playing upon them from the land. This they did with such effect that one day I saw some of the ships set on fire by the shells from the batteries, and I believe two or three of them were quite burnt. At another time, about fifty boats belonging to the English men of war, commanded by Captain George Balfour of the *Aetna* fireship, and Mr. Laforey, another junior captain, attacked and boarded the only two remaining French men of war in the harbor. They also set fire to a seventy-gun ship, but they brought off a sixty-four, called the *Bienfaisant.* . . .

At last Louisburg was taken, and the English men of war came into the harbor before it, to my very great joy; for now I had more liberty of indulging myself, and I went often on shore. When the ships were in the harbor, we had the most beautiful procession on the water I ever saw. All the admirals and captains of the men of war, full dressed, and in their barges, well ornamented with pendants, came alongside of the *Namur.*

The Vice-Admiral then went on shore in his barge, followed by the other officers in order of seniority, to take possession, as I suppose, of the town and fort. Some time after this the French governor and his lady, and other persons of note, came on board our ship to dine. On this occasion our ships were dressed with colors of all kinds, from the topgallant-mast head to the deck; and this, with the firing of guns, formed a most grand and magnificent spectacle.

The Citadel Falls
by Louis Antoine de Bougainville

On June 3 [1758] the British with 24 ships of the line, 20 frigates, and two fire ships, and about 150 transports entered Gabarus Bay [at Louisburg]. The same day they fired on the defenses made to prevent this landing.

The fifth and six they tried in vain to prevent this landing.

On the eighth at four in the morning two ships and six frigates, moored very close to shore, delivered a continuous fire on the defenses until eight o'clock. The landing force in 150 barges in two divisions, under command of Generals Amherst, Wolfe, and Whitmore; that of General Wolfe made its landing in a place accounted impracticable. The French troops, only too fortunate in not being cut off in their retreat, re-entered Louisburg the next day with a loss of about eighty men killed or captured.

The night of the seventeenth to eighteenth the enemy opened the trenches. . . . The landing made, the capture of the city was inevitable. . . . The place surrendered July 26 [1758]. . . . During the siege we had 1,500 men killed and the English lost 3,400 [actually 195 dead and 363 wounded]. Three sorties were made, one of 1,500 men, the other 1,200, the third 600. The number of our prisoners, soldiers, habitants, and sailors comes to about 8,000 men.

At the start of the campaign the English, not believing that Louisburg would hold them up so long, expected, immediately that it was taken, to come and besiege Quebec. Their plan was to establish their supply depot at Gaspé and their warships were to cruise between Gaspé and the Seven Islands. The frigates with the transports would have ascended the river, anchored at the capes, and the troops would have landed in barges at St. Joachim [on the north bank of the St. Lawrence, off the Isle of Orleans]. Louisburg being taken only at the end of July, they gave up the Quebec expedition and formed the plan of establishing themselves at Gaspé. On August 10, hearing of the Battle of Carillon, they sent six thousand men to New York. . . .

Canadians and Frenchmen, although having the same origin, the same interests, the same principles of religion and government, with an urgent danger facing them, cannot agree among themselves. It seems that these are two bodies which cannot be amalgamated together. I even believe that a few Canadians pray that we do not succeed, hoping that all blame will fall on the French. . . .

I reached Quebec May 10 [1759], after having been for ten days in the ice between Cap Nord and Cap Ray. The Bordeaux fleet arrived there three days after me, and on May 23 the advance of the British fleet was at Bic.

Then all prepared for the defense of this so-exposed frontier. The troops assigned to this defense were five French battalions and about five to six thousand militiamen. M. de Bourlamaque, with the other three battalions and a thousand Canadians, was charged with covering Montreal on the Lake Champlain side, and the Chevalier de la Corne, with twelve hundred men of *la marine* and the militia, on the Lake Ontario side. MM. de Vaudreuil, de Montcalm, and de Lévis had returned to the capital.

On June 3 I was detached with five companies of grenadiers and five hundred militiamen to build redoubts and lines from the falls of Montmorency up to Quebec.[16] My camp was enlarged day by day up to the

---

[16] Montcalm and Bougainville now devoted all their efforts to preventing a British landing on the north bank of the St. Lawrence, especially upriver of Quebec.

twenty-eighth, as the entire army came to occupy it, and as the English army, arrived a few days before, landed on the Isle of Orleans and two days later put a body of three thousand men at Pointe Lévis opposite Quebec. From this time on the English tried several manœuvers to make us abandon our position. The batteries established at their Pointe Lévis camp smashed and burned the city. In mid-July the troops camped on the Isle of Orleans moved to the left bank of the Montmorency Falls, while we occupied the right. Mr. Wolfe there put nearly fifty guns which, through the shape of the terrain, swept all the plain which was held by the left of our army under the command of the Chevalier de Lévis. The Marquis de Montcalm was at the center, and I was in charge of the right under the Marquis de Vaudreuil.

On July 31 the enemy anchored three vessels broadside in front of our camp on the left, one with sixty guns; their artillery and the batteries at the falls delivered upon us for hours a fire which there are few examples, for in this space of time there were nearly four thousand shot, bombs, or grenades thrown. At two in the afternoon the troops at Pointe Lévis got into their landing craft and came at four o'clock to land and form columns of attack opposite our left, while the troops camped at the falls came down to attack at the same time. The Chevalier de Lévis had made his dispositions to receive them, and the Marquis de Montcalm had joined him with a party of troops from the right and center. The enemy was repulsed with a loss of six or seven hundred men, and in retreating they burned two of their anchored vessels.

The Chevalier de Lévis then was sent to defend the Lake Ontario frontier, threatened by a considerable army which was coming after having taken Niagara.

Meanwhile, several English vessels had passed up above Quebec, and measures were taken to prevent their inroads on our communications. August 5 the number of these vessels was increased and a landing force of fifteen hundred men was put on board them. I then was detached with a company of grenadiers, a light company of regulars, and one of militia to guard the communication of the army and of Quebec with the vessels from which the provisions were drawn, and with Montreal. There were about five hundred men spread out over these lines of communication, and they were to be under my orders.

I followed the English squadron as far as Pointe aux Trembles, where it anchored. This parish is seven leagues from Quebec [toward Montreal]. I there assembled about 250 men and I had three-quarters of a league from me on my right a troop of 150 volunteer cavalry under the command of M. de la Rochebeaucour, organized at the start of the campaign, instructed and disciplined by this officer, who has served with the greatest of distinction.

The afternoon of August 8 the enemy anchored broadsides before the landing place at Pointe aux Trembles a frigate of twenty-two guns and several bomb ships [boats carrying high-angle mortars] which fired on the shore. The landing place was a smooth beach without any covering heights or any defenses; I had not time to make any. Their first landing was made at low tide; their troops, to the number of fifteen hundred men, formed there and marched against me. The cavalry was advanced on my right and I might have had three hundred men in the action. This first attack did not succeed and they re-embarked. My horse was hit. They came on a second time to the attack at high tide and were again pushed back with a loss of three hundred men killed or wounded.

On the tenth the enemy camped opposite on the south shore. My detachment was increased by a company of grenadiers and two hundred militiamen. On the seventeenth the enemy made a night movement in barges and landed at Deschambault, seven leagues above me [forty miles upstream from Quebec]. I at once marched there with my two companies of grenadiers, my light company of regulars, one hundred cavalrymen, and sixty militiamen, and forced them to re-embark. Then they broke camp, took to their boats again, and their squadron was left downriver and anchored opposite St. Augustin, three leagues below Pointe aux Trembles and four above Quebec. I followed them there. The next night they were reinforced with about one thousand men and came to attack me from ten in the evening until half-past twelve. They made a great bombardment from their ships' cannon and muskets, attempted a landing without success on my left, and never dared set foot ashore.

These efforts on their part proved that they had designs on our communications, a thing essential to us, but difficult to guard, [we] being obliged to follow on foot with much inferior forces the movement and rapid advances of their vessels and barges.

At the beginning of September the English evacuated their camp at the falls, went to Pointe Lévis, and the largest part of them went on board the squadron which was opposing me. Then I was given the five grenadier companies, Duprat's volunteers, three light companies of our regulars, and a few militia light companies, which gave me a corps of fifteen hundred men, in addition to the various posts I had placed along the shore. The English anchored opposite Cap Rouge, three leagues from Quebec, where I went. They made several moves to keep me on the move and a few offensive demonstrations.

Between the night of the tenth and that of the twelfth, the troops camped on the Isle of Orleans, those at Pointe Lévis, and on the ships entered their barges and surprised a post half a league from Quebec.[17] I was not informed of it until nine in the morning. I marched at once, but when I came within range of the battle, our army was beaten and in retreat [and Montcalm was gravely wounded]. The entire English army advanced to attack me. I retreated before them and posted myself so as to cover the retreat

[17] Wolfe discovered a path from the river shore at Anse de Foulon up the bluffs to the Plains of Abraham. The post referred to here stood at the top.

of our army, to join with it, or to march again against the enemy if it was judged proper.

The Marquis de Montcalm died the next day of his wounds. He had conducted a campaign worthy of M. de Turenne, and his death caused our misfortunes. It was believed necessary to abandon the Beauport camp all standing and to withdraw behind Jacques Cartier River, eleven leagues from Quebec, which the enemy at once besieged. I took it upon myself (and the Marquis de Vaudreuil approved) to remain with my corps at Cap Rouge and Lorette. There I reassembled the remnants of our army and got provisions into Quebec.

On the eighteenth I marched with six hundred men to throw myself into [Quebec], and the Chevalier de Lévis, arrived before from Montreal, advanced the army to get within range of attacking the English. I was only three-quarters of a league from Quebec when I learned that the city had surrendered. It had been bombarded for sixty-eight days. I was forced to retrace my steps, for the English army moved to march against me.

Such was the end of what up to this moment was the finest campaign in the world. We spent three months in bivouac. Just the same, the English hold only the [outer] walls and the King [still] holds the colony.

MONTCALM WAS DEAD. Bougainville, his loyal lieutenant, struggled to fight off the despair that surely gripped him in this grim hour. Until the climactic battle (which Bougainville missed), the French had conducted a brilliant defense in the face of overwhelming odds. Yes, they had lost the west—but Indian diplomacy was changeable, and that situation might be reversed easily enough. Yes, the British had finally captured Fort Niagara—but the main force on Lake Champlain had yet to break through. Yes, the French had lost Louisburg, and with it control of the St. Lawrence River—but Montcalm had collected his forces and fortified the northern bank, while Bougainville raced up and down to fend off British landings.

The critical break in the St. Lawrence campaign occurred when General Wolfe discovered a treacherous path up the 150-foot cliff at Anse de Foulon. With the same skill he had shown at Louisburg, he landed his men at night on the narrow beach below. They climbed the bluff, drove off the surprised French guards, and poured onto the Plains of Abraham above Quebec on the morning of September 13, 1759. The plan was daring: if Wolfe lost the battle, he would have no retreat. Nor could he bring many cannons with him up that steep trail. But Montcalm reacted with uncharacteristic haste: he could have gathered overwhelming numbers from the garrison of the city and the Canadian militia, but instead he abruptly attacked with half his men. Using safe, sound, conventional tactics, Wolfe carried the day—though the commanders on both sides fell mortally wounded.

The British had captured the city of Quebec, but they had not yet conquered New France. Montreal still held out. Furthermore, the British camps and occupied towns formed mere islands of control in a sprawling colony: tens of thousands of hostile inhabitants and Indians occupied the country-side. So when winter brought the conventional campaign to a halt, the invaders decided to do something about those diffuse, dangerous enemies all around them.

In September 1759, Major General Jeffrey Amherst delivered a set of remarkable orders to Major Robert Rogers, commander of the colonial rangers. As mentioned earlier, the British lacked Indian scouts; they relied instead on the services of a handful of backwoods frontiersmen under the leadership of Rogers (a latter-day Benjamin Church). Though national myth, fed by James Fenimore Cooper, depicts the colonists as a set of sharpshooting trackers and hunters, in truth the wilderness terrified most Americans. Virtually all were farmers, most comfortable when plowing cleared fields outside of nice, safe towns. Rogers was one of the very few who actually fit the myth.

When Amherst issued his orders to his ranger subordinate, the general was in command of the army on the southern end of Lake Champlain; the French had abandoned forts St. Frederic and Carillon. Winter came fast that year, and Amherst's force would have to wait yet another year before breaking through to Montreal. But Rogers could still move across snow and swamps—and the general knew a target particularly ripe for a ranger attack. He ordered the rugged frontiersman to strike deep into the Canadian wilderness and destroy the Abenaki village of St. Francis.

Amherst's decision seems odd, even pointless. The British were clearly winning the war: why attack a settlement filled with women and children? But the general brought two considerations to bear: first, he (and all regular officers) dreaded the thought of this splendid conventional war turning into a guerrilla struggle. No one wanted to muddy the glory of defeating Montcalm in honorable battle with a drawn-out campaign against wilderness-savvy Indian warriors. As Benjamin Church had ruthlessly shown at the turn of the century, as the French had shown in their wars with the Iroquois, attacks on villages made effective strategy in dealing with Indian raids. And a firm blow at the strongly pro-French Abenakis might weaken the commitment of New France's remaining allies.

The second consideration was revenge: simple, cold revenge. The St. Francis warriors had gone on the warpath with the French in every war. They had raided New England frontier villages for generations. Most important, they had taken part in the destruction of Fort William Henry (and Amherst believed, mistakenly, that they had played a large role in the ensuing massacre). Fighting Indians frustrated conventional soldiers such as Amherst; he wanted very much to get back at them.

The Rangers Attack
by Robert Rogers

The General, exasperated at the treatment Capt. Kennedy had received from the St. Francis Indians, to whom he had been sent with a flag of truce and proposals of peace, who had been by them made prisoner with his party . . . , determined to bestow upon them a signal chastisement.

He gave orders as follows:

> You are this night to join the detachment of 200 men which were yesterday ordered out, and proceed to Missisquoi bay, from which you will proceed to attack the enemy's settlements on the south side of the St. Lawrence, in such a manner as shall most effectually disgrace and injure the enemy, and redound to the honor and success of His Majesty's subjects. Take your revengence, but remember that although the villains have promiscuously murdered women and children of all ages, it is my order that no women or children should be killed or hurt. When you have performed this service, you will again join the army wherever it may be.

> YOURS ETC.,
> JEFF. AMHERST
> *CAMP AT CROWN POINT*, SEPT. 13, 1759
> TO MAJOR ROGERS

The account of the expedition to St. Francis is contained in a despatch to Gen. Amherst, as follows.

I cannot forebear making some remarks[18] upon the difficulties and distresses which attended the expedition under my command, against the village of St. Francis, situated within three miles of the river St. Lawrence in the heart of Canada about halfway between Montreal and Quebec. While we kept the water, it was found extremely difficult to pass undiscovered by the enemy, who were cruising in great numbers upon the lake, and had prepared certain vessels armed with all manner of mischievous implements to decoy English parties on board, and destroy them.

But we escaped their designs, and landed at Missisquoi bay in ten days. Here I left my boats and provisions sufficient to carry us back to Crown Point, under the charge of two trusty Indians—who were to remain there until we came back, unless the enemy should discover the boats, in which case they were to follow my track, and bring the intelligence.

The second day after this, they joined me at night, informing that 400

[18] These remarks on the Rangers' march to St. Francis have been moved for narrative continuity.

French had discovered my boats, and that 200 of them were now following my track. This caused us some uneasiness. Should the enemy overtake us, and we have the advantage in an encounter, they would be immediately reinforced, while we could expect no assistance, being so far advanced beyond our military posts, our boats and provisions likewise being taken, cut off all hope of retreat by the route we came. But after due deliberation, it was resolved to accomplish our object at all events, and return by Connecticut River. Lieut. McMullen was despatched by land to Crown Point to desire Gen. Amherst to relieve us with provisions at Ammonoosuck River, at the extremity of the Coos intervales; that being the way we should return if we ever should return.

We now determined to outmarch our pursuers, and destroy St. Francis before we were overtaken. We marched nine days through a spruce bog, where the ground was wet and low, a great part of it being covered with water a foot deep. When we camped at night, we cut boughs from the trees, and with them constructed a kind of hammocks to secure ourselves from the water. We uniformly began our march a little before day and continued it until after dark at night. The tenth day after leaving the bay brought us to a river fifteen miles south of St. Francis, which we were compelled to ford against a swift current. The tallest men were put upstream, and holding each other, the party passed over with the loss of several guns, which were recovered by diving to the bottom. We now had good marching ground. . . .

On the evening of the twenty-second day after our departure from Crown Point, we came in sight of the Indian town of St. Francis, which we discovered by climbing a tree at three miles distance. Here my party, consisting of 142, officers included, were ordered to refresh themselves.

At eight o'clock Lieut. Turner, Ensign Avery, and myself reconnoitered the town. We found the Indians engaged in a high frolic, and saw them execute several dances with the greatest spirit. We returned to our camp at two o'clock, and at three, advanced the whole party within 500 yards of the village, where the men were lightened of their packs, and formed for action.

Half an hour before sunrise, we surprised the village, approaching it in three divisions, on the right, left, and center; which was effected with so much caution and promptitude, on the part of the officers and men, that the enemy had no time to recover themselves, or to take arms in their own defense, until they were mostly destroyed. Some few escaped to the water, but my people pursued, sunk their canoes, and shot those who attempted to escape by swimming. We then set fire to all their houses except the three reserved for the use of the party. The fire consumed many Indians who had concealed themselves in the cellars and lofts of their houses and would not come out.

At seven o'clock in the morning the affair was completely over. We had by that time killed 200 Indians, and taken twenty of their women and children prisoners; fifteen of the latter, I suffered to go their own way; and brought home with me two Indian boys and three girls. Five English captives were also found and taken into our care.

On parading the detachment, Captain Ogden was found to be badly wounded, being shot through the body, but still able to perform his duty. Six privates were wounded, and one [allied] Stockbridge Indian killed.

I ordered my party to take corn out of the reserved houses, for their subsistence home, there being no other provisions there; and while they were loading themselves, I examined the captives, who reported that a party of 300 French and some Indians were down the river four miles below us; and that our boats were way-laid. This I believed to be true, as they told the exact number, and the place where they had been left; that 250 French had three days before gone up the river, to "Wigwam Martinic," supposing that I intended to attack that place.

A council of war now concluded that no other course was left us, than to return by Connecticut River and [Fort] Number Four. The detachment therefore marched in a body eight days upon that course, and when provisions grew scarce near Memphrémagog Lake, it was divided into companies with proper guides to each, and ordered to assemble at the mouth of Ammonoosuck River, as I expected to find provisions there for our relief.

Two days after we separated, Ensign Avery of Fitche's regiment, with his party, fell upon my track, and followed in my rear. The enemy fell upon them, and took seven prisoners two of whom escaped and came to me next morning. Avery with his men soon after joined us and we proceeded to the Coos intervales. . . .

This tribe of Indians was notoriously attached to the French, and had for a century past harassed the frontiers of new England, murdering people of all ages and sexes, in the most barbarous manner, and in times of peace, when they had no reason to suspect their hostile intentions. They had within my knowledge during the six years past, killed and carried away more than 600 persons. We found 600 scalps hanging upon poles over the doors of their wigwams.

It is impossible to describe the dejected and miserable condition of the party on arriving at the Coos intervales. After so long a march over rocky barren mountains, and through deep swamps, worn down with hunger and fatigue, we expected to be relieved at the intervales and assisted in our return. The officer despatched to the General reached Crown Point in nine days, and faithfully discharged his commission; upon which, the General immediately ordered Lieut. Stevens to Number Four, and to proceed thence with provisions up the river, to the place I had designated; there, to wait so long as there were any hopes of my return.

The officer thought proper to remain but two days, and returned carrying with him all the provisions, about two hours before our arrival. We found a fresh fire burning in his camp, and fired guns to bring him back, which he heard, but would not return, supposing we were an enemy. . . .

Capt. Ogden, myself, and an Indian boy embarked upon a raft of dry pine trees. The current carried us down the stream in the middle of the river, where we kept our miserable vessel, with such paddles as could be split and hewn with small hatchets. The second day we reached White River falls; and very narrowly escaped running over them. The raft went over, and was lost; but our remaining strength enabled us to land and march by the falls. . . . I attempted to construct another raft. Not being able to cut the trees, I burnt them down, and burnt them at proper lengths. This was our third day's work after leaving our companions. The next day we floated down to Watto-quichie falls, which are about fifty yards in length. . . . The next morning we floated down within a short distance of Number Four. Here we found several men cutting timber, who relieved and assisted us to the fort. A canoe was immediately dispatched up the river with provisions, which reached the men at Coos in four days after.

THE ST. FRANCIS raid showed that the war was far from over, even after the fall of Quebec and the death of Montcalm—a fact driven home by the account that follows. Once again, Louis Antoine de Bougainville would be in the thick of the fight for the survival of New France. Command of the French forces fell to the daring Lévis, an outstanding young officer who has appeared frequently in this and the preceding chapter. Faced with defeat on every front, Lévis and Bougainville launched a bold counterattack in the winter of 1759–60: once more, French skill and audacity met British numbers. Despite all the disasters, despite all the territory lost, Lévis made a gamble that just might work—if only the French fleet could break through the blockade and bring vital reinforcements to Canada.

The Final Surrender
by Louis Antoine de Bougainville

The campaign did not end as happily as it began. It cost us Quebec, Carillon, St. Frederic, Niagara, Frontenac, and the Marquis de Montcalm. This general was killed at the battle lost on September 13 before Quebec, and the colony was brought to bay.

These then were the frontiers of the Quebec region: a little fort hurriedly built at the Jacques Cartier River; Isle aux Noix organized for defense on Lake Champlain; and a fortified island in the midst of the rapids which on the Lake Ontario side form the head of the St. Lawrence River.

During the 1759 campaign I was almost always on detached duty in command of the companies of grenadiers and volunteers guarding the army's communications with its supply depots, which were eighteen leagues away. I had several special advantages; I even hoped to throw myself into Quebec to defend it after the battle, [but] Ramezay, King's lieutenant who commanded there, never wished to give me the opportunity. . . . This man surrendered without having tried a cannon shot, and the enemy not even having started their trenches.

In the month of March 1760, I was sent to Isle aux Noix to defend it; Desandrouins, engineer officer, was charged with the defense of Fort Lévis at the rapids, and the Marquis de Lévis left to besiege Quebec, the snow not yet having melted. The speed of his march surprised the enemy. Murray, [English] Governor of Quebec, came out with his troops, was well beaten on the same terrain where we had been September 13, 1759, lost his field artillery, and was forced to re-enter the place. They at once started the siege, that is to say in order to be open to no reproaches in case aid came from France, they started the trenches in the snow and put in position a dozen twelve-pounders (there were no others) against a place defended by a numerous garrison and more than one hundred cannon of heavy caliber.

The arrival of an English squadron decided the matter.[19] It was necessary to raise this siege of a sort, leaving Bourlamaque with a body of troops to follow along the river the movements of Murray, whose troops had been reinforced. The Marquis de Lévis prepared some defenses at Isle Ste. Helene, opposite Montreal.

In the month of August I was besieged at Isle aux Noix which I had strongly entrenched, and I evacuated it on the twentieth day by order of the Marquis de Vaudreuil. I retreated through the woods to St. Jean. Two days later we had to shut ourselves up in Montreal, General Amherst already having arrived on the island of that name, after having taken Fort Lévis; Murray having landed there on the other side, after having forced Bourlamaque to fall back there, and the army which had laid siege to Isle aux Noix occupied Longueuil and La Prairie [Kahnawake], ready to join the other two. It was more than needed against a paltry town, overpowered on all sides, which had only a shirt and ten or twelve bad cannon; we were reduced to less than three thousand men.

I was charged by the generals to carry to General Amherst the articles of a general capitulation for Canada.

The country was well-treated, the English well knowing that it would remain theirs; the troops badly, since the English General demanded that they should lay down their arms and not serve for the rest of the entire war. We presented a memoir to the Marquis de Vaudreuil containing sharp protests against these humiliating conditions and the offer to attack the enemy at once or to defend Isle Ste. Helene. The Canadian [Governor] Gen-

[19] The British ships arrived in May 1760.

eral gave us written orders to lay down our arms, and at the end of the year
we returned to France on English transports.

ON THE AFTERNOON of November 20, 1759, a British fleet under the
command of Admiral Sir Edward Hawke fired the first broadsides in the Battle of Quiberon Bay—and instantly destroyed all hope for saving New
France. The French fleet, under Admiral the Comte de Conflans, was attempting to break the British blockade and launch an invasion of Ireland;
had it succeeded, the government of William Pitt certainly would have
poured forces into the island, perhaps breaking off its assault on New
France. But Hawke cut off Conflans's escape, and the French ships broke
formation and fled back to port. In the end, the Royal Navy captured or destroyed a third of the French fleet, bottling up the rest for good.

Lévis and Bougainville could not know of the disaster at Quiberon Bay;
thanks to the vigilance of the Royal Navy, New France, or what was left of
it, was sealed off from all contact with Europe. So they acted as soldiers must
act: they assumed that help would be forthcoming, and launched their daring winter attack on Quebec. Then came the British relief squadron up the
St. Lawrence, severing even that slender thread of hope. On September 8,
1760, Governor-General Vaudreuil and his officers agreed to surrender.

The final victory over New France represented nothing less than a revolution to the American colonists. For New Yorkers and New Englanders, it
meant the end of nearly a century of warfare: there would be no more expensive expeditions against Canadian fortresses, no more scourging raids on
their frontier towns. The war changed life for the middle and southern
colonies as well. In the past, Pennsylvania, Maryland, and Virginia had ignored the conflict with Quebec; as far as they were concerned, they managed
their own Indian diplomacy quite well (especially in the case of the Quaker
government in Philadelphia), and the struggle against New France did not
concern them. But this war had changed all that: the fighting over the Ohio
valley threw them together with the northern colonies for the first time, and
the French-inspired Indian raids brought the war home.

In other words, the French and Indian War gave the colonies a new set
of common interests by giving them a common foe (as shown by Franklin's
interesting but pointless conference at Albany, with his doomed plan for
colonial union). Soon after the collapse of Quebec, Native Americans
stepped in to take New France's place. Fighting began even before Montreal
fell: the Cherokees waged a fierce and effective war on the southern colonies
from 1759 to 1761, capturing Fort Loudon and 200 men. Elsewhere a brief,
uneasy peace settled in as the British took control of French forts in the west
(Britain's seizure of Canada was ratified by the Treaty of Paris in February
1763, which ended the Seven Years' War, as the conflict was called in Europe). But Indian discontent grew rapidly, fed by a new faith that spread

from tribe to tribe. The Master of Life, it was said, called for a return to tra-ditional ways. And deft diplomacy by the Ottawa and Seneca convinced nu-merous nations that only the French had held American settlers back; with the French gone, the Indians themselves had to drive the enemy away.

Starting in May 1763, thousands of warriors from dozens of tribes at-tacked British forts all across the west. No less than seven posts fell in the Great Lakes region; farther east, the Indians captured forts Venango, Le Boeuf, and Presqu'ile. Forts Pitt (formerly Duquesne), Niagara, and Detroit endured prolonged sieges, as the Native Americans ambushed relief columns. More than 2,000 colonists died in widespread raids. Peace finally returned in early 1765, when British delegations spread word of the Royal Proclamation of 1763: the king had forbidden the colonists from settling on the western side of the Appalachians.

When the British government conquered New France, in a sense it con-quered its own American colonies. Since the founding of Jamestown a cen-tury and a half before, these diverse settlements had largely taken care of themselves. The colonists' own assemblies had handled their own defense (along with other expenses). The crown had made a number of attempts to assert greater control, placing royal governors in charge of most (but not all) colonies, enforcing the Navigation Acts, and fighting to get permanent salaries for royal officials. But the French and Indian War suddenly changed the situation. The conquest of Canada demanded a massive commitment of military power; and the war with the Indians that followed (marked by a number of embarrassing defeats) showed that the crown could not walk away—it must garrison a healthy number of troops in North America for the first time.

A continuing military commitment to the American colonies meant a continuing (and heavy) expense. This came on top of an enormous debt, built up by more than seven years of war on both sides of the Atlantic. But a solution suggested itself immediately. With more than a million subjects living in North America, surely the colonists could pay for royal troops to de-fend their own homes. Government ministers quickly drew up plans for un-precedented taxes on the previously self-taxing Americans. And to keep the defense bill as low as possible, land-hungry settlers would be restrained from moving into Indian territory.

Nothing creates unity like a shared opponent: the French and Indian War demonstrated that clearly enough. But no one in the colonies would have predicted that the British government itself might become the common foe. Indeed, as fighting with the Indians died down, everything indicated a return to customary disunity. In New England, the children of the Great Mi-gration preserved their identity and culture; the fractious Anglo-Dutch fam-ilies of New York maintained their commercial bent (and patroonesque estates up the Hudson River, inhabited by tenant farmers); Quakers and Ger-mans made Pennsylvania a land apart; while Virginia, the Carolinas, and the new colony of Georgia hosted a drastically polarized society ruled by great planters and served by enslaved Africans. And all down the line, families from Ulster, Scotland, and the English border counties pressed into the backcountry. Indeed, the only thing they had in common was their king: young George III, who succeeded his late grandfather in October 1760.

This was a rich, diverse landscape—a far cry from the impoverished, disease-ridden, besieged settlements of the early seventeenth century. But was it a new nation in the making? In 1765, only a fool would think so.